Ranger Raid

RANGER RAID

*The Legendary Robert Rogers and
His Most Famous Frontier Battle*

PHILLIP THOMAS TUCKER

STACKPOLE
BOOKS
Guilford, Connecticut

Published by Stackpole Books
An imprint of The Rowman & Littlefield Publishing Group, Inc.
4501 Forbes Blvd., Ste. 200
Lanham, MD 20706
www.rowman.com

Distributed by NATIONAL BOOK NETWORK

British Library Cataloguing in Publication Information available

Library of Congress Cataloging-in-Publication Data

Names: Tucker, Phillip Thomas, 1953– author.
Title: Ranger Raid : the legendary Robert Rogers and his most famous
    frontier battle / Phillip Thomas Tucker.
Other titles: Legendary Robert Rogers and his most famous frontier battle
Description: Guilford, Connecticut : Stackpole Books, [2021] | Includes
    bibliographical references. | Summary: "This book digs deep into Robert
    Rogers's most controversial battle: the raid on St. Francis in Canada
    during the French and Indian War. Phillip Thomas Tucker refreshes this
    story, combining the biography of Robert Rogers, the history of his
    Rangers, and the history of the native peoples in this region"—
    Provided by publisher.
Identifiers: LCCN 2020049680 (print) | LCCN 2020049681 (ebook) | ISBN
    9780811739733 (cloth) | ISBN 9780811769716 (epub)
Subjects: LCSH: Rogers, Robert, 1731–1795. | Rogers' Raid, Québec, 1759. |
    United States—History—French and Indian War, 1754–1763—Atrocities. |
    Abenaki Indians—Québec (Province)—Saint Francis River Valley. |
    Rogers' Rangers—Biography. | United States—History—French and Indian
    War, 1754–1763—Regimental histories.
Classification: LCC E199.R74 T83 2021 (print) | LCC E199.R74 (ebook) |
    DDC 973.2/6/092 [B]—dc23
LC record available at https://lccn.loc.gov/2020049680
LC ebook record available at https://lccn.loc.gov/2020049681

Contents

Introduction

S⊤. Francis! S⊤. Francis! No name throughout the early history of the settlements of New England and across America's frontier was more terrifying to generations of settlers than that of the legendary center, for nearly an entire century, of seemingly countless raids launched from the Abenaki community of Odanak, located on the St. Francis River in Quebec, Canada. The Saint François de Sales Mission, or St. Francis, had long been viewed as the heart of darkness and the author of a lengthy list of evils by long-suffering settlers across America's northern frontier. The infamous place deep in Quebec was known as Saint-François in French during the imperial struggle of Europe's two major powers, England and France, to gain possession of the North American continent in the French and Indian War.

Known as the Seven Years' War in Europe, America's first major war forever altered the destinies of North America's inhabitants, including Native Americans and especially the Algonquian peoples, who lost their greatest white supporters, the French. After the French signed a peace treaty with England in 1763 and were eliminated from most of North America, the tragic fate of Native American people was sealed, because nothing could now stop the tide of migrating settlers, who sought the best Indian lands for their permanent possession.

Like no other American of his day, Robert Rogers garnered his enduring fame by having become America's premier "special forces" leader (considered today to have been the revered father of America's Special Operations Forces of the United States Army), developing a new way for Americans to wage war that was unimaginable to generations of Europe-trained military leaders, who considered this kind of fighting not taught in Europe's military schools "barbarian" and "uncivilized." Like a proud father raising and nurturing his children, Rogers carefully molded his Rangers—America's first elite force of

I

fighting men—into some of the most invaluable and indispensable soldiers in the British-Provincial Army during the French and Indian War, while fighting the French, Canadians, and Indians in the remote wilderness. With boldness and skill, he led the hard-hitting "special forces" Rangers of his own creation into some of the remotest deep forests and mountains located between New France and New England, garnering celebrity status on both sides of the Atlantic.

In a masterful way, Rogers utilized his innovative tactical thoughts and novel warfighting ideas about the art of Ranger warfare in the severest weather conditions, including in the depths of wintertime, and amid the thickest northern forests of mostly virgin spruce and pine, while battling a highly skilled opponent. Making an original contribution to the art of war, Rogers then wrote America's first wilderness warfighting manual of twenty-eight rules, including those that he employed during the 1759 St. Francis expedition: golden rules for effectively waging Ranger warfare in the unmapped wilderness of the northern lake country and against a resourceful foe considered invincible. Significantly, Rogers's innovative and insightful axioms for waging a highly effective brand of warfare have applied to unconventional warfighting to this day.

But no success of this ambitious frontiersman, the enterprising son of a lowly Ulsterman from the northern end of the Emerald Isle, was more sparkling in overall tactical terms than his audacious raid on St. Francis. Consequently, Rogers is still revered and idolized by today's Rangers of America's Special Operations Forces, which now have a global presence to safeguard United States interests and those of the American people in foreign lands around the world. Major Rogers's exceptionally bold strike on the Abenaki "town" of St. Francis, located more than 150 miles (the return journey was more than 200 miles) slightly northeast of Crown Point, where the secret expedition began with high hopes not long after sunset on September 13, 1759, was one of the most remarkable feats in the annals of American military history. The war waged by Rogers and his Rangers was a total one in its sheer ruthlessness. And Rogers's raid, which was nothing less than an American epic, that destroyed St. Francis was just one chapter in a bitter struggle for survival on America's most untamed frontier, where this conflict for the heart and soul of America was dominated by the simple alternative of kill or be killed. At this time, the Rangers' ranks were dominated by a good many

Scotch-Irish fighters who still embraced distinctive Celtic and Gaelic ways, including the Gaelic language and even headdress (blue Scottish bonnets), when they waged war in an innovative way.

Contrary to romantic myths, what happened at St. Francis on October 4, 1759, was a shocking example of barbarism—a massacre of mostly non-combatants and innocents in which women, children, and the elderly were victims. In this context, white Rangers had completely evolved to the brutal ways of the enemy, whom they hated, in a thorough transformation created by the war's excesses and horrors. The full extent of the savagery demonstrated by both sides had not been seen in the annals of Western warfare since the dark days of antiquity. Given this heightened fight for survival with no holds barred, it was only natural that each side looked upon the other as the epitome of evil and as the devil's disciples, who had to be extinguished.

In the annals of American history, Rogers's raid has been long presented as a decisive blow that broke the considerable power and will of the western Abenaki, who had long called St. Francis home, in a climactic showdown of good versus evil in the traditional nationalist narrative dominated by romance and distortion. But in truth, this rosy scenario of a pristine victory in Quebec and a decisive result with long-term strategic consequences of supreme importance was certainly not the reality. In a classic irony, Rogers attacked a town that was largely devoid of warriors, who were away and active elsewhere, and almost all of the Abenaki warriors continued to fight on against the encroachment of settlers long after the raid and until the war's end in 1763.

As noted, however, the American public has been long presented with the much-embellished and romantic view that Major Rogers struck a decisive strategic blow that wiped out the Abenaki as a formidable fighting force, as presented in official reports, popular histories, and Rogers's own self-serving accounts. Nevertheless, this popular misconception about a climactic raid in terms of overall decisiveness has still served as the standard view of the St. Francis raid in the twenty-first century: one of the most enduring myths about one of the most famous chapters of the French and Indian War. The ambitious Rogers, born on the untamed New England frontier in November 1731 to lower-class Scotch-Irish immigrant parents from Ulster Province in the north of Ireland, sought recognition and promotion from his highly placed British superiors through his fanciful accounts, which included his battle reports. These official army reports concealed Rogers's true losses and errors while often significantly exaggerating enemy losses.

As a career-minded officer of outstanding promise, Rogers hoped to win promotion and increase the size of his Ranger command by presenting the most positive possible accounts to impress his British superiors. Even more, Rogers was often mired in debt, even having equipped and paid his men out of his own pocket and failing to be reimbursed, and he eventually resorted to writing as a means of solving his financial woes. Therefore, he desperately needed a literary success when he went to London in the hope of reversing his sagging financial fortunes with the 1765 the publication of his journals— the pressing need for profits, reputation, and future advancement that created a situation not ideal for fostering a great degree of honesty and truth telling.

For such reasons, therefore, I have decided to rely only sparingly on the *Journals of Robert Rogers of the Rangers*, because it is clear that they are primarily a memoir written by Rogers to flatter himself, in contrast to a more authentic journal like the one written by Captain Louis Antoine de Bougainville, the Marquis de Montcalm's trusty aide-de-camp, who served from 1756 to 1760. For these reasons, I have focused more on telling the dramatic story of Rogers's Rangers from the historical gold mine of contemporary newspaper accounts, especially those overlooked by previous historians, which have been long forgotten.

In addition, this current book has explored the most forgotten aspects of Rogers's Rangers in greater detail, including the key role played by Africans, both freemen and former slaves, who fought in the ranks and served with distinction as part of America's first integrated combat force of elite fighting men. This more inclusive approach has helped to overturn past historical myths and one-sided interpretations of a romantic nature. The traditional myopic, ultranationalistic, and even white-first focus on this subject has long obscured these other key players, both black and Indian Rangers, to a lesser degree, in the telling of the Rogers's Rangers' story.

The fundamental basis of the dramatic saga of this slashing raid has primarily derived from Rogers's sanitized and self-serving account in his book that became popular across America. Covering up less savory factual aspects of the attack, including atrocities stemming from the major's no-quarter order, and the lengthy and costly withdrawal, including the horrors of cannibalism, south through an uncharted wilderness, Rogers's work was published in London two years after the French and Indian War ended with the 1763 Treaty of Paris. Therefore, Rogers became even more famous on both sides of the Atlantic based on what he had written about himself—or, in truth, what was written by one of his better-educated aides-de-camp or one of his friends, who served as basically a ghostwriter. Rogers only emphasized successes, which were duly exaggerated, to enhance his accomplishments and leadership abilities, laying an extremely narrow and one-sided foundation for what we know about the raid on St. Francis today.

In addition, instead of focusing on the heroic odyssey of the Abenaki people during their struggle for survival and to retain their lands, and in basically following Rogers's one-sided focus on a sanitized version of events, generations of white American historians and writers have been guilty of some of the same distortions and xenophobia, telling this remarkable story from the most narrow and romantic of perspectives, partly due to the traditional hero worship of their idol. Even more in the absence of Abenaki voices and Native American historians, generations of American historians have focused more on the overall story of the historic western push of American expansion and battling the Indians, especially the Great Plains tribes, long after the colonial period.

The audacious raid of 1759 was distinguished by a ruthlessness and harshness that not only equaled but sometimes even surpassed the brutality and desperation of the Indian opponent. (To be entirely fair to Major Rogers, his superior, British major general Jeffery Amherst, who was known for his xenophobia and hatred of the Abenaki, had specially directed him to inflict a terrible retribution on the inhabitants of St. Francis with the written orders "Take your revenge.") The ritualistic and customary brutality of the Abenaki in wartime was firmly rooted in the traditional values of a warrior culture, ethos, and spiritual faith that was alien to the white man.

A most disturbing fact that needed to be hidden from the colonists and the British-Provincial Army for morale purposes was that the raid never effectively ended future Abenaki raids—as long alleged and as had been the very reason that Amherst had originally ordered Rogers's bold strike—and resulted in an absolute fiasco for the elite Rangers. However, the glorification and romanticization of the raid disguised the fact that Rogers lost a large proportion—around 50 percent—of his command during his long withdrawal from St. Francis.

Indeed, at least 69 out of the 142 men who had descended upon St. Francis with fixed bayonets on that fateful early October morning in Quebec were lost in what the French could rightly claim as a victory in the end. (Most—forty-three men—died of starvation during the long journey from St. Francis, and only one fighting man, an Indian ally, was killed in the attack because of the lack of resistance, given the absence of warriors who were elsewhere.) Most revealing of all, the stunningly light losses among Rogers's men highlighted the full extent of the lack of opposition, because St. Francis was virtually defenseless at the time of the attack.

In the end, the severe physical demands stemming from the ordeal of the raid's aftermath, not the combat prowess of Abenaki warriors, had eliminated a large percentage of America's elite of the elite: the primary objective of French leadership for years. In this regard, the much-celebrated raid on St. Francis was very much a self-inflicted wound of immense proportions, and Rogers was fortunate to escape with his life. Clearly, a shockingly high price (the loss rate among Rogers's Rangers was far higher than losses of a military force fighting on a conventional battlefield on both sides of the Atlantic at this time and especially on today's modern battlefields, especially among the Special Operations Forces) had been paid in full for the wiping out an infamous Indian town, despite the fact that it was almost completely barren of fighting men (Canadians, French troops of La Marine, and Abenaki warriors who were elsewhere) and lacked legitimate defensive capabilities. In another example of the concept of total war, the physical presence of St. Francis was totally obliterated, much as the ancient Romans had wiped out all physical remains of the defeated mercantile city of Carthage—Rome's great commercial and imperial rival on Africa's north coast in 146 BC.

Such gruesome facts as the frightfully high cost of the raid in crucial Ranger manpower, especially the loss of fine commissioned and noncommissioned officers, had to be carefully hidden from the public on both sides of the Atlantic for morale purposes and so that the French would not know that their opponents' most lethal fighting men had been so thoroughly decimated in what was, in truth, an overly ambitious and disastrous mission so deep into an uncharted wilderness of Quebec, although the primary tactical objective had been achieved. At Crown Point on September 12, 1759, Major General Jeffery Amherst had accepted Major Rogers's audacious plan of taking the war to the enemy as never before and emphasized the urgent need to raze this vital strategic position, which had never before been attacked by white soldiers. Amherst issued his official orders the following day, not long before Rogers and his men embarked upon their perilous journey just after sundown on September 13. And as noted, the raid on St. Francis can be viewed as a disaster because it failed to end Abenaki raids, and so many valuable Rangers were lost forever. Of course, Rogers was responsible for so many of these sacrificed men, who could not be readily replaced, and he experienced considerable guilt for having lost so many good soldiers, especially to starvation.

Even more contrary to popular perceptions, a large percentage of Rogers's attackers were not Rangers but Provincial troops and British soldiers, who had bravely stepped forward to volunteer to serve with the Rangers on the most dangerous mission of the French and Indian War. From the beginning, the raid's one-sided success was exaggerated in regard to eliminating the most fearsome enemy of the frontier settlements, especially the number of warriors ("at least 200," in Rogers's words), to bolster the morale of settlers and soldiers on both sides of the Atlantic. In truth, and according to the best primary sources, around 140 Abenaki people—mostly women, children, and the elderly—were killed, and very few of these were warriors: that it was a massacre of innocents has been the most overlooked and forgotten aspect of the attack on St. Francis.

Of course, Rogers's estimated number of two hundred enemy warriors killed was a gross exaggeration that appeared in his often inaccurate and self-serving *Journals*. Instead, as noted, the vast majority of victims were innocent noncombatants; the war parties were elsewhere, including having recently played a part in Quebec's defense when the city was under great threat from Major General James Wolfe. Again, there was no conventional fight or even legitimate battle, especially an epic one, as long portrayed, for possession of St. Francis, because the town was defenseless when the surprise attack came in the early morning light of early October. All evidence has revealed that the attack on St. Francis resulted in a massacre—not the traditional epic battle—on a bloody scale not previously committed by soldiers of the British-Provincial Army, thanks to the orders of not only Amherst but also Rogers. Quite simply, Rogers's men did what they had been ordered to do, resulting in the bloody reckoning at St. Francis.

The alleged destruction of the town's sizeable manpower base in a legitimate battle became a prominent part of the romantic legend and myth about the raid that has long endured: a gross distortion of the historical facts based mostly on a morality tale of good vanquishing evil in what was basically a feel-good story created for propaganda purposes in 1759. Most Abenaki warriors of St. Francis were either out hunting or assigned to French forces elsewhere, including Quebec's defense. Not even Joseph-Louis Gill, the white chief (the son of two captives from the settlements) of the Abenaki village located on the placid river, was present at the time, ensuring that no leadership galvanized any kind of resistance in the defense of St. Francis—the most commonly overlooked aspect of the famous attack on St. Francis.

In the end, consequently, what happened at St. Francis was the antithesis of the lengthy epic battle between attackers and warriors depicted in the romantic legend of white fighting men triumphing over a large number of Abenaki warriors in a moral showdown in which good vanquished evil as in an epic moral clash from the pages of the Old Testament. Quite simply, the myth of a glorious battle and great victory, long celebrated by generations of white America, replaced the ugly truth and unpleasant reality of a massacre of mostly noncombatants. In consequence, a good many complexities, contradictions, and fundamental truths about the most famous raid of the French and Indian War have remained hidden, lost, or forgotten to this day: the genesis for the writing of this current book.

From the beginning of America's settlement of the English colonies along the fringe of the Atlantic coast in the seventeenth century, threatened on every side by the French and their large numbers of Indian allies, the historic fear had long existed that white (English and Anglo-Celtic) civilization would be overwhelmed by a tide of dark-skinned native inhabitants—or the so-called barbarians as the ancient Greeks had long called the Persians and other non-Greeks—in a racial apocalypse: the most horrific and ultimate New World nightmare in the minds of generations of white settlers that recalled for some history-minded colonists the tragic fall of ancient Rome to the hordes of barbarians who had swept down from the north.

In one sense, Major Rogers's raid on St. Francis has served as a biblical racial narrative and morality tale to reveal how white soldiers, with God's help and a good deal of courage, ultimately triumphed over darker-hued Native American warriors, thereby countering this longtime historic fear, if not obsession, among whites of their potential defeat and annihilation when three races—white, black, and red—collided in a bloody racial showdown.

After all, if America's enemies prevailed during the French and Indian War, then what transpired would be not only a religious (Catholic) success but also a racial and cultural victory for the enemy, who would then dominate North America.

Perhaps the ultimate tragedy was the fact that the Indians and white settlers, especially the lowly Scotch-Irish, who mostly inhabited frontier regions, fought and died as mere hapless pawns in the vicious struggle for the possession of the North American continent, serving the imperial ambitions and interests of aristocratic, upper-class elites of the major European powers. But a host of immediate concerns and fears, including racial, of the average frontier colonist of little means obscured these larger strategic realities of a global conflict that separated lower class from upper class.

Therefore, in the end, the colonists' solution to possible extermination by a dark-skinned people—the worst of all fates in overall psychological and emotional terms—called for extermination of their enemies, like the Abenaki, because it simply became a case of one or the other surviving the nightmare of the French and Indian War. What has been generally forgotten about the popular legend of Rogers's attack on St. Francis is the fact that it was also a morality tale with broad psychological and racial implications, which influenced generations of Americans.

Defeating the Abenaki was all about extinguishing long-existing racial anxieties and fears posed by Native American warrior societies that sought to destroy white yeomen farmer societies in a profound clash of not only races but also civilizations and cultures. As the New Englanders and Rogers viewed it, their struggle against New France and its Native American allies was also directed against the ultimate horror if they lost: New England and the rest of America eventually becoming French, darker in color from inter-mixing between whites and Indians, and Catholic, with an ancient feudal system instead of representative government dominating the land, which was viewed as the ultimate political, social, racial, and cultural apocalypse.

What has been most forgotten about the dramatic story of the attack on St. Francis was the fact that Rogers, unlike almost all officers of the day, was exceptionally egalitarian and enlightened to an inordinate degree when it came to the Rangers, both enlisted men and the officer corps, which was one generally overlooked factor that played a large role in explaining the raid's success against the odds. Therefore, the ranks of the Rangers included blacks (free and slave), mulattoes, and Native Americans, both full-blood and mixed race, who hailed from the Christianized Indian community of Stockbridge, Massachusetts. These lower-class minorities served and fought beside the primarily Scotch-Irish Rangers with distinction. As in the other English colonies, slavery was a legal institution in the colonies of New England and throughout the British Empire.

The longtime ignoring of the role of black Rangers—a silencing based on race that has long existed in history books—was unfortunate in regard to the overall historical record, because some of Rogers's finest fighting men, including in the St. Francis raid, were not whites but blacks and Native Americans, who also hated the Abenaki. Therefore, one focus of this current book has been to tell the forgotten story of these forgotten black Rangers as much as possible, despite the lack of documentation and information about them.

According to the traditional story of the raid, the Abenaki people of St. Francis and their rich, vibrant culture, which had existed for centuries— much longer than Europeans had been in America—were worthy of nothing more than systematic and cruel elimination in a righteous crusade by white soldiers vanquished the so-called children of the Devil. Conveniently overlooked was the historical fact that the Abenaki had been longtime victims of a relentless white expansion and exploitation that threatened their very existence, and in consequence their largely refugee community of St. Francis had long thrived along the banks of the St. Francis River by the time that Rogers launched his surprise attack.

In the process of generations of historians presenting a one-sided and romanticized version of events, Major Rogers became a sainted hero and idol for the American public, especially in New England. And, of course, heroes needed the evilest of foes to vanquish in the name of the moral right and the harsh delivering of a righteous form of justice—the sword of the Lord to the Holy Bible–reading settlers along the frontier—that justified not only cruelty but also massacre. And, of course, the Abenaki filled the requirement of the perfect villains in the most simplistic view of the raid on St. Francis, which suffered God's wrath according to the traditional white version of events. Like the Abenaki warriors, when at war and in the tradition of their revered ancestors according to the warrior ethos, Major Rogers and his men scalped their victims and dispatched wounded opponents, both Indian and French, with an undisguised zeal in the name of God and country, revealing a white barbaric and dehumanizing side that was no less savage than that of Abenaki warriors. In many ways, experienced Rangers became even more savage than the so-called savages during this most vicious of wars, including at St. Francis on that bloody autumn day in Quebec.

This current book has incorporated more honest viewpoints of the Abenaki people, including those that have come from the words and views of captured whites, who viewed the Abenaki in an entirely different light. A number of new views and fresh perspectives have also been presented in this book in regard to the Rangers, the St. Francis raid, blacks in New England, the complex racial dimensions of the conflict, and the Abenaki people in general to restore a much-needed fairer perspective and balance to counter the harsh Eurocentric viewpoints—including that the Abenaki were basically little more than animals only worthy of extermination—of the self-serving winners, who have so often distorted history for their own benefit.

As mentioned, the daring raid on St. Francis was excessively brutal to the point of genocidal. To Rogers's credit and to be fair, he was under direct orders of his English superior, Major General Jeffery Amherst, who in his official orders directed Rogers to "take your revenge." As noted, the majority of Rogers's victims at St. Francis were women and children in a massacre of innocents. Quite simply, Major Rogers had brought hell itself to St. Francis, and he and his men delighted in their own Dante's Inferno in wreaking a righteous vengeance.

Indeed, what happened at St. Francis on the morning of October 4 was an extremely dark event that has been unworthy of its lofty celebration and widespread memorialization, as has been so enthusiastically emphasized for more than 250 years. Clearly, in the dramatic story of the slashing raid on St. Francis, the differences between motivations (high-minded and commend-able) and results (slaughter of innocents and an outright massacre) must be considered separately today with the advantage of hindsight. However, contrary to common stereotypes, the destruction of St. Francis was part of a war that was as much religious as it was racial within the overall context of a larger international conflict—the first global war that stretched as far away as India. On that bloody morning in the first week of October, the darkest of motivations of Rogers and his men only reached new heights at the sight of the hundreds of scalps, including small ones bearing the hair of children and even infants, hanging from the tops of poles above the dwellings of St.

Francis in the early morning light: a grisly sight that fueled their resolve to kill without mercy, as ordered by the major.

All in all, Major Rogers was an extremely complex figure and a striking contradiction in many ways. Derived from his frontier and combat experiences, because he was literally a child of the Massachusetts and then New Hampshire wilderness and without a formal education (military or civilian), he left an enduring written legacy. As noted, Rogers wrote America's first manual of twenty-eight golden rules for the successful conducting of irregular warfare (guerrilla or Indian warfare) ever created in the New World, which greatly deviated from the standard practices of European warfare: a case of breaking with the past and tradition to formulate something entirely new in the art of warfare by combining the best of European tactics with the best Native American tactics, and Scottish and Irish border tactics to a lesser degree, to create a wise guide about conducting unorthodox warfare, while containing tactical and innovative truths about how to best succeed in the art of asymmetrical war fighting in a hostile environment of unmapped woodlands when far from support. Significantly, these rules of successful warfighting still apply today, especially in regard to America's Special Operations Forces, who fight for America around the world.

Most important, Rogers had been most responsible for the creation of a new type of warfare in America based on the stern realities of a small, independent command battling in the wilderness during all seasons of the year. In the end, even the conquest of St. Francis—the high point of Rogers's career—was forgotten on both sides of the Atlantic after the American Revolution. However, the irrepressible Rogers, who accomplished his most unexpected and unimaginable military achievements in the art of "ranging" war when the challenges were the greatest, is not forgotten today.

Today, the young men of America's elite Special Operations Forces have continued to bravely serve around the globe, in the name of making America and the world a safer place, never forgetting their true father from long ago. In a classic case of history having come full circle, this reality is most symbolic and appropriate because Major Rogers had helped to make America safe during its darkest days during a brutal war of survival, when everything had hung in the balance. Rogers was once hated far and wide as Wabo Madahando (White Devil), a name bestowed by the Abenaki in what was actually the ultimate compliment for having struck fear into the hearts of so many of America's enemies.

Significantly, this current book is also the story of the rise of the lower-class Scotch-Irish of the frontier, especially the Rangers, and their significant contributions in the making of early America. Most important, the majority of the Rangers at St. Francis were Scotch-Irish. By complete coincidence, ironically, this book was mostly written during the 260th anniversary—a historic event that was ignored and forgotten in both the United States and England—of Rogers's daring raid on St. Francis, when he demonstrated to the world what mostly American soldiers, long ridiculed by the British (especially the officers) as nothing but contemptible "Yankee Doodles," could accomplish against the odds.

Like Rogers himself, the raid on St. Francis became legendary in its own time, when it was covered extensively by many colonial newspapers (fully utilized in this book) in major urban centers like Boston and New York City and in other small cities across the colonies. Even after more than 260 years, Rogers's raid on St. Francis is nothing less than an American odyssey with as much courage, pathos, and drama as seen in the idealized tales of the ancient Greeks of legend, including Homer's immortal story (*The Iliad*) of the Trojan War. But unlike the ancient folklore of the Greeks from centuries ago, the ample primary evidence—diaries, memoirs, journals, letters, and colonial newspaper accounts—has revealed that Rogers's raid on St. Francis was one of the most remarkable chapters in American military history. Most of all, it is now time to take a new and fresh look at Rogers and his Rangers and the raid on St. Francis in the making of early America for the twenty-first century.

To bestow greater balance and fairness on the traditional narrative, I have also focused on telling the other side of the story, as much as possible, from the Indian, French, and Canadian perspective. Therefore, I have also included the wartime journal of the Marquis de Montcalm's brilliant aide-de-camp, Captain Louis Antoine de Bougainville, as well as the memoirs of Captain Pierre Pouchet and an account by a French common soldier named Charles "Jolicoeur" (a fond nickname meaning "sweetheart," bestowed upon the young man by the ladies of Quebec) Bonin, all of whom were born in France. In addition, Native American voices and views have been included in this work. It is my view that the voices of the other side need to be heard for an overall better understanding of not only the war but also the unforgettable story of Rogers's Rangers.

But this winner-take-all struggle for North America was much more than a fight over the possession of the land and even the clash of religions and civilizations. Most of all, this conflict was very much like a war against terrorism—America's first struggle against the day's greatest terrorist threat. Generations of settlers along the northern frontier lived in absolute fear of war parties of New England's Native American enemies suddenly emerging from the dark forests or out of the night to lay waste and kill all inhabitants in sight, including women and children, except those relatively fortunate ones whom the raiders decided to take back to Canada as captives to ransom to reap a sizeable cash reward. No European, not even during the religious wars that had long devastated Europe, had previously faced such a deadly and brutal foe as the warriors who ravaged the frontier year after year.

Warriors like the Abenaki brought hell on earth to the frontier settlers for generations, and no amount of prayers or resistance could stop them from unleashing an unprecedented destruction on the settlements for the better part of a century. Becoming saviors of the hard-hit frontier, Rogers and his men struck back in the same brutal manner after they had evolved into the most lethal fighting men of the British army in North America. The dramatic story of Rogers and his devastating raid on St. Francis was truly an American saga, and it is still an important one today in multiple ways, partly because he was truly a founding father—not in a political sense—of the American military tradition at the very beginning and at one of the most troubled times in American history.

Rogers was destined to command seventeen Ranger companies, which consisted of an entire corps, at different times during the French and Indian War, not as America's first Ranger captain (there were other Ranger captains in New England before Rogers) but certainly as the most famous one in the annals of American history. Rogers had become the undisputed master of what the French called *la petite guerre* (little war), which reached its highest form with Rogers, who firmly believed that he and his men could accomplish anything, especially those military feats that seemed impossible to almost everyone else, especially the enemy.

To reap dramatic victories, Rogers waged a kind of war that was absolutely ruthless, vicious, and brutal—to match that of his opponents—to a degree unseen on such a wide scale in America's wars. And in such a nightmarish conflict that was Darwinian, there was no glory, like in America's other wars, except an extremely grim one in relative terms. Indeed, none of America's wars—past or present—were either uglier or more inglorious than the struggle of Rogers and his Rangers year after year, when one mistake might result in the command's annihilation. It was a brutal conflict defined and dominated to an inordinate degree by the most nightmarish elements of human warfare: mercilessness on both sides, rife with beheadings, mutilations of the living and dead, scalping for bounty money (including by the Rangers), disembowelments, and killing without thought or remorse on a scale not previously seen in America. There was no question that Rogers and his Rangers were hardened professional killers who dispatched their victims with businesslike efficiency and ease in a true holy war.

When Rogers gave orders to kill French, Indian, or Canadian prisoners about to be liberated by their countrymen and to ensure escape, the captives were systematically murdered and scalped by the Rangers. And of all conflicts, racial wars—Native Americans against whites and vice versa—have always guaranteed the most hideous of war crimes and atrocities, which were played out in full throughout the course of the French and Indian War. Quite simply, this was America's evilest conflict at a time when dark hearts dominated the motivations and actions of both sides in a true Darwinian war of survival of the fittest, in which Rogers, who represented a moral force of good to tens of thousands of Americans, especially the Scotch-Irish on the frontier, across the colonies, and his Rangers rose to the fore like no other American fighting force: ironically, an apocalyptic struggle for possession of the North American continent was played out in full.

In the end, Rogers symbolized the essence of the early American experience in all of its unique forms. Most of all, he personified something entirely new and special: the rise of a new man and the American spirit fueled by the unprecedented possibilities for the conquest of the vast North American continent, which was the key to America's future greatness. Even before the official shaping of the nation by the American Revolutionary generation and experience, the saga of Rogers and his crack Rangers, America's premier wilderness fighting men, was also very much the story of the rise of early America. These men came to represent the core of the American frontier experience and America's core meanings and very essence, including a heightened sense of independence, resourcefulness, and self-sufficiency, rooted in the Darwinian struggle of survival of the fittest during the bitter contest to gain possession of a truly majestic land that was as boundless as it was beautiful.

New France's eventual defeat in 1763 was also the defeat of its Native American allies, setting the stage for their eventual collapse in the face of the relentless tide of western expansion, when the numbers of white settlers and soldiers were too great to stop and never ceased coming in the future: a case of literally opening the floodgates for large numbers of land-hungry settlers across the Appalachians and into the Ohio and Mississippi River Valleys with the rise of America's first sense of Manifest Destiny, after the decisive French defeat.

There has long existed not only a mythical Major Rogers but also a mythical story of the raid on St. Francis steeped in seemingly endless layers of romance, because both the man and the most hated place in Quebec have become enduring legends surrounded by fables and myths to this day. Therefore, by the use of as many first-person and contemporary accounts as possible, I have sought to separate facts from fiction, while presenting the historical Rogers and his Rangers in the most accurate manner possible. Consequently, reliance on contemporary accounts, especially from colonial newspapers, including previously unpublished ones, from both sides, especially about the devasting raid of St. Francis, has made this the true story of an incomparable American saga of Major Robert Rogers and his Rangers.

The popularity of the romanticized story of the famous raid has silenced historical facts, including those pertaining to New England slavery; to reliable black Rangers like Private "Duke" Jacob of New York, Private Boston Burn of Massachusetts, and other forgotten black Rangers; and to the key contributions of Captain John Stark. Therefore, in a corrective analysis and in telling the forgotten story of black Rangers as much as possible, this current book will place a much-deserved emphasis on the remarkable Captain John Stark, who truly deserves recognition very close to that of Rogers himself. Rogers's fame has grown partly because the key roles and contributions of Stark and other top lieutenants have been consistently kept in the dark shadows by not only novelists but also historians since 1759. Symbolically, Stark and Rogers—who had been more like brothers than close friends since the more innocent, carefree days of their youth in the Merrimack River country—were the heart and soul of Rogers's Rangers from beginning to end. Unlike most books about Rogers's Rangers and the raid on St. Francis, this one will give credit where it is due and finally place the remarkable Captain Stark, who was Rogers's top lieutenant for years, in a proper historical perspective for the first time in a work focused on Rogers and his most famous raid.

In regard to the evolution of tactics, a thorough revolution in thought had taken place because of the advent of Rogers's novel mode of warfare, which not only matched but also often prevailed over that of the tough irregulars of New France, including some of the fiercest Native American warriors. Rogers proved to one and all that the best way to thwart the original masters of irregular-style, or Indian warrior, warfare in the untamed wilderness was basically not only to utilize their own tactics and strategies but also to take them to an even higher level: the winning formula over a savvy opponent long considered invincible because Rogers and his men fought more Indian-like than the Indians.

Of course, conventional European warfare and powerful British-Provincial armies were still key to capturing Quebec and Montreal to defeat New France, but it was the evolution in the art of Indian warfare as perfected by Rogers that ultimately allowed for conventional warfare, such a sieges and battle tactics, combined with the Ranger Corps to prevail in the end. Indeed, it was Rogers and his unique brand of wilderness warfare that paved the way and allowed for the conventional tactics of the British war machine, including the use of light troops modeled after the Rangers, to achieve decisive results and succeed in a long-overlooked symbiotic relationship that eventually led to the fall of Montreal and Quebec and the winning of the war during the great imperial showdown over possession of North America. In overall terms, the Rogers revolution in tactical thought helped to transform the British army, especially the novel concept of light troops and the employment of large numbers of Rangers, to adapt to the new realities of warfare in North America. Quite simply, the key to decisive success lay in waging war in the manner perfected by Rogers, who pointed and led the way for British generals and the British armies in the key transformation.

Rogers's story is also the story of the rise of colonial America, the decline of the Native American people, and the dramatic maturation of the American people, especially the Scotch-Irish from Ulster Province in north Ireland. This current book will present a "new look" perspective about Major Rogers, the Rangers, and the war itself. Therefore, the overall purpose of this book has been to present the fascinating story of St. Francis, Rogers's Rangers, and Native Americans in general in a fresh and more realistic perspective. During America's most unheroic and irreligious age in the third decade of the twenty-first century, now is certainly the right time to take a new look at America's first hero and the most audacious raid in American history.

A fresh and more honest look at Rogers and his men is long overdue at this time. Even Rogers has remained very much a mystery man to this day. Most misleading of all have been the stylized and romanticized portraits of Rogers created by his London publishers from their vivid imaginations to sell books to an eager public: more fantasy than fact, much like the myths about the raid on St. Francis. In this most popular image of Rogers, he appears more like a plump Quaker preacher than the most dynamic and boldest American leader of the French and Indian War.

In much the same way, the man himself has been elevated into the realm of fantasy by his many admirers, seeming more an eighteenth-century superman than a real person with weaknesses and vulnerabilities as a commander, which sometimes cost the Rangers dearly in an exceptionally high number of lives lost. However, like those of his Rangers in general, Rogers's role and accomplishments shaped America in fundamental positive ways, including instilling a measure of newfound pride and confidence in the American people, who found their inspirational hero in Rogers during the darkest days of the struggle for survival.

In the end, Rogers himself became a casualty of one of the most brutal wars in American history, because the conflict's searing memories never left him, however. Understandably, he became hardened, cynical, and jaded, having been severely traumatized by the haunting visions and nightmares about a horrific war that never ended for him. In consequence, Rogers was also a victim of his own successes until his dying day in May 1795, having seemingly lost his soul in fighting a savage war with his heart and soul to defend his people. Therefore, Rogers left a big part of himself—especially the humble son of Scotch-Irish immigrants who had loved the pristine beauty and freshness of the northern wilderness like a good wife on a nice farmstead along a New England river on the frontier—in many bloody clashes in which he had shown no mercy, including at St. Francis. Like his enemy, Rogers scalped not only Native Americans but also Canadians and Regular French soldiers, killed prisoners who he feared might be recaptured, ordered that no mercy be shown at St. Francis, and even killed a Native American woman to provide food for himself and his starving men on the long, nightmarish march back from St. Francis.

Most of all, this book tells a distinctly and uniquely America story: that of the dramatic rise of the Americans as a dynamic new people in a new land, of the tragic fall of Native American peoples in part because of the role played by Rogers and his Rangers, who fought, looked, and thought more like Indians than the Indians themselves in America's most brutal conflict, and of the key developments that led to a new epoch in history in which representative government persevered over the ominous threat of the feudal system of New France.

Much like the dramatic rise of America in general, that of Rogers and the raid on St. Francis possessed both a brutal and a heroic side, representing a host of complexities, nuances, and paradoxes well beyond the simplistic and romantic stereotypes that have long existed. First and foremost, Rogers and his men were not racists in the traditional sense, as often alleged by today's modern dictates of political correctness and fashionable perspectives, because they primarily fought to defend homes, families, and the land they loved against a most serious Indian threat, when white Rangers served beside respected black, mulatto, and Indian Rangers, who were some of the finest fighting men in Rogers's command.

In the end, the British and Americans prevailed in 1763 to ensure the writing of the winner's history for generations to present an extremely one-sided view of this all-important struggle over the possession of North America. However, this book will present the full story (the good, the bad, and the ugly, including a massacre, the killing of large numbers of Abenaki women and children, cannibalism, no-quarter warfare, racism, genocide, the looting of St. Francis, including of a Catholic church, and much more) of this especially brutal chapter of American history in a proper historical context without the usual romantic myths and excessive glorification. Therefore, in exploring both the myths and the realities, this book has taken an extremely close look—the most detailed ever—at the full story of the famous raid on St. Francis and not just at the glorified story presented by the winner.

As much as possible and especially through the use of an abundance of colonial newspapers and in the words of surviving Rangers, I have sought to make Rogers and his world come alive to the modern reader to provide an honest and realistic portrait of this remarkable, but controversial, man of destiny, before the birth of the United States of America in the forge of a people's revolution. Of course, Rogers was neither a saint nor a "White Devil," as he was called by his enemies. In addition, this book has focused on the dramatic story of the forgotten common people, the Scotch-Irish and the other common folk, who tamed a frontier and created a nation out of the wilderness. Consequently, I have also presented the ordeal of the frontier's common people, both everyday black and white men and women, mostly of the lower class, who were without the benefit of privilege, education, wealth, or political connections, because they, like Rogers, played their part in rising to the stern challenge in the overall making of America.

With the winning of the French and Indian War in 1763, the American people and their British allies sealed the fate of Native Americans in what was part of a bitter struggle for possession of the land in a Darwinian-like conflict that had very little, if anything, to do with race, as has long been assumed: the antithesis of today's modern environment in which seemingly everything has been explained and analyzed in terms of the simplistic factor of race. Consequently, modern Americans need to rethink the true meaning of their early past by actually getting to know some of the first Americans, such as Rogers and his Rangers, who helped to pave the way for the birth of a new nation. Even more, these mostly lower-class men serve to remind modern Americans of the frightfully high cost of freedom in a truly dark time: one of the reasons for the writing of this book.

At the time, and like no other American previously or during the course of the French and Indian War, Rogers symbolized and personified the most breathtaking and egalitarian ideal of the bold promise of America—that any man, regardless of birth, class, education, or social status could rise up on his merits for a better life and even to make a profound change in his world, including on behalf of his people, the American people, during their most difficult and tortuous trial of all, when everything was at stake. In this way, Rogers and his men represented an entirely new kind of fighting man and hard-hitting elite combat unit not seen before—an American command, including blacks, Indians, Hispanics, Scots, Welsh, Irish, and other ethnic groups of the lower class, that embodied the spirit of the frontier, a representative democracy, and a nascent American nationalism that was on the rise.

Most of all, this book not only is about a true American odyssey and epic that resulted in a remarkable 350-mile round-trip journey 262 years ago to St. Francis but also will explore the exceedingly difficult and bloody process of the making of America in the forge of the greatest global war of the eighteenth century. And most important, the painful growth of a new people in a new land resulted in the creation of a nascent American nationalism from seemingly endless hardship and adversity, when the frontier world was an exceptionally dark and dangerous place.

This unforgiving and Darwinian frontier environment was the harsh world of Robert Rogers, who emerged on his own at the right time and place to protect his people and strike back at their longtime tormentors, who posed a most serious threat, while becoming a master of the art of wilderness warfighting to compile an unforgettable chapter in the annals of American history. Even more, this is the story of the unforgettable Ranger leader and his men, who played a distinctive role in the making of America during the bloody struggle to win America's first frontier.

Chapter One

America's First and Bloodiest Frontier

IN THE DECADES BEFORE THE AMERICAN REVOLUTION, THE THIRTEEN English colonies in North America were prosperous and thriving to fulfill the idealistic vision of the rise of a better world in a new land. However, it was only a matter of time before the lives of the English colonists were changed forever by the arbitrary decisions of the aristocratic leaders of the European powers and the eruption of a new global conflict and America's first major war, the Seven Years' War. This world war was destined to change the world.

As it was known in America, the French and Indian War (1754–1763) was the world's first global war and a life-and-death struggle of survival for the thirteen English colonies during the intense European rivalry between England and France for possession of the North American continent and the imperial right to determine America's fate. A long list of outstanding French successes had early piled up in astonishing fashion until large numbers of colonists asked if America was destined to be conquered by New France, the largest overseas colony of France, which seemed likely to be the case in the conflict's early years.

At this time, the power of New France, centered on the St. Lawrence River cities of Quebec and Montreal, both former fur-trading posts in the early days of settlement, had generated the all-consuming fear of total conquest that haunted the English colonists, especially those settlers located along the remote northern frontier that lay in the path of unrestricted French aggression.

As an experienced leadership in Quebec fully realized, the French had to be especially aggressive in this war because of their small numbers compared to the thirteen English colonies' 1.5 million people. However, the English colonies were surrounded to the north by Canada, to the west by the French-controlled Mississippi and Ohio Valleys and the Illinois country along the "Father of Waters," and in the south by Louisiana and all the way to the mouth of the Mississippi River. Therefore, with the French early winning the French and Indian War on all fronts, the survival of the English colonies along the Atlantic became very much in doubt. Not only the sprawling chain of the Appalachian Mountains but also the vast lands of New France had the English colonies hemmed in along the Atlantic coast. As late as 1720, the settlement of the colonies had been confined within one hundred miles of the Atlantic coast until a flood of Scotch-Irish immigrants from Ulster Province in north Ireland began pushing west and north onto Native American lands to create America's first frontiers in the wilderness.

Devastating raids led from deep inside Canada by Canadians, French soldiers, Native American warriors of the First Nations (Canadian tribes), and occasionally even zealous Catholic priests struck year after year to cause extensive devastation along the vulnerable frontier. These slashing raids were so bold and audacious that they came within sight of English centers of power, including America's largest cities of Philadelphia, Pennsylvania, and Boston, Massachusetts.

These hard-hitting French, Indian, and Canadian raids were so effective in spreading death and terror to the English settlements across hundreds of miles that the English feared they would be pushed into the sea. This brutal conflict was not only part of a global war but also a clash of civilizations, cultures, and religions, ensuring an exceptionally savage brand of warfare and heightened passions on both sides. At this time, English civilization, language, culture, and value systems were all under severe threat and lay on the verge of extinction, because the more experienced and better organized forces of New France—Native Americans, especially Abenaki warriors, Canadians, and the French—proved vastly superior to anything that the divided, bickering colonies, which were too independent and quarrelsome for their own good, could muster.[1]

A citizen of Easton, Pennsylvania, a town nestled in a picturesque valley surrounded by forested mountains where the blue waters of the Delaware and Lehigh Rivers intersected, described the dire situation in January 1756: "The Country all above this Town, for 50 Miles 'tis mostly evacuated and ruined [and] The people are chiefly fled into [New] Jersey. . . . The Enemy made but a few Prisoners, murdering almost all that fell into their Hands, of all Ages and both Sexes."[2] Indeed, this was a merciless conflict, especially on the remote frontier, that early "took on a tone of barbarism perhaps not witnessed in the Western world since antiquity."[3]

By the end of 1755, one Boston newspaper reported the undisputed ugly and dismal reality in overall strategic terms: "So the French have, on the whole, triumphed over us on the North American continent [and] Britain is a great loser by this Years Work."[4]

In many ways and for the most part, this vicious struggle for possession of the North American continent was actually a transplanted religious war like those that had ravaged Europe for centuries—another dramatic showdown between Protestantism and Catholicism that had long inflamed such intense passions, including seemingly endless atrocity and slaughter.

In the seventeenth century, for instance, there had been only seven years in which no war existed between European states divided primarily by religion, which had long fueled their holy wars. During this bloody period, which witnessed the mass devastation of the Thirty Years' War and included the Seven Years' War (known as the French and Indian War in America), the factor of religion was more decisive as a motivator than anything else in an extreme religious age in when the average person, of both sides, was not only far more religious than the average person today but also consumed by religious faith to a degree unimaginable to modern Americans.

A latecomer to the world's great religions since its rise in the sixteenth century in defiance of the ancient rituals and autocratic tendencies of Roman Catholicism, the Protestant faith allowed a greater freedom of worship to the individual. Protestantism formed the basis for the rise of a new sense of freedom among the English colonists, who believed that they were serving God's will in both war and peace in a true holy war. From the beginning, the colonists had strongly felt that they had found their biblical promised land and New Israel in the virgin lands of the New World. These hardy settlers, especially the Puritans of a dissenter faith, were convinced that God "directed the venture" in the New World. However, God's kingdom in this beautiful, seemingly limitless and pristine land was now threatened as never before by the advance of the aggressive Old World feudalism and Roman Catholicism of the French enemy, who seemed invincible like their Native American allies.[5]

For such reasons, a journalist of a New York City newspaper looked back on the course of history in an attempt to understand the dire situation that seemed to be dooming the English colonies to extinction, which he compared to when the "Huns, Goths, and Vandals, savage Banditti, not unlike our Indian, [had] over-run the vast [ancient] Roman Empire, and crumbled it to Pieces."[6]

THE OMNIPRESENT THREAT OF FRENCH "SLAVERY"

A sense of fear overwhelmed the often-defeated colonists, despite the British army's best efforts. On March 8, 1756, a New York newspaper editor emphasized what was at stake in no uncertain terms, because the downward spiral of English fortunes, from the beginning of the French and Indian War, was "drawing pretty near to a Crisis; and . . . the issue [was will Great Britain continue to] reign Master of North America."[7]

In April 1756, the crisis became especially severe on the frontiers around Philadelphia. It seemed that all Pennsylvania was under serious threat from New France's raiders, who waged war with "a macabre intensity." In the words of one alarmed journalist in a war-torn land whose frontier had early gone up in flames, "The Indians have returned in greater Numbers [and have driven] in all the Inhabitants on the Frontiers for fifty Miles [and now threaten] to advance within Twenty Miles of this Place, to commit their Depredations."[8]

In December 1756, a history-minded New England editor of a large colonial newspaper took a broad view of the timeless cycles of history and America's sinking fortunes, which now "resemble those of the [ancient] Romans, when by their Dissensions were on the Brink of Servitude [because] The Enemy are at our Gates [and] We are surrounded with a dark Cloud [because] the Enemy entering our Borders, laying waste to the Inhabitants . . . by Fire and Sword [and] upon every Side the Enemy are rushing in upon us."[9]

This grim assessment was no exaggeration about the overall dire situation because the devastation, which could not be stopped, was so extensive. One pragmatic colonist estimated that the Native American allies of New France "do us more harm" than ten times as many troops of a traditional European opponent.[10]

Inherited from the mother country, the militia tradition of the colonies proved totally inadequate in protecting the settlers across the frontier on every possible level. Also inherited from the mother country, the popular concept of citizen-soldiers successfully defending this vast land early proved a failure; American colonists were too individualistic and independent minded, largely because of the greater freedom of the New World, to be effective. These colonials proved no match for the professional warriors from Canada's forests in red and black war paint. One frustrated colonial official, Lieutenant Governor Cadwallader Colden, of the Colony of New York, explained the militia's deplorable state and shocking inefficiency to officials in London: "Our militia is under no kind of discipline [and] There is licentiousness, under the notion of liberty, [that] so generally prevails, that they are impatient under all kind of superiority and authority."[11]

After devastating French, Canadian, and Indian raids had ravaged the frontier all spring and summer of 1756, seeming to herald the doom of permanent English settlement, one distressed Pennsylvania concluded with a dark gloom, "The Affairs of the Province [of Pennsylvania] are now come to a Crisis. Our important Day very nearly at Hand, will decide the Fate of Pennsylvania's poor remains. Whether she shall any longer enjoy the inestimable Blessings of British Liberty, or become Subjects to the Yoke of arbitrary Power.... [H]ow little has been done to repel the inroads of Savage Barbarity, or frustrate the more pernicious Schemes our treacherous Enemies are now carrying into Execution against us," seriously threatening "an eternal Farewell to Religion, to Liberty, nay, to Life itself."[12]

In a New York newspaper in May 1757, one writer worried about the worst of all possible fates for America because the English colonists were threatened by conquest from "a Mongrel Race of French Papists and Indian Barbarians [and the New World French now] clank the Chain of Hereditary Slavery," which threatened "a Free Country" that had been established in North America, which was now the bone of contention between imperial powers.[13]

Royal governor of Massachusetts William Shirley, one of the most talented of the colonial governors in North America, lamented in the spring of 1754 how the "French seems to have advanced further toward making themselves masters of this continent within these last five or six years, than they have done ever since the first beginning of their settlements" in North America.[14]

But even more on target were the words that echoed among the politicians in the Council Chamber of the Colony of Massachusetts in late August 1757: "The War is no longer about Boundary, this or that Mountain, this or that River; but whether the French shall wrest from the British Hands the Power of Trade; whether they shall drive us out of this Continent; And this War is now brought to a Crisis that must determine the future and perhaps the final Fates of the British or French Government."[15]

Clearly, a great fear existed across the hard-pressed people of the colonies, England's most prosperous overseas possessions outside the sugar islands in the Caribbean, that end times were nearing. The writer of New York's popular *American Country Almanack* wrote gloomily in January 1758, "Slavery with Giant-like Strides seems to be approaching: Where is the British Lion? alas! I fear he's dead. . . . The Alternative seems left to us, whether we shall once more attempt to preserve our Liberty, or quietly submit to Ruin [because] The Crisis of our Fate is now. . . . In some old Almanacks [which] were printed in London just half a Century ago, there were several Accounts laudably told of the glorious victories won by the Duke of Marlborough, over the French [but now] the Tables seem to be turned."[16] Indeed, during the hysteria of the time, the real fear existed among the colonists that they were facing the threat of the imposition of French slavery, because conquest seemed all but inevitable.[17]

With the same sense of alarm that was destined to grow over time with additional British-Provincial defeats, the editor of the *London Chronicle* wrote in July 1757, "Our enemy has already over-run all North-America in a manner, and taken every Place that might be convenient for them to secure the whole; and to draw our Forces from thence in order to prevent us from recovering our Losses, or Making Head against them, they threaten us with Invasions at Home."[18]

This disastrous situation and the realization that the British and Provincials were losing the war caused a distressed colonial citizen to write with heartfelt pain and incredulous disbelief, "Our cruel and crafty Enemy the French are rushing on us from every Side, brandishing the Sword with Insolence [during] a Scandalous Inaction, while we see our Country ransack'd, Wives killed, innocent Children murder'd, and aged Parents Destroy'd. . . . Let us consider how dearly our Country concerns us, which if the Enemy get Possession of, yet save our Lives, we shall be doom'd to perpetual Slavery."[19]

The Native American raiders, including the Abenaki, were masters of the art of waging not only the most destructive possible warfare but also psychological warfare by way of a brutal form of terrorism. In fact, in regard to this highly effective band of psychological warfare, the warriors of the war parties that struck south without mercy were "probably the most adroit practitioners of the art that Europeans had encountered since their sixteenth century battles with the [Islamic] Turks in eastern Europe."[20]

Knowing the weaknesses of their opponents, Indian warriors focused on an especially gruesome kind of terror that even included the desecration of the private parts of victims, male and female, to the shock of Europeans. The severed sexual organs of white victims were cast across the ground, even flaunted in the faces of captured survivors, and strewn along the path of their bloody and destructive incursion to ensure the greatest amount of shock.[21]

In fact, such devastation and slaughter along the vulnerable frontier had taken place long before the French and Indian War during previous conflicts in a desperate effort of Native American tribes to halt the tide of white migration into Indian lands. And, as usual, it was the lower-class settlers of the northern frontier who suffered the most. At Lancaster, Massachusetts, on February 9, 1676, Reverend Joseph Rowlandson, his family, and neighbors watched from the man of God's garrison house while

> *the Indians pierce one garrison and drag five villagers from their compound [and engaged in] tomahawking a man, then a woman and a child. Helpless, the garrison [at the Rowlandson house] watched two children being dragged into the forest. Soon two other villagers were captured [and] One was quickly murdered [and] A moment later a man dashed for safety from an adjacent compound. . . . He was brought down by a single gunshot [and we] saw the wounded man plead for his life, but a moment later a native split his head with a hatchet. Other natives stripped off his clothing and mutilated his remains, holding his entrails aloft for the mortified residents to see.[22]*

But for the beleaguered English colonists, the ominous threat of an authoritarian feudal system—basically slavery in their minds since they lived under a representative government based on a sense of individualism and a freedom-loving Protestantism—imposed by the victors of New France's feudal society was an all-consuming fear with the winning of one sparkling French victory after another. It seemed to many colonists that end times were drawing near and that the English colonies were facing extinction.

One distraught Virginian summarized not only the extent of the danger but also the primary causes of one English defeat after another in what was a failed war effort on all fronts: "Much more discouraging and alarming than the united Power, Cruelty and Policy of our Savages and perfidious Enemies [was the reality that] the Fate of our Country [is now] approaching, and [if] this favourable Spot of the Globe, Land of Plenty and Liberty, shall become a conquered and enslaved Province of France [then] The tyranny, Perfidy and Cruelty of a Mongrel Race of French Papists and Indian Barbarians [will force the colonists to] clank the Chain of Hereditary Slavery."[23]

As emphasized in numerous colonial accounts in this splendid land of plenty that seemed about to be lost forever to such a superior opponent, the danger existed of the possible establishment of the Catholic Church in the thirteen English colonies, if vanquished, and the transformation of their inhabitants into Catholic subjects against their will: a replay of the historic fears that had been the genesis of seemingly endless religious wars over the centuries in Europe between Protestants and Catholics, especially in regard to Europe's ancient enemies, England and France.[24]

A Healthy Peculiar Institution in New England

It was truly ironic that so many English colonists feared enslavement by the French, while practicing their own slavery across the colonies from New England to the South. A close look at America's beginning during the 1600s in New England has shattered a host of romantic stereotypes and myths that have long existed because of the existence of a healthy institution of slavery across New England long before the French and Indian War. Because of the romanticized and idealized mythical story of the making of America and because generations of American historians have excessively focused on slavery in the South, slavery had been the most consistently absent subject in the history of early New England in a thorough silencing of historical truths. The 1861–1865 sectional conflict between North and South played a large part in the silencing of how slavery had been central in the early development and overall prosperity of New England from the beginning, because the North and its armies extinguished slavery in 1865. The year 1638 was the earliest documented appearance of the first shipment of African slaves to New England.

Slavery—first the enslavement of Indians and then of Africans, who were more lucrative and effective workers compared to captured Native Americans—was nothing less than the most overlooked factor that led to the dramatic growth, success, and overall prosperity of New England's leading families, mostly merchants at the Atlantic seaports. Slavery thrived across the allegedly stainless and sinless Puritan colonies, which had been founded on a new morality and a reformed Protestant Church in the New

World. From the beginning, New England's close links to the Atlantic slave trade served as a central foundation of the economy, fueling growth and development for generations.

Slavery and slave trading were deeply interwoven into the fabric of New England life—both in the economic sphere and in social and cultural terms—throughout the colonization process. New England possessed early economic ties not only to England's Caribbean colonies of Barbados and later Jamaica, after it was captured from Spain, but also to other sugar islands of the West Indies, fueling the lucrative slave trade. New England's early leading colonists, such as Cotton Mather and John Winthrop Jr., not only owned slaves but also sold fellow human beings for a nice profit, because slavery was big business.

Indeed, the success of even the Puritans, the most religious of America's early colonizers, who were obsessed with the concept of spiritual purity, can be partly explained by the economic benefits of slavery. Indeed, contrary to popular perceptions, New England possessed more slaves than the lucrative tobacco lands of the Chesapeake in Virginia and Maryland by the middle of the seventeenth century—a forgotten fact that has overturned traditional stereotypes about slavery and its early importance.[25]

The existence of a healthy, if not thriving, institution of slavery in seventeenth-century New England has not only led to one of the great paradoxes of the New England experience but also allowed for a new perspective about the French and Indian War at this time. Ironically, the English colonists were consumed with fear of the imposition of French slavery if they lost the war for possession of the North American continent, while the institution of black slavery existed in every colony as an unquestioned cultural and racial inheritance—the ugliest of all inheritances from the mother country at a time when the colonists took little, if any, notice of the striking moral contradictions, because a virgin land needed to be developed.[26]

For such reasons, especially the fact that New England slavery was most vibrant in eastern urban areas, especially the bustling Atlantic port cities, a European visitor to Boston in 1687 was astounded by the fact that "you may also own negroes and negresses [throughout New England and] there is not a house in Boston . . . that has not one or two" black slaves.[27]

Like the other twelve colonies, the Colony of Massachusetts possessed a bustling institution of slavery, and it was simply accepted as a fact of life throughout the breadth of the British Empire, especially in the rich Caribbean islands that fueled the British economy based on the lucrative commerce in slaves and sugar. New England's primary rivers, like the Connecticut and Merrimack, flowed to its thriving port cities, especially Boston, and then out to sea and to the Caribbean, serving as avenues for the slave trade. New England's crops and products, especially salted cod, were traded with the West Indies' planters, who used every acre to grow the day's most lucrative crop of all, sugarcane, instead of food to feed the ever-growing number of slaves.

To be fair to the colonists, slavery was absolutely necessary for the development of a fertile new land in part because black manpower and labor were needed for the time-consuming process of taming the wilderness and the frontier in a vast land of almost unimaginable promise. Therefore, the so-called Moorish slaves or blackmoors from Africa became the ultimate solution not only for development but also for prosperity across New England.

The grim legacies of slavery could be seen across New England at an early date. Just outside the busy port of Boston, an iron cage had stood since 1755 in the common of Charlestown, Massachusetts, to provide a grisly remainder that this was a land of slavery. Inside the iron cage, the decomposing body of a former slave named Mark hung from a gibbet to serve as warning to any slave who contemplated killing his master. Of course, it had not mattered that Mark's master, a grizzled sea captain who had long plied the Atlantic, had been a brutal man. Mark and his wife, Phyliss, had been so severely abused for years that they had no choice but to save themselves. The two slaves, consequently, finally took desperate action and poisoned the sadistic sea captain, earning Mark's death sentence from an angry white jury.[28]

Of course, most slaves received much less severe punishment because of their monetary value, but what many received was certainly harsh enough. For instance, Katherine, a female slave in the port town of Salem, Massachusetts, was sentenced to a public whipping for having a child out of wedlock, a common punishment for sexual indiscretions among slaves, reflecting white concepts of morality based more on theological dogma than any hint of humanism.[29]

Ironically, John Winthrop's Puritan vision of a bright and shining "City on a Hill" had not only been corrupted but also become a hell on earth for captive Native Americans, who were sold into slavery in the West Indies, with Africans imported to replace them. Winthrop's idealistic dream had been cynically financed by the New England colonists' warm embrace of slavery that served as a sturdy foundation of that righteous hill upon which the Puritans' holy mission rested from the beginning.

Influential Puritans, including Winthrop's associates, even believed that it was God's holy design to vanquish Native Americans for the express purpose of "deliver[ing them] into our hands" for trading them to the Caribbean's sugar islands in return for black slaves. After all, black slaves were cheaper (an estimated twenty times) than white English indentured servants. For such reasons, the Pequot War (1636–1638) led to mass enslavement of Native Americans by New Englanders to fuel the lucrative slave trade with the full approval and support of the colonial legislatures and community leaders, who sat in the front rows of their churches every Sunday morning.

Partly because even the Holy Bible confirmed the belief in the wisdom of lifelong servitude, which was then echoed by the words of Puritan ministers, the lucrative institution of slavery, based on exporting captive Indians for sale to the West Indies to rid New England of its longest-existing internal threat and importing Africans, who were viewed as less threatening, by way of the Atlantic slave trade, was a key factor that led to the astounding success of the idealistic "City on a Hill."[30]

Winthrop, the most respected religious leader in Massachusetts, revealed his hypocrisy, which made a mockery of his righteous concept of a golden "City on a Hill," when he described in 1638 how the ship *Desire*, which sailed out of the port of Salem north of Boston, had taken Indian slaves to be sold in the Caribbean and returned with "some cotton and tobacco, and negroes, etc."[31] Winthrop had recorded the first documented case of African slaves arriving on the shores of New England: a thriving trade in untold misery that ensured the Massachusetts Colony's economic development and success.[32]

THE ENEMY'S MOST SUCCESSFUL TACTICAL FORMULA

As if they were fighting yet another one of the seemingly endless religious wars in Europe in the New World, success for the forces of New French in North America during the early years of the French and Indian War had been based on the effectiveness of a wise strategy of relying on the best tactics of European traditional warfare, combined with the best tactics of New

France's Native American allies: an unbeatable and lethal combination that delivered a hard-hitting one-two punch for which the British and Provincials had no defense or answer.

The secret to the remarkable success of the French in utilizing the numerous tribes of their lethal Native American allies to reap maximum benefits was based upon the wise policy—the antithesis of historic English treatment of Native Americans in general—of treating them with respect and allowing them to fight their own kind of war without attempting to dictate rules and strategy and without displaying the traditional European arrogance and xenophobia that had long dominated English dealings with Indians. Therefore, savvy French and Canadian leaders smartly allowed their Indian allies to wage war on their own terms and as their ancestors had done for centuries. This wise strategy paid immense dividends when the Native American warriors were supplied with French muskets and black powder from the forts that guarded New France, especially Fort Saint Frédéric and Fort Carillon, which dominated the Lake Champlain Valley, and war parties were augmented with French marines, including experienced officers, and Canadian frontiersmen, who fought in a masterful fashion like Indians.[33]

As fate would have it, there was only one solution to stem this crisis, and that called for a radical transformation of the traditional English way of fighting that had proved so disastrous in defending the land and its people. One high-ranking professional soldier who had been born in Scotland, British brigadier general John Forbes, correctly understand what was needed, which explained the eventual rise and success of young Robert Rogers and his Rangers: "Wee [sic] must comply and learn the Art of Warr [sic], from the Enemy Indians or anything else."[34]

Largely because of the inherent deficiencies of the inadequate militia system, inherited from England, that relied on untrained citizen-soldiers, the American fighting man was thoroughly mocked and looked upon as little more than a joke by both the French and the British. Quite simply, there was no central authority for an organized and coordinated offensive effort between the separate colonies when it was most needed. But the fallacy of the popular militia concept of part-time citizen-soldiers—untrained and nonprofessional—had proved ineffective, almost to the point of uselessness, while the French primarily relied on experienced professional soldiers, the

French Regulars, Canadian frontiersmen, and the consummate warriors of their Native American allies.

Clearly, the average American, or colonial, fighting man on the frontier—the individual citizen-soldier who relied on his own abilities instead of his government, colonial or British—had to quickly adapt and catch up to the enemy's superior combat capabilities by evolving, mostly, from a yeoman farmer to a legitimate fighting man to match the magnificent fighting machine, although an irregular one, of the Canadians, Indians, and French. Otherwise the prosperous English civilization in the thirteen colonies thriving along the Atlantic coast and farther inland might well become extinct. However, this evolution toward parity with an aggressive and resourceful enemy would be a long and painful transition that successfully reached its highest point with the rise of a new concept in warfare: the tough and resourceful fighting men of the ranging companies, or Rangers, led by a young man named Robert Rogers.

Indeed, in time and after having long been at the mercy of their enemies from Canada, the colonists, before Rogers's and the Rangers' dramatic rise, eventually evolved and learned to fight in the seemingly endless forests and in the highly effective manner of their opponents, especially Native Americans, who had long relied on the deadly art of ambush, stealth, and hit-and-run raids to vanquish the enemies of their own race centuries before the arrival of the first Europeans. This all-important successful adaptation to the warfighting ways of America's more experienced and most lethal and ruthless enemies was most thoroughly achieved by Rogers on a permanent basis during the French and Indian War.

Learning to excel at Indian ways of warfare like no other fighting man on the British side, Rogers was a product of an exceptionally harsh, unforgiving environment of the untamed northern frontier and of one of the most vicious conflicts in American history. Especially on the remote frontier, this was a time when life was exceptionally cheap and short for many settlers of the New England colonies, which occupied a precarious perch when boxed in by the Atlantic Ocean to the east and the Appalachian Mountains to the west. But these searing wilderness and wartime experiences of settlers across the frontier were a fiery forge that molded Rogers into one of the most distinguished leaders of fighting men in America not only during the French and Indian War but also in American history.

Most important, Rogers's men had early evolved into masters of the ranging service. They believed in him and would follow Rogers to hell and back if necessary. A resourceful and innovative leader with a charismatic personality, Rogers led the way into a seemingly endless number of unprecedented challenges and dangers to inspire his men to do the impossible. This vicious fight for the possession of the continent to determine the future of the English colonies was no ordinary struggle: it was the most devastating of all global contests that had spilled into the New World. For the colonists, the French and Indian War (1754–1763) was a living nightmare straight out of the Dark Ages and the old religious wars of Europe, which was distinguished by a destructiveness that was Darwinian in its excesses. No chapter of American history was darker and bloodier than the bitter struggle on America's northern frontier by the time that Rogers and his Rangers, mostly men from the Merrimack River country like their commander and other northern frontier regions, took center stage in this brutal contest for the heart and soul of America.

UGLY RACIAL CONFLICT: THE DARKEST SIDE OF HUMAN NATURE

The so-called better angels of our nature were almost entirely absent from the war-ravaged northern frontier during the French and Indian War, because the conflict was starkly Darwinian and all about survival of the fittest. The darkest side of man and the evil that lay deep in dark hearts triumphed at unprecedented levels during the life-and-death struggle of each side to develop the best strategy and tactics to vanquish the enemy in what was basically a race upon which life and death depended. The birth of Rogers's Rangers in 1755 as the best company of a New Hampshire regiment, under Colonel Joseph Blanchard, evolved out of this evolutionary race to outfight the enemy before it was too late.

Ironically, Robert Rogers's dangerous northern frontier of New England was the by-product of the most idealistic and enlightened intentions because the original English colonists had believed that God had bestowed upon them the righteous mission of settling in the New World. Having broken away from the main Church of England, or the Anglican Church, deeming it too much like the Roman Catholic Church, the Puritans—Pilgrims—were die-hard dissenters who had gone their own way.

Ironically, however, the pious newcomers from the Old World threatened to plunge the vibrant Algonquian world, culture, and language, which was dominant among Native American tribes in the East, into the same kind of darkness that they had left behind in Europe. The ravages of disease, fire, and sword and the profound changes they brought threatened to forever change the Native Americans' traditional way of life. Even more, the idealistic newcomers believed that they had the God-given right to possess this bountiful land, setting the stage for America's longest war against indigenous people, destined to last nearly to the twentieth century.

In 1629, in the stark biblical terms of the Old Testament, John Winthrop, who was a primary leader of Boston's strict Puritan theocracy of the Massachusetts Bay Colony, asked the key question that was answered by the theft of large amounts of choice Native American lands by swarms of land-hungry squatters, mostly poor settlers, who simply carved their own homes out of the wilderness: "Why may not Christians have [the] liberty to go and dwell amongst them in their waste [undeveloped] lands and woods . . . as lawfully as Abraham did among the Sodomites?"[35] Indeed, English preachers of what they believed was the only true faith had long emphasized to settlers the biblical words that had long inspired the chosen people of the Hebrew faith: "I will appoint a place for my people Israell [sic]."[36]

The morally intoxicated Winthrop early labeled Native American people as Sodomites. Even more, he emphasized Christian-versus-non-Christian dynamics to partly justify the sale of captured Native Americans to the hellish sugarcane plantations of the West Indies for profit rather than for purely racial reasons because the obsession with skin color only arose later in America. Meanwhile, the Native Americans saw themselves as "the real people," whom their God had allowed to dominate this virgin land of incomparable beauty. Immensely proud and largely correct in their analysis of their special place in the world, the Algonquian people considered themselves culturally and morally superior to the new settlers, who had invaded their lands with impunity, as if the Indians simply did not exist.

Unlike in Europe, both sides embraced a war of terrorism—a conflict that was modern in the sense that it was total because it was waged with a "macabre intensity" not seen on other side of the Atlantic. In the most forgotten chapter of this bloody war more than a century before the French and Indian War, many Pequot captives were sent to the English Caribbean colony of Barbados in the lucrative Atlantic slave trade: the systemic process of ridding New England of Native Americans and replacing captured Indians with black slaves. In September 1638, a treaty signed at Hartford, Connecticut, officially ended the once proud existence of the Pequot tribe, which had long ruled their ancestral homeland without rivals in southern New England. Incredibly and in short order, the Pequot had gone out of existence, like the fading away of a summertime dream. Finally, the last Pequot people were sold as slaves to the rich sugar islands of the British West Indies, including Jamaica, after their crushing defeat in the Pequot War to complete the process of a thorough ethnic cleansing.

During King George's War (1744–1748), the Abenaki continued to raid the English settlements along the vulnerable northern frontier, including strikes on Saratoga, New York, and communities near Boston on the East Coast. All the while, the colonists remained on the defensive instead of organizing their own strikes into Canada during a series of wars: Queen Anne's War, known in Europe as the War of Spanish Succession (1702–1713); the War of the Austrian Succession, or King George's War (1744–1748); and the Seven Years' War, or the French and Indian War (1754–1763). Except for the French and Indian War, these wars began in Europe and then spilled over to North America like a spreading cancer.

Therefore, out of the carnage and ethnic cleansing of multiple wars in the wilderness, a bloody borderland had been created where vastly different civilizations, races, and cultures had long violently clashed. In consequence, the refugees of vanquished tribes, which were decimated by the ravages of disease, the curse of slavery, and the swords and bullets of the white man, had migrated north, including to St. Francis in Quebec, to escape the tide of land-hungry New Englanders. These imperial struggles for empire, which stemmed from the cynical manipulation of Europe's ruling class and ebb and flow of European imperial rivalries that had long existed between royalty, the elites, and the wealthy upper classes of Paris and London, claimed untold lives on both sides for generations.

In consequence, a good many poor settlers of the lower class and equally poor Native Americans were destined to die in an especially vicious struggle that continued to rage for generations during bloody wars for empire between England and France with a degree of barbarism not seen since the days of antiquity. Many frontier settlers had seen captives butchered before their eyes, chopped up with tomahawks, and severed heads and entrails held aloft by triumphant warriors to terrify other whites. No small wonder that the settlers early viewed these fierce warriors, who were far superior fighting men than the English, as "Children of the Devil." In the process, dark skin color became increasingly identified with evil in what might be described as the birth of racism on American soil.

Like most of his neighbors, after having learned the ways of the Native Americans, Robert Rogers was fated for the life of a soldier and a special destiny. Setting aside the wooden plow in the fields of the Upper Merrimack River country of New Hampshire, and with it his existence as a lowly Scotch-Irish yeoman farmer without expectations, he embarked on his military career (first militia, then Rangers of his own creation), having acquired an abundance of knowledge about the deep forests of the untamed frontier of the Merrimack River country and about Indians and their warfighting ways that had long proved so successful: the very antithesis of European ways of waging war.

Rogers had been born in "this bonny Country" of beauty and plenty on November 7, 1731, in the small frontier settlement of Methuen, in northeastern Massachusetts. Amid a pristine wilderness, Rogers enjoyed his most carefree years in the location around the family log cabin, which was situated just beyond the northwestern outskirts of the small farming town on a grassy knoll within sight of the blue waters of the Spicket River. Robert was the fourth son of his loving parents, who spoke with the distinct Irish brogues of the north of Ireland, James Jacob Rogers and Mary McFatridge Rogers. Mary gave Robert six brothers and four sisters in total. Symbolically, amid the rich, black soil and virgin timber in the Upper Merrimack River Valley, Robert was the first member of the family born on America soil. The frontier was dominated by the lower-class Scotch-Irish, and the Rogers family, with its Ulster roots, made an ideal fit with these natural frontier settlers.

Like other Scotch-Irish settlers who dominated the northern frontier, the Rogers family worshiped as faithful Presbyterians. This fiery faith was far more individualistic and democratic than that of the Anglican Church (the official church of England) in the village of Methuen. Here, Robert first learned the spiritual teachings of the Holy Bible from his parents and began to read in the privacy of the family cabin located on the western outskirts of Methuen. Robert also learned about the cultural and folk ways of north Ireland from his Ireland-born parents and perhaps longed to see the native homeland so far away.

Incorporated into a town in 1725 and located on the north bank of the east-west flowing Merrimack River before it turned north to follow a north-south course toward the higher ranges of blue-hazed mountains, Methuen was largely a Congregationalist community of mostly British stock. Its Holy Bible–reading members viewed Scotch-Irish immigrants as not only outsiders but also foreigners. No evidence has been found that the Rogers family worshipped on a regular basis at the Congregationalist church that stood atop Meeting House Hill in Methuen. However, because the nearest Presbyterian church was located in Londonderry around seventeen miles to the northwest, Robert was baptized by a young Congregationalist minister, Reverend Christopher Sargent, on November 14, 1731—only seven days after his birth. He was the first member of the Rogers family, which was Scotch-Irish to the core, to have been baptized on American soil.

Then, after Robert's birth, two other children of Mary and James (including brother Richard, a future Ranger captain who was born on May 6, 1734) were baptized in the rustic church on Meeting House Hill. In total, Mary Rogers gave birth to five additional children on America soil. Therefore, from the beginning, Robert was an American, with a close family of two parents and four siblings who had been born in Ulster Province, north Ireland. Rising higher from hard work and a determination to make their American Dream come true, the members of the Rogers family were on their way to middle-class status, which allowed Robert and his siblings a better overall upbringing than would have been possible if this Scotch-Irish brood had been hampered by lower-class status, like most other immigrants from the old country. The Congregationalists, whose faith was closer to that of the Anglican Church than the more individualistic style of worship of Presbyterianism, had allowed a nearby squatters' community of Ulster immigrants to be established in a rough-hewn village of rustic log cabins located just beyond the town's western edge: a convenient mostly Scotch-Irish and lower-class buffer against the inevitable next Indian attack from the north.

The Scotch-Irish Rogers family found this place to their liking, the northern frontier community of Methuen, located in the northeast corner of the Massachusetts Bay Colony around thirty miles north of Boston and situated on the 117-mile-long Merrimack River that rose from springs that flowed east down the White Mountains and then ran south to eventually empty into the Atlantic near Boston. Far north from unfriendly Boston and its anti-Irish environment, the untamed frontier was a breath of fresh air—the sweet taste of far greater freedom than found in the coastal lowlands of the upper-class elites and wealthy merchants—to Scotch-Irish immigrants compared to the self-righteous Puritans, who were members of Boston's autocratic theocracy.

As for other Scotch-Irish immigrants of humble background after they had trekked north up the Merrimack River from Boston, this was a place where the Rogers family had secured their land as opportunistic squatters. Achieving middle-class status and leaving his Irish immigrant squatter status behind, James shortly bought forty-four acres on the Spicket River several miles from the northwestern edge of town. Here, he worked in clearing and improving the land. Most important, this enterprising Scotch-Irish immigrant family of former lowly tenant farmers, who had been victims of rich English landlords increasing rents and other abuses in Ulster Province, north Ireland, worked hard to make their dreams come true. Clearly, history had come full circle for the Rogers family of Irish exiles, who had become the victims of English colonialism, greed, and imperialism on the Atlantic's east side, which in part eventually rose to the fore to cause the French and Indian War on the west side to change the life of young Robert Rogers forever.

Greener Pastures

Then, in the spring of 1739, James and Mary Rogers, who were Presbyterian natives of County Antrim in Ulster Province and might have earlier migrated from the Emerald Isle's picturesque Sperrin Mountains region, made another move to the wide, open spaces to the northwest in the Upper Merrimack River Valley: more fertile and luxurious lands in one of the remotest areas of the frontier in south-central New Hampshire. This special place in the wilderness for the Rogers family was located around forty miles northwest of Methuen and west of the narrow band of mostly Scotch-Irish settlements situated along the wide Merrimack River. James and his friend Joseph Pudney made a good deal to purchase 365 acres apiece from Zacheus Lovewell of Dunstable. The head of the Rogers family obtained the deed for his property of virgin lands on November 24, 1738, after having paid the first installment to Lovewell.

The Rogers family pushed north until they finally stopped at a broad open space of grasslands surrounded by pristine forest: a magical place of promise that was distinguished by a beautiful meadow and beaver pond of clear water surrounded by rows of yellow birch trees in today's southeast New Hampshire. This broad meadowland of tall grasses beside a clear trout stream was bestowed by the new Scotch-Irish settlers with the name Mountalona because it reminded James and Mary Rogers of Ulster Province's beauty just southeast of Londonderry. Surrounded by forested hills of virgin timber, this beautiful place in the pristine wilderness was also called "Great Meadows." Members of the Rogers family never forgot north Ireland's beauty, especially the Sperrin Mountains in Tyrone and Londonderry Counties, where a green forest of birch trees, which thrived in cold weather, grew high in the relatively few extensive woodlands in this part of Ulster Province. By this time, most Native Americans, including the Abenaki who had concentrated in their St. Francis sanctuary in Quebec, had fled north, leaving this ancient hunting ground open to the most adventuresome squatters.[37]

Robert Rogers summarized the formation of New Hampshire from the Colony of Massachusetts in 1740, when pioneers "settled themselves to the north-east, between the rivers Merrimack and Kennebeck, and formed two distinct colonies, one named New Hampshire, and the other Maine."[38] Along with their fathers, the sons and daughters of the Rogers and Pudney families worked overtime—from sunrise to sundown—to transform a wilderness into productive farmland, while keeping an eye out for prowling Abenaki warriors, whose well-known taste for revenge knew no bounds.[39]

AN UNTAMED NORTHERN WILDERNESS

With his considerable insight into the natural world of the vast backcountry seen by few whites, which revealed Rogers's insatiable curiosity and love for the world of nature, especially when trekking alone during many of his sojourners north into the wilderness toward Canada when hunting and trapping, Rogers described the dominant physical characteristics of the Colony of New Hampshire:

> *The most considerable mountains of this province [New Hampshire], and indeed in New England, are those called the White Mountains, so called from their appearance, which is like snow, confiding, as is generally supposed, of a white*

flint, from which the reflection of the sun is very brilliant and dazzling, and
by their prodigious height are to be seen at a very great distance [and] I cannot
learn that any person was ever on the top of these mountains. I have been told by
the Indians that they have often attempted it in vain, by reason of the changes of
air they met with, which I am inclined to believe, having ascended them myself
till the alteration of air was very perceptible, and even then I had not advanced
half-way up; the valleys below were then concealed from me by clouds.[40]

Rogers also partly described the northern lands of the Abenaki: "The great part of it towards the province of Quebec being mountainous, is entirely unfit for agriculture; and that towards [the east] is low, covered with spruce, and white and yellow pines, and some oaks, excepting near the banks of rivers, which fall from the mountains [and into the rich lands to the south] would have been better improved, had not the inhabitants for many years past been kept in almost continual alarms, and sometimes driven from their plantations by the savages," especially the Abenaki.[41]

Having been early forced off their ancient homeland and hunting grounds had only made warriors, especially the Abenaki of St. Francis and other refugees from other areas and tribes, into the most bitter of enemies. Therefore, these revenge-seeking warriors from French Canada, especially the sanctuary of St. Francis, continued to trek down their well-trodden war trails, such as those along the Connecticut River, which snaked through the wilderness. They raided the northern frontier with complete impunity and caused a massive amount of death and destruction when least expected, especially among the mostly Scotch-Irish settlers who had carved out homes in the fertile Upper Merrimack River country.[42]

But this extremely harsh war unleashed by the Abenaki and other Native American allies of New France was not as simplistic or one-sided as it seemed, because it was about much more than hatred or race, as usually portrayed in the most basic terms by generations of traditional historians. Long before they decided to launch their raids on the settlers, indigenous populations along the Atlantic coast and farther inland, including in the Merrimack River Valley, once home to the western Abenaki, had been thoroughly decimated by an unseen enemy more merciless than any Native American enemy war parties or the whites. This unseen enemy was epidemic disease, caused by the deadly germs brought by Europeans who had early spread viruses like smallpox and measles among the indigenous peoples. Native Americans possessed no immunity to these lethal illnesses, which were the grimmest of reapers—more so than the white man's guns or armies—ever seen in North America.[43]

These so-called virgin soil diseases that raged in an unspoiled land eventually decimated as much as 90 percent of the Native American population in North America in a true, but largely forgotten, holocaust that wiped out whole villages and very nearly entire tribes. Before long, the very existence of the indigenous peoples was at stake because of the cruel ravages resulting from innocent contact between such vastly different races and cultures.[44]

With everything at stake during the decimation of one tribe after another, Native Americans early realized that they had to acquire new tribal members—natural reproduction was much too slow, and Indian infants died as readily from the white man's diseases as adults—to ensure the survival of their sophisticated cultures and civilizations, which now lay on the verge of extinction. In consequence, the ultimate solution for the disease-ravaged people was entirely sensible under the circumstances: to conduct "mourning wars" in honor of lost family members in which raiding expeditions were launched more to secure captives than to kill in order to gain large numbers of prisoners, either whites or members of other tribes. These captives were then adopted into the tribe to replace dead family members and replenish the ravaged population. In the annals of American history, this has been the most overlooked reason for the seemingly endless raids that devastated the northern frontier and explained the disappearance of hundreds of whites, especially infants and children, who had been carried north by returning war parties to become part of these melting-pot societies deep in the wilderness.[45]

The devastation, slaughter, and abduction of large numbers of white captives (men, women, and children) was so extensive that it seemed almost as if the entire northern frontier—much of it already deserted to escape the murderous raids—would be depopulated, with large numbers of settlers fleeing to safe havens at forts or closer to the Atlantic coast, even to the friendly confines of Boston. All the while, the number of killed and captured settlers continued to grow to frightening levels, because the frontier was decimated over hundreds of miles. With British fortunes continuing to sink during a losing struggle between 1755 and 1758 during the years of the French and Indian War, an angry, frustrated American wrote, "The Crisis of our Fate is now. . . . We have little Room to hope for a Deliverance from our Distress."[46]

Bringing hell on earth to the scattered and isolated frontier settlements, Native American raiders were unstoppable, continuing to strike with the bloodiest of results and proving that they were masters in the art of terrorism because, in the words of one resigned colonial, "we may as well goe [sic] to War with Wolfs and Bears."[47]

Paris-born Captain Louis Antoine de Bougainville, a most promising French officer who served as the trusty aide-de-camp of the Marquis de Montcalm, the finest French commander of the French and Indian War, was shocked by his first close look at the Native American allies of New France and their viciousness toward unarmed whites, both prisoners and settlers, including women and children, on the northern frontier: "The cruelties and the insolence of these barbarians is horrible, their souls are as black as pitch."[48]

In reprinting a letter first published in Philadelphia, a Boston newspaper revealed an undeniable truth of the widespread slaughter that had become the ultimate horror:

The Scalping of the Frontier Inhabitants by the Indians is not peculiar to Pennsylvania, but common to all the Colonies, in Proportion as their Frontiers are more or less extended and exposed to the Enemy[, and no colony has] been able to secure its Inhabitants from Scalping by the Indians; who coming secretly in very small Parties skulking in the Woods, must sometimes have it in their Power to surprise and destroy Travellers [sic] or single Families settled in scattered Plantations. . . . How much Care must it be for such an Enemy to destroy a Ploughman at Work in his Field?[49]

But, of course, the interloping whites, including the Pilgrims, committed their own long list of atrocities, solemnly believing, like the idealistic European Crusaders who had marched from Western Europe to the Holy Land to slaughter Muslims because they were unbelievers, that they were fulfilling the will of God, thereby justifying their own slaughters. The killing of Indians by many frontier whites for little more than sport only made Native Americans more determined to wreak a bloody revenge in a nonending cycle of extreme violence. The early common view of settlers was that the Indians were nothing more than "the devil's instruments"—or fair game—to ensure the most vicious of reprisals.[50]

In early fights against the Pequot in New England, Indian dead were decapitated, and their heads, including those of both men and women, were set atop poles with eyes and mouths wide open as grim trophies. Such was the ill fate of the unfortunate King Philip. His rum-preserved hand was kept as a trophy, and his bleached skull was displayed atop a tall pole in Plymouth, the center of Pilgrim religious authority and power, where it stood high in full view, just like hundreds of white scalps that waved over the residences at St. Francis for decades.[51]

The massacre of the Pequot at Mystic witnessed the horrors of blood-thirsty English soldiers having "received and entertained [the men, women, and children fleeing their burning homes and coming out into the open fields lined with whites] with the point of the sword."[52] Even Pequot dogs were ordered killed by English officers, who seemingly thought of everything in waging their total war and spared nothing, "so that they might not be eaten to prevent starvation" among the defeated tribe.[53] This genocide of the Pequot thoroughly shocked Native Americans of neighboring tribes because the white man's ruthless total war was "too furious, and slay[ed] too many men."[54]

A gifted intellectual who personified the Age of Enlightenment, Bougainville was a sophisticated French officer who easily quoted inspiring words from the ancient classics, including Homer's *Iliad*. He had even authored, before he was twenty-five, a celebrated treatise on calculus that was respected across Western Europe. Captain Bougainville had few good words to say about the most lethal of New France's Native American allies, the Abenaki, who often struck in the remote northern frontier area where the Rogers family lived, calling them "one of the most unmanageable and insolent of all."[55]

Like the Abenaki warriors he fought year after year when the leader of the Rangers, Rogers never forgot his lower-class roots—in his case, in the rolling hills of Ulster Province, north Ireland. While facing the omnipresent threat of Abenaki attack from the depths of French Canada, the Rogers family took pride in the fact that they were descendants of some of Ulster Province's first Scottish settlers, who had migrated south to north Ireland from the Lowlands of Scotland. As noted, the Rogers family, transplanted sons of Erin, had bestowed on their home the name Mountalona to honor the green Presbyterian hills of County Derry, Ulster Province, north Ireland.

The long-suffering refugees from the bloody borderlands of the trauma-tized Celtic world had also poured into the frontiers of the Colony of New York, west of Massachusetts. Besides the omnipresent Scotch-Irish settlers,

Scottish Jacobites of the clans from the Scottish Highlands, defeated by the British in 1746, penetrated north up along the west side of the Hudson River and into New York's highlands. Proud Celtic names of the places where they settled in the wilderness, New Scotland and Irish Corners, reflected their unique history, culture, and ethnicity.

Scottish refugees who had suddenly found themselves situated in the Green Isle's northern lands of the Celtic-Gaelic people, who were hostile to the Protestants (Scotch-Irish) because their finest lands—like those of the Abenaki—had been stolen by the interlopers, these once again transplanted Protestant Scotch-Irish, like the Rogers family, had settled all along the northern frontier. Ironically, like the Abenaki of St. Francis on the Atlantic's other side, even the Irish Catholics were refugees who had fled from England's conquest and settlement of north Ireland in England's so-called Ulster Plantation.

Like the ill-fated Pennacook people, who had been uprooted from the Lower Merrimack River country by the surging tide of white settlers and fled north in a perfect exodus to St. Francis, Native American people had been pushed off ancestral lands by the mostly Scotch-Irish waves of settlement, which was relentless. Indeed, a lifetime of battling hostile neighbors in the borderlands was nothing new to the Scotch-Irish but merely part of everyday life for them and generations of their ancestors.

After all, the Scotch-Irish had fought an extremely "wild war," which was often no-quarter warfare, over the course of generations in Ulster Province to keep their land and religion safe from the native people, Irish Catholics. In this regard, for America's northern frontier Scotch-Irish, the Abenaki had seemingly replaced the Irish Catholics as lifelong antagonists in two distinct worlds and experiences separated by the Atlantic.

In an accurate analysis of the Scotch-Irish of the frontier by one historian who was not guilty of overstatement, "They were a hardy race, and fought stoutly for the pleasant valleys they dwell[ed] in" across the breadth of north Ireland.[56] But the New World wilderness was even more dangerous because the untamed frontier was so remote that one colonist described the situation of a frightening aloneness, far from any kind of assistance: "We were quite out of Christendom."[57] And the enemy they faced was the fiercest of foes because "they act like wolves," in the words of a shocked Increase Mather, who believed that they needed to be treated accordingly because it was God's will.[58]

Here, in the isolated wilderness of the Upper Merrimack River country, Rogers's Scotch-Irish family thrived in the new land, but it came at another price. Robert had little opportunity to receive a proper education, except what his father or mother taught him from the pages of the Holy Bible in the privacy of their log cabin nestled in the wilderness. There was little time for such societal niceties as the refinements of higher education and culture, because the Scotch-Irish were living on the wild frontier, where simple survival was the primary concern of each day.

The mostly small farmers of the New England frontier were in a no-win situation in simultaneously battling man and nature, both as heartless as they were unforgiving, but this situation was nothing new in living on a dangerous frontier, where death could come at any time. This situation had been much the same in the past for their Protestant ancestors in seemingly endless Scottish and Irish rebellions and struggles over culture and race and for the possession of both Scotland and north Ireland—two embattled and bloody borderlands, where the common people's dreams seemingly always died early, ugly, and tragic deaths at the hands of powerful invaders with superior weaponry and unbridled lust to kill men of a different culture, religion, and society. Scotch-Irish families across the breadth of the northern frontier, like the Rogers family in the Upper Merrimack River Valley, possessed "no other alternative but to push or be pushed" off the land that they loved.[59]

But more important, the Scotch-Irish had early learned the key lesson that had ensured their survival as a hard-pressed people in the troubled Old World, and this time-honored axiom now applied to New England's northern frontier as the only means of survival in the New World and the harsh realities of forging a decent life on the ever-dangerous edge of empire: if anyone "should strike or offend them, it was their credo to strike back twice as hard."[60]

And they had much to fight against from the beginning (before Native Americans) in a new land dominated only by the cruel laws and arbitrary dictates of a capricious nature, because the Scotch-Irish were discriminated against by other whites, from the Puritans to the English, who unfairly looked upon them as almost subhuman for a host of reasons. In the words of one Scotch-Irish immigrant, he "was looked upon as a barbarian" because he hailed from the Emerald Isle, which had become England's first colony by way of bloody conquest, often featuring the horrors of no-mercy warfare.[61]

More than in the case of Irish Catholics back in picturesque Ulster Province, the humble farmers of the northern frontier faced no ordinary enemy but the most magnificent fighting men in the land, especially the Abenaki, whose professional warrior ethos celebrated warfare and its horrors to an inordinate degree and even possessed a spiritual aspect incomprehensible to the European mind, especially a religious one.

By this time, the Native Americans themselves had fallen victim to an excessive love of war that had corrupted the better part of their natures. Cruelty, ritualistic torture, and horrors had become a celebrated way of life, which they believed was necessary for their peoples and their tribes to persevere and survive in a cruel world: an evolution from the wartime experience that hardened the hearts and minds of generations of utterly ruthless warriors in a process that was necessary, because only the strongest and most heartless had survived centuries of brutal conflict long before the arrival of the first European explorers, who were shocked by the enemy's viciousness that so numbed their senses.[62]

And no people in all New England were more determined not to be pushed off a land that they loved and worked hard to make productive than the feisty Scotch-Irish, who returned ferocity with ferocity, as part of their own distinctive heritage of struggling for survival across the sea. Therefore, when the raiders from New France waged a war of terrorism on the settlers, the settlers returned the favor by waging their own unique brand of fighting fire with fire.

After all, the Scotch-Irish people possessed their own dark legacies of having battled past enemies in almost unending bloody warfare for centuries when caught between the border of Scotland and England in a nightmarish past that they considered heroic, such as in the heady days of Scottish freedom fighter William Wallace—a common man who became a dynamic leader of the Scottish people after having risen on his own merit and ability, like Rogers—whose hatred of the British occupiers of his ancestral homeland knew no bounds. These die-hard Presbyterians also well understood from their own history of seemingly endless tragedy that life was a bloody struggle calling for great sacrifice because only the strong survived in a harsh world. Therefore, partly from a love of God, to whom they prayed for deliverance from the evildoers who sought to destroy them, the Scotch-Irish settlers embraced the ancient stories of vengeance from the pages of the Old Testament with a passion born of righteousness and desperation blended with vengefulness, because these qualities were the keys to survival in a harsh land.[63]

A question not adequately explored by generations of historians for whatever reason—almost certainly a lack of interest in the Scotch-Irish experience—is just how significant his own Scotch-Irish heritage was in shaping the heart and soul of Robert Rogers. Perhaps the best evidence can be seen in the fact that so many of the men of Rogers's Rangers were of Scotch-Irish heritage and also that he formed close associations with other Irish and Scotch-Irish officers and soldiers—a Celtic brotherhood of ethnic warriors—who were not Rangers. During the French and Indian War, Rogers informed some Irish officers, including Ulster Province–born Captain-Lieutenant Henry Pringle, that he had been "born in the County of Antrim" in Ulster Province.[64]

This notable example has indicated that Rogers fought not only for New Hampshire and America at an early date but also for his people's native homeland across the sea. For all practical purposes, and although he had been the first American-born member of the Rogers family, Ulster Province, north Ireland, still meant something very special to Rogers by the time he commanded the most famous fighting force of Americans during the French and Indian War. Clearly, having revealed a good deal of ethnic pride, Rogers considered himself an authentic Celtic and Scotch-Irish warrior like of old, because he was certainly one in regard to his tenacity and never-say-die qualities of a warrior leader, deeply rooted in the Celtic and Scotch-Irish experience, which he repeatedly demonstrated on the battlefield. Like an ancient Celtic warrior of the Scottish Highlands, Rogers thought of himself as a member of a hard-fighting clan from the old country in a distant past. Like so many other hardy Scotch-Irish, he had grown up on the northern frontier, but the legacies of Ulster were still with him because they had never vanished. He was described as "a handsome giant with red hair and blue eyes"—a typical Celtic look.[65]

But during the dark days ahead, when so much hung in the balance for his frontier people, it became the primary mission of Rogers and his Rangers to do much more than simply push back against the raiders from the north in the cherished Scotch-Irish tradition but also to take the war to the enemy by launching their own raids deep into the hostile territory of an uncharted wilderness. Besides the lofty esprit de corps and close camaraderie of Rogers's Rangers, the overall motivation was exceptionally high among these crack fighting men from the forests and mountains, especially at a truly brutal time, when "it was very shocking for the husband to see the wife of his bosom her head cut off, and the children's blood drunk like water, by these cruel savages."⁶⁶

Such graphic firsthand accounts of the tragic fate of so many frontier settlers have long been dismissed as exaggerations or propaganda by cynical modern historians who have found such atrocities to be almost beyond rational belief because they defy the imagination. However, this was not the case, as fully realized by the traumatized and war-weary people of the frontier, who endured horrors that are almost incomprehensible to the modern mind. Regardless of age or sex, everyone with white or black skin found in the fields attempting to raise or harvest crops or located in an isolated log cabin was a potential victim of New France's fierce raiders on the unforgiving frontier, where life was so often short and cheap when the warriors struck. The Abenaki and the warriors of other tribes made no distinction when it came to killing and taking scalps for trophies to show off their combat prowess to the people of their home communities. One rare account based on first-person testimony has revealed how one party of Provincials was ambushed in the summer of 1757 and roughly handled by their more experienced Native American foes, who were masters of wilderness warfare. Among the war-painted attackers streaked in red and black who unleashed "Hideous Yells" were hard-hitting warriors "of the Tribe call'd Cold-Country [from Canada;] they not only kill, but, if they have the Opportunity, suck the Blood out of the Bodies of the dead; our Men were scalped and mangled in a most Barbarous Manner."⁶⁷

Even in the civilized environment of Montreal, which was New France's second-largest city, French Regulars were astounded by a nightmarish spectacle in 1746, while they and leading French and Canadian officials, including the revered governor of New France, watched the cruel fate of a prisoner who had been taken in New York: "The Dutchman was perfectly naked, tied Hand & Foot, chain'd to the Post, and the Indians, dancing, singing, roasting, stabbing, gashing and tormenting him. . . . [A]n Indian Woman tho't it not enough but took a Wire, scalt it red hot, and run it thro' his Penis into his Body, to his unutterable Anguish."⁶⁸

All in all, the strategy of a war of terrorism ultimately backfired on the Native Americans, in part because they had taken on an incredibly tough and resourceful people who also placed a supreme value on the importance of revenge, the Scotch-Irish, who never forgot or forgave. The Native American atrocities only made the settlers more determined, and they fought back more frantically instead of being cowed—a forgotten explanation for the high motivation and resolve of Rogers and his Rangers, deeply rooted in the overall Scotch-Irish experience on both sides of the Atlantic.[69]

Brave Frontier Women, Black and White

As noted, hardy frontier women, both black and white, who helped to settle the land and ultimately to make America, were not spared by the war parties that so suddenly swarmed out of the forests to overwhelm isolated farms, log cabins, and villages nestled in the wilderness. Even pregnant women were routinely cut down by the slashing of steel tomahawks and scalping knives, because this, most of all, was a war of terror as a well-calculated and deliberate strategy of the French and their Native American allies.[70]

An entry in a Philadelphia newspaper described the horror of one raid, which achieved its intended results, in the Lancaster, Pennsylvania, area during the spring of 1757: "5 Men and one Woman (who was with Child) were killed and the Scalped [and] the Frontier Inhabitants are in great Distress, and moving from their Plantations [south and east] as fast as they can."[71]

What resulted from the hard-hitting raids was systematic slaughter regardless of age or sex. A Philadelphia newspaper reported how "the Widow Ramasay and Two Children, and two of the name of Clugston, were all killed by the Indians . . . at the Foot of the South Mountain [and] the Woman's Head were cut off, and her Body mangled in the most Cruel Manner."[72] In New York, a raiding party of warriors found easy victims when "a Man was kill'd . . . as he was tilting up a Cart of Dung [to fertilize the fields], after which the Indians went to his House and kill'd and scalp'd his Wife, and carried off his six Children" into the dark forests that led to French Canada.[73]

Even worse, a main eastern newspaper, the *Maryland Gazette*, published in the port of Annapolis, Maryland, described the ultimate horror of when an isolated frontier fort was overwhelmed by Indian attackers during the spring of 1756. Among the killed Marylanders on the colony's western frontier "was a Woman big with Child, whom they rip'd open and scalp'd the Infant, and a young Girl, one of the Prisoners, who is suppos'd was not able to travel fast enough with them, was found at the foot of the Mountain."[74]

Another letter from the war-ravaged Pennsylvania frontier in April 1758 revealed the tragic fate for women, whose long-flowing hair was highly prized as making exceptionally fine scalps by the warriors, including the Abenaki from St. Francis: "A Woman was killed and Scalp'd last Night by the Enemy . . . a Widow woman carried off [to Canada and] In Tulpehocken [in southeast Pennsylvania and located northwest of Philadelphia], one Levergood, and his Wife killed [and] At Northkill [in Berks County, Pennsylvania, named after a cold and clear trout stream of the same name], the Wife of Nickolas Guiger and two Children, and the Wife of Michael Titlefer, all killed and scalped."[75]

But the women of the frontier often fought back with spirit against the Native American raiders in part because they knew about the enemy's cruelty and penchant for torture, while also fearing the prospect of gang rape, which they had heard about from their relatives. At such times, female courage and survival instincts, especially to save their children, often rose to the fore across the frontier in dramatic ways.

A major Boston newspaper reported how Massachusetts settler John Smith,

> *being at Work at a small Distance from his House, was beset by 3 or 4 Indians, who killed and scalp'd him, and took his Ax and split his Skull leaving the Ax in his Head; and then went to his House, where was only his wife; and her Son sick in the bed, whom she was sitting by; one of the Indians went in and . . . he took his knife, and attempted to stab him; but the Woman resolutely took hold of the Indian and turn'd him out of the House and fastened the Door against them; telling her Son to take Care of himself, who immediately got down in the cellar and hid himself and so escap'd but they firing into the Window shot the Woman and kill'd her, and then enter'd the House, scalp'd her, and split her Head with a Hatchet; and plunder'd the House of Money, Clothes, Provisions, and other Things.*[76]

A frontier woman was not even safe when riding a swift horse along a dusty country road cut through the wilderness while on her way to visit a friend on a neighboring farm. As revealed in a Philadelphia newspaper about a tragic incident in August 1757 in Lancaster County, "Last Thursday, John Andrew's Wife going to a Neighbor's House, was surprised by six Indians; had her Horse shot [from] under her, and she and her Child were carried off."[77]

During this same period on the bloody frontier, where the number of victims steadily increased to appalling levels, "ten Indians surprized [*sic*] Isaac William's Wife, and the Widow Williams, alias Smelley, killed and scalped the former, in sight of the House, she having run a little Way, after three Balls had been shot through her Body; the latter they carried away Captive."[78]

Along with white women on the frontier, black women (both slave and free) became victims of the Indians' wrath, and they also fought back with desperation against war-painted raiders. Black women living and working on the frontier as slaves and who became victims also revealed how slavery was part of early New England life from the beginning. Though it is entirely forgotten today, black and white men, women, and children often died side by side in the making of early New England.

During the legendary French and Indian raid on Deerfield, Massachusetts, on the morning of February 29, 1704, one of the first victims was a female slave named Parthena, owned by John Williams. Williams also lost a black male slave named Frank, who was later killed when the warriors, including Abenaki, became drunk on captured supplies of alcohol. The raiders from New France were entirely colorblind and "made no distinction between English colonists and their enslaved servants, coerced colonists."[79]

Another Indian attack, reported in the pages of the *Maryland Gazette*, proved devastating near the end of July 1757: settler "Alexander M'Keakeasy [of Irish descent] was shot near his own House by an Indian, in the Knee [and] At the same time his Son was carried away Prisoner; and a Negro girl, whom an Indian had by the Hand, leading off, escaped by the Assistance of two Dogs, whom she set at the Indian, but he flung his Tomahawk at her, and cut her very Much in the Neck, tho' it is thought she will recover."[80]

But the largest loss of female lives occurred during the massacre of hundreds of members of the garrison of Fort William Henry, at the southern end of Lake George, after its surrender to forces under the Marquis de Montcalm on August 10, 1757. During the most infamous massacre of the French and Indian War after still another French victory in capturing the strategic fort, "the throats of most if not all the Women [soldiers' wives and lovers and camp followers, such as laundresses and cooks] were cut, their Bellies ript [*sic*] open, their Bowels torn out and thrown upon the Faces of the dead and dying Bodies [and] the Women were murdered one Way or another...."

[T]he Children were taken by the Heels, and their Brains beat out against the Trees and Stones" in a great orgy of bloodletting.[81]

But far more pioneer women were killed on the frontier than at Fort William Henry. Like so many other women settlers who became victims, Mrs. Philip Call "had her head scalped and almost entirely chopped off" from the repeated blows of an Abenaki tomahawk. Her killer later boasted with callowness and amusement how the poor woman "squealed like a pig when he tomahawked her" to death.[82]

However, a white woman's life on the frontier could become extremely complicated for a variety of reasons having more to do with whites than with Indians during the clash of white cultures and civilizations in this wilderness war. For instance, one

> *English Woman, Wife of one of the Soldiers [and] having been taken Prisoner by the French at the Time of the [July 1755] Defeat of General [Edward] Braddock, and supposing that her Husband was slain at that Time, during her Imprisonment married a French Subaltern, by whom she had had one Child, being with her Husband coming Prisoner thro' Albany [New York] was there discover'd by her former Husband, who was then on duty there:—He immediately demanded her, and after some Struggles of tenderness for her French Husband, she left him, and closed again with her First:—Tho' 'tis said the French Husband insisted on keeping the Child, as his Property, which was consented to by the Wife and her first husband.*[83]

Fortunately for them, captive white women generally received far better treatment than male prisoners, because they were needed to bear children to keep the tribe healthy by replacing fallen warriors after they were adopted and then incorporated into tribal life. If a white female was captured at a young age, the transformation was almost seamless to a surprising degree. In relative terms, most white women captured by Native Americans across the colonies embraced the morals, values, and ethos of the Native American community, as if they had been the offspring of Indians and had never known white society.

Apparently almost fascinated by the Native Americans' depths of depravity, which seemed to have no end, even when Native Americans were known for their excessive indulgence of their children—no severe punishments such as spanking—even more so than whites, Captain Bougainville, the respected aide-de-camp to the aristocratic Montcalm, described how, to his horror, an Indian "child of six danced without a breechclout [and] his parents gave him an Englishman to kill to stop him crying."[84]

This shocking incident was no far-fetched story or idle camp rumor among the French. An ill-fated Provincial corporal named Turner, who had been captured at Fort Granville, located on the Juniata River in central Pennsylvania, had been taken back to a Delaware village, Kittanning, located on the east bank of the Allegheny River. Here, Turner was tied "to a black Post, [where the Indians] danced round him [and] made a great Fire, and having heated [steel] Gun-Barrels red hot they run him through; they tormented him thus near three Hours, then scalped him alive: and at last held up a Boy, with a Hatchet in his Hand, to give him the finishing Stroke."[85]

LIFELONG TRAUMAS

Around the summer of 1755, before the British government dispatched General Edward Braddock's ill-fated expedition west through the wilderness in the vain hope of capturing Fort Duquesne, located in today's Pittsburgh, Pennsylvania, to dominate the strategic Ohio River, known to the French as "Beautiful River," a lonesome Pennsylvania Ranger named Captain Jack became a legendary figure on the frontier. He had formed a company of Pennsylvania Rangers during the early phase of the French and Indian War. Jack's dream of living on the frontier with his family in peace and prosperity had turned into a nightmare. After returning from a hunting trip in the Juniata River country of central Pennsylvania, he found his log cabin burned to the ground and his wife and two children slaughtered like cattle for market. Jack thereafter lived in the wilderness by himself, fueled with the burning desire and "the single purpose of killing the red man [and] He was seldom seen in the settlements [because] He roamed the forest in search of Indians. . . . [T]he extermination of Indians [was the] goal" of his life.[86]

By comparison, nothing in the historical record has indicated that Rogers shared such a pathological hatred for Native Americans as long assumed by historians and writers, exposing still another myth about the Ranger leader. After all, friendly Native Americans near Rogers's boyhood home had been the young man's early mentors in learning about wilderness ways.[87]

As could be expected, Rogers eventually became traumatized by the brutalities and horrors of war, especially after his costly raid on St. Francis and the heavy loss of life among his men at the Second Battle on Snowshoes on March 13, 1758, and during the long withdrawal from the site of his greatest victory, reaped deep in New France. In this sense, Rogers was fated to become a tragic victim of the war's dehumanizing process and even his greatest successes, where extreme excesses in the art of killing fellow human beings became part of the overall equation for victory in this cruelest of all of America's wars.[88]

Located at the forks of the Ohio River, Fort Duquesne was the key to the Ohio country and had long been a thorn in the side of the English settlements. Rogers described how Fort Duquesne, a launching pad for countless raids on the frontier, stood "upon the point of land between the river Monongahela and Ohio. From this the general course of the river is west, inclining to the south for near a thousand miles, as the river runs, where it joins the Mississippi."[89]

But, as noted, battling the ever-resourceful raiders from New France was no small challenge for the settlers, because they were more focused on raising crops on their farms to provide for families than waging war on the frontier: the difference between professional fighting men and amateurs. As mentioned, no one fought more skillfully or better in the deep woodlands than Native Americans, before the dramatic rise of Rogers's Rangers, who basically evolved into white Indians in terms of their extensive warfighting skills. One aristocratic and well-educated French officer, who had just arrived in New France, described the faithful Native American allies of New France as presenting an "extraordinary spectacle, more suited to terrify than to please; curious, however, to a philosopher who seeks to study man in conditions nearest to nature. These men were naked save for a piece of cloth in front and behind, the face and body painted, feathers on their heads, symbol and signal of war, tomahawk and spear in their hand."[90]

He also later described the Native Americans of French Canada as consisting of warriors who proudly stood "erect, well-made, and almost all of great height."[91] But this above-mentioned French officer, the erudite Captain Louis Antoine de Bougainville, penned with bitter frustration in a September 1757 letter how these warriors had committed such awful cruelties that

he was forever haunted by their horrible deeds: "Spectacles still more frightful have befouled my eyes and left an ineffaceable bitterness in my soul. May
the memory of these abominations vanish. What a land! What a people!"[92]

But despite their many faults as allies, which Bougainville routinely
emphasized from the utterly perplexed European perspective, these Native
Americans were the consummate fighting men and natural killers of a professional warrior society that honored a stoic courage above all else. Because
of trade with the French, they had made warfare more lethal by combining
the skillful use of muskets and steel weaponry, tomahawks and knives, with
the best tactics of irregular warfare ways—or guerilla-style fighting that
especially featured ambushes and hit-and-run raids—to become the most
lethal warriors in North America.[93]

Therefore, for generations, Native American warriors, armed with
French muskets and black powder, proved invaluable as the frontline fighters of New France because they seldom met with defeat: the key in keeping
English settlement confined east of the Appalachians and mostly along
the East Coast for decades, despite the much larger English population, in
part because they were well rewarded by the French for their atrocities and
scalps in gold and brandy.[94]

Ironically, these hard-hitting raiders of New France were fueled by a
burning faith that was Western European–based and founded on the Holy
Bible. The ties of Catholicism bound together Canadians, Indians, and
French in what was a holy war against the Protestant heretics of the frontier settlements. Captured by the French in 1756, Robert Eastburn, born in
England but raised in Philadelphia in a Quaker family before he converted
to Robert Rogers's Presbyterianism, described the religious-inspired united
efforts, as if they were still engaged in a religious war and righteous crusade from centuries back in Europe: "Our enemies leave no stone unturned
to compass our ruin; they pray, work, and travel to bring it about, and are
unwearied in the pursuit. . . . O may the Almighty awake us, cause us to feel
our danger, before it is too late, and grant us salvation!"[95]

In another bitter irony, the English colonies possessed a vast superiority—
around ten to one—in manpower not only to defend themselves but also to
take the war to the enemy, if they properly organized and conducted effective
offensive operations, which were not seen in the early years of the French
and Indian War. However, they faced the sprawling French Empire on all

sides and a resourceful and smart opponent, who was extremely aggressive because of the considerable numerical disparity because the best defense was the offensive. The imperial rivalry over the limitless potential and financial gains of the Ohio country had originally sparked the war, which broke out in full force in 1755.

Indeed, the imperial ambitions and greed of upper-class politicians, leaders, and investors on both sides of the Atlantic had early sowed the seeds of bitter conflict and the destruction of so many lower- and middle-class settlers on the frontier, especially the Scotch-Irish, for years to come. With the French enjoying the advantages of geography that confined their hapless opponents and hampered their defensive and offensive efforts, the English settlers not only had to fend off the unstoppable war parties of Native American warriors but also were forced to confront a harsh natural environment: multiple challenges on dual fronts that were simultaneous and most daunting, when only the strong survived the harrowing ordeal in the untamed wilderness.[96]

CHAPTER TWO

Quebec's Infamous Jesuit Missionary Town of St. Francis

AFTER FAILED BRITISH OFFENSIVE EFFORTS IN EVERY SINGLE CAMPAIGN season from 1755, beginning with General Edward Braddock's defeat, to the disastrous year of 1758, which was a low point of British-Provincial fortunes during the French and Indian War, Prime Minister William Pitt, a brilliant strategist and the architect of decisive victory in the end, concentrated a massive amount of British and Provincial manpower for the 1759 campaign. Even more, he chose the right man for the job of delivering a decisive blow, Major General Jeffery Amherst. The careful and meticulous Amherst advanced thousands of his British Regular and Provincial troops north up the strategic Lake Champlain corridor in a mighty flotilla during the summer of 1759 to fulfill military ambitions not realized since the war's beginning.

Like Pitt in finding the capable Amherst buried in the British army establishment, so Amherst had found his man in Robert Rogers, who had been promoted to "Major of the Rangers," now a corps that had been desig-nated Rangers because of the growing list of Rogers's successes, on April 6, 1758. As usual, Amherst depended heavily on the talents of Major Rogers and his hardened Rangers to lead the way north in the mightiest offensive effort yet mustered by England in this war.

Without Rogers out in front and performing with his usual skill during his Rangers' advance, Amherst would not have been able to launch his great offensive of late July 1759 with confidence and any realistic possibilities for success. He now possessed the comforting assurance that the army's best intelligence gatherers and most reliable men would ensure that he did not stumble into a clever French ambush.

Faced with overpowering British might, the French prudently abandoned Forts Carillon and Saint Frédéric to focus on saving the vital center of French power, mighty Quebec. However, Amherst then committed the folly of remaining too long at Crown Point instead of advancing farther north, because he had no knowledge of General James Wolfe's progress before Quebec. Most important, and as never before, to the opportunistic Rogers and his Rangers, the fall of Forts Carillon (the future Fort Ticonderoga) and Saint Frédéric at Crown Point on Lake Champlain in the early summer of 1759 "meant that all the northern colonial frontier would soon be free for settlement [and now only one single] obstruction remained [and it was] the St. Francis Abenakis."[1]

Ironically, in the end, Major Rogers would never have been able to strike the legendary Abenaki sanctuary at St. Francis had the original French plan for the refugee community remained intact from the earliest date. In 1687, the primitive Fort Francois, also known as Fort Crevier, had been built in a much stronger and more strategic position, on the south bank of the St. Lawrence River at its intersection with the St. Francis River, than the present and final location of the Abenaki town of St. Francis less than ten miles to the south.[2] Enjoying longtime security because of its remoteness, this initial Abenaki sanctuary had been positioned to serve as an advance post to thwart Iroquois war parties, which originated from the Six Nations of the Iroquois Confederacy in New York and the southern Great Lakes region, heading to Quebec or Montreal, acting as a buffer for these two most important urban centers in Canada.[3] Symbolically, with the arrival of a new century, fate had intervened in August 1700 when land was ceded to the most lethal allies of the French, the Abenaki, for the creation of a Jesuit mission located on the St. Francis River: the genesis of the St. Francis where Major Rogers was destined to deliver his most famous attack in early October 1759.[4]

And in still another irony and twist of fate, Rogers would not have been able to launch his best-known raid had the more recent ambitious plan of the missionaries, known as "black robes" to the Native Americans, of the Society of Jesus been allowed to enact their planned move of the town to a better and safer location. At that time, Captain Louis Antoine de Bougainville wrote in his journal, "The Marquis de Vaudreuil has received representatives from the Abenakis of St. Francis ... that the Jesuits wish to move their village to the lands of the Belle Riviere. The pretext of these zealous missionaries [at St. Francis] was go get them [the Abenaki] away from commerce with the French and the use of brandy, and their object to profit from the lands which the Indian cleared [for raising crops along the St. Francis River but] the Abenaki do not at all consent to this change of abode."[5]

In the end, Pierre de Rigaud, the Marquis de Vaudreuil, the savvy governor-general of New France, who knew that appeasing some of New France's most faithful Native American allies was all-important for delivering punishment to the English frontier settlements, decided upon the future of the Abenaki in early February 1757. He allowed them to stay on the St. Francis River not only because that was their own heartfelt wish but also because they were a refugee people, in part from the Lake Champlain Valley but primarily from the east in Maine and to the southeast in New England. A good many pressures, going all the way back to 1675, including attacks by Mohawks and other Six Nations tribes, ravagement by European diseases (especially smallpox), and the relentless advances of English settlement had created a refugee people. Quite simply, the Abenaki, a hardy but seemingly ill-fated people, were on the brink by the time of the French and Indian War, a situation that fueled their desperation and ferocity.

Vaudreuil also had been influenced by the pleading words of "Jerome," the "chief of the villages of the Abenakis." In eloquent terms, the chief had explained to the Canada-born governor, who detested the English with a passion, how "the black robes [Jesuits] wish to make us leave our native hearthstones and carry our council fire elsewhere. This land we inhabit is ours. What it produces is the fruit of our labor. Dig into it and you will find the bones of our ancestors. Thus, it is necessary that our ancestor's bones rise up from the ground and follow us into a foreign land."[6]

In his journal, Bougainville concluded, "The Jesuits finally renounced" their attempt to move the Abenaki, and the refugee community of St. Francis remained on the St. Francis River—to the knowledge of Robert Rogers, who possessed a good deal of information about this mysterious place in Quebec from Ranger Captain John Stark, who had been a captive at St. Francis in 1752.[7]

French common soldier Charles Bonin briefly described St. Francis when he saw the village in the spring of 1759: "Near the River St. Francois . . . there is a rather populous village of Abenaquis savages [and freshwater] Fish are plentiful in the River St. Francois."[8]

For generations and the better part of a century, the most feared enemies of New England settlers along the unprotected frontier were the western Abenaki of the Green Mountains region in today's Vermont. Like most Native Americans, the Abenaki had a good many old scores to settle with the white interlopers, having long possessed a host of legitimate grievances because their native homeland had been taken over by the white tide, whose numbers had only continued to increase, like their relentlessness to gain additional acreage of ancient Abenaki hunting lands at any cost. Consequently, the Abenaki had been steadily pushed northwest into the wilderness of Canada, where they had largely concentrated at St. Francis for survival in an ever-changing world to their detriment. Although their prehistory is shadowy because of the lack of written records, the Abenaki were an ancient people with original roots in today's eastern United States. Seemingly endless warfare with other tribes, the spread of fatal European diseases, especially the ravages of smallpox, and the ceaseless encroachment of English expansion had forced them to seek the help of the French, who promised protection, arms to fight the hated English, and Catholicism.

The white newcomers from across the sea, who believed that God had brought them to their own promised land, had put down roots along the fertile meadows and creek and river bottoms across the New England frontier, where the Abenaki had long grown crops in the rich soil and hunted seemingly countless game in the past. The Jesuits had early converted the Abenaki to Roman Catholicism, and these long-suffering people had embraced it with a passion, after having long clashed with interloping Protestants. Consequently, the Abenaki were not entirely uncivilized in the traditional sense, like the tribes much farther to the west, which were well beyond contact with whites, including missionaries, except for some hardy Canadian and French trappers who had ventured into an uncharted wilderness.

New England's population steadily grew, and new settlements were hacked out of the forests on even more expanses of Abenaki lands. Abenaki warnings not to trespass—both in their own words and left in traditional tomahawk markings on trees that denoted their territory—were ignored by land-hungry settlers. As early as 1690, therefore, revenge-seeking Abenaki and other warriors, led by the French, had trekked south up the St. Francis River, by Lake Memphremagog, and then down the great length of the Connecticut River—ironically, Rogers's route of retreat from St. Francis after he destroyed the town in early October 1759—which pointed like a dagger into the heart of the New England settlements that were vulnerable: a long-distance strike, or deep raid, that "marked the beginning of systematic French-directed Indian attacks on the New England settlements, in which Abenaki served as the shock troops of the French war effort."[9]

The Abenaki and other Algonquian peoples of the New England region, like the Pennacook, or Pawtucket, of the Merrimack River Valley in western Massachusetts, before they were devastated in the genocidal Pequot War, had suffered greatly at English hands. They had been driven north and west (a gradual "exodus" over time that ended for many refugees at St. Francis, where they had formed a refugee community with seemingly endless grievances against the white man who seemed to want to own everything) by the relentless tide of settlement until establishing their village strategically in the St. Lawrence River country. Here, between Montreal to the southwest and Quebec to the northeast, St. Francis was strategically located to strike back at the interlopers to the south.

Based on official land grants issued by the central government in Quebec, this Jesuit mission settlement had long provided a safe haven for Abenaki war refugees, who had fled out of necessity after their traditional world had collapsed: the situation guaranteed that they became the staunchest allies of the French and the most merciless killers of the English for generations to come. For the Abenaki, there would be no understanding or truces with the ever-aggressive Protestant settlers of New England, especially the Scotch-Irish frontiersmen who had Abenaki blood on their hands and lived on choice Abenaki lands.

It was a supreme irony of history that the longtime center of countless raids and murders along the frontier of New England had been partly created in the beginning by the harshness of the religious-minded Puritans in search of a New Canaan. And there was no place in this New Canaan for the original inhabitants of the land. St. Francis had been considered the epitome of evil for generations, although it was a place of God. The Jesuit missionaries who had founded the Saint François de Sales Mission at the town of Odanak (St. Francis), Quebec, at some point during the period from 1660 to 1670 on the St. Francis River, just six miles, south or upstream, from the St. Lawrence River, had long encouraged the warriors to strike without mercy at the Protestants who were surging north and west to threaten New France.

From the beginning, the Abenaki were fueled not only by hatred of the encroaching settlers but also by the Jesuit teachings to destroy the Protestant heretics by driving them into the sea. Inflamed by a burning desire to settle old scores, the Abenaki and other warriors had unleashed the most famous strike by New France's raiders in late February 1704 at Deerfield, Massachusetts. Ironically, the legacy of the slaughter at Deerfield, when the entire community had been caught by surprise in the predawn blackness, was still very much with Rogers's Rangers, which included good fighting men from Deerfield whose relatives were no more because of the Abenaki's wrath—seasoned Rangers like Captain Simon Stevens and brothers Martin and Matthew Severance, among others.

As high up as Governor-General Vaudreuil, top French political, religious, and military leaders had early played a key role in inflaming the Abenaki people to show no mercy. These insidious activities by French leadership had been conducted behind the scenes since early 1730 to fuel the unleashing of countless Native American raids across the broad expanse of the frontier. Vaudreuil, a cynical realist and gifted politician, did whatever he could to ensure that the Abenaki and English settlers became the most "irreconcilable enemies" to the very end, because he needed Abenaki ferocity since it paid high dividends in the overall military effort during a war of attrition. The governor of French Canada bragged in a letter about the success of one war party that had been sent "towards the region of Boston" and "laid waste" to a wide area: "More than three hundred [English] persons [were] captured and killed."[10]

Abenaki ties with the French, already very close because of the lucrative fur trade and religion, were additionally strengthened when the English retaliated and killed warriors who raided south. Abenaki representatives, consequently, journeyed to Quebec and requested additional French support, which the governor, who was supremely satisfied that his highly effective strategic plan to make the valley of the St. Lawrence less vulnerable to invasion because of the presence of the fearsome Abenaki at St. Francis, was delighted to provide. Decade after decade, St. Francis had never been threatened by either British or Provincial forces and had come to symbolize French invincibility and Abenaki success by 1759.[11]

Ideally situated in a picturesque setting, the "town"—according to Rogers's view; it was certainly not a traditional Native American village, as long assumed—of St. Francis was strategically located between Montreal and Quebec, serving as a key linchpin in the overall defense of Quebec. The warriors enjoyed the advantages of the natural avenue of the Connecticut River and its valley, after first following the St. Francis to its headwaters, to journey south to attack the New England settlements for generations. Here, in a wilderness sanctuary, the French had long served the Abenaki as missionaries, suppliers of weapons and black powder, trade partners, especially in furs, and protectors of a distinctive culture and way of life.

Quite unlike the English, especially along the frontier in New England, the French had long maintained a very close relationship with the Abenaki that included intermarriage and the rise of a mixed-race people. French trappers, traders, and missionaries had long entered into the mainstream of tribal life with an ease not seen among the more xenophobic English. For instance, Pierre Hertel de Beaubassin, born in 1715, had been raised among the Abenaki at St. Francis, where his father had served as an interpreter and trader. All in all, by 1759 St. Francis was very much a melting-pot ethnic community, where whites, Indians, and intermixtures of the two peoples lived together for generations along the banks of the St. Francis River and without racial animosities.

Throughout Rogers's lifetime, the Abenaki never relinquished the bitter feud with the invading English settlers, who had long surged up the Connecticut and Merrimack River Valleys to clear the forests for farms and kill game and Indians in their path. The greatest threat to the tribe's existence was the fatal combination of the relentless advance of white civilization and European diseases (measles and smallpox were the deadliest epidemics), for which the native people possessed no immunity, which, if unchecked, would destroy the traditional culture and ancient ways of a distinct people.

Ironically, and to their amusement, the Abenaki knew that the whites feared and hated them, though not some of their cultural ways, especially their dress. New England's settlers on the northern frontier had evolved over the decades, adapting to Indian ways, including learning and adhering to their highly effective warfighting ways as best symbolized by Rogers. Abenaki losses from decades of combat and the ravages of disease had cruelly culled the population without mercy. In addition, the early New England frontiersmen and militiamen had learned how to fight back and waged a savage war of "unbridled terror," resulting in a series of bitter reprisals by both sides that had descended into darkness and depravity. Therefore, the Abenaki had long burned with desire to obtain revenge for lost family members and regain their former hunting lands now occupied by yeomen farmers, who squatted and cut down the virgin timber for fields without paying anything to anyone, as if God had ordained them as the rightful owners.

All in all, the development of St. Francis represented a remarkable success story. Whereas only twenty families had lived at the picturesque site located just south of the St. Lawrence River in around 1660, the time of the village's birth, St. Francis had emerged as the main western Abenaki population center in Quebec because of the seemingly endless threats and pressures from both whites and their Indian allies. Relentless pressure from not only New Englanders but also their primary Indian ally, the Mohawks of the Iroquois Confederacy (especially during King Philip's War of 1675–1676, "a horrific race war"), resulted in the destruction of Native American people in southern New England. As much as the settlers complained of the horrors of Indian brutality, the Abenaki could make a strong case that they had been wronged first and even more grievously than the whites.

As mentioned, these brutal conflicts over land and race disrupted traditional Native American life in every way, forcing large numbers of Abenaki to flee to Canada to settle at French Jesuit missions like St. Francis, but also at a number of others, like Wigwam Martinique, located seven miles southwest of St. Francis, that provided safety and a chance for people to start their shattered lives anew. The largest number of refugees headed north along well-established trails of traders, trappers, and war parties, which had long struck the frontier settlements and then returned along the same well-trodden route that cut through the seemingly endless woodlands. These hardy survivors became the so-called French Indians.

Strategically located just before the St. Lawrence River to the north, St. Francis and its mixture of various Indian peoples had long symbolized Native American unity forged by the quest for survival and desire for retaliation. More important, St. Francis became the symbolic center of Native American resistance to English encroachment, fueled by the desperate hope of halting the Anglo-Celtic tide, which only grew stronger, like a plague of locusts, and had overwhelmed their beloved ancestral homeland and hunting grounds to the south and east.[12]

As if so deemed by fate and the gods of war, the Abenaki and the Scotch-Irish, like the Rogers family, were all victims of a toxic mix of English imperialism, ancient religious hatreds between Catholics and Protestants, clashing cultures and races, settlement patterns, ignorance on both sides, epidemic disease (including venereal diseases), deep-seated prejudices, and colonialism, ensuring that they were mortal enemies forever more. England and its opportunistic ruling class had discovered the key to successful expansion and colonization around the world to exploit its riches to their maximum benefit: the future source of national wealth, greatness, and superpower status for a small island nation well into the twentieth century. This successful model of conquering entire peoples to strip them of their homelands, which had allowed England to gain its first colony in subjugating Ireland with fire and sword, was simple: push aside the native people in brutal fashion, including by terror that spared neither women nor children in an early form of ethnic cleansing, to deprive fighting men of their familial and logistical support systems and take their rich lands of bounty and beauty.

What the English had early learned to commit in the name of God (Protestantism and Puritanism) and country in Ireland's savage conquest was a winning formula faithfully continued in the New World. These war-fighting lessons from the Old World paved the way for the conquest of New England's tribes with the same kind of unmerciful brute force. Caught in the twisting contours of history beyond their control, which made them little more than pawns in war, transplanted northern Irishmen, or Ulstermen, like Robert Rogers, actually had more in common with the Indians than the aristocratic and large landowning English elite, who arbitrarily dictated the fates and futures of the common people, regardless of color, with a callous stroke of a pen or by conquest: the tragic story of the struggles of two poor people who were manipulated and exploited by the greedy ambitions of the ruling powers and aristocratic elites of Europe.

No doubt, the most thoughtful Ranger and Abenaki warrior understood this paradoxical and strange alikeness born of a host of commonalities as deemed by fate during the most vicious war in American history. In truth, without the hatred and prejudice that seemed to have no end, frontiersmen and Abenaki warriors might well have been friends in less killing times because they loved the same things: family, friends, children, and this beautiful land of boundless promise, where they engaged in the same pursuits of hunting and fishing in a special place that both believed had been bestowed on them by God.

Nevertheless, for a wide variety of reasons, and as noted, Scotch-Irish frontiersmen mostly filled the Rangers' ranks and contributed the most to the overall quality and character of Rogers's Rangers—America's most elite fighting force during the French and Indian War, which was second to none.[13] Throughout the French and Indian War and especially during the 1759 campaign, in which decisive success was won, Rogers and his crack Rangers were able to achieve more than "thousands of the British regulars," who were considered the best European fighting men on earth.[14]

And as mentioned, a distinctive Scotch-Irishness, with deep roots in the hardworking people and rich culture of the green hills of County Antrim and other counties of Ulster Province, north Ireland, most of all defined the character of not only the Rangers in general but also Major Rogers. Despite Rogers's elevated rank and fame across the colonies, he often acted and fought in the front ranks like a common soldier to inspire the men to believe that they could beat any enemy and perform any mission. Rogers always led the way in an attack or scout to the amazement of his followers.

Rogers had escaped so many brushes with death from seemingly countless arrows, bullets, and tomahawks that he and his men truly believed he was destined never to be killed in this war—another factor that explained the desire of so many men, including volunteers from the British and Provincial ranks, to join the Rangers on even the most dangerous missions. In fact, Rogers had so many narrow misses with death that he had been reported killed numerous times, to the delight of the French leadership. As noted, Rogers's men absorbed his unique brand of unbridled confidence as if by osmosis, inspiring them to perform beyond the call of duty. The Scotch-Irish major's inspirational leadership style, aggressive nature, and confident swagger were key ingredients that would lead him and his men in audacious bids to do what everyone, except Rogers, believed was impossible.[15]

One of Rogers's rules of survival in the art of ranging war revealed why he was so often successful on the battlefield and during the conducting of deep raids: "If your rear is attacked, the main body and flankers must face about to the right or left, as occasion shall require, and form themselves to oppose the enemy, as before directed; and the same method must be observed, if attacked in either of your flanks, by which means you will always make a rear of one of your flank-guards."[16]

In addition, Rogers was motivated to excel by a host of very personal reasons that stirred deep inside him and fueled his tireless actions against the enemies of his people. The Abenaki, including warriors from St. Francis, had played a leading role in the massacre at Fort William Henry in the summer of 1757 during an orgy of bloodletting that sent shock waves reverberating on both sides of the Atlantic. Even more, Rogers believed—correctly—that it had been Abenaki warriors who dug up the body of his brother Captain Richard Rogers, who had died of smallpox on June 22, 1757, at Fort William Henry before the infamous massacre, just for the grisly honor of taking his highly prized scalp. Knowing or assuming that the culprits were from St. Francis and emphasizing the horror that haunted him for the rest of his life, Rogers never forgot how "such was the cruelty and rage of the enemy after their conquest that they dug him up out of his grave and scalped him."[17]

While traumatized and brutalized by the seemingly endless horrors of this murderous war, Major Rogers was at the peak of his fame because of successes throughout 1759, including the fall of Forts Carillon and Saint Frédéric to Major General Jeffery Amherst's British-Provincial Army in the summer. With the eventful summer nearing its end, he was now about to unleash his wrath, including for the deaths of his brother and a good many friends, neighbors, and comrades, on the most tempting of all targets, which he had obsessed about for years, St. Francis.[18] Indeed, he had long proposed delivering the punishing blow to St. Francis to a "succession of British leaders under whom he had served [but] His arguments had had no effect; nor did the fear gripping the New England frontier."[19]

Realizing that he had become an enduring symbol to the American people because of his leadership of the Rangers for years, the rawboned New Hampshire frontiersman of Scotch-Irish heritage with little education and a lowly background rejoiced in the publication in colonial newspapers of his exploits as "the famous scouter," as early as February 1756, and long thereafter as "Famous Rogers"—the resourceful, hard-hitting commander of an elite American fighting force that made people across the colonies, especially along the frontier, extremely proud to be Americans. Most important, the seemingly impossible feats of Rogers and his Rangers played a part in the initial development of a distinctive sense of American nationalism, which was destined to rise to the fore in a people's revolution from 1775 to 1783.[20]

TRAGIC PAWNS CAUGHT BETWEEN THE INTERNATIONAL RIVALRY OF ENGLAND AND FRANCE

The home of the western Abenaki village of St. Francis was more properly known to the Native American people for generations as Odanak. Historically, the Abenaki people were not only hunters and gatherers but also farmers, proficient at growing maize and other traditional crops, including beans, squash, and even sunflowers, in the broad fields that lay before the nourishing waters of the St. Francis. Because the community of St. Francis was located on a wide and placid point of the river, the soil was black and rich. Here, crops flourished under the bright Quebec sunshine, and they were harvested in the late summer and fall before the arrival of a six-month-long winter.

As noted, the Abenaki's world had fallen to pieces by the time that St. Francis had become a refugee center. In contrast to the eastern Abenaki of Maine, the smaller branch of the tribe was originally known as the western Abenaki of today's Vermont and New Hampshire. Belonging to the same linguistic group as other Algonquian peoples of many northeastern tribes, including those that had once inhabited the fertile lands of New England before the Europeans' arrival that forever altered their world, the Abenaki were Algonquian speakers, with a rich culture and ancient civilization based on living in perfect harmony with nature. Of course, the Abenaki's harmonious view of the natural world and maintaining a perfect balance with the land and everything in it was the antithesis of the white man's ethos, which basically waged war against nature to conquer and tame it to their maximum advantage.

The word *Abenaki* meant "people of the Dawnland," or the "Dawn Land People," or easterners who prayed to their god to honor the rising of the sun in the east each morning. The Abenaki called themselves Waanaki. These people lived closely with and were one with the land, the timeless rhythms of the natural world, and the mystical ways of nature in a symbiotic relationship. The western Abenaki of St. Francis were related to more distant groups of Native American people from other tribes, such as the

Maliseet and Passamaquoddy of eastern Maine. Central and eastern Maine were the Abenaki tribes' ancestral homeland, before they were pushed west by the settlers and their lives become dominated by the rhythms of war. These nature-loving people with loving families and deep beliefs in God had formerly prospered based on a harmonious existence with nature on the Atlantic coast, before the arrival of the white man.

In overall terms, the Abenaki were fortunate. During the first genocidal conflict in America, the Puritans destroyed the Pequot tribe of Connecticut in a climactic preemptive strike on the principal village along the Mystic River. The New Englanders unleashed a brutal brand of no-quarter warfare, a horrific genocide. Most of all, the Abenaki of St. Francis were true survivors of not only past encounters with whites but also the ravages of disease, especially smallpox, which had thoroughly culled their numbers in a cruel decimation. Consequently, the Abenaki embraced the Catholic faith with a passion in part because of having early received harsh treatment from the Puritans, convincing them that they needed to bolster their traditional spiritual faith. While they wore traditional dress and retained old cultural ways by the time of the French and Indian War, the Abenaki were widely considered Christian Indians because they had embraced Catholicism for three generations. French missionaries had long lived with the Abenaki to spread the word of God and earn their respect, including at St. Francis. The warriors of the community of St. Francis—named for St. Francis of Assisi, the revered Italian Catholic saint canonized by Pope Gregory IX during the summer of 1228—symbolically served on behalf of the flourishing of the Catholic faith.

In a classic irony, Rogers and his Rangers had reaped their lofty reputations when mostly serving in the ancestral hunting lands of the Abenaki in the Lake Champlain region, battling their Native American nemeses year after year. The western Abenaki had long occupied today's Vermont and New Hampshire, especially in the picturesque Connecticut River Valley and Lake Champlain areas, before the coming of the white settlers. It was the misfortune of the Abenaki not only to have been caught in the path of westward and northward expansion of New England's settlers but also to have been pawns trapped between the imperial rivalries, ambitions, and jealousies of France and England, who had transferred their ancient struggle for power and religious dominance from Europe to the New World. Consequently, the Abenaki ultimately became the tragic victims of aggression, ambition, and greed that thrived on both sides of the Atlantic, especially after the ancient cross-channel feud between England and France, ongoing for three centuries, had spilled over to become the religious-like struggle for possession of North America.

With their lands, people, and culture under severe threat from multiple directions, ensuring a hard-hitting backlash, the Abenaki raided south in a vain attempt to halt the tide of light-skinned interlopers who were seemingly destroying everything that they touched to forever change the Abenaki's world. Quite simply, the Abenaki's war was in defense (and, of course, offense was the best defense; hence the incessant raiding of the frontier) of everything they loved and that had made them the proud "People of the Dawn."

All the while, the relentless push of New Englanders, who lusted for the best Abenaki lands of immense beauty and promise, was still another migratory cycle of history that was played out to force the Abenaki from their ancestral homeland of mostly northern New England—the sacred "Dawnland"—during the seventeenth and eighteenth centuries: a guarantee of the eventual growth of St. Francis into the major Abenaki center of resistance and a stronghold situated in the remoteness of Quebec's wilderness.

From this community on the St. Francis River, war parties of revenge-seeking Abenaki warriors were supplied and basically led by the French since at least 1690, while they waged a holy war against their hated enemy with lighter skins and strange ways never understood by them. In striking back, the war parties had long journeyed south along the Connecticut River to enter vulnerable settled areas of northern New England. A magnificent river of destiny, the Connecticut was New England's longest river. It was known to the Abenaki people as Kwini tekw, or "the long river," after rising near today's United States–Canada border and flowing south over four hundred miles, through first Vermont and Massachusetts, then Connecticut, and eventually into the Long Island Sound on the Atlantic coast.

In a desperate and spirited defense of their sacred homeland, way of life, and religion, both Catholicism and their traditional spiritual beliefs, the Abenaki had long raided the isolated cabins and remote settlements of New England settlers: ugly and grim realities that were just part of ever-risky life on the frontier, which served as key motivators for Rogers and his Rangers to fight longer and harder because they possessed seemingly countless old scores to settle. Many Rangers remembered what had happened at Deerfield, Massachusetts. Part of a contingent of two hundred warriors, which included fighting men of the western Abenaki and experienced warriors from St. Francis, participated in the famous raid that had brought so much death and destruction. Deerfield lay on the fringe of western settlement in northwest Massachusetts, nestled in the Connecticut River Valley, leaving it especially vulnerable.

In this infamous bold strike led by French officers during Queen Anne's War, warriors journeyed south down the Connecticut River on snowshoes, while moving swiftly over a snowy landscape. The attackers struck the sleeping town on the early morning of February 29, 1704, some fifty-five years before Rogers's attack on St. Francis. More than one hundred New Englanders were taken prisoner, including women and children, and hurried back through the forests to Canada; some of the captives ended up in St. Francis.

The Abenaki of the northern Vermont region, southeast of Montreal, had fought their own war to determine their own destiny, because their existence depended upon stopping the encroachment of the white tide into their ancestral homeland, including their sacred lands. This holy ground included Lake Champlain, where western Abenaki creation stories, myths, and cultural heroes were based around Bitawbagok (Lake Champlain) and traditional hunting lands located mostly east of the lake. Lake Champlain had long served as the border between the western Abenaki of Vermont and the Iroquois of New York west of Lake Champlain. According to the Abenaki, their special world under the sun had been created and bestowed by the god Tabaldak, who had given Gluskab the power to create a pristine, virgin wilderness for the people to thrive and prosper in.

Another powerful Abenaki god, Odzihozo, known as "the Man Who Made Himself," had created Lake Champlain, which became the most beautiful place in existence, the center of the spiritual world for the Abenaki people. However, these picturesque lands were threatened by the tide of migrating settlers, which the Abenaki needed to stop to preserve their own way of life, values, culture, and holy grounds. Majestic Mount Katahdin, the highest point in Maine, was also part of mystical, spiritual, and religious legends of the Abenaki before they were pushed into Canada, including to St. Francis.[21]

FORGOTTEN ABENAKI VIEWS

Previous books and historians have ignored the richness and complexities of Abenaki life by presenting the usual one-dimensional caricature of the sadistic and cruel warrior that has only focused on the worst aspects—the traditional demonization. The white-based version of the St. Francis story has long reduced the Abenaki people and their sophisticated culture to the most simplistic negative racial stereotypes that have continued to exist to this day. History books and novels have presented the Abenaki as unhuman, so-called red devils, deserving of not only destruction but also genocide.

Indeed, previous books about the St. Francis raid have presented the Abenaki people as nothing but obscure background players who completely fulfilled the one-dimensional villain role in the traditional sense. But, as mentioned, the struggle known as the French and Indian War was actually much the same for both people because this was a war of simple survival in a savage land—a brutal fight for possession of a beautiful and bountiful land and the future of the North American continent.

However, and fortunately for modern readers, it is still possible to reveal (or in this case reclaim), by digging deeper into the historical record and beyond the traditional narrative long presented by American historians, the overall humanity of the Abenaki people, whose communal society ensured that all members shared in the bounty of hunts and harvests and enjoyed a rare equality unlike in the white world. Because of generations of culturally biased and outright racist writings about the Abenaki, the fundamental truths about this remarkable people have been long hidden from view.

Therefore, many of the central mysteries about the Abenaki have remained alive and well to this day to distort the historical record. Fundamental truths have been long obscured because the distortions of biased and race-based white accounts have almost always painted the Abenaki as the epitome of evil and worthy only of extermination. Unfortunately, because they were an illiterate people, the Abenaki left no accounts, allowing the one-sided perspective of the winners concerning what happened at St. Francis to be perpetuated by generations of writers, including novelists, Hollywood screenwriters, and historians.

Because the Abenaki were not a literate people, their words and thoughts have been long absent from the historical record, allowing fantasy and fiction to fill in the missing pieces. And naturally, the Abenaki—like people of any culture and race—have deserved a more realistic, accurate, and overall positive view of their way of life and general existence. Most of all, their longtime fight with the English was very much a righteous holy and noble war to save themselves and their culture from the onslaught of the land-greedy people who had stolen their ancestral territories, including even ancient burial grounds of their revered ancestors and some of the best hunting grounds that had long sustained their families.

Ironically, perhaps the best (if not the only) way to ascertain the truth about the Abenaki and their cultural ways and humanistic qualities has been to look at the accounts of white captives of the Abenaki. These accounts of captive white men and women have revealed a great many fundamental truths about the Abenaki people beyond the negative stereotypes, including with regard to warriors. Setting aside the white warfare-based accounts that have described the Abenaki only in the most demonic terms, captive accounts often show a compassionate culture with deep spiritual, philosophical, and intellectual roots.

The forgotten side of even the most seasoned Abenaki warrior was in fact a surprising amount of compassion and love that stunned captive whites, especially those individuals who had been adopted into the tribe. Indeed, instead of torturing and killing all white captives (as long assumed then and even still believed today), the Abenaki treated large numbers of whites extremely well and adopted them into the tribe at St. Francis. Especially after European diseases had killed so many Abenaki men, women, and children, this process of strengthening the tribe by adopting white captives was absolutely vital to the continued existence of the people. Consequently, many white captives enjoyed the same fate among the Abenaki as captives of rival tribes for generations: successful assimilation.

In this sense, the Abenaki were color-blind, and without the traditional kind of mostly color-based racism prevalent in the English colonies, when they adopted whites as readily as Indian captives without a hint of cultural bias or xenophobia. Families across New England assumed that their loved ones had been killed by the captors during the long journey into Canada's dark depths, when in fact they spent the remainder of the lives in contentment as full-fledged and equal members of the tribe—an unthinkable and unimaginable reality for whites, especially grieving relatives of missing family members.

A good deal of kindness and compassion were means employed by Abenaki warriors and family members to win over white captives to a new life, paving the way for them to become part of a new people, who now called the land of Quebec their home. These chosen whites replaced lost Abenaki family members, especially sons or other relatives killed in war, becoming appropriate surrogates in what had become tribal custom according to a revered tradition, which was all about survival of the tribe in the long term.

A young white captive of the Abenaki of St. Francis named Susanna Johnson revealed views that have overturned some of the most fundamental negative stereotypes about not only the Abenaki but also Native Americans in general. In summarizing her long period of captivity at St. Francis, Susanna presented basic truths in her fascinating book that shocked white readers, who had never previously encountered such a thorough overturning of racial stereotypes about Native Americans. She wrote honestly and with sincere conviction about the St. Francis warriors who had captured her and her family, including her husband and children, on August 24, 1754 (barely five years before Rogers's devastating attack on St. Francis), at the northern-most settlement near Fort Number Four in Charlestown, New Hampshire, located on the east bank of the Connecticut River.

Most significantly in Susanna's revealing memoir about her experiences, including at St. Francis, she advised white readers to alter their prejudiced thinking and views based on popular racial stereotypes:

> In justice to the Indians, I ought to remark, that they never treated me with cruelty to a wanton degree; few people have survived a situation like mine, and few have fallen into the hands of savages disposed to more lenity and patience. . . . Can it be said of civilized conquerors, that they [Europeans], in the main, are willing to share with their prisoners, the last ration of food, when famine stares them in the face? Do they ever adopt an enemy, and salute him by the tender name of brother? And I am justified in doubting, whether if I had fallen into the hands of French soldiery, so much assiduity would have been shewn, to preserve my life.[22]

This distinct sense of consideration and compassion of the Abenaki warriors for white captives was displayed from the beginning of her capture. When first taken captive after having been aroused from her sleep by the Native American attackers who crashed through the front door, a naked

Susanna was surprised when "an Indian had plundered three gowns, who, on seeing my situation, gave me the whole."[23]

Clearly, Susanna's overall experiences as a captive had made her open-minded toward people of a different race and culture to a remarkable degree, because what she had personally learned about the Abenaki people, including even battle-hardened warriors, in their own home settings completely shattered the long-existing racial stereotypes and fears that she had learned on the northern frontier before her capture. But Susanna's enlightened transformation of racial thought and the erasing of racial stereotypes about Indians had not come easy or in the beginning of her period of captivity. Of course, her experiences were most difficult in the beginning before their arrival at St. Francis. The attack on her home and family could hardly have been more traumatic. Fleeing the scene of the devastating attack before the arrival of militiamen from the nearby Fort Number Four, the Abenaki and their terrified captives, including Susanna's husband and small children, had moved north at a brisk pace through the dark woodlands. During the first halt, Susanna, who was in a late stage of pregnancy, was surprised when "the savages, supposing that we, as well as themselves, might have an appetite for breakfast, gave us a loaf of bread, some raisins and apples, which they had taken from the house."[24]

When Susanna was about to give birth one early morning during the long trek north to St. Francis, the war-hardened Abenaki warriors stunned her with their completely unexpected acts of compassion and deep concern for her well-being: "I was taken with the pangs of child-birth. The Indians signified to us that we must go on to a brook. When we got there, they shewed some humanity, by making a booth for me." The "Indians kept aloof the whole time [and] About ten o'clock a daughter was born. They then brought me some articles of clothing for the child, which they had taken from the house."[25]

The first published account of Susanna's amazing odyssey all the way to St. Francis and her miraculous return from captivity was printed in a Philadelphia newspaper in January 1758:

A few Days ago past through this Place [New Haven, Connecticut] in her Way home, Mrs. Johnson, with her Sister and two Children: they with the rest of their Family being nine in all, were taken Captive by the Indians at No. 4, in August 1754, and were carried from thence to Crown-Point, where they arrived in

nine Days after they were taken: In the Wilderness between No. 4 and Crown-
Point, Mrs. Johnson was delivered of a Child, having no Woman with her but
her Sister of about 14 Years old; yet by the Help of her Husband [Captain James
Johnson] she and Child arrived safe at Crown-Point, and from thence proceeded
to Canada [and St. Francis].[26]

Susanna provided other examples of Abenaki compassion toward the white captives upon reaching St. Francis. After an exchange of goods, Susanna passed from the possession of her warrior captor and became part of a new family, which had the highest standing in all St. Francis:

I was taken to the house of my new master, and found myself allied to the first
family [of St. Francis]; my master, whose name was [Joseph-Lewis] Gill [whose
white parents had been captured separately on the northern frontier and brought
to St. Francis, where they had eventually married], was son-in-law to the grand
sachem [the tribe's spiritual leader], was accounted rich, had a store of goods, and
lived in a style far above the majority of his tribe.—He often told me that he had
an English heart, but his wife was true Indian blood. Soon after my arrival at
his house, the interpreter came to inform me that I was adopted into his family. I
was then introduced to the family, and was told to call them brothers and sisters,
I made a short speech, expressive of gratitude.[27]

Like other white captives, Susanna was surprised by the genuineness and warmth of her new Abenaki family, which included Antoine and Sabattis (or Xavier) Gill, who were destined to be captured in Rogers's raid and taken back to New England. As she wrote, "My new sisters and brothers treated me with the same attention that they did their natural kindred."[28]

In fact, Susanna was impressed by the overall peacefulness and happiness of the Abenaki people, of both pure and mixed blood, especially the family of Chief Gill. Born in St. Francis in 1719, blond-haired Joseph-Louis Gill, who had been baptized as a Roman Catholic like his captive parents (including his father of Irish heritage), had become "the White Chief" of the Abenaki by the time of Rogers's attack. It was most appropriate that this rather remarkable white man with blond hair, who had married an Abenaki woman, was the chief, because St. Francis was a mixed-race community that included English captives, Frenchmen, French Canadians, and their offspring with Abenaki women.

Ironically, the most hated Indian community in America was more open-minded about matters of race and racial intermixing than the so-called civilized white communities in New England and elsewhere in America. Susanna described other common features of Indian life that surprised her: "The inhabitants lived in perfect harmony, holding most of their property in common [and] They were extremely modest, and apparently adverse to airs of courtship."[29]

Indeed, completely in tune with the world of nature, the Abenaki people of St. Francis were deeply spiritual and even more devout than most whites because of not only their native religious beliefs but also their Catholicism. Missing the mark like the generations of white novelists, historians, and Hollywood writers who have focused on the evil qualities of the Abenaki in relation to the St. Francis raid, Francis Parkman almost casually concluded that the Indians at St. Francis had been long targeted by Major Rogers for destruction: "They were nominal Christians, and had been under the control of their missionaries for three generations; but though zealous and sometimes fanatical in their devotion to the forms of Romanism, they remained thorough savages in dress, habits, and character."[30] Of course, Parkman's words reflected his racial views, conservative background, and New England heritage, as well as his times that were known for racial intolerance.

For instance, in denouncing the savagery at St. Francis, he emphasized how white captives were subjected "to the torture of 'running the gantlet'" between a row of warriors swinging sticks and clubs at the runners.[31] However, the experiences of Susanna Johnson and a good many other white captives have told a much different story from that related by generations of white historians. Susanna tells us in her own words about the event endured by herself, her husband, and another male captive. In a symbolic running "thro' the gauntlet" at St. Francis upon their arrival, she emphasized, she and the male captives were treated gently because "each Indian only gave us a tap on the shoulder."[32]

An editor of the newspaper in New Haven, Connecticut, reported in January 1758 about Susanna's liberation: "Mrs. Johnson, with her Sister and two Children ... after living [at St. Francis] for some Time, among the Indians, they were bought [by additional money that filled the coffers of St. Francis in what was a most lucrative business transaction] by a Frenchman, and last July 17 sailed from Quebec in a Cartel Ship for England, from which they came to New-York [and] The Child which was born in the Woods . . . is still alive, and returned with its Mother."[33]

Indeed, Susanna's story was destined to continue with history coming full circle not long after Rogers raided St. Francis. Chief Gill's two sons, Antoine and Sabattis, survived the long retreat of the starving Rangers from the destroyed St. Francis in early October and into the biting cold and rains of November. A remarkable reunion occurred at, of all places, Fort Number Four, after Susanna had returned from Massachusetts to live in her old hometown of nearby Charlestown, New Hampshire, on the Connecticut River. Here, the tattered and worn Rangers, including Rogers, came in with Sabattis, who, when he saw Susanna, yelled in excitement, "My God! My God! Here is my sister!"[34]

Susanna Johnson never forgot one of the happiest moments of her life: "It was my little brother Saba[t]tis [Xavier], who formerly used to bring the cows for me when I lived at my Indian masters [the Chief Joseph-Louis Gill family]. He was transported to see me, and declared that he was still my brother and I must be his sister. Poor fellow! The fortune of war had left him without a single relation [but his father]; but with his country's enemies he could find one who too sensibly felt his miseries. I felt the purest pleasure in administrating to his comfort."[35]

In truth, and contrary to what generations of Americans historians, including Francis Parkman, have maintained in their reliance on simplistic and popular racial stereotypes, the Abenaki, including the warriors, "were deeply devout" as a people in general, because a deep sense of spiritualism reigned supreme along the banks of the St. Francis River.[36] And, as mentioned, this solemn devoutness and spiritualism among the Abenaki also included a passionate Catholicism. However, because of their separate legal status while living in the government-sanctioned mission community of St. Francis, the Abenaki continued to retain their own language, distinctive cultural ways, communal government, and separate identity, almost as if the mission priests and Catholicism in their midst were nonexistent.[37]

Indeed, Abenaki devotion to the Catholic faith, which helped to fuel a savagery seldom seen when the warriors raided the settlements, was a key quality that made the Abenaki warriors the most formidable opponents year after year. The Abenaki had long prospered in their pristine world along the blue waters of the St. Francis River, while their reputation as consummate warriors spread far and wide.

Here, these resilient people of strong faith believed that they benefited from the overall general harmony and beneficence of their universe with the blessings of their God. But this delicate balance and harmonious relationship with the pristine world of nature and Abenaki guardian spirits had been dramatically disturbed and thrown badly off balance by the interloping whites, who took their lands, cut down the tallest trees, and chased the deer and moose away from ancestral hunting grounds. By the time of the French and Indian War, consequently, the world was badly out of sync for the Abenaki, who only wanted to return to a past without the hated English and their evil ways. In part, they fought to restore the long-lost balance that was necessary for the tribe's future survival and a bright future for their people.

Therefore, the large numbers of Abenaki warriors who struck at the New England settlements year after year were not simply killing for killing's sake in a blind rage. For the most part, they were attempting to restore the overall harmony of their universe, which had been turned upside down by the ceaseless tide of white interlopers who brought disease—including venereal disease but especially smallpox and measles—as well as trade goods and alcohol (the last two had created a dangerous dependence and invisible chains that tightly bound them to white civilization, eroding tribal values and customs). All of this threatened to destroy the Abenaki's very existence as an independent people.[38]

As Susanna Johnson and other captured whites had learned, the social life of the Abenaki was rich and complex, differing remarkably from their own European-based society in ways that the transplanted whites at St. Francis could have never imagined. Unlike in the capitalist world that sought to destroy nature partly by waging an exploitative war of conquest upon it, the Abenaki lived in perfect harmony with the natural world, while family life thrived in an open society, without the curse of racism, based on sharing in a communal existence with their equally sharing neighbors regardless of color.

Therefore, no Abenaki, young or old, went hungry, like in white society and even England's great capital of London on the Thames River, because there were no class or racial distinctions among the people, who shared both good times and bad times as one: the antithesis of European societies, in which the wealthy ruling class of the large landowning elites dominated the lower-class of mostly landless peasants, who were little more than slaves.

Greed and selfishness, which were known only too well in the white world, were frowned upon in Abenaki society, while sharing and generosity were viewed as the most virtuous traits—stemming from time-honored tribal values rather than traditional Catholic values—that defined the true character of an Abenaki man or a woman. To the shock and horror of white society in general, the admirable qualities and virtues of Abenaki society were so many that white captives easily and relatively smoothly fit into the overall stream of daily life of an agrarian people, acclimating with loving adopted relatives. Unruly, impolite, and inconsiderate behavior brought great shame to a person who upset the cherished harmony in this communal society, which put a premium on good and decent behavior toward fellow human beings.

However, Catholicism likewise played an important role in Abenaki life. A favorite design utilized by spiritual-minded Abenaki women on artwork was the Christian cross, and warriors wore silver and gold crosses and other symbols of Roman Catholicism in both war and peace, unlike most frontiersmen, who placed more of their faith in their trusty muskets or rifles.

To preserve all that they valued and loved about their close-knit societies of loving individuals that were literally on the brink long before the French and Indian War, the Abenaki struck exceptionally hard at New England's settlers with a ferocity seldom seen. Like in the world of nature, where a perfect balance dominated as if seemingly by the dictate of a benevolent God, the maintaining of harmony among tribal members was all important. Most of all, the thriving Abenaki community located on the St. Francis River was a loving society in which even many white captives, like Susanna Johnson, were fully accepted and treated exceptionally well, including being addressed as brother and sister and treated affectionately as such.[39]

Even the captives taken at Deerfield in the bitter cold of February 1704 were "treated well by their captors" at St. Francis and then on the long trek to Montreal. One captive, Reverend John Williams, who survived his ordeal, was surprised to see white children, adopted by the tribe and fully acclimated to Indian life, living as well as the longtime members of the extended community at St. Francis.

Captain John Stark, Rogers's longtime top lieutenant who, like the major, was a proud son of the Upper Merrimack River Valley, might well have decided not to embark upon the St. Francis raid in September 1759 because he "felt somewhat loath to attack a village that had treated him well" when held a captive in 1752.[40] Indeed, Stark would be unable to "muster the necessary lust for vengeance against people who had shown him so much 'genuine kindness' during his captivity" at St. Francis.[41]

Stark's odyssey became legendary. The youngest of the group, John Stark hailed from the Scotch-Irish family farm that bordered Amoskeag Falls near Harrytown in the Merrimack River Valley (located near today's Manchester, New Hampshire), and he, like Susanna Johnson, was destined to undergo an amazing ordeal and transformation. He and three companions, including his older brother William Stark, had been hunting and trapping on the clear waters of the Baker River, around seventy miles north of his Merrimack River home since March 1752, when they were captured by ten Abenaki warriors of a hunting party on April 28, 1752. A large supply of furs, especially lucrative beaver pelts, were eagerly taken by the warriors, wiping out months of hard work. He and his other surviving comrade—William Stinson had been killed, while his brother William had escaped—were forced to run the gauntlet at St. Francis on June 9. Amos Eastman was savagely beaten by warriors with wooden clubs during his desperate run between two files of Abenaki in part because he had foolishly repeated a phrase (not in English) that he would beat all of the young men, which, of course, incensed the proud warriors, especially the younger ones.

But Stark smartly knew better than to repeat the phrase as instructed, deciding to let his actions speak for themselves during his ordeal. Instead, he "declared, in a loud voice, [that] he would kiss all the young women [in a song]; and, being athletic, the few buffets he received were returned with such earnestness and interest that some were knocked down, and others, alarmed at his boldness and prowess, [then] allow[ed] him a peaceable transit" through the gauntlet.[42]

Thereafter, during his five weeks of captivity at St. Francis, Stark "became a great favorite with the Indians"—the elders of the tribe had been especially impressed by his bravado and feisty nature and called him "Young Chief"— for the aggressive qualities that later helped to make him Rogers's top lieutenant, fighting primarily against the Abenaki in the wilds far north of the northern settlements.[43]

Especially after Stark had gained the respect of the warriors, including the wise elders, before he was ransomed thanks to a Massachusetts initiative headed by Captain Phineas Stevens—the father of Captain Simon Stevens of Deerfield, Massachusetts, and his older brother Lieutenant Samuel Stevens, both members of Rogers's Rangers—who had become a legendary hero for his defense of New England's northernmost fort (Fort Number Four), he long appreciated the Abenaki kindness he had received at St. Francis, particularly after he was adopted into the tribe by the sachem.

Having benefited from being "treated . . . as one of their own," Stark never forgot the undeniable reality "that he had experienced more genuine kindness from the savages of St. Francis, than he ever knew prisoners of war to receive from any civilization nation."[44] However, purchases by the French for servitude and sizeable ransoms paid by the English secured a good many white prisoners, both males and females, before they became fully acclimated into Abenaki life. During July 1756, for instance, Rogers learned from a French prisoner "that the [English] prisoners were sold in Canada for 50 crowns each."[45]

Captive Robert Eastburn, who was raised in Philadelphia, would have agreed with Stark and Susanna Johnson's admiration for their captors and the Abenaki's better qualities, which rose to the fore and were on full display at St. Francis. He described one of numerous examples of Indian kindness when he was ill clothed and sick in freezing weather: "The Indians perceiving I was unwell, and could not eat their coarse food, ordered some chocolate [a French favorite] to be boiled for me, and seeing me eat that, appeared pleased."[46]

Stark's good treatment while a captive in St. Francis in 1752 was no exaggeration or embellishment, because he came to so greatly admire the Abenaki in multiple ways. To the shock of white civilization, revealing a deep-seated fear of the acclimation process of whites, especially females, into Native American society, which was viewed as the worst of all horrors, some white captives even refused to return to white society when given the opportunity. The fact that many white captives declined to return to so-called civilization was unimaginable on every level to people across the colonies and for generations thereafter.

Reflecting mankind's historic adaptive and melting-pot nature—different people have naturally mixed regardless of race and intermarried (mostly in

common-law unions) wherever they have met from the beginning of time—
and how the white and Native American worlds had become intermixed by the
time of the French and Indian War, this relatively smooth acclimation process
of so many white captives at St. Francis was the ultimate white nightmare.
This development heightened the longtime fear among the English that the
American wilderness was fully capable of corrupting and eroding Europeans
by reducing them to the so-called barbaric level of the hated "savages," who
represented all that was evil to generations of settlers.[47]

During the early colonial period on the northern frontier, including
during periods between the wars, the intermixing of whites (both captives
and noncaptives) and Native Americans was easier because the modern racial
concept of whiteness had not yet become a powerful force to discourage intimate interaction between different races on the melting-pot frontier, as later
would be the case during the course of western expansion. Instead of embracing the intolerant concept of whiteness—in part because the British had long
been viewed as the enemy by Celtic people, especially the Irish, since English
invaders had subjugated their ancestors and native homelands—settlers at
this time generally viewed themselves more as Scotch-Irish, Scottish, Irish,
or Welsh than as white.[48]

PRIVATE ROBERT KIRKWOOD'S AMAZING SCOTTISH ODYSSEY IN THE NEW WORLD

Like Captain John Stark, Ranger Robert Kirkwood, a young Lowland
Scot who had formerly served as a private in a Scottish Highland com-
mand (Colonel Archibald Montgomery's 77th Highland Regiment), also
learned intimately about Native American ways as a captive. And like Stark,
Susanna Johnson, and so many others, he also grew to greatly admire his
captors from the northern wilderness. He had been captured by Shawnee
warriors in mid-September 1758 when Major James Grant's advance of
Brigadier General John Forbes's expedition was repulsed at the outskirts of
Fort Duquesne—today's Pittsburgh—and mauled by a tide of angry Native
Americans and French.

Wounded by a warrior with buckshot in the leg and at his captor's mercy,
Kirkwood was just about to be tomahawked when a warrior interceded and
saved him at the last second. This compassionate warrior believed that Kirkwood had been divinely ordained to replace his dead brother. Consequently,

the much-surprised Scotsman was viewed as a surrogate brother and treated with great kindness, especially after his adoption by the tribe. Along with his life, Kirkwood gained a tribe, brother, and wife, including her son.[49]

Private Kirkwood said of his spiritual Shawnee brother, who had saved his life and altered his fate forever, "He then informed me that . . . they were at war with a neighboring nation called Cherokies [*sic*], and that in an engagement they had his brother killed, but that the good man, i.e., God, had sent me in his place [and] they hugged me and called me in their broken english, Brother; they then gave me the name of him, in whose place I was adopted [and] They used me with so much affection, that at first I could not help regarding them very much."[50]

Then Kirkwood recounted how

> *I was presented to my adopted wife and a fine boy who my brother told me was my son [and] While I was among them, I lost all knowledge of the time, the Indians calculating all by Moons. . . . I asked [my adopted Shawnee brother after learning to speak some of the Shawnee language] what was the reason, he and the rest of his nation had so much regard for the French, and such an antipathy to the English, and why they acted with so much inhumanity towards the settlers; he answered, because the French were kind to them, and dealt in every thing towards them with honesty, whereas the English used them quite otherwise, several having [been] wrong'd [and] He added, that the lands now possessed by the English, formerly belong'd to them, and that the French promised they should be restored; he remarked that the English instead of making this restitution were daily encroaching, and curtailing them of what was left, that this, together with the insinuations of the French, gave them great encouragement to murder those that fell into their hands.[51]*

When Kirkwood told his adopted Shawnee brother that "the Good Man" (God, also known to many pro-French Native Americans as "the Master of Life") was not pleased that "such murders should be perpetrated," the warrior then explained how "he did not like such murders, but that revenge was sweet, and that a bad warrior was esteem'd no better than an old woman [and] that the Good Man was certainly angry with the white people for taking their lands."[52]

When asked about God and the afterlife, this Shawnee warrior who had saved Kirkwood's life answered his adopted white brother that "at his death he should go to any place that God or the Good Man should appoint, where if his conduct was approved, he should never feel either hunger or cold, or undergo any other hardship."[53]

As fate would have it, when the opportunity finally arrived, Kirkwood eventually escaped from the Shawnee in late May 1759 while part of a hunting party along the Ohio River, just in time to rejoin his Scottish regiment and to then volunteer to serve on Rogers's expedition to St. Francis. Kirkwood was just the kind of young and durable Celtic fighting man whom Rogers needed on his daring raid to St. Francis. His expertise in Indian ways and wide-ranging experiences would have astounded the major, who had never been captured despite many close calls, if he and Kirkwood engaged in private conversations.[54]

PRIVATE THOMAS BROWN'S HARROWING ORDEAL

When young Private Thomas Brown enlisted in the Rangers in May 1757, he had no idea that he had made a pact with the devil because he was about to enter into a surreal hell during his Ranger service—the disastrous Second Battle on Snowshoes. After having been victimized by a deadly ambush, Rogers had left the wounded survivors, who were cut off on the battlefield in the thick woods and on their own under a veil of darkness, escaping to fight another day. At this time, Private Tom Brown was in bad shape, having been wounded in three places during the hot firefight and then left helpless on the body-strewn battlefield like most of his immediate comrades. The small group of fallen Rangers around him included his company commander, Captain Thomas Speakman of Boston. Lying nearby, Ranger Robert Baker also had been left alone in the depths of the dark woodlands and high snow just west of Lake Champlain on the night of March 13, 1758.

Brown described the horror of watching as an "Indian came to Captain Spikeman [Speakman], who was not able to resist, and stripped and scalped him alive; Baker, who was lying by the captain, pulled out his knife to stab himself [to commit suicide], which the Indian prevented and carried him away. . . . [N]ot being far from Captain Spikeman, he saw me and begged me for God's sake! to give him a tomahawk that he might put an end to his life!"[55]

Private Brown, only a fresh-faced teenager with a spunky attitude, was astonished when he attempted to escape the following morning after the bloody battle in which the Rangers had been slaughtered and had suffered frightful losses: "I heard the shouts of Indians behind me [and] four came down the mountain, running toward me [and] When they were within a few rods of me they cocked their guns, and told me to stop; but I refused, hoping they would fire and kill me on the spot; which I chose, rather than the dreadful death of Captain Spikeman [who was scalped alive and beheaded]."[56]

However, the wounded Brown was finally captured. After surviving a harrowing ordeal, Private Brown wrote, "On the 1st of May [1758] we set off to go to the Mississippi, where my Indian master belonged [and whose village was reached in August.] When we came here I was ordered to live with a squaw, who was to be my mother. I lived with her during the winter, and was employed in hunting, dressing leather, &c., being cloathed [sic] after the Indian fashion."[57]

In the end, Private Thomas Brown was officially exchanged in November 1759. Ranger Brown's odyssey was a remarkable one, and he only survived because of, as he said, the "kind appearance of a good God for my preservation."[58]

THE RANGERS' DESIRE FOR REVENGE

Of course, Rogers, like the fierce Achilles, who had been the best warrior among the ancient Greeks during the Trojan War and not unlike the burly New Hampshire major of Scotch-Irish antecedents in regard to his larger-than-life leadership style in heading the Rangers year after year, possessed quite a different view of St. Francis than John Stark, Susanna Johnson, Robert Kirkwood, and other captives of the Abenaki. Indeed, Rogers had been obsessed with a burning desire to destroy St. Francis for years.

As Rogers explained in his November 5, 1759, report to Major General Jeffery Amherst, "This nation [Abenaki] of Indians was notoriously attached to the French, and had for near a century past harrassed [sic] the frontiers of New England, killing people of all ages and sexes in a most barbarous manner, at a time when they did not in the least suspect them; and to my knowledge, in six years time, carried into captivity, and killed, on the before mentioned frontiers, 400 persons."[59]

As noted, Major Rogers also possessed personal reasons that explained his obsession with dealing St. Francis a knockout blow. He wanted to obtain a measure of revenge for the desecration of his brother Richard's body at the soldier graveyard at Fort William Henry. Either Abenaki warriors—the most likely culprits—or members of another tribe had "dug him up out of the grave and scalped him," in Rogers's own words.[60]

Echoing the common view, the editor of the *Boston Gazette* emphasized how the Abenaki of St. Francis were "guilty of more Inhumanities, Bloodshed, and Murders, than perhaps any Tribe on the Continent."[61] In truth, the Abenaki had largely become pawns, if not victims, of the fiery teachings of zealous Jesuits, who lived at St. Francis. The endless anti-Protestant rhetoric of the militant priests had been effective in creating holy warriors eager to take heretic scalps. The Jesuits had even relied on the much-emphasized story that the English—and not the ancient Romans stationed at Jerusalem—had killed Jesus Christ. Clearly, ugly aspects of so-called European civilization had come to the Abenaki to shape their perceptions of the world, while helping to make them the most lethal killers on the frontier.[62]

For such reasons, the world of Robert Rogers was a surreal one on multiple levels, because of the striking contradictions and paradoxes that were truly astonishing. There was the breathtaking beauty of the unspoiled land of virgin wilderness, blue lakes, and clear streams that had been untouched by man and appeared exactly how God had intended them to be in all their natural glory. The awe-inspiring beauty of this magnificent land was seemingly mocked by the surreal horror and immorality—in white eyes—of the native inhabitants, who fought for their homeland with a ferocity that had long appalled the colonists.

But it was precisely the beauty of this pristine land, loved by the Abenaki and by settlers for the same reasons, that caused the Native Americans to commit the most horrific acts of cruelty and brutality. The Abenaki hoped that this unrestrained brand of terrorism might drive these English interlopers off their ancestral lands in panic. However, most Scotch-Irish settlers were not the kind to be scared away or give up. Instead, they fought back even harder with their own ferocity and brutality, which matched that of their enemy. During this nightmarish war of unparalleled horrors, Rogers's Rangers served as the symbolic spearhead of this sharp backlash against the settler's longtime tormentors who had so often come sweeping down from the north: the fundamental genesis of the upcoming raid on St. Francis calculated to wipe out the most infamous Native American sanctuary in North America.

Consequently, it was the great beauty and unspoiled nature of this wondrous land of the north country that provided the primary catalyst for the Abenaki's unleashing of a brutality on a scale that defied the imagination, including horrors directed against white women and children. And it was all committed largely in the name of something that was beautiful and God's own masterful creation that was awe-inspiring: the possession of a truly magnificent land of seemingly endless promise.

Major Rogers intimately understood the subtle nuances of this strange symbiotic relationship between pristine natural beauty and man-made horrors that had been magnified to unprecedented heights in this war. Indeed, everything that happened between the fighting men on both sides in this nightmarish war was all about the land and its irresistible appeal, because it had always been the primary bone of contention between empires, civilizations, and vastly different peoples—English, French, Native Americans, Scotch-Irish, and Canadians—who actually thought much the same in fundamental ways, and much more than has been emphasized by modern historians.

But it was the poorest settlers, mostly the Scotch-Irish on the ever-dangerous frontier because they could not afford land anywhere else, and the poorest of all inhabitants, the Native Americans, who were truly caught in global events beyond their control in the unpredictable ebbs and flows of this brutal struggle between imperial empires, which was waged to secure the riches of North America—not gold or silver but this vast land itself because it equated to limitless riches that could be harvested for centuries to come. In the larger scheme of things, and as a cruel fate would have it, the settlers on the northern frontier and the Native Americans were all nothing more than tragic pawns who slaughtered each other year after year, while being cynically used and manipulated in the great imperial game of empire building by the kings, political elites, and aristocrats of the European Powers.[63]

CHAPTER THREE

The Most Audacious Raid
of the French and Indian War

FULLY UNDERSTANDING THE SUPREME IMPORTANCE OF STRIKING THE
Abenaki in their most secure sanctuary, the ever-eager Scotch-Irish major,
referred to in colonial newspapers as "the brave Rogers" and "the Famous
Rogers," had been thinking about the most daring of raids for a considerable time by the summer of 1759. He had been lusting to strike the great
enemy sanctuary of St. Francis for almost as long as he could remember.
Quite simply, no place stood out more in Robert Rogers's mind than St.
Francis, because this had been the legendary staging area for the seemingly
endless number of devastating raids on the New England settlements for
generations. No Native Americans had so thoroughly mastered the art of
unleashing surprise attacks with such lethal effectiveness than the Abenaki.
In having thoroughly adapted to the ways of Indian warfare, Major Rogers
had himself become a master of innovative tactics designed to catch the
opponent by surprise, and he was ready to put them to use in his pet project.

Rogers's eagerness to attack St. Francis was well known. With both written and oral proposals, Rogers had implored John Campbell, the Fourth Earl
of Loudoun, who had taken over command of British forces in North America after Governor William Shirley had stepped down, to be allowed to attack
St. Francis. In August 1756, Rogers had "applied" to the Earl of Loudoun,
who had just gained command of the British army in North America, that he
"might attempt to penetrate Canada, and distress the inhabitants, by burning
their harvest (now nearly ripe) and destroying their cattle."[1]

Rogers's most formal proposal to Lord Loudoun to be allowed to attack St. Francis had been rejected on October 19, 1756, but the setback had only made him more determined to succeed in the end.[2] Indeed, as if possessing a fine wine from an ancient vineyard that had matured with age, Rogers "had harbored for several years" a bold plan for the most audacious small-scale offensive operation in the entirety of the French and Indian War.[3]

As noted, Rogers had been long contemplating a bold strike on St. Francis, which meant going into the dark heart of New France, and it had never left his heart and mind. No one had performed such a daring tactical feat of this magnitude because no one had possessed the combination of vision and raw courage Rogers did. Positioned in the wilderness between Quebec and Montreal in protective fashion, St. Francis seemed to have been located too far into the depths of hostile territory of Quebec for any possible strike by a party of raiders. Rogers thought otherwise.

In his agile mind in which nothing was impossible, Rogers had long thought about rowing north down the broad expanse of Lake Champlain to its northeastern head to reach a mysterious place in the unmapped wilderness called Missisquoi Bay: he could not be followed along this water route unless spotted by French patrol boats, which he knew that he could elude as he had so often in the past. Then, from this advanced point on the northeast of Lake Champlain, a band of fast-moving Rangers could then trek around seventy-five miles, as the crow flies, north to St. Francis. Incredibly, despite the knowledge that such a mission would be the most daunting and dangerous of his career, Rogers was not deterred by the notable fact that St. Francis was, in the major's own words, "situated within three miles of the river St. Lawrence, in the middle of Canada, about half way between Montreal and Quebec."[4]

As demonstrated during dozens of past missions north in and around Forts Carillon and Saint Frédéric for years, Rogers had evolved, in his focus on killing French, Canadian, and Indian fighting men and their leaders, into a master of waging economic and logistical warfare rather than the traditional war of attrition. This was not the case with the Abenaki when it came to Rangers, whose scalps were always the most prized possession. In the hope of destroying not only settlers but also the economic foundations of their encroaching civilization in order to push back and force the abandonment of entire settlements, the warriors, who knew that the

demographic odds were against them, had long relied on terrorism. Therefore, large numbers of settlers had long been killed in the grisliest fashion,
livestock slaughtered in the fields, trees of fruit orchards cut down, and the
barns and storage bins containing food necessary for survival through the
harsh New England winters torched.

But because the French population of French Canada—concentrated
in Montreal, Quebec, and the thin line of small settlements in the St. Lawrence Valley—was many times smaller than that of the English colonies and
received less support from France, which had long focused more on the war
in Europe, than the thirteen colonies from their mother country, Rogers's
especially devastating kind of economic warfare was an effective means of
reducing New France's limited war-waging capabilities and eroding the will
of the civilian populace in a harsh northern environment.

Although not yet in his mid-twenties, Rogers had early learned firsthand about the ugly ways of economic and psychological warfare, which
were classic tenets of guerrilla, or Indian, warfare. In April 1748, the Rogers
family farm at Mountalona, which reminded these Scotch-Irish settlers of
the grassy meadows and green hills of Ulster Province, had been destroyed
by an Indian and French raid almost certainly launched from St. Francis.
The attackers had wiped out a decade's worth of sweat, sacrifice, and hard
work. Robert saw his family's burned-down cabin, slaughtered livestock,
and razed orchard. It was a lesson that the young man from the northern
frontier never forgot, because the farm had represented the family's principal capital and future.

Rogers's unsurpassed skill in waging his own special brand of economic
war of attrition on New France's southernmost defensive bastions was well
honed by the battle-hardened Rangers by the beginning of General Jeffery
Amherst's summer campaign of 1759. Rogers's longtime logistical war had
been focused on destroying supplies of food in the hope of inducing the
abandonment of French advance positions of Fort Carillon and Fort Saint
Frédéric (basically the same longtime strategy of the Abenaki in regard to
attempting to force back the tide of settlement) in the strategic Lake Champlain corridor during what was a total war.

When around Forts Carillon and Saint Frédéric, therefore, he had long
targeted French storage bins, granaries, barns, and supplies of cordwood for
destruction in wintertime, burned fields of grain, and killed livestock. In the

process, the Rangers became experts in efficient and swift destruction. Most important, this was no random destruction on Rogers's part in what was a well-conceived logistical and economic war, of which he had been a master for years. As early as January 26, 1756, Rogers wrote in his journal, "We employed ourselves while we dare stay in setting fire to the houses and barns of the village, with which were consumed large quantities of wheat, and other grain; we also killed about fifty cattle, and then retired, leaving the whole village in flames."[5]

On February 29, 1756, Rogers struck again to catch the enemy by surprise, waging a hard-hitting and effective logistical war that proved highly effective. He led a force of Rangers north toward Fort Carillon on another daring mission "to distress the French and their allies, by sacking, burning, and destroying their houses [and] barns [and] by killing their cattle of every kind."[6]

Therefore, by 1759, Rogers and his men possessed more experience than any soldiers in the British army in the refined art of raiding over long distances to wage a frontier brand of economic warfare with a thorough effectiveness. In this sense, the upcoming raid on St. Francis, where the products of the Abenaki harvest by women and children had been stored for the winter by October 4, should also be seen as an offensive effort directed at waging economic warfare and terrorizing the opponent by destroying not only his home but also his economic support system.[7]

Contrary to existing stereotypes about the Rangers as nothing more than ruthless killers, Major Rogers had long acted in accordance with his orders to wage a war of destruction that was less about the grim business of killing as many of the enemy as possible. William Shirley emphasized how one of Rogers's primary missions was to "destroy their out Magazines and Settlements" of the French situated around their forts. General Jeffery Amherst's orders to Rogers on September 13, 1759, to destroy not only small settlements along the St. Lawrence River Valley but also St. Francis were largely economic and logistically focused.[8]

If any troops in America could perform this seemingly impossible mission all the way to "the middle of Canada to destroy St. Francis," in Rogers's words, it was the Rangers, whose level of experience in waging effective economic warfare and in the art of Indian warfighting ways was unmatched in Major General Jeffery Amherst's army or anywhere else. By this time, Rogers and the Rangers had become indispensable to the overall war effort. For ample good reason, therefore, the reputation of Rogers's Rangers and their resourceful commander had grown to considerable heights, including among the French and the Indians, who hated the troublesome Rangers, who often outthought and outfought them in their own territory.

Ironically, Rogers's first regimental commander, Colonel Joseph Blanchard—who had led his New Hampshire regiment with distinction when Rogers first served as a private in 1754 and then possessed a captain's rank in the spring of 1755, when he led the command's best company, which was "the genesis of Rogers's Rangers"—wrote prophetically in a letter to Rogers of the situation that now applied to the St. Francis expedition instead of General James Abercromby's 1758 campaign, while praising the overall high quality of the Rangers on March 10, 1758:

> *I rejoice, as well as for the signal Honour you've acquired by your martial Attempts and Success, in Defence of Country. May you Live, and that Spirit not depart from you, so long as a Frenchman in this Land dare own himself an Enemy. The enterprising Youths from our Frontiers who have and are joining you for the Ranging Service, are not the Gleanings, but the first Fruits of North-America, by their Loyalty, Courage and Activity, it seems by Instinct, as well as Principle, are fitted to be thought to rob a Bear of her Whelps—or enter those effeminate—unmolested Dens, in your Neighborhood, which have (to our Dishonour) stood too long in our Way. . . . I heartily wish you a favorable Opportunity and successful Attack against those mongrel Disturbers of the publick Peace, and a full Reprisal in Honour, Profit and Revenge, for all their perfidious Treatments [while] the Enemy's County filled with Scalps, Captives, Money, private Plunder, war-like Stores and Provisions. . . . For a New England Man [has] to reflect on the past horrid Scenes of Devastations and Murders perpetuated by those tawny cloven footed tribes [especially the Abenaki], hurried on by these satanical French invaders.[9]*

THE LUCRATIVE BUSINESS OF SCALPING

By this time, no English target was more eagerly sought by the average Abenaki warrior than the much-touted Rangers, whose scalps were rightly considered a great prize above all others. Acquiring a reputation that had spread far and wide by this time, Rogers and his men had long fought the enemy on their own terms with a success that had early astounded the once overconfident enemy. Wearing a mixture of Indian garb and nondescript civilian clothing, green coats, and hunting wear that blended in with the northern forests, Rangers of every rank, including Rogers, took scalps as readily as the Abenaki and at the first opportunity.[10]

By this time, scalping had been transformed into a business venture. During a July 1756 mission to gain intelligence from Forts Carillon and Saint Frederic at Crown Point, Rogers learned to his shock from a French prisoner that "60 [French] livres was the reward for an English scalp" paid by the government of New France.[11]

And, of course, no scalp was more eagerly sought by the Abenaki than that of Major Rogers, and achieving this great goal would have made an Abenaki warrior famous across the land. Ranger leader Captain Jonathan Burbank was killed on May 11, 1759, and scalped in the mistaken belief that he was Rogers. The warrior who scalped Burbank "held up the trophy with great exultation, thinking it to be that of Major Rogers [and] the [Ranger] prisoners informed him of his mistake and the Indians appeared to be sorry" for the missed opportunity.[12]

The major European powers had long sanctioned the taking of scalps and paid bounties for scalps of both whites and their Indian allies. Therefore, the fact that Rangers took scalps was an accepted part of life and wilderness warfighting in a brutal conflict in which all manner of atrocities were the norm. As early as 1755, five pounds sterling were paid by the colonial government to a Ranger for each enemy scalp taken.[13] Even private individuals of means offered bounties for dead Indians with no consideration for whether they sided with the French.[14]

To his credit, French common soldier Charles "Jolicoeur" Bonin wrote with historical insight about the art of scalping, while displaying disgust that "the French and English were accustomed to pay for the scalps, to the amount of thirty francs' worth of trade goods. Their purpose was then to encourage the savages to take as many scalps as they could, and to know the number of the foe who had fallen. . . . It is shameful for the human race to use such barbarous methods."[15]

When Rogers and his men took Canadian, French, and Indian scalps, they were only committing bloody acts that were customary and fully accepted by both sides—just an ordinary feature of everyday life for a fighting man in the French and Indian War. Again, the tradition of scalping had been fully established well before Rogers's birth on the northern frontier. In the 1690s, northern colonies, including Massachusetts, voted to give forty pounds to anyone who brought in the scalp of a Native American warrior. Massachusetts then extended scalp bounties to any inhabitant of New France and nineteen pounds for "every scalp of such female or male" children in what was evolving into total war.[16]

In the astute analysis of a modern historian born in Montreal that was right on target, "With such narrow margins between the dead or living [bounties for captives and scalps that were set at about the same price], these bounties were in fact an invitation to systematically kill Indigenous, Canadian or French captives of all ages and both sexes."[17]

In striking contrast, the French paid smaller bounties for scalps than the English colonies, usually around one-tenth less, because they preferred captives to scalps, unlike the English. In this sense, the English were actually crueler, although it seemed that the Abenaki were the epitome of evil because they fought on the front lines of New France, launching incessant raids year after year. Clearly, two vastly different civilizations of rival European monarchies and imperial powers had placed different societal and military values on the taking of scalps, which reflected different historical legacies and cultural backgrounds.[18]

The relatively few soldiers' diaries—illiteracy was widespread—during the French and Indian War have revealed the results of some of Rogers's activities when it came to scalping in 1756. On June 1, one soldier wrote how Rogers and his men returned on a typical mission to the north "with a French Prisoner and 1 scalp," while another man penned on July 19 how the Rangers came back with "eight Prisoners and four scalps."[19]

In Rogers's own words about Captain Jacob Cheeksaunkun, the elder, and Lieutenant Jacob Naunauphtaunk, the younger, and the return of a company of warrior "Wolves" hailing from Stockbridge, Massachusetts, they "took ten prisoners, and seven scalps, out of a party of fifty French."[20] Revealing a macabre fascination that equated to victory over the English Protestants whom he utterly detested, even Governor-General Pierre de Rigaud, the Marquis de Vaudreuil, "faithfully chronicled in his dispatches every English scalp they brought in" as trophies.[21]

On March 13, 1758, to initiate the bloody Second Battle on Snowshoes not far from Fort Carillon, Rogers's experienced men ambushed only part— the initial advance party—of a much larger force of French, Canadians, and

Indians not far from Fort Carillon, cutting down a good many of the foe with an initial close-range volley. Then, with the enemy in full flight in the first phase of what evolved into a disastrous battle for the Rangers, when visibility was low amid the tall timber of a creek valley, around "half of Rogers's men gave chase; others began to scalp the fallen."[22]

This brutal practice in America's most cruel war became fully accepted by many Americans, including in major cities on the East Coast. Even George Washington, as an extremely ambitious, young lieutenant colonel of the Virginia Regiment, was almost casual about the scalping of Frenchmen in reporting to Virginia's governor, Robert Dinwiddie, who had ordered the mission to warn the French about trespassing on Virginia's claimed territory after having established Fort Duquesne at the strategic forks of the Ohio. In a June 3, 1754, letter, after the recent skirmish at Jumonville Glen on May 28, 1754, in southwestern Pennsylvania that had sparked the French and Indian War because of the most colossal blunder of his military career, Washington described the horror. While the tall Virginian could only helplessly watch, the Indians under his small command "knock[ed] the poor, unhappy wounded [Frenchmen] in the head, and bereiv'd them of their scalps."[23]

From the beginning, financial rewards certainly played a part in the process of whites of all classes adapting to Indian warfare in this grisly manner. During Queen Anne's War of 1702–1703, the Massachusetts Colony offered forty pounds for an Indian scalp. In 1723 during the next war, the Massachusetts government in Boston promised the Iroquois warriors a good many guns, ammunition, and presents "for the scalps of males aged twelve and over," and this, of course, included the Abenaki. At the same time, colonists of the Bay State Colony were offered a bounty of 105 pounds for the scalp of any male Indian above the age of twelve.[24]

Most horrifyingly, this lucrative bounty system of the colonial government also included the payment of fifty pounds for the scalp of an Indian woman or child under the age of twelve, because every Native American had become fair game.[25] Then Massachusetts governor Shirley placed the lucrative bounty of one hundred pounds on every Indian scalp taken.[26] But bounties for Abenaki scalps had in fact been part of the aggressive English war against the Abenaki long before Governor Shirley made his lofty pronouncements from the comfort of Boston.[27]

In 1724, Captain John Lovewell and his men from the Dunstable, Massachusetts, area reaped a hefty reward of $500 for their first scalp. This lucrative development then served as a powerful motivation for money-hungry recruits to enlist and serve in the war against the Pequawket or Pigwacket, a subtribe of the western Abenaki (Sokoki), who had fled to St. Francis for safety. Lovewell and his men gained another ten scalps to reap a fantastic reward of $5,000.[28] Scalping was evolving into big business among whites on the money-scarce frontier at an early date.[29]

At this point and despite their eagerness to reap financial rewards, these well-armed Massachusetts men of the frontier militia were not yet savvy like Native Americans, including the Abenaki, who had been able to collect the most possible money, becoming richer by turning one scalp into two or three. In July 1757, Captain Louis Antoine de Bougainville exposed this savvy Native American trick in his journal. Cheating about the number of scalps to collect more money was revealed after one reconnaissance that had resulted in a bloody fight: "The English had eleven men killed and four wounded, two of whom since died of their wounds. The Indians, however, brought back thirty-two scalps; they know how to make two or even three out of one."[30]

"Jolicoeur" Bonin, who had been born in France and had seen all the Native American tricks, also wrote about another deception when it came to the taking of scalps: this situation "gave rise to a trick among the savages, either native or suggested to them. To increase the compensation [from the government of New France] for the scalps, they got the idea of making them of horsehide, which they prepared the same way as human scalps. The discovery of this fraud was the reason they were more carefully inspected before a payment was made."[31]

The high bounties recently paid to the greedy scalpers of the Penobscot people by the Massachusetts governor before Shirley, Spencer Phips, was one forgotten reason that played a part in the infamous massacre at Fort William Henry, where a bloody revenge was wreaked upon the surrendered garrison: forty pounds' payment for a warrior's scalp, while the scalps of women and their children under age twelve brought half that amount, or twenty pounds. Penobscot warriors, who were part of the Marquis de Montcalm's Native American contingent, obtained a measure of revenge by attacking the column of helpless white men, women, and children after Fort William Henry's surrender. These revenge-seeking warriors still recalled the killing of

Penobscot men, women, and children by Massachusetts militiamen who had collected a nice payment in bounty money: a cruel history coming full circle with each new atrocity leading to another in a seemingly endless cycle in an increasingly vicious war.[32]

In March 1759, a Boston newspaper reported one success over the enemy that proved more lucrative, including the taking of the scalp of a non-warrior because of the cash bounty: "Capt. Cargill shot one of them (an old Squaw) and brought in her scalp, and brought in about 100 Dollars worth of Beaver" pelts.[33]

However, taking scalps became risky business for careless warriors, if their white victims at English farms or settlements had been infected with smallpox. By December 1756, during the early phase of the French and Indian War, some warriors had gotten wise to the dangers of removing the scalps of sick settlers. Therefore, when Native American raiders in Pennsylvania struck by surprise to catch the settlers napping, "a Boy was killed and scalped, and another who had the small Pox, was dangerously wounded by the Indians. . . . The wounded Lad says he saw but two Indians, one painted red [and] the other black, they cut him badly, but would not scalp him [for] fear of taking the infection" themselves.[34]

Scalping was a highly prized and an almost ritualistic act often committed by Rogers and his Rangers that revealed how thoroughly they had become acclimated to the ugly realities and war-hardened value systems of not only the northern frontier but also the Native American world. But in truth, the cultural and societal value system allowing the taking of "body parts as war trophies has been part of virtually every human culture that ever raised a weapon in war [and] scalping among Natives was a culturally complex means of demonstrating bravery, gaining prestige, and appeasing the dead. In some cultures, scalps could even be ceremoniously 'adopted' as a replacement for deceased relatives."[35]

Since time immemorial, the taking of a prize from an enemy's body by a victorious warrior has been a means of celebrating victory and displaying one's combat prowess. Just as Rogers and his Rangers eagerly took scalps, which they viewed as symbolically important, at every opportunity, the warriors of the Trojan War and other ancient battles, especially the Greek hoplites, also assigned great importance to the comparable act of stripping prized bronze armor—breast plates and greaves—off the corpses of vanquished opponents:

the taking of the ultimate trophy. Stripping the armor from the body of a dead foe was comparable to stripping a scalp from the head of a fallen enemy by the eighteenth century: a harsh wartime tradition that transcended races, centuries, and cultures because it was part of a cherished warrior ethos and the overall human experience from time immemorial.[36]

Even the famed ancient Chinese heroine Mulan, who had disguised herself as a male to serve god, country, and emperor and fight as a warrior and become an enduring legend to the Chinese people, had sworn, "I've come to compete in the number of heads of slain fighters."[37]

TEMPTING FATE TOO MANY TIMES

Quite remarkably, Rogers never considered or cared about the great personal risks of such a long-range and dangerous mission to St. Francis, which would be his deepest penetration of New France and most daring mission to date. However, he certainly knew that the odds of survival were stacked against him as more time passed. To date, Rogers's closest brush with death had come in a bloody showdown in January 1757. No mission of the Rangers had seemingly begun so harmlessly. Frustrated that he had been denied permission in October 1756 to attack St. Francis by haughty Lord Loudoun, who prized the Rangers too much too risk them and wanted them to stay closer to home and continue to gather intelligence for his forces, Rogers was at least allowed to increase his activities in the strategic Lake Champlain Valley, where the two southernmost French forts (Carillon and Saint Frédéric) safeguarded the entry into Canada.

A practical Lowland Scot, Lord Loudoun was right. Most of all, he knew that the experienced Rangers—his elite corps of fighting men who always led the way—were simply too valuable to risk on what would have been the most dangerous mission of the war. On January 15, 1757, as if to compensate for the setback of not gaining permission to attack St. Francis and deferral of a dream, Rogers had then led an intelligence-gathering reconnaissance mission out of Fort William Henry, located at the southern end of Lake George.[38]

This intelligence-gathering mission into the wilderness had suddenly turned dangerous when Rogers and his men uncharacteristically blundered on returning from gaining additional information near Fort Carillon. On the return march along their approach route, as ordered by Rogers, with Captain John Stark covering the rear of the single-file column with his company, the

Rangers approached the site of ambush cleverly conceived by French, Canadians, and Indians. Under fine partisan leaders with ample experience, a good
many enemy soldiers were deployed in a half-moon formation on the brow
of a hill. Under excellent cover behind tall trees, they hoped to surround (as
Rogers long knew and told of his opponents' usual tactic in his rules of war)
and then destroy the Rangers to the last man. This grim tactical possibility
was enhanced because Rogers was not aware that he had walked into a trap
aligned across the high ground until it was too late. All hell suddenly broke
loose with the unleashing of a close-range volley that wounded the major,
who was leading the way as usual, when a bullet grazed his head in the first
fire and dropped Rangers all around him.

The nightmarish combat at the Battle of La Barbue Creek (also known
as the First Battle on Snowshoes) on the bitterly cold afternoon of January
21, 1757, was especially intense and bloody. Rogers was wounded twice on
this ill-fated day, and another bullet clipped off the tip of the long red hair
of his stylish queue. When it appeared that their heavily pressured position
was about to be overrun by a larger number of attackers who now sensed the
kill, Rogers ordered a hasty retreat through the dense woodlands under the
cover of darkness to save themselves before it was too late. To buy time to
ensure their stealthy escape, the surviving Rangers had turned on prisoners
and systematically dispatched them without a second thought because these
veterans knew what had to be done in such a situation: they were "knock'd
... on the Head [with musket butts or hatchets or both]" because of the fear
that they "should Escape and give Information to the Enemy."[39]

Taking along any prisoners from Five Mile Creek (La Barbue Creek
that was situated just southwest of Fort Carillon) would have endangered
the entire force, slowing the Rangers down when a rapid retreat was the only
salvation even at night. Savagery was the order of the day on the northern
frontier in a conflict as merciless as the harsh winter weather, and few clashes
were as bloody as the First Battle on Snowshoes.[40]

Quite simply, this struggle had evolved into a total war in the wilderness for both sides, and Rogers and his men fully realized as much, when
everything was at stake in their fight against a merciless foe. In the words of
one historian who was right on target, "The savage forest fighting in North
America allowed no safety for noncombatants, no pity for the wounded, and
no mercy for prisoners."[41]

The supreme importance of scalping in his frontier culture—as harsh and unforgiving as the land itself—was emphasized with considerable insight by one white man who had lived with Native Americans after his capture as a soldier of one of the king's regiments: "He who has most fortune in the war, and takes the greater number of scalps, has by the voice of the whole, this dignity conferred on him. And every Indian is esteemed according to the number of scalps he takes; if he exceeds five, he is graded a captain, and commands the like number of inferior Indians. Hence it is, they are always ambitious for war, and to this circumstance alone may be attributed their perseverance and resolution in the midst of great and imminent danger."[42]

Besides the warrior ethos on both sides, and as mentioned, the lure of a good deal of money also played a large factor in the taking of scalps among Native Americans and whites. One warrior explained that scalp taking was big business and absolutely necessary for the maintaining of trade and the exchange of money that fueled the tribal economy: "They [the French] paid them well for all the scalps they took, which induced them the more, as by that they were enabled to provide themselves with many necessities, which they should otherwise be in want of."[43]

EXACTLY THE RIGHT TIMING

In perhaps the greatest irony of all in regard to the upcoming strike on the infamous Abenaki sanctuary, Rogers had long planned to unleash his great raid on the hated St. Francis in the dead of winter. He had advocated this plan to Lord Loudoun back in 1756, because, in Rogers's mind, winter was the perfect time to strike a lethal blow. At that time, Rogers had worked out every detail for a winter raid in his mind, and he had always been ready to implement his heart's desire. Rogers, however, had to wait for the right British superior to see the urgent need to eliminate St. Francis and give the order that he had long wanted to hear. Therefore, Rogers did not have to spend the usual extensive amount of time in planning the raid by the late summer of 1759, because he had in fact planned it long ago, and those details had remained fixed in his head. Under these circumstances, he could unleash his expedition to attack St. Francis in less than twenty-four hours if only given the go-ahead by a visionary superior.

As the New Hampshire major from the frontier fully realized, no additional time could be wasted during this final push north under General

Amherst, who was now stalled at Crown Point, to win it all after the fall of Forts Carillon and Saint Frédéric in the summer of 1759, if his great dream was destined to become reality, before winter's arrival. As Rogers fully realized from his days as a hunter during his youth in the wilds of the Merrimack River country and from the sight of great flocks of honking Canadian geese heading south up the broad expanse of Lake Champlain, both day and night, winter would come early that year, and only a few weeks were left before the descent of colder weather. Summer was slowly dying, but not Rogers's ambitions, which continued to burn brightly.

With the meadow grass along clear streams already starting to turn brown, white-tailed bucks rutting and hunting for does in heat, and the hardwood trees—beginning with the birch trees along the lakes—gradually gaining a more colorful cloak before the arrival of full autumnal hues, Rogers saw the first indications of winter already closing in around him in the depths of the Lake Champlain country. With mid-September fast approaching and the night growing cooler, he knew that the icy and snowy hand of old man winter would soon tightly grip the picturesque region—a dangerous no-man's-land—like a cold vise.

However, the slow dying of late summer and nearness of early autumn in 1759 offered a host of advantages for stealthy Ranger operations, which were fully appreciated by Major Rogers, who only saw the opportunities in keeping with his optimistic nature. First, the thick green foliage of summer had yet to tumble gently to the ground from the hardwood trees of the seemingly endless forests, providing concealment for raiders like in June and July. However, by this time, some trees, the clusters of birch and the taller, stately cottonwoods along Lake Champlain's shores, had already begun to turn lighter in color, a distinctive yellow amid the seemingly endless carpet of summer green that covered this northern land of lake country like a blanket.

By the time Rogers reached St. Francis—no small feat by any measure, if they managed to make it at all—the Abenaki would have already brought in the fall harvest to provide a bounty for the raiders, if they captured the infamous town situated in picturesque fashion on the St. Francis River: another key factor not lost on Rogers for his most-dreamed-about wilderness strike, with another harsh Canadian winter on the horizon and destined to begin about a month earlier than in his native New Hampshire. Rogers had already noticed how the squirrels high in the treetops were already in the process of gathering acorns for the long winter that would shortly descend in full fury.

But the final details, including a secret departure based on the British-Provincial Army's advance location at Crown Point after the fall of Fort Carillion and Fort Saint Frédéric, had been completed in Rogers's head by September 12, when he had been called to headquarters. If he found the opportunity, if Major General Jeffery Amherst was in a receptive mood, Rogers planned to attempt to get his approval to strike the most audacious blow of the French and Indian War. As Rogers knew from his past experience, one could never know the mood of any British general before entering his headquarters because of politics and personal factors that had long fueled rivalries among commanders in scarlet coats.

As Rogers hoped, Amherst would certainly be able to realize that a raid on St. Francis at this time would certainly throw a major scare into Montcalm and other French leaders while they faced the serious threat of General James Wolfe, who was attempting to capture Quebec, because Rogers's strike might well be seen by them as the spearhead of Amherst's long-awaited advance north in an attempt to gain Montreal on the St. Lawrence. Even more, such a deep penetration all the way to St. Francis, located between the major urban centers of Montreal, to the southwest, and Quebec, to the northeast, by Rogers would cause French leaders to overreact in panic and draw attention and defenders away from Quebec, which had to be protected at all costs for New France to survive this war, while providing security for Wolfe's southwestern flank.

To guarantee a degree of secrecy, and as noted, the final planning process already existed in Rogers's mind, having been in his thoughts and prayers for years. Rogers hoped to depart Crown Point before anyone in the British-Provincial Army or the French army realized what was happening in overall strategic terms, because secrecy equated to not only success but also survival, if and when he was allowed to go forth on his most ambitious enterprise.

In fact, and contrary to Rogers's earlier judgment, attacking St. Francis in winter was not the best time to unleash the most daring Ranger raid of the major's career. Instead, and quite by accident, a strange fate had been kind to Rogers and his men by bestowing the best of all times to conduct the raid and reach St. Francis—in early October in 1759 and not 1756—because General Wolfe was now at the gates of Quebec, where the French had concentrated men and resources in a final defense of the pulsating heart of New France.

At this time, King Louis XV and the French government across the sea continued to focus on the war in Europe, as if the continent were the key to victory in this global conflict. In consequence, French forces had been stretched exceptionally thin across Canada and by clever design because of Prime Minister William Pitt's strategic maneuvering to exploit French weaknesses. Indeed, the multi-prong British offensive effort—Amherst was only one arm—during the 1759 campaign was the greatest threat ever faced by Quebec and New France. All in all, the fickle gods of war had finally turned against New France, allowing Rogers even more of an opportunity to succeed in his long-desired expedition to St. Francis, if he gained General Amherst's approval.

During this dramatic showdown in 1759, French, Indian, and Canadian forces were no match in numbers because of their opponents' superiority in manpower, ships, and resources. New France's defenders were strewn out at various posts and forts, especially in regard to protecting Quebec, which was the key to New France. By this time, Wolfe and his mighty army of British and Provincials, including Rangers, and armada of ships had closed in on the mighty bastion of Quebec, which was long thought to have been impregnable.

But, most important, Pitt's excellent strategic plan of unleashing Amherst and Wolfe in simultaneous advances had been correctly calculated to divide French forces, which were already depleted by the lack of much-needed reinforcements from France, which continued to be focused on the war in Europe. In the vital Lake Champlain strategic corridor, the most unexpected of all developments had astonished General Amherst when Forts Carillon and Saint Frédéric were both evacuated without a fight, falling into his hands like gifts from above: another strategic situation and development indicating to Rogers that now was the time to raid St. Francis given that the British-Provincial Army had not advanced from the abandoned Fort Frédéric at Crown Point.

In an entirely unexpected development to the British during the summer, French leadership had decided to sacrifice its two key forts in the Lake Champlain Valley to defend Quebec at all costs. At Quebec, three-quarters of New France's manpower had been concentrated for a last stand when everything was at stake for France's largest colony. This strategic reality now worked to Rogers's advantage during this cooling September at Amherst's sprawling encampment at Crown Point, because St. Francis was more vulnerable than ever before, with warriors far from their village deep in Quebec and defending other points. Therefore, Rogers was chomping at the bit during the balmy days of September, because St. Francis now presented "the soft underbelly of New France," which was more vulnerable than ever before, as Wolfe's threat to Quebec had reached a high point.[44]

Clearly, the strike on St. Francis that Rogers had long envisioned was destined to be no haphazard or ad hoc raid of any strategic significance. Because Amherst had failed to advance north beyond Crown Point in closer support of Wolfe, which was his top priority and that of Prime Minister Pitt, the meticulous and cautious major general, who had no news of Wolfe's situation and feared that New France's forces would be united against him if Wolfe was defeated, needed the raid on St. Francis to demonstrate that he was still on the offensive and for pressing strategic considerations.

After all, Pitt had long emphasized from London that close coordination of the dual offensive efforts of Amherst and Wolfe was the key to decisive victory, and he was entirely correct, as usual. If Rogers won his long-awaited final approval to go ahead at Amherst's headquarters to fulfill his greatest ambition, then the raid on St. Francis would fit neatly into the overall scheme of the larger strategic interests and priorities at a time when the French had concentrated most of their forces to protect Quebec and Paris remained obsessed with the war on the European continent.[45]

In May 1756, an insightful journalist with a New York City newspaper had boldly advocated a new aggressive policy that he saw would finally have decisive results and that conformed to a strategic conviction long held dear by Rogers: "to attack them in their Towns [because] a little Smattering of History will inform us, that a few hardy, resolute and enterprising Fellows" could often perform the impossible in wartime to help to turn the tide of war, just as Rogers and his men were about to demonstrate.[46]

A Smiling Fate

Because of the overall strategic situation, with New France threatened as never before by a mighty British army before Quebec and the vast majority of Abenaki warriors far away from St. Francis in Quebec's defense, unlike if Lord Loudoun had allowed the Ranger attack on St. Francis when he was formally asked on October 19, 1756, now was exactly the right time for Rogers to gain permission to be unleashed.

In the upcoming winter, when the campaign would be over for both armies, the Abenaki warriors, if not conducting still another devastating raid on the northern settlements, would be back at St. Francis for the traditional winter respite from having assisted the French army in conventional warfare before fighting started up again in the spring of 1760. But now the warriors were absent from St. Francis to face the new threats posed to New France, especially to Quebec by Wolfe, unlike in October 1756, when French forces were winning the war on all fronts and their prospects had never looked brighter for winning the North American continent.

Due to the considerable difference in the overall strategic situation, the late summer and early fall of 1759 offered the best time to strike a blow on St. Francis, whereas success might not have been possible in late 1756, because the French were much stronger at that time and more successful on all fronts. Indeed, this present time with autumn drawing near offered a narrow window of opportunity that Rogers knew he needed to exploit in full also because he realized that Amherst needed to open communications with Wolfe before fortress Quebec, because Pitt had emphasized coordinating offensive efforts as closely as possible for the winning of decisive victory.

In terms of fulfilling the great dream that had consumed him for years, Major Rogers was actually now very fortunate because General Amherst was in an exceptionally foul mood that was entirely uncharacteristic of this methodical and cerebral man, who always closely guarded his emotions. On September 10, by way of a French flag of truce that had arrived at Crown Point, he had just learned from a French captain, who brought a letter from the Marquis de Montcalm, that his naive attempt to send a small party to reach Wolfe by trekking through Abenaki country and very close to St. Francis, also under a flag of truce, had badly misfired.

The general's anger over the embarrassing failure of the mission of Lieutenants Quinton Kennedy and Archibald Hamilton, which Amherst had optimistically dispatched on August 8 from Crown Point, had actually paved the way for the granting of permission for Rogers to unleash the most famous raid in the history of Rogers's Rangers. In a classic case of outsmarting himself that garnered him a reprimanding letter from Montcalm for using men—the two British officers in this case—out of uniform to attempt to get his message to Wolfe, Amherst had launched the Kennedy-Hamilton mission in an ill-fated attempt to ascertain developments before Quebec, since he had not heard anything from Wolfe since the end of June: Should Amherst advance to assist Wolfe at Quebec or had he been repulsed before the great fortress city to warrant caution?

In his letter and as noted, the Marquis de Montcalm severely chastised Amherst because these two British officers, who had volunteered (no Ranger had volunteered when given the second opportunity after Ranger ensign Benjamin Hutchins of Boston, a former member of "Rogers's Own" and of Captain Moses Brewer's company, had volunteered for Amherst's first attempt to reach Wolfe by a long land-water route that was too time-consuming), were caught by Abenaki uniforms out of uniform. Additionally, the respected Captain Naunauphtaunk Jacob, the junior and the son of Captain Cheeksaunkun Jacob, had been captured deep in Abenaki country in leading this doomed party. Because Hamilton and Kennedy were out of uniform (they were dressed as Native Americans), they could technically be considered spies by the French and shot. The sullen captives had then been taken to St. Francis at a brisk pace.

The mission's failure and resulting embarrassment for the proud, if not vain, major general, who valued his image and honor above all else, had finally allowed Rogers the long-awaited opportunity to revive his old 1756 plan of striking his long-anticipated blow in a bid to forever destroy the most troublesome Native American sanctuary during the course of the French and Indian War. Fortunately for Rogers, the overall strategic situation now presented the best of all times to make a great dream come true by catching the Abenaki of St. Francis by surprise, if all went according to the well-laid plain of the ever-opportunistic Rogers, who also rejoiced in the fact that Major General Amherst—unlike so many other British officers—was open-minded and respectful of the successful American fighting man, especially Rogers.[47]

At this time, Rogers had no idea that the dynamics of New France's Native American allies had dramatically changed compared to previous campaigns. Smallpox had decimated Vaudreuil's Upper Great Lakes and other western allies. For the all-important 1759 campaign, the governor-general and Montcalm now possessed a much-diminished force of Native Americans and were forced to rely more on the Abenaki of St. Francis and other Christianized warriors for the 1759 campaign and the defense of Quebec.

Therefore, in 1759, the largest number of warriors from St. Francis were utilized to resist Wolfe's invasion and not in the defense of their own homeland in the vast wilderness northeast of Missisquoi Bay, especially their infamous community located on the St. Francis River. As fate and strategic developments would have it, St. Francis was left virtually defenseless exactly when Rogers planned to strike a blow at his target more than 150 miles slightly to the northeast, if unleashed by Amherst. Clearly and for once, in regard to his pet project of destroying St. Francis, timing had been kind to Rogers and his men even before the war's most daring mission was launched, because the gods of war were smiling upon him, after the passing of frustrating years that seemed endless to the major.[48]

But in truth, the exact timing of the raid, the perfect time to strike St. Francis, which was the period from mid-September to early October, was crucial for the success of the riskiest of missions yet conducted during the French and Indian War. A master woodsman and lifelong frontiersman who intimately knew the ways of the forests as well as the ways of the Abenaki from so many years of experience, Major Rogers tailored his most daring raid to conform to the advantages of the geography, the season, and the overall strategic situation, which were destined to form the fundamental basis for Major General Amherst's forthcoming September 13 orders to strike St. Francis and destroy it. With the knowledge of a hunter or trapper perfectly at home in the wilderness, Rogers fully realized that he needed to strike before the autumn leaves fell from the trees to denude the forests, because the Rangers would need all of the natural cover that they could find to exploit this advantage during the lengthy journey north to St. Francis.

Therefore, and above all, Rogers knew that St. Francis must be attacked before the falling of the leaves from the tall maples, oaks, and birch trees that thrived in the moist, cool woodlands and before the end of the sunny days of the warm Indian summer just before the arrival of bad weather of late fall. Indeed, Major Rogers knew to launch his attack before the arrival of harsh weather that came around mid-October in the Quebec region. At that time, dropping temperatures and bitter winds sweeping south from an Arctic cold front would end traditional campaigning of European military leaders on both sides, while making the waters of wide Lake Champlain especially choppy. If Rogers's luck held true, then the first days of October, perhaps even the first week or two deeper into autumn, might see a continuance of the delightful weather of a late "Indian summer," or so he hoped.

Even more, Rogers also needed to strike just after Abenaki harvest time, when the gathered crops had been stored in corn granaries at St. Francis—all necessary for the tribe's survival in the depths of the harsh Canadian winter of around six months. Again, exact timing was crucial; the return of the warriors to St. Francis from hunting and war parties was only a matter of time after the fall harvest, when the armies went into winter quarters for the season.

The remaining Abenaki men, who were relatively few in number, at St. Francis focused on their main responsibilities of hunting for food to stockpile before the long winter. But, as noted, most Abenaki warriors were absent because of their faithful service with French and Canadian forces as scouts and fighting men. And according to custom, it had been the women and children who traditionally gathered the harvest primarily from the broad cornfields along the fertile bottoms of the St. Francis River and on the higher ground around the community itself.

As he well understood, Rogers needed to attack the legendary village on the St. Francis River before the warriors returned from hunting and military service and after the harvest had been stored in warehouses: a narrow window of opportunity that Rogers was determined to exploit to the fullest.

This last consideration was most important. The white raiders, if they made it so far north deep into Quebec, would be traveling extremely light, and resupply could only come with the capture of St. Francis's granaries, which would be filled by women and children with corn from the fields to feed the tribe through the winter. Rogers also hoped to strike at a time when it was generally believed by the Abenaki that the most serious warfare had ceased for the year. All in all, Rogers's planned attack was an ideal time to hit St. Francis—more than 150 miles slightly northeast of Crown Point—with the cooling weather of early fall and before the harsh winter arrived in full fury, while the vast majority of Abenaki warriors were concentrated at Quebec.[49]

Quite simply, the timing of the launching of the raid was now exactly right because the enemy would have his guard down as never before. Both armies were already beginning to take the first steps of going into winter quarters in the long-established European tradition, including the issuing of woolen winter coats, but not Rogers and his men. Ironically, the popular name "Indian summer" had been bestowed by New England settlers because this was the perfect time—the last warm spell in the early fall before winter's arrival—for the warriors to more easily descend south along their ancient war trails and strike at the frontier settlements.

And now, Major Rogers planned to employ the time-honored Indian tactics of stealth and surprise at the very time when generations of Native Americans usually attacked the settlements. This time of year, the last period of warm weather of "Indian summer" just before cold Canadian weather covered the land in a white shroud, could be utilized by Major Rogers, who was thoroughly acclimated to Indian ways on all scores. Clearly, this beautiful Indian summer presented a narrow window of opportunity for Rogers not only to strike St. Francis but also to withdraw south and back to safety before the worst winter weather swept over the land.[50]

But most fortunately for Major Rogers, and as noted, General Wolfe's ever-growing threat to Quebec was invaluable in the overall strategic picture to provide cover, bestowing a greater opportunity for the Ranger chieftain to be ordered by General Amherst to go forth to St. Francis. All in all, Rogers's timing could hardly have been more fortunate.[51]

Historian Francis Parkman failed to give exact numbers, but he repeatedly emphasized that Native Americans, including the Abenaki, were a large part of the mostly Canadian garrison that defended Quebec. Because of the lack of reinforcements from France, the French now relied more heavily on the Canadians and Indians in their brave attempt to defend the key to French Canada, Quebec.[52]

FINAL APPROVAL

After having thoroughly pleaded his case to the major general with conviction, intelligence, and insight at Crown Point headquarters on the previous day, Major Rogers was about to receive his final secret orders on Thursday, September 13, from Amherst, who had long championed Rogers and his Rangers, whom he knew were second to none as warfighting experts in the wilderness. He had complete faith in what Rogers could accomplish against the odds when ordered to strike a blow so far north in an unmapped region of Quebec.

For such reasons, the major general from an old aristocratic British family, who was new to warfare in North America, often deferred to Rogers's expertise, judgment, and "opinion in relation to" the fine art of forest warfare. In no uncertain terms, Amherst made sure to emphasize to Rogers that this upcoming expedition into the wilds of Quebec was to be a vengeful raid and harsh in the extreme. In truth, therefore, blame for any future excesses, which were inevitable for a variety of reasons, deserved to be laid squarely on

Amherst and not Major Rogers, who would only be following his September 13 orders, when he finally attacked St. Francis.

Issued almost immediately before Rogers was to begin the long trek north, in order to ensure a greater degree of secrecy, Amherst's September 13 orders issued from his headquarters at Crown Point, located around two hundred miles southwest of Quebec, for Rogers to attack St. Francis emphasized in no uncertain terms,

> *You are this night [September 13] to set out with the detachment as ordered [orally] yesterday, viz. of 200 men, which you will take under your command, and proceed to Misisquey Bay [the northeastern end of Lake Champlain] from whence you will march and attack the enemy's settlements on the south-side of the river S. Lawrence, in such a manner as you shall judge most effectual to disgrace the enemy, and for the success and honour of his Majesty's arms. Remember the barbarities that have been committed by the enemy's Indian scoundrels on every occasion, where they had an opportunity of shewing their infamous cruelties on the King's subjects, which they have done without mercy. Take your revenge, but don't forgot that tho' those villains have dastardly and promiscuously murdered women and children of all ages, it is my orders that no women and children are killed or hurt.*[53]

All in all, this is a fascinating order from a highly respected major general on a number of levels, especially because of its fundamental cynicism and extremely dark overtones, which rarely came from this polished and diplomatic man who hailed from a privileged family of the English aristocracy. Even as an official document, Amherst's order is full of striking contradictions and ambiguities that basically left Rogers with the discretion to do pretty much as he pleased and saw fit under the circumstances, within certain broad guidelines. After all, he was to embark on a lengthy mission far from headquarters and well beyond Amherst's control for an extended period. First and foremost, Amherst had designated a target for destruction that was not a fort or a military installation of any kind in the traditional sense. St. Francis was a community that contained more women, children, and elderly people, even when most warriors were present, which was now not the case.

Despite its overall strategic importance for an extended period, no French garrison or fort—not even a wood palisade wall—protected St. Francis. The overall vulnerability of St. Francis was a rather remarkable development given the strategic importance of this position, which was basically part of New France's first line of defense in the south and situated between the two vital points of Montreal and Quebec. But because the Abenaki possessed such a fearsome reputation and had won so many successes year after year, a great confidence, if not hubris, dominated St. Francis and its people, who had long won nothing but victory in this war. Except for the ever-optimistic Rogers, St. Francis was considered completely untouchable by one and all, including a smug French leadership and especially the Abenaki people, who believed that their God smiled upon them.

As fate would have it, Quebec was shortly about to surrender when Wolfe (who was destined to be mortally wounded, like the Marquis de Montcalm, in the climactic battle that determined the mastery of an entire continent) won his great victory on the Plains of Abraham just outside the city's gates on the same day Rogers finally obtained his fondest wish of all at Crown Point when he gained his official orders on September 13, 1759—a turning point in not only British but also American history.

For the most part, the development that led to St. Francis's complete vulnerability had been born of an unprecedented amount of contempt for the English Regulars and colonial fighting men. Likewise, for mostly the same reasons, no permanent warriors or French or Canadian troops were assigned to St. Francis on a regular basis. And, as noted, the largest number of Abenaki warriors now served with French forces in Quebec's defense. Then another sizeable group of warriors was away from the village on hunting expeditions for extended periods. This situation was especially the case in late September and early October 1759, when warrior-hunters were out securing game for the tribe's survival for the upcoming winter. For such reasons, St. Francis was depopulated of warriors and any sufficient body of defenders.

However, Major Rogers faced a moral quandary of a serious nature because he had basically been ordered by Amherst to commit what might be considered a war crime today. How exactly was he to obey the major general's orders to "take your revenge" in attacking a community of mostly noncombatants after Amherst had reminded Rogers to "remember the barbarities that have been committed by the enemy's Indian scoundrels on every occasion"?[54]

As issued at Crown Point by Amherst on September 13, these orders were very nearly a green light for the Rangers to commit atrocities. Basically, Amherst had employed a false moral facade to separate an upcoming

English genocidal action from the French responsibility for what had accidently happened in the aftermath of Fort William Henry's surrender without Montcalm's prior knowledge or consent. But this political game of both sides attempting to maintain the moral high ground for public consumption during what they viewed as an honorable war does not hide the ugly fact that as early as 1706, and which still now applied in full to St. Francis, Abenaki leaders had bragged to Iroquois and Mohegan delegates at Albany, New York, "Our wigwams are full of English scalps blowing in the wind."[55]

But yet, as if to clear his name of all blame in the event of negative publicity or charges of killing Indian woman and children, which was inevitable in attacking a large Indian town, in the future, Major General Amherst then emphasized, "It is my orders that no women or children are killed or hurt."[56] In no uncertain terms, and without the expected moral facade for a proper English commander who symbolically represented the king and the empire, Amherst recorded the true nature of the mission by emphasizing how Rogers and the Rangers were "to go & destroy the St Francis Indian Settlements and the French settlements on the South side of the River St Lawrence."[57]

But how were Major Rogers and his men to take revenge, as directed by Amherst, on the enemy at St. Francis if no large body of warriors or French forces were present there? Perhaps when he first received the orders from the major general at Crown Point headquarters, Rogers either did not notice the discrepancies or did not pay much attention to the fact that the orders seemed almost to have been written by a crafty English lawyer to ensure that Amherst could not be held responsible for any future atrocities. But the truth was that he had indeed ordered the most lethal killing machine in the entire British-Provincial Army to take full revenge on a community of mostly non-warriors, and that ugly fact cannot be denied.

Clearly, thinking with a well-honed legal and political mind, Amherst was making sure that he was not held responsible for whatever moral transgressions might occur at St. Francis, which were inevitable and only a matter of time when Rogers successfully attacked his most dreamed about target, because it was only an Indian village—the most infamous one in North America—and not a military target like a fort or a garrison. From intelligence gained from prisoners, Amherst and Rogers almost surely possessed some prior knowledge that the attackers would not be encountering any French troops or sizeable number of warriors, especially because Quebec was under threat and had drawn away a good many defenders from a wide area for its defense, including from St. Francis.

After all, and although he possessed the best fighting men in Amherst's army for succeeding in this dangerous mission in faraway Quebec, Major Rogers was about to go forth with too few men to strike a target deep in enemy territory by doing what he did best of all: leading a deep raid far from the army and straight into the dark heart of the enemy's country, because he was an expert at conducting such dangerous expeditions and better than anyone else on the English side in the struggle to win the North American continent.[58]

PRIOR INTELLIGENCE

Knowing that stealth and secrecy were the keys to a successful mission, Rogers was fully accepting, in his final discussion with General Amherst at Crown Point's headquarters, of embarking on his most dangerous mission with barely two hundred men—Rangers and volunteers from British and Provincial regiments. Rogers knew that a small force was necessary to achieve the best results when stealth and secrecy were most important of all. Of course, Rogers preferred to command a contingent consisting entirely of Rangers, who knew how to move with care and lead with ease, but such was not to be the case.

As often in the past, British army politics had once again come into play, and Amherst made the final decision about the composition of the task force. Rogers possessed authority to pick the men he wanted with him on the expedition, but Amherst had made it conditional. Therefore, Rogers was ordered to choose the best men not just from the veteran Ranger companies but also from the entire army. And, of course, like a good soldier, the major followed orders to the letter on busy September 13 to keep in the good graces of a superior who fully supported him and his efforts.

However, Rogers felt better about not leading an all-Ranger force because he knew that he would not find a French garrison, a fort, or a large number of defenders at St. Francis, which was located so deep in enemy territory. Consequently, Rogers was about to prove the fallacy of the longtime assumption that St. Francis would never be targeted and successfully hit with a devastating blow that the Scotch-Irish leader now envisioned with clarity.

As mentioned, St. Francis was not fortified because of its lofty reputation and remoteness and since it was a community center of mostly

Abenaki families in the St. Francis River Valley. In fact, in geographical terms, the town was vulnerable more by water than by land. As noted, not even a protective wooden palisade, like around many Native American villages in the Northeast, protected St. Francis. Like almost all of his warriors, even St. Francis's "White Chief" of Irish blood, the blond-haired Joseph-Louis Gill, was destined to be in another location (at the Yamaska River with a small contingent of his warriors in ambush positions once the raiders' presence in Quebec had been discovered) by the time Rogers eventually struck his long-awaited blow.[59]

Unlike in attacking a traditional military target, no prior scout or reconnaissance of St. Francis was necessary or required under the circumstances, because the great distance involved made it impossible and because Rogers already possessed an intimate knowledge of the village. And any such Ranger scouting expedition into Quebec to gather last-minute intelligence might allow the secret operation to be early exposed to the French: a risk that simply could not be taken.

Among generations of New England settlers, St. Francis had become almost a legend, but an exceedingly grim one, and a mysterious place of endless lore and tales. But, of course, the past horrors committed by Abenaki raiders had left the most searing legacy of all, and it still burned deeply in the tortured soul of New England and its long-suffering people across the frontier. Partly explaining what eventually happened in terms of a righteous retribution at St. Francis on October 4, 1759, because it was a certain inevitability, "there was scarcely a man among [Rogers's Rangers] who had not had a family member or friend killed or abducted by the Abenaki."[60]

As mentioned, Rogers had long possessed an ample amount of information about St. Francis, including from firsthand sources such as white captives taken to the most infamous Native American community, including Captain John Stark. Whites, men and women, who had been captured and held at St. Francis had survived and returned after having been bought and ransomed by the French, who had paid off the Abenaki to secure captives in this lucrative business arrangement.

A hero of the 1747 defense of the Fort Number Four, Massachusetts-born Captain Phineas Stevens, who had lost two brothers in an Indian ambush and who became an early Massachusetts frontier legend in his own time, had quite a harrowing story to tell. Significantly, the captain's sons, officers Simon and

Samuel Stevens, served in the ranks of Rogers's Rangers to continue a distinguished military legacy. As a younger man, Phineas had been captured by the Abenaki in 1723. Then "he was taken prisoner and carried to St. Francis [and] This informed him of the Indian customs, and familiarized him with their mode of warfare."[61]

As noted, Rogers received the most intimate information about St. Francis from Captain John Stark, who still savored some of his novel and unforgettable experiences at the town as a captive. He had been captured while trapping for furs in the northern wilderness and held at St. Francis in 1752. Here, he had been treated much better than he had ever expected, including with a distinct measure of respect that had to be earned the hard way by this remarkable young man from the Merrimack River country. Indeed, Stark's extensive knowledge proved invaluable, because he "provided Rogers with critical information about the village's immediate geography and specific layout."[62]

Benefiting from good treatment at St. Francis, like John Stark, Susanna Johnson had survived her harrowing ordeal of capture, despite having been forced to march with her Abenaki captors all the way to St. Francis. In Susanna's words about the white captives' arrival at St. Francis, "Two hours before sunset, we came to the landing, at the village. No sooner had we landed, than the yelling in the town was redoubled; a cloud of savages, of all sizes and sexes, soon appeared running towards us" in what turned out to be a friendly greeting.[63]

Susanna and her infant had lived "in a large wigwam" with three warriors and the same number of women at St. Francis. This remarkable young New Hampshire woman from the Connecticut River country mentioned the number of French houses that were located in the Jesuit mission village pleasantly situated on the St. Francis River.[64] Five years before Rogers's raiders descended with fixed bayonets on the community on the early morning of October 4, 1759, she described the Indian community located on a bluff overlooking the St. Francis River in the following manner: "St. Francis contained about thirty wigwams which were thrown disorderly into a clump. There was a [Roman Catholic] church, in which mass was held every night and morning, and every Sunday [while] the hearers were summonsed by a [church] bell [from a bell tower]; and attendance was pretty general. Ceremonies were performed by a French friar [Roman Catholic priest], who lived in the midst of them for the salvation of their souls."[65]

But five years later, St. Francis was much larger than in Susanna Johnson's day, because the war had caused the relocation of additional Abenaki people and refugees from other tribes. For such reasons, St. Francis had evolved into the major center of the Abenaki and their resistance effort, which was second to none in terms of effectiveness and lethality.

Ironically, this community located on the picturesque river did not consist primarily of traditional, conical-shaped Abenaki wigwams or the larger longhouses that were well-known features of Native American life in the Northeast. Instead, St. Francis was most distinguished by the look of a very traditional-style community of regular French houses and other European-like structures. Serving also as centers for social events and religious observations, the longhouses, which housed multiple families or large extended families, had been traditional structures located in large permanent Abenaki communities for centuries. These traditional Native American structures were absent at St. Francis.[66]

And this wilderness sanctuary of angry warriors located just below the St. Lawrence River had been dominated by a single motivation for nearly a century: revenge on the people who were most responsible for having caused the loss of their sacred homeland, best hunting grounds, and ancestral grave sites, which were a central focus of Abenaki spiritual life.

In his journal, Captain Bougainville described how at Fort Carillon on July 22, 1757, before the unleashing of a flood of warriors who reached their all-time peak during the campaign directed at capturing Fort William Henry, "Father [Pierre Joseph Antoine] Rouband, Jesuit, arrived with 112 Abenakis and St. Francis Indians" and the revenge-seeking warriors of other nations, and these fighting men were determined to take as many English scalps as possible, which had been accomplished in grisly fashion.[67]

KEY QUESTIONS ABOUT MAJOR GENERAL AMHERST'S SEEMINGLY IMPOSSIBLE ORDER

As mentioned, the key catalyst that had fueled Major General Jeffery Amherst's rage and explained why he had readily given permission for Rogers to finally go forth on this risky mission was the disastrous fate of the Kennedy-Hamilton mission. One soldier who was stationed in the "Camp at Crown-Point" on September 13 described the dismal news about Amherst's special mission, which had filtered in from the north and from Montcalm himself: "The two Officers [both lieutenants] and Indians that went from hence to Quebec, were all taken" prisoner by the Abenaki of St. Francis.[68]

As the insightful Pitt had long emphasized, the key to decisive success in the 1759 campaign was for the close and simultaneous offensive effort of Amherst and Wolfe to force the division of the limited manpower of New France: the ages-old concept of divide and conquer that was destined to determine the fate of the North American continent. In consequence, Amherst had long been desperate to communicate with Wolfe to determine the most recent developments before he resumed the advance to coordinate their offensive efforts. Amherst realized that if Wolfe had failed before Quebec, then he could not push forward with confidence because he would then become a victim of divide and conquer himself.[69]

At Crown Point headquarters on September 12, Major Rogers had seen firsthand how Major General Amherst was extremely upset about recent developments pertaining to his most recent attempt to establish contact with Wolfe, especially after having received Montcalm's note of admonishment. Following Pitt's directions for a closely coordinated advance on two fronts and as mentioned, Amherst had been attempting to establish communications with Wolfe (who was equally in the dark about Amherst's progress in his ordered advance into Canada by way of the Lake Champlain strategic corridor as planned), beginning with Ranger Ensign Hutchins's effort to acquire information, for some time.

Fuming at his Crown Point headquarters, the general was most of all frustrated and seething because his recent August mission had resulted in the failure of the small party under the two British officers, Kennedy and Hamilton, who had volunteered for the dangerous mission, to communicate with Wolfe: a harebrained scheme of the major general that had badly backfired, causing him great personal embarrassment.

As noted, Amherst had first gained the stunning news of the capture of the Kennedy-Hamilton mission on September 10 with the arrival of the Marquis de Montcalm's scathing letter that had been received under a flag of truce—the twenty-seven-year-old Rogers had seen a golden opportunity and taken full advantage of it at Amherst's Crown Point headquarters on September 12.

As he explained, Rogers knew that Amherst

was exasperated at the treatment [which he believed was more severe than was actually the case, but he was a fellow British officer and gentleman] which Capt. [Quinton] Kennedy [a highly capable Lowland Scot of the 17th Regiment of Foot married to a Mohawk woman, who was so fascinated by Mohawk culture and dress that he copied for himself and had compiled a list of wilderness exploits well known on both sides of the Atlantic] and another British officer Lieutenant Archibald Hamilton [likewise not wearing a scarlet coat and disguised as an Indian] had met with, who had been sent with a party under a flag of truce [with longtime Ranger captain Jacob Cheeksaunkun, the younger, who was in charge of a half dozen Stockbridge Mohegan Rangers who were known as "Wolves"] to the St. Francis Indians, with proposals of peace to them, and was made by them a prisoner with his whole party; this ungenerous inhumane treatment determined the General to chastise these savages with some severity, and, in order to do it, I received from him [orders to attack St. Francis].[70]

But was this situation actually the case in regard to an anger that burned deep inside Major General Amherst, who was not previously known for open displays of anger of any kind? The rumored (rather than actual) rough treatment of two Regular British officers—out of uniform, in Indian disguise, with a small escort of Mohegans and a hidden message from Amherst to Wolfe—by the Abenaki of St. Francis hardly seemed a proper justification for launching a risky raid with the army's most dynamic leader and best fighting men who were highly prized by the major general, needed by Amherst for the push farther north as ordered by Pitt.

Of course, Amherst's real priority had been that the Kennedy-Hamilton mission would establish communications with General Wolfe outside Quebec under the guise of a flag of truce for the alleged purpose of establishing a peace with the Abenaki, which was an absolute impossibility and a ploy. As noted, the real mission to St. Francis, after having proceeded north down the length of Lake Champlain and trekking overland after leaving Missisquoi Bay located at the northeastern corner of Lake Champlain, had been to establish communications with General Wolfe, who was just outside Quebec with a formidable army and naval force. Therefore, the two ill-fated British officers had carried letters from Amherst to Wolfe, which were taken by the

Abenaki when they were captured. The white captives had then been sent to Montcalm, who rightly could have executed them under the rules of war.[71]

Therefore, the supposed justification—the alleged bad treatment of Kennedy and Hamilton, which was not the case—for unleashing the attack was nothing more than a convenient excuse. Indeed, this situation was so undeniable that Rogers even took the opportunity in his journal to utilize the well-known Scotch-Irish cultural trait of unbridled sarcasm at Amherst's expense. After all, none of Amherst's truce bearers had been roughly mishandled or hurt by either the Abenaki or the French.

Because of his overriding concern to communicate with Wolfe so that they could coordinate their offensive efforts as expressly ordered by Pitt, Amherst had been guilty of abusing the accepted rules of warfare in regard to the white flag of truce supposedly carried by the Kennedy-Hamilton party in a not-so-clever ruse. Amherst was supremely embarrassed because not only the Abenaki but also the French had immediately seen through the phony peace mission. Like the Marquis de Montcalm, Major General Amherst, who was ever sensitive about his status as a proper gentleman and pristine image of an honorable military officer in the eighteenth-century tradition, had been astounded by the sharp words of Montcalm's letter, basically questioning his honor and integrity because of the underhanded nature of the Kennedy-Hamilton mission, which had fooled no one. Of course, the marquis (an aristocrat who had been born in France of a noble family) was exactly right. Clearly, Amherst had deceitfully and crassly exploited the core principle of the flag of true, which was considered sacred by both sides.

Instead of receiving harsh treatment, as was rumored to have enraged Amherst by the time of his headquarters meeting with Rogers on September 12, the two British officers had been treated relatively well by the Abenaki and especially by the French, who generally treated fellow European officers with delicacy and decency. But while the two bungling British officers were eventually released, veteran Indian Ranger leader Captain Jacob, the junior, who hailed from Stockbridge, Massachusetts, remained imprisoned.[72]

Therefore, in the months ahead, Amherst was destined to launch a vigorous public relations campaign, including in colonial newspapers, to justify his controversial actions. And, of course, the news of Rogers's destruction of St. Francis in the fall of 1759 would place this scandal in the shadows, to Amherst's relief. New England and New York periodicals explained to its readers how

> notwithstanding the many reports that have been spread some Time ago of Capt. Kennedy's being sent by Gen. Amherst with an Express to General Wolfe, that it was not so, but that he was sent with a Flag of truce to the Indian town of St. Francis, with overtures of Peace, proposed to them by Gen. Amherst, and try to bring them over to English Interest: But they, contrary to all the Rules of War, (even the Savages themselves have heretofore held Flags of Truce sacred) immediately on his arrival, seized Capt. Kennedy, and the few others that were with him, and carried them Prisoners to Montreal: Intelligence of which afterwards coming to the General's Ears, he was so exasperated against them for their inhumanity, that he immediately propos'd the destruction of their Town to Major Rogers [it had been Rogers who made the proposal], who willingly undertook the Adventure.[73]

Nevertheless, Amherst had believed the worst about the alleged harsh handling of Kennedy and Hamilton, feeling a sense of guilt for their treatment because of his folly. In the end, therefore, the general needed to launch a strike on St. Francis for a variety of reasons that were valid and pressing to him on a personal level. The mounting pressures of the existing strategic situation on numerous fronts had resulted in the general ordering Rogers to go forth on his mission within only forty-eight hours of learning about the miserable failure of the Kennedy-Hamilton mission. But instead of having been the key catalyst as long assumed by historians, the news of the Kennedy-Hamilton mission's failure had only been the final straw that had broken the camel's back in Amherst's mind.[74]

As revealed in the major general's journal, Amherst penned how Rogers had been ordered to "go & destroy the St. Francis Indian Settlements and French [white Canadian] settlements on the South side of the River St Lawrence."[75] But the single-minded, if not obsessed, Rogers was wise in his careful calculations about his most dangerous mission, with his Scotch-Irish common sense rising to the fore. He had no intention of taking the war to the scattered French settlements nestled in the fertile valley of the St. Lawrence after destroying St. Francis, because it was much too dangerous, if not suicidal. He had only one focus, and this top priority was the one that had long consumed his heart and soul for years, the destruction of St. Francis; everything and anything else paled in comparison as an objective, regardless of what had been written in Amherst's September 13 orders. Significantly, Rogers's attitude mirrored that of his Rangers when it came to the urgent need to wipe out St. Francis.

Likewise, Major General Amherst's orders to Rogers disguised basic and fundamental realities, especially in regard to emphasizing that no harm should come to women and children at St. Francis, after he had strongly denounced in writing the many years of atrocities committed across the frontier against white women and children, as if to the justify harsher treater destined to be played out in full in bloody fashion at St. Francis. After all, in the heat of combat, and despite his heightened sense of upper-class morality common among the British military elite, Amherst, like Rogers, knew exactly what would happen and the grim implications of the revenge-seeking dynamic, which the major general had emphasized in his orders, once Rogers unleashed his men, because an atrocity of a significant nature was as inevitable as the rising of the sun. After all, the target of Rogers's mission was the longtime center of too many devastating raids to count and the manifestation of pure evil to generations of settlers along the vulnerable frontier: the most combustible of all situations in the heat of combat.

In consequence, there would be only one possible result in the upcoming attack on St. Francis, which was now inevitable for a variety of reasons. Therefore, Amherst was only covering his own rear, so to speak, when he stressed that no harm should come to noncombatants at St. Francis. Considering that the hard-bitten warriors of New France had long employed a war of terrorism that had caused destruction along the frontier for generations, this was almost a comical form of subterfuge on the general's part (not unlike the harebrained Kennedy-Hamilton mission that had caused so much embarrassment) to clear himself of any wrongdoing by Rogers—the inevitable slaughter at St. Francis—for his own benefit. After all, the French would eventually report the killing of noncombatants at St. Francis with the major general's strongly worded orders to destroy an entire community: all part of the long-existing propaganda war of words between England and France that was played out on both sides of the Atlantic throughout the French and Indian War.

VENGEANCE FOR THE SLAUGHTER AT FORT WILLIAM HENRY

A more realistic explanation of Major General Amherst's true motivation for ordering the attack on St. Francis, rather than the convenient excuse of alleged anger over the treatment of two British officers who had been treated well, actually lay in what had occurred two summers ago at Fort William Henry, located at the southern end of Lake George. Therefore, while Amherst was unsettled by the Marquis de Montcalm's recent letter of censure because his honor was challenged, he knew that what was needed to ease his profound personal embarrassment and take the focus off the ill-fated peace mission was to score a spectacular victory that would garner headlines across America. And the colonial newspapers covered no one more than Rogers and his daring exploits for a fascinated readership across the colonies.

As he fully realized, such a sparkling success by Rogers would pay personal dividends to the austere major general whose reputation had been tarnished, demonstrating to Pitt that he was doing more than simply remaining inactive with his sizeable British-Provincial Army at Crown Point, where he was busily constructing a new fort that would dwarf Fort Carillon and Fort Frédéric for an extended period during good campaigning weather. Most important and even more pressing, Amherst now needed to create a hard-hitting diversion in support of Wolfe, whose offensive effort had stalled before Quebec's walls. Ironically, Amherst did not know of Wolfe's dramatic victory on the Plains of Abraham on September 13, which won Quebec on the same day that he wrote Rogers's orders to attack St. Francis.

And the ever-opportunistic Major Rogers, who had made his dramatic proposal on September 12 to an upset Amherst at exactly the right time at headquarters, especially since the major general needed to make some kind of a forward movement from Crown Point, had just the right aggressive plan— the one he had been thinking about for years, maturing in conception in his mind, and first proposed to Lord Loudoun years before. A successful strike on St. Francis would wash away the recent embarrassment felt by Amherst and steal the headlines since Rogers was one of the most popular military figures in America and had been for years.

Even more, if successful, a raid on St. Francis would be a punishing moral and psychological blow to the enemy at a time when French fortunes were finally at low ebb, and it would almost be like driving a nail in New France's coffin. As noted, and from beginning to end, this was Rogers's ambitious plan, not Major General Amherst's, as assumed at the time, including as published in colonial newspapers for the general public across the colonies.

Indeed, in short order, Rogers's anticipated victory at St. Francis would also wipe out the humiliation of the loss of Fort William Henry in the bloody summer of 1757 and the shocking slaughter of a good many defenseless soldiers, including camp followers and wives, whose "bellies [had been] ript open [and] their Bowels torn out" by the unleashed warriors, including Abenaki. Amherst had relatively little personal knowledge of the raids on the New England frontier, as he emphasized to Rogers in his orders, but he was well aware of the most infamous Indian atrocity to date after Fort William Henry's surrender.

As mentioned, the Marquis de Montcalm had led a mighty force, including Abenaki warriors, who scouted and led the way for the French army's advance to the southern end of Lake George, that surrounded the doomed fort in early August 1757. Montcalm's ample amount of artillery had made the fort's surrender inevitable before the arrival of the cooler weather of autumn, especially after Colonel Daniel Webb refused to send reinforcements, which became known to Montcalm from a captured letter from Fort Edward's commander.

And it was common knowledge that the Abenaki had played a leading role in the atrocities, beginning with dragging sick and wounded soldiers out of their hospital beds to be tomahawked and scalped before the eyes of their surrendered comrades. Although Major General Amherst did not specifically mention the massacre at Fort William Henry in his September 13 orders to Rogers, it could not have been far from his mind. When the column of surrendered British and Americans had begun the march southeast from Fort William Henry to Fort Edward, the warriors had butchered women and helpless men, who only carried unloaded muskets, according to the surrender terms, in a bloodlust run wild. Abenaki warriors led the way in killing and scalping men, female camp followers, and soldiers' wives and children, unable to defend themselves, after the French "let their Indian Blood Hounds loose upon our People."[76]

Lieutenant Nathan Brigham, a zealous volunteer on Rogers's most dangerous mission who had left his Massachusetts regiment behind to serve beside the Rangers, was determined to avenge his unfortunate Bay State comrades in the aftermath of Fort William Henry's surrender because mostly

Massachusetts men and noncombatants (wives, camp followers, and family members) had been slaughtered.[77]

Even Bougainville, the highly capable aide-de-camp to Montcalm, was shocked, writing in his journal, "A great misfortune which we dreaded has happened. . . . [T]he capitulation is violated and all Europe will oblige us to justify ourselves [after some prisoners,] hoping to put them [the warriors, including Abenaki] in a good humor, had given them rum, which despite all our warnings, they had kept in the flasks." The drunk warriors, because brandy "is the god of the Indians," then slaughtered many English paroled troops and took even more as captives back to the wilds of Canada.[78]

Drawing a sad conclusion about a lethal equation that had cost the lives of hundreds of soldiers, including some Rangers, and civilians, Captain Bougainville simply summarized how the Indians "get drunk, and the English die a hundred deaths from fear every day."[79]

Father Pierre-Joseph-Antoine Roubaud of St. Francis

Perhaps the most overlooked factor that explained not only the slaughter at Fort William Henry but also the devastating Abenaki raids that had for so long vomited forth from St. Francis was the powerful influence of Catholicism. In general, modern historians and writers have minimized this key factor because Christianity and Indian savagery had been generally viewed as separate entities because of their inherent incompatibilities than portrayed by period writers.

Significantly, the influential spiritual and Catholic leader of St. Francis, Father Pierre-Joseph-Antoine Roubaud, had trekked south with the Abenaki warriors to Fort William Henry. Ironically, he joined the war party from St. Francis in the hope of ensuring that his so-called Christianized Abenaki fighting men, who had joined Montcalm's army to kill as many Englishmen and reap a grim glory based on the final tally of blood-stained scalps, would not be corrupted by the wilder ways of the non-Christianized warriors from the far western Great Lakes region.

However, the dedicated Jesuit missionary from St. Francis, who spoke fluent Abenaki, was about to learn that when it came to slaughtering helpless Englishmen and ripping their scalps from their bloody heads in the most efficient fashion, the good father's Abenaki were no different from the warriors of the western tribes, especially when alcohol drove them—both

Christianized and non-Christianized—into spasms of an orgasmic blood-letting. Roubaud had preached to the warriors in French from his mobile chapel before the attack, as if they were involved in a religious war in Europe. Rogers and his Rangers knew that Father Pierre-Joseph-Antoine Roubaud, a relatively new missionary to St. Francis—having been working there for just over a year—and a die-hard Jesuit, like Father Sebastian Rale, who had led the Abenaki of Norridgewock in raids against New England settlers, was a young Catholic zealot of a militant bent. He equated the viciousness of Abenaki attacks with the proper religious duty to stop the advance of Prot-estantism from moving farther north.

Known for his zeal and intensified teaching skills, which proved effective when indoctrinating Indians in the proper faith to fuel their ferocity against the hated Protestant heretics, he was a native of Avignon, France, and in his mid-thirties. He had entered a local Jesuit college in France at the age of thirteen, becoming thoroughly indoctrinated in Jesuit teachings. He not only preached a terrible retribution to halt the insidious spread of Protestantism, as if it were a deadly disease, but also encouraged Abenaki war parties to thoroughly punish the heretics and pagans, equating raids with holy missions in support of the true faith.

Father Roubaud, therefore, represented everything that Rogers and his Rangers—not to mention the settlers across the frontier—hated about this brand of militant Catholicism and the troublemaking Jesuits, because they had long fueled the fierce fighting spirit of generations of Abenaki war-riors to kill New Englanders with a perverted religious-based relish that bordered on sheer joy. To be fair to Roubaud, in somewhat of a paradox, he was not supportive of the worst excesses of Indian warfare demonstrated at Fort William Henry. Badly underestimating the number of Protestant losses when a witness to the massacre of so many helpless whites, Father Roubaud wrote how "the massacre [of Fort William Henry] was not of long continuance [but also] the number of killed was hardly more than forty or fifty."[80] Unfortunately, the Abenaki singled out blacks (free and slave) and Indian Rangers for special ill treatment and to take back to their villages as prisoners and slaves.[81]

With the distinctive tribal markings of the African motherland on each cheek, Ranger Private "Duke" Jacob faced a cruel fate, perhaps even enslave-ment if captured, because some of the savviest Indians realized the financial value of men with dark skins to Quebec's upper-class French, who adhered to the luxurious lifestyles of wealthy French planters in the West Indies. Compared to whites, Indian Rangers likewise shared a dismal fate if captured, death or slavery, because they were seen as race traitors by the Native American allies of New France.[82]

As noted, Rogers immensely benefited from the utilization of his Indian Rangers, including Indian officers, especially Captain Jacob the younger (and also the elder) and his Stockbridge warriors, since the beginning of their service in the late summer of 1756. These tried veterans of a darker hue from western Massachusetts wore both traditional attire and those elements of European clothing that best suited them as tough fighting men whom Rogers greatly appreciated during his wilderness war.[83]

Therefore, in the end, Rogers's audacious plan of attacking St. Francis had finally been embraced in full by Major General Amherst because of a host of valid factors and circumstances that had conveniently combined together as one near mid-September 1759 to present the perfect opportunity for which he had long waited. Now widely known as "the Famous Rogers," he was about to take this widespread fame even higher—no small accomplishment for a remarkable individual, who was already viewed as the hero of the common man across the breadth of the colonies, especially on the northern frontier. Rogers's great dream of striking deep into French Canada and destroying the notorious Native American village of St. Francis was about to become the most beautiful of realities to him, after he had experienced one frustration after another during the passing of the better part of half a decade.[84]

ATROCITIES CONTINUE UNABATED

The desire to strike St. Francis for revenge's sake was powerful on many levels, serving as a chief motivation among the Rangers. As expressed by British captain James Abercromby, aide-de-camp to Major General James Abercromby (his uncle) and an early admirer of Rogers's aggressive style of warfare, in early February 1756, more than two and a half years before the attack on St. Francis, "The memories of this country, particularly, are full of the unheard-of cruelties committed by the French, and the Indians, by their instigation, for which I think every brave man ought to do his utmost to humble that haughty nation."[85]

This young British captain from the upper-class elite had captured the exact sentiment of not only Rogers and his Rangers but also almost all the residents of New England, especially along the war-ravaged frontier. Philippe de Rigaud Vaudreuil, the capable governor-general of French Canada from 1703 to 1725, had long secretly encouraged the Abenaki to strike at the New England settlements, while his successor and brother, Pierre Francois de Riguad, who served as the last governor from 1755 to 1760, enjoyed his perverse fascination in having "faithfully chronicled in his dispatches every English scalp they brought in" as a trophy to be admired by one and all.[86]

By the summer of 1756, when both sides (including the Rangers) were killing without mercy and taking scalps at every opportunity, Major Rogers described in his *Journals* how "60 [French] livres was the reward for an English scalp, and . . . the prisoners were sold in Canada for 50 crowns each."[87]

Significantly, Rogers never made any comparable complaints, like so many French officers in regard to New France's Native American allies, about his reliable Ranger Mahicans and Mohegans, including a contingent that was ultimately bound for St. Francis with their white counterparts. These savvy wilderness warriors, including the fabled "Wolves," would be needed for the deepest penetration of enemy territory to date. Fluent in numerous Indian languages and intimately understanding various aspects of Native American culture, the major knew how to speak with diplomatic care and deal fairly with these ultra-sensitive warriors, who seemingly never forgot even the most minor slight, with a rare skill that included a measure of respect, which these proud warriors fully appreciated.

In terms of leadership abilities and command presence, Rogers had a winning way with his dark-hued Rangers, including African Americans like "Duke" Jacob, Provincials, and Indian Rangers, which partly explained his highly effective leadership style, while molding them into respected members of North America's most elite fighting force.[88] Quite simply, by this time, and unfortunately for the people of St. Francis, the Rangers were nothing less than "the most formidable body of men ever employed in the early war of America."[89]

Rogers's extreme tact and diplomacy was one forgotten secret of his amazing success as a leader. For instance, in early 1759 in preparation for that year's campaign, Rogers had written a carefully worded letter to Uncle Uncas, the chief of the Connecticut Mohegans, who were Christian warriors like the Stockbridge "Wolves," to raise a Ranger company of fighting men for which he would gain the rank of captain and full British pay. The letter was full of a high level of courtesy and respect for Uncle Uncas and his people. Even more, Rogers wrote that if this revered Indian "uncle" was not interested in serving in the new Indian Ranger company of around fifty good fighting men, then "I shall expect Doquipe and Nunnipad [to serve but] I leave you the choice of an Ensign and two Sergeants"—an almost unprecedented designation of key personnel of a military unit by an Indian leader in Ranger service.[90]

Displaying far more respect for Native Americans than most white men, the open-minded and racially tolerant major, long unfairly viewed by historians and writers as an Indian-hating racist, ended the letter as if writing to an esteemed British general: "Brother Uncas, Your most obedient humble servant."[91]

Too Little, Too Late in Overall Strategic Terms

Stretched to the limit in overall strategic terms, New France had little realistic chance of a successful resistance effort to counter Amherst's formidable might or that of Wolfe, who commanded thousands of troops, far outnumbering the French, and a formidable British fleet of warships—the largest ever seen in North America's waters. In desperation, French leaders in Montreal had prudently dispatched reinforcements south to the strategic Lake Champlain sector because of the overwhelming strength of General Amherst's army, but it was not enough.

Viewed by Louis XV from the luxurious comfort of Versailles as being of relatively little value because it was located seemingly at the end of the world, the vast expanse of Canada was the most neglected front during the course of the Seven Years' War. Seen as hardly more than a snowy wasteland of little, if any, importance as compared with Western Europe, where the Seven Years' War was waged, Canada's overall obscurity in the apathetic minds of Frenchmen of all classes and the ignorance of the wealthy ruling elite, especially the king, sealed New France's fate.

France's largest overseas colony was destined to be abandoned for the imagined more important concerns and interests in Europe, which were the top priority of the king of France and his short-sighted ministers who lacked Pitt's strategic vision. Like other members of the French elite, whose arrogance allowed them to look down on France' largest overseas colony, Canadians in general, and the most successful colonization effort in the nation's history, Voltaire believed that the war was fought over nothing more than "a few acres of snow."[92]

France-born Charles "Jolicoeur" Bonin was among the reinforcements of around 150 French soldiers who had been dispatched to the strategic Lake Champlain corridor, when he saw this dominant place of strategic importance for the first time. He wrote how they were sent to "Fort Carillon, which the English called Ticonderoga. We are bound for this post, the last French post in this sector, because it is threatened by the English at Fort George only four leagues away. . . . At the time of our arrival, there was only two hundred and fifty men under the command of General [Francois-Charles de] Bourlamarque in the garrison at Fort Carillon. . . . [T]he commander [one of the top lieutenants of Francois-Gaston Duc de Lévis, who was Montcalm's second in command] had laid mines under the fort and bastions to blow up the whole structure, if it was found necessary to abandon it" to the superior might of the British army under Amherst that advanced from Fort George on July 21, 1759.[93]

As mentioned, Major General Amherst needed to gain a smashing success that would make the headlines on both sides of the Atlantic, due to his own failure, in this decisive campaign, to advance farther north from Crown Point to more closely support Wolfe before mighty Quebec. Even after his key success in having captured Fort Carillon, Fort Saint Frédéric, and Crown Point, which the French had evacuated in a strategic withdrawal to consolidate defensive positions to better protect Montreal and Quebec, he had failed in his overall strategic mission to push any farther north to support Wolfe with an aggressive offensive operation designed to capture Montreal to the northwest by this time.

When time was of the essence, Amherst had wasted valuable time and resources constructing a massive new fort at Crown Point and not promptly advancing farther north down Lake Champlain and into Canada, as expected by Pitt in London, to support Wolfe before Quebec. Ironically, the evacuation of these key defensive positions, Fort Carillon and then Crown Point and Fort Saint Frédéric, had caused Amherst more unease than elation, fueling caution because of his fear of French trickery or an ambush, despite an ample number of Rangers (nine companies under

Rogers), who could provide timely and accurate intelligence and invaluable protection as usual. Therefore, Amherst had ordered Major Rogers to go forth into Quebec on his pet project, which had brought a sense of relief to the gifted major general.

After all, Amherst had no idea of the extent of Wolfe's progress against the cliff fortress that dominated the St. Lawrence where the great river significantly narrowed, and he feared that Quebec could not be taken by the young general. If Wolfe was repulsed before Quebec, then Amherst worried that resurgent forces of New France would then take the offensive to target his army in the strategic Lake Champlain corridor. Quite simply, for a host of reasons, Amherst had failed to display the requisite aggressiveness and now needed a spectacular success to mask his failure as a result of having stubbornly remained in place at Crown Point, as if his once-glorious campaign were already over. All in all, Amherst had fallen victim to his fears: the antithesis of Rogers's determination to score a victory by undertaking the most dangerous expedition to date.

Pitt had originally ordered Amherst "to pursue any other enterprise which in his opinion would weaken the enemy, without detriment to the main objects of the campaign," which was to capture Montreal and then to assist Wolfe at Quebec, the key to Canada.[94] In essence, Pitt's orders had emphasized the importance of aggressiveness and gave Amherst the opportunity to finally order the strike in the general direction (north) of Montreal on St. Francis, as Major Rogers had long envisioned with clarity.[95]

As mentioned, Amherst gave his final acceptance of Major Rogers's bold plan on at headquarters on September 12, 1759, only because the general was now the key player and architect in the war's most crucial campaign, and he needed to demonstrate some degree of aggressiveness. All in all, this was an ironic and unexpected development, because Amherst commanded more troops than even commanded by Wolfe, who possessed the most important mission of capturing Quebec, while Amherst was to have captured Montreal as directed by Pitt.

Too much success gained too quickly and easily seemed to have befuddled the naturally cautious Amherst, who continued to be fearful and excessively methodical at Crown Point, when dash and aggressiveness were required to secure decisive victory over a badly outnumbered opponent. Glory had been reaped early, boding well for this campaign. The general's ambitious offensive plans of eventually marching on Montreal had begun promisingly with the capture of Fort Niagara, which was located to the west on the Niagara River, in upper New York, where it entered Lake Ontario, by Ireland-born Sir William Johnson and his army, which included Iroquois warriors. Bestowed with the burden of main responsibility by Pitt when the eyes of the British nation were upon him, Amherst had capably led "the grand central advance" in the Lake Champlain strategic corroder with his usual methodical care since July, and the overall strategic results had been impressive, but not from any tactical brilliance displayed on his part.[96]

After all, the French had willingly abandoned Fort Carillon, Fort Saint Frédéric, and Crown Point, which Amherst had easily taken possession of in the mid-summer of 1759. After gaining these two strategic French points with such relative ease and suffering just a handful of losses—news of which "was received with universal joy through the whole Fleet and Army," penned one soldier in a letter, because of the carefully calculated French withdrawal north to consolidate their overall strategic positions by abandoning these southernmost positions—Amherst held all the high cards. However, he kept them too close to the vest. After all, he was in an ideal position to keep his promise to Pitt "to make an irruption into Canada with the utmost vigor and despatch," especially when Wolfe was positioned before Quebec.[97]

But in the end, Amherst continued to remain more tentative than was necessary because he imagined that young Wolfe might fail in his ambitious undertaking of conquering Quebec, and then New France's forces, under the wily Montcalm, would resume the offensive by striking south. In that case, Montcalm would certainly exploit the opportunity and concentrate on him—a possibility that made Amherst even more cautious.

This growing fear had caused the general to needlessly postpone the northward offensive of the most powerful force in the 1759 campaign, while wasting too much precious time at Crown Point. As conceived by Pitt and in the end, Amherst did not lead the grand central advance into Canada in a timely manner to first subdue Montreal, as so optimistically envisioned by London strategists because it was vulnerable, when Wolfe needed such timely support to win decisive victory at an earlier date. In fact, Amherst had never even aggressively pursued the withdrawing French forces after they had evacuated the twin strategic positions that had long guarded Lake Champlain: a key role that Rogers and his men would have played in leading the way for the British-Provincial Army north down Lake Champlain and very likely all the way to Montreal.

Therefore, instead of taking advantage of the French withdrawal north toward the St. Lawrence River and the heart of Canada, Amherst remained obsessively focused on his pet "construction projects" at Crown Point. Therefore, he wasted weeks of fine weather that were ideal for active campaigning in rebuilding forts and roads instead of advancing north in pursuit of a reeling enemy, as everyone had fully expected on both sides of the Atlantic. Compensating for his considerable failings (which would have enraged Pitt, had he known about the sad state of developments in the strategic Lake Champlain corridor), Amherst found a timely alternative by finally becoming very receptive to Rogers's concept of striking deep into French territory.

Therefore, Amherst's September 13, 1759, orders to Major Rogers to descend upon St. Francis—more than 150 miles distant—not only masked (if successful) considerable campaign failings on his part but also fit into the larger strategic objective of maintaining the offensive effort as ordered by Pitt, if only by creating a diversion to assist Quebec. However, to achieve the central objective of an effective diversion to assist Wolfe, Rogers's raid into Quebec should have been launched much earlier in the year, because it was already too late in the campaign to make any strategic difference by this time.

Indeed, Pitt's planned offensive to finally proceed north just before mid-October was much too late for success, because Amherst had wasted so much valuable time at Crown Point. Therefore, Amherst's offensive was destined to be cut short by the arrival of winter weather. As one soldier penned about the future delayed offensive effort, Amherst's much-belated initial movement north down Lake Champlain was fated to be thwarted by "high contrary Winds, and, in general, bad Weather," which forced a hasty return of the expeditionary force back to Crown Point, after a completely wasted offensive effort.

Even more, and as mentioned, symbolically, on the very day (September 13) that Major Rogers received orders for his men to push forth from Crown Point and north toward the ultimate rendezvous with destiny at St. Francis, Wolfe finally captured Quebec. But the promising British general, exposed on the Plains of Abraham, in one soldier's words, "was shot as he was charging his Men to keep down, being squatted, till the Enemy gave 3 Vollies, and was mortally wounded by the Canadians." Wolfe won his glory on the Plains of Abraham on September 13, because Fortress Quebec was now doomed.

Nevertheless, and as noted, any success, especially in destroying St. Francis, gained by Rogers would become widely publicized on both sides of the Atlantic, and Amherst would reap the credit for what this determined major in a green uniform and his Rangers accomplished—at no risk to the general's lofty reputation. The major's failure, if that proved to be the case during the St. Francis expedition, would be entirely his own (an American was a perfect scapegoat during this period), while Amherst would still be viewed as a great hero for having captured the two strategic forts on Lake Champlain. Therefore, because Quebec had already fallen in September, the objective of the mission to St. Francis was primarily to deliver a psychological blow in the hope of continuing to weaken the enemy's will to resist, especially in regard to ceasing Abenaki raids.

Clearly, Rogers's luck had finally turned in his favor in a number of ways, after he had gained a coveted major's rank in 1758, when he officially commanded nine Ranger companies. In overall strategic terms and as mentioned, Rogers's raid was destined to serve as a diversion to assist Amherst as much as Wolfe by providing a convenient cover-up for his considerable failings. Ironically, in regard to the overall strategic situation, the raid on St. Francis was destined to be launched too little, too late to alter or affect the overall strategic picture as originally envisioned by Rogers and Amherst on September 12, when expectations could not have been higher: the ultimate irony in the story of the most famous raid of the French and Indian War.[98]

Unfortunately for Major Rogers, the belatedness of Amherst's ordering the raid resulted in another significant drawback that boded ill for the mission's success. The sizeable garrison of Quebec was released by the British victors, according to the articles of capitulation and the traditional honors of war, after the city surrendered. This strategic situation now meant that French, Canadian, and Indian fighting men, including Abenaki warriors and fighting men who had escaped, from the Quebec garrison and area were now free to return south and face Amherst's anticipated advance.[99]

Meanwhile, Amherst's impotence was sorely felt by the entire army of fighting men, whose spirits had reached new highs after the fall of Forts Carillon and Saint Frédéric, despite the heady success. As lamented by one soldier with prophetic insight at Crown Point before mid-September, "We are still here, great Preparations for going on [in advancing], but not ready yet. Many People begin to think we shall not go further this Year."[100]

A MASTERFUL MISINFORMATION CAMPAIGN
Most important of all, a clever plan was designed on September 12 to ensure that this vital secret mission to St. Francis remained secret. Above all else, Amherst and Rogers fully realized that the daring mission all the way to St. Francis would never have a chance of succeeding if any word about it was prematurely leaked to the French. The French, of course, would galvanize every available soldier and warrior to destroy Rogers and his men, who would never be more vulnerable than when so far in the far north country.

From his comfortable Crown Point headquarters to ensure secrecy, Amherst had possessed the wisdom to present Rogers with his official orders on Thursday, September 13, directing him to depart from Crown Point that very night, long before the sunrise of September 14, within twenty-four hours. Again, this was possible because Rogers had his plan already well conceived in detail in his head, as he had emphasized to the major general on September 12. As Amherst penned in his secret orders—with one exception, only the major general and Rogers knew of the final destination—for the night of September 13, "You are this night to set out with the detachment as ordered yesterday."[101]

Like in military operations, updated and accurate intelligence was the key to success on multiple levels. Consequently, Major General Amherst had earlier ordered small parties of Rangers north to gather intelligence, and this information now paid dividends. During one of his last intelligence-gathering efforts in early September, which appeared in the pages of the October 4, 1759, issue of the *Maryland Gazette*, an officer at Crown Point wrote, "A small Party of our Rangers have brought in three French Prisoners, from the other End of the Lake [Champlain]; they are Soldiers and Germans by Birth [and they] bring no Intelligence that can be depended upon. However, they say, that for a long time they heard nothing from Quebec. . . . General Wolfe's and [Vice] Admiral [Charles] Saunders's long Silence surprise all very much."[102]

Amherst had hoped that Rogers would be able to gather timely information from French prisoners about Wolfe's situation, but nothing had been gained. But more important for the upcoming success of the St. Francis expedition and demonstrating insight about the art of deceiving the enemy, Amherst planted articles in newspapers to throw off the French about the unleashing of Rogers's secret expedition and its ultimate destination: a propaganda campaign that was most likely forthcoming from the efforts of Amherst's talented and well-educated staff officers at Crown Point headquarters.

Consequently, the major general shortly had a British officer write a letter on September 18, 1759, from Crown Point for publication in American newspapers. This letter, written five days after Rogers had already departed Crown Point for his raid on St. Francis and printed in the October 4, 1759, issue of the *Maryland Gazette*, read, "I have the Pleasure to inform you, that Major Rogers, who left this [Crown Point] a Day or two ago [September 18], with a Scout of about 120 pick'd Men of the whole Army, fell in with, and after a smart Engagement of some Time, defeated a Party of French and Indians (about 10 miles from this Place) consisting of 300; and has taken 200 Prisoners and Scalps, with the Loss of three Men killed."[103]

In a masterful example of misinformation, the writer of this anonymous letter then provided the information that was sure to comfort French leaders far and wide, especially with regard to the future safety of St. Francis and even Montreal: "It is said [that Major Rogers] himself is either killed or wounded."[104] Clearly, this was a clever ruse that seemed to ensure even greater safety for strategic points to the north.[105]

If French leaders saw no subterfuge in still another English propaganda trick, then they would have wildly rejoiced in the fact that the ever-troublesome Major Rogers was perhaps now dead, as seemingly everyone in New France wished. No doubt a good deal of fine Madeira wine was drunk in celebratory fashion among relieved French leaders, perhaps even the governor in Quebec, if they had read this account that appeared in the pages of the *Maryland Gazette* on October 4, 1759—ironically, the very day that Rogers was destined to attack St. Francis![106]

On the same day, in this same newspaper, another story (from a letter dated September 20) was placed next to the above-printed September 18 letter written from Crown Point. It read, "The brave Major Rogers has been out on a Scout with a Party of his own Men, and Draught from the Regulars amounting in the whole to 200; he by some Means or another got Intelligence of a Scout of the Enemy's, of 300 Men and Way-laid them; when a smart Action happened between them, in which our People have got a complete Victory. The Major, it is said, has brought in with him 100 Scalps, and upwards to 100 Prisoners, with only a trifling Loss to his Party."[107]

Of course, this intense battle allegedly fought north of Crown Point was a complete fabrication because there had been no fight whatsoever. Even more, the letter was written when Rogers and his men were already well on the journey to St. Francis. This latest flurry of English propaganda intended not only to fool the enemy but also, and most important, to disguise the fact of Rogers's push on St. Francis.[108]

However, some of this propagandistic fraud was exposed when a soldier at Crown Point wrote how the information of "Major Rogers's bringing in 200 Scalps and Prisoners, proves not to be well-founded, tho' 'tis said, the Account was wrote by a Regular Officer at Crown-Point."[109] In addition, rumor of a false destination for Rogers and his men was spread far and wide in the hope that it became known to the French. For instance, the editor of the *Boston Gazette* reported on October 1, 1759, the rumor that Rogers was moving west across the Adirondack Mountains, just west of Lake Champlain, as part of an ambitious plan to link with General William Johnson's forces for a planned offensive operation that targeted the Iroquois town of Oswegatchie in upper New York near today's Ogdensburg.[110]

But if given the opportunity, and as French leaders and America's reading public already knew from the Rangers' past missions that defied the imagination, Rogers's men would have relished nothing more than the opportunity to take so many scalps while serving under the Ireland-born Johnson. Rogers and his Rangers were much like savages because such brutal qualities were necessary for the waging of a successful wilderness war, as they were shortly to fully demonstrate in the attack on St. Francis. The seemingly endless horrors of this war had a thoroughly dehumanizing affect like few other conflicts, especially Rogers's rough-and-tumble wilderness war. All in all, it was a very easy, if not inevitable, development for a fighting man, regardless of race, color, or which side he fought on, to sink into the moral morass of the depths of depravity of this most brutal of conflicts, which had stripped away all aspects of humanity, the longer that it lasted.

In an indirect tribute that was most complimentary because of his lethal effectiveness in this war, especially in regard to what he was destined to demonstrate at St. Francis in the near future, the Abenaki were about to bestow on Rogers the well-deserved nickname "the White Devil," or Wabo Madahando, or Wobomagonda. But in truth, the fighting men of both sides were devils when it came to waging the wilderness war, and Abenaki as well as Rangers were guilty of seemingly countless atrocities. In the depths of wartime, the community and societal values of the frontiersmen and the Abenaki were actually fundamentally much the same: destroy the enemy and every part of his civilization by any means and at any cost. And it was the job and nasty business of Rogers to accomplish his longtime goal, because the destruction of St. Francis was perhaps the most universally popular military objective among the common people, especially along the frontier, in the history of the English colonies before the American Revolution.[111]

VITAL MEETING BETWEEN ROGERS AND STARK AND A MUCH-NEEDED MAP

There would have been no Robert Rogers (he might well have been earlier killed in battle, especially at the bloody Second Battle on Snowshoes) as we know him today without the superior leadership abilities and skills of his top lieutenant, Captain John Stark. And even more, without Stark's influences and indirect contributions, there perhaps would have been no successful raid on St. Francis, although he was absent.

Stark was an old, faithful friend from the Merrimack River country and the finest Ranger leader in the outfit after the major himself. Rogers was most fortunate because he could not have possessed a more capable top lieutenant than the rough-hewn Stark. In fact, if anyone could compare favorably to Rogers, it was Captain Stark. If Rogers had been killed or died of disease, Stark would have taken command of the Rangers in seamless fashion. Just as "the Famous Rogers" was America's first war hero of the common people across the colonies, then Stark might well have been the second greatest American hero of the conflict. However, he was one who never received the headlines or lavish press like his boyhood friend, partly because of his retiring and modest nature compared to the brash Rogers.

For a variety of reasons, therefore, Stark has become the forgotten player in the story of the St. Francis raid, as if he had no influence on or connection to it whatsoever. However, such was simply not the case. He had thoroughly informed Rogers about the details of St. Francis, especially its general layout and the Abenaki war trail along the Connecticut River that led to and away from the town. To be sure, Rogers's finest captain was not on the raid to St. Francis, much to the major's regret, but fate had deemed otherwise. This fact ensured greater obscurity for Stark in the popular imagination and in the one-sided view of Rogers-worshiping historians. However, Stark was certainly one of the most gifted Ranger officers in the command's history, and this general obscurity has been entirely undeserved on every level. But most important, and although he was not present on the raid, the dynamic captain's inspirational legacies and influences were alive and well to play a key role in the St. Francis story.

Ironically, in the late summer of 1759, partly because he had proven competent in obeying Major General Amherst's orders in completing his recent road-building assignment to the east, Stark would not become a member of the great raid. He had just completed his critical mission in record time, after another job well done. Fortunately for the overall orchestration of the raid on St. Francis, Captain Stark had just returned to Crown Point, after his assignment with two hundred Rangers to cut a road east through the wilderness from Crown Point across the rugged Green Mountains, part of the Appalachian Range, and all the way east to Fort Number Four on the Connecticut River. If Stark had not been so proficient in this road-building mission and returned to Crown Point ahead of time to talk about St. Francis in detail with Rogers, then there might not have been a successful raid on St. Francis.

Even more, the timely return of Stark's two hundred "road builders" provided Major General Amherst with the luxury of keeping two hundred Rangers with him at Crown Point when he finally decided to advance north, which then allowed Rogers to go forth on the mission to St. Francis with his approximately two hundred men. Stark had just returned on September 9, earlier than expected by anyone, because he had overcome the extreme difficulties of the assignment in splendid fashion. Quite simply, the captain's timely return to Crown Point in essence opened the door and set the stage for the launching of Rogers's raid.

Of course, Stark's lofty reputation had also played a role in the general's final decision, because Major General Amherst knew that he needed the captain's skills and abilities, which were certainly on a level with those of Major Rogers, for his upcoming advance farther north down Lake Champlain. Thanks to Stark's arrival at Crown Point, and almost like presenting a gift to his friend, Rogers was at long last free to fulfill his greatest ambition by the time General Amherst gave his final approval to forge ahead on September 13. Indeed, with Stark and Rogers once again reunited as a highly effective leadership team at Crown Point, Major General Amherst was fully aware of the undeniable reality that even his mighty army would be "helpless" without the Rangers in leading the way during the advance north.[112]

Amherst so greatly trusted the gifted frontier captain, the son of Scotch-Irish immigrants like Rogers, that he could afford to allow Rogers to depart and fulfill his ambitions in his riskiest mission to date. As Amherst fully appreciated, if Rogers was killed or captured, then Stark would neatly fill in the gap left by the major without lowering Ranger capabilities. Clearly, Major General Amherst possessed as much faith in Stark as in Rogers. After all, Stark had been a key player in the overall success of Rogers's Rangers from beginning to end, helping to make them a more effective fighting force over an extended period of time. Indeed, without the tactically gifted Stark's many past contributions to Ranger successes for years, Rogers's distinguished career might well have ended much differently, with more glaring defeats and perhaps his death. Stark was very much Rogers's guardian angel, especially during the heat of combat.[113]

Basking in having his great dream of finally receiving the official order that unleashed him to attack St. Francis, which had been rejected by apathetic British leaders for years, Rogers was elated on September 13 like it was his birthday. He ordered hasty, but thorough, preparations not only on September 12 but also the following day for his most important mission to date. He had almost certainly departed Amherst's headquarters with a broad smile on a ruggedly handsome face that he could not hide from his men and others, even had he wanted to maintain the proper soldierly composure of a legendary leader.

Seventeen whaleboats began to be loaded with supplies for the long journey north into the remote vastness of Quebec, including the army's traditional rations. Sacks of cornmeal and barrels of salt pork were stockpiled in the deep bottoms of the sturdy vessels. Also, barrels of pitch and tar were also loaded upon the boats to repair any damage to the wooden hulls, if they crashed into rocks or logs during the watery journey northward.

At this point, nothing could dampen Rogers's spirits, not even the cold rain that began to fall during the afternoon of September 13—perhaps an ominous sign to the most superstitious Rangers, who were always on the lookout for omens. After all, and at long last, the major had finally gained the long-awaited approval to strike a blow that neither the Abenaki nor the French would ever expect or forget, and it all stemmed from the strategic mind of a rugged frontiersman of promise from the backwoods of the Merrimack River country. Rogers had secured nothing less than permission from the leading British commander in North America to turn a dream into a moment of glory that, as he and his men saw it, was such a long time in coming.

Thanks to a host of special circumstances that had unexpectedly and suddenly come together at the right time and place and under the right commander, the attack on St. Francis had been given renewed vitality by the major general to fulfill Rogers's loftiest expectations. It was a moment that Rogers never forgot. With relatively little time remaining before departure from Crown Point, Rogers continued to dispatch a flurry of orders for last-minute preparations, because the movement would begin in only a relatively few hours to guarantee secrecy, not long after darkness descended upon the land on September 13 and at a time when the loons' mournful cries echoed across the dark waters of Lake Champlain.

As noted, the most ambitious and audacious plan in the history of Rogers's Rangers had to be kept a perfect secret for obvious security reasons: a situation ensuring that the major and his command were destined to depart with the dropping of the veil of darkness only a relatively short time after Amherst had penned the delighted Scotch-Irishman's orders from his large wooden desk at headquarters. Maximum security shrouded the boldest of plans for ample good reason, as Rogers and Amherst fully realized. Too often in the past, deserters and prisoners on both sides had talked openly in the hope of winning the favor of their captors, almost as if conversing freely with friends back home or at a country inn.

Therefore, one of the long-existing myths about the St. Francis raid was that only two men knew about it before it was launched: Rogers and Amherst. In fact, a third man knew all about what was happening and the final objective: John Stark. In consequence, he made invaluable contributions that helped to ensure the overall success of the St. Francis raid. Stark's many thoughts and views were now needed by Rogers because they were invaluable not long before the final departure: still another example of how Stark and his important contributions to Ranger success have been so often cast into the dark shadows in the historical record, especially in regard to the daring strike on St. Francis.

Rogers and Stark were not only like brothers but also soul mates. Indeed, Rogers trusted no one more than his faithful top lieutenant, other than his brother Captain Richard Rogers, who was no more, having died of smallpox at ill-fated Fort William Henry in late June 1757. And as noted, Rogers and Stark—twin spirits from the northern frontier—had grown up together in the Merrimack River country, where they had hunted, fished, and trapped together in the pristine wilderness.

Consequently, at some point after his meeting with Amherst on September 13, Rogers met with Captain Stark, who was informed about the boldest mission ever about to be undertaken by the Rangers. Rogers needed to obtain additional information that his fellow Scotch-Irishman still retained in his head about St. Francis—a good many vivid memories of his six-week odyssey as a captive at St. Francis, where he had been held in 1752. But Stark had not been a prisoner in the traditional sense. After having demonstrated his courage under the most adverse of conditions, Stark had been adopted into the Abenaki tribe.

Most of all, at this time just before embarking upon his own personal rendezvous with destiny in faraway Quebec, Rogers needed a good map of the town and the area from the northeast end of Lake Champlain (Missisquoi Bay) to just below the St. Lawrence River, where the St. Francis entered Canada's mightiest river—the dark heart of Abenaki territory. After all, no extant British or Provincial maps detailed the more than 150 miles of unknown terrain that lay in the lengthy stretch of landscape located between Crown Point and St. Francis.

This was an uncharted, primeval wilderness and one of the most dangerous stretches of no-man's-land between New France and English forces. Few Rangers, including Rogers, knew anything about the northern end of Lake Champlain, a French lake dominated by enemy vessels that had long constantly patrolled this strategic waterway leading north into the heart of New France. This area was not only French territory but also Abenaki territory, considered a sacred homeland by these warriors and their people. The lengthy trek north down Lake Champlain would take Rogers dangerously close to Montreal, which was located on the St. Lawrence River northwest of the northeastern head of Lake Champlain at Missisquoi Bay. As the British had no maps of St. Francis and the surrounding area, Stark's knowledge and expertise was invaluable to Rogers.

Eager to ask many questions about the lengthy, mysterious stretch of land that led to St. Francis and about the town itself, Rogers evidently met with Stark in his own personal headquarters at Crown Point. This ad hoc meeting took place most likely on September 13, while Rogers was making preparations to embark down Lake Champlain not long after the sun set over the western horizon of the Adirondack Mountains. However, if this important meeting between Rogers and Stark was held at night on September 12, then there was ample time for the two old friends to discuss matters at length in a private setting, while perhaps enjoying an evening cup of tea or even a pewter goblet of good old New England rum.

This forgotten key meeting was conducted in an informal manner in a last private session between the two natives of their beloved Merrimack River country, for which they fought year after year, on the eve of Rogers's launching of his most ambitious expedition to date. Both old friends realized that it might well be their last meeting on this earth because of the immense dangers involved in this mission, if Rogers was killed or captured on the riskiest raid ever conducted by the Rangers.

At some length during the meeting, Captain Stark informed Rogers of all that he knew about St. Francis, which he had once called home at a time that seemed like an eternity ago. Stark told him about what to expect in regard to the lay of the land and the approach to the town. And he described the general contours of the St. Francis River, which continued to widen during its descent into the St. Lawrence. This longtime river of life in Abenaki lore would be Rogers's most formidable natural obstacle, which had to be crossed by the entire command to reach St. Francis. Because the town of the same name was located on the St. Francis River, Stark knew a great deal about the river just below where it flowed into the St. Lawrence.

As Rogers learned, St. Francis stood on the river's high bank, which was also covered with grain fields, mostly corn, that lay around the town. By this time of year, and as noted, the corn had already been harvested by Abenaki women and children in preparation for the upcoming winter. Therefore, the hardened frontier captain, whose father had been born in Scotland, might have told Rogers that these fields would have been harvested by the time he reached St. Francis, which might be around the end of September—a journey of around two weeks from Crown Point, if they made it at all. Most important, Stark emphasized how once Rogers struck the river, it was a simple matter of following it north to St. Francis—a natural watery avenue leading straight to the major's long-elusive goal and prize.

During the meeting of the longtime friends, Stark provided a good many intimate details about the town that Rogers could not have previously known. To his delight, Rogers was acquiring invaluable firsthand information—it was almost like gaining intelligence from an Abenaki tribesman because of the extent of Stark's broad range of knowledge gained from personal experience—that could be obtained nowhere else, even in regard to the best possibilities of Rogers's final approach to St. Francis and the overall plan of attack.

Clearly, an old friendship from their boyhood days in the Scotch-Irish frontier community was now paying immense dividends for Rogers when he needed them the most. Rogers was most of all focused on acquiring every last detail from Stark's fine memory about one of the most vivid chapters of his life. Quite simply, these two dynamic frontier leaders—the two Rangers who had accomplished the most in having molded the Rangers into an elite fighting force—were now having the most important meeting not only in relation to the upcoming raid but also in the history of Rogers's Rangers, after the recent Rogers-Amherst meeting.

After this crucial informal meeting between Rogers and his top lieutenant, the major certainly felt a greater degree of confidence in having gained a wealth of firsthand information from someone who had lived at St. Francis, and Stark knew the most intimate details about this remote place in Quebec like no other white person. For the major, the fact that St. Francis was no longer just a name but also a target that he could now envision in his head with more clarity and in greater detail—the area around and the terrain leading to the town—was critical if his bold masterplan were to succeed against the odds. A host of unknown questions that had long nagged the Scotch-Irish major had suddenly disappeared while he listened to the descriptive words about St. Francis uttered by his best captain.

Symbolically, in a crucial hour of need and as often in the past, Captain Stark had once again come to the aid of Rogers on the eve of launching his raid. In regard to the captain's contributions, this kind of timely rescue of Rogers in the field of intelligence was not unlike that at the first Battle on Snowshoes in early 1757, when Stark had literally saved the day for the reeling Ranger command with sterling leadership that rose splendidly to the fore after Rogers had uncharacteristically stumbled into a deadly ambush. If not for Stark's tactical skills in that hard-fought battle, Rogers and his men might well have been completely overwhelmed and wiped out to the last man—including Rogers, then a captain, who had been wounded twice, forever ending his career and his obsessive dream of destroying St. Francis.

Therefore, Stark had very likely not only saved Rogers's life during the greatest disaster in the history of Rogers's Rangers but also now allowed him a much better chance of achieving what would become the most famous exploit of his career. Unfortunately, the overall importance of Stark's key role in this initial planning and intelligence-gathering phase of the St. Francis raid has been minimized and all but forgotten, including by leading historians.

Other than vital intelligence gleaned from a vivid memory of a most eventful chapter of his life when living with his Abenaki brothers and sisters at St. Francis, Stark gave what Rogers needed the most of all: a map of St. Francis and the surrounding area, drawn from what he remembered. The captain recalled enough significant details and geographical information that he was able to draw a good map of a wide area that Rogers needed to know about: not only the St. Francis River country but also the Upper Merrimack River country, where he had been captured as a younger man, and the Upper Connecticut River country to the west. Both were parallel river valleys that ran north-south through virgin wilderness and lay south and southeast of the strategic Lake Champlain corridor.

After Stark had been captured by the Abenaki in 1752 at age twenty-three, he had been brought up the ancient war trail that ran north along the Connecticut River and then the same path through the uncharted wilderness that followed the north bank of the St. Francis River to the village of the same name. This old, well-trodden trail led up the Connecticut River to Lake Memphremagog and then to the clear-flowing headwaters of the St. Francis: the exact route that Rogers would eventually choose for his withdrawal from St. Francis after its destruction on October 4, 1759, because it was the only route then open to him for escape.

Thanks to Stark's timely contributions in providing invaluable intelligence, Major Rogers would no longer be blind in regard to some of the basic geography in and around St. Francis. Instead, he would have in his possession the two most important items that he needed for his mission to succeed—besides a good deal of luck—which were destined to pay immense dividends to him: his trusty compass and a detailed map drawn by Captain Stark.

Stark's vital contributions during the raid's final developmental stage have been forgotten or minimized, almost as if they were of no importance, or else ignored entirely by historians, who have too often cast the captain as an obscure, shadowy figure. However, Stark's contributions were crucial to the overall success of the upcoming raid. To be fair, the fact that Stark was not a member of the expedition has played a leading role in why his key contributions have been overlooked for so long. But in the end, and as mentioned, Stark made timely contributions that greatly enhanced Rogers's chances of success.

Ironically, Captain Stark made his invaluable contributions to St. Francis's destruction while still feeling a sense of belonging to and admiration for the Abenaki people of this place located on a gently flowing river. There is no doubt that Stark still possessed some empathy for the Abenaki, especially since he had been adopted into the tribe and almost certainly still had some adoptive relatives there. Of course, Major Rogers realized as much, which might have explained why Stark remained behind with the majority of the Rangers, around two hundred men, while Rogers forged ahead with a lesser number of Rangers, along with British Regulars and Provincials who had volunteered their service.

Most important, Stark's inspirational influence and example, despite his absence on the raid itself, remained with the Rangers during their upcoming odyssey. In this special way, it was as if Captain Stark would be beside his close friend—the major—during his most dangerous mission in the weeks ahead. Indeed, Captain Stark's legacy was an important one, and it was carried by Major Rogers and his men all the way to St. Francis. For all of these reasons, the inspirational moral force and influence of Rogers's top lieutenant would be with the Rangers every step of the way during their greatest adventure in faraway Quebec.

For as long as anyone could remember, and because their very name—like that of St. Francis itself—had for so long struck fear across the frontier settlements, the Abenaki never imagined that any white soldiers would ever possess the necessary courage and audacity to attack them in the longtime safe sanctuary that the Great Spirit had expressly created for them. Rogers was about to make a forceful statement about frontier daring and courage of a determined white commander that would leave a deep and lasting impression among not only the Abenaki but also the French leadership. The major shortly demonstrated that no place in New France was safe from his reach because of the hard-hitting and wide-ranging capabilities of his men in this war for survival during the struggle for possession of the North American continent.

Like a good commander who always looked after his men's welfare, although absent on the far-flung raid, Stark played a key part in allowing Rogers and his men to achieve their full potential in the upcoming mission. In Captain Stark's heart and mind, while he was destined to remain with his Rangers at Crown Point with Amherst and the main army, he was still very much with Rogers and his men during their greatest challenge, and he would be with them every step of the way to St. Francis, which he had once called home.[114]

CHAPTER FOUR

Final Preparations for the
Odyssey North to St. Francis

RECONFIRMING WHAT JEFFERY AMHERST HAD TOLD HIM AT THE RECENT meeting in the major general's headquarters at Crown Point on the previous day, Major Rogers took the time to carefully read his official orders as penned on September 13, which were issued just before he departed under cover of darkness for secrecy's sake:

> *You are this night to set out with the detachment as ordered yesterday, viz. of 200 men, which you will take under your command, and proceed [north] to Misisquey [Missisquoi] Bay [located at the northeastern end of Lake Champlain], from whence you will march and attack the enemy's settlements on the south side of the river St. Lawrence, in such a manner as you shall judge most effectual to disgrace the enemy, and for the success and honour of his Majesty's arms. Remember the barbarities that have been committed by the enemy's Indian scoundrels on every occasion, where they had an opportunity of shewing their infamous cruelties on the King's subjects, which they had done without mercy. Take your revenge, but don't forget that tho' those [Indian] villains have dastardly and promiscuously murdered the women and children of all ages, it is my orders that no women and children are killed and hurt. When you have executed your intended services, you will return [to Crown Point] with your detachment to camp, or join me wherever the army may be.*[1]

Of course, the fulfillment of these orders was much easier said than done when Major General Amherst was sitting at his desk in the comfort of his headquarters at Crown Point and still fuming about the dismal failure of the Kennedy-Hamilton mission. Contrary to the confident and cocksure words that were written by the respected British general who burned with vengeance that had played a part in the creation of these go-ahead orders, which were an obvious case of strategic overreach in regard to also attacking St. Lawrence River settlements, Rogers interpreted his orders in his own way out of necessity. As a pragmatist, Rogers viewed the realities that existed for this far-flung mission rather than what had suddenly emerged from the overactive imagination of Amherst. After all, Amherst possessed little knowledge about the mysterious region to the north and the art of wilderness warfare, Canadian geography, and St. Francis.[2]

First and foremost, Rogers instinctively knew that the mission of destroying St. Francis would be the most demanding endeavor in Ranger history, especially because the 1759 plan was more convoluted and dangerous because of present circumstances than his 1756 plan, which would have yielded an easier, less costly success. Although Rogers now possessed "the flower" of the Rangers, he lacked the manpower and time for any secondary mission of striking at the more distant settlements, north of St. Francis, in the St. Lawrence River Valley: an absolute impossibility, especially as almost twice as many Rangers under John Stark remained at Crown Point than he would take with him to St. Francis.

Indeed, if almost by a minor miracle he managed to reach St. Francis without incident and destroyed the town, then Rogers would be very fortunate to outdistance the inevitable French and Indian pursuers, who would be shortly alerted to the presence of the hated Rangers in the heart of New France. Clearly, as revealed in his overly ambitious orders to Rogers, Major General Amherst had no idea of the geography around St. Francis, the challenges of campaigning so deep in enemy territory, or the toll that such a lengthy expedition would inevitably take on the men, who would be at their physical limit, if not their breaking point, by the time they reached St. Francis, if they were so fortunate as to evade the enemy during the arduous journey north.

The mere thought that any English raiders might march north down the St. Francis River, where the town of the same name was located, and so far into the depths of the wilderness and enemy territory filled with so many of the enemy seemed nothing short of folly. If Rogers had decided to comply exactly with Amherst's order—and he did not from the beginning because he better understood what this most dangerous of missions would entail—then his entire command would have been almost certainly destroyed.

In his wisdom, therefore, Major Rogers simply immediately put any thought about striking the St. Lawrence settlements on the river's south side and nestled in the fertile river valley (more than 150 miles distant) completely out of his mind, because it was simply unrealistic and a dangerous case of mission overstretch. Upon reading Amherst's orders, Rogers must have longed for the relatively more simplistic qualities of his well-conceived October 1756 plan to attack St. Francis, which was devoid of such complications that compromised chances of success.

In regard to dismissing any thought of continuing north to strike the French settlements because it was totally unrealistic, this was an all-important decision that ultimately saved him and his task force of Rangers, Provincials, and British soldiers, who had completely put their trust in the major's wisdom, experience, and expertise: one key reason that explained why so many Rangers and Provincial and British soldiers were so eager to join and follow Rogers to hell and back if necessary, because they trusted his ability to make smart decisions that would ultimately save lives. By far and without question, Rogers's wisest decision was not considering taking the great risk of committing the folly of proceeding farther north from St. Francis, after it was destroyed, to the St. Lawrence settlements, as directly ordered by the highest-ranking British officer in the land: a classic case of Rogers's Scotch-Irish common sense and a degree of self-sufficiency rising to the fore to save the lives of his men, as it had so often in the past.

Finally, all was ready after a good many zealous volunteers from both British Regular and Provincial regiments had descended upon the Ranger encampment at West Bay on the afternoon of September 13 to sign up for the expedition. Because of Rogers's lofty reputation, there was no shortage of eager volunteers who had been born on both sides of the Atlantic. With a good eye well honed by experience, the major, who was a keen judge of men, closely interviewed and picked only the fittest and best men for the mission deep into New France.

On the evening of September 13, not long after General Amherst had presented his secret orders to Rogers, he was already on the verge of embarking that very night. The handsome twenty-seven-year-old Ranger chieftain's face was pockmarked, as he had been stricken with smallpox while in the service, and scarred by an Indian bullet that had grazed his forehead during the First Battle on Snowshoes on a frigid January 21, 1757. At that bloody time, Rogers's top lieutenant, Stark, who commanded the rear guard with his usual skill, had saved the day by keeping a good many attackers at bay by making a courageous last stand on high ground to buy precious time to save the ever-dwindling command, while Rogers was wounded multiple times. Rogers and his Rangers owed a great deal to Stark, who only became more determined in a crisis in the Scotch-Irish tradition of fighting even harder against the odds.

With his long hair tied in a queue, or a stylish ponytail that was popular and hung down his neck and onto his upper shoulder, which was wide, in keeping with his imposing physicality of a rawboned frontiersman, Rogers was about to lead 190 men—132 Rangers, both white soldiers (108 men) and Stockbridge warriors (24 men); the other handpicked soldiers were quite literally the best and the brightest of a highly motivated task force that contained soldiers from a total of five Provincial regiments and five British regiments—from Crown Point on the most dangerous secret mission of the French and Indian War not long after the sun of September 13 had set. They were about to conduct the most daring raid in Ranger history, while defying the odds that were stacked frighteningly high against them.

Appropriately, at this time, Major Rogers was in his prime and possessed more experience than any other Ranger officer in North America, having survived wounds and the ravages of disease, including smallpox and scurvy, over his years of the most demanding service. He was now at his physical, intellectual, and moral peak, which all came together at this time as he embarked on his greatest challenge and longest mission deep into the dark heart of enemy territory. Most of all, Rogers and his men were determined to strike a devastating blow against the "heathens" and "papists" who had long banded together—a hellish and unholy alliance of warriors and Roman Catholics in the ultimate nightmare for generations of God-fearing Protestants living on the northern frontier—to unleash their holy war in the name of God and country.

But as noted, these were not just white Rangers, who were the best men of an elite corps in terms of overall experience levels, making them the most formidable fighting men in the British-Provincial Army, but also twenty-four Mohegan and Stockbridge Mahican Ranger warriors, who were destined to prove invaluable as usual. Because of past heavy attrition and the fact that Captain Stark had recently been detailed with his sizeable command of Rangers by General Amherst, after the capture of Forts Carillon and Saint Frédéric at Crown Point, to build the wilderness road across the seemingly impassible Green Mountains from Crown Point to Fort Number Four on the Connecticut River, as well as the fact that Major General Amherst desired to keep Stark's 200 men with the main army after their road-building assignment, the number of veteran Rangers available to Rogers were relatively low at only 132 men. This low quota was certainly not what Rogers desired at this crucial moment.[3]

The number of Provincial volunteers, who had now become basically adopted Rangers, consisted of thirty-seven men. In fact, the number of volunteers who had originally come forth to join Rogers's next far-flung adventure in the wilderness was more than the major could handle, and many American volunteers walked away disappointed because there were simply not enough vacancies. But this situation worked in Rogers's overall favor. He possessed the luxury of choosing the best and brightest, fittest, and healthiest of the throng of eager volunteers who had poured forth with considerable enthusiasm.

In a letter, one participant of the raid wrote of the command's unique composition: "Major Rogers, with a Party of Rangers, and Capt. [Amos] Ogden, of the New-Jersey Regiment [consisting of crack light infantrymen known as the Jersey Blues], with a Detachment from 5 Provincial Regiments [under the highly capable Captain Ogden who led nine members of] Col. [Peter] Schuyler's [New Jersey Regiment, which had gained its nickname of "The Blues" from the blue collar of the uniform], [and half a dozen men of] Col. [Eleazar] Fitch's [Third Connecticut Regiment under the command of Ensign Elias Avery], Col. [Nathan] Whiting's [Second Connecticut Regiment]; Col. [Henry] Babcock's [Rhode Island Regiment], and [Lieutenant] Noah Grant and a few men of Col. [Timothy Dwight] Ruglass's [Ruggles, who led a Massachusetts regiment, or battalion], and Lieut. [William] Dunbar, with a Party of Light Infantry, the whole consisting of 230 Men, when they departed from Crown-Point."[4]

Another ten men had volunteered from the Provincial regiment commanded by Colonel David Holm and fourteen Provincials under Captain Leonard, or Leo, Butterfield, including Lieutenant Jenkins, who failed to survive this risky mission. Significantly, these Provincials were "all seasoned woodsmen," most of whom had been "on party with Rogers's Rangers" in the past.[5]

A contingent of twenty-one British Regulars, including cadet volunteer Hugh Wallace, had also volunteered for the mission to St. Francis. These Britons were under the command of Captain Manley Williams, who was a member of the 60th Royal American Regiment. Of this group, Lieutenant William James Dunbar, a member of the 80th Regiment of Foot, was one of the best British Regulars on this mission.[6]

By leaving the redcoat ranks of revered British regiments in volunteering for this special mission into an unmapped wilderness, the English volunteers, like the Provincials, relished the fact that they were joining a unique fraternity of fighting men. Indeed, Rogers had long ago "shaped the changing landscape by instilling esprit de corps [because a new] volunteer found himself joining an institution already full of shared stories, as well as resolute expectations and warrior ambitions."[7]

All in all, while this contribution of Provincial and British Regular volunteers who had come forth on September 13 seemed overly significant in overall numbers and influence at first glance, the heart and soul, character, and core elements of this expedition were thoroughly dominated by Rogers and his Rangers.[8] Indeed, for his riskiest mission, Rogers took comfort in the fact that he now possessed more than 130 Rangers, who were "the flower of his Rangers."[9] Of course, Rogers's staff officers were ordered to remain at Crown Point, such as Adjutant William Stewart, who had served in the British army for more than a quarter century. By this time, he was too old and more needed at headquarters than on the dangerous mission to St. Francis.[10]

Most important, the fact that so many non-Rangers had volunteered to join the Rangers' ranks was not the liability that it seemed at first glance. After all, Rogers was an expert in the art of choosing only the best men from all of Amherst's army as ordered by the major general. The key to a successful mission was that Rogers now relied on his Rangers, who served as the dependable nucleus of the expedition to St. Francis, despite decimation from the ravages of disease and costly fights like the Second Battle on Snowshoes. This last nightmarish battle in the snowy wilderness not far from Fort Carillon had led to the deaths of more than 140 Rangers in a battle that more resembled a slaughter.

At this time, two distinctive qualities now most distinguished Rogers's ad hoc force: the youth of the ranks and the color composition of his command, which made it stand apart from both British and Provincial regiments. Most Rangers were young men in their physical prime. These fighters in the ranks were in their teens or twenties, thanks to the brutal attrition that had unmercifully culled the ranks over the years to eliminate older men and hardened veterans.

However, by this time, many Rangers no longer looked young after their hard and demanding service under Rogers, which made them appear older than their years because they had often been to hell and back. These young Rangers had long ago lost their innocence and naive illusions about the glory of war. Unlike any other command in the British-Provincial Army, this was a racially integrated Ranger force of blacks and Native Americans, including twenty-four Mohegan and Mahican warriors. These veteran dark-skinned Rangers stood proudly in the ranks with young white Americans from across the colonies and volunteers from the British regiments.

In terms of uniforms and an overall look, Rogers's men presented a motley appearance that was deceiving at first glance. They almost looked more like a group of hunters or militiamen than soldiers, because the men of each unit wore a different kind of uniform or no uniform at all. One of the greatest myths is that Rogers's Rangers all donned neat green uniforms, including shirts and trousers, as long depicted in film, television, books, and artwork. But such was not the case.

Because the Rangers were not an officially recognized British Regular command that served and fought together like other units, and instead consisted of independent Ranger companies within the British army, an official uniform was never adopted for Rogers's Rangers. As Rogers realized, all that really mattered was that they wore the clothing that best accommodated and suited service in the dense woodlands in which they fought in all seasons of the year. Therefore, the much-imagined brightly colored uniform, including green overcoats, for every soldier would have made Rangers ideal targets against a snowy background.

Of course, in ideal terms, the Rangers most of all needed a white uniform for winter, a brown uniform for autumn, and a green uniform for spring and summer. Therefore, in the end, the partial solution to this dilemma had been no regular uniform at all, although green was the most popular color and the one worn by Ranger officers, including the major, and noncommissioned officers. Consequently, the common soldiers in the ranks simply wore the most durable, practical garb fitted for woodlands warfare, which blended in with the natural surroundings depending on the season: a practicality and flexibility that best suited Rogers's men whenever they confronted the enemy and regardless of time of year.

Only the best Provincials had volunteered because they felt honored to serve with the "famous" Ranger leader, as he was known across the colonies, which also indicated the rise of a new sense of pride in themselves as Americans that had been forged in the wartime experience. However, in general, while Ranger uniforms were varied and almost civilian-like in overall appearance, they often had certain commonalities that were best suited for the deep raid into the enemy's homeland: short green coats for the officers and noncommissioned officers and some enlisted men, Native American moccasins, tomahawks, and leggings, which bestowed an Indian-like appearance.[11]

At long last, Rogers was on the verge of fulfilling his greatest dream of embarking upon the lengthy journey in a determined bid to destroy St. Francis, if all went well and according to his well-laid plan. He must have been ecstatic in finally obtaining his long-awaited opportunity, while also feeling burdened by a host of new priorities and concerns, because he knew that this new mission would be the most demanding of his career to date.

First and foremost, Major Rogers was no doubt concerned by the fact that his trusty top lieutenant, Captain John Stark, was not going with him on this journey. The uncomfortable reality that Stark would not be part of the major's most audacious expedition was almost inconceivable because he was the heart and soul of the Rangers, like Rogers. Due to Stark's unique experience of having been adopted to become a full-fledged member of the Abenaki tribe and a young warrior, he still had friends and kin at St. Francis. Stark, therefore, had very little, if any, desire to join the attack on St. Francis, where, if he went north with the command, he might have found himself in the undesirable position of having to kill an old friend and perhaps even an adoptive family member.

With Stark having excused himself from any vexing moral dilemmas by not joining the St. Francis expedition and obeying General Amherst's orders (the latter was almost certainly the case) to remain with the main army at Crown Point to scout and screen the army's upcoming advance farther north, Rogers was fortunate in having to choose a top lieutenant to replace his old friend since childhood days from among a cadre of highly capable veterans who had served with the Rangers for years. These tried veterans included men who had survived a host of bloody encounters, including the life-and-death struggle known as the Second Battle of Snowshoes.[12]

Indeed, Major Rogers benefited from possessing not only good enlisted men but also an experienced and trustworthy group of top lieutenants, whose superior qualities partly made up for the absence of Captain Stark and the relatively low number of Rangers who would be journeying north. Rogers would not have been so effective during this upcoming expedition without experienced and high-quality officers in the ranks of his Rangers as well as the Provincial officers, who possessed wilderness warfare experience and had volunteered to join Rogers on his upcoming journey to exactly where the volunteers had no definite idea.[13]

CAPTAIN JOSEPH WAIT

Massachusetts-born Captain Joseph Wait was just the kind of experienced and capable officer now needed to replace the incomparable Captain Stark. Wait served as second in command during the expedition to St. Francis, and he proved an excellent choice. He was one of Rogers's most seasoned and best officers, having engaged in "border scouting service" in a Massachusetts Provincial company in 1754. Hailing from the town of Sudbury, Massachusetts, located just west of Boston, he was the second son of Anna and John Wait. The hard-fighting Wait had served as a corporal in a Provincial Ranger company led by Captain John Burke of Scotch-Irish heritage. Captain Wait had performed "with distinction" in the strategic Lake George sector of this vicious wilderness war for possession of the continent.[14]

Reflecting Rogers's astute ability to pick the best men, Wait had languished as only a lowly corporal in Captain John Burke's company of Massachusetts Provincial Rangers, where any possibility of his rise higher in the ranks had been effectively thwarted. Wait, whose name is sometimes spelled Waite, had acquired such a distinguished reputation for courage and leadership ability that Rogers knew he had to have still another reliable Massachusetts man by his side to enhance the overall quality of the Rangers, especially on this mission. Therefore, Rogers had eagerly sought out Wait because of his growing reputation and list of accomplishments, and he then offered him a Ranger commission.

On January 10, 1758, the Scotch-Irish major recommended Wait for a lieutenancy in a proposed new Ranger company. However, only four days later, Wait was officially commissioned ensign by Lord Loudoun in Rogers's "Own Company" of elite Rangers. Once free of his stunted career with the Provincials, Wait continued to perform with distinction, especially on the field of strife at the bloody Second Battle on Snowshoes, where his abilities rose to the fore. Rogers could not have been more satisfied with the overall performance of Wait, who had emerged as one of the finest Ranger officers in the command.

Therefore, on April 7, 1758, Wait was promoted by Rogers to a lieutenant's position, filling in a vacancy left in "Rogers's Own" company of crack fighting men. Then, at last, Wait gained the lofty position that he most deserved, becoming captain on May 11, 1759. As a sad fate would have it, Wait died a hero's death in battling for the great dream of American independence near the end of September 1776—more than a decade and a half after the attack on St. Francis, where he played a starring role from beginning to end.[15]

Captain Wait hailed from a family of tough-minded and hard-hitting Rangers, who had likewise excelled as leaders. The captain's younger brother, Sergeant Benjamin Wait, was another fine soldier who served in the company of Captain James Rogers. He gained recognition for effective leadership during the Louisbourg Campaign in 1758, when he served in the captain's Ranger contingent. It must have been a reassuring thought, with Captain Stark's absence, that Rogers could count on the ever-reliable Wait brothers, Joseph and Benjamin, during the expedition to St. Francis.[16]

Indeed, Wait was one of the closest officers to Stark in terms of overall exceptional leadership ability, resourcefulness, and tactical skill. On the eve of launching the raid, the major fully understood not only the strengths but also the weaknesses of the men of his officer corps. As noted, Captain Stark was an irrepressible officer who was second to none, but Captain Wait was nearly as tactically astute and capable as Stark: no small accomplishment, which spoke extremely well of Wait's leadership skills, as Rogers fully recognized and appreciated.

Like Stark, Captain Wait was a fortunate survivor of the most ill-fated and bloodiest day in the history of Rogers's Rangers. In March 1758, Rogers had blundered when he led his men straight into a deadly ambush during the Second Battle of Snowshoes. But the combined leadership abilities of Rogers, Wait, and especially Captain Stark, as well as other skilled fighting men who fought tenaciously to save their own lives, had risen to the fore in splendid fashion during a true emergency situation, after a large percentage of the command had been cut down in the snowy wilderness west of Lake Champlain.

One notable fact was that Captain Wait had survived this nightmarish slaughter, when the large force of Canadians, Indians, and French fighters from nearby Fort Carillon had nearly wiped out every single Ranger. As with Rogers and Stark, Wait's superior performance proved his valor and expertise as a natural leader in the fine art of survival in a no-win situation. By the narrowest of margins, Wait, Stark, and Rogers had escaped after sunset with only relatively few members of the decimated Ranger command in a brutal fight that no survivor ever forgot. Consequently, Captain Wait was exactly the kind of seasoned top lieutenant needed as Rogers's right-hand man on this most daring expedition to St. Francis. Rogers knew that he could count on the courage and combat prowess of the ever-dependable Captain Wait in any emergency situation in the days ahead. The ever-resourceful Wait was destined to save "many Ranger lives" during Rogers's expedition to St. Francis and into the great unknown.[17]

Naturally, even when everything was now going according to the major's plan, Rogers fully understood how he and his men were about to face a long list of unprecedented challenges and dangers during their upcoming strike so deep into the heart of Canada. However, as mentioned, Rogers felt greater confidence for a sparkling success on this expedition because of the overall high quality of the men in the ranks, especially the trusty officer corps, consisting of the best and brightest Rangers.[18]

Lieutenant Noah Grant, Ulysses S. Grant's Great-Grandfather

A veteran leader of Connecticut, who had scouted and waged war in the Lake Champlain Valley sector since 1756 while leading his own scouting parties that ventured toward Fort Carillon, Captain Noah Grant was one of Rogers's indispensable men. Rogers counted on this fine officer from Tolland County, in northeastern Connecticut, during some of his most daring of raids and scouting missions, going all the way back to October 1755. A volunteer from the Massachusetts regiment of Colonel Timothy Dwight Ruggles of Boston and a mature officer born in July 1718, Grant was just the kind of man Rogers knew he simply needed by his side if his great dream of destroying St. Francis was to become a reality this fall in Quebec.

Grant's sterling leadership qualities included reliability and steadfastness, especially under a hot fire and in desperate situations. Like Rogers, Grant remained cool and calm in the heat of combat, while other soldiers lost their heads under the intense stress of not only close-range fighting with Native Americans (including the Abenaki) and Canadian frontiersmen but also no-quarter warfare against their most capable opponents. He had even survived capture when taken by some of the fiercest warriors in America in August 1756 and lived to tell the tale like relatively few others.

In barely a hundred years' time in America, it would no longer be young Americans battling against Canadians, Indians, and Frenchmen but brother versus brother in the Civil War. Of all the soldiers of the more than two million men who served in the Union Army of President Abraham Lincoln from 1861 to 1865, one man was destined to emerge as the North's winningest general, who prevailed in some of the most decisive battles in both the western and the eastern theaters. The name of this remarkable man was Hiram Simpson Grant, better known as Ulysses Simpson Grant. Known for his shyness, superior horsemanship, and courage on the battlefield, he was a West Pointer and hero of the Mexican-American War.

Significantly, like Captain Noah Grant of Connecticut, the Ohio-born Ulysses possessed the same coolness under fire, dynamic leadership ability, and tactical stills, which made him President Lincoln's most successful commander of the Civil War. Some of the New England captain's most sterling qualities were comparable to those of his famous great-grandson, but to a lesser extent. When General Robert E. Lee surrendered his battered Army of Northern Virginia at Appomattox Court House on Palm Sunday 1865, it was Grant who accepted the unconditional surrender of the South's principal army, ensuring that the Confederacy lost the war and was destined for the ash heap of history.

Major Rogers possessed a gifted lieutenant in Grant, who proved to be a worthy ancestor of Ulysses, when the Rangers were engaged in attempting to save North America from an opponent that lost few battles.[19] By the spring of 1760, Grant would be promoted to the captain's rank, while continuing to retain the supreme confidence of Rogers and Amherst.[20]

Lieutenant Noah Grant could not have been more highly motivated. He never forgot the cruel fate that had been suffered by his brother, Lieutenant Solomon Grant, on the northern, or Lake George, front in June 1756. At that time, Solomon and a small mounted party of thirteen Connecticut men had been ambushed. The unfortunate Grant had been found with a "Sow Hogg [war club] in his Back," while his arms and legs had been cut off and "scattered here and there."[21]

Captain Noah Johnson

Captain Noah Johnson was the most experienced man in Rogers's officer corps: no small achievement, after having survived so many battles and skirmishes, which had included narrow escapes. He was the oldest soldier on the expedition, and his high level of experience seemed to have no end. Born in the community of Dunstable, New Hampshire, Johnson had first gained combat experience as a first sergeant in Captain John Lovewell's war against Native Americans in 1725. He then served as a private in Captain John Goffe's ranging company during the King George's War of 1745, gaining additional invaluable experience.

This vast amount of Indian-fighting experience ensured that when Noah Johnson enlisted in Rogers's scouting company—the so-called Winter Company in 1755–1756—of Colonel Joseph Blanchard's New Hampshire Regiment, he gained the rank of sergeant. For the same reasons, Johnson became an ensign in Rogers's new company, which had then gained invaluable experience in wilderness warfare. He then advanced to the rank of a lieutenant in the expanded command of Rogers's Rangers, serving in Captain Richard Rogers's company by 1756. At around age fifty-four, he was the oldest officer who participated in the St. Francis raid, outperforming more physically fit men in their twenties to the amazement of one and all.

However, fate was not kind to the elder frontier statesman and battle-scarred warrior of Rogers's Rangers, who was so thoroughly respected by the major and his men. Tough as nails, grizzled, determined to do his duty to the end, and ever-resourceful, Johnson was mortally wounded by the enemy on June 5, 1760.[22]

Captain Amos Ogden

For the most daunting and seemingly impossible of expeditions launched in the annals of American military history, one destined to thrust all the way into the heart of New France like a dagger, Major Rogers gained one of his finest Provincial officers in Captain Amos Ogden of New Jersey. Ogden volunteered with nine well-qualified men from Colonel Peter Schuyler's fine regiment of Provincials from the fertile land later known as the "Garden State."

He had gained ample officer experience as a captain of Schuyler's New Jersey Provincial Regiment, the elite light infantrymen of the "New Jersey Blues," since the siege of Oswego, New York, in 1756. Ogden had served extremely well in this capacity all the way up until the time of the St. Francis raid: more than three years of faithful service, while gaining invaluable experience as a captain and leader of New Jersey boys, who liked to fight the enemies of their country.

All the while, Ogden's reputation for inspirational leadership and courage in the face of dangers had grown considerably over the years. He was fearless and just the kind of seasoned officer Rogers early realized that he needed with him on the long journey to St. Francis. All in all, Ogden was a special officer who had long desired to join the elite Rangers because his well-proven abilities over an extended period were tailor-made for Ranger service. At long last, Ogden had fulfilled his longtime hope of transferring out of the "New Jersey Blues" and gaining his dream of becoming a Ranger, when he volunteered to serve on this mission to St. Francis.

The capable captain of the "Jersey Blues" had petitioned General Thomas Gage in the hope of securing a permanent assignment and a captain's rank under Rogers's command during the spring of 1759. Ogden's chance to serve with the Rangers became a reality when he received news on September 13, 1759, that volunteers were needed on a special mission without anyone mentioning its ultimate destination. As he shortly discovered, Rogers was extremely well served in having Ogden in command of the Provincials during the upcoming mission. The Provincials who joined Rogers were high-quality fighting men with frontier skills. They were all volunteers from five regiments and from various colonies that had long suffered from Indian raids, including the hard-hitting war parties from St. Francis: a unique fighting force of highly motivated young American volunteers who fought for God and country. The Provincials were generally as young as the Rangers.

These zealous volunteers—especially the boys from the New Jersey Blues, whose uniforms were trimmed in blue, hence their regiment's distinctive nickname—possessed considerable pride in themselves and their abilities.[23]

Second Lieutenant William "Bill" Hendrick Phillips

Second Lieutenant William "Bill" Hendrick Phillips was one of the finest Ranger officers who accompanied Rogers on his most famous raid where few imagined that he dared to go. He now led the elite company of hard-fighting Rangers known as "Rogers's Own," after having been promoted to an officer's rank for heroics and leadership skills demonstrated in full at the hellish First Battle on Snowshoes. Born around 1719 and representing a high level of frontier maturity and wisdom in the ranks among the generally young Rangers, Lieutenant Phillips hailed from a diverse ethnic background, which helped to make him one of Rogers's finest officers of outstanding ability.

In many ways, he was torn between two worlds, white and Indian, because Phillips had been part of both diverse environments for his entire life, which had been most unconventional. He had been raised in the area around Albany, New York, by an Indian Mohawk mother and French father. His mother also had some Dutch blood. She almost certainly was a Pennacook of the Abenaki tribe. They were a distinctive people who had lived in the Merrimack River country before the Europeans' arrival. Clearly, Phillips was very much a melting-pot soldier. With a measure of pride in his heritage, he represented the common mixing of races on the frontier and the creation of a new man in the New World.

While growing up in a wilderness area located about halfway up the Merrimack River toward its source in the mountain springs far above, or north, he embraced his Indian side with a passion. He became extremely knowledgeable about the wilderness and an expert hunter. Soon, "Bill" Phillips, from Concord, New Hampshire, was as proficient in the thickest woodlands as Native Americans, who were the people of his own blood: the perfect qualifications for the making of an ideal Ranger officer, who knew the wilderness and its ways like the back of his hand.

A single man fond of drink, like Rogers, which was a common feature of life on the northern frontier, Phillips had turned his back on life as a hunter and did some blacksmithing to earn income on the side before he became a Ranger private in "Rogers's Own" company on June 1, 1756. And he had distinguished himself ever since that time. Phillips's outstanding skills and abilities in the art of wilderness warfighting shortly became obvious to Rogers and others. Not surprisingly, he won promotion to sergeant in October 1756.

Very likely, a friendship developed between "Bill," who was of a darker hue because of his Indian heritage, and Rogers, since they both hailed from the Merrimack River country and had explored so much of this wild region since the days of their youth. On December 11, 1756, Rogers recommended Phillips for an officer's rank. To Rogers's delight, Phillips won promotion to ensign in late February 1757: still another example of Rogers not having been cursed with any of the stereotypical Indian hating or racism that was such a common feature of life on the frontier.

"Billy" continued to prove his outstanding leadership abilities both on and off the battlefield, where he had displayed combat prowess and wilderness savvy. Then a second lieutenant's commission was gained by this ambitious mixed-race Ranger in August 1757, and higher advancement was yet to come for this talented man of the wilderness. Knowing that he had an ideal officer, Rogers recommended Phillips for promotion to the rank of first lieutenant in early 1758.

By this time, Phillips had proven himself to be one of Rogers's finest officers. During the fight at Rogers's Rock (Second Battle of Snowshoes) on March 13, 1758, Phillips, then in his late thirties, was captured after "a heroic land stand" against the screaming tide of French, Canadian, and Indian attackers who were eager for Ranger scalps. Although tied to a tree after his capture, Phillips was lucky. Unlike almost all of his men, who lost their scalps during the slaughter, he was not tortured or scalped by the Native American victors in their bloodlust. When he found the opportunity, Phillips escaped his Canadian captivity before the year's end and rejoined the Rangers to continue the fight with an even greater reputation for resourcefulness and skill. Like Rogers, Second Lieutenant Phillips now had plenty of old scores to settle with the Abenaki, after losing his men (whom he considered his white brothers) at the bloody Second Battle on Snowshoes.[24]

Phillips's supreme devotion to the Rangers and Rogers was once again demonstrated when he discovered that his officer's position had been filled in his absence after the Second Battle on Snowshoes—it was assumed that he had been killed, like so many Rangers, on that most ill fated of days. Undaunted, Phillips took the career setback in stride and then proudly served as a volunteer in "Rogers's Own" company while battling the enemies of his people and country.[25]

Lieutenant William James Dunbar

Major Rogers was destined to benefit from the leadership abilities of a remarkable soldier, who was a British Regular of Gage's 80th Regiment of Foot (a light infantry regiment that had been modeled after the Rangers), Lieutenant William James Dunbar. Dunbar was a blue blood with lofty upper-class ties. He was first cousin to an English lord and related to General James Abercromby, but he had the heart and soul of a true Ranger. The New Hampshire major from the frontier with winning ways and plenty of charisma to ensure a good many faithful followers was delighted to have Dunbar with him on his most dangerous expedition.

Displaying the usual good judgment when it came to fighting men, Rogers knew his man well. And he fully appreciated Dunbar's sterling leadership abilities, which helped to make his command more formidable on the eve of embarking north into the vastness of the great unknown. Lieutenant Dunbar had already learned the ways of wilderness warfare under Rogers, making a perfect fit with the cocky and confident Ranger command of sturdy individualists. He had served as a cadet "on party" with the Rangers in the past and had essentially become one of them in the close-knit Ranger brotherhood by the time of the St. Francis expedition, when only the best men, especially officers, were needed by Rogers.

As fate would have it, Dunbar was destined to become the highest-ranking and only British Regular officer left on the mission after Captain Manley Williams, who was a British Regular and second in command of the expedition, was hurt and sent back to Crown Point early in the northward trek down Lake Champlain. The replacement of Williams with Dunbar gave the major a most worthy replacement when one crisis after another was on the horizon.[26]

Solid and Dependable Veterans of the Enlisted Ranks

It was much more than a veteran officer corps of talented and experienced men that made Rogers's task force quite formidable at this time. After all, some men in the enlisted ranks were as qualified and experienced as the officers, including the African American private "Duke" Jacob. At age twenty-six (nearly the same age as Rogers) and in the prime of life, "Duke" had volunteered for this dangerous mission and was more than willing to follow Major Rogers wherever he led the command. Having recently obtained "Duke's" release from an unjust confinement in jail by white authorities in Goshen, New York, in another example of Rogers's fatherly efforts in always taking care of his men, the major delighted in the fact that this elite black Ranger would be by his side during the upcoming expedition, because Jacob was "a gifted fighting man," and his courage and never-say-die attitude in battle were well known throughout the command.[27]

Ranger Peter "Pete" Bowen was another dependable fighting man of the enlisted ranks. He possessed ample experience in the art of wilderness warfare. He had been a proud member of Rogers's original company in 1755, protecting his people from the wrath of the northern raiders, especially the Abenaki. Bowen was known as "One-Eye Pete" by the boys in the ranks. Ranger Bowen had been injured by the accidental firing of a fellow Ranger's musket that resulted in the loss of one eye.[28]

Needing every resourceful and reliable Ranger he could lay his hands on for the many challenges that lay ahead, Rogers also benefited from the fact that some men of Captain Stark's company had volunteered and also joined the expedition. Stark's Rangers did so, despite needing rest from their recent arduous road-building assignment to link Crown Point with Fort Number Four on the majestic Connecticut River.[29]

Because so many Rangers had been killed and captured in the last couple of years, especially at the horrific Second Battle on Snowshoes, which had unmercifully culled from the ranks more than 140 men—all fatalities whose scalps now hung high in front of Indian lodges in villages across Canada and especially at St. Francis—and because Major General Amherst had decided to keep Captain Stark and his detachment of two hundred Rangers with him to serve as his army's trusty eyes and ears in the future, Major Rogers now relied on a sizeable contingent of Provincials, including fine officers, like Lieutenant Noah Grant and Captain Amos Ogden, in keeping with the army's politics and Amherst's strict orders: a situation that now gave the expedition almost an entirely American one.

Rogers was about to take only 108 trusty white Rangers with him on the upcoming mission, which was only about half the number of Rangers that Amherst had decided to keep under Stark at Crown Point. However, these men whom Rogers now commanded were among the finest men and officers of the Rangers—a sturdy nucleus of elite fighting men who now served as the sturdy foundation of the task force. Clearly, after Rogers's departure, the major general was looking out for and acting in the best interests of his army and his overall strategic objective when he eventually decided to continue to advance north, as expected by Prime Minister William Pitt, in a bid to capture Montreal, whose garrison was weak because reinforcements had been dispatched to Quebec.

But he had left Rogers at somewhat of a disadvantage in the name of army unity and decided to have all three contingents (Ranger, Provincial, British Regular) of his army represented in the expedition: a divergent force that the major would have to fuse together as a single command to ensure overall effectiveness in record time. However, the major felt fortunate to have 108 white Rangers and another 24 Stockbridge Rangers, for a total of 132 Rangers with him at this time: his ace in the hole.

As noted, thirty-seven zealous Provincials had volunteered on September 13 for the most dangerous mission of their lives, as had twenty-one British Regulars, to the point that only about half of Rogers's force was Rangers. Largely, the past attrition—not only from enemy bullets but also from the spread of deadly disease, especially smallpox, which claimed the life of the promising Captain Richard Rogers—had dramatically reduced the Rangers and their overall effectiveness to a degree. However, after the tragic culling of the ranks on multiple fronts, in which disease was always the most lethal foe, what was left for Rogers was the pick of the Rangers.

In a brutal Darwinian process that Rogers had seen all his life in the world of nature, the weaker and less resilient Rangers, men of poorer eyesight and slower reflexes, had been weeded out of the ranks in past actions over the years. Now left were the most experienced, resourceful, and battle-hardened Rangers, who were the elite of the elite. Therefore, in this sense, the Ranger force could afford—to some degree—to be augmented by many non-Rangers without significantly compromising the overall hard-hitting capabilities of Rogers's Rangers, because they made the British Regulars and Provincials better fighting men in a classic case of osmosis, since these volunteers were now serving with crack fighters with lofty reputations: a realization that not only raised the morale and motivation of these enthusiastic volunteers who hailed from both sides of the Atlantic but also enhanced their own combat prowess, and this was especially the case in the upcoming trek north and the attack on St. Francis.

Captain Ogden, a seasoned and savvy officer of immense value, commanded the sizeable Provincial contingent of thirty-seven men who had volunteered from five Provincial units. These highly motivated fighting men hailed from the New Jersey regiment (including soldiers of Ogden's own company from the New Jersey Blues) of Colonel Peter Schuyler, cousin of Philip John Schuyler of future American Revolutionary War fame when he served as one of George Washington's generals; a Massachusetts battalion (under Timothy Dwight Ruggles); a Rhode Island regiment; and three Connecticut regiments.

For the same reason, a total of twenty-one dependable Britons from British light regiments, consisting more of woods-savvy fighters than British Regulars proper because they had learned from the Rangers, now served with Rogers. As mentioned, Lieutenant William James Dunbar of Thomas Gage's 80th Regiment of Light-Armed Foot was foremost among these Britons. This was the first British light regiment, which had been organized in May 1758, and the pride of the English.

In fact, Rogers was very much the symbolic influence and architect of the concept of British light troops in many fundamental ways because the most enlightened British leaders had modeled the light infantry on the Rangers: one of the highest compliments to Major Rogers and one of his lasting legacies to the British military establishment. Since the time of the formation of the light troops, these tough British soldiers had learned a great deal about fighting Indian style in the wilderness. Therefore, they had improved immensely in overall quality in having distanced themselves from the traditional ways of European warfighting, acclimating to the stern demands of wilderness warfare by following the innovative warfighting ways of Rogers.

Like the Indian Rangers and primarily because of Rogers's lofty reputation and democratic style of leadership, the Provincials and Britons merged as one into the brotherhood of the Rangers because Rogers led an elite command. Indeed, most of all, it was Rogers and his inspired leadership style that served as the all-important glue that held all them and the command together in the weeks of unprecedented challenges and dangers ahead.

Significantly, Rogers's command represented one of the rare examples of American and British soldiers serving together not only capably but also in relative harmony in this war, almost as if they hailed from the same side of the Atlantic that divided divergent cultures and societies that were destined to go to war against each other in less than a generation: a rather remarkable development that spoke eloquently and volumes about the lofty leadership ability of the dynamic son of Scotch-Irish immigrants, when Rogers was commanding so many divergent individuals in his rare democratic style that bestowed an unprecedented degree of equality to each man.

Another primary factor that allowed for this unusual harmony and cohesion between the Rangers and volunteers from British army regiments, especially the men from the Scottish regiments like the famous Black Watch and Montgomery's Highlanders, was the commonality of a shared Celtic heritage and culture. All in all, in regard to overall demographics, Rogers was about to lead forth a mostly Celtic expedition, which was disguised by the fact that a large number of men were officially members of the British army and from the five Provincial regiments, which contained a good many men of Irish and Scottish descent.[30]

As far back as 1757, Scottish volunteers of the 42nd Regiment of Foot had been assigned by Lord Loudoun to the Rangers "to be trained [by Rogers] to the ranging, or wood-service under my command," penned Rogers.[31] These Scottish soldiers from the British army included mostly men from the rugged Scottish Highlands of legendary freedom fighter William Wallace, with the common Scottish names of Campbell (three) and Frazier.[32]

A soldier at the "Camp at Crown-Point" noted in a September 14 letter what seemed like a routine development, but this was certainly not the case, when Major Rogers was about to lead his men forth to the beach of Lake Champlain with confidence in the darkness of September 13 just after sunset, as so often in the past. Before marching his troops to the beach where the seventeen whaleboats lay loaded and ready for the journey north when daylight remained on September 13, Rogers closely inspected every fighting man with a keen eye to make sure that everything about him and his equipment, especially the regulation issue firearms and the condition of the firing pans, was in proper working order.

Rogers also made sure that the leather cartridge boxes of each man of the British Regulars and the Rangers contained sixty rounds and that the leather shot pouches that hung from the leather belts of the Provincials were full of lead balls. He also checked that each man had plenty of fresh musket flints of a dark color (French flints were amber, unlike British flints) to guarantee the necessary spark to ignite the black powder charge in their Brown Bess flintlocks. Powder horns were slung over the Rangers' left shoulders. These powder horns were both plain and decorated with fancy inscribed designs like the one Rogers carried either now or in the past. One of Rogers's first powder horns had been skillfully carved by a talented free black soldier from Massachusetts named John Bush.

Each Ranger also wore a sheathed knife in a wide leather belt that also held a tomahawk for close-range combat. The steel tomahawk proved extremely handy and effective when confronting Abenaki warriors, who were armed to the teeth, fighting on their own terms and in their own homeland. Haversacks, slung over the shoulders of each soldier, carried the army-issue provisions—salt pork, cornmeal, and biscuits—while canteens were slung over the right shoulder. Rogers also inspected other necessary gear worn by the men. Like a good commander, he had to make sure that everything was right and correct.

Not long after sunset on September 13, Rogers prepared to lead his men past the ruins of Fort Saint Frédéric, which hugged the shore of Lake Champlain, and down the sharp slope to the beach of the broad lake of blue. Before Rogers and aligned on the beach, which was sandy at this point, lay a lengthy row of seventeen whaleboats, full of provisions and extra gear. A soldier, most likely a British officer, at the army's "Camp at Crown-Point" shortly wrote in his September 14 letter about the secret mission whose destination was known to only three men: Major General Amherst, Captain Stark, and the Ranger major, who was still only twenty-seven at this time but carried with him the maturity and wisdom of an older man: "Rogers went out [of Crown Point under the fall of darkness on September 13] with a large Scout of 250 Men."[33] This estimation was an exaggeration of the strength of the task force by a fairly large percentage: ironically, Rogers would certainly need those additional men in the dark days ahead.

At this time, the majority of Rangers, mostly Scotch-Irish and other Celts, including good fighting men from Scotland and Wales, which the British had conquered by crushing past independence movements of the common people, were "all lusty, stout men, six feet high," which ensured stamina and strength for the arduous demands that lay ahead. These durable qualities mirrored the outsized command presence and imposing size of the talented major from the Merrimack River country.[34]

All in all, this was not only a significant ethnic demographic but also a source of pride among the men, especially the Scotch-Irish soldiers like Rogers, which helped to explain the most overlooked factor that helped to define the ultimate success of the St. Francis raid in the end. If ever the Scotch-Irish, who had been long discriminated against and defamed for generations on both sides of the Atlantic by whites, Britons and colonials, because of their lowly background and distinctive race, had good reason to be proud, then it was on this occasion in embarking on this special mission.

History had come full circle for the Scotch-Irish men from some of the bloodiest borderlands in European history. All in all, the French and Indian War was basically just another vicious border war on the fringe of empire for the Scotch-Irish. They were a border people originally from the Lowlands of Scotland, who had long fought the fierce Scottish Highlanders, when they had been armed with broadswords, to defend their homeland in the Low-lands, before migrating south to England's Ulster Plantation colonization effort in the rolling hills and valleys of north Ireland.[35]

FORGOTTEN CELTIC AND SCOTTISH CONNECTION

If the Scotch-Irish connection was not only the most forgotten dominant demographic aspect of Rogers's Rangers but also the overall dominant demographic of the raid on St. Francis, then the Scottish connection was the second most forgotten demographic. This Celtic contingent included the Scotland-born volunteers of the British light infantry, such as the Black Watch regiment and Colonel Archibald Montgomery's Highlanders. Like the Scots, especially the Highlanders from the picturesque landscape of northern Scotland, which was most distinguished by its mountainous terrain and deep lochs, the Scotch-Irishmen from Ulster Province had been a war-rior people with a reputation for ferocity since ancient times. In defense of their ancient homeland, the Scots had battled the ancient Romans and then fought with tenacity for Scotland's freedom from English rule under popular leader William Wallace, a self-made commoner of extraordinary military ability—like Rogers, who was Scotch-Irish to the core and proud of it—in a desperate bid to win equality and establish a free Scotland.[36]

A Scotch-Irishman himself from the green hills of Ulster Province, who greatly admired Rogers and his Scotch-Irish and Irish, including immigrants who had been enlisted from the port of Boston by Ranger recruiters and dominated the Rangers' ranks, Captain-Lieutenant Henry Pringle described Rogers's Rangers as consisting of "independent Companies . . . in short, they are created Indians & the only proper Troops to oppose to them [and] They dress & live like the Indians, & are well acquainted with the Woods.—There are many of them Irish [and] They shoot amazingly well . . . mostly with riffled Barrels."[37]

Interestingly, Pringle also named the origin of Rogers's parents as Antrim County, Ulster Province, as revealed to him by Rogers himself.[38] If this was indeed the case, then Major Rogers was a more true-blue Irishman than has been generally thought in the past, including by generations of historians.[39]

Most appropriately, while this was predominantly a Scotch-Irish and Celtic raid because of the ethic demographic of Ranger leaders and the common soldiers in the ranks, it was also very much a traditional Scottish borderland raid of old because of its overall ethnic composition. The ever-shifting currents and contours of history in the blood-soaked Scottish borderlands had long ago set the stage for the rise of Scottish fighting men in redcoats. The British army and its combat leaders had early learned about the ferocity of the Celtic warriors of the Highland clans of Scotland in the bitter conquest of Scotland, and they early realized that their combat prowess could prove to be an invaluable asset for England.

In a strange, paradoxical development, the very British leaders who had so ruthlessly crushed the Jacobite fighting men of Culloden, where a brutal no-quarter policy was embraced by the redcoats, and then razed the Celtic homeland in the picturesque Highlands during a brutal counterinsurgency, spoke highly of their ferocity on the battlefield. Therefore, wise British ministers, who faced a manpower crisis, then took the necessary step of incorporating far more Celtic fighters, wearing traditional Scottish Highland garb, into the British army for service in America.

Therefore, two Highland battalions—the future 77th and 78th Highland Regiments of Foot—were authorized and raised in 1757. These culturally distinctive Highland regiments were filled with tough fighting men who spoke Gaelic, sang ancient Scottish tunes and war songs that told of battling a long list of old enemies, and proudly carried the old Celtic and Gaelic warrior ethos with them to America: Celtic cultural legacies and traditions that were now more fully represented in Rogers's command for the upcoming raid on St. Francis, fitting in with the predominant Scotch-Irish demographic of the Rangers.

However, feisty Lowland Scots also served in these new Highland regiments, including one young man who had been one of the first volunteers to serve in Montgomery's Highland command, Private Robert Kirkwood. Like his comrades, he was proud of his Scottish Lowland heritage—like that of the Scotch-Irish who filled Rogers's ranks—which was as distinctive and unique as that of the famed Highlanders. Hailing from the small port of Ayr on Scotland's west coast and a cooper (barrel maker) without a promising future, young Kirkwood had volunteered with typical Celtic enthusiasm to serve with Rogers on September 13. And he was now a member of the St. Francis expedition with other Lowland Scots who were eager to fight the Abenaki.[40]

Like Rogers's Rangers, who were largely Scotch-Irish in overall composition from beginning to end, mirroring the basic demographics of the northern frontier, a good many of these tough Scottish fighting men from the British Scottish regiments had already met grisly fates at the hands of Native Americans from almost the very beginning of their service in the New World. Indeed, during the advance on Fort Duquesne in the Ohio country during the autumn of 1758, when near the strategic French fort, Scottish Highlanders in red uniforms "were goaded to fury at seeing the heads of their slaughtered comrades stuck on poles, round which the [Highland] kilts were hung derisively, in imitation of petticoats."[41]

As noted, the upcoming raid on St. Francis was very much a Celtic one because of the most dominant demographic in Rogers's ranks. Scotch-Irish and Scottish fighting men still thought very much like Celtic warriors of old, while remembering the beauty of the green hills of Ulster Province and the Scottish Highlands, and yet embraced their ancient cultural ways like a holy shroud. This was an appropriate development, because Rogers, the son of Scotch-Irish immigrants from north Ireland, was the ideal commander of such tough Celtic fighting men, who fought with their hearts and with ferocity: a perfect match for battling the Abenaki on their own terms in the uncharted wilderness and trekking all the way to the infamous missionary town of St. Francis.

Therefore, it was most appropriate that these largely Scotch-Irish fighting men were led by a handsome, large-sized man of Scotch-Irish heritage with red hair, blue eyes, and a light complexion that reflected his Scottish and Irish heritage. Throughout the course of history, the key explanation that was a secret to the past successes of the Scotch-Irish on the Atlantic's east side was that the Celtic and Scottish clans had long rallied behind a dynamic ancient Celtic chieftain or a "great captain" in the New World. And most of all, Rogers was now that transplanted "great captain," whom the Scotch-Irish and Celts—both Rangers and volunteers—had gathered around for the audacious strike on St. Francis.[42]

Most of all, and as in the past, Rogers and his large number of Scotch-Irishmen were once again about to demonstrate in the upcoming attack on St. Francis the axiom that had long explained the survival of the hardy Scotch-Irish as a people in one bloody borderland after another and on both sides of the Atlantic and why they had acquired such a combative reputation, since the days of the ancient Romans and their mighty legions, which had invaded the ancient Celtic homeland: if attacked by anyone at any time, it was then time to "strike back twice as hard"![43]

Ironically, General James Wolfe had served as a young aide under the Duke of Cumberland, the blood-thirsty "butcher of Culloden" because of the massacre of so many Scottish Highlanders, whose Jacobite rebellion was crushed forever during the slaughter, including of the wounded Scotsmen as they lay helpless on the grassy moor. During the campaign that resulted in Quebec's fall in September 1759, it was ironic that Wolfe now counted on his tough Scottish Highlanders in red uniforms, and his trust was repaid.[44]

Most symbolically, a good many of Rogers's men had chosen—a flexibility and freedom of choice allowed by the major to enhance fighting spirit and esprit de corps—not to wear any kind of regulation British army headgear, especially the fancy silver-laced caps for officers and sergeants, during the upcoming long-range raid.[45]

Instead, a good many of Rogers's men, especially the Scotch-Irish and Scottish Rangers, now wore "Scottish Bonnets, as the Rangers [often] wear nothing else when they go out" into the field, in the words of one contemporary.[46] Indeed, these popular woolen blue bonnets, flat and lying close to the head that were ideal for wilderness warfare, were worn by both Lowland and Highland Scots with pride, and they were seen throughout the ranks of Rogers's Rangers.[47]

Noticeable at first glance was a distinctive jaunty look about the Celtic and Scotch-Irish soldiers who wore this headgear of whatever variety, including some fur hats of fox or lynx skins. This free-spiritedness among Rogers's men was also revealed by a protruding hawk or turkey feather or an evergreen sprig from a pine or spruce branch that extended above the soldier's headgear at an angle.[48]

Displaying wisdom, Prime Minister Pitt had early placed a high value on these Scottish warriors, making sure that two Scottish regiments served in North America to confront some of the fiercest fighters ever faced by England. In his own words, revealing how he thought much like Rogers in regard to the legendary Celtic fighting man, Pitt said, "I sought for merit wherever it could be found [and] found it in the mountains of [Scotland's] north. I called it forth, and drew it in the service a hardy and intrepid race of men."[49]

A Special Destiny Calls to Major Rogers

Ironically, Rogers's first phase of his unleashing of the war's deepest raid, the lengthy journey north down Lake Champlain, which had been the longtime watery avenue of the Mohawks and their Iroquois Confederacy allies for striking north into Canada, including Montreal and Quebec, was about to begin. This body of water was nothing less than the lake of destiny on the northern front in this war. In this regard, it was most appropriate that Lake Champlain was the setting for the first part of journey to St. Francis that lay around 150 miles to the northeast.[50]

Significantly, Rogers's raid was much more than simply a mission of revenge for too many past atrocities to count over the decades, as generally assumed by American historians in the most simplistic explanation. Most of all, Rogers's long-range raid deep into the heart of New France was part of the overall British offensive plan that was keenly focused on capturing Quebec—much as the ancient Romans had long been dedicated to the destruction of their great rival, the city-state of Carthage on the coast of North Africa. Like Rogers's vison of destroying St. Francis, this great Roman goal of wiping mighty Carthage off the map had been eventually achieved after decades of bitter fighting and strenuous imperial efforts. And now a comparable obsessive conviction dominated the Rangers and fueled their resolve: "Canada must be demolished—Delenda est Carthago,—or we are undone."[51]

As mentioned, Rogers's objective, which was the hated wilderness "Carthage" of the French and Indian War among the frontier settlers, now had to be kept a closely guarded secret that could not, at all cost, be allowed to slip out. Therefore, no one said a word to anyone about his ultimate target, while wild speculation among the soldiers increased at Crown Point. But like the French leadership, no one could imagine that St. Francis was destined to be the ultimate target.

From the beginning, only Rogers and General Amherst—and then lastly Captain Stark—were in the know for fear that the great secret might leak out. In an effort to keep the precious secret, Rogers penned how "it was put in public orders that I was to march a different way [but] I had private instructions to proceed directly to St. Francis."[52] Most of all by this time, Major Rogers fully understood that the key to success was rooted in an undeniable truth that was revealed by his own words: the supreme importance of "secrecy in all his operations" against the enemy.[53]

Thinking like a modern operational leader, Major General Amherst prudently disguised the most secret of missions to enhance the survival of Rogers and his command. As noted, one of these rumors was that the expeditioners were on their way to link with General William Johnson's army, which was about to be taken over by General Thomas Gage. Even more, to fuel the rumor mill and camp talk that was always active when a task force was about to move out, Rogers's objective was said to be a fictional place called "Suagothel." In addition, rumors (including those initiated by Amherst from his Crown Point headquarters) were spread that Rogers commanded five hundred men, which was more than double the size of his task force, and that the expedition was certainly not bound for such a faraway objective located on the northeast side of Lake Champlain, the remote Missisquoi Bay.

One soldier speculated that Rogers and his men were planning to strike an Indian town known as St. Jean that was situated north of Lake Champlain and sandwiched between Fort Chamby to the north and Fort Isle-aux-Noix to the south on the Richelieu River that entered the St. Lawrence just west of where the St. Francis joined Canada's mightiest river. But only the most intelligent soldiers in Amherst's army—especially those from New England, who had long dreamed of St. Francis's destruction until it became not only an obsession but also a fantasy—saw through the rumors and reasoned that St. Francis might be the target, because Rogers's men were issued rations for at least a month.[54]

In the days ahead, a series of rumors filtered from Crown Point to the newspapers. It became common knowledge, thanks to the swirling camp gossip mill, that Rogers was about to depart with a sizeable force and head north into the vast unknown of an unmapped wilderness on a mission of destruction because of the expedition's large size. From a September 14 letter, for instance, the *Boston News-Letter* reported on September 27 (when Rogers was destined to be nearing St. Francis) in an overestimation of the size of the expedition from Crown Point: "Rogers went out Yesterday with a large scout of 250 Men."[55]

Undaunted by the seeming impossibility of it all, Rogers now faced his greatest challenge in the longest-range mission of his career because, in his own words, St. Francis "was situated within three miles of the river St. Lawrence, in the heart of Canada, half way between Montreal and Quebec."[56] But because of a recent development to the north, he now faced a greater danger than usual during what would be the first phase of the mission before he had departed Crown Point. Rogers might not even have been aware of this unexpected development to the north on Lake Champlain, which now jeopardized the mission.

Both Major General Amherst and Major Rogers had been so eager, albeit for different reasons, to strike a blow on St. Francis that one important point had been overlooked. On the night of September 11, one of the boldest acts ever undertaken by any Ranger, especially a noncommissioned officer, had transpired on the waters of Lake Champlain just north of Crown Point. On this suitable dark night, Sergeant Major Joseph Hopkins, an audacious and experienced soldier in Rogers's mold, who later was destined to break with the major for selling overpriced rum to the men for a nice profit, led an incredibly bold mission against the French sloop *L'Esturgeon* and almost fulfilled his lofty goal of burning the vessel.

This daring attempt by the sergeant major had naturally placed the remainder of the French fleet, which patrolled Lake Champlain with complete authority, on high alert. All of this ensured that the enemy, who patrolled the lake like a hawk, was even more vigilant than usual on the eve of Rogers's leading his men into the midst of exactly where the French vessel had been attacked. Clearly, the ever-unpredictable twist and turns of fate were already early working against Rogers's boldest design.

Almost certainly, therefore, French leaders had bolstered the fleet by perhaps including ground patrols to guard strategic points along the lake's shores or from nearby hilltops for added security. Quite simply, Rogers was about to take his men straight into a beehive of renewed French activity and defensive preparations on water and perhaps on land. However, not even this recent development was enough to deter the passion of Amherst, who had ordered the daring Sergeant Major Hopkins to embark upon the mission on September 4, less than a week before Major Rogers received his instructions to descend upon St. Francis and destroy the town.

Clearly Amherst and Rogers should have been more prudent by wisely delaying the launch of the expedition by at least a week. However, both men were too anxious to initiate the process of delivering the blow on St. Francis as soon as possible in the hope of weaning the Abenaki from their longtime alliance with New France partly because of the lateness of the season.

From the beginning, therefore, a measure of prudence and caution had been swept aside, including by the usually careful Rogers because he had nurtured his great dream of striking St. Francis for years. Nothing would now deter Rogers and his burning desire—an obsession second to none for him—for a single moment by September 13, 1759, after he had received his final orders from Amherst. Indeed, nothing at all could stop Rogers—not even the most feared Indian ally of New France, not even a newly alerted French leadership and lake fleet, not even the great expanse of an uncharted wilderness, and not even hundreds of miles of enemy terrain that had to be covered in a round-trip journey by a task force of barely two hundred hardy souls serving God and country with a young man at the helm.[57]

With late summer slowly dying, the sheer willpower and resolution of Major Rogers was about to propel him and his rustic expeditioners, full of confidence and high hopes, on the most daring enterprise in the history of the Rangers. If everything went according to the most ambitious of plans, then it was now only a matter of time before a bloody reckoning was destined to come to St. Francis and its people, who were about to receive the greatest shock of their lives.

CHAPTER FIVE

Relying on the Stealth of
New England's Sturdy Whaleboats

WITH THE LATE SUMMER SUN OF SEPTEMBER 13 BEGINNING TO DROP OVER the forested mountains and a greater chill in the air along Lake Champlain, the great adventure, although a most dangerous one, of a lifetime was about to begin for these young men and boys from across America—the deepest raid ever launched by Rogers that almost defied the imagination because of such a long distance involved and the seeming impossibility of this mission on a scale not yet seen in this war from any troops of the British-Provincial Army.

Indeed, St. Francis lay more than 150 miles almost directly north but slightly to the northeast of Crown Point and just south of the St. Lawrence, which linked Montreal, to the southwest, and Quebec, to the northeast. According to standard procedure found in Rogers's twenty-eight rules of ranging, which he had composed in 1757 and followed to the letter as much as possible, Rogers's handpicked men of high value and experience—108 white Rangers, 24 Stockbridge Rangers, 21 British Regulars, and 37 Provincials—had looked fit and ready during the so-called parade for a final inspection before marching to the whaleboats. Each Ranger had appeared eager for duty "with a Flintlock, sixty rounds of powder and ball, and a hatchet, at which time an officer of each company is to inspect the same, to see they are in order" for the great challenge that lay ahead immediately before Rogers ordered his men to march for the vessels.[1]

In the cold darkness of September 13, not long after the sun had set over the dense forests of the towering Adirondacks on the western horizon, Major

Rogers then led less than two hundred men—Rangers, British Regulars, and Provincials—to the seventeen loaded whaleboats aligned along the beach, after descending the steep bank with minimal noise.

Without the usual clatter of gear and equipment like more heavily equipped British Regulars on the move, these veterans marched in silence to the muddy beach of the peninsula of Crown Point, where the land leveled to the water. In the haunting darkness, the clear waters of Lake Champlain seemed unseasonably cold so far north at this time of year even before the arrival of mid-September. But thankfully, the lake's waters were not rough from bad weather or the high winds that often swept up Champlain from the north and Canada's depths that stretched to the Arctic: ideal conditions for a stealthy and silent push north in the night, down Lake Champlain toward the heart of New France.

Indeed, as Rogers now realized to his delight from his vast expertise in all aspects of the outdoors experience, including during nocturnal hours, there was no hint in the night air of rain and colder weather that might be shortly coming. Naturally, this was one of the major's primary concerns, especially during the first part of the journey, when the whaleboats were filled to capacity with rations and gear. Of course, the arrival of bad weather, especially high winds to create choppy waters, would have slowed progress down Lake Champlain toward the broad lake's northern end, where the land of Quebec continued to gradually drop toward the St. Lawrence and its fertile valley.

As usual, Rogers had led the way to the sandy beach of the lake bathed in a quiet stillness and to the flotilla of whaleboats. In a kind of soldier's ritual, the major was naturally the first to enter the lead boat, loaded down seemingly with everything imaginable for the long journey toward where the North Star already twinkled in the night. With hardly a sound in the lead whaleboat, Rogers pushed off into the watery blackness and the lake's quiet waters. Even here, at the shallow beach of Lake Champlain amid the night air that continued to grow colder in the chill of mid-September, Rogers made sure that a perfect silence was maintained among his men.

The overall cumbersome process of pushing the whaleboats off into the lake was completed as quietly as possible. In the blackness, the eerie silence was faithfully maintained by the Rangers, Provincials, and Britons, just as Rogers desired and had ordered. Only the night sounds from the nearby wooded hills and the slight noise of the men working the wooden oars in unison could be heard in the night, while the whaleboats cut through the deep waters on the journey north. Perhaps Rogers and his men now wondered whether they would ever again see Crown Point.

Nevertheless, the formidable challenge of such a lengthy expedition—of which the men were aware due to the excessive number of rations that had been issued—only seemed to motivate the major's followers, while also lifting spirits for what they anticipated would be a grand adventure. At this time, some expeditioners believed that this journey would ultimately take them to La Galette to link with General Thomas Gage's forces, after disembarking and then pushing west to cross the heavily forested Adirondack Mountains. For this extremely ambitious mission to St. Francis that suitably began at the beginning of a dark night without a full moon whose light would have shimmered off the waters to make the seventeen vessels visible to the enemy, the confidence among Rogers's men was exceptionally high, despite the fact that no one, except Rogers, who maintained his silence, knew where they were bound.

One measure of Rogers's unique leadership style was his uncanny ability to instill higher morale in his men, regardless of the situation or setting. Even the volunteers, like Scotland-born Private Robert Kirkwood, took confidence from the major. Everyone trusted Rogers's judgment, believing that he could navigate this mission to a successful conclusion, while saving as many lives of his command as possible, unlike the usual commander, who was too often obsessed only with winning personal glory and gaining promotion at his men's expense.

In his most revealing memoir, published in Scotland in 1775 at the beginning of the American Revolution, Private Robert Kirkwood, the Scotland-born volunteer from Colonel Archibald Montgomery's regular Scottish regiment of the British army, which was known as the Royal Highland Regiment, wrote, "Under the conduct of Major Rogers, we set out for St. Fransway in whale boats on Lake Champlain, and [eventually] came very near Montreal," which lay just northwest of the lake.[2]

All the while, Rogers remained true to his rules of conducting effective ranging warfare in the wilderness, especially in regard to an emphasis on stealth and secrecy that were so necessary for survival. In his Rule Number XXIV, the major penned, "If you are to embark in canoes, battoes, or otherwise, by water, choose the evening for the time of your embarkation, as you will then have the whole night before you, to pass undiscovered by any parties of the enemy, on hills, or other places, which command a prospect of the lake or river you are upon."[3]

In a letter, a participant of Rogers's most ambitious raid, who like the others had no idea of the extent of the odyssey that lay before them, described how "on the 13th of September, with 30 Days Provisions, they embarked in Whale-boats, and proceeded down [north] Lake Champlain" in high spirits and confidence.[4] Another soldier at Crown Point spread the news of yet another Rogers mission into the wilderness, writing on September 18, "I have the Pleasure to inform you, that Major Rogers . . . left this a Day or two ago, with a Scout of about 120 pick'd Men of the whole Army."[5]

In the same newspaper, the *Maryland Gazette*, printed in the port of Annapolis, on the same day in another rare account, a published letter revealed how the "Brave Rogers has been out on a Scout with a Party of his own Men, and Draught [draft] from the Regulars, amounting to the whole to 200."[6] Later, still another man's September 14 letter was published in the *Maryland Gazette* on October 11, explaining how "Rogers went out [from Crown Point] with a large Scout of 250 Men."[7]

Plying quietly through the lake's calm waters, which gradually widened as they progressed farther north under the protective veil of darkness, this flotilla of seventeen whaleboats filled with young men and boys remained under Rogers's tight discipline and security from the journey's beginning, because French patrol vessels might suddenly appear at any moment. Rogers's Rule Number XXV, which applied to the beginning of the expedition down the vast length of Lake Champlain, which pointed straight into the heart of New France like an English dagger, stated, "In paddling [in canoes] or rowing [in whaleboats], give orders that the boat or canoe next the sternmost, wait for her, and the third for the second, and the fourth for the third, and so on, to prevent separation, and that you may be ready to assist each other on any emergency."[8]

In his rules for properly conducting ranging warfare in the wilderness, Rogers also emphasized in Rule Number XXVI another priority that came into play on this cold night on Lake Champlain, but only to a limited degree because there was no intention for the Rangers to make an attack during this secret journey north because secrecy had to be maintained at all costs: "Appoint one man in each boat to look for fires, on the adjacent shores, from the numbers and size of which you may form some judgment of the number that kindled them, and whether you are able to attack them or not."[9]

While the row of whaleboats maintained their alignment in a neat and tight formation that eased noiselessly through the dark waters like a line of cautious Rangers trekking through the forest when deep in enemy territory, the night's blackness shrouded the broad lake surrounded by hills and dense forests. The brisk night air felt almost freezing cold to the men, who had just left the warmth of their quarters not long ago, including in British Regular encampments, in the open whaleboats.

By this time, the chill of autumn had already arrived by the second week of September to provide an early hint of the harsh winter on the way from the north. Winter now lingered like a ghost on the northern horizon toward the Arctic, from which bitter winds and lower temperatures would shortly descend upon the Lake Champlain Valley with a vengeance. In this regard, the major and his men were in a race to beat winter's arrival, hoping to strike St. Francis before the descent of harsh cold weather that would wrap the land in the first snowy shroud of white and subzero temperatures.

But now these beautiful days of early fall along picturesque Lake Champlain were still warm and balmy in the afternoons, when skies remained clear of threatening dark clouds filled with snow. The pleasant autumn weather had invigorated the spirits and hopes of the men in the ranks. However, it had just recently turned unseasonably cold for this time of year in late summer, which reminded Rogers of the urgent need to push north as rapidly as possible toward the St. Lawrence River. However, this was only a brief cold snap before more seasonable and warmer weather shortly arrived.

Therefore, with the cold snap that the night only made more severe, each man—Provincials, Rangers, blacks, Indians, Scotsmen, Irishmen, Britons, Welshmen, mixed-race fighting men (various degrees of mixtures between Indian and white, and black and white), and others of a truly melting-pot fighting force that had been seamlessly united under the easy authority of the major's leadership—wore blanket rolls behind their backs to keep dry, while rowing ever northward down the wide lake, which led toward the enemy. These woolen army blankets were essential for protection from the steady creep of winter that was on the way from the same direction that these sojourners were now headed with confidence for a successful mission, despite the odds stacked against them.

Major Rogers's ultimate objective was an obscure bay, located the northeastern arm of Lake Champlain around seventy-five miles straight north as the crow flies, over which the chevron-shaped formations of honking Canadian geese surged north across the skies in the spring. Known to Rogers but not extremely well, because he had not seen it previously, this targeted site was Missisquoi Bay, which took its name from an Abenaki word meaning "a great grassy place" and "a great marshy place" in the wilderness.

Like a good shepherd tenderly nursing his flock when pushing north through the night and even more hostile territory, Rogers made sure that each whaleboat closely followed the previous in a long file of vessels. As usual, the major was at the head of his contingent in the lead vessel, moving down the lake in the blackness and between hills of a virgin wilderness in which enemy war parties lurked like thieves in the night.

Any kind of separation between the steadily moving vessels that eased through still waters in a haunting silence might well prove fatal. Therefore, as if they possessed a life of their own, the long row of seventeen whaleboats flowed as one down the wide lake in a disciplined line. The movement was so efficient that it was as if these rough-hewn landlubbers had been veteran sailors from the leading ports of New England, looking out for whales in the Atlantic's waters instead of watching for signs of Indians, Canadians, and Frenchmen, who might be lurking along the timbered shoreline.

Symbolically, the sturdy whaleboats that carried Rogers's men—about a dozen men apiece in each vessel now moving smoothly over dark waters—represented an amazing American success story of can-do spirit that was one key to the economic success in the Northeast. And in many ways, this New England success story was comparable to the overall success story of the Rangers' themselves, because it primarily stemmed from American self-reliance and courage. It was no coincidence that so many of Rogers's men, both New England Rangers and Provincials, now served in the ranks that reflected the distinct regionalism of New England, which had long suffered the brunt of Native American raids.

Whaling was a major American industry and staple of New England's thriving economy, like the slave trade. By this time, whaling had become part of American life and culture. And Rogers's men, Rangers as well as Provincials, had long demonstrated that same kind of can-do spirit amid the wilderness environment during wartime. Just like on this risky mission all the way to St. Francis, New England blacks and Native Americans, with dark hair (kinky and straight, respectively) tied behind their backs in stylish queues, or ponytails, and wearing gold earrings and jaunty sailor-like attire, had long served together in the pursuit of the migrating whales across the seven seas. Significantly, unlike on land, while working in pursuit of whales on the rolling waters of the world's oceans, the color of the black or Indian seaman's skin was not as important to the practical New England captain, his top officers, and the crew as his abilities aboard ship.

In that regard, therefore, traditional life at sea in New England's whaling industry had long brought a unique sense of equality not seen on the land in any of the thirteen colonies—just like in the case of the blacks and mixed-race fighting men (mostly the products of black mothers and white fathers, both slave owners and random whites, who had united as one out of wedlock) who served with distinction in the ranks of Rogers's Rangers—because one's character and ability mattered the most while working at tough jobs on the sea.

Consequently, a good many whites—whalers and Rangers—who hailed from New England's ports along the Atlantic's rocky coast, already knew about the natural equality of the black man. They understood that a man of African descent was as good as themselves in either chasing down whales on the so-called Nantucket Sleighride or fighting the veteran Canadians, Indians, and Frenchmen in the wilderness. And in general, this rare sense of egalitarianism that existed between blacks and whites at sea was something not seen farther inland from the coast, where racism—born mostly of a xenophobia from a longtime isolation from different cultures and peoples—thrived in far larger dosages.

In this regard, and as in America's rich seafaring tradition, service for blacks in Rogers's Rangers was an overall liberating experience when it came to race relations, because they were all a band of brothers who served, fought, and died together with a high esprit de corps, camaraderie, and sense of pride. It was appropriate that this rare equality that existed between black and white was increased not only from the wartime environment but also from service on the frontier, which, like on the sea, became a birthplace of greater equality for blacks who served with pride in Rogers's Rangers.

Therefore, this unprecedented development of greater racial equality occurred in Rogers's Rangers at a time when slavery was alive and well in all the colonies and across the breadth of New England, which was another tragic inheritance from the mother country: just as the integrated crews of New England's hardy seafarers of the whaling crews, which had long made a livelihood by going "a-whaling" for sperm, humpback, and bowhead whales, had long been distinguished by multiethnic and multicultural traditions. And this egalitarian tradition of New England was seamlessly continued in the ranks of Rogers's Rangers in the form of a melting-pot soldiery of a wide variety of ethnicities during the expedition to St. Francis.

Significantly, Rogers's Rangers were America's first professional integrated combat force, and this remarkable development had been due to the major's open-mindedness in racial matters, especially the enlightened concept of black Rangers serving side by side with white Rangers. As the son of lowly Scotch-Irish immigrants, regardless of rank, Rogers never felt that he was too good or superior to sleep and eat beside a man of African descent, as did so many other whites, especially from the wealthy upper class, who were surrounded by black domestics and slaves all their lives.

While the American whaling industry was ever on the rise to dominate the world market in the seventeenth century, the British whaling industry was in a state of decline: symbolically, Rogers's Rangers and their resourceful Scotch-Irish commander and the common man in general—the American— were also on the rise by 1759 to herald the arrival of a new day for a new people in the New World.

While Rogers and his 108 white and black Rangers, who served beside 24 Stockbridge Indian Rangers on this expedition, were destined to reach their peak of performance at St. Francis, so the colonists were destined to shortly reach their own peak with the issuing of the Declaration of Independence on July 4, 1776, because of the direct results, influences, and legacies of the French and Indian War: both developments stemmed from the rise of the common man in the New World from the dual wilderness and wartime experiences that had resulted in the creation of a new man, the American.

Ideal for plying the often treacherous waters of Lake Champlain whenever there might be a sudden change to stormy weather blowing in from the north, Rogers's seventeen whaleboats (between twenty to twenty-five feet in length and with round bottoms and keels, built from strong cedar clapboards, and made for speed in cutting through the ocean's waters) were in good shape, thanks to Major General Jeffery Amherst's meticulous nature and farsighted concerns, which now paid dividends to the Rangers.

Designed for moving swiftly through the rough waters of ocean swells, these vessels were sturdy and light—a rare combination of unique qualities that bestowed a perfect balance in uniting much-needed dual strengths—and hence ideal for navigating the often choppy waters (thanks to brisk northern winds blowing south from the Canadian Arctic) of this wide lake nestled in a virgin wilderness of spectacular natural beauty. And, importantly, the shallow draft of these light vessels allowed for the whaleboats, when rowed in unison and with vigor by men working closely together on each side of the boat, to ease gracefully along the lake while swiftly cutting through the waters like a knife.

Significantly, during this all-important 1759 campaign, in which the British were going for broke as never before, with Prime Minister William Pitt skillfully directing the overall war effort, the thoughtful Major General Amherst, who was exceptionally meticulous in regard to intricate details and obsessive about taking all necessary precautions to enhance the chances for success, had recently ordered a hardworking team of "Calkers" to repair any leaks found in the light cedar planking of the whaleboats. Maintenance was needed in part because these whaleboats had been brought all the way from principal whaling ports of New England, like Cape Cod, Nantucket, New Bedford, and Martha's Vineyard. These well-constructed whaleboats had already been broken in to enhance their overall water worthiness, having already cut through the Atlantic's waters in chase of whales. However, some whaleboats had possibly been built in Albany, New York, on the Hudson River and Schenectady, New York, on the Mohawk River.[10]

In an incredible logistical success story all in itself, the whaleboats had been transported from the Atlantic coast and north up the Hudson River and then to Albany, before the long-distance portage north for use on the lakes (Lake George and then Lake Champlain, from south to north) located above Fort Edward: quite a logistical accomplishment that now paid immense dividends to Rogers for the fulfillment of his water-land journey deep into the wilderness of Quebec.[11]

Second Lieutenant William "Bill" Hendrick Phillips knew all about the Albany area, where he had been born around 1719 to a white French father and Native American mother. This fertile region along the Hudson was Mohawk country of the Iroquois Confederacy. Bill had Mohawk blood running through his veins from his mother's Native American family, who loved their native land as much as the Scotch-Irish like Rogers loved the Merrimack River Valley.[12]

It has long been thought that the sturdy bows of Rogers's solidly constructed (in the high-quality New England shipbuilding tradition) whaleboats had been marked with the name of his Ranger corps, but such was not the case. The distinctive marking of boats with specific unit designations had been ordered by the detail-oriented Major General Amherst at Crown Point on September 20, 1759, after Rogers and his men had departed with high hopes and a degree of unfounded confidence in a true mission impossible.[13]

After thorough preparations for the daunting challenges that lay ahead, the weapons of the Rangers had never been in better shape by this time: Rogers's own requirement, which he had excessively emphasized for this far-flung mission. First and foremost, the army's standard smoothbore musket, the Brown Bess, was the weapon of choice for most of Rogers's men. Of course, the Rangers' fewer rifled muskets, blessed with greater accuracy and longer-range capabilities because of the length and rifling of the barrels, always received the most careful attention over the less delicate (in overall relative terms) but more sturdy Brown Bess. Rogers possessed a group of lethal riflemen, who were experts at neatly clipping off a turkey's head or hitting a bounding deer racing through the woodlands.

From countless arms inspections conducted by the detail-oriented Rogers who seemingly never missed any detail, the Rangers knew that a well-oiled and rust-free weapon with a clean barrel often made the difference between life and death in the bloody showdowns with the enemy. Therefore, Ranger weapons—both smoothbore and rifled muskets—were in excellent shape by the time that Rogers's men headed north in their whaleboats as silently as possible. When loaded with the rounds of "buck & ball," the Rangers' smoothbore muskets were especially deadly—basically a mini shotgun—that was far easier to load than a rifle, which often fouled and took too long to reload, especially in a close-range firefight amid the tangled woodlands along Lakes George and Champlain. In the heat of combat, a single second might well mean the difference between life or death. And, most important, the Rangers' smoothbore Brown Bess muskets came with a long bayonet that was ideal for close-range combat, unlike the rifle, which had no bayonet, presenting a severe liability in close combat.[14]

Evidently for logistical reasons, some volunteers of Rogers's expedition had received less than the required thirty-day supply of provisions, when most men had received the correct amount. Scotland-born Private Robert Kirkwood wrote how they possessed "23 days [worth of] provisions" during the push north down Lake Champlain from Crown Point and ever deeper into the watery unknown, surrounded by high ground covered in dense forests. This seven-day difference in the amount of rations issued to a minority of Rogers's task force held grim implications in the days ahead for those men, evidently mostly the British volunteers, who had been short-changed. This wild region of virgin lands through which Rogers now journeyed still looked the same as when in 1609 Samuel de Champlain, the father of New France, had first explored the lake and surrounding area and been astounded by the natural beauty of a pristine land.[15]

In a letter, one of Rogers's men described how stealth and care were the hallmarks of the push north down the lake that seemed to expand forever northward, with the men quietly working in rowing relay teams that maintained a rhythm that ensured a good pace. This tactic guaranteed the utilization of the oarsmen's maximum strength, endurance, and vigor, "only rowing in the Night, for Fear of the Enemy's Vessels on the Lake."[16]

Although the target of this dangerous enterprise was secret, members of Rogers's command realized from the beginning that they were on an exceptionally long mission deep into enemy territory because of the usually large number of rounds and provisions that had been issued—a situation that only fueled wilder rumors of no validity. Meanwhile, the danger that existed in the eerie blackness on this broad lake amid the wilderness began almost immediately for the major and his men on Lake Champlain.

At some point in the journey north, the seventeen New England whaleboats would have to run a gauntlet of armed French vessels, brimming with cannon and vigilant men—Indians, Canadians, and Frenchmen—who wanted nothing more than to wipe out a large force of waterborne Englishmen, especially Rangers. As Rogers knew from prior experience and the latest intelligence, the French patrol boats lay somewhere to the north farther down the lake. These French vessels, with their vigilant crews, routinely patrolled Lake Champlain for the express purpose of stopping audacious incursions like that of Rogers, while protecting Canada, especially Montreal to the northwest and Quebec to the northeast.

In the whaleboats—the same kind that had long departed from America's leading whaling ports, like Cape Cod, Martha's Vineyard, and Nantucket in Massachusetts, and plied the ocean's rough waters in the killing of sperm and bowhead whales to obtain their precious oil to light lamps and lanterns across New England, Rogers's men rowed hour after hour in the cold blackness of a night that seemed almost menacing because of the hushed quiet. Of course, Rogers allowed no lights of any kind—not even a pipe or cigar for either an officer or an enlisted man. He had ordered the tightest of security measures, which were necessary for this mission to succeed in the face of extremely high odds.

Consequently, there were no lanterns on Rogers's seventeen vessels, while the weary men rowed deeper into the night and throughout the early morning hours for safety's sake. The seemingly mysterious loons, while gracefully plying the calm waters of small, hidden inlets surrounded by dark forests, occasionally unleashed their eerie, mournful cry, which echoed hauntingly over the lake's cold waters and the surrounding hills like a trumpet, when widely separated mates attempted to locate each other in the night.

For the superstitious men in the ranks or Britons who hailed from the cobblestone streets of London or Liverpool, the cries of the loon echoing over the lake seemed absolutely unearthly. Urbanite Englishmen of Captain Manley Williams's contingent had never before heard the ghostly wails of the loons—a large water bird with black and white plumage that dove deep into blue waters in the pursuit of fish. It was the strangest cry that they had ever heard, sounding almost like an ill omen suddenly erupting out of the blackness. But the Irish Rangers from the rural countryside of pristine lakes on the Green Isle knew this fish-eating bird as the "diver" because of its artful fishing methods. These Irish soldiers were familiar with its mournful wail—lengthy, loud, and piercing—which they could never forget from their childhood days.

To avoid detection from the menacing French patrol boats—a schooner and three sloops possessing thirty-four cannon in total and more mobile swivel guns, which could unleash a deadly spray of small iron projectiles—located somewhere to the north, Rogers basked in the relative safety of only traveling Lake Champlain at night. Clearly, Rogers was not taking any chances because no mistakes could be made, or the entire expedition might be doomed.

Especially after the losses of Forts Carillon and Saint Frédéric the previous summer during Amherst's relentless advance north, the French vessels had long carefully roamed these waters with undisputed authority, but they had now shouldered the primary responsibility of guarding the way north by water into the heart of Canada. Of course, the cannon of these French vessels could literally blow Rogers's little whaleboats out of the water to quickly end the expedition before it had barely begun. Therefore, in moving ever closer to his ultimate objective of Missisquoi Bay located at the lake's northeast corner, Rogers and his men would be forced to run a gauntlet of omnipresent risks and dangers for the nearly eighty-mile journey down the lake.

As during past expeditions, Major Rogers had taken seemingly every precaution. He even had the oars muffled by covering them in sheepskins or wool, which effectively deadened the noise except for the creaking of long, wooden oars. Eight oars propelled each whaleboat, four on each side for a perfect balance when rowing in harmony down the lake in the cold night. Rogers's men rowed with a careful and disciplined silence in rhythmic unison hour after hour. All the while, a lengthy line of seventeen whaleboats steadily moved north up the broad expanse of Lake Champlain's dark waters. Everyone was conscious that any loud sound, like the mishandling of an oar from an insidious weariness or a clumsy mistake by a rower, might give away the entire secret enterprise that was as bold as it was dangerous.

All the while, the biting cold of an Arctic wind descended from the north, whipping down the broad lake in the darkness. Former seafarers and whaling men in the ranks no doubt delighted in Rogers's reliance on maritime vessels and skills that fueled this expedition into the depths of the dark unknown. It was obvious that Rogers was an expert familiar with plying Lake Champlain's waters from his past experience of so many prior waterborne expeditions deep into French territory, in contrast to the simplistic frontier stereotype of a woodsman without experience in naval operations.

A Hidden Place Called Otter River

Finally, Rogers spied what he was looking for from the bow of the lead whaleboat that hugged the timbered eastern shore of Lake Champlain: the westward-jutting peninsula, extending into placid waters, that had been created by the sediments of a westward-flowing river. With sore and weary arms from hours of rowing throughout the miserable night, the Ranger, Provincial, and British Regular soldiers far from their homes and families finally halted before daylight on September 14, after entering a secure inlet of shallow, swampy water surrounded by dense pine and other hardwood trees.

Located on the lake's eastern side and situated fifteen miles north of Crown Point, this cozy inlet was basically a small, narrow bay: an ideal spot in Rogers's mind for sound security reasons during the first stage of his plan of leapfrogging northward up the lake. The headwaters of Otter River tumbled down from the Green Mountains that dominated the eastern horizon, where the New England homeland of so many of Rogers's men lay. One by one and still extended in a lengthy row, the seventeen whaleboats, of a relatively light weight, from New England were pulled and dragged onto the river's banks by Rogers's weary sojourners.

Then the boats were turned upside down and carefully concealed with brush to hide them from prying Indian and French eyes in the daylight hours. Here, under a brushy and tree-covered bank of the river, which provided good concealment, with the reversed lightweight boats providing shelter, Rogers and his men slept the sleep of the weary. Lying low and making little sound, they spent the day attempting to stay warm in their woolen blankets, while lying under the protection of the deep hulls of their wooden vessels.

Rogers's men were exhausted, their muscles strained and sore, after their painful ordeal of rowing throughout the long night. Mental anguish and heightened tension of the expeditioners throughout the night had ended, at least temporarily. Hour after hour, everyone in the seventeen whaleboats had been tense and nervous, rowing northward with care, making sure that they made no unnecessary noise. Just losing grip of an oar for it to clank loudly off the cedar edge of the whaleboat might prove fatal if a vigilant enemy were nearby. The backs, upper arms, and shoulders of the rowers ached to the point of numbness on September 14 while they slept under their whaleboats just east of the mouth of Otter River.

Even while asleep, some Rangers no doubt dreamed that they were still rowing in a rhythmic, seemingly endless unison that seemed to have continued forever. However, some soldiers, especially landlubbers, might have still marveled at how quickly and easily they had become one with the movement of the long wooden oars. No enemy had been encountered, and the expedition had not been sighted. For this, Rogers had good reason to feel thankful. The rumors that French boats had been moving in this area proved false.

The French patrol boats had transformed Lake Champlain into the most dangerous of places for an isolated English task force farther and farther from Crown Point as it pushed north. Rogers now realized that this greatest danger lay north of Otter River.

While never knowing when the French patrol boats to the north might suddenly appear to discover the bone-tired trekkers from Crown Point, Rogers basked in the security provided by his first encampment. He knew that Otter River (located in the east-central section of the Lake Champlain Valley) was the southernmost river to enter the lake from the east during Rogers's waterborne journey. Rogers also realized that the river, the home of families of playful otters—hence, its appropriate name—entered the lake from the east from its spring-fed waters in the Green Mountains covered in a dense carpet of evergreens.

Naturally, Rogers continued to be extremely careful, becoming warier because they were now farther north, well beyond the friendly confines of Crown Point. Consequently, just as he had done during prior missions, the major prudently dispatched his best scouts north to ascertain the terrain and to keep a sharp lookout for any enemy patrol boats on Lake Champlain in preparation for the next step that would come with nightfall of September 14 to continue the leapfrogging process of cautiously venturing farther north down the lake. North of Otter River, prowling French vessels jealously guarded the waterway against all interlopers. Meanwhile, Rogers's men felt safe and secure, because they had carefully disguised their whaleboats with underbrush and tree limbs, allowing a sense of relief.

FRENCH PATROL BOATS!

Sharp-eyed Ranger scouts, panting and out of breath, returned to Rogers from exploring the lake's eastern shore to the north. They presented Rogers with the startling news that he had been dreading: while his hidden men slept and gave sore muscles and stiff backs a much-needed respite from the hard work of what seemed like the physical nightmare of endless rowing in the enemy's country, French boats were patrolling just north of the swampy mouth of Otter River. Ironically, this was almost the same scenario that had been encountered in July 1756, when Rogers had attacked a lone French schooner anchored about a mile north of the mouth of Otter River.

Now, unlike during the earlier expedition, Rogers prudently decided to remain in his hidden position on Otter River on the night of September 14. In addition, Rogers determined that the night of September 14, when the skies had cleared to allow moonlight to shimmer off the lake, was too light to risk continuing north. But most of all, he hoped to buy time for the danger posed by the menacing French vessels to pass, knowing that he could not afford to take any chances when so far north of Crown Point—a smart and wise decision by the carefully calculating major.

Located fifteen miles north of Crown Point, the swampy mouth of Otter River, which was surrounded by a carpet of tall, green reeds that rustled gently in the winds blowing from the north across the broad lake, was an ideal buffer for concealment only a short distance east up the river. Otter River, which flowed west straight into Lake Champlain, could not have been better placed for Rogers's purposes of hiding for two consecutive days.

Clearly, Rogers's plan of spending time at the mouth of Otter River was a good one. Only a short distance from the river's mouth, this remote location provided a perfect hiding place for the seventeen whaleboats and the entire task force. Even more, this secure spot allowed the men the much-needed opportunity to rest, which made a careless mistake from weariness less likely once they resumed their journey north. Here, not far from Otter River's entrance, Rogers's men slept all through the daylight hours of September 14 in carefully concealed positions amid the evergreen thickets along the brushy riverbank.

The exceedingly careful major possessed the best of reasons to buy precious time in a safe position for another day, because the French vessels loomed just north of the swampy mouth of the Otter River, as reported by the faithful scouts. Even more, and as noted, the French were now on high alert, after Ranger Sergeant Major Joseph Hopkins had recently attempted to burn one of the French vessels, the sloop *L'Esturgeon*, which was out of its staging port at Isle-aux-Noix to the north. Hopkins's daring mission had occurred where the lake narrowed like a river (the Richelieu River) on the gradual descent to the St. Lawrence River and beyond the lake's northern end only two nights before Rogers and his men had embarked from Crown Point.

Rogers therefore needed for the excitement of the Hopkins's raid to die down and desired the arrival of a darker night or more favorable weather conditions, either a hard rain or dense fog to cover the lake's waters, to provide the opportunity to ease past the three ominous French sloops, which had been spied just north of Otter River by the expert scouts—most likely some of the Stockbridge Mohegan Ranger "Wolves." Major Rogers now waited for the opportunity to slip past the Gallic vessels by allowing them to return to their base for resupply. Quite simply, Rogers's mission was now thwarted before it had hardly begun because he was forced to buy time near the mouth of Otter River out of prudence and urgent necessity.[17]

It now seemed like Rogers's Irish luck had finally deserted him, especially if the French vessels anchored just north of Otter River to protect the watery avenue leading into the heart of New France remained in their guardian positions for an extended period, while continuing to thwart the raiders' objective of pushing north down Lake Champlain.

A Strange Series of Mishaps

Still other signs seemed to indicate that Rogers's legendary luck had indeed turned, and not for the better. He had already been forced to send back one Indian Ranger to Crown Point because of illness. But this was only the beginning, because the germs of the virus had already spread to other members of the expedition, especially among the warriors. Further unsettling for the major, a number of mishaps descended upon Rogers's command with a surprising suddenness that was least expected by the ever-optimistic Scotch-Irish commander during this lengthy period of staying under good cover at the mouth of Otter River, while awaiting the arrival of the first moonless night or bad weather to mask the forthcoming attempt to move past the French patrol vessels to the north.

Because Rogers had no choice, the inactivity and hiding close together of his men in the thickets along the Otter River allowed for the spread of disease in the cramped quarters. It is not known, but perhaps the sickness had been first contracted at Crown Point because of the concentration of thousands of troops. Wherever the sickness had first gained its foothold, it had now descended upon Rogers's command in full force when the expeditioners were on their own and far from support.

Already, seven men had fallen ill by only the second day of the mission, which was an ominous sign of future trouble because of the men's close proximity to each other while lying in hiding for two days near the mouth of Otter River. Rogers immediately ordered the sick and injured men to return to Crown Point, which was relatively easy because no French vessels or land patrols lingered in their rear to the south. These men were ordered back under the command of Provincial captain Leonard Butterfield, who had been accidently wounded along with Captain Manley Williams.

The frontier major was not shocked by this development, because this seemed to always happen during the first stages of any expedition—as if nature were weeding out unfit men (culling the herd) in a Darwinian process—when soldiers set out from one of the forts, where disease was commonplace. As mentioned, Rogers already had been forced to send back one sick Stockbridge Ranger warrior on the first day out of Crown Point. Rogers also knew that having men of an ad hoc task force together for the first time from different units—Rangers, Provincials, and Regulars—and divergent backgrounds was always a recipe for the spread of disease. But he never expected to lose such a large percentage of his men (thirty-four disabled soldiers and seven healthy escorts) in the beginning stage of this ambitious expedition—all within two days—before he finally departed Otter River, because of not only illness but also a series of mishaps beyond Rogers's control.

Divided into three parties to avoid a possible French ambush on the return trip, they were dispatched back to Crown Point by Rogers in staggered stages. The first group of eight soldiers under Captain Butterfield, who hailed from Massachusetts, were sent south along the lake's eastern shore on September 15. The forty-one men, who could no longer proceed any farther north than Otter River, in total would eventually reach Crown Point on September 18 and 19. There, they would inform General Amherst, who would be discouraged by the arrival of many of Rogers's followers so early in the trek north, of the dismal situation and sudden wave of bad luck, especially that the mission had been thwarted at the mouth of Otter River for an extended period within fifteen or so miles of Crown Point.[18]

THE MYTH OF CAPTAIN MANLEY WILLIAMS

Rogers lost his top lieutenant in rank and seniority. Captain Manley Williams was the highest-ranking British Regular officer in the command. He was dispatched back to Crown Point with three white Rangers, thirteen Indian Rangers, four British Regulars, and two Provincials on the night after Captain Butterfield's party had departed. Historians have long confused Captain Samuel Williams of the Royal American Regiment, who had been a Rogers antagonist since March 1759, with Captain Manley

Williams. Both men were British officers and proud of that fact. When Captain Manley Williams was accidently injured at the mouth of Otter River when he tripped over a log and his flintlock musket discharged, wounding him in the hand and arm, Captain Butterfield of the Colony of Massachusetts also had been wounded.

Some friction between Rogers and Manley Williams, who was fated to be killed by the Cherokee in the summer of 1760, might have already developed because Williams was officially second in command of the entire expedition, and the two men represented two different branches of the service, which almost always ensured rivalry. Amherst had assigned Williams to the expedition, and the Briton was not Rogers's ideal choice.

However, Rogers had known better than to complain or challenge his firmest supporter in high places on such delicate matters—a political and personal savvy of the astute frontiersman that was almost instinctive and revealed his skill in getting into the head of his British superiors. Amherst and Williams were fellow Brits and shared a bond that meant a great deal to them. Worst of all for Rogers, if he was wounded (and especially if he was killed), then Captain Williams would reap the credit for a successful raid, if everything went according to an extremely ambitious plan—the major's pet project for years—while Captain Joseph Wait would then take command of the Rangers in Rogers's absence.

In addition, ultra-sensitive matters of seniority were in play because Williams held a British officer's commission in the British regular army, unlike Rogers. Rogers was a major of Rangers, whose command technically existed outside the British military establishment in the form of independent Ranger companies of the British army. Even more, Major Rogers might well have believed that the ambitious Williams was scheming to take his place and lead the Ranger force that he had created, which was very likely the case.

Most galling of all, Rogers realized that Williams lacked the healthy stamina and the necessary Ranger experience to command the expedition. However, the British captain had been tolerated because of Amherst's desires and orders. No doubt at this time, Rogers would have given anything to have his top lieutenant, Captain John Stark, with him on this dangerous expedition as second in command instead of the aristocratic Williams.[19]

Therefore, under the circumstances, Rogers might have felt some relief when Captain Manley Williams, long assumed to have been incapacitated by an alleged accidental explosion of a powder keg in some mysterious way instead of by the accidental firing of his own musket when he tripped over a log, had to be transported to Crown Point in a whaleboat. Two injured Highland volunteers were also dispatched south to Crown Point in the last party of nine men, including seven Rangers who were sick, exhausted, or lame. So far, Rogers's men had sustained far more casualties and losses (thirty-four disabled men and seven healthy escorts in total, and all within only two days) inflicted by themselves than by the enemy during the ill-fated stay along Otter River.[20]

An increasing amount of evidence has revealed that there was no powder keg explosion, as long alleged and assumed by historians, writers, and novelists. A more truthful account appeared in a soldier's letter that was printed in the October 1, 1759, issue of the *New-York Mercury*: "Capt. Williams of the Royal [American Regiment led by British officers] & a few more were wounded, in stepping over some logs by their Pieces going off, but slightly [and] They were sent back" to Crown Point.[21]

Fortunately for Rogers, he possessed an ideal officer—more experienced and having all the necessary qualities of an excellent Ranger leader, which were needed on this expedition—present to take Captain Williams's place: Lieutenant William James Dunbar. In this sense, the overall quality of the command increased significantly with the departure of Captain Williams. The highly capable Lieutenant Dunbar had learned the trade of an excellent Ranger leader as a bright-eyed cadet under Rogers's tutelage, which was destined to pay dividends in the desperate days ahead.[22]

Consequently, the overall composition of the command had changed dramatically since Rogers had first gained a safe sanctuary in the heavily wooded environs of the mouth of Otter River. Before the mission had hardly began, Rogers had lost numerous men to accidents, aliments, exhaustion, sickness (perhaps measles or smallpox among the Ranger Indians), and injury—nearly one-fifth of his entire command.

Significantly, thanks to the spread of the sickness, Rogers had lost half of his Stockbridge Indian Rangers, who were badly needed for the many challenges that lay ahead, making his force more white (Rangers, Britons, and Provincials) in the process. All forty-one men—an invaluable manpower resource for successfully accomplishing the mission—were now headed back to Crown Point only days after embarking from there. If Rogers was not a more determined leader, then losing such a large percentage of his command might well have given him second thoughts about the wisdom of continuing onward as if nothing had happened.

As mentioned, and unlike Major Rogers, the British major general at Crown Point felt discouraged by the large manpower loss because the chances of success had dimmed considerably. It was becoming increasingly clear to Rogers and Amherst that the task force sent forth from Crown Point with so much optimism had been too small for the daunting mission, because no one could have predicted the loss of so many fighting men without yet having fired a shot at the enemy.[23] However, Rogers had lost precious manpower and valuable time to bad luck, ill fate, injury, and disease through no fault of his own, because of an entirely unforeseen number of sudden mishaps and developments well beyond his control.[24]

Any other commander, British or Provincial, would have almost certainly abandoned what now seemed destined to become the most ill fated of missions, after having lost such a sizeable percentage of his task force when still relatively close to the home base. But Major Rogers was not that kind of a commander. He never allowed reversals to discourage him in any way, which was one of the most forgotten secrets of his success. Such sharp setbacks only served as a challenge for Rogers to rise higher and above the adversity and obstacles to fulfill his assigned mission: a rare and unique quality, based on willpower and strength of mind, that had long made Rogers the most active and dynamic leader in the British-Provincial Army.

Major General Amherst fully appreciated the Scotch-Irish major's unique talents and such special leadership qualities seen in no other commander. Amherst's undying faith in Rogers was so strong that he wrote to Prime Minster Pitt that, despite the loss of so many good men so early in the expedition, who then staggered back to Crown Point from the Otter River's mouth, and knowing Rogers's tough can-do mentality, which he admired, the highly motivated major from the New England frontier still possessed "men enough to Execute the Service he is sent on."[25] Although seemingly too optimistic, Amherst's words revealed his conviction that Rogers could do almost anything that he set his mind to achieving.

Meanwhile, Major General Amherst gained additional proof of his wisdom in having ordered Rogers to go forth, despite the hefty odds that were stacked ever higher against the mission's success. On September 18—five days after Rogers had departed Crown Point with his typical confidence and sense of optimism born of the frontier experience—Amherst received a dispatch from Brigadier General Thomas Gage that was far more disturbing than the reports that Rogers had lost so many of his men hardly before the mission to St. Francis had begun. Proving that he was a commander who was better suited for a desk job, Gage's letter informed Amherst of bad news that infuriated the general: Gage had failed to fulfill his orders in the only part of Amherst's campaign that took the offensive other than Rogers's expedition. Incredibly, with relatively little justification, Gage had called off the offensive effort to capture La Galette based on Amherst's well-conceived plan—that both he and Gage would advance on Montreal from different directions. Amherst's one-two punch would have certainly brought success. But this shocking news deflated the commanding general's optimistic forecasts for success of an offensive operation that had been calculated to assist General James Wolfe before Quebec.

With the news of Gage's missed opportunity to capture La Galette, an important post located on the St. Lawrence River, and the wasted effort that was to have been a catalyst for his own offensive effort north toward Montreal, Amherst's disgust reached a new high. With Amherst still stationary at Crown Point in building a new fort near the site of old Fort Saint Frédéric, he had counted on his twin offensive efforts—Rogers's mission to destroy St. Francis (a raid that was partly calculated to keep the French from reinforcing La Galette) and Gage's offensive to take La Galette on the St. Lawrence—to compensate for his long period of inactivity before he resumed the offensive by pushing northeast to Montreal.[26]

Consequently, as fate would have it, and to Amherst's delight, his continued confidence in Rogers now paid dividends because the mission to St. Francis represented his only offensive effort when he had been ordered to take Montreal in conjunction with Wolfe's effort to capture Quebec. Whereas General Gage had failed to fulfill his orders because he had encountered setbacks and aborted his mission without ever unleashing a maximum offensive effort, Rogers was not deterred in the least by his reversals and those of others. While Pitt and the king himself expressed displeasure at the shocking news of Gage's failure in the face of relatively few obstacles, they heard that Rogers was on the move as ordered, despite having encountered an unprecedented number of sharp setbacks when least expected, including early on losing a large percentage of his command.

Once again, Rogers proved that he was a tough-minded commander who could succeed against the odds and despite reversals because of the strength of his determination and vibrancy of his can-do spirit, while other commanders—General Gage in this case—failed precisely because they lacked the same sterling qualities that made the Scotch-Irish major such an exceptional leader in the struggle for the possession of North America.[27]

THE GOLDEN OPENING TO PROCEED FARTHER NORTH

Then, all of a sudden, the bad luck that had thwarted Rogers's ambitions and significantly reduced the size of his command to darken his future prospects—the mysterious factors of luck and fate seemingly orchestrated by the gods of war for their own fickle amusement—vanished. Without the sudden turning of the major's fortunes when the French vessels pushed farther up Lake Champlain on September 15, his expedition "would have gotten no farther than Otter Creek [River]," and Rogers's great dream would have ingloriously faded away forever.[28]

In addition, at this time, Rogers and his men were most fortunate because the weather suddenly turned rainy and colder, and then, at long last, a moonless night arrived after two days of waiting near the gloomy mouth of Otter River. These developments opened a small window of opportunity for the now sixteen whaleboats—after the injured Captain Manley Williams's departure back to Crown Point in one vessel—to proceed north and pass any lingering French vessels, when the Gallic sailors in the patrol boats could hardly see their hands before their eyes. Rogers now prepared to slip north past any remaining French boats that jealously guarded their watery domain, as if it were the Seine in Paris.

At long last and most of all, Rogers's luck had finally turned for the better because of the fact that three French vessels, with ample cannon aboard to blast English whaleboats out of the water, had moved south up the lake in menacing fashion. The patrol boats had eased past the mouth of Otter River in silence and toward Crown Point to check to determine if General Amherst had moved north or dispatched troops closer to Montreal. Finally, the way was now open for Rogers to proceed down Lake Champlain on his vital mission.[29]

With the way now clear through where the lake was still relatively narrow to the north before opening out into a much wider body of water around twenty miles north of Crown Point—a great relief to Rogers that decreased the possibility of ambush or running headlong into a French vessel—Rogers ordered his men to haul out the hidden whaleboats shrouded in greenery not long after sundown on September 15. He then directed his whaleboats to enter the cold waters of Otter River for the short trip with the west-flowing current into the eastern side of Lake Champlain with the veil of the first descent of darkness on the late evening of September 15.

Initially a shock to Rogers that he simply shook off because it would not deter him from reaching his faraway objective to fulfill his fondest ambition, the drastic reduction of manpower (forty-one men) meant there were now two, sometimes three, fewer soldiers in each whaleboat to man the oars, which forced a greater overall effort in rowing the sixteen whaleboats northward—another sixty miles or so needed to be covered by water before they reached their objective at the northeastern end of Lake Champlain, Missisquoi Bay. Consequently, the journey north in the night was more difficult and slower because of the loss of manpower that reduced the overall manpower strength at the oars. In addition, the bad weather—which proved a blessing because the pounding rain obscured visibility—slowed the pace of Rogers's push down the ever-broadening lake that proved choppier and more temperamental than smaller Lake George to the south below Lake Champlain.

During the downpour of cold rain, the New England whaleboats, with the men keeping in a disciplined formation, the stern and bow of each boat close to its neighboring vessels, hugged the lake's tree-lined eastern shore under the even darker shadows provided by the edge of the dense forest of virgin timber. All the while, Rogers's men steadily rowed north and closer to Montreal, located to the northwest, in the blackness.[30]

With the French vessels now patrolling to the south, Rogers and his men eased north along the east bank under the tall hardwood trees for security reasons, although the whaleboats had no masts or canvas sails for any breeze, if the wind had been blowing from the opposite direction, to assist the bone-weary rowers, who might have felt that they were like the slaves of ancient Roman galleys on the Mediterranean long ago. Around twenty miles north of Crown Point, Lake Champlain widened to become a much broader expanse of water. Just as it seemed as if everything was on track when the rain ceased on September 18, the trekkers met with the wrath of Mother Nature on the nights of September 19 and 20, with more deluges of cold rain and even frost when temperatures dropped.

While churning the long wooden oars in unison, Rogers, in the lead whaleboat as usual, and his men were pelted with nature's harsh offerings from the depths of the frozen Arctic. Night after night, the sharp wind swept down the open waters of the broad lake without mercy. The icy rain fell to create a hellish mix with the cold winds, which cut through thin coats and uniforms of the men like a knife. All the while, Rogers had his men prepared for action, in case they suddenly encountered a French vessel with cannon loaded and ready to fire at the first sighting of the hated English. Then, in such an emergency situation that might come when least expected, the men had been informed by Rogers to grab their weapons and gear, hurriedly row toward land, and seek safety in the thick woodlands along the eastern shore of Lake Champlain.

Without extra coats and keeping up the same coordinated rhythm of rowing in unison that required muscularity and vigor, the bone-chilled men could not pull on any extra clothing (winter garments had been left behind at Crown Point) in the colder and stormier weather. Thin woolen jackets and Scottish blue bonnets that reminded them of the majesty and beauty of the Scottish Highlands became thoroughly sodden in the downpour, while buckskin pants and Indian-style leggings were similarly drenched. Rain and sleet hitting faces and the stubble of unshaved beards caused misery and additionally hampered what little visibility remained on the most miserable of nights.

Soaked Rangers in the bows of the whaleboats strained their eyes to make sure that their vessels did not plow into the rear of the boats in front of them. The wetness and cold only added to the pain of sore muscles from the seemingly endless rowing in the night, when danger could emerge at any moment. The nagging realization haunted the relentless rowers that once they landed on the eastern shore under good cover before the next sunrise, they would not be allowed to light campfires to dry themselves. After all, the sighting of a Ranger fire by a Frenchman, Canadian, or Indian would all but doom the mission, already seemingly the most ill-fated one to date for Major Rogers and his men.[31]

The grueling, if not torturous, routine was the same: demanding and arduous rowing all night long and then hiding out in the shadowy woodlands in the day, which left worn muscles of arms, shoulders, and buttocks aching because the stormy weather had made the rowing even more difficult and tortuous. Having joined the Rangers the previous spring, Second Lieutenant George Campbell recorded in his diary the men's progress and daily encampments, hiding in the dense woods from prying French, Canadian, and Indian eyes: Shelburne Bay on the sixth day from Crown Point (September 19); Wallets Bay on the seventh day from Crown Point (September 20); St. Alban's Bay on the eighth day from Crown Point (September 21); the southeastern end of Hog Island on the ninth day from Crown Point (September 22), when the cold rain resumed, after only a relatively brief respite from the cold deluges that soaked everyone, including the major, to the skin.[32]

GAINING THE FIRST KEY OBJECTIVE: REMOTE MISSISQUOI BAY

Meanwhile, the mind-numbing pain of rowing the lengthy oars like ancient Vikings in their slender and sleek longboats, which had possessed an unprecedented grace, on a raid in the darkness seemed to have no end for Rogers's weary men. Wet to the skin from the cold rain, the sojourners were badly in need of rest and warming fires, but there was no time for such luxuries. Rogers was pushing his men hard and to the very end of their endurance, because time was of the essence, and even colder weather lay on the horizon of an early winter in Quebec.

Most of all at this time, after having pushed north for eight nights beyond Otter River and the first hideout in the evergreen forests, the major's immediate objective was Missisquoi Bay. Located at the northeastern end of Lake Champlain, this strategic location now had to be reached as soon as possible and without additional mishaps that had boded ill for the mission's success. However, this final stretch along the lake was the most dangerous part of the watery trek as Rogers and his men pushed closer to Missisquoi Bay in the pouring rain.

Major Rogers knew that he had to reach his chosen point and solid ground at all costs after his men had rowed north around sixty miles since having departed the swampy mount of Otter River. But was Rogers now heading straight into an ambush in his eagerness to reach a landing site? At this time, no one had any idea of the location of the enemy—a fact of grave concern for the major.

Therefore, the seemingly endless routine of rowing ever farther north up the broad lake, which had become still wider as the sixteen whaleboats eased ever closer to Missisquoi Bay, had continued unabated on so many consecutive nights—eight since departing the Otter River with nightfall of September 15—that they all ran together for bone-weary men. Consequently, Rogers's exhausted soldiers lost a sense of time and space while rowing night after night with vigor to make the best time possible. With Montreal almost on the northwestern horizon, the Rangers must have wondered whether they were going to row all the way to Montreal. All the while, Major Rogers kept his secret about their ultimate destination nestled in the Quebec wilderness, fueling his passion to keep moving ever northward.

But, finally, the night of September 23 was destined to be the last night of the watery sojourn in downpouring rain that seemed to have no end for the long-suffering men in wet moccasins, leggings, and uniforms, which remained soggy and icy cold. After the rocky start of this far-flung expedition into the north country, they had made frustratingly slow time, covering only about seven and a half miles each night, while continuing to hug the eastern shore and the edge of the omnipresent woodlands now that they were so deep in the heart of New France.

At the north end of Lake Champlain, the long line of whaleboats—moving with a weary, if not mind-numbing, pace somehow maintained by the rowing men while the vessels kept close contact in the pounding rain—at last entered the placid waters of East Bay on the night of September 23. Reaching this wide bay located just off the main channel of Lake Champlain brought a sigh of relief to Rogers, despite the coldness that reminded him and his anxious men that no large expedition of British or Provincial solders had ever been so far north before.

The ever-optimistic major knew that the worst of the dangers were already behind them and no doubt thanked God for having successfully dodged numerous close calls, especially the three French patrol boats armed with plenty of cannon and carrying sharp-eyed fighting men from France and Canada. Thankfully, this remote place known as East Bay was too shallow for the entry of any lurking French patrol vessels, which were always on the prowl, like hungry hunters in the forest, for any English task force.

The dark waters of East Bay led northeast to Missisquoi Bay, which was the most extreme northeastern corner of Lake Champlain. Large numbers of migratory birds found this secluded bay, filled with edible floating aquatic plants—wild rice, tall grasses, and especially the clusters of cattails on its borders—an ideal stopping place on their journey south at this time of year, and it served as such now for Rogers and his men. Quiet Missisquoi Bay was isolated and remote. Shallow (a maximum depth of only fifteen feet) and surrounded by heavy forest and thick underbrush, it was an ideal sanctuary that sheltered the isolated command from harm like a benevolent natural guardian, especially from menacing French vessels. This area was known for having long been the home of the great blue heron that stalked the water's edge in the hunt for frogs, small crustaceans, and fish in the swampy lowlands of Quebec.

Most important, Missisquoi Bay was ideally suited for Rogers's purpose of finding a good secret landing site, located just below a wooded ridge to the northeast. These wetlands along the bay were secluded and hidden by the surrounding swamps that seemed to stretch forever to the north. This isolated area was sacred Abenaki territory, and the mystical-sounding name of Missisquoi suited this "a great marshy place" amid an uncharted wilderness located slightly southwest of St. Francis: Rogers's Holy Grail at this crucial stage of the expedition.

All the while, Rogers kept his most immediate objective in mind, because it represented the end of the exhausting journey by water: a safe landing site, or so it seemed. The northeastern arm of Lake Champlain at its farther northernmost extension was a perfect dead-end and remote place that went nowhere—ideal for Rogers's goal of finding an obscure place to disembark and hide the sixteen whaleboats and the vital provisions for the return trip, after they succeeded in their all-important mission far to the northeast, if they were so fortunate.

During the last few days of cold rain, after a week of moving steadily north down the seemingly endless expanse of Lake Champlain, Rogers and his men noted how the high ground on the eastern shore had gradually become more level as they neared the expanse of lowlands that lay before the St. Lawrence River Valley to the north. The landscape had leveled out as they had gradually approached the fertile lowlands of Quebec south of the St. Lawrence River and its wide valley, unlike farther south where Lake Champlain had been surrounded by forested mountains, the Green Mountains to the east and the Adirondack Mountains to the west.

As Rogers had realized for days, based on what the ever-reliable Captain Stark had told him, the appearance of more level ground the farther north they traveled indicated that they were getting ever closer to one of the mightiest rivers on the North American continent: the Mississippi River of Canada, the St. Lawrence. Basically, this remote region, in which St. Francis lay to the northeast and just south of the St. Lawrence, was part of the southern lowlands of the St. Lawrence. And most important, these lowlands now pointed and led all the way to St. Francis, which was around eighty miles distant, slightly to the northeast of Missisquoi Bay.

Meanwhile, the cold rain continued to fall on the dismal night of September 23, soaking everyone in the sixteen whaleboats that stretched out in a lengthy line over dark waters. However, the vessels moved slowly onward and relatively close together for security's sake, just in case they ran into trouble.

Reaching an Ideal Landing Site in the Wilderness

Feeling a measure of relief for having miraculously reached this remote point that offered comforting shelter after slipping out of East Bay and into Missisquoi Bay in the darkness during the cold night of September 23, Rogers continued to look for the right place to ensure a successful landing. After having gained prior knowledge about this place, since he had never been so far north down Lake Champlain before, and after his lead whaleboat had angled to the right, or east, into the northeastern edge of Missisquoi Bay, Rogers neared his immediate objective.

Meanwhile, the other sixteen whaleboats dutifully followed Rogers's whaleboat, easing into the placid bay shrouded in blackness. Perhaps one of the Stockbridge "Wolves" had once visited the site of this old Abenaki village on the bay to provide Rogers with some information about the lay of the land—flat ground of a mostly swampy region with few distinguishing features—and the obscure location of Missisquoi Bay, which was the northeastern arm of Lake Champlain.

Finally, amid the expanse of shallow waters of Missisquoi Bay, the hard work and endless high anxiety of the last ten days finally came to an end for the weary Rangers, Provincials, and Regulars, who detested having been reduced to the menial role of rowing sailors during this seemingly endless journey to only God and Major Rogers knew where. Symbolically at this point, and as the major realized, the northeastern head of Missisquoi Bay pointed directly toward St. Francis, as if Providence were pointing the way to Rogers's ultimate objective.

For the water-soaked Rangers, southern Quebec was a strange-looking land without hills and mountains, unlike the beloved picturesque homeland of New England of so many Rangers. This was the first time that any of these men, including Rogers, had been so far north. Major Rogers now possessed some misgivings that the forthcoming march slightly northeast toward St. Francis might result in encountering both a sizeable enemy force and a vast expanse of marshy country covered in a concentrated mass of stagnant water from decades of spring rains and snowmelt. This flat northern bog country in Quebec would be almost impossible for a large body of soldiers to march through, or so it seemed.

Amid the darkened expanse of Missisquoi Bay and hoping to ascertain a firm spot along the swampy shoreline, covered in a thick carpet of tall cat-tails and reeds, and with the eye of a natural topographer, Rogers looked for the best place to land on Canadian soil. This quiet bay of smooth waters was shrouded in an eerie stillness and quiet, which gave the major more confidence that the interlopers had not been discovered. But as Rogers realized, this peaceful serenity could all change in a single moment with an explosion of gunfire erupting from hidden ambushers.

When on the verge of making this crucial landing on Quebec soil, Rogers and his devout men, who had long worshipped mostly in log churches and even outdoors across America, hoped to God that they were not entering an ambush, if any war party of French, Indians, and Canadians, led by savvy partisan commanders, had followed them north along the eastern shore of Lake Champlain. If so, then Rogers and his men would be sitting ducks in their sixteen whaleboats, which slowly proceeded across the bay's dark waters, as if expecting the worst from the darkened woodlands lining it.

But the thickets along the shore remained silent, and nighttime creatures continued to make their nocturnal sounds since they had not been disturbed by any men on the shore, offering a sense of relief to these young men and boys, who were so weary that they perhaps now doubted if they could even put up much of a fight, if a close-range volley suddenly exploded from along this low-lying shore in Quebec.

However, Rogers knew that it would have been impossible for large numbers of the enemy to take positions for an ambush in the dense marshes because of the deep mud and heavy underbrush lining Missisquoi Bay. Therefore, the brush-tangled swamps acted like a buffer that provided a comfortable degree of safety to the anxious major, who continued to strain his eyes for any sign of movement and his ears to catch any faint sound, like a seasoned woodsman hunting in the fading light of day. Sighing with relief upon detecting nothing unusual, therefore, Rogers directed that the sixteen boats row toward the shore. He then ordered that the whaleboats be hauled through the late summertime maze of reeds, cattails, and lily pads as quietly and quickly as possible and into the dense underbrush and thickets along Missisquoi.

The men acted automatically, like on every previous morning in the predawn darkness just before sunrise since having departed Crown Point a seeming eternity ago. Rogers made thorough efforts to find the best hiding spot because the boats would have to be hidden for an extended period. After ten nightmarish days of rowing night after night through gusty winds, sleet, and slashing rain to the point that the arduous journey and endless demands on aching muscles and hardship-numbed minds could hardly be endured any longer, Private Robert Kirkwood must have wondered about the strange fate that had brought him all the way from Scotland to this obscure place called Missisquoi Bay. He wrote of the mission, which had finally reached the northeastern end of Lake Champlain, that they then "went into a small creek [off Missisquoi Bay on the lake's far northeast side] in the lake," which was surrounded by thick forests, and then dragged the whaleboats up the small creek.[33]

On their difficult sojourn up the wide, wind-swept lake during the last ten consecutive dark nights filled with nerve-racking tension and fear of being spotted by the French, Rogers's men had been denied the sight of the beautiful Lake Champlain Valley, when the surrounding hills were draped in bright autumnal colors ravaging to the eye. In daylight hours, the lake of deep blue waters was known for its beauty in fairly "sparkling like a jewel" in the bright sunshine.[34]

Now no time could be wasted, as Rogers fully understood and emphasized. Finally, the long journey by water north up Lake Champlain was over for the wet sojourners. Even at this seemingly happy end of the watery journey, however, the landing on the muddy, blackened shore of Missisquoi Bay was not without danger. Rogers had taken the risk of boldly entering the shallow waters of Missisquoi Bay, which was located northeast of East Bay, and in his eagerness to gain solid ground, he had not sent out a party of scouts to investigate the shoreline for dangers. However, Rogers's gamble at Missisquoi Bay had paid off.

Surrounded by swamps and hardwood trees, including towering pines and virgin oaks that cast even darker shadows on the black waters, this quiet, shallow bay seemingly situated in the middle of nowhere was an ideal hiding place for the boats. One of Rogers's men described in a letter how, after having "proceeded down Lake Champlain 10 Days, they then landed, and hawled [*sic*] their Boats out of the Lake" at its northeastern corner, which provided shelter and a blessed respite from the long journey up the lake.[35]

Here, the whaleboats continued to pay dividends because they were so light and maneuverable that they could be hauled ashore with relative ease and carefully hidden even by worn men with diminished physical capabilities and when nearing the end of their endurance, which had been so severely taxed during the lengthy journey north.[36]

Ironically, on the bay five miles to the south of Rogers's landing site, an Abenaki refugee community of around twenty families had once been formed and now included a sacred burial ground. This mission village had once thrived along the wide bay, which often teemed with waterfowl in more peaceful days, before the start of the French and Indian War, when it was abandoned. Here, a Jesuit mission had been established in 1744, before the refugees had then moved slightly northeast to St. Francis and other French mission towns in Quebec.

Many Abenaki warriors had remained with French forces at Isle-aux-Noix on the Richelieu River just to the northwest of Rogers's landing site. However, these facts, if he knew them at the time, were of no concern to Rogers, who already had far too many other things on his mind. He now was only thankful that no Abenaki, especially a war party, had decided to remain on the bay or to reoccupy the old village site, where the bones of buried Abenaki still lay in eternal peace in a pristine land that they loved.[37]

What was now of much greater concern to Rogers was the fact that Amherst's recent mission in the failed attempt to communicate with Wolfe had taken this exact route to St. Francis. Quinton Kennedy and Archibald Hamilton, the two ill-fated British officers who had been dispatched by a naively confident Major General Amherst on their mission of folly to communicate with Wolfe, had also disembarked at this northeast corner of Missisquoi Bay. This small party, including Captain Cheeksaunkun Jacob, the younger, had made the mistake of moving overland along an established trail until captured by the party of Abenaki hunters from St. Francis. As fate would have it, the prisoners had been then taken to this most infamous of all Native American communities in North America, St. Francis. To some degree, therefore, Rogers was concerned about taking the same route, but he had no choice at this point—this was the quickest and easiest way to St. Francis through the uncharted wilds of swampy country.

If Rogers had any misgivings—and there is no evidence or record that he did—then he would have been right on target as this area was now riskier to enter because of recent developments. Indeed, as mentioned, Kennedy and Hamilton had also landed at Missisquoi Bay and proceeded far north along the Yamaska route into the depths of Abenaki territory before their capture. French leadership had then realized that security measures were inadequate in this key sector far behind the old French front lines at Fort Carillon, because it was the southern approach not only to St. Francis but also, and more important, to Montreal and Quebec.

Consequently, a concerned Governor-General Pierre de Rigaud, the Marquis de Vaudreuil, a former soldier who still thought like one and now worried about the vulnerability of the southern front, which left an open avenue to Montreal from the south, dispatched a courier to François-Gaston de Lévis because of his increasing security concerns. He ordered Lévis, a capable leader of noble blood in France in 1719 and the Marquis de Montcalm's second in command, to increase security measures with regular patrols to be conducted around Missisquoi Bay and the surrounding area. French leadership knew that this was the neglected point that Kennedy and Hamilton, seemingly aware that this was the Achilles' heel of their enemy's southern sector and forgotten backdoor to the heart of New France, had recently entered with impunity not long ago.[38]

Here, in the heavy underbrush a short distance up the creek at the head of the crystal-clear bay surrounded by swamps, when French concerns about the vulnerability of the Missisquoi sector had reached a new high, Rogers felt secure by what he had seen so far—absolutely nothing to cause any concern at this point. With hand signals and without saying a word, he directed his men, who must have thanked God to have survived the long watery journey and finally reached solid ground for the duration of the expedition, exactly where to hide their sixteen whaleboats in the thickets. Rogers continued to communicate with his men in whispered tones in preparation for moving out to where destiny itself led.

A good supply of provisions for an entire month were hidden under the overturned whaleboats for protection. These rations of cornmeal and salt pork would sustain Rogers's men on the return trip south from Missisquoi Bay all the way to Crown Point, if luck and the gods of war favored them, after they successfully completed their mission at St. Francis and escaped along the same route. At long last, the watery odyssey of Rogers's men was finally over because the first phase of this operation so far from Crown Point had ended, and the next phase, which was equally risky, was about to begin.

With the men continuing to maintain a disciplined silence, the Rangers, Britons, and Provincials worked fast to conceal the whaleboats in the thick underbrush—now a habit performed with skill and efficiency in order to beat the sunrise, after so much recent practice on the journey north. Underbrush and the branches of certain trees, like maples, were not cut by the Rangers' tomahawks to be used to cover the whaleboats. After all, such an inappropriate natural covering would shortly turn brown in the September midday heat to indicate to a sharp-eyed Abenaki warrior that something was badly amiss amid the natural greenery of the thickets. Because their lives often depended upon such wilderness skills and commonsense procedures, these dark-hued Abenaki fighting men, especially those from St. Francis, were experienced in ascertaining even the slightest discrepancy in the natural setting, such as a broken twig or branch not caused by the deer of these swamps and forests.

Therefore, pine and spruce boughs were quietly cut with knives and bayonets and used for cover by the fast-working Rangers, Provincials, and British Regulars, like Lieutenant William James Dunbar, now the only Regular officer left remaining with the command. He therefore now led the British Regulars after Captain Manley Williams's departure by whaleboat due to injury from the accidental firing of his own musket. Here, at this good but careful pace, Rogers's men worked briskly and almost mechanically to cover the sixteen whaleboats. Pine and spruce branches, the most common evergreen in this part of southern Quebec, which consisted mostly of flatlands, were used because they would not shortly turn brown to expose the location of the hidden boats and invaluable cache of provisions, which were absolutely necessary for the return trip to Crown Point, if and when Rogers's mission succeeded.

Rogers also certainly sent out a small detail to take possession of the forested ridge—known today as Pigeon Hill because passenger pigeons had long roosted on this high perch overlooking the peaceful bay to the northeast—just in case an enemy force occupied these heights to then wreak havoc on the 156 men (after the return of 34 sick and injured men, accompanied by 7 healthy escorts) once they moved out to begin the long-distance cross-country trek across lower ground.

Detected by the Abenaki

Unbeknownst to Rogers at this time, several sharp-sensed Missisquoi Abenaki hunters had already heard the soft splash of a long, wooden whaleboat oar on Missisquoi Bay in the dead of the previous night (September 23). Knowing the world of nature, these experienced hunters from St. Francis realized, because of the lateness of the hour, that the splash was not made by a fearful beaver or otter sending a warning or a loon diving for fish.

Fearing the worst, and not taking any chances, the Abenaki warriors wisely reported what they believed had to be nothing less than a daring party of English interlopers prowling around in the waters of Missisquoi Bay to Brigadier General Francois-Charles de Bourlamaque, who was located at French headquarters at Isle-aux-Noix to the northwest, just southeast of Montreal, where Lake Champlain narrowed on its journey to the St. Lawrence. Never forgetting the earlier unsettling news about how Kennedy and Hamilton and their party, including Captain Jacob, the younger, had slipped with ease down the length of Lake Champlain and then proceeded overland along the Yamaska River trail completely undetected, Bourlamaque reacted quickly from his Isle-aux-Noix headquarters.

He immediately responded to the latest intelligence of this obvious English activity on the bay. He prudently ordered a thorough reconnaissance of Missisquoi Bay by the highly competent Ensign Langy (Jean-Baptiste Levrault de Langis Montegron), the son of a Frenchman and an Indian mother, whose skills and leadership abilities had become legendary by this time and were even well known to the Rogers. Serious trouble was already brewing because of the seemingly unlimited talents of the cagy Langy, who had early emerged in this war as the primary nemesis of Rogers. The master Canadian partisan delivered his greatest defeat—and it was a brutal one that had resulted in the slaughter of more than 140 Rangers—upon the Ranger leader at the nightmarish Second Battle on Snowshoes. In the snowy wilderness near Fort Carillon, Rogers had been wounded twice and was lucky to have escaped with his life.

Most of all, Major Rogers had already been most fortunate not to have been detected amid the increased French activity because of the growing concern for the security of the Missisquoi Bay sector, whose embarrassing vulnerability had been thoroughly exposed by the hapless Kennedy-Hamilton mission. But through no fault of his own, Rogers's presence was about to be detected because of what had been left behind in Missisquoi's waters: part of a damaged oar, which had perhaps slipped from the blistered or sore hand of a weary man who had already expended almost every ounce of strength during the lengthy journey north, and later a wooden fragment of a whaleboat hull—confirmation of the soft and barely audible splash of a single oar that had alerted the keen-hearing of Abenaki hunters, whose ears and instincts had long been trained to detect such anomalies in the pristine wilderness environment.

The years of a cruel attrition among Rogers's command had reduced overall combat capabilities, while boding ill for future success. Therefore, the infusion of new blood—the highly qualified Provincials and British Regulars who had volunteered for this mission with considerable enthusiasm—was more positive than negative, as generally assumed by historians.

As mentioned, the journey of Rogers's task force had been so arduous that his force had been significantly reduced to only 156 men by this time, after those soldiers who had been unable to continue north down Lake Champlain were sent back to Crown Point by the major because of health, accidents, injuries, and excessive weariness. Ironically, Rogers's task force had been steadily reduced, which would ultimately prove an asset by increasing the stealth and maneuverability of this small task force when it was needed the most.

Ominously, Rogers was destined to lose a quarter of his command (forty-eight men) hardly before the trek on land had begun from the landing site at Missisquoi Bay, and the greatest challenges and difficulties still lay ahead. Perhaps Rogers now entertained doubts about the wisdom of his most ambitious mission to date, but that was unlikely given his past record of overcoming obstacles. In keeping with his personality and character, Rogers was determined to forge ahead regardless of the cost. When the released sick and injured men had finally staggered unexpectedly into Crown Point after their return journey, Major General Amherst had known that the chances for a successful mission had been significantly reduced: a situation that made him appreciate his wisdom in having kept Captain Stark and two hundred Rangers at Crown Point, because they were too valuable to the army to risk.[39]

As noted, the miserable journey of ten days all the way to the marshy northeastern end of Lake Champlain had proved most costly for the expeditionary task force almost from the beginning, far more so than Rogers had anticipated: an initial culling process of separating the weak from the strong that usually occurred but not to such an extent. As Rogers penned of the ordeal and severe adversity in his November 5, 1759, report to General Amherst,

> *Our party was reduced by the accident which befell Capt. [Manley] Williams, the fifth day after our departure, and still farther by numbers tiring and falling sick afterwards. It was extremely [difficult and challenging] while we kept the water (and which retarded our progress very much) to pass undiscovered by the enemy, who were then cruizing [sic] in great numbers on the lake; and had prepared certain vessels, on purpose to decoy any party of ours, that might come that way, armed with all manner of machines and implements for their destruction; but we happily escaped their snares of this kind, and landed [on] the tenth day at Misisquey [sic] Bay.[40]*

Thinking ahead as usual, Major Rogers now made another smart decision that demonstrated his wisdom and insight when deep in enemy country—a wise precaution that might well spell the difference between victory and disaster. After his men had concealed the sixteen whaleboats not far from Missisquoi Bay, Rogers took a masterful step for his own future preservation and that of his command if the French found his hidden whaleboats and supplies of provisions for the return journey to Crown Point.

In a hushed tone at a time when the lack of noise was also key to survival, he ordered two of his Stockbridge warriors of Captain Jacob's company of Rangers to remain at a vantage point a good distance from the boats, just in case French and Indians, under the ever-resourceful Ensign Langy (of course, Rogers did not know that his old nemesis had been ordered to investigate Missisquoi Bay and would be on the prowl in search of Englishmen) discovered the concealed boats and vital provisions.

This important mission bestowed on the two Stockbridge "Wolves" a key role and an opportunity to avenge the recent capture of their beloved company commander, Captain Jacob, the younger, in the nearby woodlands. Meanwhile, Rogers's men maintained their discipline by not saying a word, as ordered, when so deep in enemy territory, as when they had been journeying north day after day on the water.

Because Rogers had specifically ordered the two trusty Stockbridge "Wolves" to watch the hidden whaleboats and provisions from a safe distance, they could escape in time and follow the Rangers' tracks east to catch up with Rogers, before the men turned northeast, in Quebec's wilderness, to inform him that the whaleboats had been captured, if that much-dreaded scenario developed.[41]

Feeling more confident that he had been able to reach this advanced position without detection so far north at the northeastern corner of Lake Champlain at Missisquoi Bay and around seventy-five miles south of St. Francis on the river of the same name, and despite having suffered a significant reduction in manpower, Major Rogers actually faced a most daunting route through an uncharted wilderness that was actually closer to one hundred miles than the seventy-five to eighty miles as the crow flies over this unmapped wilderness.

As was his custom, Rogers wasted no time because time was now of the essence on a crucial mission that was already behind schedule and remained one key factor in the overall equation for victory in this early fall in Quebec. Early on the morning of September 24, relieved that they could return to normal daylight hours, despite still being sore and weary from the previous night's toil and the lengthy journey, Rogers's 156 men quickly formed a line, or regular parade. Not aware that the Abenaki hunters were now taking word of their presence to General Bourlamaque at Isle-aux-Noix, the upbeat major spoke some brief encouraging words in a whispered tone to his men, which revealed that he was taking no unnecessary chances at this point slightly southwest of his great goal of St. Francis.

Wearing bulging packs and in full gear, Rogers and his commandos, stiff and sore, began their trek east from the bay that would continue for around twenty-five miles before turning northeast toward St. Francis, averaging eight to ten miles per day (ironically, about the same pace that they made each day during their northward journey by water from Otter River) and moving farther away from the greatest threat at Isle-aux-Noix. Although it would delay reaching St. Francis by days, Rogers was now moving overland through the hardwood forests east of the bay (an unmapped wilderness) following no trail—the key mistake of the Kennedy-Hamilton party had been to follow the Yamaska River trail upon which they were captured by Abenaki hunters. Rogers most likely followed a thin game trail made by deer and moose that led east from the bay before turning north toward St. Francis.

Ironically, to these men, including Rogers, who had never been so far north before, it hardly seemed that they were in Canada because it was not any colder than it had been at Crown Point. Everything looked rather strange to the sojourners in this unknown area around Missisquoi Bay because it was different from what they had seen before. No Rangers, or any men of Amherst's army for that matter, had seen this land before or been so far north, unless they had been taken prisoner by the Abenaki and then escorted roughly to St. Francis in the past. However, few of those men were still alive to tell the tale.

Despite all the setbacks and the mind-numbing weariness from the arduous journey north, Rogers had become even more determined to march all the way to St. Francis and destroy the infamous place in part because this goal had been his all-consuming desire year and year. The major's resolution, now a burning passion, remained powerful and never faltered, despite the fact that no one knew of the exact nature and lay of the land before them because no British army or Provincial troops had ever marched through this wild area that was the sacred land of the Abenaki. No white man on his own had ever entered this forbidding region that was as strange as it was dangerous, because to do so was a virtual death sentence.

The major's little command of Rangers, Provincials, and Regulars, who had been rowing all the previous night in the pounding rain, marched briskly through the forest, while wearing their usual gear of blankets, knapsacks, and packs. As noted, they steadily surged east before turning northeast based on Rogers's limited knowledge gained from studying John Stark's hand-drawn map. In Private Robert Kirkwood's words summarizing the beginning of the final push inland, the bone-weary troops, with Rogers at the head of the column in the early morning light of September 23, had "proceeded over land to St. Fransway," which these men had heard about their entire lives because of the horrors that had long stemmed from the most infamous place in North America.[42]

As usual, when the major led the way and pushed deeper into southern Quebec, all of Rogers's 156 men were determined to follow him wherever he might lead and ever farther into the hardwood forests that stretched over such a great distance toward the St. Lawrence River and St. Francis. These men were betting their lives and fates in the confident gamble that they were in good hands with the experienced Scotch-Irish major when so far from Crown Point and safety.

In a letter written on November 26, 1759, from Fort Number Four, another soldier described how the confident command, which might as well have been following the irrepressible Rogers to the end of the earth, much as Alexander the Great had led his ancient army of Macedonians into India and all the way to the Indus River, because of his inspirational leadership style that even radiated a sense of equality in his words and actions, boldly proceeded "on their March for St. Francois, an Indian town, so called, on the River St. Francois."[43]

This letter was much more accurate than a letter penned from Amherst's army at Crown Point and published in the *Boston Evening Post*, stating that the ultimate objective of Rogers's raiders was Montreal.[44] Actually, in terms of direction after Rogers turned north to march straight toward St. Francis, this objective had almost seemed to be the case because, in Rogers's words, St. Francis was located "in the heart of Canada, half way between Montreal and Quebec."[45]

Located around eighty miles from the reed patches and thorny thickets along low-lying Missisquoi Bay, St. Francis seemed to French leadership the most unlikely of places to be attacked by English raiders not only because of its infamous reputation known for generations across the colonies but also because it was situated the farthest away from Missisquoi Bay of the five Indian missionary settlements in the general area. For nearly a century, and as noted, St. Francis had acquired an outsized reputation that none of the other of the Indian towns could approach because of the extensive damage and terror caused by the Abenaki across the frontier for so long.[46]

In consequence, no French leaders expected an attack on St. Francis of all places in the beginning. On September 27, General Bourlamaque, who was primarily responsible for defending the vital Lake Champlain strategic corridor, believed that the unleashed English force might even be heading for Quebec. But thinking more about how Hamilton and Kennedy had recently entered Quebec by way of Missisquoi Bay before having been captured by the Abenaki hunters from St. Francis, and considering recent intelligence, he finally concluded to his superior that "all appearances indicate that they want to punish Saint-Francois for its loyalty."[47]

Consequently, the capable general flew into action, especially after the Indian scouts of Ensign La Durantaye's routine patrol of Missisquoi Bay, while Rogers and his men trekked onward through the wilderness, had found part of a wrecked oar of English design from a New England whaleboat floating on the water. He also notified the commander at Montreal about the alarming situation in the vulnerable Missisquoi sector, as well as the governor, a respected La Marine officer, of Trois-Rivières, which was located on the St. Lawrence River south of Quebec and about halfway to Montreal. Bourlamaque emphasized that reinforcements needed to be dispatched to St. Francis as well as the Indian village of Yamaska, which also might be the raiders' objective.

Then the astute General Bourlamaque, who was proving his leadership abilities in attempting to thwart this new threat that had so suddenly and unexpectedly materialized out of thin air, sent a courier to warn St. Francis before it was too late. But, in fact, it was already too late to either warn St. Francis or stop Major Rogers, who was forging ahead despite the increasing number of setbacks and escalating odds against a successful strike on St. Francis.[48]

After all his efforts, Bourlamaque, a savvy professional officer who had been Montcalm's top lieutenant when the two dynamic French leaders had captured strategic Oswego, New York, on Lake Ontario in August 1756 to stun the English and Provincials with still another French victory, felt satisfied that he had done all in his power to stop these English raiders and ensure their destruction in a judicious repayment for their sheer nerve in having orchestrated a bold penetration so far into Canada. To an experienced French leadership, this rare audacity demonstrated by the English was an alarming development in itself, because they had not previously demonstrated such a confident boldness, as if they held the hard-fighting Canadians, French, and Indians in utter contempt: an extremely dangerous attitude.

Even more, General Bourlamaque now relied on a forty-man force, under the highly experienced Ensigns Langy and La Durantaye, to ascertain exactly where the raiders had landed on Missisquoi Bay's shores to follow the tracks of these crazy Englishmen, who had dared to trespass on not only the sacred ground of New France but also the ever-dangerous, if not fatal, Abenaki territory with an unparalleled impunity. Even more, if these audacious raiders—

it was still not known that Rogers had been unleashed from faraway Crown Point—succeeded in their unknown mission and returned in triumph to their hidden whaleboats on Missisquoi Bay, in the hope of gaining their stored provisions for the return trip to Crown Point, then the French would have suffered the greatest of humiliations.[49]

DARK DEPTHS OF THE SEEMINGLY ENDLESS SPRUCE BOGS

What Rogers and his men were about to encounter shortly after beginning their arduous march from Missisquoi Bay was a hellish natural landscape. This was a forbidding place that even animals had long shunned because of its overall uninhabitability: mostly a vast expanse of low-lying black spruce bogs, an uncharted quagmire of dank waters filled with decaying vegetation and a distinctive stench that rose above this wide stretch of swamps that seemed to have no end. This remote region was eerie and strange looking, having once been the northeastern part of Lake Champlain in prehistoric days. Ancient glaciers that had scoured the earth more than ten thousand years ago had left these lowlands overflowing with water, after the glaciers had finally receded and the ice melted to form the St. Lawrence, which emptied into the sea. Mother Nature herself now presented a formidable natural obstacle to the far-flung expeditioners that was guaranteed to sap morale, take lives, and slow the march to St. Francis at a time when colder weather was on the horizon and when provisions were already limited.

These watery bogs of Quebec, seemingly devoid of animal life, were situated amid an uncharted wilderness and began in an isolated location northeast of Missisquoi Bay, as if they had been especially made to present still another challenge to the interlopers from faraway Crown Point. Far more than Rogers and his men had first imagined upon entering this strange landscape, the vast expanse of spruce bogs lying at sea level presented a new nightmare for the trekkers, who had only a short time to celebrate their relief upon leaving their watery journey, the dreary place known as Missisquoi Bay, and the sixteen whaleboats to march on dry land toward their ultimate target.

Fortunately, besides Lady Luck, who continued to be on his side, Rogers possessed the two most important items that he needed for a successful journey to St. Francis: his trusty compass, which proved invaluable amid the forbidding terrain of the hellish spruce bogs, and Captain John Stark's map, drawn from memory on the same day, September 13, that the major had received orders from General Amherst to launch his expedition not long after the sun dropped below the horizon.

All in all, the sprawling spruce bogs were a truly hellish and forbidding terrain that was a typical northern type of wetlands unlike those that were located farther south on the higher ground of New England's northern frontier. Trekking through the dirty waters of the spruce bogs, Rogers and his men were immediately soaked because the water level nearly reached the top of the Rangers' deerskin Indian leggings and the volunteers' trousers.

This was an alien land to even the most experienced Rangers who were unfamiliar with this type of most challenging terrain, where the land as far as the eye could see was covered in cold, murky waters distinguished by floating vegetation in an uninhabitable setting. The spongy soil under these dark waters often gave way underfoot, causing men to sink deeper into the morass. But, most important, Rogers knew that their tracks could not be followed even by the best Abenaki scouts in this uncharted wilderness, encouraging him to push onward with confidence.

The tall spruce trees, coniferous evergreens also known as the swamp spruce or bog spruce of the pine family, and larch trees had been severely stunted in their natural growth in such a forbidding landscape that seemed unearthly to the interlopers. The Celtic lads in the Rangers' ranks had never seen such a hellish natural environment even in the moors of Scotland or the watery peat bogs of Ireland. Ironically, in a bitter mockery, these seeming endless spruce bogs might have reminded the Rangers of more carefree days during the army's recent advance on Fort Carillon, when they had met with little resistance.

During this period, Amherst had ordered out Rangers to protect details of spruce-tip-gathering soldiers, who then used the tips to brew spruce beer to allegedly combat the ravages of scurvy. Worst of all, the nearly impregnable spruce bogs were a harsh environment for vegetation, animals, and especially Rogers's followers, who trudged onward through a hellish environment. Even game—that seemingly had more good sense than mortal men—was scarce, shunning this strange land that barely supported life in any form. Trekking onward, attempting to keep up with the ever-energetic major, who was leading the way as usual, was a daunting physical struggle for the expeditioners in the black spruce bogs that seemed to have no end.

Relying on a trusty, but small, compass that was located at the bottom of his powder horn, Major Rogers had led his 156 men first east and then northeast, while pushing deeper into the depths of the nightmarish landscape of a mysterious region of the forbidding spruce bogs. But most of all, Rogers continued to move farther away from Isle-aux-Noix and its sizeable garrison, situated near the northern head of Lake Champlain, as they trekked north through the stinking bogs.[50]

As emphasized in his rules of ranging service, which were now necessary in the midst of the spruce bogs when simple survival had become a top priority, Rogers made sure that when "you march over marshes or soft ground, change your position, and march abreast of each other to prevent the enemy from tracking you (as they would do if you marched in a single file) till you get over such ground."[51]

Ironically, and fortunately for Rogers, this low-lying swampy region northeast of Lake Champlain almost all the way to the St. Lawrence—a moat-like region in its protectiveness—had long served as a natural buffer that protected St. Francis on the south. In every single war to date, the complacent Abenaki of Odanak had been secure from any English attackers coming from the south or southwest via Lake Champlain—the main artery that led to this remote region because, of course, there were no roads of any kind in this vast land covered in virgin wilderness. Consequently, believing in the promises of their French protectors and relying on their isolation amid the unmapped wilderness to protect them, the confident Abenaki had long felt secure to the point of carelessness.

Indeed, for generations, the Abenaki had felt totally safe because they were well beyond the reach of the hated whites, especially the often-defeated British army, including the troublemaking Rogers and his men, despite the fact that the Rangers had thoroughly adapted to Abenaki warfighting ways in a masterful manner. In this sense, the raid on St. Francis can be viewed almost as a classic Abenaki-like strike that had long devastated the frontier, but in the opposite direction. Indeed, instead of the revenge-seeking raiders moving south and possessing dark skins, Rogers and his determined men of mostly Scotch-Irish descent moved steadily north with holy retribution on their minds in a case of history, death, and tragedy coming full circle.

As usual, because the life of his command depended upon it, the insightful Rogers continued to think ahead, anticipating the many possibilities that might endanger his small command during a mission so far north and nearly all the way to the St. Lawrence River. Despite not knowing the exact lay of the land before him, because the major had wisely avoided the well-established Yamaska route for safety's sake (the Abenaki town of Yamaska was located seven miles southwest of St. Francis), the major still basked in a confidence born of his earlier wise decisions that had increased the overall chances for success.

Even while toiling through the clinging mud and cold water of the spruce bogs, Rogers proceeded north with a self-assured confidence that destiny awaited him at St. Francis, while encouraging everyone to keep moving at a brisk pace. The New Hampshire major felt that he had taken the necessary wise precautions to ensure a successful mission. After all, at the northeast corner of Missisquoi Bay, he had smartly left two of the most reliable Mohegan "Wolves" from Stockbridge to keep a distant eye on the hidden whaleboats and cached provisions just in case.

Rogers wrote in his report to General Amherst, "Here [at Missisquoi Bay amid the lowland at the northeastern arm of Lake Champlain], that I might with more certainty know whether my [sixteen] boats (with which I left provision sufficient to carry us back to Crown Point) were discovered by the enemy, I left two trusty Indians to lie at a distance in sight of the boats, and there to stay till I came back, except [if] the enemy found them; in which latter case they were with all possible speed to follow on my track, and give me intelligence."[52]

THE MOST ALARMING OF ALL NEWS

Clearly, the ever-careful major, who had never been so far north and deep into enemy country before, was not embracing any assumptions or ill-founded illusions when the existence of his command was at stake. By expecting the worst-case scenarios and taking necessary precautions in consequence, Rogers was setting the stage for his command's survival. He therefore felt confident in moving steadily north toward his coveted target because of another key factor about which he had no doubt at all. The decision to trek through the bogs—known as the "Drowned Lands"—guaranteed that Rogers was now not leading his troops into an ambush, because he was moving along no established route in a truly forlorn region. And, as noted, the frontier major knew that his tracks could not be followed. Amid the dark waters and the density of the spruce bogs, the major realized that no high or solid ground existed for the enemy to prepare an ambush on this least expected approach to St. Francis. Therefore, while pushing through an unknown country that no white had seen before, Rogers was assured that the spruce bogs provided a degree of safety against the most dreaded possibility: the ambush that had been so masterfully orchestrated by the Indians, Canadians, and French, who were experts in this dark tactical art that had taken so many Ranger lives in the past.

But, of course, Rogers could hardly control events, despite taking the best possible precautions under the circumstances. He received a stunning blow in the second night's encampment amid the spruce bogs with the arrival of two panting Stockbridge Rangers, who gave the proper password, on the cool evening of September 25. Mud-covered and totally exhausted at this point about eighteen miles north of Missisquoi Bay, the two faithful warriors reported a stunning development that would have completely undermined all hopes for future success in the mind of any other commander. But such was not the case with Rogers when the most shocking of news was conveyed to him by the trusty "Wolves." Indeed, "it happened the second day after I left them [at Missisquoi Bay], that these two Indians came up to me in the evening" with the intelligence that Rogers most of all dreaded to hear.[53]

As if the ordeal of relentless toiling through the dark waters, around a foot deep on average, of the spruce bogs in wet leather moccasins and soggy Indian deerskin leggings, which extended up to Ranger thighs, for most of the last two days was not bad enough, the two Stockbridge Mahican Indians had somehow—no small feat—managed to reach the main body in the midst of the swamps, after following what little could be seen of their trail at a brisk pace, revealing the extent of their woodcraft talents, which were little short of miraculous. All in all, it was now clear that Rogers's foresight had paid immense dividends, as he had envisioned with clarity days before.

Here, in the late evening cold of September 25, a dramatic meeting with his officers took place. The two Stockbridge Rangers dutifully informed Rogers that the hidden whaleboats and around five days' worth of provisions had been discovered on September 21 by a party of around four hundred French, Indians, and Canadians from Isle-aux-Noix. The Ranger "Wolves" did not know that this task force was under the command of the ever-troublesome Ensign Langy (Jean-Baptiste Levrault de Langis Montegron) and Ensign La Durantaye of La Marine.

This strong contingent of Canadians, French, and Indians had been dispatched from Isle-aux-Noix by General Bourlamaque after the discovery of pieces of a wooden whaleboat hull and the shattered oar that had been found floating in Missisquoi Bay. It is not known definitely if this was one of Rogers's boats or that of an earlier scouting mission. But the fact that these items were found floating in Missisquoi Bay seemed to reveal some kind of recent activity. However, one of Rogers's sixteen whaleboats may have hit a rock or log during the long journey north. If so, then one whaleboat may have been in bad shape upon entering Missisquoi Bay, and pieces of its damaged hull might have fallen off.

Regardless of the mysterious source of the whaleboat debris floating like a buoy in the clear waters of Missisquoi Bay, the stunning news of this fortuitous find had acted like a French alarm bell that had sounded far and wide. As mentioned, General Bourlamaque had ordered the four-hundred-man task force south, which eventually led to the discovery of Rogers's precious boats and provisions hidden in the underbrush near the bay, and he issued his warnings to nearby garrisons and towns.

Indeed, the sharp eye of Ensign Langy, as cagy as he was a tough fighting man who fairly lusted for the opportunity to once again whip the hated Rogers, had discovered the hidden sixteen whaleboats stashed in the thickets and covered with underbrush that seemed out of place to the Canadian woodsman's trained eye. By any measure, Langy was no ordinary partisan leader. He had played the leading role in thoroughly decimating the Rangers at the Battle on Snowshoes, transforming a hard-fought battle in the snowy wilderness into an unprecedented slaughter of Rangers. When Langy and his Indians, Canadians, and French were finished cutting down one man after another on that bloody March 1758 day, nearly 150 Rangers lay dead among the tall timbers on a hellish battlefield in which Rogers had been thrashed on a scale not previously seen.

As could be expected, Rogers's old nemesis was delighted in finding the hidden whaleboats in the thickets. He burned with the desire to ensure that these vessels would never be used by the enemy. Ensign Langy promptly ordered them broken up with tomahawks, while others were hauled to the portage site in the shallow bay. Historians have long maintained that Ensign Langy set fire to the boats and provisions, but this scenario makes no sense. Langy knew better than to set the whaleboats on fire, because the black smoke would have warned Rogers of what had happened and especially because he planned to set up an ambush for when the Rangers returned, if they proved so foolish as to retrace their steps.

Even more, Langy and his men also needed the ample fresh English provisions (enough for around fifteen days) since they were stationed at the far southern end of the lengthy French logistical line. Foodstuffs from Montreal and Quebec were always in short supply because of the mother country's weak logistical links to New France. Consequently, burning the provisions would be pointless. Even a relatively small hole chopped by the steel tomahawks in the bottoms of the whaleboats was sufficient to wreck the hulls to render them useless. All in all, setting the whaleboats on fire would have been an illogical and irrational act committed by the hard-fighting ensign, who was known for his sound judgment.

Most important, Ensign Langy dispatched a messenger to General Bourlamaque with the good news of his unexpected discovery of the whaleboats, and the dashing French general hurried south with still another task force of three hundred men, who were eager to kill Rangers and take their scalps. Prudently, the alerted Bourlamaque had been thorough. As mentioned, he had smartly dispatched messengers to alert the governors of Montreal and Trois-Rivières, located on the St. Lawrence just below Quebec, as well as French army commander the Marquis de Montcalm and even Father Roubaud, the missionary priest at St. Francis who was now at Trois-Rivières and absent from his devoted flock.

After receiving the warning, Montreal governor Francois Pierre de Rigaud de Vaudreuil, who was the privileged son of the governor-general of New France, anticipated Rogers's expected route north from Missisquoi Bay to St. Francis. Therefore, Rigaud ordered a three-hundred-man task force placed between the Yamaska's mouth and the St. Francis River just before these waterways entered the waters of the St. Lawrence.

Overwhelmed with the lustful desire of possibly destroying Rogers and a good many Rangers, General Bourlamaque dispatched another 100 men to bolster the ambush established at the whaleboat discovery site on Missisquoi Bay to increase the number of ambushers to 360 men. The fact that Ensign Langy was left in charge of these 360 fighters indicated that the French fully expected Rogers's return because they knew that he would be needing provisions and the sixteen whaleboats for the return journey to Crown Point. But of course, this might well prove to have been only a case of wishful French thinking if Rogers decided not to return. For Langy, who had wanted so badly to destroy Rogers and his hated Rangers for years, this was a dream come true: the possibility of wiping out Rogers and his men in yet another clever Langy ambush, which would win him greater fame across New France for not only defeating Rogers but also perhaps capturing or killing the legendary Ranger leader.

In fact, Major Rogers, who naturally did not know about Bourlamaque's precautions and swift actions in his determined bid to counter the suddenly emerging threat so deep in New France, was now even unluckier than he imagined and in even greater danger than he anticipated. The recent fall of Quebec to General Wolfe, who never lived to see the fruits of his decisive victory on September 13, had unleashed large numbers of French and Canadian troops and warriors, including Abenaki fighting men, who had escaped the fiasco to the northwest.

Therefore, General Bourlamaque now possessed an ample number of troops to negate the belief of Amherst at Crown Point headquarters that Rogers had a better chance of succeeding in his perilous mission because of the concentration of French, Indian, and Canadian defenders at Quebec. But the entire strategic situation had changed dramatically when Quebec fell on September 13. And now trekking north through the wilderness toward St. Francis, Rogers was destined to learn nothing about Quebec's surrender for a considerable amount of time until his capture of St. Francis on October 4, when struggling against the odds to get his command to his objective in one piece.

The tactically astute Langy, who was one of the finest Canadian officers in the art of irregular warfare and who had bested Rogers at the Second Battle on Snowshoes and other close-range clashes in the wilderness, now knew that a large force of Englishmen was on the move deep in the home territory of Quebec. But the French—not even Ensign Langy, who never acquired a level of fame comparable to the "famous scouter" (a widespread renown gained by Rogers in colonial newspaper as early as February 1756) in buckskin and a green uniform coat—did not definitely know that it was the famed Rogers but almost certainly expected as much. As noted, and as long assumed by historians, there were no Ranger markings on the bows of the sixteen whaleboats, like in 1760, to enlighten the French about Rogers's presence, however.

Indeed, Ensign Langy of La Marine, like his father before him, who was a career soldier and had four sons who became proud officers, almost certainly knew that only Major Rogers had the right amount of audacity for leading such a long-range expedition deep in the heart of New France. But he certainly did not know that his vigorous work in the systematic destruction of the whaleboats had been seen by two of Rogers's best men—the Stockbridge Ranger "Wolves," whom Rogers had prudently left behind. Therefore, by thinking ahead to remain one step ahead of the enemy, Rogers had already outfoxed Langy, who clung to his glorious illusion of the raider's possible destruction upon his expected return to Missisquoi Bay, when he had stationed the two Ranger warriors at the right place on their special mission, which paid great dividends.

Even more, and as the two Stockbridge Rangers had told Rogers, about half of this force from Isle-aux-Noix, around two hundred French, Canadians, and Indians under the veteran fighter La Durantaye, were even now in fast pursuit of Rogers's command, after it had entered the broad expanse of spruce bogs. The eager fighting men of this revenge-seeking French war party began pushing east and then northeast on the morning of September 26, following Rogers's tracks in the mud on the swamp's edge and any broken branches that told a story to sharp-eyed Indian scouts.

Ensigns Langy and La Durantaye believed that the Rangers were headed for either Quebec to reinforce Wolfe or St. Francis, or perhaps both, since St. Francis, situated just below the St. Lawrence, was on the way to Quebec on the St. Lawrence to the northeast. As Langy and La Durantaye knew, if it is was Rogers who was now on the loose so deep in a part of Canada that had been long secure from any English interlopers, then almost anything was possible from the most daring leader in the entire British-Provincial Army.

Of course, Major Rogers had been stunned by the shocking news of losing his sixteen vessels and so many provisions for the anticipated return trip to Crown Point, sabotaging his well-laid plans upon which his entire mission was based. But no record exists of the Scotch-Irish major's erupting in anger or unleashing a string of obscenities, and he remained calm, as if he was sitting in a cozy New England tavern and drinking hot-buttered rum on a cold winter night with friends.

Expecting the raiders to return by the glaring tactical mistake of following their own previous route (the best of all ways to fall into a deadly ambush), the other half of this formidable Canadian, French, and Indian force set up an ambush at Missisquoi Bay, which Langy orchestrated with his usual skill. Langy felt sure that this mysterious English expeditionary force would make the fundamental error of returning to secure their whaleboats and provisions, which were necessary for the raiders' survival for their return trip south to safety.

Therefore, in the midst of the most dangerous mission that they had ever undertaken and far from the safety of Crown Point, Rogers and his men now realized that they were in far more serious trouble than imagined and more than ever before. Under the circumstances, Rogers's outstanding leadership abilities now rose to the fore, because he continued to inspire a high level of confidence among a divergent group of men, many of whom—British Regulars and Provincials—he had never before commanded.

Continuing to outwit the enemy, the major was about to require his weary men to not only march away at an accelerated pace from the heightened danger posed by their pursuers but also head straight into the lion's den and into the midst of far greater danger. Rogers had already made up his mind about his final decision to forge ahead at any cost, resisting the temptation of aborting the mission to save lives, perhaps his own. However, he needed to keep up a bold democratic facade at this crucial point and convince his top lieutenants and his men to continue north in the hope of outracing their pursuers and achieving a remarkable success, despite the ever-lessening chances for an optimistic outcome.

This desperate situation for the ad hoc command of Americans and Britons in the middle of nowhere was discussed during the hasty commanders' conference of grim-faced and low-speaking officers in the traditional manner of frontier decision making among the ultra-democratic Rangers, who were proud of hailing from representative governments of the colonies as part of the greater liberties gained as part of the British Empire: the ultimate dilemma and seemingly impossible situation of a good many hostile warriors, with their French and Canadian allies, now not only behind but also before them at St. Francis and lurking on their left flank, while they were far from any support.

This grim tactical reality could not be denied by the New England major, who attempted to overlook the worst-case scenario before his fellow officers, whom he treated as equals instead of lowly subordinates. The entire supply of provisions that had been carefully cached under the over-turned whaleboats had been either destroyed or taken to be consumed by the French Regulars, Indians, and Canadians, who certainly enjoyed free English rations at the expense of King George II, who now basked in the luxury of the longtime royal residence at Windsor Castle in the county of Berkshire. Their precious rations for the lengthy return trip to Crown Point were no more, like the balmy weather of a past hot summer in the Lake Champlain country. A good many of Rogers's men (and perhaps the major himself) wondered whether they would survive this arduous mission and live to see the arrival of the spring of 1760.

As a cruel fate would have it, in a development that almost certainly made Rogers laugh grimly at the old saying "luck of the Irish," now "barely into the raid, the rangers' presence was known and their planned avenue of escape [back to the safety of Crown Point] closed" by the recent turn of bad luck. No doubt, Rogers now wished to God that his old 1756 plan to destroy St. Francis had been utilized by Amherst instead of the new September 1759 one that had too many of the major general's fingerprints, but such was the strange fate that had long seemed to protect New France's most hated Indian town among generations of New Englanders. Ironically, the major and followers were now haunted by the grim realization that the enemy lay not only before them and on their left flank but also behind them, with a burning desire to take as many Ranger scalps as possible: the most disturbing of developments that might have caused a less resolute commander to think about surrendering to the foe.[54] In a classic understatement that revealed his tough mentality and positive way of thinking, a stoic Rogers merely con-cluded how this monumental setback was an "unlucky circumstance."[55]

Indeed, in his report to Amherst, Rogers described how he had to quickly adjust his overall strategic plan to the new, extremely dismal reality, after the two Stockbridge Rangers had

informed me that about 400 French had discovered and taken my boats, and that about one half of them were hotly pursuing my track. This unlucky circumstance (it may well be supposed) put us into some consternation. Should the enemy overtake us, and we get the better of them in any encounter; yet being so far advanced into their country, where no reinforcement could possibly relieve us, and where they could be supported by any numbers they pleased, afforded us little hopes of escaping

their hands. Our [sixteen] boats being taken, cut off all hopes of a retreat by them;
the loss of our provisions left with them, of which we knew we should have great
need at any rate, in case we survived, was a melancholy consideration.[56]

This unnerving situation that had so suddenly developed was nothing
less than disastrous, and there seemed no realistic tactical solution that made
any sense under the circumstances. Such was especially the case if Rogers
decided to turn and face their pursuers under the hard-hitting La Durantaye
from Missisquoi Bay in a full-fledged battle on unfamiliar ground far from
support: a tactical scenario that invited certain annihilation. Even if Rogers
succeeded in ambushing the pursuers, he risked the arrival of additional
French reinforcements if he made a time-consuming stand and fought a long
battle against expert wilderness fighting men, who were deft at killing Rangers. Major Rogers was now ever mindful of one fact: he knew that his raiders
could never return the way he had come with high hopes not long ago. If
Rogers had known that the savvy Ensign Langy, who had gotten the best of
him in the past, was now on the loose in this area, then he would have been
even more concerned for the ultimate fates of his mission and command.

As noted, this tactical situation as it now existed in the wilds of Quebec
was only the latest chapter of the ongoing personal duel between Rogers and
Langy that had long raged along the strategic Lake Champlain corridor.
However, Ensign Langy decided to remain at the site where he had found
the sixteen whaleboats, because he believed that an unprecedented opportunity awaited him to score a great triumph, if by only remaining patient in a
good ambush position. Since he had been so successful in the art of setting
up ambushes that had ensnared Rogers and his men in the past when snow
had been on the ground, so Langy had set up another clever ambush at Missisquoi Bay, where the whaleboats had been hidden in vain, while Ensign La
Durantaye was leading the pursuit north through the nightmarish spruce
bogs and moving as fast as possible.

And the major from the Merrimack River country shrewdly knew that
he could not engage in a fight to his rear because St. Francis beckoned far
to the north like a young, attractive virgin lover on a soft April afternoon
lying invitingly in a green patch of springtime clover under the warm sun. As
noted, Rogers worried about the possibility of large numbers of the enemy
who might suddenly arrive to attack his rear. After all, this was very much

a personal war between Major Rogers and Ensign Langy, who had so often matched wits and tactical skills on the field of strife. Naturally, each man possessed a healthy and well-earned respect for the other. But, of course, each expert partisan commander also possessed a good deal of pride in himself and his command, wanting to destroy the other at the first opportunity.

However, at least initially, Rogers had to curb his innermost desires in this most vexing of dilemmas when he thought about turning to fight his pursuers because he was aggressive by nature. Quite simply, Rogers and his command were now just too deep into Canada, relatively close to not only Isle-aux-Noix but also Montreal, to the northwest, to engage in a full-scale battle in an unfamiliar wilderness in the middle of nowhere. As was customarily the case when facing a crisis, the Ranger officers discussed the situation in whispered tones. Here, in the cold darkness and stinking swamps that they had never seen before, and when so far from Crown Point, a new plan had to be quickly hatched by desperate men, who had been significantly slowed down in trekking through the swamps.

While veteran officers discussed a host of possibilities during the commanders' conference, Rogers already knew what he had to do. Nevertheless, key questions were up for debate. Should this secret mission be aborted because of so many sharp setbacks encountered when so far in enemy territory? Had the original plan to push so far north and attack St. Francis been too ambitious from the beginning, because the risks had steadily increased while the number of men decreased in a seemingly fatal development? Because of the great distance involved in having pushed so far north into Quebec, was this seemingly no-win situation nothing more than a classic case of tactical overreach, which was little more than folly committed by the major? Had Rogers's optimism and confidence led him to take the road to certain disaster for the entire command?

Had Rogers committed the sin of overreaching in attempting to accomplish too much—an absolute impossibility in the view of the military experts on both sides, especially in the most respected European military schools of the day—to fulfill his greatest ambition that had consumed him for years? Was still another disastrous Second Battle on Snowshoes and against the same hard-hitting opponent, the talented Ensign Langy and other veteran partisan officers, now in the making, with half of the enemy task force, which exceeded in number that of Rogers's entire command, waiting in ambush, and with Ensign La Durantaye, an excellent La Marine officer of outstanding ability, now leading the pursuit north? After all, these were two of the finest partisan officers in Canada, and they were driven by the burning desire to take as many Ranger scalps as possible.

Since it now seemed as if Rogers and his men were virtually trapped, the French leaders fondly hoped to end the ambitions of these raiders in gory fashion. Consequently, were the scalps of the hated Rogers and his followers soon to wave in the October breeze above the lodges and houses of St. Francis, like those of hundreds of other victims—men, women, and children? Such nagging thoughts racked the brains of Rogers and his men at a true moment of crisis when they seemingly faced certain annihilation.

Surely with the provisions for the return trip and whaleboats destroyed by Langy, who experienced great joy in his destructive work to thwart the raiders' well-laid plans for future escape, it now seemed the right time to abort the mission and sensibly embark upon escape from what had become a disastrous situation. Was surrender a viable option because French officers generally followed the long-accepted European rules of honorable conduct? Or would the captured Rangers, after they had surrendered and been promised mercy by the French, be slaughtered like in past bloody encounters?

Clearly, as Rogers fully realized beyond all doubt, this final option of submission was the least desirable because it was much too risky: the enemy, especially Ensign Langy, had been long intent on wiping out the hated Rangers to the last man. Consequently, the ever-sensible Rogers was not about to risk the lives of his men—even if his officers favored capitulation—based on a rosy set of French promises that had often proved entirely worthless in the past and might well result in the slaughter of his entire command.

Likewise, setting up a clever Ranger ambush to surprise Ensign La Durantaye's overly aggressive pursuers, who were not far behind the slogging command, was not realistic under the circumstances, because the Rangers possessed only a limited supply of ammunition and potential ambushers, after having already lost so many good men on the northward journey. Quite simply, Rogers knew that they could not punish the pursuers as he instinctively desired, because his command was too far from Crown Point, and there was now no margin for error.

CUTTING THE GORDIAN KNOT

Clearly, the grizzled major faced a true Gordian knot that seemingly could not be untangled or cut in the manner of Alexander the Great long ago in a heroic age that was no more, regardless of what decision he made or whatever was believed by his top lieutenants, who consisted of his best leaders. To this Spartan-type leader in a short green uniform coat, Indian leggings, and no sign of his major's rank to be seen by the enemy, only one possibility remained in such a no-win situation, and this was the boldest option of all under the circumstances: despite the major setback of losing any possibility of the planned withdrawal south down Lake Champlain, subsisting on provisions for the journey back to Crown Point, and now facing a no-win situation, Rogers was not deterred in the least. He continued to maintain a confident facade before his anxious men, as if nothing disastrous had happened and everything could be overcome.

On his own, Rogers had already decided in his own mind to outmarch his pursuers in a desperate race, not away from the enemy in a lengthy withdrawal with his tail between his legs, but forging ahead and ever deeper into enemy country, straight toward the legendary heart of darkness, St. Francis, to destroy the entire community, before the arrival of French, Indian, and Canadian reinforcements bolstered the town. He and his men would then push south for New England (must farther east and parallel to Lake Champlain) through an uncharted wilderness of mountains, swamps, raging rivers, and the densest forests.

Here, amid the stench of the putrid spruce bogs, Rogers was now determined to "prosecute our design," in the major's own words: to continue the grueling march north through the swamps to strike St. Francis as originally planned. Once again, Rogers's determination to adhere to a definite course of aggressive action during an active campaign in enemy territory in his relentless pursuit of a key tactical objective revealed that he rarely deviated from the original plan.

Clearly and most of all, Rogers would not allow his great dream of destroying St. Francis to die an early death in the spruce bogs of Quebec because of a series of sharp setbacks, regardless of how severe that they happened to be: a situation that would have certainly deterred an average commander of a task force so far from home on such a dangerous mission. During this hushed Ranger conference on this chilly night in the forbidding swamps, when the fate of not only the command but also the mission were being determined in the democratic tradition, the top officers, like Captain Amos Ogden and Lieutenant William James Dunbar, agreed with Rogers's opinion to proceed as if none of the alarming setbacks had occurred. But as noted, Rogers would have decided to continue onward, regardless of the advice of his top lieutenants, because he would never turn back.

Despite his own firm conviction, which he would allow no one to over-turn, Rogers continued to adhere to the cherished democratic tradition in the face of a disastrous situation, even if it was only an egalitarian facade at this time. But, most of all, if he was fortunate enough to reach and destroy St. Francis, then Rogers now knew that the only possible return to safety was to follow the St. Francis River in a generally southeastern direction to its forks, reaching the eastern side of Lake Memphremagog by following its southerly branch, and then following the Passumpsic River Valley that led south to the Lower Coos Meadows along the Connecticut River and to Fort Number Four at the northern edge of New England.

To Rogers, this was a familiar route through the wilderness that provided the best possibility of escape, after he succeeded in destroying St. Francis, if everything went according to plan. Major Rogers had now resurrected his old 1756 plan of withdrawal from St. Francis, which he knew was feasible for making his escaping after destroying the infamous place. But this plan of withdrawal was a most daunting one—around two hundred miles through an uncharted wilderness before reaching safety, if they survived the wilderness's challenges and the inevitable vigorous enemy pursuit.

To ensure that the new plan of withdrawal had a chance of succeeding, the major relied upon First Lieutenant Andrew McMullen, of Worches-ter, Massachusetts, by way of a sailing ship from Ireland. He was another dependable soldier with Scotch-Irish roots like Rogers and an immigrant like Rogers's parents. The major dispatched more than a half dozen other men, who had become increasingly lame and injured (like First Lieutenant McMullen, who was hobbled after having stubbed his toe at the first hidden bivouac near the mouth of Otter River) and sick by this time.

McMullen's contingent—7 men in total to reduce Rogers's command to 149 men—was ordered to make its laborious way overland more than one hundred miles back to Crown Point (a nine-day mission destined to be completed on October 3, which was the day before Rogers's attack on St.

Francis) to inform General Amherst of their dire situation and the major's new desperate, but feasible, plan upon which the very survival of the Rangers now depended: after the destruction of St. Francis, returning to safety by way of pushing up the course of the St. Francis River, marching south on the east side of Lake Memphremegog (another beautiful Abenaki name for a sacred place), and then south down the Connecticut River, beginning near its headwaters, which led to the safety of Fort Number Four and New England.

As mentioned, Major Rogers realized that this was the only possible route of escape, and he knew that it was a good one, because this exact same route had formed the basis of his 1756 plan to attack St. Francis and then withdraw, which had been rejected by the inflexible Lord Loudoun (to Rogers's great disappointment). Most important, Rogers emphasized to First Lieutenant McMullen for Amherst to send provisions north from Fort Number Four up the Connecticut River (called "Ouoneh-tu-cut" or "the Long-Tide River" by the Abenaki) to meet the survivors.

He even told the dependable Irishman that the vital provisions should be sent north up the river by Second Lieutenant Samuel Stevens of New Hampshire. Rogers knew that Stevens was very familiar with the wilderness north of Fort Number Four, where his father had become famous for its spirited defense with only a relatively few men against New France's raiders long ago. Even more, Stevens had been a former private of John Stark's company, after having enlisted in late February 1758. Rogers believed that he had made the ideal choice of a man who might well play a key role in saving his command, when they reached the Connecticut River, after the destruction of St. Francis.

The carefully calculating New Hampshire major, who had decided to go for broke, realized that Second Lieutenant Stevens knew this area well and had demonstrated reliability in the past, which was crucial if the final phase of this plan was to succeed.

Therefore, Rogers directed that the provisions should be sent north to where the Lower Ammonoosuc, or Amonsook, River (known to the Abenaki as "the narrow fishing place") entered the Connecticut River and above the upper end of the Lower Coos Intervales (Cohase Intervals or Coos Meadows) about sixty miles north of the remotest and northernmost English fort on the New England frontier, Fort Number Four. The provisions, as directed by Rogers, were to be taken to where the Wells and Lower

Amonsook Rivers entered the Connecticut River—the best logistical site because of the intersecting rivers.

All in all, Rogers's alternative plan was a good one based on years of planning. An Irish immigrant who had only been in America for five years and a future patriot in the struggle for liberty during the American Revolution, First Lieutenant McMullen was given the most crucial of all assignments. Everything now depended upon McMullen's reaching Amherst at Crown Point and the urgent dispatch of provisions from Fort Number Four and north up the Connecticut River, before it was too late for Rogers's returning command, if they survived and were even fortunate to reach this point so far south.

Major Rogers understood how the Rangers would certainly be out of food, especially if they failed to capture St. Francis and the supplies stored after the seasonal harvest, because the approximately two-hundred-mile journey south by foot from their target would take them across a hostile countryside largely devoid of game and one of the poorest hunting grounds imaginable. Clearly, this last phase of Rogers's plan was extremely risky, because even Fort Number Four was located more than sixty miles north of the nearest New England settlement, and the tight grip of a harsh winter would have already descended upon the tranquil Connecticut River Valley. Rogers had to wonder how many of his men could possibly survive the lengthy journey south, but he had no choice in the matter because of the most disadvantageous of circumstances well beyond his control.

First Lieutenant McMullen, who joined the Rangers as a private, had served capably in the ranks of the elite company known as "Rogers's Own" since February 1757 and then advanced to gain an officer's rank because of his impressive leadership qualities in 1758. He could be depended upon to get through and deliver this all-important information to Amherst, as the Scotch-Irish commander fully realized. Embracing what was nothing less than a sacred trust and in command of six injured and sick men, McMullen was determined to get through at any cost to deliver Rogers's crucial message of the new route of withdrawal from St. Francis, because he fully realized that the lives of his comrades and friends were at stake.

Still another motivation fueled McMullen's determination to succeed in his crucial mission of reaching Crown Point, which he was destined to accomplish on October 3, after a grueling nine-day march of around one hundred miles, just in time to ensure that provisions were sent up the Connecticut River under Second Lieutenant Stevens, in whom Rogers had obviously placed great faith. The trusty, tenderhearted son of Erin burned with the desire to once again embrace his future wife, pretty Hannah Osgood.

She awaited the Irishman's return to her arms at Rumford (today's Concord), New Hampshire, in the Merrimack River country, which had once been the ancestral homeland of the Pennacook Abenaki. As fate would have it, some members of this tribe were now living at St. Francis, and they had never forgotten their harsh displacement by whites from their ancestral land, which they had loved for so long. Hannah was another reason that explained why McMullen was determined to get through and reach safety, and her love helped to give him the strength to carry on.

BOLDLY FORGING AHEAD AND ON TO ST. FRANCIS!

By this time, and as noted, Rogers possessed only one realistic solution for his vexing dilemma of having too few men—now reduced to only 149 followers after Ireland-born McMullen and a half dozen men departed for Crown Point—so deep inside the enemy's country and so far from support of any kind. And, most of all, as Rogers fully realized and as noted, this no-win situation of enemy war parties swarming around him now called for a desperate race ever farther north and deeper into Canada to reach St. Francis in time, before being attacked or ambushed: the case of a desperate sprint through the spruce bogs in an attempt to outrun pursuers, who knew that the raiders were in serious trouble and delighted in the knowledge.

If the French, Canadians, and Indians struck out of the spruce and pine forests, then such an attack guaranteed the direst of consequences for the diminutive command, including the slaughter of a good many men and the prisoners hauled off to St. Francis to be tortured and killed in ritualistic fashion for the immense entertainment of the entire village. Quite simply, this was one race that Rogers could not afford to lose, because it was the most important one of his life.

Consequently, to avoid this tragic fate, which was all but inevitable if Rogers made a single blunder, a monumental effort of endurance was now required for any chance of successfully reaching St. Francis and then withdrawing from it to reach safety nearly two hundred miles to the south: "We determined if possible to outmarch our pursuers, and effect our design upon

St. Francis, before they could overtake us," in Rogers's words, and destroy the command that had been drastically reduced by steady attrition: the ugliest of encroaching grim possibilities that could be easily accomplished by large numbers of French, both Regulars and La Marines, Canadians, and Indians led by experienced commanders, who skillfully fought in the wilderness like Rangers and knew all of the tactical tricks.[57]

All in all, this was a courageous final decision to proceed, despite the growing list of sharp setbacks that revealed the iron will and determination of Major Rogers to complete the mission at any cost. Counting the recent departure of Lieutenant McMullen and his band of six worn-out or lame men, who were no longer up to the stiff challenge, Rogers's expeditionary force had already been reduced well beyond anything that he could have imagined possible back at Crown Point.

Clearly, the drastic reduction of manpower was nothing less than a cruel culling and potentially fatal attrition for the entire command: a staggering total of 48 officers and men, who were ill, lame, or too exhausted to continue the difficult trek that promised little rest, had already been lost to Rogers at the exact time when he needed as many men as possible because the overall situation had reached a crisis point, leaving only 149 physically fit men for the final push on St. Francis.

A stunning one-fourth of Rogers's entire command was no more even before the first shot had been fired in anger or the first sighting of an enemy, after McMullen's party headed south on their own perilous journey to Crown Point. Indeed, to date and nearly a week and a half after having departed Crown Point, not a single man of Rogers's task force had been lost in any actions with the adversary in a bizarre development. In fact, Rogers and his men had not even been sighted by the foe during the lengthy journey north. As noted, they had left behind ample evidence of their presence, however. Clearly, fate had not been kind to Rogers's mission or his command at this point, so far north of Crown Point and so deep in Canada.

In a systematic reduction in only a relatively short period, Rogers could no longer count on seventeen Rangers, fourteen Stockbridge warriors, ten Provincials, and seven British Regulars, who had departed the command. Without the Canadians, Indians, and French ever having fired a shot at Rogers's trekkers, this terrible attrition rate had drastically reduced Rogers's command by a total of forty-eight men for the strike on St. Francis, if they successfully reached this advanced position still far to the north: a stunningly high number that was far too large of a loss for the enormity of the most daunting of missions. As mentioned, however, Major Rogers was not discouraged and remained true to his pet plan and project.

Indeed, Rogers was now replying to an unprecedented crisis situation with the best solution of all in his mind, and it was simply to forge ahead without looking back or entertaining any debilitating fears or nagging doubts about his ultimate success. Thanks partly to his frontiersman's willpower and Scotch-Irishman's stubbornness, qualities absolutely necessary for survival in a bloody borderland for the adversity-hardened people from Ulster Province, he remained totally committed to reaching St. Francis, even if he was the last man standing and had to charge into the town by himself with flintlock pistols blazing.[58]

Despite the seemingly insurmountable dangers and with no illusions, fully realizing that the extent of the risks had never been greater than at this crucial time, Rogers later wrote to Major General Amherst—in the message to be carried by Lieutenant McMullen—of his eventual escape route much farther east by land than his advance route by Lake Champlain's waters, if the mission proved successful, emphasizing "that being the way I should return, if at all."[59]

In his November 5, 1759, report to Amherst after he had just miraculously survived the most harrowing of ordeals during the withdrawal from St. Francis, Rogers wrote how despite the long list of setbacks and increasing disadvantages that seemingly should have led to an aborted mission, "It was, however, resolved to prosecute our design at all adventures [and hazards], and, when we had accomplished it, to attempt a retreat (the only possible way we could think) by way of No. 4"—the northernmost fort on the Connecticut River and the New England frontier in New Hampshire.[60]

With the whaleboats and provisions for the return trip no more, thanks to Ensign Langy's timely discovery at Missisquoi Bay, there was now no turning back, especially along the same route, because Rogers was not the kind of commander who ever turned back, especially when his life's dream of destroying St. Francis—part of his heart and soul by this time—still strongly beckoned him onward toward his longtime objective. As noted, even the severest setbacks only emboldened the iron-willed major and made him more determined to continue forward and succeed in the end. Indeed,

Rogers liked nothing more than a stiff challenge to demonstrate to one and all that even the most daunting of obstacles and setbacks could be overcome by his own strength of will and abilities.

But Rogers's bold decision to continue what now seemed like a collapsing mission that had suddenly become more dangerous would result in the most arduous of land journeys, first on to St. Francis and then a long retreat to safety of more than two hundred miles south, lasting for around the next month and a half in increasingly cold weather and through an uncharted wilderness that the Rangers had never seen before.

In the words of Private Robert Kirkwood about the brisk forward movement now ordered by Rogers, who knew the immense value of not wasting a single moment in such a dire situation, "We penetrated through a vast track of woody country" of which there were no maps except what Captain John Stark had provided to Rogers on the eve of the departure from Crown Point, which proved invaluable to the major in forging ahead with greater confidence.[61]

Now that the enemy had been alerted to the interlopers' presence somewhere in the wilds northeast of Missisquoi Bay, Rogers knew that French leaders would certainly rush all available reinforcements to protect St. Francis before it was too late, if they ever determined that this point was his primary target, because other targets seemed more obvious for the raiders to strike. Montreal, a far larger and more vital target located on the St. Lawrence River, which needed to be taken in conjunction with Quebec, according to Pitt's grand design for reaping decisive victory, was closer to Rogers than St. Francis and easier to reach.

Therefore, some French leaders wondered whether Montreal might be the target, since it was the second-largest and most strategic town in Canada after Quebec. Indeed, might the English raiders turn northwest, instead of continuing northeast toward St. Francis, to strike Montreal? But while Montreal lay on the north side of the St. Lawrence, St. Francis stood just below the greatest river of destiny in the turbulent history of New France. Rogers and his Rangers, if this were the identity of the exceptionally bold English interlopers who had secretly landed at Missisquoi Bay, were known for their resourcefulness, and a direct threat to Montreal could not be discounted by the French leadership.

Unbeknownst to Rogers, Montreal had already benefited from Quebec's fall, gaining greater protection from the arrival of a good many of Quebec's

defenders, whose presence made New France's second city on the St. Lawrence more formidable. But Rogers continued to have only one thought and
target in mind—St. Francis—after having early dismissed Major General
Amherst's unrealistic orders to strike the French settlements located on the
south side of the St. Lawrence River just north of St. Francis.

DESPERATE RACE FOR LIFE

Therefore, the desperate Scotch-Irish major and his men faced a deadly
race (Rogers had a seventy-two-hour head start before the vigorous pursuit
of a couple hundred French, Canadians, and Indians under the highly capable Ensign La Durantaye) of nearly one hundred miles in total, or about
seventy-five miles as the crow flies, from Missisquoi Bay northeastward
and then over some of the worst imaginable terrain—low-lying, sunken,
and covered in thick brush and stagnant water that was around a foot deep
on average but often deeper at spots. All the while, Rogers encouraged
everyone onward through the dark and cold waters, knowing the supreme
importance of moving as rapidly as possible in the hope of getting out of
the nightmarish spruce bogs.

However, continuing to toil north through the spruce bogs was the
smartest route because Rogers possessed the good sense to avoid the
Kennedy-Hamilton party's Yamaska route, where the French, as the major
realized, would surely lay a clever ambush of experienced fighting men eager
to destroy every last Ranger if possible, thanks to the actions of Montreal's
governor, Rigaud. Governor-General Vaudreuil ordered war parties from not
only St. Francis but also the mission village of Becancour to link with Canadian militia to protect the Yamaska Valley southwest of St. Francis.

And, as feared, a force of around two hundred French, Indians, and
Canadians was now in fast pursuit at a time when the day's heat in late September reached the searing temperatures of late summer. During the difficult
trek through the dark, foul-smelling waters of the spruce bogs under a hot
sun, sweat stained the Rangers' uniforms, while also wetting their buckskin
leggings, which darkened and became softer from the mixture of rain, sweat,
and bog water.

All the while, rations were eagerly consumed by the men until supplies
ran low, while providing relatively little nourishment. A cold sweat also
poured from some of Rogers's raiders because of the growing fear of the

encroaching dangers that hovered around the exhausted trekkers like a dark cloud. If anyone could gain Rogers's rear and deliver a punishing blow, it was the veteran troops, with experienced Indian scouts leading the way, under the La Marine's Ensign La Durantaye, who was one of the best partisan commanders in the entire Lake Champlain Valley sector.

Therefore, with La Durantaye and his French, Indians, and Canadians close behind them, Rogers drove his men harder through the clinging mud and muck of the stinking swamps. Day after day, the major continued to push his men onward through the spruce bogs of acidic water the color of coffee: up every morning before sunrise and marching at a pace of less than ten miles per day, then continuing to push onward through the mire even after the sun dipped below the horizon. But since the men knew that their lives were at stake, Rogers had to rely less on inspirational example and encouraging words than usual. Most important, everyone continued to move onward at a steady pace in the hope of preserving their lives, which called for fulfilling their mission of destroying St. Francis (where storehouses of food could be gained) as soon as possible.

Thoroughly soaked men, sweating in the unseasonable heat so near the St. Lawrence River in late September, steadily trudged through the seemingly endless bogs, which were bordered by towering spruce trees on the flat horizon on all sides. To some trekkers, especially men from New England's mountains, it must have seemed like they were floundering onward in the muddy bottom of a watery bowl that they could not see beyond. Major Rogers hoped to strike the south bank of the St. Francis River at some point downstream from the town that stood on the north bank, which would allow him to follow the river north to his target about three miles south of the St. Lawrence River.

All the while, Rogers and his men might have wondered about the paradox of the sight of so many spruce trees that grew in such profusion in this wet, lower ground unlike in New England. After all, clumps of spruce trees of New England were normally located at higher elevations, including the White and Green Mountains, where the hardwood forests ceased to be supplemented by spruce forests. For ample good reason, the exhausted Rangers, Provincials, and British Regulars cursed the stinking bog that made their lives miserable with every step forward, with mud clinging to feet that tripped over submerged roots and logs that could not be seen below the surface of the acidic waters.

Fortunately for the major and his faithful followers, who continued to toil north as if following the North Star, they were now following the needle of Rogers's trusty compass that pointed directly to his objective. The seventy-five-mile flowing waters of the St. Francis, after rising in a mountainous lake to the northeast, angled northwest toward St. Francis to deviate from their usual north-south course, resulting in an overall *V*-shape from beginning to end at the St. Lawrence. This meant that Rogers could strike the river when it made its final descent just before reaching St. Francis and then the St. Lawrence just to the north and its valley filled with a narrow stretch of farmlands owned by hardscrabble Canadian and French agriculturalists.

But Rogers had no idea that this desperate race northward would take a total of nine grueling days, which turned out to be a living nightmare for his slogging followers, who only dreamed of reaching dry land. For Rogers and his men to win this life-and-death race from a tide of angry pursuers, they would have to cover more than fifty miles, from beginning to end, of mostly spruce bogs. This water-soaked land was one of mystery to whites and even the Abenaki, who possessed the good sense to not venture into such a nightmarish region. Even more, the desperate race of Rogers and his men to St. Francis might yet prove to be folly, because the French might have set up an ambush at St. Francis. Rogers could only hope that St. Francis had not been reinforced, assuming French leadership had correctly determined his ultimate target in Quebec's wilds.

With energy and stamina running low, the exhausted men floundered through the nightmarish spruce bogs, whose dark waters lacked sparkling clarity, unlike the spring-fed streams and rivers of Rogers's native Merrimack River Valley. All the while, the inevitable wear and tear on the wool uniforms, buckskin leggings, and moccasins of Rogers's men continued to take a toll during the arduous trek that was destined to last for a full week and a half. Fortunately, however, Major Rogers had long ago made a series of smart decisions to meet the stiff challenges of the hellish trek through an uncharted wilderness, almost as if he had somehow anticipated gaining Amherst's approval for this mission, well before even that of Kennedy and Hamilton. At the cost of nearly 340 pounds (Colony of New York currency) on credit—later reimbursed by the British government—he had made sure that his men were well equipped and supplied with as much new gear as possible.

Significantly, Rogers knew the supreme importance of gaining a new issuance of durable gear, which was almost as valuable as ample combat experience, for the stern challenges that lay ahead. He therefore had spared no expense in good New York currency in providing four hundred pairs of new moccasins (two for each Ranger), and the accompanying two pairs of footings for each man to fit snugly inside each moccasin for added durability in trekking through the wilderness. The Rangers' footwear of choice from the beginning, these deer leather moccasins were comfortable but snug, even for the Scottish volunteers from Colonel Montgomery's Highland regiment. After all, the Indian moccasin closely resembled a soft Scottish Highland shoe known to generations of Celts as the *cuaran*.

Thinking ahead as usual, Rogers also purchased two hundred pairs of thigh-high deerskin Indian leggings (to replace worn-out ones whenever necessary during the trek north), which distinguished Rangers from other troops in the British-Provincial Army. This special Native American feature of the typical Ranger attire provided good protection against thick underbrush, especially thorn bushes, and sharp tree branches when trekking through the woodlands.

Best of all, these tough and durable deerskin leggings were light, unlike most standard army-issue clothing. More important, Rogers had purchased a supply of 202 new hatchets, or tomahawks, with matching leather cases, and the Rangers had also been issued these new weapons and other essential new gear needed for inevitable hand-to-hand combat in the upcoming attack on St. Francis.[62]

Because he knew that his mission would be so demanding on every level, Rogers also made sure that his men wore the more durable high-topped moccasins with sturdier soles rather than the low-topped moccasins for summer use—a switch for cooler and more inclement weather that might well spell the difference between victory and defeat at the final climactic moment of the upcoming attack, while also ensuring that Rogers's men were able to more quickly reach their long-anticipated objective of St. Francis.[63]

VENGEFUL FRENCH LEADERS

But, of course, not all the new equipment in the world to enhance combat capabilities would make any difference if Rogers and his men encountered a large force of the enemy, especially when aligned in a traditional crescent-shaped ambush. After the discovery of the hidden whaleboats at Missisquoi Bay, and as noted, the word had gone out far and wide that an audacious force of Englishmen was on the loose deep in their own territory. Governor-General Vaudreuil, in Montreal, would write on October 3 with confidence, "I have sent all the St. Francis Abenakis and a number of sturdy Canadians out in search of the English who were in these barges," or whaleboats.[64]

The Canada-born governor, who hated Protestant settlers and their endless encroachments on French lands, desired nothing more than to have Rogers and his followers destroyed to the last man by his favorite fighting soldiers, the sharpshooting Canadians and the well-trained fighters of La Marine, because they were not only more lethal but also more blood-thirsty, like the Native American warriors.[65]

As mentioned, Governor-General Vaudreuil also ordered the best of the Canadian militia, including hardened frontiersmen who had been raised in the northern woodlands, to link with the St. Francis Abenaki, who had been part of Quebec's defenders before the city was recently captured by Wolfe, to destroy the audacious raiders. This contingent of Canadian militia was sent to join the Abenaki from both the town of St. Francis and the mission community of Becancour, located on the south side of the St. Lawrence across from Trois-Rivières on the river's north side, to destroy the raiders should they attempt to attack Becancour.[66]

Seemingly everyone had flown into action with the startling news. General François-Gaston de Lévis, who was of "poor but noble birth" and now extremely eager to wipe out every single English soldier who had dared to penetrate so deeply into New France, thoroughly mocking the celebrated level of French intelligence, wrote to the governor of Trois-Rivières to dispatch troops to St. Francis before it was too late.[67]

The likelihood existed that Rogers and his command would be destroyed in totality in a matter of days, because it seemed as if he and his men were trapped on three sides because of the rapid reaction of the French leadership, especially the governor-general of Canada. Like other leaders, Governor-General Vaudreuil felt that any interlopers north of Missisquoi Bay and so far from Lake Champlain could be easily destroyed by multiple task forces of experienced fighting men. The governor and other French leaders believed that they had developed a good plan to nab the English raiders and end their lofty ambitions on the sacred soil of their beloved Quebec.

First, it was assumed by some French leaders that the raiders would not be able to cross the St. Francis River, which was Rogers's most formidable natural obstacle, especially because it was swollen by recent rains. Therefore, it seemed to them that St. Francis was safe and secure, unlike Yamaska, which was also known as Wigwam Martinique and located just to the southwest by about half a dozen miles. And, as noted, they were convinced that these English raiders would follow the same route that had been taken by the ill-fated members of the Kennedy-Hamilton party down the Yamaska River and its lush valley, because this was the most direct route to take for descending upon St. Francis, if that might be the target and not Yamaska.

But outthinking the enemy, Rogers also early realized as much, which had made him even more determined to have embarked upon another route of his own making that the enemy possessed no knowledge about—straight through the spruce bogs that were considered impassable and the last place on earth that an Englishman would go. After all, part of Rogers's amazing successes year after year were the result of his uncanny sixth sense and well-honed instincts to get into the minds of his opponents and anticipate their next move, while keeping them guessing and off balance.

This unique quality of a true great captain had already served Rogers extremely well during this mission that had already defied all expectations, because the French leadership had decided not to reinforce St. Francis in the mistaken belief that no raiders would dare march so far north—it was simply impossible, or so it seemed. They believed the raiders could be easily ambushed on the march in their anticipated attack on Yamaska or Becancour. Clearly, Rogers had not only fooled his opponents but also outsmarted them by staying away from the risky Yamaska route, because he made the necessary decisions to negate their best leadership decisions without firing a shot in anger. Rogers's uncanny ability to outwit his experienced and older opponents should have given him renown as the "Wilderness Fox" of the French and Indian War.

Therefore, a large force of Abenaki, including some warriors from St. Francis (most of whom had originally been dispatched to help to defend Quebec earlier in the year), and "the elite of the colony's [Canadian] militiamen" were now patiently waiting in ambush (ironically, like Ensign Langy and his idle task force at Missisquoi Bay) at Yamaska less than ten miles to the southwest, while Ensign La Durantaye and his vengeful Canadians,

Indians, and Frenchmen continued their relentless pursuit behind Rogers's steadily trudging men to fulfill their lust to slaughter the hated Rangers.[68]

ROGERS'S NEVER-SAY-DIE ATTITUDE

Now, when facing their ultimate crisis situation and pushing steadily north through the forbidden terrain of the nightmarish swamps, the task force of 149 Rangers, Provincials, and Regulars continued onward with visions of a future victory looming ahead, after the departure of McMullen's contingent of seven men. The Scotch-Irish major now possessed two key advantages that were destined to prove invaluable. First and foremost, Rogers's inspirational leadership was a key factor that enabled the men of different backgrounds, multiple branches of the service, radically differing regional and national attitudes, and races—a truly disparate fighting force of Indians, blacks, and whites from across the colonies and both sides of the Atlantic—to come together as one in believing the Rogers-inspired faith that they would succeed in their secret mission to destroy the very foundation of France's most loyal and lethal Indian ally and then get back safely with newly won laurels.

Quite simply, in a reciprocal way, Rogers believed in not only his Rangers but also his collective group of Britons and Provincials, whom he had handpicked for this special mission, like no other such integrated force that he had commanded in the past because of their overall high quality and high motivation. And in a reciprocal relationship that in itself was special, these fighting men believed in him, especially in regard to his making the right decisions in order to secure the final decisive victory and then getting them back home alive and well. As a lower-class product of the frontier and the son of immigrant parents, Major Rogers made sure that no social, class, economic, or racial distinctions fostered any hint that this unique and divergent group of fighting men was anything less than a band of brothers.

From the beginning, Rogers's inspirational leadership style had already heightened the overall unity among these mostly lower-class men, including a good many Scotch-Irish. Rogers not only was admired and respected to a degree not enjoyed by other leaders but also served as a benevolent father figure to the young men and boys in the ranks. In fact, they fairly idolized the brash and confident major, who never gave up once he had embarked upon a mission, regardless of the difficulties encountered along the way.

Despite this task force's consisting of so many different individuals from a wide variety of units of the British and Provincial armies, they were bonded by the knowledge that they were the best fighting men in Amherst's army. In the midst of severe adversity and hardship in toiling through the knee-deep waters of the spruce bogs, the well-honed esprit de corps of Rogers's command—a direct reflection of the major's outstanding leadership abilities—remained surprisingly high among these men who were on the most dangerous mission of their lives. For the volunteers, they had undergone something like a transformation that had come from serving beside the legendary Rangers and their famous commander.

While they trudged wearily through the cold waters of the spruce bogs, knowing that an unkind fate had seemingly trapped them in a no-win situation that seemingly spelled their doom, these young men and boys gamely kept their faith in the future. They hoped for the best and prayed silently to God that he would bless them with the sweet taste of victory in the days ahead. After all, St. Francis had been long viewed as the epitome of evil, and they saw themselves as righteous warriors, like the Crusaders to the Holy Land long ago. Therefore, Rogers and his men, most faithfully read the pages of the Holy Bible, felt that God was on their side and would not betray them in their darkest hour.

Forged in countless fights in an uncharted wilderness with the cruelest of enemies in America's most brutal war, the Rangers were members of a special fraternity of elite fighting men, and they were proud of that fact. There was an air of desperation about the Rangers that was one forgotten factor that made them elite fighting men who combined toughness and high morale. Like Rogers, the Rangers possessed a certain cockiness that made them believe that the setbacks which they had already encountered could be overcome with a superior fighting spirit and sheer determination.

The rest of Amherst's army had long known as much, resulting in jealousy among British officers, including commanders like Colonel William Haviland, who denounced the Rangers with the deep-seated contempt of the members of the English upper class, who were known for their hatred of the lowly Irish and the Scotch-Irish from the conquered Emerald Isle. The arrogant colonel had denounced the Rangers as nothing more than a "Riotous sort of people" (another way of basically saying that they were Scotch-Irish, an innuendo not lost on Rogers, who basked in his ethnic heritage) and not worthy to serve his majesty.[69]

But, of course, Rogers knew much better than members of the the British ruling class, because he judged men only on their personal abilities and skills, not their social status, family background, or color. Beyond the myths and romantic legends that have long glorified the Rangers to no end, they were in truth hardened professional killers: a quality now especially appreciated by the major and necessary for another successful mission as expected by headquarters and by people across the colonies. During this most daring of missions far from support of any kind, Rogers swore without exaggeration that he "never saw a better Command of Officers and Men" than at this time.[70]

But now some of these mud-streaked Rangers struggling through the boggy wilderness worried if their ultimate fate was destined to be that of many of the surrendered men of Fort William Henry, when the "Indian Blood Hounds [were let] loose upon our People [to massacre soldiers and civilians and even engaged] in the Murder of all the Sick and wounded" in the hospital.[71] If so, as often evident after past fights against a merciless foe in the wilderness, then almost certainly the triumphant warriors, especially those from St. Francis, would leave the "Bodies [of the Rangers] cruelly mangled [and] their Heads cut off and stuck on Poles."[72]

All the while, despite the recent setbacks that had now placed them in such serious jeopardy when so deep in Quebec, the Rangers continued onward with an undying faith in their commander and the ultimate success of their far-flung mission into the dark heart of New France. While following the relentless major, who seemed to never tire or get hungry, to wherever he led them through these seemingly unending spruce bogs, these tough-minded men were proving that they were the antithesis of a "Riotous sort of people" at a time when it counted the most.

This blind, unthinking faith of Rogers's men in their dynamic frontier leader had been well placed, while he was leading them deeper into Canada. Even more, Rogers continued to draw the best traits and qualities from his followers when the going got especially tough, which was now in trudging through the stifling spruce bogs with the enemy in fast pursuit. As usual, the young major led by example, which was now especially important in encouraging his men onward and keeping faith in ultimate success. Despite hell and high water, Rogers always marched at the forefront to inspire his mud-streaked and soaked men, who kept following behind the major farther into the vast unknown of the eerie spruce bogs that stretched all the way north to the St. Francis River Valley.

As the miserable setbacks had continued to pile up to a level that would have discouraged any other commander, who almost certainly would have aborted the mission and embarked upon the journey home in angry frustration, Rogers only became more determined to succeed in reaching St. Francis at any cost: the rarest of leadership qualities that served as a source of inspiration to the men in the ranks. The major's men marveled at his most admirable qualities, which forged a bond with their rough-hewn leader that encouraged them to keep moving straight north: Rogers's never-say-die determination to finally obtain his longtime goal had only been intensified by the seemingly insurmountable obstacles that he had already encountered, as it would be by the unknown nasty surprises he would inevitably encounter in the future.

Even in this most desperate of situations—a winner-take-all race to outmarch his dogged pursuers when his precious provisions and whaleboats for the return trip to safety had been lost—failed to dampen Rogers's spirits. All the while, Rogers was consumed with a laser-like focus on his target. The harsh forge of adversity and string of bad luck only steeled the resolve deep inside him to persevere against all the odds, while bringing out the best in Rogers both as a man and as a leader.

And now, amid the watery nightmare of the muddy spruce bogs, when it seemed like this was the darkest of times for the expeditionary force under Rogers's care, when the Canadians, Indians, and French, under Ensigns Langy and La Durantaye, were already gloating about the inevitable end of "the famous" major, who was the hero of not only New England but also the colonies in general, Rogers was now actually at his best. His eager enemies fondly envisioned how many fresh scalps they would shortly take, including that of the major himself. However, to thwart such lofty enemy ambitions, Rogers continued to be at his most resourceful and innovative to defy expectations. The awful knowledge persisted that the pursuing enemy was lusting for the long-sought opportunity to kill as many Rangers as possible in the most horrific manner, including ritualistic torture when the Ranger victims had been tied to trees and burned at the stake for amusement: a harsh realization that only fortified Rogers with greater resolve to thwart the enemy's best-laid plans to end his career in the most inglorious fashion.

Indeed, in such a no-win situation that seemed to have no solutions, Rogers should have been discouraged, especially when he and his men were completely exhausted, wearing tattered, dirt-streaked uniforms and covered in scratches from underbrush and thorn bushes. Some of Rogers's men had already succumbed to a dark mental state, being at the end of their rope. However, Rogers remained upbeat and cheerful when the going got especially tough. While encouraging everyone onward through the mire, he cracked jokes and repeated old Scotch-Irish and frontier witticisms, beaming a broad smile that brought smiles in return.

With the arrival of each new day, the same weary routine continued for the major's followers. The difficult trek, seemingly always harder than the previous day, began before daylight and ended only when daylight faded away in the dark spruce bogs to the sounds of croaking frogs and night birds. All that anyone knew was that St. Francis lay somewhere on the distant northern horizon, which remained flat and lined with spruce trees to guarantee some disorientation among Rogers's men seemingly trapped in an untamed wilderness.

All the while, Rogers continued to issue forth all manner of encouragement to instill his trademark never-say-die spirit in others in tones that were just loud enough for his men to hear above the continuous sound of splashing bog water. Rogers steadily motioned for everyone to continue to move onward and even faster through the mire during a life-or-death race to reach St. Francis, before being overcome by revenge-seeking pursuers who wanted to forever end the distinguished legacy of Rogers's Rangers in the remoteness of the dismal spruce bogs.

FAMILIAL BONDS AND FORGING A NASCENT AMERICANISM

However, it was much more than simply Rogers's leadership ability that kept everyone moving onward with hopes for a successful outcome, despite all the setbacks that seemed to have no end. During this crisis time, the firm ties of community, friendship, and family bonded these young men and boys tightly and kept the Rangers together and optimistic during the arduous trek north through the spruce bogs. Many of Rogers's men were close friends, neighbors, and relatives who had grown up together in the frontier communities of northern New England, especially in the largely Scotch-Irish communities like Derryfield (today's Manchester in southcentral New Hampshire), which were nestled into the picturesque beauty of the Merrimack River Valley.[73]

Of course, ties of blood were some of the firmest bonds among the Rangers, such as between Captain James Tute and his brother Amos Tute. James Tute was held in high esteem by Rogers and Major General Amherst. The two brothers had embarked on the 1759 campaign and remained closely together just like when they had grown up together in Hardwick, west of Boston in central Massachusetts, with loving parents, James and Kezia Tute.[74]

Likewise, Massachusetts-born Captain Joseph Wait, who was Rogers's second in command in the absence of Captain John Stark, who remained behind at Crown Point to command around two hundred Rangers (whom Rogers now desperately needed if a large fight now suddenly erupted in Quebec), and his Massachusetts-born brother Sergeant Benjamin Wait also inspired their men ever northward through the swamps. They were destined to fight at St. Francis and stay together during the difficult journey home. The Wait brothers, who hailed from the wilds of frontier New Hampshire, were two of the finest Rangers in Rogers's command, having displayed courage and leadership abilities in the past.[75]

Almost as much as the fact that they were united by a deep bond, a high-spirited sense of camaraderie, their Protestant faith, especially Presbyterianism, and a sky-high esprit de corps, these mostly Scotch-Irish Rangers were also fused together by a powerful emotional and psychological ethnic tie: the fact that they were free citizens of the British Empire and also Americans, or the cousins of the Britons. And, as mentioned, they were also united in a mutual desire for revenge, ensuring that they were about to deliver a devastating blow much like the ones long unleashed by countless Abenaki war parties on the isolated settlements in a classic case of poetic justice and karma coming full circle.

But these seasoned expeditioners in soiled buckskin, hunter's garb, and short green coats that blended in so well with the landscape were also unique in still another way. When the Abenaki and other Native American allies, who had long trekked south down their historic war paths—first along the St. Francis River and then the Connecticut River (the basis of the planned route of Rogers's 1756 raid on St. Francis)—had struck exceptionally hard, they had often been accompanied by experienced French marines and younger marine cadets, who were mostly Canada-born, leading the way. Just like the cadets who had long served in Rogers's ranks, these French cadets were training on the job to become officers. These highly motivated Frenchmen were now devoted to destroying every last Ranger on the soil of Quebec with relish.

Battle-hardened members of independent companies (ironically, Rogers's men were also members of independent Ranger companies within the British army), these well-trained French marines of the Compagnies Franches de la Marine (better known as La Marine) had been recruited by France's Ministry of the Marine. In contrast, the men of Rogers's command were quite the opposite compared to the overall composition of the war parties even now lying in ambush or pursuing them: not a majority of Indians with relatively few whites but a hardened strike force of mostly whites with only a few Indian allies—the Stockbridge Mohegan Ranger "Wolves."[76]

Most important, during long-distance missions, what Rogers and his men were even now in the process of helping to create was a distinctive sense of a nascent American nationalism, because the major had evolved into an authentic wartime hero across the colonies by this time, America's first. And although the Rangers served in the British army in separate, independent companies, they possessed a distinctive look, manner, and style that was uniquely American and all their own.

They had long been incorrectly seen as nothing more than misfits and "outsiders" by the British Regulars and their elitist officers, but the development of a separate identity and esprit de corps was due more to the rise of their distinctive Americanism, because they now represented the heart and soul of America. Therefore, the people of the home front, especially along the frontier, expected great things from the Rangers. However, no one could conceive that these young men and boys were now on the grueling march to St. Francis. By this time, Rogers and his Rangers symbolized America and represented a distinct and unique identity of a can-do soldiery to an entire generation of colonists.

For such reasons, Major Rogers was well known across the colonies as "the famous scouter," and the people of America were extremely proud of this inspirational New Hampshire frontiersman and his unorthodox fighting men who fought like Indians and outsmarted them in their home territory.[77] Despite all the setbacks of this seemingly ill-fated mission, Rogers was now in the process of overcoming all adversity and enhancing his already high reputation, while orchestrating the most daring raid of the French and Indian War, one that "would live in history."[78]

THE NIGHTMARISH ORDEAL CONTINUES

Meanwhile, the harrowing ordeal of trekking through the vast expanse of Quebec's eerie swamplands, which looked like a primeval landscape straight out of prehistoric times, could not have been more difficult for Rogers's men day after day. For most of the distance of around one hundred miles that had to be trekked to reach their objective on the north bank of the St. Francis River, Rogers and his followers continued to trudge through the thorn bushes, thickets, and watery spaces of the nightmarish spruce bogs. The swamps, on average, contained around a foot of dark water, which smelled of decay and rot because they consisted of a stagnant drain-off without freshwater, except for rainfall.

For the weary expeditioners in tattered uniforms from both sides of the Atlantic, each halt called by Rogers after darkness fell finally provided the Rangers, Provincials, and Regulars with well-deserved rest amid a hellish landscape. The ever-dwindling supply of meager rations of now-soggy dried beef, cornmeal, and sausage were taken out of packs and eagerly consumed by ravenous men, who had been pushed to the limits of human endurance by this time.[79]

Then, even before the first light of day began to peep over the low eastern horizon and through the tall spruce trees before the cold of another late September night had faded away, the Rangers were up and on move in the early morning darkness, when cold mists still hung over the bogs to reduce visibility even after the dawn. At a steady pace, they surged through the cold waters of the swamps while Rogers implored his men to move faster; there was no time to lose as St. Francis to the north beckoned. As usual, Rogers was in front, leading the way through the stinky waters filled with rotting vegetation, heading steadily toward a rendezvous with destiny on the St. Francis River.

With time of the essence, when the French, Indians, and Canadians, under Ensign La Durantaye, were very likely close behind them, for all they knew, with sharpened knives and a lust to take the scalps of Rogers and his men, the daily toil through the swamps often continued in the cold darkness and half-freezing water after sunset, when the major sought to cover as much ground as possible, before settling in for the night.

Occasionally during the grueling trek north, they spied a bald eagle, an osprey hunting for fish, a flock of fast-flying ducks, or a majestic, chevron-shaped formation of Canadian geese—easily identified even at night by Rogers's men from a chorus of honking in the distance—high in the fall sky heading south in their own race (like Rogers's own but in the opposite direction), before the arrival of harsh winter weather descended upon the land. No doubt, Rogers's slogging men must have wished to have the ability to fly forever out of the miserable cold wetness of the spruce bogs, while they sneezed and coughed from the ill effects of the increasingly cold weather. Knowing only too well that a cruel fate had turned against them as they suffered from fever, chills, and hypothermia, Rogers's exhausted men thought of home so far away and wondered whether they would see it or their families ever again. At this time, Rogers's followers could not imagine how few of them would ever return from this mission into the dark heart of Quebec.

But at least the thoughts of loved ones, mothers, siblings, wives, and fathers kept these men somehow moving onward through the swampy muck that filled nostrils with a suffocating stench, even when it seemed like the weary process of simply putting one foot before the other in trudging through the watery quagmire was no longer possible for these totally exhausted Rangers, Provincials, and Regulars. But somehow these men kept going and followed the major, who was still in the lead, knowing now that they were headed for St. Francis because of the number of mind-numbing days spent in pushing north toward a great prize situated in the middle of a vast wilderness: a realization that had lifted spirits to fuel a faster pace.

Sleeping amid the haunting landscape of the spruce bogs during these eerie nights, which were cold and damp, called for considerable resourcefulness among the raiders. Crude but effective floating rafts were created by cutting saplings and then setting moss and underbrush in place to form a makeshift green mattress. These were carefully fashioned on the major's orders to keep men dry and, hence, healthy. At night, half of the command slept, and the other half remained alert and ready for a surprise attack, while the loons' eerie calls that sounded like a mournful lament and the repeated chorus of hoots from the great horned owls high in the spruce trees echoed over the swamp.

These frontier-style stationary "rafts"—basically temporary hammocks—kept the men relatively warm, while they slept above the bog's stinking waters of dark brown, especially after the weather turned even colder, accompanied by high winds, on September 29. Sleep came easily to these thoroughly exhausted men, who needed rest to replenish worn bodies (which had been wet all day) and to restore energy for the next day's ordeal. Rogers's men dreamed of homes and lovers they might never see again, or they suddenly awakened in a cold sweat from a fever-induced nightmare in which an Abenaki warrior was scalping them alive. But it could even be worse for a captured Ranger, as the grizzled veterans from past campaigning with Rogers fully realized. At least Rogers and his men were thankful to be safe from the swarms of biting mosquitoes, gnats, and black flies that tortured a man in spring and summer to no end. The first killing freeze of the early autumn had already descended on this land on a previous night to relieve them of the presence of these troublesome pests.[80]

Then, at long last, and unbeknownst to them, Rogers and his men supremely benefited from the major's decision to trek through the spruce bogs in the most hoped-for development of all. Ensign La Durantaye and his men, including the best Abenaki scouts, who had been doggedly tracking Rogers since ordered to do so by General Bourlamaque from Missisquoi Bay to the southwest, were simply unable to follow the nonexistent tracks of the Rangers through the bog's dark waters and black mire.

By this time, the hunger pangs had grown severe, as some wet and mud-splattered soldiers had consumed their rations far too quickly. Rogers's men could only curse the disturbing fact that more rations had not been brought with them, especially after they had been destroyed along with the whaleboats by the French. Consequently, famished soldiers even ate what little remained of their deerskin moccasins after they had consumed all their provisions, despite Rogers's repeated warnings about the wisdom of moderation when it came to eating their limited rations.

As careful as during a typical approach on Fort Carillon in an intelligence-gathering mission as so often in the past, Major Rogers had early issued orders neither to leave anything behind, such as broken branches, nor to step on rare spots of dry land to leave behind a footprint while toiling through the spruce bogs, which would provide telltale clues for pursuers: orders that had already paid dividends by frustrating the pursuers. To the pursuing French, Indians, and Canadians, it had seemed as if the raiders had vanished off the face of the earth.

Prospects for a successful mission were looking up. As noted, a frustrated La Durantaye, unable to ascertain Rogers's route or location, reluctantly ordered his pursuit to end. Clearly, Rogers had gotten the better of this respected partisan chieftain, demonstrating his wisdom in having decided to take his command into the worst possible landscape to pass through in all Quebec. If Rogers had known of this thankful development when Ensign La Durantaye finally called it quits after much effort that had proven in vain, he would have almost certainly celebrated to some extent on two accounts: the merciful ending of the pursuit and having bested the veteran partisan leader La Durantaye.[81]

In his journal, a frustrated Captain Nicholas des Meloizes, who was part of Ensign La Durantaye's pursuit party, which had finally been forced to return to Isle-aux-Noix with regrets at having been outwitted by Rogers, wrote how they had not discovered "anything" about this mysterious group of English raiders, who had come from so far away and seemingly out of nowhere to have magically appeared on Missisquoi Bay and then vanished into thin air. All the while, Rogers and his men now continued to push toward St. Francis with a mixture of confidence and an audacious impunity, while assuming that they were still being followed.[82]

As planned, Rogers's desperate gamble of entering the watery vastness of the unmapped spruce bogs had actually proved a godsend that covered his tracks and disguised his movements to ensure that the command could not be followed by some of the best Abenaki trackers. Time and time again, the analytical major had tactically outthought his pursuers and eluded the well-conceived ambushes cleverly setup by the enemy to destroy the expedition.

But, of course, the men of Rogers's command paid the highest personal price for having escaped the pursuers since embarking on this harrowing ordeal in the spruce bogs. By this time, the men had lost considerable amounts of energy and physical capability, which translated into diminished overall combat capabilities, when fighting lay ahead at St. Francis in a bloody reckoning that they eagerly anticipated. However, that made no difference to the major, whose top priority had been to outrace the vigorous pursuit, and this feat had been accomplished, when it had seemed as if no hope remained.[83]

All the while, Rogers maintained the correct bearing of marching directly north in steadily approaching his target, thanks to his trusty compass located at the bottom of his powder horn. But if something bad happened to Rogers during this arduous trek straight north, or he and his compass became lost, the far-flung command could still move in the proper direction, because, according to one contemporary account, the Ranger "officers usually carr[ied] a small compass fixed in the bottom of their powderhorns, by which to direct them" at all times.[84]

Lost Men Who Died in the Spruce Bogs: The Forgotten Casualties

Meanwhile, danger was an omnipresent factor even when no enemy was nearby. Major Rogers was destined to lose more men in the maze of the swamp bogs—7 in total to reduce the command to 142 men—than in the attack on St. Francis. With the merciful relief of darkness after each day's march, bringing much-needed rest of the worn expeditioners after the continuation of their daily agonizing ordeal, Rogers and his officers then called roll to make sure that everyone was present, an event met with greater dread with each passing day, and for good reason. It was at this time, in the early darkness that descended like a curtain over the spruce bogs, after the men had marched all day from sunup to sundown, that the awful truth became known about who had failed to make it to the night's cold bivouac amid the swamps in the depths of Quebec.

During the seemingly endless trek of pushing ever onward in a northerly direction with limited visibility when surrounded by a green wall of tall spruce trees, few, if any, Rangers knew which of their comrades had gradually weakened physically and psychologically or become injured during their silent individual treks. Hour after hour, the men became more widely separated in toiling through the dank waters, while suffering under the midday heat and searing sun. By that time, the foremost task among the slogging soldiers was simply performing the task of taking one step at a time through the morass of mud and cold water.

Experienced Rangers, even the strongest men, were primarily focused on the simple goal—challenging in itself under the circumstances—of attempting to keep up with the seemingly tireless major, who continued to lead the way, as if not weary in the least. Less durable Rangers, which was almost everyone at this point, marveled at Rogers's seemingly endless stamina, as he never seemed to tire throughout the ordeal.

Therefore, with each soldier engaged in his own personal struggle in pushing forward at a brisk pace, no one had noticed if a man suddenly fell behind or was hurt—for instance, suffering a nasty cut on the bottom of the foot or injuring a leg. Such injuries meant that the unfortunate soldier became hobbled and slowed his pace, gradually losing contact with the rear-most Rangers—a virtual death sentence. And, of course, Rogers never saw what was developing in the rear or who had fallen far behind because he continued to lead the way in the front throughout the expedition.

Fever, disease, and lameness proved fatal to some men, who could go no farther. Even a slight injury to the bottom of the foot or a cut on a toe could cause a Ranger to start to limp and then fall farther behind the main body. It is not known, but the possibility existed that a kind comrade might have mercifully put an end to the life of a dying or injured man to spare him the cruel fate of capture, torture, or perhaps even being scalped alive by a cruel enemy who showed no mercy.

In toiling through the acidic water of a dark color, which alone might have led to a fatal sickness if swallowed, an injury to a foot or leg then became infected and more painful with each step, until a soldier could go no farther north from where the flights of Canadian geese continued to depart with winter's cold on the way to a pristine land draped with bright autumn colors—reds, yellows, and oranges—unlike the dreary spruce trees of dark green. Because of the flatness of Quebec's forbidding terrain and the density of the stands of spruce trees growing in the so-called Drowned Lands, which had been created millions of years ago by an ancient sea, no one could see for a long distance amid the thick vegetation and green oppressiveness that was claustrophobic.

A veteran Ranger, Provincial, or British Regular was not seen if he suddenly dropped from exhaustion or even fainted from excessive hunger after having early consumed all his supply of rations or from weariness in the September afternoon heat to sink below the dark waters, especially if he had been limping from a foot or leg injury after having tripped over a submerged root or log. Even the slightest cut on the bottom of the foot or toe, especially the big toe on either foot, caused imbalance and disability.

Or if a deerskin moccasin was lost in the sucking muck, or cut by a submerged root or sharp branch, or simply fell apart from having been wet for so long, then a Ranger had only one replacement in his pack. If both pairs of moccasins became unusable or lost, then a Ranger could go no farther. And if such misfortunates happened, then a tragedy resulted: a completely worn-down trekker simply could no longer keep up with his comrades, lingered ever farther in the rear, and then became lost in the spruce bog, because he could not see the rear of the command or follow his comrades' tracks. And no one who moved onward before these unfortunate victims, lingering ever farther behind, could see their tragic plights when far to the rear and while darkness descended over the land. The unlucky Ranger then eventually succumbed to a lonely death in the alternating dense growth and watery expanse of spruce bogs, while the rest of Rogers's followers continued to move onward as fast as possible through the morass.

Thereafter, just a lonely blue Scottish bonnet—only worn by the Rangers, especially those men of Scotch-Irish descent from the northern frontier—or perhaps a fur or leather cap floated atop the bog's dark waters to tell a tragic tale of a new widow and orphans back home in some remote settlement or frontier log cabin situated on an isolated hilltop in the wilderness. Like Rogers, the Scotch-Irish soldiers in the ranks certainly appreciated the symbolic significance of wearing Scotch bonnets even at this time during their greatest challenge. This unique soldier headgear reminded these Celtic warriors of their distinctive ethnic and cultural heritage, the many struggles (especially for freedom) of their ancestors from Scotland and Ulster Province, north Ireland, while engendering a sense of pride in themselves and their long-suffering people, who had persevered on both sides of the Atlantic.

Again, the fear that the Indians, Canadians, and French were pursuing close behind Rogers's men kept everyone moving at a brisk pace, except the exhausted and hurt soldiers, who fell even farther behind with each passing hour. Fortunately, to maintain the proper direction, Rogers and his top officers continued to rely on their compasses. However, the average enlisted man possessed no compass. Therefore, when he fell behind in the nightmarish spruce bogs, the common soldier was truly lost and on his own in a strange land in which everything looked the same.

In the time-honored tradition of a frontiersman always keeping his black powder dry above all else, a compass in the butt end of the powder horn was least likely to get wet during a heavy rainfall. Danger only came for this powder reserve when a soldier fell completely underwater in the swamp after losing his footing in the spruce bog's dark waters, laced with a crisscrossing maze of submerged roots of trees, or amid clumps of vines or water lilies that ensnared feet in the shallows. In contrast to top Ranger officers, the average common soldier and enlisted man in Rogers's command, without a compass, faced a serious liability that might well have cost more than one life.

For all practical purposes, consequently, it was over when a soldier lost sight of the fast-moving rear of Rogers's expeditioners, who continued to push northward with a relentless determination. While Rogers's men wearily trekked through murky waters—tea colored from the nearby tall spruce trees, clumps of underbrush, and thick vegetation—some of these young men and boys increasingly thought of God and family, neither of whom could help then. Therefore, it was easy for even healthy men to tire out and then lose sight of their comrades. Especially during a cold downpour of rain, additional soldiers lagged behind because they were unable to follow the tracks of those men who had gone before them. After all, and as noted, this situation of leaving no tracks behind them that could be followed had been Rogers's primary reason for having entered the unmapped vastness of the spruce bogs in the first place. All traces of the command's movements were now hidden under the expanse of dark waters, as the major had envisioned from the beginning.

Clearly, Rogers had been correct in having chosen his smart strategy for the march to St. Francis along the route least anticipated by the enemy. And this requirement meant trudging through the spruce bogs that acted like a protective cushion that had safely separated him from his eager pursuers, who wanted nothing more than to cut the throat of a hated Ranger before Ensign La Durantaye decided to turn back. Consequently, the arduous push through the spruce bogs for more than a week was very much about winning a life-or-death race to St. Francis to escape pursuers.

However, and as noted, Rogers's bold decision was nothing less than a death sentence for his most exhausted and injured men (seven in total), who never reached the night's encampment on different days. In what was actually a cruel Darwinian exercise of the survival of the fittest, which separated the weakest from the strongest men in the ranks, these unfortunate soldiers simply disappeared forever in the cold wetness of the spruce bogs. They were never seen again by their comrades or families far away.

Overwhelmed with exhaustion, these lost and injured soldiers, who could not keep up with their comrades who continued to move as fast as they could through the morass, were the forgotten casualties of Rogers's raid on St. Francis. And, as Rogers and the hardier survivors knew, it was already too late to go back and search for lost comrades who never reached the night's bivouac amid the hellish bogs. Almost as discouragingly, the Quebec swamps provided little protection from the night's biting cold of late September, which told Rogers's men that Old Man Winter was on the way and would arrive more than a month earlier than in their New England homeland.

Far from home, friends, and family, these seven unfortunate men, who found themselves all alone behind the main body, died slow, agonizing deaths amid a vast expanse of the wet lowlands: the gloomiest of all surroundings for the tragic ending of good men. The remains of these forgotten soldiers, who succumbed to lonely deaths during the most famous raid of the French and Indian War, were never recovered. Today, the bones of these seven soldiers— Rangers, Provincials, or British Regulars—still rest in peace at unknown places in the trackless swamps of Quebec, after having been left behind by their comrades who continued to forge ahead.

The tragic loss of missing men, who had simply disappeared forever in the spruce bogs, was lamented by their friends and comrades at the next night's encampment, when the company commander's roll call of their names brought no answers. Instead, only a haunting silence dominated the scene, sending a pall of gloom over the survivors, who realized the cruel meaning of the eerie quiet. Those soldiers fortunate enough to have reached that night's bivouac must have wondered whether they would be the next to be absent at the nightly roll call, because this punishing march had now turned into a case of survival of the fittest even for the healthiest men and the least accident-prone.

In purely psychological and emotional terms, when the names of lost men echoed through the blackened spruce bog and were not answered at roll call at night, an ugly reality of an awful truth sent chills down spines of the survivors. All the while, these fighting men, who found themselves in the middle of nowhere, were once again reminded of the omnipresent dangers of an accident or single misstep. As on so many past missions, only the strongest and most fortunate Rangers were destined to survive this most harrowing of ordeals.

Consequently, the deaths of these missing men only reinforced the conviction among the survivors that a complete victory now had to be won in the upcoming attack on St. Francis, so that these lost souls would not have died in vain. In consequence, because of these seven missing comrades, whom they would never see again, Rogers and his men now possessed a fresh motivation to strike exceptionally hard, when the time came to attack St. Francis so that this nest of longtime evildoers was entirely erased from the earth for all time. Such deep-seated motivations guaranteed that whenever Rogers and his followers finally neared their ultimate target located on the St. Francis River, all of their pent-up emotions would be unleashed with a terrible fury against the longtime tormentors of their people, just as the handsome Scotch-Irish major had long hoped and prayed.

In summarizing the nightmarish ordeal, which he would never forget, in his November 5, 1759, report to Major General Amherst, Rogers wrote, "In nine days through wet sunken ground; the water most of the way near a foot deep, it being a spruce bog. When we encamped at night, we had no way to secure ourselves from the water, but by cutting the bows of [spruce] trees, and with them erecting a kind of hammocks. We commonly began our march before day, and continued it till after dark at night."[85]

In his diary, one Ranger lieutenant described, "We encamped in ye bogs & contriv'd hammocks of yet Spruce above ye rotten wet ground. We are oligd'd each nite to cut saplings & lay them across each other, not unlike a raft, then spread boughs & leaves over ye top & & thus escape yet moors wetness below as we slept."[86] And, of course from the beginning, Rogers had made sure that no one ever lit a fire on any night in the freezing spruce bogs, which might betray their location to the ever-vigilant French and Indians, who might be anywhere.[87]

Meanwhile, like an experienced sea captain of a ship journeying in the vast expanse of the ocean, Rogers continued to navigate his men in the proper direction—straight north—by the trusty compass located at the bottom of his powder horn and by checking moss on the north sides of tree trunks at night. In fact, the march through the cold swamp waters, which sapped the strength and spirits of thoroughly soaked men like an insidious cancer, might well have continued longer by several days than the standard figure of nine days long used by writers of the St. Francis story.

A newly discovered letter from an expedition member, written after the raid, explained how the interlopers from faraway Crown Point had "marched for 12 Days" through the wilderness of Quebec.[88] Indeed, in one historian's words, "The time from September 23, the day they left Missis-quoi Bay, to October 4, the dawn of the St. Francis attack, comprised twelve days [and] Total mileage via Rogers's map route was 103 miles afoot to the village of St. Francis."[89]

Best of all, before returning to the fort at Isle-aux-Noix, Ensign La Durantaye, in the belief that Rogers would utilize the Yamaska trail in the river valley, linked up with the two other French, Indian, and Canadian units positioned on the Yamaska's banks in eager anticipation of the raiders' eventual arrival. However, Rogers had already outsmarted his opponents and would not fall into their trap, as if knowing exactly what his opponents were thinking and anticipating their tactical moves calculated to destroy him and his command.[90]

Then the spirits of Rogers and his men were lifted when they suddenly happened to see a flock of ducks flying swiftly south overhead and in silence, except for the slight sound of the beating of their wings when close overhead. They flew so low that the beating in unison of their wings was distinctly heard to draw the attention of men toiling through cold waters. Like a hunter during his youth in the wilds of Merrimack River country, Rogers knew what this sight meant.

Based on years of experience, the major took the sight of the small flock of waterfowl on the move in a low flight just above the spruce trees as a clear indication that the freshwaters and edible vegetation, unlike in the spruce bogs, for these ducks lay just ahead and farther north, because the St. Francis River was nearby. Rogers's astute observation and analysis based upon his keen knowledge of the mysterious ways of nature cheered his 142 followers, because they now knew that their great objective lay nearby and that the most arduous of journeys was finally nearing an end, which brought prayers and thanks to God for his mercy.[91]

A WILD, RAGING RIVER TO CROSS

Finally, on October 3, the battered spirits of the worn Rangers, soaked with nasty bog water and streaked in dirt and mud, were lifted when they finally struck firm ground—which they had thought that they would never see again—that was level and easy to cross under a green canopy of the tall trees, after emerging from the stagnant waters of the spruce bogs. At long last, Rogers and his men departed a watery hell on earth and never looked back.

Best of all, this slightly higher ground was solid and dry, without any stretches of dank water that stank to high heaven from the stench of decaying vegetation and debris. Here, in the fertile valley of the St. Francis, virgin stands of sweet-smelling pines had replaced the stale water of the dreary swamps that they had endured in misery for the past nine days or more. In consequence, Rogers's spirits now soared like those of his rejoicing men. In his heart of hearts, the major now knew that St. Francis lay just ahead and only a bit farther north. A great sense of relief spread through the weather-beaten ranks with the knowledge that they had avoided the vigorous enemy pursuit and that they had not walked into an ambush; however, if St. Francis had been alerted and reinforced by the French, the most unpleasant of welcomes imaginable would have awaited the raiders.

Reaching firm ground amid the stand of towering virgin timber, including stately pines, located just before the St. Francis River guaranteed that soaked and torn moccasins and deerskin leggings would finally get a chance to dry without being taken off by the men, who now wore what little was left of ragged clothing. Clinging mud and muck were cleaned off makeshift uniforms, gear, and weapons by the survivors. As usual, Rogers naturally insisted that all weapons be as clean as possible in preparation for the challenge that lay ahead.

Even the wet woolen blankets, soaked and dirty from the nastiness of bog slime and stale water distinguished by a foul smell, would have a chance to dry. Now heavily bearded, the haggard survivors were sweat stained and tattered from their harrowing ordeal. The once jaunty turkey and eagle feathers that had protruded from the blue Scottish bonnets, likewise stained, of these elite fighting men had either broken or been lost by this time. The soggy deerskin moccasins of the trekkers were falling apart, and the soaked Indian leggings, mostly of a blue color, were also in bad shape, after the torn originals had already been replaced by extra pairs, thanks to Rogers's foresight.

Sick and sneezing men with aching head colds from the near-freezing nights also had a better chance of recovering their health once clear of the swamps that stank from the decaying vegetation and water. Most of all, the knowledge that the St. Francis River flowed north to the town of St. Francis, which was now located about a dozen miles away to the northwest, filled Major Rogers and his men with a sense of jubilation.

However, their elation was tempered by the realization that pursuit might be right behind them. If they did not get across the river as soon as possible to the St. Francis, or northern, side of the river, then the entire command might be wiped out on its banks if a horde of screaming Indians, Canadians, and French suddenly poured out of the dense forest, after following their tracks on the firm ground.

Not taking any chances on the clear morning of October 3 and taking all necessary precautions, Rogers hurriedly formed his men into three files for the final advance toward the river that lay ahead, while also sending out parties of reliable men to guard the flanks and rear. Scouts were also dispatched straight ahead to make sure that the command would not walk into an ambush. Then the advance of 142 Rangers, Provincials, and British Regulars across the firm ground continued north, after having lost seven men in the spruce bogs.

Finally, Major Rogers spied the thin ribbon of blue through the tall pines and could hear the rapid flow of water over boulders. Even more, he could almost smell the freshness of the pristine flow of the clear waters of the St. Francis, after having breathed the stagnant air of the spruce bogs for the last week and a half. Rogers now knew that all he had to do was to cross and then follow the river north to St. Francis, while moving his command with care and defying the odds.

However, this picturesque river presented still another formidable obstacle, after they had just conquered the formidable obstacle of the spruce bogs and emerged like drowned rats from the morass. But how could Rogers get the entire command across a raging river to reach St. Francis on the other side? Quite simply, there was no time to build wooden rafts, as Rogers had originally contemplated as a possible solution to the dilemma. In addition, the construction of rafts would make too much noise. And the young major could not risk staying in one place too long when so near to St. Francis. Rogers knew that his command could still become a target of a raiding party striking from the rear or of St. Francis warriors hurriedly dispatched upriver striking from the front.

However, in overall tactical terms, Rogers rejoiced in knowing that he still possessed the element of surprise because no Abenaki war party had appeared on either side of the river, and all was perfectly quiet and still in the area. Most of all, he also realized that the enemy in the town situated on the river was overconfident from so many past successes over the years, believing that their sacred river protected their secluded sanctuary and its people for all time.

As in years past, the Abenaki remained entirely convinced that no English force would ever dare to advance so close to their longtime safe and secure haven located so deep in the unmapped wilderness. While the Abenaki had long viewed the St. Francis as the river of life and a living benevolent and protective spirit that deserved reverence like other aspects of the world of nature, the major meant to turn it into the river of death until its waters ran red with blood if he succeeded in his bold plan.

Significantly, past writers and historians have written without sufficient explanation—it has been described as a remarkable occurrence—about how Rogers had the good fortune to have suddenly emerged from the spruce bogs to strike the south bank of the icy, fast-flowing waters of the St. Francis River very close to an ideal crossing point around midday on October 3. Here, the St. Francis was still relatively shallow and fordable in normal conditions, unlike farther north downriver toward St. Francis. Farther north, the St. Francis gradually widened and deepened to become a much more formidable river, while rushing north to enter the St. Lawrence River.

However, the recent rains had swollen the river's waters to heighten the water level at summer's end, before the arrival of colder temperatures: a fact that caused a sense frustration for Rogers, who was an expert in the ways of rivers since the days of his youth along the Merrimack River and other northern New England watercourses that he knew intimately. Quite simply, the St. Francis's waters were now too high for a crossing at this initial point gained, and it would cost more valuable time to find a suitable crossing site at a narrower point.

Nevertheless, Rogers had reached a most advantageous point on the river. For instance, the banks of the St. Francis farther north grew stepper and higher as the river gradually descended toward the lowlands of the St. Lawrence River. Therefore, the only realistic place to cross the river lay to the south, or upriver, because it was an impossibility farther north where the river widened and became deeper, which Rogers realized because he knew that the St. Francis entered the St. Lawrence just to the north. Most important, for Rogers to have struck the river so far south—an estimated fifteen miles (actually only around a dozen miles) because he was now actually several miles closer to the community of St. Francis—was absolutely crucial in overall geographic terms.

In addition, to provide another key advantage, Rogers had gained the south bank so far south that it was off the beaten path for the normal travel patterns of the villagers of St. Francis. Here, so many miles south of St. Francis, there was none of the usual river-related activity of young swimmers, older Indian fishermen, or women washing clothes, as there would be much farther down the river and closer to St. Francis.

Consequently, at this point in the river, so far below St. Francis, Major Rogers and his men did not have worry about encountering any Abenaki children or women. At this time of year, no fish, including the schools of shad, were spawning, like in the spring, guaranteeing no gatherings of villagers along the riverbank to net the fish. And the recent harvest, especially from the bountiful fields of corn around the village, meant that the Abenaki no longer relied upon a diet of fish, because they were already stocked up for the winter.

Most important, Abenaki war parties were elsewhere. As noted, they had spent all summer defending Quebec until mid-September. In consequence, Rogers's expeditioners had not seen anyone, not even an advanced scout or guard at any point so far. And, fortunately, no warriors were now pushing southeastward from the village down the ancient warrior path that continued a long distance up the St. Francis, then down the Connecticut River, leading south down the river toward the New England settlements. In addition, at this point, the St. Francis was too shallow and narrow for any French armed vessels, and the rough waters of the rapids also guaranteed that no Abenaki warriors were moving up and down the river in their traditional birchbark canoes in this area.

Rogers also benefited from another key factor at this time, which helped to screen his upcoming crossing of the St. Francis River. The tall trees, now cloaked in the bright red and yellow colors of a beautiful early autumn in Quebec, especially the majestic maples in full color, still retained most of their leaves to provide good cover for the interlopers, like the evergreens, including the pines and spruce. Therefore, in this picturesque setting, the tall timber in full foliage on both sides of the St. Francis would provide a band of desperate men crossing the raging river with excellent natural cover.

To gain a shallower crossing point, because the recent rains had swollen the river's waters, Rogers ordered his three columns to turn to the right and march south until he found exactly the right place to cross. With plenty of light remaining in the day, and fearing the arrival of an enemy war party from multiple directions, Rogers knew that he needed to conduct a crossing with the sun still high in the sky, which went against the more careful axioms of the major's own rules, especially waiting for nightfall to provide a veil of cover. Quite simply, he was too close to St. Francis to waste any additional time after expending so much effort in having reached this advanced point.

Therefore, all in all, after having suddenly emerged from the spruce bogs, how could Rogers have possibly reached an area that had provided the ideal crossing point before the river widened and deepened after having crossed nearly one hundred miles of unmapped terrain that he had never seen before? Significantly, it was certainly no accident or blind luck that could be contributed to the Irish in this case.

Indeed, two distinct factors had ensured that Rogers and his men gained almost exactly the right spot to cross the St. Francis without spending much time searching for a crossing point. First, the major possessed his trusty compass—certainly Rogers's most valuable instrument on the expedition. Rogers had often relied on his trusty compass to always point north—toward St. Francis itself—when the skies were too cloudy to follow the North Star at night. But even this invaluable compass was perhaps not the most important factor in having guided Rogers and his men in the proper direction to ensure that he gained the river just before it significantly widened and deepened to become unfordable, while flowing north toward St. Francis and then on to enter the St. Lawrence River.

One of the most important factors that explained Rogers's success in gaining the south bank of the St. Francis River and shortly reaching his most advantageous point for crossing the river farther south, below his ultimate target, came from the past contributions and efforts of the major's top lieutenant, John Stark. As mentioned, Stark had thoroughly filled Rogers in on everything and anything that he could remember about St. Francis, the river's course and nuances, and the topography of the surrounding area, just before Rogers and his men departed Crown Point on September 13.

Captain Stark knew all about St. Francis and the entire area from the weeks that he had been a captive of the Abenaki. As noted, he had been captured in the wild Baker River country of New Hampshire in 1752 and then adopted into the Abenaki tribe at St. Francis on the elders' decision. For five weeks in Quebec, Stark had called St. Francis home, and many good memories of that memorable experience continued to linger throughout his eventful life and well into his old age.

Most important, Stark knew exactly where the St. Francis narrowed to provide a good crossing point below St. Francis to the southeast, which was almost exactly where Rogers and his men eventually crossed the river at this fordable point, after Rogers moved farther upriver to the south away from the village: definitely no coincidence or happenstance. As noted, Stark had drawn a detailed map of St. Francis and the surrounding area for Rogers at Crown Point. Of course, such a well-drawn map showed Rogers exactly where the river narrowed before growing much wider and deeper the closer one moved downriver and north toward St. Francis.

Consequently, based on the hand-drawn map of what Stark had remembered from his younger days, Rogers had been able to find exactly the right location farther south to cross the river in regard to size and depth, including without the presence of Abenaki women and children at the river at this point so far from St. Francis or moving along a trail leading to this fordable point to detect his presence: all key considerations that Stark would have informed Rogers about at Crown Point.

In this respect, it was almost as if Stark, the former resident of St. Francis in what now seemed like a dream to him, was with Rogers and his men at this point on the river, which was a southern tributary of the St. Lawrence. As noted, although Stark was not present, this was very much a special mission that continued to have all the hallmarks and unique qualities of the formidable Rogers-Stark team of inspired leadership that had led to past successes. In this sense, it was almost as if Stark were still by the major's side because of the invaluable map that had been drawn by the captain, offering sound advice and wise council like so often in the past, because the inspirational legacy of Rogers's top lieutenant was alive and well in multiple ways.[92]

While leading his men south and away from St. Francis, Rogers also knew that he needed to find good natural cover for a stealthy crossing as soon as possible, when he believed that the pursuit was not far behind. Quite simply, this river was the most formidable natural obstacle that lay before St. Francis on the river's north side and just south of the mighty estuary known as the St. Lawrence, the key to Canada.

With keeping black powder and weapons dry a top priority, disaster could result if the river was not properly crossed and in timely fashion at a location that provided good cover. If Rogers and his men wasted too much time on the south bank, then it was feared that Ensign La Durantaye—if he had continued his pursuit, which was not the case, unbeknownst to the major—could gain the greatest victory of his career by catching Rogers and his men with their backs against the river: the recipe for annihilation.

As throughout this odyssey, a good deal of resourcefulness would be required for a successful crossing in the wilderness. Fearing that pursuers were close behind, Rogers knew that he had to get his men farther south and across the river as soon as possible, which was vital to success. All the while, Rogers was haunted by the fact that if the French, Canadians, and Indians reached the river, he and his band would be either annihilated or forced to surrender—most likely the former.

Rogers consequently continued to follow the course of the St. Francis south, because he knew that the river would narrow in this direction. Most of all, Rogers realized that he only needed to move his command a relatively short distance upriver where it narrowed. Also, at this time it made good sense for the entire command to keep moving just in case the pursuers were not far behind. Therefore, Rogers refused to give the command a much-needed rest, because everyone had to keep moving because their lives might well depend upon it. In a hurry, as if still expecting the worst because that kind of thinking was always the key to survival, Rogers marched his men southeastward and upriver because, in the words of a Ranger lieutenant from his diary, "ye River very wide here so we went [south] and up stream where it appeared narrow."[93]

In a classic example of frontier resourcefulness in a crisis situation, he was searching for a place to cross where the river was suitably narrow but swifter, upriver where the ground was higher in elevation. He finally found exactly what he was looking for, including a narrow gully by which the men could file down to the river, after having pushed around two miles southeastward throughout more unfamiliar territory to ensure less chance of detection by the villagers of St. Francis.

Thinking fast and keeping his priorities in perspective, the major developed a novel solution for crossing the river as quickly and as quietly as possible. First, Rogers ordered his men to strip naked to avoid getting their clothing and powder wet. Weapons, powder horns, and gear were placed atop packs, which would be held high above heads for the precarious crossing.

Rogers then gathered his tallest and strongest men and sent them out down the wooded gully and into the raging water, where they formed a long line—a sturdy foundation—that served as a chain for the men to cross. The major ordered his followers to cross by holding on to the largest and stoutest men of the initial line that now extended from the south bank to the north bank.

Fortunately, at this point, the river's bottom was rocky instead of muddy, allowing the men firm footing against the rushing current in water that was around five feet deep. By "hooking their arms together for mutual support, [they] forded [the river] with great difficulty": another one of the major's ingenious decisions that played a part in leading to the success of the St. Francis mission.[94]

In his November 5, 1759, report to General Amherst, Rogers summarized in his usual concise fashion the ad hoc crossing of the river around fourteen miles from his target: "The tenth day after leaving Misisquey [sic] Bay, we came to a river [located] above the town of St. Francis to the south of it; and the town being on the opposite or east side of it, we were obliged to ford it, which was attended with no small difficulty, the water being five feet deep, and the current swift. I put the tallest men up stream, and then holding by each other, we got over with the loss of several of our guns, some of which we recovered by diving to the bottom for them."[95]

After crossing the ice-cold waters of the swift-flowing river that was the home of trout, soaking wet Rangers, Provincials, and Regulars dried off as best they could in the shelter of the narrow timbered ravine on the north bank. Of course, when so close to St. Francis, there was no way that Rogers would allow his men to build fires that might give away their location. Therefore, the Rangers, Provincials, and British Regulars shivered in the cool early October air when chilled to the bone from the dangerous river crossing.

However, the rapidly flowing water was refreshing, washing the dirt from bodies scarred by briars and thorn bushes from toiling through the spruce bogs for a week and a half. The location of this ravine—an ideal hiding spot and safe from prying Abenaki eyes—on the opposite north bank was another reason that explained why Rogers decided to choose this key point to cross the river. As usual, the experienced major was not taking any chances and thought only about the welfare of his men and the overall safety of the command, like a good shepherd watching over his flock.

Here, in the comforting shelter of the wooded ravine on the St. Francis side of the river, after dressing in dry clothing, Rogers's men now devoted attention to making sure that their smooth-bore muskets and black powder were dry, blowing into firing pans and wiping moisture off the firing mech-anisms of their Brown Bess flintlocks and rifles. Rogers had early sent out scouts, including his Stockbridge warrior "Wolves," to check the thick woods of colorful hardwood trees, towering high into the blue early autumn sky, for any lurking war party, while keeping their eyes open for a possible ambush.

In truth, Rogers's command was still vulnerable on the north bank and just upriver from St. Francis, despite the successful crossing, because this was unfamiliar territory, and no one knew what to expect. If suddenly attacked by an Abenaki war party from St. Francis, then Rogers's command could be easily destroyed on the St. Francis side of the river, where the raging river was still situated to their backs, leaving them most vulnerable, because there was now no escape or spruce bogs to hide their tracks as on the river's south side.

Most of all, this remaining band of brothers—Rangers, Provincials, and British Regulars who were united as one—were fortunate survivors, unlike the seven men whose bodies remained in the vast expanse of the spruce bogs because they had become lost in the swamps, injured, or sick. After the suc-cessful crossing of the troublesome St. Francis, spirits lifted to new heights among Rogers and his chilled men in the hidden ravine on the north bank. Most important, they had crossed to the river's north side without detection, and no enemy had been seen or encountered, not even a scout—positive proof that the enemy had still not deciphered Rogers's movements or even discerned their exact location so deep in the heart of the Abenaki's own homeland and so near to the legendary town of St. Francis.

Here, in the sheltered ravine near the river's rapidly flowing waters, Rog-ers's followers quickly consumed some of the few remaining rations. To the raiders, it seemed like a minor miracle that they had escaped a full-fledged fight with enemy warriors, who coveted the scalps of every interloper who had been bold enough to enter into their home country. Best of all, future prospects never looked brighter for Rogers and his men at this time, after the gaining of the north bank without a shot fired in anger. The luxury of not having to fight a costly battle that would have warned St. Francis brought a new lease on life to invigorate the major and the entire command.

Thankfully, the terrain on the river's north side consisted of solid and "good dry ground," in Rogers's words. The living nightmare of toiling day after day through the spruce bogs that seemed to have no end was finally over on this glorious October 3, when the bright sunshine and beauty of early autumn in Quebec was in full splendor. And now the way was open all the way to St. Francis, like a gift presented by the smiling gods of war for Rogers and his men.

CONTINUING THE PUSH TOWARD ODANAK, OR ST. FRANCIS

Safely on the river's other side, hidden in the timbered hollow, and still concerned that the enemy might still be in pursuit and appear on the opposite bank at any moment, the men enjoyed a short respite while eating what precious little rations remained. All the while, Rogers was anxious and impatient, anticipating the worst. Consequently, they were soon once again on the move, since Rogers knew that no time could be wasted and that it was too dangerous to remain stationary for too long.

In three separate files, with his vigilant flankers out to protect the forward movement on each side and in the rear to guard the backdoor, Rogers then hurriedly formed his much-relieved men, whose spirits were high. The major and his soldiers then headed at a brisk pace in a northwestward direction. As usual, Rogers led the way in following the course of the raging river that led straight northwest to St. Francis and a fatal reckoning with its inhabitants. The river's cold and fresh waters had acted as not only a tonic but also a cleanser. As mentioned, some of the bog's stench, scum, and dirt had been partly washed off in crossing the river, which was reinvigorating to weary men who had worn no clothing in the cold crossing.

By this time, everyone had uniforms that were tattered and in overall bad shape, which provided still another motivation for capturing St. Francis in one bold rush to catch the town by surprise: the securing of well-made and dry Abenaki clothing, especially deerskin moccasins, shirts, and leggings, to replace what was already worn out. Meanwhile, Rogers and his followers made good time over solid ground in the final trek northwest in following the river through the pine forest to reach St. Francis, which was just ahead downriver, while the sun dropped lower in a clear autumn sky that was about to bestow a red Quebec sunset over the land.

It was almost too good to be true, or so it seemed to Rogers. Thankfully for the men in the ranks and Rogers's overall progress toward his target, no more spruce bogs were encountered along the entire length of forested and solid ground on the river's north side. Still no war parties, scouts, or villagers were seen anywhere during the trek upriver and ever closer to St. Francis. As could be expected, this situation caused confidence to soar in the ranks for a successful operation, when this mission had so often recently seemed like folly under the most disadvantageous of circumstances.

Almost certainly, the most devout men in the ranks believed that a kind Providence had finally smiled and turned a kind eye upon what they knew was the most righteous of missions to destroy St. Francis. Major Rogers was extremely thankful that, against the odds, he had successfully dodged all enemy parties and still retained the element of surprise, after the most harrowing of ordeals. However, he was still wary and kept his instincts on high alert and his eyes open for danger, while flankers and scouts were out searching the woodlands for any signs of trouble.[96]

After crossing the raging river and following his own rules of ranging service, Rogers had made sure that the group of sojourners secured "a piece of ground that may afford your centuries [*sic*] the advantage of seeing or hearing the enemy some considerable distance, keeping one half of your whole party awake alternatively through the night."[97]

Now finally situated in a secure position on the river's north side, and with his men moving onward at a good pace but with caution, Rogers continued to be fueled by the desire to inflict extensive damage on the ancient enemies of his people, especially the lower-class Scotch-Irish, who had suffered so much and for so long across the northern frontier: "The histories of this country, particularly, are full of the unheard-of cruelties committed by the French and the Indians, by their instigation, which I think every brave man ought to do his utmost to humble that haughty nation, or reduce their bounds of conquest in this country to a narrow limit."[98]

According to a September 26 letter written from the northern frontier town of Albany, New York, and printed in the October 11, 1759, issue of the *Maryland Gazette*, when Major Rogers's mysterious whereabouts were still unknown to the French and Amherst, "This may be depended on a Fact, that the Major is going out on a Scout with a large Party which our Accounts mostly fix at 500 picked Men, and we make no Scruple of judging, that this Conduct [in this unknown mission] will be such as to perpetuate the Character which has been so justly given him of being a brave Man."[99]

One of these so-called picked Men of experience and trustworthiness was Private Robert Kirkwood. A young Scotsman from the old country across the sea and who still closely embraced Celtic attitudes and ways, Kirkwood emphasized how he proudly served in "a force of volunteers under the command of brave Major Rogers, against a place called St. Fransway" in faraway Quebec, Canada.[100]

A faithful Presbyterian born in Scotland who loved his beautiful land of the ancient Celts, Kirkwood knew of the brutality of unleashed Native American warriors. He had already witnessed "to my unspeakable grief and terror . . . five out of my nine [fellow soldier captives] burned in the most cruel manner. . . . [H]aving purposely collected a number of the roots that grow in fir-trees, they stick these to the fleshy parts of the unhappy victims, and then set them on fire, which consumes them in a slow and lingering manner . . . and, as if this was not enough, they frequently use the barbarity of tomahawking them, i.e., striking a tomahawk into their skulls."[101]

Ranger Thomas Brown, an intelligent, young man of promise who had grown up in his parent's home at Charleston, Massachusetts, located just outside Boston, had been haunted by the horror of seeing the body of his friend Lieutenant Samuel Kennedy "much tomahawked by the Indians" to present a gory spectacle on the blood-stained snow, after the Second Battle on Snowshoes.[102]

For such reasons, and knowing of the savagery of merciless warriors of the bloody Abenaki raids, which had long brought fire and death across the northern frontier for years with impunity, Kirkwood explained his primary motivation for having joined Major Rogers and his expedition deep into the dark heart of New France during the most dangerous experience of his life: "I went upon this party being stimulated with the hope of revenge."[103]

Like the physically imposing Scotch-Irish major who simply never gave up when the going got tough, hard-bitten Celtic fighting men like Kirkwood saw their goal of the destruction of the Jesuit mission at St. Francis as a righteous act for God and country to protect the people of the long-ravaged frontier settlements.[104]

Most important, the way was now open to St. Francis, and Rogers reveled in the realization that he and his men were now moving easily northwest across good ground that was dry and solid, while closing in on fulfilling his greatest dream of all: the destruction of St. Francis to forever end all the nightmarish horrors that had been inflicted on generations of settlers across the frontier.

To the visionary and ever-optimistic major, who had long defied the odds with his die-hard determination and sheer willpower—which his followers then inherited as if by osmosis during the most arduous of campaigning and in the midst of the greatest dangers—it now seemed as if nothing could stop him from realizing his greatest ambition, which had consumed him for so long.[105]

When he allowed himself the luxury, Rogers already basked in the realization that the long-awaited bloody day of reckoning for St. Francis was now in the near future, because destiny continued to call him and his men onward through the tall timber that stood along the St. Francis River and ever closer to the most infamous Native American town in North America.

CHAPTER SIX

Rogers Determined to Fulfill His Special Destiny in the St. Francis River Country

UNTIL THE HIDDEN NEW ENGLAND WHALEBOATS THAT HAD BEEN BROUGHT all the way from the whaling ports of New England along the Atlantic coast had been discovered by Ensign Langy's Abenaki, Canadian, and French in the thick underbrush just up a small creek off Missisquoi Bay, not only completely altering but also sabotaging his well-laid plans, Major Rogers was most fortunate in part because it had long seemed absolutely impossible to everyone—especially the Abenaki—that any white soldiers, English, Ranger, or Provincial, would dare march so far north and deep into the heart of Indian country to threaten the very center of Abenaki power and prestige.[1]

Major Rogers, consequently, still benefited from the initial advantage of surprise because preparations to destroy his command had been belatedly and hurriedly formulated only recently in somewhat of a panic among an alarmed French leadership, after the expedition had departed Crown Point twenty days before. Rogers was motivated by the knowledge that no single place in North America was more symbolic as an omnipresent threat than St. Francis.

Therefore, pushing several hours down the ever-widening river known as the St. Francis, a southern tributary of the St. Lawrence, and in a northwesterly direction, Rogers was able to approach relatively close to St. Francis with his remaining 142 men without being detected. Thankfully, the largest enemy force, around two hundred men as estimated by Rogers, was now concentrated at Yamaska (Wigwam Martinique) only around seven miles to the southwest.

Here, with loaded flintlock muskets, the eager soldiers of New France waited patiently in a well-conceived ambush that would never be sprung by

281

them. Governor-General Pierre de Rigaud, the Marquis de Vaudreuil, had miscalculated by stripping St. Francis of most of its relatively little remaining manpower in the mistaken belief that these bold English raiders would pass through Yamaska. Again, and as mentioned, in a supreme irony, no French leader knew for a fact that Rogers was on the loose in part because it still seemed impossible. They evidently believed that the incomparable Rogers was too valuable to Amherst for his anticipated offensive effort down the strategic Lake Champlain corridor and farther north toward Montreal to risk the major's life in the seemingly most insane of missions imaginable.

By this time, the community of St. Francis consisted of more than sixty well-constructed houses, including windowed wooden structures—regular French residences—like those that now stood in Montreal or Quebec. The conical-shaped wigwams and rectangular longhouses of the Algonquian peoples were more prominent in the Northeast throughout the past, but most St. Francis Abenaki lived in these structures of a distinctive French style.

The largest buildings in the community were the Jesuit mission Catholic church and the grand Council House, which stood on a central plaza at the town's head. The Council House was the largest structure located at St. Francis. Amazingly, there were still no roving parties of warriors in the vicinity, which allowed Rogers's smooth approach from the southeast. It was almost too good to be true. Obviously, Rogers still possessed the element of surprise, which he had long dreamed of obtaining in order to fulfill his fondest ambition: the most lethal tactic of the deep raid that had been thoroughly mastered by the Abenaki as long demonstrated across the frontier.

At this time, perhaps Rogers might have suspected an ambush because the approach to St. Francis had been so easy, which no doubt only made him warier. Even at this advanced point just southeast of St. Francis along the swift-flowing river, which was now much wider than where they had crossed to the south, Rogers could not afford any unnecessary risks at this time, as he fully realized. With St. Francis now in easy reach, he realized that one small mistake or even a momentary slip of judgment might sabotage all that had been accomplished so far.

From his broad knowledge of Indian ways and habits, Rogers knew that parties of warriors might be moving between him and the village, returning to St. Francis from successful hunts to secure meat for the long winter that lay ahead. Most of all, the major realized, based on prior experience, that there had to be some guards, both young warriors and elders, such as their fathers, located closer to the village.

This infamous town was situated on a bluff above the level bottoms—ideal for growing the seasonal corn crop—of the flood plain of the St. Francis River. Unfortunately for Rogers, he could climb no nearby elevation to gain a view of the village to ascertain Abenaki security measures or to count the number of warriors. Rogers and his men were also located in the slight valley of the timbered river bottoms. Even more disadvantageous, as the major later discovered, a wide clearing, or field now free of recently harvested crops, lay before the town, so that Rogers could not sneak through underbrush and trees to obtain an extremely close look at the village, as he would have preferred, and like when he had so often surveyed Fort Carillon and Fort Saint Frédéric at close range and boldly scalped Frenchmen within sight of the appalled French garrison.

With time of the essence, Rogers searched for a solution to his vexing dilemma, because he now needed to know the exact location of his most tempting of targets and its overall strength. He must somehow get into a good elevated position to obtain a full view of this mystical place not only to satisfy his curiosity but also, and more important, to develop the best tactical plan suitable to the terrain and to fulfill his ambitions of catching the community completely by surprise.

A TALL PINE IN THE MIDDLE OF NOWHERE

After he had "halted [his] party" of 142 survivors for a thankful rest near dusk on October 3, after a march of more than ten miles to the northwest and parallel to the St. Francis River, the still anxious and wary Rogers knew that correctly ascertaining the exact lay of the terrain before St. Francis might literally be the key to life or death. The major, consequently, searched the area for a tall tree as the sun began to dip over the western horizon when he knew that he had reached a point just southeast of St. Francis—not just any tall tree but an almost perfect one for observation, which needed to be situated on a small patch of higher ground to observe St. Francis, with sufficient branch cover so as not be seen by any of the town's inhabitants.

With his well-honed instincts on high alert, Major Rogers had already sensed that he was sufficiently close to St. Francis, evidently after spying indications of past movements of small numbers of Abenaki women. Or

Rogers might have sniffed a hint of smoke from the Abenaki cooking fires, if the wind was blowing to the south. For all that Rogers knew, an enemy war party of considerable size might have been assigned—as it should have been after the discovery of his presence at Missisquoi Bay—the job of protecting St. Francis.

Here, about four miles southeast of St. Francis, at around twilight on October 3 and after three weeks since embarking on this mission, the major finally found exactly what he was looking for: a tall, majestic pine, with just enough branches not to obscure his vision but to hide his shape, that he could scale easily to finally gain a clear view of St. Francis, which lay before him to the northwest like an oasis. Even the shape and location of the towering pine were considerations to ensure that his large frame would not be silhouetted against the skyline, when the sun was beginning to set and the evening's coolness had already descended upon Quebec.

To the surprise of onlookers below, Rogers's large frame did nothing to hamper his nimbleness in scaling the tree, like in the more carefree days of his youth in the Merrimack River country. This large pine tree that Rogers had chosen offered a commanding position high above with no branches hampering his view to the northwest on the north side of the St. Francis River, while having just enough branches at his eagerly anticipated perch to hide his presence, when relatively close to the legendary town. From this high point at a distance of around four miles from the town in the fading light of a beautiful October day and using a pocket telescope as known as a spyglass, Rogers could finally gain a view of St. Francis that lay elevated on a bluff overlooking the wide river in the late evening, when the sun's fading light provided a screen that helped him avoid detection, if any Abenaki were nearby.[2]

The exact distance of this tree from the town is not precisely known, because accounts have varied from men who possessed no maps or had little idea about this unfamiliar area. In a letter, one of Rogers's men wrote that "just before Night [on October 3], Major Rogers climb'd up a Tree" that was sufficiently tall to command a wide area once he gained his good perch, which provided an ideal observation platform.[3] Fortunately, the land just south of the St. Lawrence and the St. Francis River was relatively flat, and this tall pine, located on a slight elevation, allowed Rogers to see a long distance without any obstacles in his way.

It is not known, but Rogers might have taken off his leather moccasins—by now ripped and moldy from trekking through the spruce bogs—to climb the towering pine tree barefoot as he had done as a mischievous boy in the mostly Scotch-Irish settlement of Methuen, Massachusetts, or at Mountalona, New Hampshire, so long ago. After having advanced before his whole party of raiders, who nervously waited, Rogers now adhered to his own written rule, which he put to paper in 1756, in getting his good look at St. Francis: "When nearing their objective one or two of the rangers go ahead to select the most advantageous observation point."[4]

As quietly as possible, and making sure that he knocked off no dead branches or clusters of pinecones that might drop and alert an Abenaki scout, if one was nearby, Rogers quickly scampered higher up the tree so that he could gain his bird's-eye view of St. Francis, or Odanak. St. Francis had been known by this name before the arrival of the Jesuits to convert the Abenaki to Protestant-hating Catholics bent on destroying heretics without mercy or remorse. Meanwhile, Rogers steadily moved up the tree ever so carefully for fear of making noise and with the graceful agility of a big cat on the prowl in the wilds. With the ease of a sprightly teenager, Rogers, age twenty-seven, climbed carefully toward the top of the tree, because St. Francis had to be viewed, before darkness settled over this part of Quebec.

Fortunately, at this time, Rogers was far removed from the spruce trees of the bogs because he was now in pine country, which was far more picturesque compared to the miserable "Drowned Lands." There the spruce trees, bunched close together in dense clusters, were too thick and difficult to climb, unlike the tall pines that towered high from the St. Francis River's rich bottoms. These fertile bottoms along the St. Francis River were less acidic, allowing the growth of a splendid forest of timber that extended all the way to the open clearing before the village situated on the broad river, whose waters at this point shortly entered the St. Lawrence three miles to the north in Rogers's estimation.

In moving higher up the tree, Rogers felt the cooler air that was refreshing on this autumn evening of October 3, from a chilly breeze that gently swept off the St. Francis River at the end of another warm day. Although he had never been so far north before, the major knew that fall came to this unmapped land much earlier than in the New England settlements, and

Rogers already felt the difference in the air's crispness. As was typical on an autumn evening in the St. Francis River country situated not far below the St. Lawrence River, a slight breeze brought a distinct chill to Rogers, but he ignored his slight personal discomfort. All that he was focused on at this point was gaining the best elevated position from which he would not be detected and catching his first good view of the town that he had heard so much about for as long as he could remember.

As the evening chill at the end of another autumn day in Quebec cut like a knife when Rogers reached the highest point on the tall pine that dominated a wide area all around, Rogers might have wished to have felt such cooler temperatures when he and his men had been sweating and toiling through the seemingly endless spruce bogs—all but impassable, or so it had been thought by French leadership—in what had been a living nightmare for the trekkers.

Atop the large pine and supported by a sturdy branch that he knew was sufficiently thick to bear his weight of around two hundred pounds, Rogers finally gained his ideal elevated natural platform. From his lofty perch, he knew better than to now attempt to swat at any insects buzzing around his face. If a mosquito—they were larger here in Quebec than in New England—now landed upon his face, then it could suck the major's blood to its heart's content, because Rogers was not now going to make any sudden move to swat it away for fear of giving away his presence to a sharp-eyed Abenaki warrior. Perhaps, while high in the treetop on the river's north side that overlooked a wide stretch of the St. Francis River country, he might have heard the sharp cries of the unseen nighthawk, which flew high overhead in the twilight to start the night's feeding frenzy in what was a perfect banquet of pesky insects flying in the blackening autumn sky.

From his commanding vantage point and peering through the large, concealing branches at his long-range view of St. Francis to the northwest on October 3 at around dusk, he saw the first thin shreds of dark smoke rising high in the sky above the town. This smoke came from Abenaki cooking fires and from the stone chimneys of the French-style houses. Rogers carefully surveyed the town from end to end as best he could from this lengthy distance, while analyzing the village's overall layout and carefully noting every detail in his eager sight.

In the fading light of the balmy October evening, Rogers had finally obtained the good view of St. Francis that he had long desired. And because St. Francis was located on the bluff and the harvested fields lay before the town situated on the river bluff, he could easily see over the tree line that lay between him and St. Francis. In his first-ever view of St. Francis, the major, already with a fair growth of a red beard that made him look almost like a Viking chieftain of old, was now surprised by what his unbelieving eyes saw: what appeared to be a regular town in the French style and not a traditional Abenaki village that consisted of the usual array of beech-bark huts, which had been used by the Abenaki for centuries. Rogers viewed not only the houses but also darkening dirt streets in the fading light of dusk because St. Francis sat atop a river bluff overlooking the wide watercourse of placid waters rolling north.

The town's dusty streets were wide, straight, and almost like a rural town in France. They now appeared to be all but deserted in the fading light. Rogers was astounded by the sight of a town of around sixty regular houses. Putting some of the frontier communities of the Merrimack River country to shame, St. Francis was a town of nice houses, with chimneys and windows, in the traditional French style that was popular across Quebec. As noted, the largest structure in St. Francis was the Council House that stood on the rectangular plaza at the head of town. From the pine's towering height, it was clear to Rogers that French leaders and the Jesuit missionaries had made a concerted effort to make St. Francis a showcase town to fortify morale and rally refugee warriors to fuel the exodus of Abenaki war parties to ravage the frontier with fire, tomahawk, and scalping knives.

This sizeable town—larger than many New England communities on the frontier—had been built around the wooden Catholic church near the large Council House on the French-style plaza, like those in the old country, where rural communities and social life had long been centered on a central plaza. At first sight, Rogers saw that the Council House and the Roman Catholic church were the two largest and most dominant structures in St. Francis. To an outsider, the startling sight of the European-like town amid the wilderness was surprising, if not a bit troubling.

Like his men, Rogers never expected to see a legitimate European-style town, for all practical purposes. However, it was abundantly clear to the major that the town's appearance symbolically complemented the prestige and strength of New France's most formidable Native American ally. But most of all, the Scotch-Irish major realized that this mission town in the wilderness was strategic because of its central location between Montreal to the southwest and Quebec to the northeast. As never before, Major Rogers and his 142 men, including officers, were now incredibly deep in enemy territory that had never been seen or touched by white raiders.

To the dirt-stained Rogers, who tried in vain to ignore the numbing soreness of his limbs and overall weariness of his entire body from the lengthy trek through the spruce bogs, the intoxicating sight of St. Francis must have been extremely invigorating. In fact, to the major, the town might have looked more like a ghostly vision of another place and time—much like a kind of mirage in the growing darkness, one that had long only existed in his imagination.

Indeed, by any measure, St. Francis certainly did not appear to be the most feared Native American town in the history of New England's colonies, for generation after generation, looking eerily calm and quiet in the dimming light of a beautiful fall day. However, the evils and surreal horrors that had long stemmed from St. Francis were deeply interwoven with the experiences of almost every family in New England, including a good many men in Rogers's ranks. Quite simply in the popular imagination, St. Francis represented the grimmest of legends filled with unspeakable horrors that had long haunted generations of New Englanders.

For such reasons, the appearance of St. Francis was both alluring and beguiling to Rogers, if not mesmerizing. The town situated on the river flowing into the St. Lawrence was most inviting and completely vulnerable to a surprise attack by stealthy Rangers and the volunteer Provincials and Britons. To Rogers, the sight of St. Francis might be described as the promised land because of its longtime centrality to this thinking, beckoning to him to come forth. At this time, the New Hampshire major from the Merrimack River country might have wondered at the striking contradiction that made him contemplate more deeply on almost a philosophical level that contradicted his reputation as the consummate backwoods frontiersman: how such a civilized-looking, peaceful, and quaint village, built on the traditional French model and more modern looking than many New England frontier villages, could have long unleashed such a vast amount of terror, more than any

Native American town on the North American continent. It all seemed like a puzzling contradiction to Rogers, who could hardly believe his eyes.

However, it is not known, but Rogers's initial surprise at his first sight of St. Francis might not have been as complete as later experienced by his men, when they eventually entered it with fixed bayonets and tomahawks at the ready early on the morning of October 4. Rogers had learned some intimate details about the overall appearance of St. Francis from prior intelligence, especially white captives, such as John Stark, who had survived their St. Francis experiences. What could not be denied by Rogers was the fact that destroying St. Francis was his life's goal, which had long consumed his thoughts and basic instincts. He therefore was entirely transfixed by his target like a bird of prey about to descend upon an unwary rabbit in an open field, while maintaining a laser-like focus on every aspect of the town.

For the first time, in soaking up every detail that he could ascertain from the treetop in the ever-decreasing amount of daylight, Rogers looked over every inch of the most prominent features of the town as best he could. At near dusk, the St. Francis River, which had given the town vitality and life from the beginning, was a dark ribbon to Rogers's eye, but it could be seen by the increasing yellow light from a rising moon that shimmered off the black waters of the wide St. Francis. The major knew that this river continued to flow a relatively short distance north to enter the St. Lawrence—the "Father of Waters," or the Mississippi River of Canada.

Beyond the bare open fields, which had only recently produced excellent crops on the fertile soil of the river bottoms for the recent harvest, a prominent one-story wooden structure—the second-largest structure in town after the Council House—had been built like other French houses of worship in small towns across Canada. Located at the front or head of the town, the Roman Catholic church towered above the surrounding houses, serving as the community's centerpiece. Here, generations of Abenaki had been indoctrinated into the Catholic faith, thanks to the dedication and tireless efforts of faithful Jesuit missionaries and priests, who had been born in France.

However, the religion of St. Francis was not the usual Catholic faith as taught to simple French farmers, including retired soldiers from regular French regiments, in the St. Lawrence River Valley. Instead, the Abenaki had been taught a most militant brand of Catholicism that was closer to something from the Roman Catholic Church's Spanish Inquisition, with the same goal—the persecution and destruction of Protestant heretics. The Abenaki had been long preached a radical theology by generations of French priests, like France-born Father Pierre-Joseph-Antoine Roubaud. He was now the respected Catholic leader of the St. Francis Abenaki, and one of Roubaud's specialties was encouraging raids on the frontier settlements to kill Protestants because it was God's will in his intolerant Roman Catholic mind.

Father Roubaud, age thirty-three, had successfully made the transition from a wide-eyed student at a Jesuit college in France to an active member of Abenaki war parties. The passionate Jesuit had witnessed the massacre of Provincial soldiers and noncombatants, including camp followers, at Fort William Henry, when the unleashed Abenaki contingent (mostly his own parishioners) had been commanded by a La Marine officer. Roubaud had long taught that the golden path to heaven for the Abenaki lay in killing large numbers of heathens and heretics to the south. The Jesuits preached that Protestant heretics who worshipped an anti-Catholic faith needed to be destroyed with fire and sword to the last man, woman, and child.[5]

For such reasons, it was estimated by one historian about the Fort William Henry massacre that "more than one hundred women, some with their brains still oozing from the battered heads, others with their whole hair wrenched collectively with the skin from the bloody skulls, and many, with their throats cut, most inhumanly stabbed and butchered, lay stripped entirely naked, with their bowels torn out" not far from Fort William Henry.[6]

Because of the militant aspects of Roman Catholicism, which was as feudal in Canada as in France, and what lingered of their old tribal spiritualism from their ancestors, the Abenaki were true holy warriors, who believed that they were waging a most righteous war to justify all manner of atrocities on a vast scale. And because of this religious and spiritual fuel that had long motivated the uncontrolled passions of countless warriors when unleashed on the frontier, St. Francis was truly the dark heart of the persistent evil of Abenaki war parties trekking down the well-trampled war trails that led south to the ultimate reality of the most devastating of raids for generations. The attackers had slaughtered large numbers of men, woman, and children without mercy for nearly a century—no white person was spared unless taken back through the dreary wilderness to Canada as a sullen prisoner to be exchanged for a nice ransom (a profitable business in itself) or in exchange for French prisoners.

During these terrorism-focused raids that possessed the overall goal of panicking the settlers and driving them off the land forever, even the cattle, hogs, and sheep in the fields were systematically slaughtered. This especially ugly, but effective, brand of terrorism was all part of the French and Abenaki strategy to destroy anything and everything connected to an insidious Protestant civilization, which possessed the potential not only to corrupt Abenaki civilization but also to destroy it in the end.

While long supported by French supplies, black powder, and muskets manufactured in France—for instance, at the modern arms factory in Tulle—and accompanied by veteran Canadian and French officers of La Marine (such as one dynamic father-son team of the name St. Ours, a lieutenant and ensign, respectively, both killed in battle against the hated English), who almost always joined Abenaki war parties in striking south, what the Abenaki had waged for decades was not only genocide but also what we know today as the grim process of ethnic cleansing in a determined bid to wipe out an entire people and civilization: a classic case of religious cleansing and ethnic purification, thanks partly to militant priests like Roubaud, who waged a holy war like his Abenaki followers.

After Rogers recovered from his surprise at the sight of sixty houses in a traditional Quebecois style that had been transferred from the mother country and the large church that dominated the entry into the town, he finally came to a set of all-important conclusions. First, and almost incredibly from his lofty perch in the tall pine, he saw that the town along the serene-looking river was bathed in the mundane and routine stillness of a typical fall evening. Rogers, therefore, could not completely be sure about the number of warrior guards at such a distance. However, it was clear that St. Francis was vulnerable and ripe for the taking. From what he had seen, the major knew that no one had been alerted to the presence of his command, setting the stage for a surprise attack and a certain victory that would become the talk of both sides of the Atlantic.

Therefore, Rogers naturally felt a sense of exhilaration, because he now realized that he had succeeded not only in making his dream come true of catching the town by surprise but also in his crucial mission of doing what almost all Englishmen, Canadians, Native Americans, and French (military and civilian) considered an absolute impossibility: advancing with stealth and secrecy by both water and land over a great distance for three nerve-racking weeks to catch the Abenaki and St. Francis completely by surprise, as he had envisioned with clarity for years. Significantly, only Rogers and his men had believed that they could accomplish the impossible against the odds when they had embarked on this expedition with high hopes from Crown Point not long after dark on September 13. Perhaps even Major General Amherst really did not believe that all of this was possible and only hoped for the best, especially after Rogers had early lost such a high percentage of his manpower from accidents and sickness.

Incredibly, to Rogers's absolute delight, no one had yet warned the Abenaki of the immediate danger that was headed their way as the result of the most secret and stealthy of approaches, which had taken nine days of moving east and then northeast to get through the nightmarish spruce bogs that were considered impregnable. So far, no Abenaki war party, hunter, or scout had seen anything of Rogers and his men, including on Lake Champlain, in a rather remarkable development. To the French, this mysterious English contingent of especially daring raiders were like ghosts in the night, who could be neither caught nor seen by anyone, including the finest La Marine partisan officers and best Abenaki trackers.

Therefore, even at this late date, neither the French nor Abenaki expected a strike on St. Francis from the south because of the lengthy distance from Missisquoi Bay and the vast expanse of spruce bogs—the very last direction considered feasible for raiders in the minds of top leaders at French headquarters at the highest levels. In this regard, an overanxious French leadership had outsmarted themselves, and Rogers had outsmarted all his pursuers by this time, with frontier savvy and common sense having risen to the fore in splendid fashion.

In addition, the general assumption among French leadership was that Englishmen and Provincial troops lacked the courage and nerve to do the impossible by brazenly entering into the heart of the enemy's country—the mystical and mysterious land of the Abenaki, who were the most feared Native American ally of New France—and striking the most audacious of blows, because St. Francis had never been touched before by attackers, and its fearsome reputation was so outsized.

The sheer sense of satisfaction for Rogers to realize that he finally had St. Francis within his grasp must have been nothing short of overwhelming to his very senses. He now realized that his boldest gamble of the all—trekking a long distance down Lake Champlain and then marching his relatively small band of Rangers, Provincials, and British Regulars through the broad expanse of the spruce bogs, which took a week and a half—had paid immense dividends, even more than he had imagined.

After all, the Abenaki had long ago concluded that English Rangers would never dare do the unthinkable and attempt to march through the spruce bogs, where only a light-footed deer or moose could nimbly traverse such a barren landscape without starving to death like a wayward human being without provisions or common sense. But the Abenaki, exceptionally smug and overconfident, were destined to shortly discover that they had been entirely wrong in their longtime strategic calculations and demeaning racial and ethnic stereotypes about their white enemy, which had long existed and never been questioned at St. Francis by even the wisest chief and sachem as long as anyone could remember.

Rogers now reached his most personally rewarding conclusion and delightful realization of his entire career because of the town's complete vulnerability, while high in the pine tree that overlooked St. Francis and the surrounding countryside draped in the fading glow of the red light of sunset. In many ways, the sense of absolute aloneness now felt by Rogers from his vantage point high above his resting men was most appropriate. Indeed, under these special circumstances, the New England frontiersman had alone masterminded this bold plan to catch St. Francis by surprise, and he was now on the verge of the most dramatic moment of his career for doing the impossible against all odds.

After all, Major Rogers was the first and only one to truly believe that the most audacious attack plan of the French and Indian War was possible, when no one else had been convinced that it was even remotely feasible, as early as May 1756. In fact, this was one of the boldest plans ever developed by any commander in American military history, and Rogers had developed it with a good deal of loving care on his own, when only he had been convinced that it would succeed year after year. Clearly, Rogers was not only a brilliant tactical mastermind and visionary when it came to warfighting in the wilderness but also a dreamer, yet one rooted in undeniable realities and truisms.

Indeed, in his agile mind for years, Rogers had envisioned what he and his Rangers could accomplish with sheer audacity if only unleashed by a senior British commander, but such highly educated and revered men of the

British military establishment had too often underestimated and devalued the Rangers primarily because of the fact that they were mere colonials and mainly lowly Scotch-Irish. However, Rogers and his largely Scotch-Irish men knew better the truth of their own bravery, combat prowess, and abilities, allowing the major to dream the realistic dream of attacking the most impossible of targets, St. Francis.

In his head, Major Rogers had long planned and imagined this precious moment and special time when he and his men were finally deep in Quebec and at last had the much-feared St. Francis within their grasp in overall tactical terms. Indeed, with St. Francis now at his mercy, Rogers planned to close his fist and squeeze it tight on the early morning of October 4. To Rogers, this unforgettable moment must have seemed like his farthest-reaching and most cherished ambition come true, because he had been hoping and praying to gain just such an unprecedented opportunity to attack St. Francis for years.

Back in October 1756, he had proposed his unthinkable tactical concept of marching on faraway St. Francis to Lord Loudoun, who had perhaps thought Rogers was a bit crazy when he requested to be unleashed to do exactly what he was now on the verge of accomplishing and precisely what tens of thousands of his long-suffering people, especially the poor Scotch-Irish on the northern frontier, had most desired for generations: the wiping out of St. Francis. As noted, Rogers's request had been refused by the aristocratic lordship because it just seemed too fantastic to possibly succeed against such astronomical odds. But Rogers had always known that this far-flung mission was not fantastic or foolish in the least and that he and his men could accomplish what everyone else, including the Abenaki, French, and Canadians, believed was simply impossible.

Now Major Rogers was closer to fulfilling that great dream than ever before, and he basked in that realization, which brought great comfort to him as a man and commander. In fact, he could almost savor the sweet taste of vengeance and righteous retribution on what would almost inevitably be a terrible morning of reckoning for St. Francis, which would at long last come to fruition with the next sunrise, October 4. In many fundamental ways, Rogers and his men and the settlers, especially the Scotch-Irish, of the northern frontier had been waiting for their entire lives for this long-dreamed about moment, because St. Francis was now deliciously ripe, like a golden pear, for the taking by men sufficiently bold to take it by force.[7]

ANOTHER TIMELY PERSONAL RECONNOITER CLOSER
TO THE ULTIMATE TARGET

For such reasons, Rogers had been immediately elated by the sight of "the Smoak [*sic*] [of the chimneys and cooking fires of St. Francis] about 5 or 6 miles distant," wrote one of Rogers's men, about what his rough-hewn commander had seen from the top of the pine tree. However, this estimation from a man who did not climb the tree like Rogers was a considerable exaggeration, because the distance was closer to four miles. Most of all, at this point within sight of the most lucrative of targets, no time could be wasted in the final orchestration of the advance to ease into close striking range, as Rogers fully realized.

In keeping with the unique spirit of democracy that thrived on the northern frontier to a degree unknown in the more autocratic New France, which had transferred its antiquated system of feudalism to Canada, Rogers immediately called together his officers in still another democratic meeting of the leading fighting men in the frontier tradition—part of the major's unique leadership style, to which he continued to faithfully adhere regardless of the situation.[8]

Scotland-born Private Robert Kirkwood, who had known no such extensive pine forests in his native land across the sea like the one in which he now found himself, described the situation after Rogers climbed down from the tree and called his men together: "A council was held, to confide in what manner we should proceed."[9]

Meanwhile, Rogers's ascent and descent from the tall pine had allowed for a much-needed respite for his exhausted men, who had reposed in the rest of the weary. Indeed, Rogers had ordered his men "to refresh themselves" for the upcoming challenge and the attack that would shortly be unleashed on St. Francis, while he had scaled the tree to make his observations. Here, during the welcome respite, soldiers consumed some of their last remaining rations, while other men went hungry, having already eaten all their provisions in the spruce bogs. Soldiers without any food now regretted their lack of discipline, with stomachs growling and hunger pangs already creeping in.[10]

In this crisis situation, the democratic spirit of Rogers and his egalitarian-minded command, consisting of so many independent-minded individualists who mirrored the mentality of their commander and the frontier's cherished value systems, continued to pay dividends. Additionally, Rogers's unique leadership ways also continued to play a role in binding the men as one with the same sense of purpose in the most dangerous of situations, especially when so near St. Francis: part of the can-do attitude and feisty fighting spirit that had created "the most formidable body of men ever employed in the early years of America."[11]

But as usual, Rogers was not taking any changes, knowing that one mistake might lead to the detection of his sizeable force of Rangers, Provincials, and British Regulars within striking distance of St. Francis. Rogers and his officers nevertheless decided to take the risk of marching closer to St. Francis in preparation for attacking the town just before first light on October 4. Indeed, despite the greater risk of running into an Abenaki war party, hunter, or villager, or even frolicking children, who would then warn the town, the major still knew that he needed to take a closer look at St. Francis to gather more accurate intelligence, just in case some kind of a trap or ambush had been set up by the wily French and Abenaki.

Therefore, as quietly as possible and with parties of reliable flankers and sharp-eyed scouts for protection, Rogers led his men in single file ever closer through the dark woodlands toward the town that was still not alerted to the nearby presence of the hated white men who had come all the way from Crown Point. With stealth, they advanced with great care as one, almost as if these experienced fighting men were now stalking game in the wilderness and about to take a well-aimed shot at an unwary deer, moose, or turkey, but with an even greater degree of alertness and vigilance than usual. Indeed, these determined soldiers were about to take their best shot in targeting the entire town of St. Francis for destruction.

In a letter, one of Rogers's faithful followers described the scenario of the renewed advance, when the major led the way, after first having "halted his Party until Dusk of the Evening [of October 3 to climb the pine tree for his first observation of St. Francis], and then march'd again, until he came within 2 or 3 Miles" of St. Francis. Actually around two miles was the proper distance to Rogers's ultimate target, because of his concern about encountering Abenaki villagers or scouts and being detected.[12]

Here, around two miles of the town, Rogers allowed his men to once again rest in preparation for undertaking their greatest challenge when nearly in sight of legendary St. Francis. Full of anxiety and fearing a possible trap of some sort because everything seemed too quiet in the pine forests and in the town—almost always a telltale sign that some kind of trouble was brewing and on the way—the wary major waited until around 8 p.m. on October 3 before he made his next move to ascertain additional information about the overall situation.

During the interim, he and his officers thoroughly checked to make sure that each man had a properly working firearm, dry black powder, a firing pan in good shape, and a trusty tomahawk by his side for the deadly work that lay ahead. Every fighting man had to be ready in every way, shape, and form in preparation for one of the hardest-hitting surprise attacks of the French and Indian War.

After all, if they were suddenly discovered by the enemy at any moment, then Rogers's attack would have to be launched immediately rather than the planned assault on the morning of October 4. For such reasons, a greater peace of mind came to the major on the cusp of his most famous success, after he had made sure that his anxious men were fully prepared for any emergency or unexpected development. It was now time for Rogers to take an even closer look at St. Francis at great risk to himself, in part because the Scotch-Irish major always led by example and never ordered anyone to do what or go where he would not.[13]

QUICKLY FORMULATING THE BEST TACTICAL PLAN

For obvious tactical reasons and to satisfy his own curiosity about this special place that he had heard about for his entire life, Rogers was itching to take a closer look at St. Francis to make sure that his earlier observations had been correct and that nothing had changed in the seemingly comatose town. From the imposing height of the treetop that overlooked the forest in bright autumn hues that stretched before St. Francis around four miles away, Major Rogers was about to gain a bird's-eye view. He had been unable to fully develop the most appropriate and best tactics based on his long-distance view of the terrain and the village of Odanak. Therefore, Rogers now needed a more thorough reconnaissance that necessarily had to be made much closer, but also still at a safe distance to ensure that he would not be seen by any Abenaki.

As noted, the sharp-eyed major had seen no hill, creek, or ridge lying before the town to slow the advance and provide the maximum advantage for a surprise attack, because no nuances of the terrain and the overall lay of the land posed any obstacles whatsoever. Because the ground was relatively level as part of the low-lying St. Lawrence and St. Francis River Valleys, which were generally flatlands, the terrain was undistinguished by any physical features that might have impeded the attack. Although the town of St. Francis was poised on the high ground of river bluffs overlooking the placid watercourse, which was around three times the width of the spot where Rogers and his men had crossed much farther upriver, this elevated position of the town had not been clearly ascertained by the major from the height of the tall pine from the distance of around four miles.

Therefore, as one expeditioner wrote in a letter, Major Rogers was determined to slip much closer to his target and perhaps a good many Abenaki warriors, who might have reinforced the town for all he knew, to more thoroughly "Reconnoiter the Town." The entire town lay before him seemingly like a gift presented to him by the gods of war, who were still looking favorably upon Rogers and his small task force, which had already overcome seemingly insurmountable odds to have even gained this golden opportunity, because no Abenaki or French defensive preparations or hectic activities were in evidence.[14]

Quite simply, St. Francis could not have possibly been more vulnerable than at this time. Later, Governor-General Vaudreuil emphasized to his disgust that he had warned the people of St. Francis "over and over again" about the town's vulnerability, but no one had listened. Clearly, a bad case of Abenaki hubris was now on Rogers's side.[15]

Located near today's small community of St. Francis on Canada's Abenaki reserve, the town had looked ripe for the taking even at a long distance to Rogers, when he had been perched atop the tall pine. However, it was still much too quiet in the dark woodlands of early autumn and the open fields before St. Francis: an unsettling fact to the ever-suspicious major when he reflected more on what he had seen, raising more doubts and questions. Smoke from a good many Abenaki cooking fires of boiling corn and freshly killed game told Rogers that Abenaki women were preparing the evening dinner for families that included a good many black-eyed and dark-haired children of all ages. Everything about St. Francis appeared normal on that early October day, which made the major even more uneasy because of his well-honed survival instincts.

Indeed, Rogers was still worried about dire possibilities. To survive this wilderness war, he always had to consider the worst-case scenario, and this situation, of course, was no exception to the rule. After all, how many Abenaki warriors of prime fighting age were about to partake in the evening meal on this October 3 more than one hundred miles northeast of Crown Point, which was now much farther away from Rogers than Montreal on the St. Lawrence? How many, if any, warriors had been ordered northeast to help to defend Quebec when General Wolfe had knocked on the door of New France's capital city? And had any warriors earlier left St. Francis to serve in other sectors, including Montreal, Isle-aux-Noix, or Trois-Rivières to the southwest of Quebec? Even more, how many warriors were dispatched from St. Francis to the south by French leaders when the command's whaleboats were discovered on Missisquoi Bay?

Of course, such pressing questions were now great unknowns that disturbed Rogers's peace of mind. To answer such nagging questions, he needed to know as much as possible, as soon as possible. Most of all, because he knew that Wolfe was threatening Quebec, he wondered how many of these lethal warriors from St. Francis were now playing roles in the defense of Quebec, which had long been the primary target of the British war effort? Was it a majority? Rogers could not be sure. However, Rogers began to sense that he now possessed a far greater opportunity than if he had been allowed to attack St. Francis in 1756.

At this time, Rogers had no idea about the current strategic situation at Quebec, after having been away from Crown Point and the last up-to-date intelligence for three weeks. He did not know that a great victory had been won on the Plains of Abraham on September 13. Consequently, Rogers no doubt was reasonably sure that at least some warriors of St. Francis were at Quebec at this time. But had General Wolfe been repulsed and retired back down the St. Lawrence and returned to Halifax, after still another humiliating British setback, to allow the warriors to return? This was a serious concern to Rogers because if so, then the warriors would have returned to St. Francis.

In truth, Rogers could not be completely sure about anything at this time. Nevertheless, the grizzled and rugged-looking major, who looked older than his years after the recent ordeal of trekking through the spruce bogs, realized that he still faced his most formidable challenge, despite the fact that St. Francis, by all appearances, seemed unprepared for an attack. However, the major's recent observation of St. Francis from high in the pine tree had told him a great deal about the intervening lay of the mostly level land, covered in dense pine forest that would conceal his command's approach to his ultimate target, because Rogers had been able to get a good feel for the general terrain and overall topography on the river's north side with the experienced eye of a longtime woodsman and natural topographer. Allowing him to develop his tactical thoughts, the major had already gained an intimate sense of the nature of the ground that lay on the river's north side and about this infamous place that had become the stuff of legend across the frontier because of the surreal horrors that had long stemmed from this mission town.

Most important, Rogers knew that he would encounter no high-ground position of hidden warriors in ambush on a timbered hilltop or ridge, when he advanced his command through the lush woodlands and over the generally level ground to the northeast, while inching ever closer to St. Francis. As noted, the thick forest that lay between the major's command and St. Francis was not a cause of concern in this situation and from what Rogers had seen so far, because the pine woods, with a carpet of soft, brown pine needles on the ground, guaranteed a stealthy approach on the unsuspecting town, which was situated in an uncharted wilderness—exactly the setting that had long ensured a perfect sense of safety for St. Francis and its smug inhabitants, who still basked in their longtime security and sense of invincibility.

Therefore, Rogers had already formulated his initial set of time-proved thoughts for the unleashing of the tactical offensive in his mind to overwhelm the village as quickly as possible with his available 142 men even before the first light of the upcoming day, October 4. Clearly, Rogers had learned his past lessons well in the wilderness war about how to catch the enemy by surprise. He was about to descend upon St. Francis with a fury seldom seen and, ironically, in the same manner as countless Abenaki war parties had long descended on isolated log cabins and vulnerable settlements across the frontier from Pennsylvania to Virginia with devastating results.

After Rogers had climbed down from the towering pine tree in the steadily cooling half-light of near dusk and then resumed his northwestward advance to ease ever closer to his unalerted target and unsuspecting victims, he already felt more assurance about what he had to accomplish and exactly how. However, Rogers still needed a closer look at the town to answer the many questions that were swirling in his mind at this time.

However, and as noted, the major's initial sight of St. Francis from the pine tree and its delightful vulnerability in its calm certitude of normality raised Rogers's hopes for success, while meeting his most optimistic expectations, almost as if his own prayers and those of his frontier people had finally been answered. As far as Rogers had been able to ascertain from the treetop, and as mentioned, the village situated along the picturesque river of blue was still undefended to a degree that had been unimaginable to him even in his fondest dreams when he had been leading his men from the nightmarish spruce bogs. So far, and almost incredibly to Rogers and his men, not a single party of French soldiers, Abenaki warriors, or Canadians had been seen on either side of the St. Francis. No footprints of any Abenaki warrior, deer hunter, or scout had been ascertained by the Indian Rangers from Stockbridge, Massachusetts, who had thoroughly searched for any signs of the enemy.

But if the community looked deserted at a time when few people were in sight, then where were the lethal defenders—the veteran warriors who had long slaughtered countless settlers without mercy across the frontier—of St. Francis? Despite his recent assurances of what seemed almost like an inevitable success looming on the horizon, this key question tormented Rogers to no end and like no other in the haunted darkness of October 3. Therefore, the major feared that the enemy's strength might be hidden in some kind of a ruse.

Rogers felt that he risked running into another disastrous tactical situation that had gotten his command, the vast majority of more than 140 Rangers, including some of his finest men, cut to pieces by Ensign Langy's fierce fighting men—Indians, Canadians of the woodlands and who were known for deadly accuracy with their favorite rifles, and veteran French of La Marine—during the terrible Second Battle on Snowshoes. Or had a large war or hunting party suddenly returned to St. Francis to thwart Rogers's well-laid tactical plans at the last minute?

At this time, Rogers had no way of knowing that the last remaining warriors of St. Francis were now far away. Few of these legendary Abenaki fighters, who were known to take relatively few prisoners in what they viewed as a war to the death, were at St. Francis at this time. The horrors committed by these warriors were the stuff of nightmares in the frontier settlements for successive generations, and Rogers and his men never forgot exactly why they were now about to strike St. Francis.

When given the opportunity, which was often, the Abenaki had beheaded English soldiers and then had carried the grisly remains on their belts as trophies, still dripping blood, as if a scalp were no longer sufficient proof of warrior courage. At Fort William Henry, Father Roubaud had been present to fortify the militant Catholicism—an especially lethal brand—that helped to make the warriors even more ferocious, including conducting Mass for his St. Francis flock. Here, the Abenaki had played a leading role in the slaughter, although the Marquis de Montcalm and French officers had attempted to stop the orgy of bloodletting. And this was another shocking atrocity that Rogers and his men never forgot, especially on the morning of October 4.

As noted, most of these famed warriors of the mysterious village of St. Francis had been long ago dispatched to reinforce the Marquis de Montcalm and especially Quebec, when under Wolfe's threat, to aid in its defense of the fortress city that dominated the St. Lawrence at this strategic point where it narrowed. Then the last large body of St. Francis warriors had been recently dispatched to deal with Rogers by Governor-General Vaudreuil, who had done everything in his power to thwart this strange band of English raiders on the loose in Quebec.

And now these dispatched warriors waited in vain for Rogers and his men to emerge from the expansive spruce bog, the so-called Drowned Lands, at Yamaska, southwest of St. Francis and elsewhere, in part because no French, Canadian, or Indian warrior, woman, or child could believe that an English force would possess the audacity to march so far north and attack the legendary St. Francis. Thanks partly to the hellish expanse of spruce bogs in which his tracks could not be traced during the watery trek in what had seemed like an eternity, Rogers had not only eluded the enemy but also won his race to defy his opponents' expectations and imaginations.[16]

Of course, Rogers did not yet know of the enemy's most recent movements and strategy, but he knew that French forces in Canada were fighting for their lives and the colony's existence in the face of Wolfe's overpowering army and mighty naval fleet: a guarantee that St. Francis was now more vulnerable than ever before. Even more, although the major did not realize it, one of his men later revealed in a letter an impending Abenaki movement: "The whole Town intended to come up [south] the [St. Francis] River on a Scout the next day," October 5.[17] But of course, and fortunately for Rogers and his plan, this intended scout by the Abenaki in Rogers's direction on October 5 would be, if launched, much too late to ascertain the raiders' location before they struck St. Francis on October 4.

With anxiety running high, and with many more questions still needing to be answered as soon as possible in the major's busy mind, Rogers selected two of his best men, who were fluent Algonquian speakers, for a special mission. He had decided to proceed forward with a good deal of care and stealth to get his much-desired closer look at St. Francis after leaving Captain Amos Ogden, an ever-dependable officer of the New Jersey Blues, in command of his surviving band of fighting men, while they were allowed rest. Exhausted men stretched out for catnaps in the cool pine thickets to restore strength and energy for the many challenges yet to come by the time the sun of October 3 dropped below the western horizon in the direction of Montreal.

In Major Rogers's words about doing what he now needed to accomplish, despite the risk of making a mistake that might alert the entire town to the raiders' presence, "At eight o'clock this evening I left the detachment, and took with me Lieut. [James] Turner [sometimes known as George and a top officer of Moses Brewer's Connecticut Mohegan company of warriors and veteran Rangers from Stockbridge] and Ensign [Elias] Avery [a trusty Connecticut Provincial leader of considerable ability as demonstrated during the course of prior service, including with Israel Putnam], and went to reconnoit[er] the town, which I did to my satisfaction, and [shortly] found the Indians in a high frolic or dance."[18]

This act was basically in keeping with Rogers's Rule Number IV for the waging of successful wilderness warfare: "Some time before you come to the place you would reconnoit[er], make a stand, and send one or two men in whom you can confide, to look out the best ground for making your observations."[19]

But, of course, Rogers himself was leading the small party for the close observation of the target instead of sending men out on his orders. Clearly, when so close to St. Francis and hoping to double-check his initial thoughts about what he had first seen, Rogers had to take another look at the most infamous Native American town in North America.[20]

In a letter written on November 26, 1759, a lucky survivor of the raid wrote about the most recent development: "He halted his Party a second Time [for his next scout and another much-needed rest of his worn men when close to St. Francis], and [then Rogers] took two Men with him, leaving the Command with Capt. Ogden, and went to Reconnoiter the Town, where he arrived about 12 o'Clock, [and soon succeeded in] finding the Indians in a great Frolick, singing and having the War Dance" in a wild celebration that echoed through the dark and still forests.[21]

Positioned in the dense underbrush of a pine thicket before the open fields, now bare after the annual harvest of corn, under the comforting veil of darkness, the major and his two trusty companions—who, if they had worn them, would have taken off their revealing green coats and blue Scottish bonnets—carefully crawled on their hands and knees through the brush toward St. Francis. Fortunately for Rogers's stealthy approach, the Abenaki's fields stood adjacent to the town. The overall layout of the community allowed the three interlopers to take full advantage of the forest and level ground all the way to the field's edge before the cluster of houses of St. Francis, which was shrouded by a canopy of the stately pines that grew especially high in the fertile soil so close to the river. Rogers himself wrote that at "8 o'clock Lieutenant Turner, Ensign Avery, and myself reconnoitred the town [and] We found the Indians engaged in a high frolic, and saw them execute several dances with great spirit and activity."[22]

Revealing his trust in Second Lieutenant James Turner, who had learned his trade under the best Ranger teacher of all after Rogers, Captain John Stark, since Christmas Day 1757, when he had first enlisted as a private, Rogers whispered to him to creep toward the sizeable Council House at the head of the town to get a better look. Turner had early proved his worth as a daring Ranger officer who knew Indian and wilderness ways, gaining a lieutenant's rank in April 1758 in Captain Moses Brewer's company of Mohegan warriors from Connecticut.[23] Likewise, Ensign Avery was an excellent officer. He had served with Israel Putnam, a fine leader who later became one of George Washington's Continental generals during the American Revolution, and his Connecticut Rangers, who, in the art of the ranging warfare, were second only to Rogers's Rangers—no small achievement and a testament to Putnam's abilities.[24]

While crawling carefully through the underbrush and ever closer to a noisy celebration that was occurring at the Council House amid the autumnal darkness of the inky-black surrounding woodlands, Turner suddenly halted before hearing unfamiliar sounds up ahead in the bushes. He strained his ears and nerves to capture additional sounds that might well spell the difference between life and death, when so close to St. Francis. Then, after remaining attentive and motionless in the blackness, the lieutenant heard grunting and panting that coincided with a rustling of bushes.

Second Lieutenant Turner wondered whether the sounds came from an animal or a human. But what kind of activity was happening right before him on a beautiful fall night? For a spell, the motionless lieutenant had no idea what was occurring in the nearby bushes, which were violently shaking. He was entirely unable to make out the source of the mysterious sounds. But yet, as more anxious seconds ticked by in the eerie blackness, he began to realize that there was something very familiar and uniquely human about this mysterious noise deep in the night. In fact, Turner realized that he himself had made such sounds in the past.

He then might have smiled to himself when finally completely sure of the exact source. Creeping closer with great care to verify his conviction that the noise came from the most human of activities, which he had engaged in with lovers and perhaps a wife in the past, Lieutenant Turner peered through the underbrush and then "saw two [Abenaki] lovers, a very fetching white lass [evidently the attractive and sexually aggressive Jane Chandler, who had been captured by the Abenaki as a child of five years of age] & an Indion sparking in ye bush."[25]

From the good natural cover, Rogers spent a good deal of time ascertaining as much as possible in looking over St. Francis. Relying on skills well known from having scouted so close to the walls of Fort Carillon for years, he had advanced close to the first houses of the town perched on the high north bank of the river. It was clear to the major (who might well have smeared his face in mud for camouflage) that the Indians had no idea that they had been targeted for destruction by the best irregular commander and tried veterans in the entire British-Provincial Army. All the while, Rogers was in the process of formulating the best plan for attacking the town, weighing tactical options and calculations for striking a surprise blow when least expected by the Abenaki.[26]

Unlike anything found in primary documentation or written by participants about the raid, Rogers's second and much closer observation of the
town did not include the most ridiculous traditions and assumptions first
perpetuated by the usually careful Francis Parkman, who played a key role
in creating the mythical Rogers of romantic New England legend in his
classic *Montcalm and Wolfe*. According to these romanticized stories, Rogers
shaved off his beard and disguised himself as an Abenaki to personally enter
St. Francis to gather intelligence. Allegedly he even walked the dusty streets
of St. Francis to gain firsthand information, since he was able to speak the
tongue of the Abenaki, which was part of the Algonquian language.

However, this popular romantic tale is implausible, because at this point
such extreme boldness by the major was entirely unnecessary, although it
would have been in keeping with his aggressive personal leadership style,
which often bordered on reckless in the face of the enemy. Such an ill-
advised stunt on the streets of St. Francis would have jeopardized the entire
mission at a time when he was on the verge of success—just another example of the romantic mythology that has long shrouded the real Rogers and
his exploits, which have become the stuff of legend. In truth, all Rogers had
to do was not be discovered, and walking into St. Francis, as alleged by his
admirers, would have risked everything for relatively little gain.[27]

But what cannot be denied is the fact that Major Rogers was not only
delighted but also amused by what he saw among the unsuspecting Abenaki
in St. Francis: merrymaking, dancing, and frolicking instead of the menacing
war dance long incorrectly assumed by historians and writers. Quite simply,
and although Rogers did not realize it at the time, the performance of a
traditional war dance was now an impossibility because there were simply
not enough warriors left in town on October 3. What Rogers viewed was a
dance celebrating a successful harvest, whose bounty now filled the houses,
including several storehouses of corn, with the necessary provisions for the
Abenaki people to survive the lengthy Quebec winter, which was much longer and more severe than in New England.

The hard-bitten major, who proudly wore the scars of past battles and
skirmishes in the wilderness against these same Abenaki, no doubt had to
force himself to contain his absolute delight because everyone in the town
appeared so unwary, just like so many settlers had been when the scalp-
seeking warriors had descended upon them without warning or mercy for

generations. Hardly believing his eyes, Rogers saw clearly that all of St. Francis was completely vulnerable and that he had succeeded in catching the town completely by surprise. What he now saw at close range confirmed what he had earlier seen from the tall pine tree.

No Abenaki war parties had returned to St. Francis, and no warriors were out guarding the community, which basked in a confidence born of an arrogance and contempt for the abilities of white soldiers, because of so many past Abenaki successes for nearly a century, when no one from the south had dared to threaten St. Francis. Almost all of the Abenaki warriors were now either far north, having guarded Quebec, or in concealed positions with the two ambushes established at the Yamaska River and at Missisquoi Bay, where they waited for Rogers's return to reclaim the sixteen whaleboats—now destroyed—and the all-important provisions for the return to Crown Point.

Ironically, the long list of past victories of these fierce Abenaki warriors over the hapless British Regulars and the frontier settlers had fueled an excess of pride in what they had achieved decade after decade: a hubris that now made St. Francis and Chief Joseph-Louis Gill's people extremely vulnerable. Rogers saw that the primary activity in the entire town was centered on the celebration, which was in full swing, at the large Council House—a special place where only social and traditional gatherings, not war dances, were held. War dances were traditionally held outside in the open air because of the large number of warrior participants.

Best of all, and as noted, the town situated along the river was even more vulnerable than Rogers had originally surmised from the top of the towering pine tree. No French La Marine regulars or Canadian militiamen, who dressed even more like Indians than Rogers's men, were seen anywhere. Not even an Abenaki warrior, with a French Tulle musket draped over his shoulder and in brightly colored war paint, was detected in the streets or coming in and out of the French-style houses. And no warriors were even guarding the Council House during the festive celebration.

Therefore, Rogers rejoiced in the absence of anyone who looked like a regular French or Canadian soldier, with no Abenaki warriors, who were the most feared Native American fighting men in North America, to be seen— precisely where they should have been seen. In the moonlight that cast a soft, whitish glow over the land, the hard-packed dirt streets of St. Francis, which passed through the rows of houses, were entirely devoid of people.

As mentioned, Captain Stark had almost certainly told him about what to expect in regard to the town's general layout. Nevertheless, Rogers still marveled at how this place was no traditional Algonquian community of longhouses and wigwams traditionally seen among the Algonquian peoples all across New England, and, best of all, no wooden palisade had ever been erected to protect the town, as at the Pequot fort at Mystic in Connecticut. Quite simply, Rogers's timing could not have been better because St. Francis could not have been more vulnerable than at this time. This French-like town of sixty houses was larger than the first log frontier communities in which Rogers had lived. Around twenty of the largest houses had been built in the traditional French style unlike anything seen in Rogers's native Merrimack River country, where crude log cabins and traditional English-style homes dominated the scenic landscape.

In 1704, near the St. Lawrence River, the French had originally laid out a detailed plan for the establishment of St. Francis, which was much like a town back in France and organized along traditional European lines. Of course, this distinctive French layout of an ancient Gallic civilization across the sea hardly seemed appropriate, given the town's dark reputation for having spawned a seemingly endless list of unspeakable horrors, after it had moved a short distance upriver to its present location. Unbeknownst to Rogers and his men, St. Francis was very much a hybrid community of Native American refugees from across New England. White chief Joseph-Lewis Gill, who lacked a single ounce of Indian blood, was the respected head man of the most infamous Native American community on the continent.

However, since the time long ago when the town had moved upriver, it had grown considerably with the arrival of a far larger number of Native American refugees. They had been pushed out of their ancient homelands by white encroachment, including north up the Connecticut and Merrimack River Valleys and elsewhere. Rogers also saw that the town included even some nice houses built of stone. Rogers had known of no stone houses while growing up among log cabins of the Merrimack River country, and this almost unbelievable fact no doubt surprised him.

Rogers did not even see Abenaki children playing in the dirt streets with small fur balls from the adults' enthusiastic games of lacrosse, which the warriors had long played in the nearby grassy fields, or later while their parents celebrated and enjoyed the festivities at the Council House. Incredibly, town members—except the infirm and elderly, who were disabled and generally absent from social activities—were almost all concentrated in the Council House, which stood prominently at the town's head, as if protecting the community, and which Rogers saw was not even guarded. The loud sounds of music, singing, dancing, shouts, and enthusiastic drumming indicated that this was a festive dance that the Indian-knowledgeable Rogers almost certainly surmised was the annual October celebration of the harvest.

Indeed, at this time of year, as Rogers had learned, the surrounding fields at the edge of the pine forest were bare of crops, especially corn. The corn had already been harvested and stored in three wooden storehouses for the community's survival during winter. During the dark days of Quebec's heavy winters from about the end of October to March, the corn would be equally distributed to each individual family in a communal and democratic manner that would have been envied by poor settlers on the hardscrabble New England frontier.

When so close to the town, and despite his extensive knowledge, Rogers could not be exactly sure what was occurring in the Council House, situated on the plaza, and why. Was this some kind of a ruse, because it all seemed suspicious? However, advancing any closer to St. Francis was too risky and dangerous and, therefore, out of the question.

As noted, contrary to the persistent myth that Rogers personally entered the town and casually spoke French and the Abenaki language to the inhabitants in gathering information, the major knew that he could not risk the entire mission, because one careless mistake or accident might lead to the discovery that more than 142 fighting men were waiting in silence on the town's outskirts for his word to attack.

Most Abenaki men, women, and children now filled the community's largest structure, the Council House, during what some accounts described as the wedding celebration of a young couple. However, as mentioned, this was actually a harvest celebration, and a great stockpile of corn was already stored in three separate log huts that served as granaries. It had been a good harvest, and the grain sheds were overflowing with corn for the Abenaki people's food during the upcoming harsh winter months.

However, the possibility does exist that this celebration was for both the harvest and the wedding. If so, like the bountiful harvest from the broad fields along the river, the wedding was also a celebration of the beginning of new life (future children) for the young woman and man; the groom had most likely already gained respect for having gone forth with a war party to raid the frontier settlements. Equally symbolic, this celebration on the night of October 3 was occurring at the exact time when Rogers and his men were planning to end life in St. Francis.[28]

Of course, this second timely and closer reconnoiter by Rogers of the most inviting of targets secured even better intelligence than he had gained from the treetop near dusk, because it revealed that St. Francis was even more vulnerable than previously imagined, while allowing Rogers to gain vital intelligence from the pine forest's edge without ever having to enter the town, as alleged by Parkman and other admiring historians. As mentioned, historian Parkman was guilty of overinflating Rogers's accomplishments in the face of danger, because the young New England scholar had become guilty of excessive hero worship of his New England idol: a romantic glorification that many historians have accepted as fact for generations.

Again, almost incredibly, no guards of any race or color were seen for the entire time that Rogers watched in absolute astonishment at the town's supreme vulnerability. Exactly where were the warriors who had earned St. Francis the most fearsome reputation of any Indian town in North America? Were they about to return to the town and appear on the early morning of October 4, when Rogers planned to launch his attack? Neither French troops nor Abenaki war parties had been spied at any point. In this sense, Rogers was still quite wary, because St. Francis had long basically served as an advanced warning center on the south between Montreal and Quebec. However, he also realized that either city could draw upon the defenders of New France.

Hardly containing his joy but not allowing it to show, because no unnecessary sound could be made when so close to St. Francis as he had already directed, Rogers realized beyond doubt that this was a dream come true—the town was ripe for the taking far beyond expectations. Along with Lieutenant Turner and Ensign Avery, from excellent cover provided by the underbrush at the edge of the open field lying before the town, the major surveyed St. Francis past the midnight hour. He even stayed watching for any new developments in St. Francis past 1 a.m., thanks to the glow of the yellow moonlight that bathed the land in a soft glow.

But like a good commander who realized that his every decision had to be exactly right at this point, Rogers still held his cards close when it came to displaying his emotions. He seldom allowed his deepest feelings to be revealed to any of his men, including Turner and Avery, who also now knew the truth of the extent of the advantageous situation at St. Francis. As always, to make the most favorable impression on his men, the major still maintained a stoic appearance with a poker face that disguised his inner joy at this time.

Second Lieutenant Turner and Ensign Avery also silently rejoiced in the fact that St. Francis was completely unguarded—the most favorable of all possible tactical situations that not even Rogers had believed possible when he had first embarked on this expedition. It seemed almost too good to be true, but it was true—the most beautiful of all realities to the mind of Rogers and his men, who had plenty of old scores to settle for many past wrongs.

Now Rogers was within easy striking distance of St. Francis, which most military people believed to have been completely impossible. Therefore, at this time, the major must have felt that he was so close to finally fulfilling his long-sought objective that he could almost reach out and touch it, feeling that his great dream nurtured over the years was about to come true—the complete destruction of St. Francis in a holy redemption for almost too many victims to count. For such reasons, as noted, St. Francis had been the place that had fueled and consumed Rogers's ambitions for years, making him fight harder and with even more determination in the name of bringing a bloody day of reckoning to St. Francis. In this sense, all paths for Rogers had led to St. Francis. Even the dreaded name of St. Francis possessed a special ring to it that sent a chill down the backbone of even the most experienced Ranger.

Paradoxically, and not lost to a large Protestant soldiery, this infamous place located on a quiet river in a picturesque setting that had caused so much destruction and death for so long had been named after a revered Catholic saint. Rogers almost certainly felt that he was now finally close to making his greatest ambition come true, after a remarkable odyssey just to reach this advanced point in Quebec. Unfortunately for the long-ravaged frontier, the seemingly insurmountable opposition to launching the dangerous gamble of advancing deep into enemy territory to destroy St. Francis in 1755, 1756, 1757, and 1758 had arisen partly because neither upper-class British leaders, from Lord Loudoun to Thomas Gage, nor their families had suffered like lower-class settlers, mostly Scotch-Irish, along the frontier.

Indeed, against the odds and against all probability, Major Rogers now stood on the threshold of accomplishing a great goal that had never been achieved. In fact, most people (especially leading British generals) had considered the novel concept of striking St. Francis utterly impractical in every way. However, Rogers had proved everyone, friend and foe, wrong. In this sense, Rogers continued his penchant for not only unorthodoxy and unconventionality but also doing the impossible. And now the Ranger chieftain was in a perfect position to deliver a severe punishment and a devastating psychological blow to an opponent and to prove to one and all what he and his men could accomplish against the odds.

After all, not even England's best and brightest, including leading generals educated the prestigious British institution at Eton, where generations of the English aristocracy had been transformed into the nation's top military leaders, could have achieved such an unprecedented feat: leading less than 150 men (only 142 Rangers, Provincials, and British Regulars now remained in good fighting shape of Rogers's task force after the grueling ordeal of the last twenty days since departing Crown Point on September 13) nearly 175 miles north through an uncharted wilderness that no noncaptive white person, other than the enemy, had ever seen before.

Even more impressively, Rogers had accomplished his amazing feat the Indian way, relying on stealth, secrecy, and a long list of well-honed wilderness skills, just like the Abenaki attackers in striking the New England settlements so far to the south. Even more, he had proven wrong the pervasive thinking of not only the Abenaki and the French leadership but also the aristocratic elite of the British officer corps, except for Major General Jeffery Amherst. Fortunately for Rogers, Amherst had possessed complete faith in the optimistic, can-do major of humble Scotch-Irish roots and unbounded confidence.

For a host of reasons, consequently, Rogers must have felt great inner relief and solace when ascertaining that St. Francis was now vulnerable as never before, because a great dream had finally been realized. However, the hardest and most challenging part of this most ambitious of expeditions still lay ahead: exploiting in full the golden tactical opportunity that Rogers had gained after so much effort. However, Rogers still had to maintain extreme caution and care, while continuing to make sure that he and his men were not detected, or all of his successful efforts would be wasted by one careless mistake.

But to make Rogers's most passionate vision come true on the cold morning of October 4 before the sun rose on another beautiful autumn day in Quebec, the major had already quietly passed the word for his men to remain as silent as possible during what was going to be the most anxious time just before he unleashed them, because all hell was about to break loose with the encroaching dawn: the eagerly awaited break of day was going to be the last one for a good many Abenaki and, hopefully, not for too many Rangers, British Regulars, and Provincials. Meanwhile, muskets—mostly the large-caliber (.75) Brown Bess—already had been loaded with fresh powder and rounds by the men, while they thanked God not only that the ground was higher, more solid, and drier on the river's north side but also that the Quebec skies were free of rain.

Indeed, Rogers's timing was ideal, because October 4 promised to be a bright, almost Indian summer–like early fall day—which very likely would not have been the case if the expedition had been delayed in departing Crown Point any longer. The major had exploited his narrow window of opportunity, and he now possessed the ability to hit St. Francis without being handicapped by bad weather. So far, almost everything had gone exactly right and according to Rogers's well-laid plans, and his good fortune needed to continue if success was to be won with the rising sun of October 4. Indeed, the mentally burdened and anxious major realized that everything had to go exactly right on this fateful morning in Quebec, if the most impossible of goals was finally to be achieved against too many odds and obstacles to count from the beginning: the complete destruction of St. Francis, until nothing was left but a memory of a past grim glory.

At this time, Rogers now had in his grasp all that he had desired for years. Miraculously, Rogers had led his men deep into the heart of New France without having had to fight a skirmish or battle, which could have culled his ranks or perhaps even led to the destruction of his command. During the last three weeks of seemingly endless ordeals, he had led his troops more than seventy-five miles by water and around one hundred miles by land since departing Crown Point in a true odyssey of unimaginable suffering, including Rogers's wise taking of the most hellish route through the spruce bogs to shake his pursuers under the capable Ensign La Durantaye of La Marine.

But a grim and harsh reality was also now in Rogers's thoughts during the early morning hours of October 4. He now not only had all of St. Francis at his mercy but also possessed his orders from Amherst, which exactly coincided with his fondest wishes and those of the long-suffering people of the northern frontier: to thoroughly chastise the enemy and destroy this infamous place and its inhabitants.

Consequently, Rogers felt an inner glow of joy that he would have found difficult to express, had he so wished, to his men, if the proper circumstances had allowed. Most important, he realized that at long last, he was finally on the cusp of achieving a sparkling one-sided success that would make him more famous not only across the colonies but also on the opposite side of the Atlantic. However, in keeping in his personality, Rogers was not concerned with fame and the future prospects of an already impressive career at this time. At this point, he was only focused on getting the job done and his mission successfully completed as ordered at Crown Point.

Even more, Rogers knew that his upcoming attack was vitally important in overall strategic terms and not just a case of unleashing long pent-up revenge in wiping out an Abenaki town, as alleged by some historians over the years. In overall strategic terms, the upcoming attack was calculated by Amherst to be an invaluable diversion to assist Wolfe in capturing Quebec, the most important target of the war, which would herald the end of New France.[29]

Unlike at any other time since embarking on this incredibly wide-ranging mission, Rogers was now even more confident of success when, as quietly as possible, he finally turned from closely surveying St. Francis from the edge of the pine forest, eased rearward with great care, and headed back through the trees from where he had come, after having gained sufficient intelligence deep in the night. In the major's own words, "I returned to my party at two o'clock [in the morning of October 4], and at three [o'clock and shortly] marched it to within 500 yards of the town, where I lightened the men of their packs, and formed them for the attack."[30]

One of Rogers's followers described in a letter how "the Major stayed until about Two in the Morning, and then returned to his Party, leaving them [the Abenaki] in the Dance."[31] In the ranks and just before the advance closer to the town, Private Robert Kirkwood recalled, "It was determined that we should [soon] march to the town that night, and lie by [and close to the town] until the morning [just before] dawn."[32]

Indeed, in hushed words and hoping that his sick men, still feeling the effects of having toiled through the seemingly endless spruce bogs for so many days, would cease coughing and sneezing on this quiet night when so close to his most desired target, the major had outlined his plan to his officers in short, concise words. In whispered tones not heard beyond the slightly fragrant pine thickets that muffled sounds on this cold night near the St. Francis River, he made doubly sure that every detail of the upcoming attack was fully understood. In addition to being fluent in the French and Indian languages, Rogers easily communicated with the Scottish Highlanders and Irish Catholics in his multiethnic ranks, whose native language was Gaelic.

Finally, Rogers then signaled another forward movement to ease as near to St. Francis as possible without risking detection, which meant advancing to near the edge of the woods. Leading the way to the northwest and perhaps with the natural-sounding hoot of a great horned owl, he signaled for his men to move through the tall pines, smelling fresh in the early morning darkness, in stealthy fashion. A single file of his men minimized any excessive noise of movement in the manner of a hunting party rather than a traditional formation of fighting men. As usual, the major was thinking ahead, while moving ever closer to his target, almost as if he were an Abenaki warrior himself on the warpath and about to strike a vulnerable settlement on the northern frontier.

One of Rogers's followers described in a letter about the final preparations, writing that the major led the way through the quiet forest and "march'd on with his Party within 300 yards of the Town, where he and all his Men threw off their Packs, and prepared themselves for the Attack" on the most hated town for generations of settlers on the isolated northern frontier.[33] Indeed, Rogers's men, in light fighting trim, were now prepared for the attack, after having moved silently onward, the tension exceptionally high as they drew ever closer to St. Francis. They then crossed the clear, trickling waters of Sibosek Brook with care to avoid making any unnecessary sounds, when nerves were taught in the night's coldness.[34]

Here, Rogers and his men occupied the last stretch of pine forest located near the edge of the open field just before the town, while the gentle pall of the yellow moonlight shined over a silent land from a cloudless sky. All the while, the faint light of fires on dirt floors in the center of houses still glowed for warmth on this cold night. It is not known, but perhaps Rogers still had some lingering doubts about what he had recently seen with his own eyes, because it was almost too good to be true since St. Francis had no guardians. And Rogers did not like the unexpected at any time and especially on the eve of battle. Was this eerie quiet and stillness nothing more than a clever setup and an ambush? Were the warriors ready and waiting in their homes and in the large-sized Council House that could be easily transformed into defensive bastions to cost a good many attackers' lives once Rogers unleashed his men? Of course, Rogers could not be sure at this time about the exact situation, and only the final attack upon the town would answer the last nagging questions and mysteries to reveal the truth of the overall situation.

However, because he had never previously attempted to attack and destroy an entire Native American village during his years of campaigning in the wilderness, Rogers failed to realize some fundamental truths about these Native American people, whom he knew almost as well as his Scotch-Irish people back home. However, the New Hampshire major did not know the daily habits of these Abenaki in their own home territory deep in Canada, having only witnessed their war making and the bloody results.

Like his comrades who served in the strategic Lake Champlain corridor, French common soldier Charles "Jolicoeur" Bonin knew more intimately than white New Englanders about the Indian allies of New France, because he had been around them and viewed their ways. In a most revealing passage in his memoir, Bonin explained a truism only recently learned by Major Rogers: "One of the reasons for the superiority of the Iroquois is that when they went to war, they would take the precaution of placing sentinels around their encampment. They remained there very quietly. This the enemy tribes [like the Abenaki] do not do [and] always let themselves be surprised, causing their defeat."[35]

In the darkness that seemed as haunted as it was eerie in the early morning hours, Rogers made sure that every man was fully prepared for the upcoming attack. In whispers, he emphasized for his men to remain perfectly quiet and as careful as possible. The resolute major almost certainly did not sleep a wink, like some of his men, because his mind was active in making sure that everything was ready. All had to be perfect in Rogers's mind, and he did everything to enhance chances for success.

Having had no opportunity on the frontier to gain anything even remotely close to a classical education, Rogers did not realize that the most lucrative target of the Trojan War, the wealthy city of Troy, had been the object of the ancient Greeks' burning desire for less time than it had been New Englanders' desire to destroy St. Francis. In this sense, in what was a symbolic moral show-down, St. Francis was basically the Troy of frontier America, and Rogers was an Achilles to the long-suffering people of the frontier.

In making a final preparation for his long-coveted attack, Rogers then hurriedly divided his force into three parts, or divisions, arranged in a wide semicircle in order to eventually surround the town once he ordered every-one forward. Most of all, he planned to hit St. Francis simultaneously from three directions—south, east, and north—to deliver three hammer blows that would be swift in the tradition of ranging warfare. The young major of boundless energy took charge of the strike force, or column, on the right, while Lieutenant William James Dunbar, the trusty British Regular of out-standing ability, commanded the British Regular light infantry in the center column. Perhaps still wearing his officer's uniform trimmed in blue or having changed into Indian, or Ranger, garb, Captain Amos Ogden, who led the handful of elite infantrymen (nine in total) of Colonel Peter Schuyler's New Jersey Blues, one of the few attackers fated to be wounded in the attack, was in command of the assault column of Provincials on the left.[36]

Calculated to acquire total victory in a hard-hitting surprise attack, these well-honed offensive tactics, especially the division of the task force into three distinct parts, adhered to Rogers's Rule Number VI of ranging warfare. As Rogers had earlier penned, "If you march in a large body of three or four hundred, with a design to attack the enemy, divide your party into three columns, each headed by a proper officer, and let those columns march in single files, the columns to the right and left keeping at twenty yards distance or more from that of the center, if the ground will admit," which was now certainly the case.[37]

In a most revealing letter, one of Rogers's men described the final prepa-rations for the attack, after having advanced "within 300 Yards of the Town . . . dividing themselves into three Divisions, himself [Rogers] on the Right, Capt. Ogden on the Left, and Lieut. Dunbar in the Center; the [total] Num-ber then reduced to only 142, Officers included."[38]

All the while, Rogers's men remembered the major's forceful orders, which had to be obeyed to the fullest. In this regard, Rogers's sense of per-fection and meticulousness was about to pay high dividends in the upcoming assault. At this time, Rogers's followers knew that every single word, uttered in hushed tones by their dynamic frontier commander, had to be obeyed unquestioningly, if a sparkling success was about to be achieved with the sunrise. In the words of Private Robert Kirkwood, "Our orders were to proceed [forward on Rogers's signal] by two and two, and place ourselves severally at each house, and on the firing of a shot by way of [a] signal from Major Rogers, we were to fire the town and at once and kill every one without mercy."[39]

This extremely harsh order was rooted in not only Rogers's deep desire to punish the Abenaki for their seemingly endless brutal raids on the frontier settlements but also his stern orders from Amherst. In his orders on September 13 issued at Crown Point, Major General Amherst had emphasized, "Remember the barbarities . . . committed by the enemy's Indian scoundrels on every occasion, where they had an opportunity of shewing their infamous cruelties on the King's subjects, which they have done without mercy. Take your revenge."[40]

Of course by this time, Rogers did not have to be reminded about what needed to be done from strictly a moral perspective when commanding a God-fearing soldiery, because he knew that Abenaki warriors had struck the northern frontier without mercy "for a century."[41] Indeed, generations of colonists had long recognized that Canada, especially St. Francis, was the "unhappy fountain from which issue all our miseries."[42]

Clearly, to Rogers, the general's order at Crown Point had given him the green light to issue his heartless orders, as wrote Kirkwood, to "kill every one without mercy."[43] Most important, Rogers's unmerciful order was simply rooted in frontier logic and pragmatism, because he now, most of all, needed to preserve the precious lives of as many of his men as possible in the upcoming attack. He knew that his command, especially with too few Rangers in the ranks, in his opinion, was too small for this far-flung and outsized mission, and he could not afford to lose any additional soldiers because they still had to trek more than two hundred miles to the safety of New England after the town's destruction; too many good fighting men had already been lost in the long trek north.

And the impossible process of attempting to sort out combatants from noncombatants in and among the houses of St. Francis in the darkness and then the half-light of early morning guaranteed that perhaps a good many men would be killed in the upcoming attack. Therefore, it was far safer to just kill indiscriminately once the killing began inside the town and in the houses now bathed in darkness. If Rogers had not made this decision to kill at random, then his men would have certainly made it themselves out of self-preservation in such a close-combat situation, because of what frontier logic and common sense dictated in the circumstances and overall situation.

But, in fact, Major Rogers, now leading the right division, had never needed any orders or approval from General Amherst to do what was now absolutely necessary to save the lives of his men because of the harsh realities of wilderness warfare, the cruel laws of nature, and the Darwinian rule of survival of the fittest. Rogers's own words indicated how this most righteous and moral of wars justified the wrath that he was about to unleash on St. Francis with a fury: "This tribe of Indians [Abenaki] was notoriously attached to the French, and had [long] harassed the frontiers of New England, murdering people of all ages and sexes, and in times of peace [between England and France], when they had no reason to suspect hostile intentions. They had, within my own knowledge, during six years past, killed and carried away more than six hundred persons."[44]

In the words of one colonial, Rogers was battling against the tide of history when destiny and the future were at stake, because "the fate of our Country [now] be approaching, and this favourable Spot of the Globe, Land of Plenty and Liberty, shall become a conquered and enslaved Province" of the king of France if this war was lost.[45]

Quite simply, Rogers's brutal orders for his men to show no mercy were rooted in both his own frontier experience and the fiery Presbyterianism, based on the Old Testament's dictates, of the Scotch-Irish on the frontier, because this was a holy war. As a means of survival in a harsh land, and in serving as the sword of the Lord, the raiders adhered to the Old Testament tenet that "Our God is a God of War."[46]

In this regard, Rogers was a true holy warrior of the deepest dye in a righteous crusade. It is not known, but perhaps Rogers recalled the words of Joshua 8:29 from his childhood days in the Merrimack River country: "And it came to pass when Israel had made an end of slaying all the inhabitants . . . so it was that all who fell that day, both men and women, were twelve thousand—all the people" of a sinful enemy city that mocked God.[47]

Even a humane French officer like Captain Louis Antoine de Bougainville would have understood the necessity of these harsh orders of no mercy
from the mouth of Rogers, who had long been engaged in a cruel war of no
mercy embraced by both sides, because he had long denounced the barbarities of France's Native American allies, especially the Abenaki, labeling them
"monsters" in his journal.[48]

When a captive, Thomas Brown of Captain Thomas Speakman's old
company, the irrepressible New England teenager of feisty spirit, described
the sad fate of one Ranger, who had been captured, like himself, and then
taken to a village of a good many people lusting to witness his demise by
the cruelest means possible: "The next night they made a fire, stripped
and tied him to a stake, and the squaws cut pieces of pine, like [skewers],
and thrust them into his flesh, and set them on fire. . . . They cut the poor
man's cords, and . . . I heard the poor man's cries to heaven for mercy; and
at length, through extreme anguish and pain, he pitched himself into the
flames and expired."[49]

Caught in a living nightmare, Ranger Brown also saw other horrors that
were all but unspeakable to the typical Englishman and American, when
one warrior "with a knife ripped open [the captive's] belly, took one end of
his guts and tied [it] to a tree, and then whipt the miserable man round and
round till he expired [while] they made their game at the dying man."[50]

For the rest of his life, and for good reason, young "Tom" Brown, who
was only age sixteen when he first became a Ranger, was haunted by the surreal horrors of this bitter fight in which he had been badly wounded by three
lead balls from veteran marksmen who had cut down scores of Rangers, who
had dropped like fallen leaves. In stunned silence, the young man from the
Boston area had watched in horror as his beloved Captain Thomas Speakman, an excellent officer from Boston, fell victim to the worst of all fates for
a Ranger during the First Battle on Snowshoes on January 21, 1757: "The
Indian came to [the badly wounded] Captain Speakman, who was not able
to resist, and stripped and scalped him alive."[51]

Brown, who was one the youngest Rangers in the ranks, with an optimistic nature, also long remembered the terrible sight of the tragic fate of
Lieutenant Samuel Kennedy, when he had been a badly wounded captive: "I
saw he was much tomahawked by the Indians."[52]

The Old Testament "An Eye for an Eye and a Tooth for a Tooth"

For such reasons, this was most of all a holy war for Rogers and his men, because they believed that even the existence of their Presbyterian faith was at stake. Scotch-Irish Presbyterians of the northern frontier had embraced what they had long read in the Holy Bible, especially in the Old Testament, that bestowed hope and faith in this vicious struggle for possession of what they believed was a promised land and a New Canaan.

Taken to heart by the Scotch-Irish across the untamed frontier, a passage in the Book of Matthew emphasized the ancient Hebrew saying that partly justified the most brutal of wars in which one atrocity had rapidly followed another in a classic case of *lex talionis* in Latin, or "an eye for an eye and tooth for a tooth," as written by ancient Jewish scholars.[53]

Best personified by John Winthrop's Puritan-based spiritual and moral idealism for the creation of a paradise in America, which held that "we shall be as a City upon a Hill, the eyes of all people are upon us," this biblical sentiment applied to the frontier experience, which had smoothly merged with the rise of a nascent American nationalism over time, which also partly explained the high motivation and warfighting mentality of Rogers and his men.[54]

Therefore, for a host of reasons, Rogers planned to treat the Abenaki exactly how they had long treated his people, especially the countless Scotch-Irish who died miserable deaths across the frontier. Private Kirkwood continued to explain in regard to the no-quarter policy and Rogers's decision to move closer to St. Francis and await the sunrise, "This being the result of the consultation, we set out to put it in execution, we accordingly proceeded and came so near, that we could distinguish the inhabitants were at a war-dance, having just returned from such a scene of blood, as was then preparing for themselves [and they] had really been guilty of the most unheard of cruelties."[55] These hard-hitting warriors of St. Francis had been long recognized as "the severest Scourges of the Frontier," and for ample good reason.[56]

Even more, and as noted, a nightmarish and blood-soaked heritage of the past now invoked a brutal day of reckoning for St. Francis. Indeed, "a good percentage of [Rogers's] detachment had lost relatives in [past] Abenaki raids on Dover, Pemaquid, Salmon Falls, Fort Loyal, York, Wells, Durham, Haverhill, Falmouth, and Deerfield [and] In their own lifetimes, hundreds more white settlers had been slain."[57]

In consequence, Rogers men had their tomahawks and scalping knives sharpened to a fine edge and ready for the necessary grim work that had to done in the hours ahead, while they made sure that they had fresh charges of black powder in the steel mechanism of the firing pans of their mostly Brown Bess muskets filled with "buck & ball rounds." A lethal determination now infused the hearts and minds of these young men and boys, because they knew that they were part of the deepest penetration ever launched into "the very vitals of New France" with the lofty goal of completely destroying a legendary enemy sanctuary long believed to be completely untouchable.[58]

And, as Rogers had long envisioned, this golden opportunity to destroy St. Francis was now possible because he had once again repeatedly outsmarted the enemy, despite having faced insurmountable obstacles. Even at this time, nearly one thousand Indians (including Abenaki warriors), Canadians, and French soldiers were quietly waiting in good ambush positions to slaughter Rangers, but in the wrong places and at the wrong times—on the Yamaska River, under Chief Joseph-Louis Gill, and at Missisquoi Bay, under highly skilled Ensign Langy. The seasoned Langy and other French partisan leaders, like La Durantaye, were eager to deliver Rogers the greatest setback of his illustrious career, if he dared to return the same way that he had come. With loaded flintlocks, ready scalping knives, and lusting at the opportunity, these haters of Rangers waited in vain for the arrival of the major and his men, who would never appear, because Rogers had always been thinking ahead to remain one step ahead of his opponents.[59]

THE STRIKING PARADOX

However, in the greatest paradox of the raid, and for all his zeal in desiring to attack St. Francis for years, the physically imposing major from the Merrimack River country did not hate the Abenaki—despite their decades of having committed all manner of atrocities, which consisted of an orgy of beheadings, torture, burning at the stake, and disembowelment of countless settlers—or the Native American people in general. This was a rare development for a lifelong frontiersman, revealing the extent of Rogers's complexities and paradoxes even in the most horrific of wars. After all, an undying hatred of Native Americans would seem beyond doubt for a man whose fame stemmed from fighting Indians and defeating them on their own terms year after year. While a good many of Rogers's men hated the enemy because of their cruel means of waging war on the hapless people of frontier settlements, which had resulted in the loss of loved ones, Rogers was not one of these hard-bitten men consumed by racial hatred.

In fact, he admired Native Americans, even the fierce Abenaki, for their nature-loving ways and powerful warrior ethos, because they were the consummate fighting men, and in general for their many redeeming qualities often lacking in many whites. First and foremost, Rogers possessed a high level of respect for Indians who fought with their hearts and a fanatical zeal because he had learned well from them over the years, especially how to fight them on their own terms and beat them in battle. Even more, in a classic case of an ingenious commander who had succeeded in the rare art of having gotten into the minds of his opponents in order to defeat them, Rogers thought very like, and adapted to the ways of, Indian warriors, who were motivated by sachems, French and Canadian military leaders, Jesuit priests, the twisted dictates of a militant Roman Catholicism, and the ancient warrior ethos of the Abenaki.

In the end, especially during the St. Francis expedition, Rogers had proved successful so far because he thoroughly understood the innermost depths of the thinking of his enemies, both leaders and the average fighting man, and their unique psychology—the key to success and central tenet of some of the most famous conquerors from the pages of history—after having gotten to know them and their ways on an intimate level, just like he understood the Scotch-Irish, who were the people of his blood. In all of his writings, Rogers revealed no hint of racial hatred or genocidal tendencies and instead expressed an affinity for Native American people, because they were true objects of admiration to him on multiple levels.

It has been most forgotten about the frontier experience, including in New England, that interracial marriage between whites and Indians was not uncommon at an early date, and these couples faced no backlash or ostracism from white society, because racial lines had not yet hardened like they became dominant in later years. In consequence, Rogers had become almost as much Indian in his own personal ways and general thinking, especially in regard to the art of warfighting, as he was a Scotch-Irishman of immigrant parents, who still loved the green hills of Ulster Province: a fusion of two distinct and rich cultures and mind-sets from opposite side of the Atlantic that combined to mold Rogers as both a dynamic man and a bold commander of Rangers.

From an early age, Major Rogers was truly enlightened—like Stark but for different reasons—about Native Americans, especially for a white man who hailed from the northern frontier of New England and the Merrimack River country, which had long felt the wrath of vicious Abenaki raiders. In this sense, Rogers was a unique New World product because he retained some of the best qualities of both the Old World and the New World.

Contrary to popular stereotypes of the most simplistic nature, Rogers possessed an inordinate amount of empathy for the Native American peoples who had been pushed off their ancestral lands by the tide of white settlement. This undeniable fact was evident in Rogers's 1766 London stage play *Ponteach*. In this work, which was ahead of its time, he complained of the evils and corruptive ways of white civilization, especially alcohol, which had often so thoroughly devastated the lives of Native Americans for generations.

Of course, neither Rogers nor the Rangers would have been successful without having thoroughly embraced Indian ways with a passion. After all, the Rangers closely emulated Native Americans, from dress to warfighting to scalping, to a heightened degree that shocked British Regulars and Provincials. In fact, some Rangers were hardly distinguishable from their Native American enemies in overall appearance, except in regard to not wearing traditional war paint.

In Rogers's own philosophical words of admiration about the Native American enemy, who had long tenaciously fought to save himself from extinction, "Most of the Indians are possessed of a surprising patience and equanimity of mind, and a command of every passion, except revenge, beyond what philosophers or Christians usually attain to. You may see them bearing the most sudden and unexpected misfortunes with calmness and composure of mind, without a word or change of countenance [and] Those advanced in years are rarely treated disrespectfully by the younger; and if any quarrels happen, they never make use of oaths, or any indecent expressions, or call one another by bad names."[60]

As a commonsense Scotch-Irishman, a complimentary Rogers, who understood Native Americans in intimate ways, also emphasized with respectful words how the "Indians do not want for natural good sense and ingenuity" to a surprising degree.[61] Most of all, and seldom admitted by whites at the time, Rogers realized beyond all doubt a fundamental truth, because of what he knew intimately about both the white and the Native American worlds. Consequently, he described how the happiest and most fortunate Native Americans in the land were those who lived in the most remote area far away from the corruptive influences of white society, which were dooming Native Americans and their rich culture and civilization to a slow death.[62]

Because he admired Native Americans and had adopted many of their ways, which he had felt were superior to white ways since the days of his youth in the Merrimack River country, Rogers was not at all prejudiced against Indians to the degree that one would imagine of a man from the northern frontier and a famed Indian fighter. Instead, and like other frontiersmen who were mostly Scotch-Irish, Rogers exhibited greater prejudice against the Hebrew people, although he was much less familiar with them than with Native Americans since the days of his youth. In his own words, "The province [of New York] is infested with a rascally set of Jews, who fail not to take advantage of the great liberty here given to men of all professions and religions, and are a pest not only to this, but the neighboring provinces" of the colonies.[63]

Thinking much the same as other people from his backwoods homeland, Rogers also displayed his frontier prejudice by writing negatively about the Hebrew people of New York City: "This city abounds with many wealthy merchants, who carry on a large trade to foreign parts, and are observed to deal very much upon honor; excepting the Jews, who have been tolerated to settle here [and] who sustain no very good character, being many of them selfish and where they have an opportunity an oppressive and cruel people."[64]

In striking contrast, and in words seldom spoken or written by any whites at the time, the major from the uncharted wilds of New Hampshire most revered the Native American people for distinctive personal qualities that he often found lacking among whites, who failed to measure up in a variety of ways to the enemy whom they had long hated. Rogers, for instance, described how "greatly are the savages influenced by a sense of honor, and the love of their country."[65]

Ironically, from Rogers's own words, which he meant with heartfelt conviction, it almost seemed as if he were more eager and willing to attack ancient Jerusalem than St. Francis. Clearly, he was hostile toward the Hebrews of New York City, including those on Wall Street where they operated businesses; of course, relatively few Jewish people lived on the frontier because they were basically a mercantile people like in Europe.

Consequently, when Rogers issued his brutal orders that set the tone for the upcoming attack in no uncertain terms, in Private Robert Kirkwood's words, to "kill every one without mercy," it was an incredibly harsh order that even violated the major's own innermost beliefs. However, it was an order based on the direct orders of Major General Amherst and actually revealed a host of frontier realities.[66]

In addition, Rogers's no-mercy order possessed distinct biblical roots that were not lost to him and his men. As mentioned, even God sanctioned the killing of men and women—sinful unbelievers and worshipers of many pagan gods—by Joshua and his ancient Hebrew warriors in their righteous war and desperate struggle for possession of the Holy Land. At this time, Joshua and his men had also faced a Darwinian struggle of survival of the fittest in their bid to lay permanent claim to the promised land, just like Rogers and his men fought for the permanent possession of their own promised land.[67]

In conclusion, and as noted, Major Rogers's order to kill all the residents of St. Francis was not issued out of a mindless or abject hatred of the Abenaki, as long assumed by historians. Instead, this well-conceived directive was practical and sensible under extremely challenging and difficult circumstances—a cynical, calculated Machiavellian act based on the command's future survival rather than emotion for the overall benefit of his men.

In truth, Rogers's no-quarter order was no different from the brutal slaying by a forward-thinking Abenaki warrior of a captive white child who was endlessly crying and might well give away the location of a war party to pursuers or of an injured adult captive, man or woman, slowing up and endangering the retiring war party. Rogers's merciless order simply represented the grim common sense and brutal logic of frontier warfare that equated to doing simply what was necessary for survival, especially when so deep in enemy territory and far from all support.

As he fully realized by this time, Rogers simply could not afford to allow a single Abenaki survivor to escape his upcoming attack, because they might then inform the French, Canadians, and Indians about the weaknesses of his command and the overall bad shape that they now found themselves in, after the lengthy ordeal in the nightmarish spruce bogs. Therefore, in the end, Rogers's harsh order to kill everyone in the town—including even angry and snapping Indian dogs if necessary—was nothing more than a case of simple struggle for survival that was as Darwinian in the extreme as it was cruel, a timeless law of nature, even among the plant life that could be seen around them, where a life-and-death struggle among countless species continued day after day.[68]

But, as noted, the upcoming assault on St. Francis was more complex than long assumed by generations of historians. The greatest falsehood about the dramatic attack on St. Francis was that it was not necessarily important because Quebec had fallen by this time. But this was not the case. The raid was more significant in overall strategic terms, including factors that were in political, psychological, spiritual, cultural, and philosophical realms, which made this upcoming fight much more than just another Indian clash of a traditional nature.

In settling Canada, which was France's largest overseas possession, the French had transferred their feudal system to the New World, with its huge class divisions and gross social inequities of an absolute monarchy that primarily ruled an oppressed peasant class without the individual rights enjoyed by Englishmen on both sides of the Atlantic: an antiquated system of a bygone age that was the antithesis of the thirteen colonies' representative governments. Canada was headed by the upper-class aristocracy of nobles and social elites, like in France, while the rest of the people—the common people, who were the vast majority—were mostly lowly peasants who farmed the extensive lands owned by the wealthy ruling class. Unlike in the case of England, the gross societal inequities and abuses of Old World France had been seamlessly transferred to the New World.

And if feudal France won the war for possession of the North American continent, then this unjust feudal system of New France would then extend south and rule the thirteen colonies with an iron medieval fist, after the elimination of British officials and leaders, both political and military. During the most crucial period of American and Canadian colonial history, therefore, Rogers and his men believed that they were fighting against the ominous threat of feudalism, autocratic government and church oppression, and the inequities of an antiquated Old World system that it was feared would impose outright slavery upon free Englishmen if North America were lost, profoundly changing their world forever.

In consequence, the motivations of the young men and boys who marched upon St. Francis could not have been greater, including the burning desire to strike a blow against "the haughty Insolence and the Pride of the

French King and Nation," the direst threat ever posed to English civilization and culture in the view of the average fighting man in the ranks.[69] Indeed, in the words of one alarmed colonial citizen who realized the enormity of what was at stake for the English colonies in this war, "Slavery with Giant-like Strides seems to be approaching" from the dark heart of New France in the form of fierce Native American allies.[70]

MAJOR ROGERS'S GREATEST GOAL FINALLY WITHIN EASY REACH

At long last, after an arduous sojourn north of nearly 175 miles by water and land, Major Rogers was about to reap the fruits of the deepest raid of his career with his typical hard-hitting style, which had been the primary secret of the outstanding military success of New France for a century: countless raiding parties of mostly Native Americans taking the horrors of war to the New England settlements with a vengeance to compensate for Canada's small population and inferior resources. Like no other American or British military man to date, Rogers utilized the most brilliant tactics of the French, Canadians, and Native American warriors against the Abenaki, fighting fire with fire. Indeed, in the supreme irony, the major was about to employ the Abenaki's own tactics to destroy them with a lethal thoroughness, but in an even more refined and heightened form, which defined this entire expedition far into the North.[71]

However, Rogers still felt a measure of well-founded concern about the size of the relatively small force that he now commanded—experienced men who had already endured a Darwinian test of survival of the fittest during a grim culling process—because it was actually in overall bad shape. Most of the invaluable provisions brought from the whaleboats that had landed on the shore of Missisquoi Bay had been consumed several days before, while the men were toiling through the spruce bogs. By this time, Rogers's followers looked more like paupers than soldiers, with scratched faces, covered with a thick growth of beard, and ragged clothing torn by bushes and sharp branches.

Even now, with victory so close, the red-bearded major was still haunted by the cruel attrition that had steadily sapped the strength of his command to leave only 142 Rangers, British Regulars, and Provincials for the upcoming attack: first, forty-one injured and sick men and their escorts had been sent back to Crown Point under Captain Manley Williams, who had sustained an accidental self-inflicted wound, hardly before the expedition had begun; then Ireland-born Lieutenant Andrew McMullen, who was hobbled, and six unhealthy men had returned to Major General Amherst to inform him of recent developments and the need for provisions to be sent up the Connecticut River for the anticipated withdrawal from St. Francis; and then seven more unfortunate men had been lost forever during the nightmarish trek through the spruce bogs. Therefore, through no fault of his own, Rogers had already lost more than fifty good fighting men, or more than one-quarter of his entire command.[72]

Confident of success, Rogers quietly passed along the last instructions in whispered tones to his top lieutenants of the right column, which he commanded. He continued to be elated that St. Francis loomed before him for the taking, thanks to the Abenaki festivities that had only ended late in the night—no guards, no war parties, no French soldiers, and no roving bands of warriors had been seen. Even at this time, the most famous major in America still could not believe that no extra precautions of any kind had been taken to safeguard the village. Rogers and his men, including the faithful Mohegans (ironically, warriors of a tribe with some ancestral and familial links to the St. Francis villagers as a strange fate would have it), were now convinced that this early morning of October 4 would be a great day of reckoning that the people of all New England had eagerly awaited for generations.

Indeed, this fourth day in October would be a bloody apocalypse for the unsuspecting Abenaki. After all, many of these battle-hardened Rangers had a relative, friend, or acquaintance killed, captured, or stolen away by the St. Francis Abenaki in the past. As could be expected, Rogers's Stockbridge "Wolves" were likewise motivated to wreak a righteous and grim vengeance, because some of their relatives had been taken by the Abenaki and were even now captives.

In consequence, the Rangers, white as well as Indian and black, had plenty of old scores to settle with the Abenaki, and they extended back for as long as anyone could remember, including for generations in some cases. But Rogers and his men hardly looked like lethal avenging angels. They were indeed a motley crew by this time, looking more like tattered beggars on a Boston street corner or on London's seedy waterfront along the Thames rather than America's elite soldiers. In fact, Rogers and his followers looked very much like the "English savages" the French had long denounced them to be.

Only what was left of the officer's short green uniform jackets—now filthy and moldy after having been soaked for weeks during rainstorms and the horrific trek through the spruce bogs—and blue Scottish bonnets revealed that the Rangers from across the colonies were members of a crack soldiery, whose reputations for hard fighting had preceded them. If not knocked off by a spruce tree branch or thorny underbrush during the slog through the seemingly endless spruce bogs, perhaps what little was left of a hawk, turkey, or eagle feather yet rakishly cocked in their leather jockey hats and Scottish bonnets still revealed a sense of pride in a distinctive Scotch-Irish heritage that stemmed from the rolling green hills of Ulster Province.

Just before the arrival of the red dawn of October 4, Rogers realized that there was now absolutely no margin for error. Rogers also knew that his men would not be hampered in any way during the upcoming attack that first required his troops charging across the wide stretch of cleared open ground—a former bean, corn, or squash field that had already been harvested—that stood before the village. Above all, these proven veterans understood that if they failed in the predawn assault that was drawing near, then they would receive no mercy, especially if captured by Abenaki warriors burning with revenge. If not fortunate enough to have been killed outright in the upcoming fight for the possession of St. Francis, any or all Ranger captives would be tortured and burned alive in bonfires, dying agonizing deaths at this mysterious place, long considered hell on earth all along the frontier.

Consequently, for the Rangers and their young commander, who was mature beyond his twenty-seven years, not only was there no turning back to find safety or solace if things suddenly turned against them and reinforcements for St. Francis suddenly arrived, but there was also absolutely no hope for them if they met with any kind of reversal, when so deep in Quebec and so far from Crown Point. Quite simply, the survival of Rogers and his men now lay in launching an overwhelming attack that had to catch the Abenaki by surprise, and it had to be as hard-hitting as it was fast paced. For Rogers and his band of faithful followers, the St. Francis River had indeed been their Rubicon, because they now faced either a complete victory or a complete defeat (if not total annihilation on Canadian soil) if things somehow went terribly wrong in the upcoming assault.

Indeed, the early morning of October 4 would undoubtedly ordain fates and make or break reputations, including the future of Major Rogers and his Rangers as the most unique and distinctive contingent of America's elite fighting men of Amherst's army. Relying on hard-hitting tactics that had been so effective in the past during the wilderness war, Rogers stayed true to his twenty-eight written rules of warfare. In preparation for the attack, and as noted, he had already divided his command into three sections: right, center, and left columns.[73]

All in all, this tactic of multiple strike columns striking at once was a good one, because each contingent of attackers would be supporting the others, while setting in place the possibility of unleashing deadly flank fires on the enemy, if necessary. If Rogers and his right column met with opposition or too many warriors, then the other two columns would strike any resisting warriors from the flank, while also "prevent[ing] the enemy from pressing hard on either of your wings, or surrounding you, which is the usual method of the savages, if their number will admit it," according to Rogers's manual about the rules of ranging war on the frontier.[74]

With their dirt-covered packs, haversacks, and blankets piled behind them in a safe place amid the dark woodlands, the white, red, and black soldiers of the task force catnapped in the thickets on an autumn night that had turned colder. Other men, too anxious and nervous to sleep, remained ready for action. Then, in the early morning hours, an anxious and wide-awake Rogers and his top officers made the rounds to the separate companies to awake the most tired soldiers, who were fast asleep in their weariness, as silently as possible. To ensure greater protection once the fighting began in St. Francis, the men were reminded to systematically operate in pairs when they entered the town and then descended upon each separate house, where they would then take their assigned position before silent dwellings in the creeping half-light before the dawn in preparation for the killing to begin.

Not taking any chances, Rogers planned to overwhelm St. Francis with his three fast-moving columns in the predawn darkness to maximize the element of surprise and, most important, to minimize losses by hitting the Abenaki from multiple directions before they even knew what was happening. If everything worked according to the major's ambitious tactical plan, then all of Rogers's men would have taken their assigned positions at all the houses in the town before the first shot was fired in anger.

However, if surprise had been lost, which still might be the case because the houses of St. Francis seemed too quiet, heightening the tension among the raiders, and a defending force had been gathered to ambush the Rangers in the upcoming attack, then one of Rogers's written rules of ranging warfare applied: "When pushed upon by the enemy, reserve your fire till they approach very close, which will then put them into the greater surprize [*sic*] and consternation, and give you an opportunity of rushing upon them with your hatchets and cutlasses to the better advantage."[75]

In this war for control of the North American continent, the surprise attack had evolved into an art form to minimize losses, but Rogers had now elevated it to its highest form by his careful orchestration and calculations. Ironically, Rogers now prepared to reap the benefits of surprise to inflict the maximum number of losses among the enemy in one bold rush, which revealed a highly effective merger of the best warfighting aspects of both Native American and European warfare, which the northern frontier major had perfected, having taken them to a higher and more refined level.[76]

In keeping with the concepts and dictates of the total war that had long raged across the frontier, Private Robert Kirkwood revealed the harshness of the major's true directives not seen in Rogers's *Journals* or official reports from General Amherst, who had emphasized to Rogers at headquarters on September 13 that "it is my orders that no [Abenaki] women and children are [to be] killed or hurt." All the while and as mentioned, the major had now made sure that there would be no escape for the doomed inhabitants of St. Francis, because he had ordered his men to charge "by two and two, and place ourselves severally at each house [and then] we were to fire the town at once and kill everyone without mercy."[77]

Private Kirkwood's more accurate words about the nature of the attack have revealed the ugly truths and realities, unlike Major General Amherst's well-conceived words for political consumption, meant to deflect blame for any deaths of women and children at St. Francis completely away from himself and onto Rogers. After all, the revered British major general, an old-school aristocrat who hailed from a stately mansion at "Brooks Place" in Sevenoaks, Riverhead, Kent, England, knew what Rogers and his men were capable of doing to the enemy, both combatants and noncombatants, when they were finally unleashed in the attack, and it would not be pretty. He was fully aware of what the army's most ruthless and lethal fighters would almost certainly do when they struck St. Francis, especially after he had ordered the major "to disgrace the enemy" and to "take [his] revenge."

Far from the general's comfortable headquarters at Crown Point, as he fully realized, this stern requirement that defined victory in a brutal total war meant systematically engaging in the grim work of destroying the people of St. Francis, including those who had either been on raids or faithfully supported these raiders, including civilians—it was the unmerciful concept of total war that had long struck terror along the frontier, and now it would be returned in full. In this bitter war for simple survival, there was now no more middle ground, because every Abenaki was a contributor to and supporter of the avalanche of devastating raids, over the years, on defenseless log cabins in the wilderness and isolated frontier communities. As Major General Amherst and everyone else knew, Major Rogers and his men were not to be denied once they entered St. Francis with fixed bayonets, when revenge and bloodlust would consume their hearts and souls. Clearly, for such reasons, an awful day of reckoning was in store for St. Francis and its inhabitants in only a short time, because Rogers was determined to deliver a stern message to every Native American ally of the French across Canada.

Indeed, at this time, "the moment of revenge was at hand [because these] Rangers and Provincials in Rogers's force were descendants of sufferers of the Deerfield Raid and other border attacks [including at the Massachusetts community of Haverhill and] Rogers himself remembered the attack on his father's farm in 1748, when the St. Francis Indians [had] left nothing standing but a lone apple tree [revealing a grim and mocking Indian sense of humor] of a struggling young orchard" in the pristine wilderness of the Merrimack River country.[78]

Final Reflections on a Chilly Autumn Night in Quebec

It is not known what final reflections on a bloody past were on Major Rogers's mind on the eve of his most successful and famous military feat during the anxiety-filled hours of October 3 just before he unleashed the hard-hitting assault. However, he might have reflected on the inspiring words of his first commander of the New Hampshire regiment near the war's beginning, Colonel Joseph Blanchard, as penned in a March 10, 1758, letter, which had helped to motivate and inspire Rogers to achieve greater feats, including at St. Francis: "Let your [Ranger] companies be not only the Glory of the Continent, but an honour to the Kingdom" forever more.[79]

And, in his own words, Rogers had sworn to always do his best in "faith-fully serving my God, my King, and Country" in what was now a great holy war that had become not only his passion but also his main pursuit in life.[80] Now at the zenith of his holy crusade against the enemies of his frontier people, the New England major recalled the seemingly endless horrors of the ceaseless Abenaki attacks, which were part of the French grand strategy of pushing the English off the continent and into the sea, and the countless victims who had been slaughtered in one devastating raid after another.

Therefore, especially now, Rogers continued to view himself as a righteous defender of his long-beleaguered people and as a frontier Joshua, the cagy Hebrew guerrilla leader who, inspired by God's commandments, had fought with his head and heart in a bloody guerrilla war against a hated enemy in the Lord's name against the believers in multiple false gods. It is not known at this time if Rogers carried a small Holy Bible, but he quite likely did, since Rogers knew that he represented the sword of the Lord and never knew when he might not return for another risky mission, and this one against infamous St. Francis was certainly the riskiest gamble of all.

At this time, on the eve of the attack, the major almost certainly thought about the talented Rangers who were no more, having faded away forever while battling for their country and people. He recalled the faces, laughter, courage, and personalities of the young men and boys of his Ranger corps, who had been slaughtered by the enemy, including after they had been taken captive on false promises that they would receive decent treatment. Today, on October 4, consequently, Rogers would be fighting for them to ensure that they had not died in vain.

In addition, Rogers might have now reflected not on his own personal past but on God and his own personal salvation, especially if he possessed any kind of dark premonition about what might happen to him in the upcoming attack. As noted, he had been very fortunate to have survived this war to still be leading the command, after having narrowly escaped numerous close calls and several wounds. As a hardened, grizzled veteran commander who could no longer be shocked or surprised by the war's surreal horrors, after having seen too many comrades, neighbors, and friends slaughtered like livestock at the shop of some mad butcher, Rogers was only too well aware that his luck could run out at any moment during an attack on an unfamiliar place far from home.

But like most soldiers devoted to doing their sacred duty, the eve of battle found these men from across America and a lesser number of Britons thinking more deeply about religion, saying silent prayers, and making solemn promises to God like never before, and certainly Rogers was no exception. After all, he had been raised on the northern frontier in the Presbyterian faith not in a traditional church but in the Rogers family cabin in the wilderness, and he first learned biblical words from his Ireland-born mother and father.

As a Scotch-Irishman from the untamed frontier of Massachusetts and New Hampshire, he had also early learned that an unmerciful brand of warfare was simply a part of life. Even the sacred words of the Holy Bible gave support for the righteous duty of a soldier in a holy war while battling for God and his people, and Rogers and his Rangers had closely embraced the moral concepts of the Old Testament during this brutal struggle against the longtime tormentors of their people. Therefore, the major perhaps recalled what God had said to David, the fiery leader of the ancient Hebrew warriors before becoming the king of Judah, from the Book of Psalms: "Fight against them that fight against me."[81]

However, the Book of Joshua was most prophetic in having provided an appropriate analogy to what was about to happen to St. Francis on the morning of October 4. At that ancient time, the courageous Hebrew leader, a true righteous warrior of God, had held the supreme tactical and moral advantage (like Rogers now just outside St. Francis) when facing a hostile town of pagans and unbelievers, while its notoriously cruel warriors had been "drawn away from the city [and] There was not a man left" to defend the place—the exact situation of St. Francis on the fateful morning of October 4.[82]

Ironically, Rogers and his men were now hundreds of miles away from home, just like this diverse group of Abenaki people were themselves now hundreds of miles from their ancestral homelands, which extended almost all the way to the Atlantic coast for the eastern Abenaki. Because of their righteous and moral rage rooted in the Old Testament, the Rangers longed to kill the nearest Abenaki without troubling themselves about the victims' age or sex, just like the Abenaki warriors would do anything to gain the scalp of the hated Rogers to prove to their people that they were the greatest warriors of all.[83]

The top Rangers were now by Rogers's side to share their greatest challenge, which was destined to become legendary in the annals of American military history. These fine soldiers with ample experience provided the major with added confidence of success in the upcoming attack on the river town. Assisting Second Lieutenant William "Bill" Hendrick Phillips, who hailed from the Albany, New York, area, in leading the crack company known as "Rogers's Own," Sergeant John Evans, who had first enlisted in early August 1756, was wrapped in his own thoughts about the upcoming fate of his men and himself. He feared that some of his men would never return from the attack, but he was determined to do his best and carry the day at any cost.[84]

An excellent leader who began his Ranger career on a cold Christmas Day 1757 as a private in Captain John Stark's company, Second Lieutenant George Turner now led the Native Americans, who hailed from Connecticut, of Captain Moses Brewer's Mohegan company. Turner had been promoted to a lieutenant's rank in late April 1757, and he served with distinction and "conspicuously" during the upcoming attack.[85]

From the town of Andover, in northeastern Massachusetts, located not far from the port of Boston, Second Lieutenant Jacob Farrington, in his mid-twenties, was also reflective, thinking about what might happen in the upcoming hours along the banks of the St. Francis River in Quebec's depths. He was now acting second lieutenant of a contingent of experienced fighting men from the company commanded by Dunstable, New Hampshire's Captain Noah Johnson. Having fought against Pequot warriors as a reliable sergeant under Captain John Lovewell in the early 1720s, the savvy Johnson was the oldest Ranger captain, who had already survived too many close calls to count. As a cruel fate would have it, he would be mortally wounded in 1760, proving to be a tough and feisty fighter to the very end.[86]

The proud owner of one hundred acres of prime land and a nice log house that he had built on it, the Lancaster, Massachusetts–born Second Lieutenant Phineas Atherton had been serving God and country since 1755. He was one of Rogers's good friends and trustiest officers.[87] Second Lieutenant Abernathan, or Abernethy, Cargill, who hailed from Boston, where he had enlisted as a private in Captain John Stark's company on Christmas Day 1757, now led the battle-hardened Rangers of the company of Massachusetts-born Captain James Tute. The captain's brother, Amos Tute, was also a Ranger. He had been captured in September 1759 when acting as a courier from Amherst to General Thomas Gage.[88]

Ironically, England-born General Thomas Gage, who was typically stiff and stuffy and entirely unimaginative as a battlefield commander, had complimented Rogers without intending to do so by emphasizing how he was "a true Ranger & not much addicted to Regularity."[89] The elitist Gage failed to realize that this unorthodoxy and irregularity rooted in the dual Scotch-Irish and frontier experiences had been one of the fundamental secrets of Rogers's amazing successes, won by a new breed of freethinking men, who relied on their own abilities and creative thinking to excel, unlike the Old World man, who lacked such flexibility and resourcefulness.

Indeed, agility and flexibility in the art of wilderness warfare were all-important not only for success in overall tactical terms but also for survival during ranging service amid the uncharted wilderness against an unpredictable foe—the antithesis of the inflexibility of this traditional British desk soldier, who was well suited for a career of shuffling papers and playing backdoor politics of a sinister nature, including at Rogers expense, since the frontier major was not that type of soldier but a man of action who allowed his achievements to speak for themselves.[90]

In many ways, this anxious period in the cold darkness just before the dawn was the tensest in Rogers's lifetime, because these young men and boys were on the verge of achieving their loftiest collective goal on their most important mission, which was destined to be a uniquely American success to its core. The relatively few Britons on this expedition almost certainly realized as much, marveling at this new kind of fighting man personified by the never-say-die Rogers and his rough-hewn men from the frontier.

All the while, high anxiety among Rogers's soldiers cut like a knife through the cold air of the St. Francis River country; nerves were as taut as a stretched deerskin on an Abenaki war drum in the haunted darkness. Although seemingly on the verge of a resounding success in the vastness of this remote part of Canada, Rogers still had a great deal to worry about just before the dawn. What if an Abenaki war party suddenly attacked from St. Francis to catch him by surprise, turning the tactical tables when least expected? After all, a nearly full moon shone brightly on this cold October night in the heart of Quebec, a most risky time to have taken an advanced position so close to a major Indian community whose reputation was legendary.

It was not known, but perhaps they had been seen by some Abenaki, like a passionate warrior and his dark-haired lover of youthful beauty, who might have already spied the Rangers' presence, after the couple had already ventured out of St. Francis to make love on the soft pine needles under the tall trees. But, of course, Rogers had no way of knowing if he and his men might have been seen or if the Abenaki might have heard the gathering of soldiers so close to the town now bathed in silence.

Hopefully, in Rogers's mind, the Stockbridge warriors, or the Mohegan "Wolves," whom he had stationed along the perimeter among the thick pines, would give ample warning of any Abenaki attack that might be forthcoming out of the darkness from St. Francis. But after the ordeal of the past three weeks, even a Ranger or revered Stockbridge Mohegan Wolf might have fallen asleep from so many past exertions and sleepless nights of the most grueling ordeal to date: Rogers's odyssey all the way to St. Francis was very much like a heroic tale of the ancient Greeks in its sheer magnitude, seemingly endless close calls, and heightened dangers over an exceptionally wide area of wilderness. So, all in all, and especially when the dawn of October 4 was fast approaching, it was a nervous night for the anxious Rangers, American Provincials, and British Regulars, because it was feared that a large number of warriors might be hidden in the town.

However, with the major's always reassuring presence and the knowledge that Rogers would lead the way in the attack on St. Francis even before the break of dawn, confidence still reigned supreme among the men who remained silent and calm among the soft bed of soft pine needles under the tall trees that felt like a cushion to weary bodies. In the haunting, cold darkness, Major Rogers passed among his band of bearded Rangers. Matted and filthy, the long hair of the Rangers, either sticking out of their blue Scottish bonnets or tied back, now gave them the look of ancient Celtic warriors, especially those red-haired men of the old Scottish Highland clans whose beards had grown since the departure from Crown Point. Because of their excessive courage that had been repeatedly demonstrated in the headlong charge, these traditional clans of the Scottish Highlands had been decimated by the rows of muskets and cannon of disciplined English soldiers, who had included a young James Wolfe, under the Duke of Cumberland on that great killing field of Culloden in Scotland (April 1746) during the ill-fated 1745–1746 Jacobite rebellion.

At that time, the great dream of an independent Scotland had been crushed forever at Culloden in bloody 1746, a turning point of history that caused another Celtic exodus to America, the British Caribbean, and elsewhere. Rogers's Scottish soldiers had never forgotten the tragic legacy of the blood-stained moor in Scotland where so many of the best and brightest

Scottish lads of the Highland clans had been cut to pieces by overwhelming firepower and then massacred, including the wounded Celts, by English bayonets, musket butts, and sabers.

But the ragged, lean looks of Rogers's young men and boys in dirty uniforms and Indian clothing could not have been more deceiving. Most of all, the Rangers of this multiracial and multiethnic command were crack soldiers known for their combat prowess in all types of combat situations, especially against the odds. And, most of all, Rogers now appreciated the undeniable fact that these veteran fighting men were ready to be unleashed to do what they did best, most effectively, and almost in an unthinking manner—killing the enemy as quickly and efficiently as possible in a brutal war without mercy or remorse.

Most of all, beyond the heady romance and glorification of Rogers's Rangers for generations by mythmaking American historians, they were ruthless and professional killers who were about to demonstrate that ugly reality. It was an immense source of pride, like their elite status, that not only the Canadians and French but also their Native American allies, including even the fierce Abenaki, feared and respected Rogers's men like no other fighting men in North America: a rather remarkable achievement by any measure.

As if stalking a deer along a clear-flowing stream in the Merrimack River country in the days of his youth, Rogers moved quietly among his men in a manner that seemed incongruous with the large size of his stout and muscular physique. Here, under the tall pines whose boughs creaked softly in the light night breeze, he spoke in soft tones to make doubly sure that everything was ready and exactly right in preparation for the upcoming challenge that was most daunting: Rogers knew that all had to be in perfect order and reassured himself that nothing was left undone.

All the while, the calm and assured major displayed an air of quiet confidence that fairly radiated from him to soothe the nerves of his men: a quiet authority that he never abused to keep the respect of his ever-individualist men and the tight bonds between this remarkable Ranger commander and his followers fully intact to a degree not seen in other commands. Most important, this rare bond had been forged by a sacred and mutual trust that was about to pay immense dividends to Rogers in the upcoming attack. Indeed, Rogers never acted like a typical British officer, especially those aristocratic and arrogant types who were forever overbearing in the typical upper-class manner of the privileged elite, and he won the hearts of the common soldiers with his easy, casual frontier sense of equality and fair play. In this sense, Rogers almost seemed to his men like a common soldier in his heart and mind, just another faithful comrade and brother who shared their hardships and fates. For such reasons, everyone obeyed the major, who also represented a father figure to the younger men and boys, without hesitation or question because they believed in him, and vice versa, especially in crisis situations.

Consequently, when Rogers moved quietly among his enlisted men, everyone welcomed his steadying presence—as they would not have for a typical high-ranking officer of Amherst's army—almost like the arrival of an old friend and benevolent father figure, who was always concerned about their welfare. Hence, they paid close attention to his advice and frontier wisdom, which might perhaps save their lives and improve the overall chances of a successful attack: keep perfectly quiet; make sure that bayonets, tomahawks, and knives were razor-sharp; see that all black powder in powder horns and brass flasks was dry; keep a fresh charge of powder in the firing pans; don't waste any precious time once the attack began and move quickly to their assigned positions in the town with as little noise as possible; don't waste time scalping Indians as in the past, despite the temptation, when there was more fighting to be done before the town was theirs; make sure that moccasins were in good shape to ensure stability of movement as a misstep might prove fatal; prepare mentally, psychologically, and physically for the greatest challenge to date; move with speed, keep eyes open, strike quickly, and then descend upon the next target; kill as many of the hated Abenaki as possible; make absolutely no mistakes of any kind; and, most important, show no mercy to anyone, because that was the enemy's way.

But now, situated so far from the safety of Crown Point and just below where the St. Francis entered the St. Lawrence, which had long been Canada's river of destiny, Rogers was still concerned and worried, even when it seemed as if he had done everything possible to make the upcoming attack a successful one. However, the lack of any threatening movement from the Abenaki proved to Rogers that his advanced position had not been detected at this point. Nevertheless, the time slowly passed in absolute quiet when so very near the Abenaki center of power situated between Montreal and Quebec, which had existed at this infamous place for more than four generations.

However, the silent calm among the pines swaying gently in the soft night breeze did nothing to ease the heightened tension and anxiety among Rogers's men, while they squatted or sat quietly on the ground covered in a carpet of brown pine needles in the early morning cold. Any sneeze or cough by any of Rogers's men, who were completely worn out after having journeyed north nearly 175 miles by water and land, was hurriedly muffled out of urgent necessity. At least the heat and humidity of summer had passed by this time, and an early morning coolness wrapped the band of raiders like a chilly shroud that cut to the bone, while they felt entirely alone and isolated when so far from Crown Point and any assistance.

Now without their Indian and army-issued blankets, which had been piled in individual clumps to the rear as ordered by Rogers, the night's biting coolness was not in the least refreshing or invigorating and rather seemed even colder to the men because of their inactivity. The chill in the predawn darkness seemed even colder than during the journey north down Lake Champlain, since the Rangers now only wore the same thin, worn uniforms and Indian dress that they had worn in summer. Here, in the inky darkness of the pine forest, some Rangers almost certainly thought about their faraway homes and the wives, lovers, parents, and children they might never see again, if they were destined to meet a cruel fate at St. Francis or during the long journey back to safety if the upcoming attack proved successful.

Rogers, of course, hoped that he had made no mistakes, and, so far, that had been the case. In fact, everything was almost too good to be true—which was troubling in itself to experienced fighting men, especially the ever-cautious Rogers. Had some kind of clever ambush and trap been laid for them at St. Francis? Only the arrival of the red dawn of October 4 over the St. Francis River would illuminate the town and the surrounding woodlands to provide the final answers to Rogers and his men.

Rogers knew only too well how the element of surprise most often resulted in disaster for the victims. The terrible day of January 21, 1757, was one that Rogers never forgot because he had received his nastiest surprise of all. Because of an unkind fate that he had no control over, Rogers and his Ranger detachment had blundered into a deadly ambush by a large group of Canadians, French, and Indians from nearby Fort Carillon. The relatively few survivors of the nightmarish fight in the snowy wilderness never forgot that bloody day. Almost certainly, just before the dawn of October 4, Rogers and some of his men thought about the awful fate of comrades when tactical mistakes had been made that had exacted a fearful price in Ranger lives, like that of Captain Thomas Speakman of Boston.

The hard-fought Battle of La Barbue Creek (the so-called First Battle on Snowshoes) had been waged in desperation by the Rangers during a last stand, orchestrated by Captain John Stark, on a forested hill covered in snow and a thick growth of virgin timber located just west of Lake Champlain, about two miles northwest of Fort Carillon. But in truth, this nightmarish encounter had been less a battle than an absolute disaster, if not slaughter, after Rogers had led his men, barely seventy Rangers, into a deadly ambush.

Here, Rogers had been wounded twice in the bitter close-range combat among the tall trees when the ground was covered in a thick shroud of snow, including when a bullet grazed his forehead in the ambushers' first volley. After fierce combat for hours on January 21, 1757, a hasty withdrawal ordered by Rogers at nightfall through the thickets to escape destruction left groups of wounded Rangers lying in clumps in the red-stained snow. One survivor, who narrowly escaped, watched a warrior first strip the clothing from and then scalp Captain Thomas Speakman, who lay helpless with serious wounds but still alive. Speakman had known that a tragic fate was inevitable for him because of the extent of his injuries, requesting in desperation for one wounded comrade, young private Thomas Brown, who was lying nearby in the snow, to give him his "Tomahawk, that he might put an end of his Life!" The handsome head of this dynamic leader of men (Speakman had first raised his Ranger company in New England in mid-1756 for service in Nova Scotia) was cut off and displayed atop a pole as a trophy in the nearby Indian village.[91]

But the most surreal horror of this unique brand of wilderness warfare that was never forgotten by survivors was the slaughter of the band commanded by Lieutenant William "Bill" Hendrick Phillips, the son of an Indian woman and French or Dutch father, during the far bloodier Second Battle on Snowshoes in the following year. Phillips and his men were forced to surrender after a fierce French counterattack. They had been surrounded by large numbers of Indians, French, and Canadians, under the tactically astute La Marine ensign Jean-Baptiste Levrault de Langis Montegron (Langy). He emerged triumphant against Rogers during the Second Battle on Snowshoes, on March 13, 1758. Rogers said of a tragic betrayal by the French, while downplaying the extent of the disaster that was truly monumental, that Lieutenant Phillips's party was "butchered by them, after they had promised them quarters."[92]

Indeed, when completely surrounded by large numbers of experienced warriors and fighters who most of all wanted Ranger scalps, Lieutenant Phillips and his men had surrendered in good faith on the French promise of decent treatment. The band of warriors became incensed when a chief's scalp—evidently identifiable by a distinctive hair ornament or perhaps even its color if he had been of mixed race and worn his hair long and in a distinctive style—was found in the green uniform jacket pocket of a Ranger officer, who clearly prized the grim trophy. In consequence, many captured Rangers were doomed. In short order, the Rangers were then "inhumanly tied to trees and hewn to pieces [with steel tomahawks and scalping knives] in a most barbarous and shocking manner."[93]

Such a grisly fate for some of his best Rangers still gnawed at Rogers and his men who had known the victims, especially now that they realized that parties of Indians, Canadians, and Frenchmen were not only pursuing them but also at some point waiting in ambush. The Rangers now understood that their ultimate fates would be not unlike that of the unfortunate men of Lieutenant Phillips's ill-fated band if they were ambushed or captured in the upcoming attack on St. Francis.

No one could forget how the Abenaki, not only warriors but also women and children, had thoroughly amused themselves in what they considered high entertainment—a perverse sort of sporting event—that was enjoyed by the entire village: the ritualistic burning to death of captured prisoners before a throng of spectators, who immensely enjoyed the torture of victims, in a gruesome ritual that was deliberately slowed down to cause the unfortunate Ranger the most intense pain possible and provide the most satisfying amusement to the entire village.

At this time, the Abenaki warriors possessed plenty of valid reasons to hate the Rangers—they had proven to be exceptional fighting men, true Abenaki killers who scalped the dead with relish—and to take out their wrath on captured Rangers. After all, under the directives of the New Hampshire legislature, Rogers was part of a group that had blazed a trail through the hunting grounds of the western Abenaki country all the way to the fertile meadows of Cowass, known as "the place of the white pines," in the Connecticut River country during March 1753. The taking of Abenaki hunting grounds by the relentless tide of white settlers was never forgotten by the displaced Abenaki, who still desired revenge.[94]

Clearly, the Abenaki warriors had a good many deep-seated personal scores to settle with Major Rogers, because his reputation had spread far and wide, and he was the champion of the frontier settlers who took their land. For ample good reason, tribal leaders had complained without exaggeration to the governor of New France of how "the English have abused us, in driving us from Our Lands, and taking them from us."[95] French leaders knew all about Rogers and his Rangers from their past performances on the field of strife. Paying a compliment to his enemy, Captain Bougainville, Montcalm's faithful aide-de-camp, wrote in his journal about "Robert Rogers [who commanded these] forest runners that the English call 'Rangers,' whose mission is to go scouting in the woods."[96]

According to Rogers and his men, including a good many Rangers who had lost relatives in the past to the Abenaki's murderous rage, it was now well beyond time that this cruel favor was returned in full force to the most loyal and lethal Indian allies of New France.[97] Even Captain Bougainville, a proper gentleman born in France, was sickened by the never-ending cruelty and slaughter committed by the allies of New France, writing in his journal how "the cruelties . . . of these barbarians [are] horrible," with no mercy shown to settlers or soldiers.[98]

Therefore, among other matters of concern at this time just before the dawn of October 4, Major Rogers no doubt was thinking about the exact wording of his stern, if not angry, orders from Major General Amherst, who had insisted that a terrible vengeance be wreaked at St. Francis. And, of course, we do not know what was spoken between Rogers and Amherst in private at the general's headquarters on September 12.

However, the official orders as written by Major General Amherst at Crown Point on September 13, 1759, were somewhat contrary, to say the least—almost certainly by design. The major perhaps now recalled—Rogers was not likely still carrying the orders on him because if he were captured, they would ensure a grisly death at Abenaki hands—that the general had said to "attack the enemy's settlements on the south-side of the river St.

Lawrence, in such a manner as you shall judge most effectual to disgrace the enemy, and for the success and honour of his Majesty's arms."[99]

Perhaps to some degree, Rogers saw the irony of fighting for King George II, or "His Majesty," in London, located around four thousand miles away in what now must have seemed another world, one that he had never seen, while risking his own life and those of his entire command in the remote vastness of the North American wilderness. Major General Amherst's orders called for harsh measures but also revealed his attempt to gain the moral high ground over his opponent—for his own conscience and in the eyes of the public on both sides of the Atlantic—which had very little to do with the brutal realities of frontier warfare: "Remember the barbarities that have been committed by the enemy's Indian scoundrels on every occasion, where they had an opportunity of shewing their infamous cruelties on the King's subjects, which they had done without mercy. Take your revenge, but don't forget that tho' those villains have dastardly and promiscuously murdered the women and children of all ages, it is my orders that no women or children are killed or hurt."[100]

After years of the most merciless conflict ever fought on American soil, Rogers hardly had to be reminded about what he had long seen with his own eyes, unlike Major General Amherst, who had been sheltered in the aristocratic elitist world of the British upper class. As noted, Rogers had been long obsessed with the urgent need to be a righteous deliverer—an avenging angel in his mind and those of his men—of a bloody day of reckoning that was long overdue for St. Francis and its warriors.

Indeed, instead of for money or glory, Rogers and his Rangers were most of all fighting on behalf of their long-suffering people, including their own families and relatives, of the northern frontier. As noted, many of Rogers's men had family members, perhaps a wife or sister or parent, who had been either killed or captured by the Abenaki. In a case of unbridled hatred and man's inhumanity to his fellow man having come full circle, the Rangers desired revenge for a good many lost friends and family members, just as the Abenaki did: an identical motivation and passionate desire on both sides that guaranteed an endless cycle of barbarity and slaughter, including on October 4, 1759.

During his closest observation of St. Francis, Major Rogers, even with his fabled hawkeyed vision well honed from the wilderness experience, had no way of clearly ascertaining what the Abenaki had fastened atop the tall poles around the individual houses, the Council House, and even the Roman Catholic church, now hanging high in the darkness as special trophies of warrior prowess: the scalps (blond, brown, red, gray, black, auburn) of between six and seven hundred white victims—men, women, children from all across the frontier.

Infants snatched from their wooden cradles and their screaming mother's arms had often had their heads bashed against trees by warriors. Mirroring the proud French tradition of hanging the prized trophies of captured English and Provincial silk battle flags in the churches of Quebec and Montreal to fortify morale and inspire greater exertion among both civilians and soldiers in wartime, these grisly trophies—the little that was left of mostly New Englanders—now swayed in the breeze sweeping off the St. Francis River just before dawn of October 4.

Clearly, the entire community of St. Francis, even the zealous Jesuit priests and missionaries, took extreme pride in these grisly trophies of wartime victims of all ages. Such savagery had long been emboldened by the fiery Jesuit exhortation to take the war to the heathen Protestants so that a Catholic God would smile upon them when they took scalps of white men, women, and children. Although Major Rogers could not see these trophies hanging so high above the buildings and houses of St. Francis, representing nothing less than the largest collection of mostly New Englanders' scalps anywhere on the North American continent, he knew that the scalps were probably in warrior houses.

However, he could not have imagined that so many scalps had become items of public display to advertise the bravery of Abenaki warriors and the fearsome reputation of St. Francis. As mentioned, hundreds of scalps were now arrayed in ceremonial and ritualistic fashion atop the tall poles above the residences, Council House, and even the Roman Catholic church of the firebrand French Jesuit missionaries and priests. Rogers might have heard about the hundreds of scalps, perhaps from Captain John Stark, who had been held captive in St. Francis in 1752. Along with so many other factors, this was still another reason why Rogers had long burned with the desire—an uncontrollable lust at this point—to wipe St. Francis out until nothing remained.[101]

Even if Rogers had been able to see the perhaps seven hundred, or more, scalps in the darkness atop the tall poles, hanging in grisly fashion above the wooden and stone buildings, he would have not been shocked in the least because of St. Francis's dark infamy, spread far and wide for generations. After all, the Rangers, of all ages and experience levels and including Rogers, also scalped with an enthusiastic zeal akin to that of even the fiercest Abenaki warrior. A persistent myth has existed since the nineteenth century that scalping was a European custom embraced by Native Americans. But in truth, scalping had been common among indigenous people in North America for centuries before the arrival of the first Europeans as a means of not only collecting trophies but also tapping into the spiritual power of the dead enemy. In this sense, the Abenaki viewed the taking of scalps as an almost religious act that was necessary for the simple survival of their people.[102]

ANOTHER FORGOTTEN KEY CONSIDERATION

With the dawn of October 4 drawing ever nearer, Rogers had other things to think about before unleashing the attack, because St. Francis still remained eerily calm and quiet. Dawn was fast approaching, and Rogers still marveled at the strange silence that made him uneasy. According to the enduring romantic myth and overall glorification of Rogers and his Rangers for more than two and a half centuries by white writers and historians, especially from New England, the major wanted nothing more than to wreak a bloody revenge at St. Francis. But in fact a variety of other factors were at work and provided a more complex explanation in regard to his true motivations.

Another popular myth was that Rogers and his Rangers were considered invincible by the French, Indians, and Canadians, but this was certainly not the case. He had committed serious errors that had gotten a good many Rangers killed and scalped in the last several years. The young major had been wounded in battling the enemy at least four times during this war to the death, and he had narrowly survived an alarming number of deadly encounters, which did not bode well for the future. More significantly, Rogers had personally led sizeable parties of Rangers that had come extremely close to complete annihilation no less than half a dozen times. In some cases, Rogers was at fault for having made bad tactical decisions and poor judgment calls. Contrary to popular romantic stereotypes, Rogers was anything but invincible.

Consequently, Major Rogers now needed a sparkling victory because of his sagging reputation from past setbacks, especially because of the terrible losses—more than 140 dead Rangers whose scalps had been removed with gusto by the victors—suffered at the Second Battle on Snowshoes. Although he was by far the best Ranger chieftain in the army and the most famous in the colonies, especially among the frontier Scotch-Irish people, who saw him as a redeeming ancient Celtic-Gaelic chieftain and a "Great Captain" in an ancient tradition, Rogers's men had suffered losses that had often reached astronomical levels. And when deep in the wilderness far from support and reinforcements, he had met his match with highly capable partisan fighters like Ensign Langy, who had mastered the art of irregular warfare like few others.[103]

As demonstrated at the disastrous Second Battle on Snowshoes, Rogers's decisions were no longer an automatic guarantee of certain success, as assumed by some historians who have glorified his role, especially after the loss of more than 140 Ranger lives, which had been a frightfully large percentage of his entire command. Many of these Ranger scalps, festooned atop tall poles in St. Francis, now waved in the gentle night breeze like grim glory flags on a ghost ship sailing the Caribbean's blue waters.

Despite the romance and glorification, Rogers was almost as often about to meet with disaster instead of success at this time: ironically, a most alarming situation that helped to ensure that he would be more careful during this most ambitious expedition, having learned a good many hard lessons in which his men had paid the ultimate price. Far too many of the best and brightest Rangers, especially among the officer corps, had been sacrificed for no gain because of Rogers's mistakes and miscalculations. For such reasons, more questions were being asked at both high and low levels of the army establishment about Rogers's abilities as a commander.

Already, before the unleashing of the attack and as mentioned, this expedition had experienced a number of close calls that might well have doomed the entire mission. However, by this time, Rogers's luck was holding firm, or he would never have reached the outskirts of St. Francis with skill and stealth. The major's sheer willpower and positive thinking had played a leading role in what had been a highly successful expedition so far, defying the odds. By this time, Rogers had become a force of nature with one thought that possessed his heart and soul: delivering St. Francis a knockout blow from which the Abenaki would never recover.

Thus, in early October 1759, for a host of reasons, Major Rogers still needed to win a great success to eliminate all doubt about his abilities among an ever-growing list of rivals and jealous fellow officers, especially among the British. The complexities and nuances of this overall situation were the driving forces and forgotten stories behind the raid on St. Francis. In a striking paradox, what was about to happen at St. Francis had been born not from past successes as much as from past defeats and high Ranger losses that were often staggering.

Therefore, nothing could now possibly enhance the major's reputation and quiet the doubters in Amherst's army more than a dramatic success at St. Francis. For personal, moral, political, and strategic reasons, the destruction of St. Francis was nothing less than a cure-all for Major Rogers. Ironically, a young man mythologized as invincible (a reputation long exaggerated by the colonial press and generations of American historians) was about to strike the most infamous place in Canada, whose own myth of invincibility was more rooted in fact—a fundamental reality obscured by the longtime romanticization and glorification of Rogers and his Rangers.[104]

THE INCENTIVE OF GREED

But how much were the desire for revenge and the wreaking of a holy retribution on St. Francis the dominant motivations of Rogers's men, as long presented in books and films glorifying the raid, which have become the stuff of romantic legend? Most overlooked has been the fact that the less noble factor of greed also played a leading role for Provincials and Englishmen in their initial decision to volunteer and serve with the Rangers.

From the beginning, some men from the Provincial regiments who had volunteered to embark on this expedition were motivated by the better Ranger pay. In this sense, there was certainly a mercenary aspect to the raid, which partly explained the enthusiasm of large numbers of volunteers. These soldiers were driven by greed or simply hailed from the lowest class. Such men, mostly Provincial volunteers, needed funds for themselves and to support families, especially on the hardscrabble frontier, where hard money was scarce. Of course, the exact factors of what most motivated the Provincials and the British Regulars cannot be determined with any degree of certainty, because of the lack of documentation and written accounts of the raid. After all, some volunteers, bored with idle camp life (where disease was often epidemic), were adventurers who desired to win fame and glory by serving under Rogers.

Perhaps one of Rogers's men said it best in letter when he explained that, for a remote Indian mission town located in the wilds of Quebec, St. Francis was actually a "vastly rich" one, because "our poor People's Scalps [six to seven hundred] had purchased riches for them." St. Francis had served as a backwoods marketplace for scalps and captives, resulting in a heavy inflow of revenue in French gold coins for generations.[105]

One of the raid's survivors revealed what they had found in St. Francis not long after the attack: "It being extremely rich for a place of that bigness, having in it English goods and vast quantities of Wampum and [also] silver and gold."[106] Later, Captain Amos Ogden, who was proud of his distinguished career with the New Jersey Blues and now commanded all Provincials with distinction, was astounded by the fact that "this Indian town was very rich"; he estimated that there were "a thousand pounds worth of Indian goods."[107]

This bountiful wealth of St. Francis was no exaggeration or myth, as long assumed, serving as a primary motivation for so many zealous volunteers, mostly from the Provincial regiments—originally a total of thirty-seven men compared to the twenty-one English Regulars who first volunteered to serve under Rogers from the Crown Point army. In fact, the taking of English scalps and ransoming of English prisoners were big business. Captives were bought by the French for domestic and farm labor in New France, primarily in the Montreal and Quebec areas, for safety considerations and due to the difficulty of escaping and making their way home over such a distance. Therefore, the Abenaki had profited immensely from this war in which killing and capturing whites, both soldiers and civilians, had become a business venture and the steady flow of captives became the major source of income for the picturesque river town.

Indeed, for generations the Abenaki had gained a good number of French and English gold coins amounting to nothing less than a virtual gold mine in the heart of Quebec's wilderness. After the attack on St. Francis fully verified as much, the victors greedily secured at least "170 guineas in gold, and probably a great deal more that was not reported."[108]

In addition, a large amount of wampum and jewelry would be taken in the capture of the town, confirming the longtime rumors that St. Francis was a place of great wealth and a modern-day Babylon. Ranger Rob Pomeroy stole, as revealed in Second Lieutenant George Campbell's diary, a valuable jewel that was only one of many stolen at St. Francis. Destined to never enjoy his newfound wealth, because he would not survive the long withdrawal from St. Francis, Pomeroy "shewed [*sic*] me a Rube [*sic*] ring he took from a [dead] savage," the ruby the size of one's eye.[109]

An unknown number of Rogers's men were consumed by the prospect of securing the valuables and treasures long rumored to exist in St. Francis. And the Abenaki were also known by the Rangers to have been long paid in French brandy—the liquor of choice among both Indians and Frenchmen during this war—besides solid gold for the taking of so many scalps and prisoners. However, all indications and accounts have revealed that the factor of greed was more prevalent in the ranks of the Provincials and English, who had volunteered for the raid, than among the Rangers, because they possessed far more old scores to settle.

Indeed, across the breadth of New England, it had been well known for a long time that St. Francis was a place that contained riches, including precious items located at the Roman Catholic church and in the community at large. Even the French-style houses contained ample English goods from the trade networks linking to the St. Lawrence just to the north and the outside world. Valuable Indian goods of a wide variety were abundant in the town, especially large quantities of belts of wampum used in trade, decorative brooches, and a tidy sum in gold, silver, and coins, including guineas.

As mentioned, it had been well known to the people of New England for years—they realized how many scalps and prisoners had been taken over the decades—that a large amount of money had been paid to the St. Francis Abenaki for scalps and prisoners, who became part of a thriving commercial enterprise. Over the years, large numbers of these captive whites, men and women, were ransomed by the French, who purchased them from the Abenaki, who had their own monetary motivation to take prisoners and keep them alive, because they represented a steady source of sizeable income.

Susanna Johnson described the money at stake when she had been a captive at St. Francis: "In the early part of November [1754], Mr. [James] Johnson [her husband, captured at the same time in the New England settlements as she was and taken to Montreal] wrote from Montreal, requesting me to prevail upon the [St. Francis] Indians to carry me to Montreal, for sale, as he had made provision for that purpose."[110]

Susanna was finally taken southwest from St. Francis to Montreal by birchbark canoe: "Here, I had the happiness to find, that all my fellow prisoners had been purchased, by persons of respectability [members of the French upper class, including the mayor of Montreal], by whom they were treated with humanity."[111]

However, this was all part of a vast money-making venture. Susanna's husband had then "obtained the privilege of two months' absence on parole, for the purpose of going to New-England, to procure cash for the redemption of his family."[112]

Some Rangers almost certainly thought about monetary rewards, and this undeniable factor of greed had served as a primary motivator as much, if not more, than service to God and country. In truth, and like the Abenaki, whites had long cashed in on the war. Even the taking of a scalp was an income-making enterprise for the Ranger or frontiersman. Governor William Shirley, of the Colony of Massachusetts, had early provided one-hundred-pound bounties for the taking and turning in of Indian scalps: a virtual gold mine to a poor settler with no prospects of any kind.[113] However, French officials likewise promoted the Abenaki to reap a rich harvest of English scalps as part of a terrorist campaign "to punish the English till they longed for peace."[114]

Additionally, the one-story Roman Catholic mission church at St. Francis contained valuable icons and religious objects, including gold or gold-plated items, that were worth a fortune to a money-short Ranger from the frontier. And Rogers's men had long fought and died by the notion that to the victors go the spoils of war, which meant that everything was fair game if St. Francis was captured.

Vivid tales from St. Francis captives had long filtered back to the frontier settlements about some of the religious objects made of gold and silver, and these seemingly fantastic stores of Abenaki riches had grown over time. Inside the Roman Catholic church, among other precious items, were ornate silver-plated candlesticks and cloth-of-gold draperies; an expensive decorative banner of the Virgin Mary and Jesus Christ was lavishly embroidered with silver and gold wire. Some of these riches had come straight from France. To spread the spiritual faith among the allies of New France, Sir Vaillant Demihardouin of France had given the Abenaki of St. Francis an exquisite statue of Notre Dame de Sous-Terre, consisting of solid silver and representing more money than any Ranger, including Rogers, had ever seen in his life.[115]

The Omnipresent Factor of Religion

More than the factor of greed, a strong religious faith of Protestantism among Rogers's men—primarily Presbyterianism since most Rangers were Scotch-Irish—was a powerful motivation in an era in which religion was far more important among the common people than it is today. Partly because he was a holy warrior and leading men in the moral fight against the steady encroachment of the ominous threat of a feudal Roman Catholicism, which moved farther south with each victory won by Montcalm and other capable French leaders, Rogers was also motivated by the idea of striking into the heart of Catholicism.

In a strange way, the centuries of bitter religious strife between Catholics and Protestants in Europe's bloody religious wars had seemingly been transferred across the Atlantic to determine who were the chosen people in the New World to forever dominate the future destiny of the North American continent. Of course, France was Western Europe's primary Catholic nation, and England was Western Europe's primary Protestant nation: ancient enemies who were seemingly forever at war because each side was determined that its religious faith would prevail.

Just as the French had believed that they were God's chosen people in the New World, so the English settlers had early embraced the same religious idealism and exceptionalism about their own special place under the sun. And, of course, both sides justified their own less noble motivations and actions, including atrocities and massacres, in a convenient cloak of morality during this brutal and truly horrible war for possession of the North American continent.

Therefore, this vicious struggle was very much a religious conflict even more brutal than anything seen for hundreds of years in Europe, including even during the religious wars. Ironically, such religious hostility and intolerance explained why Protestants had fled to the New World in the first place, but the French and Indian War had caused the cycles of history to come full circle to a new land, which had been once considered free of such international and religious turmoil.

As they realized, Rogers and his men had entered not only the land of the Abenaki but also the threatening sphere of Roman Catholicism to boldly challenge the existence of both hostile entities. But, of course, these men, mostly frontiersmen from New England, had no idea exactly how deeply this passionate faith of the Old World had been woven into the fabric of the lives of transplanted Frenchmen, Canadians, and their Native American allies, especially the Abenaki. Because of their hatred of the French, these frontiersmen under Rogers did not know about the rich history of either New France or Quebec, nor did they care to learn. Ironically, these tough fighting men with Old Testament convictions had no idea that French Canada had first come into being as France's largest colony when explorer Jacques Cartier had erected a large Christian cross to lay claim to this new land for the Gallic king and people on July 24, 1534. At that time, these bold Frenchmen of supreme faith had knelt in solemn prayer with the raising of the holiest symbol of the true faith, which also served as the genesis of a vast new colony.[116]

In much the same way, the missionary Jesuit church along the timbered banks of the St. Francis River served as a shining example of not only Catholicism but also the historic cathedral of Chartres in France. This magnificent French church of exquisite architecture was located around eighty miles southwest of Paris. Built beginning in the twelfth century, the imposing Chartres cathedral was one of the most beautiful of all houses of worship in France.

Many Frenchmen, from ruling-class nobles to peasants, who comprised the vast majority of the French people and farmed the sprawling lands of the wealthy elite, had been inspired to join the Crusades that penetrated all the way to the Holy Land in the Middle East after hearing fiery sermons delivered by revered holy men from the pulpit of this stately church. Then the people of the Chartres cathedral had become the patrons of the Jesuit mission church situated along the majestic St. Francis, donating precious religious relics to this Abenaki church more than a half century before.[117]

As noted, generations of modern historians have left out of the traditional story of the bloody surprise attack on St. Francis the importance of religious faith—mostly Presbyterianism—as a central motivating factor among the attackers, including their commander, in what was very much a religious war and not a stereotypical racial war. Indeed, for the past three weeks, this forgotten religious factor had helped to push Rogers's men ever closer to St. Francis, giving them inner strength and fortifying their moral resolve, because they were convinced that a Protestant God was on the side.

The motivations of Rogers's Rangers at St. Francis have too often been painted in the simple emotional, racial, and psychological terms that were part of America's traditional metaphysics of Indian hating and racial animosity, which later dominated the westward movement all the way to the Pacific. But this religious rather than racial motivation of the attackers, including Rogers, who greatly admired Native American people in general, was powerful, as it was in the lives of the common people on the frontier. However, the true motivations of the average Ranger were deep-seated and more complex than long assumed, lying well beyond the realm of the emotional and primeval instincts, as if only sparked by a killer instinct from deep inside or a mindless bloodlust. However, what were some of the other considerations that fueled the motivations of Rogers and his men to destroy St. Francis until nothing remained but ashes?

Long overlooked and forgotten, other key motivations have seldom been explored or analyzed by historians over the years because of the powerful process of romanticizing, mythologizing, and glorification that has long obscured fundamental truths about Rogers's Rangers. Perhaps such a negligence has been nothing more than an inevitable development, given the stereotyping of not only the raid in general but also the players on both sides—simplifications glorifying one and vilifying the other over the course of centuries and to this day.

THE FORGOTTEN SCOTCH-IRISH

Also often overlooked is the fact that the primary demographic composition of Rogers's Rangers was not English but Scotch-Irish. They were distinctive and proud people from Ulster Province, in north Ireland, known for their spirited defiance of authority for centuries. In part because they had been a rebellious race long conditioned to battling for their very existence against one invader after another in a harsh land, the Scotch-Irish had survived for generations on the borders of the empire on both sides of the Atlantic. Like the major himself, and as noted, most of Rogers's Rangers were Scotch-Irish Presbyterians, who were either immigrants or the sons of immigrants from Ulster.

Devout and God-fearing, they were a religious people who "gloried in vindicating the Presbyterian faith." Besides the Scotch-Irish settlers from the New England frontier, the Irish, mostly Catholics, hailing from the remaining three-fourths of Ireland to the south and outside Ulster, were recruited for Ranger service from the waterfront and wharves of Boston, including sailors and wharf rats of the lower class.[118]

As revealed throughout the tragic course of Scottish and Irish history, the Scotch-Irish, who as faithful Presbyterians basked in a freer form of worship as part of the Protestant Reformation, and the Catholics, the previous owners of Ulster, were ancient enemies of a blood feud. The Scotch-Irish were originally Lowland Scots who loved a sense of individualism and personal independence, in both religion and politics, as much as self-government. Significantly, the Scotch-Irish had been a borderland people in Scotland as well as Ireland, where their fundamental character and mind-set had been forged during periods of extreme hardship and adversity in a blood-drenched land. Sparking seemingly endless bloody conflicts with the native Roman Catholics of Ulster Province, the Scots had journeyed a short distance south across the North Channel of the Irish Sea to settle in the English colonization plan known as the Ulster Settlement and the Plantation of Ulster during the first decade of the 1600s.

Therefore, the Scotch-Irish along America's embattled frontier were already familiar with the bitter warfare that marked generations of ethnic and racial struggles, especially for possession of a fertile, bountiful land. In this sense, the upcoming attack on St. Francis represented only the latest round in a savage religious conflict that had been faithfully transferred across the Atlantic. Indeed, the raid on St. Francis was all about this centuries-long religious struggle that had pitted Protestant against Catholic, but now included Native Americans on both sides, including Rogers's Stockbridge Ranger "Wolves," who were Mohegans.

Consequently, Rogers and his mostly Scotch-Irish command were part of not only an Indian war on the frontier but also the bloody legacies of this old religious war on the Atlantic's other side, because both conflicts had shaped the destinies and fates of generations of these hardy Presbyterians. For a host of ample good reasons, these Scotch-Irish of the frontier had long hated nothing more than the endless troublemaking activities of zealous Catholic missionaries and priests, especially the Jesuits who had founded the mission at St. Francis. These holy men in black robes and wearing crucifixes had long incited the Abenaki to go forth and wage a brutal no-quarter war against New England's settlers in the name of God and the right religion.

In this sense, the destruction of St. Francis and its Roman Catholic church, one of the most prominent buildings in the town, and the homes of the community's priests was actually a sacred duty in the minds of the pious Scotch-Irish Protestant Rangers, because of the depth of their spiritual faith fueled by the Old Testament's fiery words. Similarly, Irish Catholics, who fought to retain not only their sacred homeland but also their faith, had burned Scotch-Irish settlements in uprisings to drive the hated Protestants, who had taken their ancestral lands, out of Ulster Province, north Ireland.

The Scotch-Irish of Rogers's command never forgot about the heroics of the ancestors who had gamely battled against Roman Catholicism in their picturesque homeland of Ulster. In this sense, the attack on St. Francis was now a simple case of the sons of those first Scotch-Irish settlers, mostly of New England, returning the favor by taking the war to a bastion of Roman Catholicism. Therefore, the hearts of Rogers's Scotch-Irish were filled with a longing not only to exact revenge for the murderous raids of the Abenaki but also to strike a blow against Catholics—the French, Irish, and converted Abenaki—as part of an ancient struggle, which had long waged on the Atlantic's other side. In this context, the distinctive blue bonnets of the Highlanders were proudly worn by a good many Rangers: reminders of their Scottish and religious heritage and past struggles against Roman Catholicism in not only Ulster but also America.

By the morning of October 4, therefore, the Scotch-Irish Rangers were supremely motivated by a host of factors that went well the beyond the traditional lens of the French and Indian War. In fact, Rogers and Major General Amherst could not have placed a better bet on the superior fighting prowess and deep-seated motivations of these mostly Scotch-Irish young men and boys of the Rangers. Under the circumstances and thanks to history's ever-unpredictable, twisting contours, burning down the Catholic church at St. Francis now represented a primary objective in the hearts and minds of these Scotch-Irish soldiers, who viewed the destruction of this Catholic holy site as a solemn Presbyterian duty to God and country. The church and its Jesuit priest (Father Pierre-Joseph-Antoine Roubaud), Roman Catholic crosses, and other religious iconography of the Old World had represented the epitome of evil to the Scotch-Irish Rangers of the New World for as long as these distinctive Celtic fighting men could remember.

Although the long-suffering people of the embattled frontier mostly viewed this conflict as an Indian war, more so than the urbanites in America's major cities on the East Coast, for the large number of Scotch-Irish Rangers in the ranks, an ancient religious war from across the Atlantic had been resumed in a new land, and the raid on St. Francis was just another chapter of the seemingly endless bloodletting in the name of God. Some Abenaki warriors wore silver crosses that reflected their love of Roman Catholicism, which they partly fought to spread, despite the traditional view that the Native Americans' fight was all about preserving their lands—the most simplistic view of the struggle of Native Americans, including the Abenaki.

It was well known that the Jesuits of St. Francis had long possessed a disproportionate and decisive influence among the Abenaki, fueling their vicious war against the Protestants because they, in theory, posed a threat to Catholicism. For a good many reasons, therefore, St. Francis and its missionary church had to be eliminated at all costs in this religious struggle. As noted, the zealous Jesuits, the so-called black robes who had been born mostly in France, had transformed St. Francis into not only a sanctuary but also the primary military staging ground for the fiercest raids ever launched by the Abenaki on the frontier settlements.

In the name of God, the Jesuits had long implored the Abenaki to drive back the tide of Protestant settlers to both preserve Catholicism in this magnificent land of promise and ensure its future spread across the North American continent. The early experiences on the frontier and their religious teachings had long told the mostly Scotch-Irish Rangers that what St. Francis represented was not only heretical (ironically, mirroring how the Abenaki, Canadians, and French looked at the Protestant settlers) but nothing less than pure evil.

And the Holy Bible, especially the Old Testament, had taught these men since childhood the moral lesson that this hellish place—a bastion of Catholic faith in the heart of the northern wilderness—had to be eliminated to make the world safe for Presbyterians, their families, and their homes scattered all across the frontier. After all, the St. Francis Abenaki "professed the Catholic faith, as a result of decades of missionary work by the Jesuits; but far from tempering their actions, this indoctrination made it all the more easy for French priests to suggest that attacks against the English would put them in higher favor with the church."[119]

The fight against the march of a militant Catholicism that threatened the northern frontier began long ago. As noted, Captain Phineas Stevens was an early Indian fighter who defended New England's northeastern frontier against this threat, emerging as a legend across the frontier for heroics performed on the east side of the Green Mountains. Symbolically, he was the revered father of several outstanding fighting men who served with Rogers's Rangers. They continued the distinguished family legacy of battling against the march of Catholicism. The hard-fighting Phineas Stevens had been captured by the Abenaki and taken to Canada, where he gained more reason to hate Catholicism in all its insidious forms.

Captain Stevens's reputation reached new heights when he led Fort Number Four's defense in 1747, and his legacy inspired many Rangers in 1759. At that time, he had boldly defied large numbers of New France's raiders with a small band of like-minded New Hampshire militiamen, boasting, "My men are not afraid to die." Knowing intimately the influential role of the French Jesuits in inflaming the Native Americans against the frontier settlers, Stevens believed beyond all doubt that "were it not for ye French [then] it would be Easy to Live at peace with ye Indians" of St. Francis.[120]

This estimation of the outsized Jesuit role in adding fuel to the fire to incite Native Americans to go on the warpath was right on target. Father Pierre-Joseph-Antoine Roubaud was just that kind of France-born Jesuit who saw waging war and slaughtering Protestants as a scared religious duty. He was now the revered spiritual leader of Catholicism at St. Francis, and this was most of all a holy war to him, as if he were a European Crusader of old in the Holy Land.[121]

An unbridled hatred toward priests, especially those born and educated in France, like the militant Father Roubaud, among the fighting men in Rogers's ranks was partly evident during the advance on Quebec, when the Rangers under Captain Moses Hazen possessed orders to "kill all, and give no quarter." Not surprisingly, therefore, when a French priest was found wounded after a hot fight in this holy war, Captain Hazen felt no pity. The bleeding priest "begged earnestly for quarters; but the Captain told the men to kill him [and] Upon which, one of them deliberately blew his brains out."[122]

It is not known with any degree of certainty, but perhaps some of Rogers's men hated the inhabitants of St. Francis for a reason other than that they were the most notorious Indians on the North American continent. There was a disturbing reality that for generations white captives had essentially become Indians after a successful acculturation into the tribe. For the average frontiersman worried about his own children becoming Indians one day if they were captured, especially at a young age, this haunting racial fear was the ultimate horror—whites turning into people who hated and fought against English civilization, while becoming full-fledged and equal tribe members, including those who then joined war parties that struck the white settlements.

The war chief of St. Francis, blond-haired Joseph-Louis Gill, the son of two white captives from New England, fought with considerable enthusiasm against the enemies (both white and red) of the Abenaki. This unsettling realization about the longtime mixing of races and the transformation of whites, especially young girls and women, into full-fledged Indians fueled a deeper racial hatred for even those Abenaki who were half white or all white, like Gill.[123]

But contrary to common perceptions, the simplistic factor of outright racial hatred based on a darker skin color was not the primary Ranger motivation to explain what was about to descend upon St. Francis with a vengeance. Most of all, a militant Catholicism was a more decisive factor than skin color in these so-called French Indians becoming archvillains to the Protestants and Presbyterians in Rogers's ranks.

Indeed, Rogers and his men possessed a far greater hatred toward Roman Catholicism than toward Native Americans in general and hating people of a darker skin color. After all, many Rangers had thoroughly acclimated to Indian ways and customs, including warfighting and the taking of Indian wives, revealing a measure of affinity and admiration for Indian people. The northern frontier, including the Merrimack River Valley, had early possessed mixed-race elements of a hybrid society, because white males had long intermingled with Native American women, which was more accepted on the frontier than in the eastern settlements and cities. Nor were the Native Americans motivated primarily by racism in their attacks on white settlements as generally assumed in the popular imagination. After all, the Abenaki had often adopted white captives and treated them with great affection like brothers, best friends, and sons. Large numbers of white captives had been part of the St. Francis community for generations.

Men like Ranger Robert Holmes had become almost as much Indian as white, adopting the cultural ways and value systems of Native Americans. One of Major Rogers's finest officers, Lieutenant Holmes was the aspiring son of a livery keeper in New Hampshire. He was destined to sacrifice his life in 1763 for the love of a young Indian girl who possessed his heart. Holmes momentarily abandoned his good judgment when he went to assist an allegedly sick Indian woman whom his young Indian lover had told him needed help. Holmes then walked into a fatal ambush.

In battling warriors who had long waged a war of terrorism and no quarter, Rogers and his men had only adapted to their enemy's ways of fighting by becoming more Indian than the Indians in perpetuating an especially vicious conflict that had thoroughly traumatized and brutalized men on both sides. In this way, white Rangers were paying the highest compliment to Native Americans and their rich culture by copying their ways and adopting their methods, which played a leading role in their rise to the lofty level of America's elite fighting men.[124]

In addition, the men of Rogers's command no doubt felt somewhat relieved that no chaplains accompanied them on this expedition, because of what they were about to do to the inhabitants of St. Francis without feeling. As members of independent Ranger companies separate from the British army, Rogers's Rangers had not been assigned chaplains like British and Provincial units. Rogers's men were about to treat St. Francis's inhabitants in the same ruthless way that the town's warriors had long waged no-quarter warfare across the frontier in a classic case of cruel frontier justice. For what Rogers and his men had in mind and were fully prepared to do without remorse, they needed no chaplains present, because as far as they were concerned, there would be no God of mercy or pity at St. Francis on October 4. Consequently, they viewed the upcoming attack on the quiet community, bathed in an early morning calm, like a righteous "crusade against the abomination of Babylon."[125]

While the white soldiers viewed St. Francis as the Abenaki Babylon, the Abenaki people of St. Francis saw their patron saint (also Italy's patron saint), St. Francis of Assisi, as protecting them from harm in the sacred Catholic tradition, especially from any attack by the hated Protestants. After all, as the

French had long told the Abenaki, this revered Italian Catholic saint would provide the people of St. Francis with safety as long as the sun shone on their picturesque land and their sanctuary town along the beautiful river.[126]

New England's fighting men, both Rangers and Provincials, across the breadth of the frontier had been raised as children on the moral dictates of the Holy Bible and its timeless teachings of ancient Hebrew scholars. The dour New England army chaplains conducted regular prayer services in camp and led the singing of favorite hymns, reminding the Provincials why they fought. After all, these pious American chaplains—worthy counterparts to the zealous and militant Father Roubaud—were engaged in a holy war against what they viewed as the epitome of evil, while remembering the great Hebrew prophet Moses, who sent Joshua against the Amalek people.[127]

Indeed, like other men, Scotland-born Private Robert Kirkwood was eager to strike a blow, crouching with his comrades in the cold pine thickets before St. Francis and motivated by "the hope of revenge."[128] He detested the Abenaki in puritanical moral terms with a naive purity uncluttered by complexities or ambiguities, because St. Francis "was a den of the most mischievous and inveterate Indian enemies the English ever had, and live in the back settlements of Canada; numberless are the scenes of bloodshed and rapine, these lawless savages had committed upon our people."[129]

Behind the longings for revenge of Rogers's men was the power of the Protestant faith, especially Presbyterianism, in what had become the most ruthlessly ungodly—in its brutality—of religious wars on American soil. A religious-minded Lieutenant Colonel Seth Pomery, a respected Provincial officer who had been a hardworking gunsmith from the Connecticut River town of Northampton in western Massachusetts, wrote in a letter to a friend, "As you have at heart the Protestant cause, so I ask an interest in your prayers that the Lord of Hosts would go forth with us and give us victory over our unreasonable, encroaching, barbarous, murdering enemies."[130]

Even more, another chaplain exhorted Provincials to fight harder because of the righteous nature of this struggle and made plain what was required of them in no uncertain terms: "Be courageous; for no cowards go to heaven."[131] Indeed, in overall motivational terms, many Rangers, Provincials, and British soldiers now with Major Rogers waged war like in the days of old during a noble "crusade against the myrmidons of Rome."[132] Making an old biblical analogy that revealed his deep readings of the Holy Bible, Dr. Thomas Williams, the physician of a New England regiment, described how the French, Canadians, and Indians fled from one hot fight in 1755 "like the Assyrians in their flight."[133]

Ironically, in waging their own crusade, Rogers and his men only utilized the harshest measures that had long defined holy war on both sides of the Atlantic. With keen insight, captive Robert Eastburn, a future Presbyterian minister, understood in 1756 how his enemies relied upon the burning faith of religion to fuel their combat prowess, while allowing them to commit the worst imaginable atrocities, without guilt or remorse, against Protestant heretics in the cruel tradition of Europe's wars of religion:

> *The enemy determined to destroy Bull's Fort [located just west of the headwaters of the Mohawk River, near the eastern edge of Lake Oneida which was just east of Lake Ontario and near today's Rome, New York] which they soon effected [on March 27, 1756], all being put to the sword [around fifty-five soldiers], except five persons, the fort burned burnt, the provision and powder destroyed; (saving only a little for their own use) then they retired to the woods, and joined the main body [which] consisted of 400 French and 300 [Huron and Iroquois] Indians, commanded by one of the principal Gentleman [Gaspard-Joseph Chaussegroes de Léry] of Quebec; as soon as they got together (having a priest with them) they fell to their knees, and returned thanks for their victory; an example this, worthy of imitation! An example which may make profane pretended Protestants blush, (if they are not lost to all sense of shame) who instead of acknowledging God, or Providence, in their military undertakings, are continually reproaching him with oaths and curses; is it any wonder, that the attempts of such, are blasted with disappointment and disgrace![134]*

Minister Eastburn heartily condemned the evils of Catholicism and how it had caused immense suffering among the Protestant people across the northern frontier. Learning as much as a captive after he had been taken prisoner because of the relentless religious-conversion efforts, which he ignored, the England-born Eastburn denounced the great "pains the Papists take to propagate such a bloody and absurd religion as theirs. . . . O! may not the zeal of Papists, in propagating superstition and idolatry, make Protestants ashamed of their lukewarmness, in promoting the religion of the Bible!"[135]

Even the French, Indian, and Canadian attackers from Fort Duquesne, located at the forks of the Ohio, who had descended upon George Washington's Fort Necessity during the summer of 1754 were partly religiously motivated. Common soldier Charles "Jolicoeur" Bonin wrote, "Before setting out the next morning, mass was said at the camp by the chaplain. After wards, we began our march" to engage in the battle that forced the surrender of Fort Necessity to bring young Washington his first defeat.[136]

For such reasons, the Abenaki became the most devoted warrior people in New France to the militant faith of Catholicism, ensuring that they became exceedingly proficient in the grim art of slaughtering settlers across the frontier in the name of God.[137] In July 1758, a Boston newspaper printed the mid-June letter of an officer who served under General James Wolfe, and he emphasized the factor of religion in motivating New France's warriors in the defense of Louisbourg, whose fate was sealed: "Our troops . . . persued [*sic*] the vile Vermin to the very Gates of Louisbourg and kill'd and took many Prisoners; among the Slain were two Indians, one of them had a Medal on his Breast, representing the French King in a Roman Dress, and an Indian shaking Hands, the Motto (Honor and Virtue) and a Crucifix with a Chain."[138]

Ironically, taking a supreme religious-based satisfaction in the work of destruction and killing like his followers, Major Rogers was about to destroy a Jesuit mission town with a brutal totality, because he detested Catholicism more than Native Americans, admiring the values and spiritual beliefs of a remarkable indigenous people, who were now fighting their own battle for survival against the odds. In his own words, Rogers wrote with a sense of respect for the spiritual beliefs of Native Americans, which were often less hypocritical than those of white civilization, which perpetrated a wide variety of abuses in the name of religion: "There is no nation of Indians but seem to have some sense of a deity, and a kind of religion among them [and] Their ideas of the nature and attributes of the deity are very obscure, and some of them absurd; but they all acknowledge him to be the creator and master of the world."[139]

MUCH-NEEDED PROVISIONS
But perhaps most of all by this time, the capture of St. Francis was absolutely necessary for the survival of Rogers's entire command, as the provisions they had brought with them from Missisquoi Bay were nearly gone, with most

having been greedily eaten by famished men during their nightmarish trek through the spruce bogs. Now, the majority of the Rangers' haversacks, which had been drawn from the English quartermasters of Amherst's army, or fashioned with typical frontier ingenuity from deer hide, or made from sail cloth or heavy linen, and the army packs of the Provincials and British Regulars, also issued from British stores, were entirely empty.[140]

Therefore, nothing was now more important—not even tasting sweet revenge by way of destroying the town—than capturing the Abenaki storehouses overflowing with food from the recent harvest, which had been a good one, duly celebrated by the Abenaki only hours before. Rogers and his men knew that capturing St. Francis's food supplies meant nothing less than survival for more than 140 men, who were engaged in a Darwinian survival-of-the-fittest odyssey of the first magnitude, because of the upcoming lengthy withdrawal to safety, if they succeeded in their mission.

But, at last, the long-awaited time had arrived for Rogers and his men to finally undo all the wrongs and savagery committed by St. Francis's warriors for nearly a century. For such reasons, Major Rogers realized that a new day was about dawn—one in which his people, especially the Scotch-Irish, of the northern frontier would no longer be butchered in their sleep with an arrogant impunity that spared neither woman nor child. Rogers and his followers never forgot how countless victims had long been horribly mutilated in the most shocking fashion possible as part of a war of terrorism to spread fear far and wide.

To inflict the maximum amount of terror, the usual Native American formula, endlessly relied upon, included beheading, dismemberment, tearing open of bowels, heads displayed atop fenceposts, and, of course, everyone (including infants) scalped. This systemic terrorism had been well calculated by the Abenaki and the French leaders, who passionately desired for the last Protestant heretic to be destroyed to force the settlers to flee for the safety of the coast. Therefore, the Abenaki had evolved into true warriors in a war of terrorism, becoming masters in this grisly art.

Heightened Predawn Tension in the Quiet Cold of the Early Morning

Meanwhile, grim-faced Rangers, Provincials, and British Regulars made their last-minute preparations to attack near the silent edge of the pine forest as quietly as possible so as not to give their whereabouts away about an hour before sunrise at around 5 a.m. This crucial time was about an hour after Rogers's last reconnaissance had been conducted close to St. Francis.

By this time, the young men and boys all the way from Crown Point looked almost like barbarians, or the so-called English savages, as the French called them, because they were gaunt, ragged, and unshaven. Dirty uniforms stank and had shrunk after being wet for so long during the torturous march through the spruce bogs. Cut by branches and thorn bushes, Ranger faces were smeared with dirt and grease, which only highlighted their beards, which had grown for more than three weeks. Rogers's men now sported black, red, auburn, and blondish beards, which were unfashionable among both the French and the English military men during this period and not at all worn by the Abenaki, because facial hair was virtually nonexistent among Native Americans for genetic reasons.

The heightened tension was now palatable among the surviving Rangers, and it had continued to rise throughout the night to reach a new high as the dawn of October 4 drew closer. Anxiety continued to mount among the men, including hardened veterans, because no one completely knew what to expect with the rising sun that at least promised some warmth to ease the cold biting into weary bodies badly in need of rest.

Best of all, the town of St. Francis still lay quiet in the autumnal darkness, and still no warriors had been seen guarding and patrolling the town. No war parties or French reinforcements had arrived in the night. No Abenaki had discovered the presence of Rogers and his Rangers positioned in the darkened pine forest just outside St. Francis, as if they did not exist at all. The overall situation had become not only strange but also inexplicable to the logical thinking of Rogers and his men, who basked in their good fortune, after having taken so many risks.

Unfortunately for the sleeping Abenaki, an undeniable bloodlust among Rogers's most experienced veterans in the ranks was also stirring in the silent pine thickets. And this deep feeling, which was about to be satisfied in the grimmest way, seemed to bring an eagerly awaited amount of warmth to the shivering bodies of Rogers's men on this tense and anxious night, when there could be no fires so close to St. Francis. Any coughs or sneezes continued to be muffled by the men on the major's orders.

With the dawn closing in, one that was destined to seal the fates of a good many Abenaki, a sense of excitement steadily heightened among the Rangers from the adrenaline already surging through their veins, while the nerves of experienced fighting men about to engage in battle against their most feared enemy were already strained. Armed with tomahawks and fixed steel bayonets for the inevitable grim business of killing at close range, Rogers's men were now ideally armed for a swift early morning strike and the inevitable close-range combat that would make October 4 the bloodiest day in Abenaki history.

The Rangers' smoothbore .75-caliber Long Land Pattern Brown Bess muskets were ready for action, their barrels having been cut down for greater maneuverability in forest combat and blackened to reduce the glare from sunlight—for instance, on the metal parts of the flintlock firing mechanism—and thereby avoid detection. These trusty firearms were loaded with "buck & ball" (deadly loads of six or seven small lead balls, which the French called "swain shot") to guarantee a shotgun-like blast that was especially devastating when fired into a Canadian, Indian, or Frenchman at close range.

With the cold dawn of October 4 fast approaching and the first morning sounds of nature just starting to make the pine forest come alive in the darkness, the steel bayonets of Rogers's men had already been slowly and silently fixed. These lengthy bayonets bestowed a distinct advantage to the Rangers when they finally came face-to-face with Abenaki warriors armed with tomahawks and scalping knives. Ranger tomahawks had been sharpened for the moment of truth that was about to come at long last. Evidently the Rangers had used parts of their clothing or their blanket edges to cover the bayonet sockets to muffle the sound when they attached steel bayonets to the ends of their Brown Bess muskets. By this time, these experienced Rangers had become experts at not making any unnecessary noises that might betray their location and intentions to the Abenaki.

Even after their most exhausting mission to date of having journeyed nearly 175 miles not as the crow flies by water and land, having marched for nine days through the spruce bogs that lay northeast of Missisquoi Bay, Rogers's men still possessed a jaunty look, revealing that their high morale and esprit de corps remained alive and well. Although hungry, tired, and half sick from their harrowing ordeal of around three weeks, they still possessed the inner confidence and resolve of elite fighting men. On the verge of striking a lethal blow, the officers of Rogers's Rangers, including the major, though not the Provincial and British volunteers, wore with pride their short, forest green jackets of wool, which now smelled moldy from the ubiquitous wetness. Quite simply and although they certainly looked otherwise, these Rangers were nothing less than the best fighting men that the entire British-Provincial Army had been able to muster for the nasty business of battling the Abenaki with the same brutal intensity.

Like other legendary elite commands, Rogers's Rangers were about to go to work with a grim efficiency with a thoroughness seldom seen. Throughout the course of the history of Western warfare, going all the way back to ancient times, elite units have played key roles. In general, these crack units can be grouped into four categories by birth, function, value, and power. Elite commands first evolved with the formation of the Theban Sacred Band of ancient Greece; the three hundred Spartans of King Leonidas's bodyguard, who rose magnificently to the challenge of defending the strategic pass against the Persian hordes at Thermopylae in 480 BC; and the Praetorian Guard, the most famous of all elite units of ancient Rome.

The distinguished legacy of distinctive bodies of elite troops continued unabated throughout the annals of military history. The Prussian Guards of Frederick the Great and Napoleon Bonaparte's Imperial (or Old) Guard had often worn different uniforms, including distinctive headgear (the Guard's famous bearskins), which distinguished them from the ordinary fighting men in the ranks. In modern times, especially during World War II, special units became elite by way of their aggressive tactics, launching deep raids behind enemy lines.

Some of these elite units were bonded by ethnicity, including Rogers's Rangers, with its largely Scotch-Irish and Presbyterian composition representing the predominant frontier demographic. In many ways, during their respective periods throughout the course of history, these elite commands and their proud members of a special fraternity evolved into the popular equivalent of Homeric heroes from the pages of *The Iliad* and the Trojan War.

This distinctive look of crack troops had long played a key part in fostering an esprit de corps that revealed to one and all, both enemies and friendlies, that they were the army's best fighting men. The short jackets of green, which blended in so well with the forest's natural vegetation, served that purpose for Ranger officers, as well as providing excellent camouflage that became more effective when slightly faded from the recent hot September weather during the trek to St. Francis. Any remaining newness to green Ranger uniforms had been worn off by this time, especially after the lengthy ordeal in the spruce bogs.

Still another unique item of the Ranger uniform also bestowed a jaunty look and signified to other troops that these soldiers were the army's elite fighting men: civilian Scottish bonnets of blue worn with a good deal of ethnic pride. Blue was the Rogers's Rangers' favorite color (ironically, the Canadian and French fighters also wore a tuque, or stocking cap, of blue) when campaigning in enemy country. However, some men also wore green bonnets that matched the color of the short uniform jackets of Rogers and his officers.

The Scottish bonnet, which was fashionable among soldiers and civilians of Celtic descent, was especially symbolic; it represented the well-known feisty spirit and hard-fighting qualities of the Scotch-Irish who dominated Rogers's ranks, both officers and enlisted men. After all, these men were mostly either immigrants themselves from the Green Isle or the sons and grandsons of Lowland Scots (as were Rogers and so many of his men), who then became Scotch-Irish, scratching out a living in the green hills of the Ulster Settlement in north Ireland.

However, Scottish bonnets were not the only popular headgear among Rogers's Rangers. Some men wore a leather jockey-style cap with a cut-down brim to enhance visibility in the dense forests. Other men wore fur caps of fox, lynx, or beaver skin, as when they had hunted and trapped in the woodlands of the frontier, before becoming Rangers. Of course, no other soldiers in North America wore the combination of green uniform jackets and blue Scottish bonnets, which bestowed on them a distinctive look that was wholly American and a source of pride. Although these tough fighting men at first glance appeared nothing more than a motley band of citizen-soldiers, the Rangers were still the elite of the elite among all of America's frontier fighters. And they were about to demonstrate as much in the upcoming attack, when Rogers was going for broke.

However, the haphazard look and unkept dress of these dirt-streaked fighting men were no longer of any importance whatsoever to Rogers. As a rule, one that had so often paid dividends, the major never picked those soldiers who were to become officers on the flimsy basis of army politics, outward appearances, or winning personal ways, especially the gift of gab, as Rogers knew all about Irish blarney as the son of Scotch-Irish immigrants. None of the major's decisions were based on first appearances deliberately calculated to impress, especially in choosing volunteers from Provincial regiments. In regard to advancing a Ranger enlisted man to the officer ranks, he first studied him closely to see what he could accomplish during the campaign and in the heat of combat: a tough and demanding test before Rogers recommended a Ranger for promotion to the officer ranks.

Rogers had long wanted only the most dependable and resourceful fighting men to serve in the ranks, especially as his top lieutenants, such as Captain Joseph Wait and Lieutenant Noah Grant, men who possessed the ability to think quickly on their feet in an emergency and crisis situations. And he had made sure that only the best noncommissioned officers, especially the experienced sergeants who could take command with a well-honed skill whenever officers were cut down or lost in battle, served in the ranks.

Major Rogers also secured enlisted men whose aim with a flintlock musket and pistol would be true when it was a matter of life or death in a combat situation. Rogers felt confident of success on October 4 because he knew that he possessed the exact kind of tough and indispensable men capable of destroying St. Francis and its inhabitants in this holy war in record time before a hasty departure.[141]

At last in the darkness of the early morning of October 4, Major Rogers was ready to fulfill his special destiny and long-awaited dream of reducing St. Francis to ashes. It is not known at this time if Rogers carried his old powder horn, dated June 3, 1756, which had seen arduous service on past expeditions deep into enemy territory. Rogers's prized powder horn was finely carved with inscriptions from the talented hand of a black fighting man of a Massachusetts regiment named John Bush.[142]

It is not known whether John Bush had served at some point as a Ranger, like Boston Burn from Westford, Massachusetts, and other black Rangers, such as Private "Duke" Jacob, both of whom awaited the order to attack on the early morning of October 4. These dependable fighting men of African heritage served as proud members of the only integrated combat force in the British army during the struggle for possession of the North American continent, in part because they trusted Major Rogers to treat them fairly and like true men of value.[143]

CHAPTER SEVEN

Final Nighttime Approach
to the Most Tempting of Targets

MAJOR ROGERS, NOW DEEP IN THE UNMAPPED WILDERNESS OF QUEBEC AND on the verge of his greatest success to date, was in his prime. He already possessed a reputation across the colonies for doing the impossible, thanks to the colonial press, including in large cities like Boston and New York. Large-sized, muscular, and stout, with both an imposing physique and a commanding presence that played role in ensuring that his men would follow him to hell and back if necessary, Rogers, at twenty-seven, was at his physical and mental zenith. He was also at the pinnacle of his career as the most famous Ranger leader in North America and very much a legend in his own time.

This dynamic Scotch-Irish leader, who was handsome and charismatic beyond what was normally expected of a homespun product from the northern frontier of the Merrimack River country, basked in a fame that was already widespread on both sides of the Atlantic. But Rogers had always defied expectations and contradicted stereotypes, and October 4 would be no exception to the rule. This burly Scotch-Irishman from the lowest level of American society, who possessed the traditional looks of the people of Scotland and north Ireland but stood taller than the average man of his day, had come a long way in life to have won fame that had spread across both America and Great Britain. And now the winning of a dramatic victory at St. Francis was guaranteed to propel that celebrity even higher, if all went well in the upcoming attack.

However, Rogers was not concerned about the lofty level of his fame, because all of that was now secondary to him. At this time, he had not been seduced by the allure of his fame, because he was still aspiring ever higher—a common man from the northern frontier on the rise by way of his own merits and accomplishments, which left him neither the time nor the inclination to dwell on more than simply keeping his men alive and succeeding in fulfilling his mission.

Instead of focusing on his rising fame, which had reached across the Atlantic to a degree that he still did not fully realize, Rogers was now more concerned about the welfare of his men and how he would have to precisely orchestrate his tactical plan to destroy St. Francis forever. And Rogers could not have known that he was about to reach the point of his own apotheosis at this remote Indian mission town in only a short time and that his life was about to change forever—ironically, not for the better years in the future, as deemed by fate—due to what he and his men were about to accomplish at St. Francis on this cold morning in Quebec.

In some distinctive ways, and as Rogers's personal destiny would have it, this situation in the pine forest immediately before St. Francis was more than simply another conventional attack, and he would never be quite the same after what he and his men were about to achieve to an extent that the young major could never imagine in totality. Indeed, after having repeatedly outsmarted his experienced opponents and trekking nearly 175 miles during the last three weeks, Rogers had no idea that the sparkling success that he was shortly to achieve in the heart of New France would eventually bring upon his head the wrath of the most powerful enemies in America (Generals William Johnson and Thomas Gage), whom he could never defeat like the Abenaki in this Machiavellian political game played behind the scenes. In the most classic of ironies, the upcoming victory at St. Francis would eventually lead to Rogers's undoing: a tragic case in which winning his greatest triumph led to his own downfall, like a classic Greek tragedy.

But the injustice of this personal tragedy that doomed Rogers and his shining career lay in the future. For now, Rogers had no time to be concerned about his personal fate, jealous rivals, or army politics because he remained too busy making sure that everything was ready. He now concentrated solely on winning the sparkling success that all New England had awaited for as long as anyone could remember.

Rogers was now entirely focused on making absolutely sure that everything about the upcoming attack would go exactly right and according to his well-laid plan, which he had formulated in his head, after his close observations of the town. He and his men fully realized that nothing could be allowed to go wrong at this point, and no mistakes could be made at the last minute. Most of all, the still-anxious major understood that everything had to flow smoothly and without a hitch, because everything was now at stake as never before.

As he hoped and prayed, Rogers was now on the verge of finally fulfilling his greatest dream and reaching the peak of his career as the leader of an extraordinary group of fighting men. Appropriately at this time and unfortunately for the Abenaki, the hard-driving major was at his physical best and most effective, which was about to be demonstrated in full. Major Rogers was about to reach his apotheosis along a river called the St. Francis in dramatic fashion.

He was now wearing a tattered green uniform and a red beard that added a distinguished, typically Scotch-Irish appearance to a handsome face, which made him look older than his twenty-seven years, while maintaining a powerful, commanding presence. Even amid a large group of rough-hewn Rangers who were expert killers and scalpers, the enemy could easily ascertain which man was the leader simply by his size, actions, and demeanor. First and foremost, Rogers certainly looked every inch the dynamic leader of men, and his imposing physicality and dominant presence were obvious to one and all.

And by any measure, these were no ordinary men who now served in the Rangers' ranks but literally the cream of the crop. The culling process year after year had left mostly tough, hard-bitten men of exceptional ability from the northern frontier. Rogers was equally tough on multiple levels, and he could as readily engage in a drunken brawl as take an Indian, Canadian, or French scalp with a quick, experienced motion and unconcealed delight. These Rangers were as rugged and rough as they were cruel in the heat of battle, which would be fully demonstrated in the upcoming attack on the sleeping town.

To effectively lead such rawboned, high-spirited, and independent-minded men and command their undying respect from beginning to end, Rogers had to be even harder and tougher than his soldiers. Rogers's toughness, both mental and physical, was one explanation for his ability to win his battles and skirmishes against the cruelest of enemies and command a sense of awe among his followers during this far-flung expedition, in which so many things had already gone wrong, to make the overall prospects for success seem especially bleak until almost the last moment.

And besides his unique leadership style—which was ultra-democratic and the very antithesis of the British military and class systems, reliant on merciless discipline and class-based authority to induce fear among the common soldiers to ensure strict obedience—which radiated a sense a fair play and egalitarianism like in no other command in North America, Rogers inspired his men to follow him to hell and back: all the way to St. Francis in this case.

In part explaining his highly effective and dynamic leadership style was the combined effect of his egalitarianism born of the dual legacies of the Scottish and Irish border experiences and his consistent concern for the welfare for his men, which were distinctive characteristics born of the frontier experience. Like the wilderness itself, the naturally unorthodox Rogers himself was untamed in regard to going his own way and doing what was least anticipated by the enemy, and he succeeded in achieving the impossible time and time again.

All in all, he possessed the ruggedness of not only the untamed New England frontier and the Merrimack River country but also the Scottish Highlands, which was a distinctive cultural legacy and a distinguished personal heritage that the major still held dear. Rogers also possessed the well-known fighting spirit, combat prowess, and audacity of the fabled Highlanders of Scotland's most mountainous region, along with the Scotch-Irish from the rolling hills of Ulster Province, north Ireland. As noted, these regions of severe adversity were blood-soaked borderlands for generations, well known for having long produced exceptionally robust fighting men from societies dominated by a warrior ethos.

With his long red hair tied behind his back in a queue (or ponytail) and a healthy red beard that had grown since he departed Crown Point on September 13, Rogers even looked much like one of these legendary red-bearded Scottish Highland warriors, who had carried broadswords and excelled at close-range combat regardless of the odds when battling British soldiers in red uniforms: blue eyes, a sturdy, stocky, and somewhat menacing build, and an even harder interior born of a difficult frontier life and years of waging bloody warfare, including no-mercy combat.

During this most dangerous of missions in the history of Rogers's Rangers, the major's men had followed him without doubt, hesitation, or reservation in part because they were following what Rogers represented like no other officer in the British-American army: an inspiring can-do spirit, a rare voice of frontier egalitarianism, the essence of a people's democracy born of the wilderness experience, and, last but not least, a budding sense of a vibrant sense of a unique Americanism, if not a nascent nationalism in its earliest and most formative stage, that motivated American fighting men to do the impossible against the odds.[1]

The Vital Element of Surprise

To his immense personal satisfaction, with the dawn of October 4 getting ever closer, Major Rogers had succeeded in retaining the element of surprise, which was revealed by the first songbirds in the forest beginning their morning chorus like it was just another fine autumn day in Quebec without the insanity and curse of war. In a striking paradox, the first English settlers, long indoctrinated in the ways of European warfare from across the sea, had once thoroughly denounced the Indians' surprise attacks as the most cowardly way to fight. And now Rogers, like no other white man in North America, had mastered the art of the surprise attack to a degree unimaginable by Native Americans like the Abenaki, as he was about to demonstrate in full on that fall morning deep in the St. Francis River country.

Ironically, French military leadership had played a large role in setting the stage for Rogers's most famous achievement, which no one had believed possible for so long, by ordering a series of countermoves to intercept and ambush Rogers's party at multiple places except for the one place where they should have focused their attention, St. Francis itself. As noted, the discovery at Missisquoi Bay of Rogers's sixteen hidden whaleboats and provisions for the return trip had acted like a magnet to the French leadership, which had mounted a clever ambush in anticipation of Rogers's return. However, the major had been too smart to make that tactical mistake after the two trusty Stockbridge "Wolves," wisely left behind by him at Missisquoi Bay to watch the boats and supplies from a safe distance, had informed him of their discovery. But with the French leadership considering various tactical scenarios for the future intentions and movements of the English raiders—all imagined and negated by Rogers's subsequent decisions and countermoves—they had overlooked a potential attack on St. Francis, because it seemed such an impossibility, largely due to the town's great distance from Missisquoi Bay and the expanse of spruce bogs lying before it, forming a most formidable natural barrier.[2]

Since ancient times, the thorough underestimation of the enemy's capabilities and intentions and an assumption of invulnerability have long set the stage for successful surprise attacks, and these errors now immensely benefited Rogers. Quite simply, the French leadership had committed the mistake of relying on assumptions and underestimating the raiders' audacity and capabilities: an attack on St. Francis seemed impossible on every conceivable level, which was exactly what Rogers's wanted the enemy to think.

However, not only French leadership but also the Abenaki themselves believed that they were invulnerable because of the remote location of St. Francis and its fearsome reputation across America. All in all, therefore, an attack on St. Francis seemed the most unlikely of possible scenarios. Surely the English raiders had a different target, the French leadership had believed. These fatal miscalculations opened the door for Rogers's stunning success on October 4.

Because of the simple realities of human nature and psychology when it came to the French leadership's march of folly that now came together to immeasurably assist Rogers and his men, St. Francis, which had never previously been threatened by anyone, was about to fall with the sudden emergence of a serious "threat, particularly of a danger not previously experienced, [and one that was] simply not believed."[3]

A BLOODY RECKONING AT ST. FRANCIS

With the cold dawn of October 4 drawing ever nearer and reminding him that winter was on the way to the Quebec country, Rogers made his last preparations before ordering the final advance—a relative short one across the broad, open field that lay before the town—from near the timbered edge of the clearing that stood before the sleeping community of St. Francis. As he fully realized, especially at this time, everything had to be in perfect order for the major's well-conceived tactical plan to succeed. At this point, there could be no mistakes or misunderstandings, and Rogers made doubly sure that everyone knew exactly what to do now that he had St. Francis in the grip that he had dreamed about for so long. Rogers's remaining 142 men would have to make up for the large percentage of the original 190-man command (forty-one sick and injured soldiers had been sent back, and seven men had vanished in the spruce bogs).

At this time, Rogers had no idea that a white man of Irish descent, just like the major himself, Louis-Joseph Gill, the son of two white captives taken from frontier settlements who had survived the arduous trek to St. Francis, was the respected sachem of the town or that what now lay before him like a golden apple to be plucked was very much a melting-pot community, where plenty of white blood flowed in the veins of many mixed-race people.[4]

After years had passed in frustration without his ever obtaining the opportunity, Major Rogers almost certainly knew that a strange fate and destiny had played a large part in leading him all the way to St. Francis, where he could finally fulfill his longtime burning ambition, because everything that he had ever accomplished in the past had now led directly to this place and time. The major might have reflected upon how many times lead bullets had barely missed him, and how several had not, all failing to hit any vital spot on his body to abruptly end his career and all his ambitions, including the destruction of St. Francis. From the beginning, fate had continuously smiled upon the young Scotch-Irishman, who had long fought with his heart like his fellow countrymen for possession of this land that they loved. Often in the past, the enemy had celebrated the supposed death of the famed Ranger leader in sharp clashes, including during this expedition, in the wilderness. The French leadership, even at the highest levels, was still consumed with the dream of eliminating its young nemesis.

The French had even killed other tall Ranger leaders, like the unfortunate Captain Jonathan Burbank. He had died a horrific death when a warrior mistakenly believed him to be Rogers and eagerly killed him to finally do away with the most enterprising of white men who had so often mocked the time-proved warrior ways and combat prowess of New France's best fighting men. Clearly, throughout the past, Major Rogers had been most fortunate, and he might have now wondered whether his luck would finally run out in the upcoming attack on St. Francis.[5]

Likewise, and as mentioned, fate and the gods of war had been extremely kind to St. Francis for an extended period before Rogers would finally bring a bloody reckoning on October 4 that would never be forgotten by the

Abenaki people. During generations of conflict and seemingly by way of a miracle, St. Francis had never been seriously threatened with harm. This legendary place located along the St. Francis River had long been a sacred and secure heaven, and the Abenaki still believed that they were untouchable because they were a special people protected by their God.

But Major Rogers was determined to prove that the deepest beliefs of the Abenaki people were badly misplaced and entirely based on lies, especially the almost casual assumption that the priests and soldiers—not to mention the Catholic God—of New France would forever protect them from all harm. While the benevolence of the blessed Virgin Mary continued to faithfully protect Montreal and its people to the southwest, such was not the case for St. Francis on the cool morning of October 4, because no kind of divine intervention would save the unsuspecting Abenaki from the wrath of Rogers and his men, who now fairly lusted to be finally unleashed by the major.[6]

With Rogers leading the right division in the upcoming attack to provide proper guidance and an inspirational example, these grim, battle-hardened men of the Rangers, with their Provincial and British comrades, of three divisions were about to demonstrate why the French had long labeled them "the English savages."[7]

Meanwhile, in the cold darkness that made nervous soldiers, especially young men and boys about to wage their first battle, shiver in the atmosphere of heightened tension just before the looming dawn broke upon the fertile valley of the St. Francis, Rogers's men were in perfect fighting trim. As noted, they had already stacked packs, haversacks, canteens, dirty blankets, and other excess gear in piles to the rear to hide them from Abenaki eyes and to be unburdened during the upcoming attack. As the major had ordered, this surplus gear had been stacked in the pine thickets beyond any well-beaten path from the village to avoid discovery. No doubt, some of Rogers's men wondered who would not return from the forthcoming attack upon the most infamous Indian village known to generations of New Englanders and if they would ever again see home and family.

At this time, when a high state of anxiety was in the air, Major Rogers knew that he needed to get his men from near the edge of the timber, mostly tall and stately pines that swayed slightly in the early morning breeze sweeping off the peaceful river, closer to the last open stretch of ground in an organized manner as quickly and silently as possible under the cover of darkness. On Rogers's signal, the troops of all three divisions moved briskly through the last cluster of trees and toward the outer edge of the extensive patch of open ground—old crop fields now bare from the reaping of the recent bountiful harvest that had brought great joy to the Abenaki—under the comforting shroud of the predawn darkness that provided shelter and safety for the onrushing men. For all the major knew, Abenaki warriors might be lying in ambush in the clusters of houses in preparation for cutting the attackers to pieces when they crossed the open ground.

With his 142 men armed with their weapons, especially Brown Bess muskets with fresh powder charges, including deadly loads of "buck & ball," which were perfectly suited to the seemingly endless challenges of Indian fighting, especially in a dangerous urban-like setting, Rogers led the way as usual. As mentioned, he was now in immediate command of the right division, which was always a comforting and inspirational sight to his men, especially in an offensive effort. In a single body that moved with discipline and swiftness about a half hour before sunrise, Rogers's men silently advanced through the haunting darkness and through the tall trees of the last stretch of pine forest on the river's level bottomlands to reach the edge of the clearing of old crop fields.

Under the comforting cover of darkness just before the sun rose over the eastern horizon, the early morning was dominated by a biting cold that continued to sting Rogers's men, especially when combined with a high degree of tension and nervousness. However, moving forward at a brisk pace through the pines warmed the stiff bodies and bones of the Rogers's men, who were going for broke as never before.

With their lengthy bayonets and large-caliber smoothbore muskets freshly loaded with "buck & ball" (basically a shotgun that was, especially at close range, ideal for Indian fighting), fresh black powder in firing pans and new flints now firmly in place in the tight, steel grips of musket hammers, these battle-hardened Rangers would be especially formidable in the upcoming close-range fight in and among the houses and streets—basically the first urban combat situation in the history of Rogers's Rangers. The doomed Abenaki at St. Francis were about to learn to their horror that Rogers's men fought just like Native Americans, paying back brutality with brutality in the most vicious war ever waged on American soil.

Standing more than six feet in height, which played a part in garnering respect from his rough-and-ready fighting men, the battle-scarred major, with his long red hair tied back in a queue, now relied on the overall high quality of his soldiers, including Mohegan Stockbridge Ranger warriors. These dark-skinned Native American Rangers, streaked in the bright colors of their favorite war paint and with heads bald except for scalp locks on top, were an integral part of Rogers's integrated fighting force. In the same manner as the Stockbridge warrior "Wolves," the Rangers also wore Indian buckskin leggings and had their trusty steel tomahawks in their hands, when descending upon the town.

But the Indian Rangers were not the only dark-hued attackers now moving toward St. Francis. Among Rogers's most dependable black Rangers, soon to be racing onward with their white comrades in the attack across the open ground, were "Duke Jacob," a few other blacks, such a "Mulatto man," and perhaps other soldiers of mixed heritage. Some of these offspring of black and white were perhaps so white in overall appearance as to be able to pass as white, especially to Indian eyes. It is not known, but very likely a black man named Prince, who was Rogers's own personal servant, may have still been with the major at this time to share the same dangers. If so, then he would have been carrying a gun in the ranks at a time when every man was needed in the steamrolling attack calculated to overwhelm St. Francis in short order.

Rogers's black men—most likely they or their parents had been captured in West Africa and transported across the Atlantic to serve as slaves in New England—were ready for action, especially Private "Duke" Jacob. Large numbers of slaves were counted in the Atlantic port cities of New England from an early date. Slaves had then moved north with white masters in the tide of settlement that had inched up the fertile Connecticut and Merrimack River Valleys: contrary to popular stereotypes, blacks and whites were early pioneers in New England's wilderness in a united effort to tame the land.

For the free black Rangers—Rogers's most forgotten fighting men of value to this day because of the general silencing of black contributions by white historians—the widespread colonial fear that defeat by France would reduce freedom-loving Americans to slaves had special meaning. After all, the French had long deemed black men and women natural chattel, as seen in the Gallic nation's large numbers of slaves, who labored from sunup to sundown on its rich sugar islands, especially St. Domingue, in the Caribbean.

Ironically, although they did not realize it at the time, the black Rangers now ran a greater risk than they realized, because Abenaki warriors especially sought to capture blacks, who fetched a higher price from members of the French upper-class elite in Quebec and Montreal. Buyers who had been wealthy planters in the West Indies readily paid gold coins for blacks to work in their households as servants primarily in the two major cities of New France, Quebec and Montreal. Among wealthy transplanted Europeans from Montreal to Boston, a black domestic servant was a status symbol and, hence, highly prized for reasons that had more to do with the egos of the rich elite than anything else. Therefore, as freemen who served in the ranks with distinction, Rogers's black Rangers now faced the possibility of learning firsthand all about slavery in Canada if they were taken captive.

Here, near the clearing's edge, where the tall pines and the brown carpet of pine needles came to an end before the village situated on the north bank of the river, whose waters could perhaps be heard flowing gently toward the St. Lawrence in the night's haunting stillness, Rogers's men of three divisions were spread out in a wide semicircle to cover a wider front. After they reached the edge of the wood line, no one could believe that there were still no Abenaki, Canadian, or French sentinels or lookouts guarding the town at this relatively late hour of the morning, even though seemingly everyone in St. Francis had been up late and involved in the harvest festivities.

These hardened veterans, who knew that close-range combat was inevitable after they entered the town, now wore what was left of Indian-style leather leggings, which were most often a stylish blue color that was sufficiently dark to blend in with the dark forests. They also wore moccasins and other adaptations of Indian garb that served as excellent camouflage to facilitate comfort and easier movement to reach the border of the wide field and especially when finally unleashed in the attack. Rogers's savvy veterans seemingly steeled themselves for the great challenge that lay ahead in the still blackness beyond the open field, where the legendary town of St. Francis stood just ahead in an eerie silence. Among the Stockbridge Ranger "Wolves" were some very good fighting men like Rangers Sergeant Phillip, Daniel Napkin and Wonk Napkin (evidently brothers), and an especially ill-fated Ranger warrior named Samadagwis.

At this critical juncture, when the woods were bathed in blackness, hiding the Rangers from any peering eyes in the town if that might have been the case, Major Rogers might have wondered whether he would ever see his twenty-eighth birthday, barely a month away in mid-November, if he fell in the upcoming fight in attempting to fulfill his most ambitious and longest-envisioned dream. If luck was not with him during the upcoming attack, as it had been so often in the past, then Rogers might be dead or spending his next birthday in an iron cage on display to the jeering crowd of French men and women in faraway Quebec or Montreal.

Everyone was in his assigned position in the formation of a wide semi-circle that stretched for a considerable distance along the forest's edge to fulfill the major's plan of surrounding St. Francis on three sides, except, of course, the river. Thinking ahead as usual in overall tactical terms, Rogers was about to detach a party of trustworthy Rangers, a special team of lethal marksmen with rifles, from the main body of attackers. Deadly marksmen with their favorite rifles, which they handled with great ease and care, like a delicate child or attractive lover, these Rangers were experts at shooting down deer and moose on the run even in the densest forest. After having surveyed the topography, the major had directed these marksmen to eventually take position on the higher ground near the river, where the river bluff stood, beyond the level fields. These expert riflemen had been told by Rogers to be prepared to shoot down any warriors who attempted to flee to the river to escape north to the safety of the small French farming settlements located in the rich valley of the St. Lawrence.

The seasoned Ranger riflemen, in contrast to the vast majority of Rogers's men, who carried the smoothbore Brown Bess muskets, were the finest marksmen in the command, and Rogers knew exactly how to exploit this advantage to the fullest. With still no sign of warriors, no warning having been given by an Abenaki scout or guard to wake the people of St. Francis, the major felt increasingly confident, despite some nagging unknowns that he could not shake. But if everything went according to Rogers's bold plan of a headlong attack from multiple directions in a lengthy line across the open field, then St. Francis would be entirely destroyed not long after the arrival of the dawn of October 4, according to his careful calculations.

At last, Rogers's and long-elusive dream seemed to be on the verge of a beautiful reality in his tactically focused mind. While the morning mists were slowly lifting through the towering pines at the clearing's edge, and after a brief pause at the timberline for final preparations and deployments for the attack, the major's men were finally ready to surge across the open ground about a half hour before the first light of daybreak on October 4. This was three weeks, the twenty-first day, since Rogers and his men had embarked from Crown Point. However, these were crack fighting men of "an elite fraternity" of the best fighters in the land, and if anyone could do the impossible, it was the Rangers and their highly motivated Provincial and British Regular volunteers, who had gambled with their lives by joining up with Rogers.[8]

Incredibly, St. Francis not only remained completely silent on this strangely still night along the banks of the St. Francis River but also was completely undefended even with the approach of dawn. All the while, the confident Abenaki now continued to repose in a blissful sleep on the assumption that their powerful French allies would always make sure that St. Francis was forever safe from the grasp of the hated English. To the very end, they never expected an attack, especially from Rogers, who was rumored to have been killed or missing in battle back in September.

However, it was always a great mistake to prematurely count Rogers out, as he was about to shortly demonstrate in full to the highest levels of the French leadership. Scotland-born Robert Kirkwood incorrectly believed that the town contained not only warriors (because of the earlier nighttime celebration he mistook for a war dance) but also Frenchmen, which was not the case. Private Kirkwood, a recent volunteer from his Scottish regiment of the British army, was wrong on all counts in part because the native Scot was still very much a fish out of water in wilderness warfighting compared to the more experienced Rangers.

Indeed, not a French soldier was now anywhere near St. Francis—nor was any Abenaki war party, for that matter—so there could have been no war dance that had continued deep into the night. During his last reconnaissance, Rogers had earlier heard a free-flowing French spoken with a familiar ease in the town, but those were bilingual Abenaki speakers who often employed the language of the Gallic people. Indeed, the Abenaki, as a Christianized people who faithfully attended Mass conducted by the Jesuits, often conversed in a fluid, rapid-fire French. Judging by sound alone in the night, St. Francis almost sounded like a quaint peasant village of peaceful farmers toiling the land on a spring-fed river located in a picturesque northern section of France, in La Havre or Brest, or in the south at Marseille and Avignon.

It is not known, but perhaps the Abenaki of St. Francis believed the old rumor that the White Devil, or Wobomagonda—as Rogers would be known far and wide after attacking St. Francis—had been killed in the Second Battle on Snowshoes in March 1758, when more than 140 of his Rangers had been fatally cut down. Symbolically, like the settlers of the northern frontier who had been victimized for generations by Abenaki raiding parties, the inhabitants of St. Francis, now mostly women and children, were completely unprotected because of their complacency and confidence that the hated English would never be sufficiently bold to advance so far north through an untamed wilderness and do them any harm.[9]

One of the primary responsibilities of the respected Abenaki shaman, or *medeoulin*, was to protect the Saint François de Sales Mission and its people, like the "Good Man," or the "Master of Life," who was the all-powerful God to the Abenaki people. Revered for interpreting the deep mysteries of the magical spirit world, much like a priest in deciphering the true moral meanings of the Holy Bible, the Abenaki shaman, who was the tribe's spiritual head, was an all-important figure idolized by the people. Most likely a highly respected man, but perhaps even a woman, the shaman was second only in overall influence in overall spiritual terms to Father Pierre-Joseph-Antoine Roubaud, who headed the Jesuit missionary community, where the Abenaki knew the Virgin Mary by the name of "Marian" or "Malian." In the end, neither this revered Jesuit priest (who might well have been jealous of, or even threatened by, the strength of the shaman's spiritual influence among the people) nor the shaman had given the people any warning of the upcoming attack.[10]

Francis Parkman concluded in a classic understatement that "many of the warriors were absent" from St. Francis.[11] However, modern historian Stephen Brumwell was more on target in this regard, when he emphasized that "St. Francis lay virtually defenceless" at this time, because of the absence of Abenaki fighting men.[12]

In the words of one raider from a most revealing November 26, 1759, letter about the large community that was about to be destroyed, "This Town had a beautiful Situation, on a fine River [known to the Abenaki as 'Alsiganteku,' or 'Abounding in Shells'] about half a Mile wide; it was regular built with Timber and Boards, in two Rows, with a fine large [Roman Catholic] Church, at the Head of the Town."[13]

Interestingly, in his official report, Rogers described St. Francis as both a "town" and a "village," but the large Catholic mission church and scores of French-style houses revealed that the former was more accurate.[14] At Crown Point, just before the expedition's departure, Captain John Stark had informed Rogers of what to expect at this missionary town, based on what he had seen when he had been a captive there during the spring and summer of 1752.[15]

Ironically, almost certainly, none of the mostly Protestant soldiers in Major Rogers's command took the time to reflect on the fact that they and their so-called barbarian enemy were actually much alike in overall religious terms, because both believed in a single God, unlike the ancient Romans and Greeks, who had possessed an entire array of gods. In fact, Rogers's men and the Abenaki embraced the same God (divided only by the Protestant and Catholic faiths), because the Abenaki, including a good many warriors, although they did not act in any way like Christianized Indians when they descended upon white settlers, were Roman Catholics under control of the priests and church when among family and friends at St. Francis. In this sense, the Abenaki were not stereotypical pagan "savages," although they were viewed as such by whites across the colonies, especially along the frontier.

No one knows the exact nature of Major Rogers's final thoughts in the tense, nerve-racking period before signaling the final order to launch the attack across the open field, after he advanced his men to the edge of the clearing and the pine thicket that smelled fresh on this cold autumnal morning.

Here, within easy sight of the village whose name was well known to every settler on the New England frontier for generations and for ample good reason, the men remained perfectly quiet at the edge of the piney woods, while catching their breath and gripping their Brown Bess muskets with fixed bayonets and their rifles without bayonets. As ordered by Rogers, they remained as still as a stalking panther or bobcat about to strike its unwary prey in the forest, feeling secure in concealment under the limbs of the tall trees, before they were ordered to attack across the open ground.

Even the thick carpet of pine needles on the forest's floor bestowed a tactical advantage on Rogers's men, who had pushed forward in silence over the cushiony brown needles that prevented loud sounds underfoot. But now the major might have wondered whether he and his bearded soldiers, who looked unlike the crack fighting men whose fame had spread far and wide, could get across the last open stretch of ground that lay before St. Francis, which continued to be shrouded in a quiet stillness. Of course, no one knew the answer, and Rogers might have been expecting the worst-case scenario.

All the while, the haze of an early morning mist continued to rise slowly up from the open fields bathed in an eerie stillness before the serene town, providing additional concealment in case the Abenaki were stirring in the village. Had the French or Indians dug any pits or another kind of concealed obstacle to impede an advance over the broad open field that lay before them, since no guards in and around the town could be seen? Of course, no one knew for sure. And it was too risky for Rogers to send any scouts forward to check, because of the wide stretch of open ground. Consequently, the major would have to just hope for the best for the final advance.

Like his men, Rogers was in no mood to be merciful because he was only focused on waging the most effective brand of warfare that he knew, and it was exceptionally brutal and unmerciful. The surreal horrors of this war haunted Rogers's mind even at this time. He had already seen far too many of his men, tightly bound to trees by a gleeful enemy, cut slowly to pieces by Abenaki tomahawks and knives. Some Rangers had been scalped while still alive, their limbs and private parts cut off in the sickest of perverse warrior amusements to leave the goriest of spectacles strewn across the ground.

Other emotions, meanwhile, tugged at the major's heart just before he issued the final order to attack across the open ground. At this time, Rogers was also motivated by the memory of the tragic death of his younger brother, Richard Rogers. He had emerged as a fine Ranger captain of whom Robert had been most proud, like a dotting Scotch-Irish father. Richard had demonstrated outstanding leadership ability in wilderness warfare. He even might have been a replacement for Robert, if the Ranger leader had fallen in battle or died of disease. Displaying uncommon promise, Richard Rogers had commanded his own company with skill. Robert's younger brother had been born in Methuen two years after Robert in the Merrimack River country as the fifth son of the Rogers family.[16]

Captain Richard Rogers and his company of Rangers had been assigned to the Fort William Henry garrison. Richard's fate was an especially tragic one, and it still nagged at Major Rogers. Richard had died of smallpox on

June 22, 1757, at Fort William Henry before the siege began and the Marquis de Montcalm captured the fort. In the end, the remains of Robert's beloved brother were not even safe from unleashed Abenaki warriors, after the surrender of Fort William Henry. Captain Richard Rogers's body had been dug up from the soldier's cemetery by Abenaki warriors for the express purpose of taking his scalp as a prized trophy. However, the Abenaki had no idea that they were digging up Richard's grave and removing the scalp of the brother of their most lethal enemy, or they would have certainly desecrated the Ranger's body even further. With a deep sense of bitterness that still burned brightly in his heart and soul, Rogers could never forget that after the surrender of Fort William Henry, "such was the cruelty and rage of the enemy [Abenaki] after their conquest that they dug [his brother] up out of his grave and scalped him."[17]

And the burly major from the Merrimack River country could never forget how the Abenaki raiding parties, as he explained, had "killed or carried about more than six hundred" settlers in just over half a decade to leave behind piles of bodies and the darkest of legacies.[18] In many ways, this most savage of all wars in America had already made Major Rogers a bitter man, but for ample good reason. Therefore, the long-overdue razing of St. Francis to the ground meant a great deal on multiple levels to Rogers.

Solomon Stoddard described in a letter the mind-set of the people on the New England frontier, explaining the hard-earned frontier philosophy that had long applied to the targeted people of St. Francis: "They use [terrible] cruelty [against all those] that fall into their hands. They act like wolves, & are to be dealt with [like] wolves."[19]

At this time, perhaps Major Rogers thought back on the April 1758 words written to him in a letter by his first regimental commander, Colonel Joseph Blanchard, who exhorted him to strike the "unmolested Dens [of the warriors] which have (to our Dishonour) stood too long in our Way [and] I heartily wish you a favourable Opportunity and successful Attack against those mongrel Disturbers of the publick Peace, and a full Reprisal in Honour, Profit and Revenge, for all their perfidious Treatments [and now] The Enemy's Country [has been] filled with Scalps, Captives, Money, private Plunder, war-like stores and Provisions."[20] None of these "unmolested Dens" of any Native American tribe had been more infamous for decades than St. Francis.[21]

Born of the most vicious conflict that had consumed America's most picturesque wilderness, viewed by both the settlers and Native Americans as their own land and worth dying to possess at any cost, this no-nonsense philosophy of the northern frontier—Rogers's own and that of the Scotch-Irish people—was embraced with considerable enthusiasm by the Rangers, especially just before the attack on St. Francis, because they were prepared to inflict maximum damage on the longtime tormentors of their people. Indeed, what Rogers and his men were about to unleash was "by the standards of European warfare [an] assault [of an] unusually ruthless" nature.[22]

Therefore, as ordered by Major General Amherst, Rogers planned to repay the Abenaki in kind without any remorse or regrets, just as these fearsome warriors, when streaked in grease and wearing war paint and decorative clan tattoos, including of foxes, turtles, and bears, to look as terrifying as possible to their victims, had long waged war on helpless civilians along the northern frontier. For this reason, Rogers's men took to heart the harsh no-quarter orders that the determined major from the Merrimack River wilderness certainly relished to an inordinate degree. Without any regret or hesitation whatsoever, he had given to his men the fateful orders that he had been waiting seemingly all his life to issue, because St. Francis had long had a central place in his life and been a major thorn in the lives of the people of the northern frontier: "Kill every one without mercy." These fateful words of an absolute destruction echoed in the minds of Rogers's men, who relished the major's directive to pay back old scores long overdue. Quite simply, the Judgment Day, and an especially cruel one, was about to come to St. Francis.[23]

As mentioned, Rogers possessed an ample number of old scores to settle with the Abenaki of St. Francis because this vicious conflict had become extremely personal for him. And these bitter memories had begun early in the major's life on the northern frontier of New England. French and Abenaki raiders had burned down the Rogers family home, a lonely log cabin in the heart of the wilderness at Mountalona, cut down the orchard—except for one solitary fruit tree left standing as if to make a mocking statement about the futility of white settlement of ancestral Abenaki lands—and killed the cattle in the pastures during the awful spring of 1748. But most of all, Rogers was now about the play the role of avenging angel for the countless men, women, and children who had been slaughtered by the Abenaki over the years, swinging the sword of the Lord with a terrible redemptive fury.

To wreak his terrible vengeance by adhering to an exceptionally hard-hitting plan of no mercy in the frontier tradition, for the many souls, especially the long-suffering Scotch-Irish people, who were no more, Rogers was especially eager to unleash the attack to strike a target that he had dreamed about destroying for years in what would be his own personal Armageddon. After it had been maturing in his mind for years, Rogers's dark vision for St. Francis was nothing less than apocalyptic, as were his world and this most brutal of wars.[24]

Of course, the Abenaki had long engaged in their own righteous war for survival, and they had suffered tremendously in vainly attempting to halt the encroaching tide of white settlement. Indeed, "if the St. Francis Indians had their own, even more powerful case against the English—against more than a century of being exploited, cheated, intoxicated, infected, plundered, displaced and fought to near extinction by them—alluding to it would have elicited nothing more than a wad of unsympathetic spit from any of Rogers' raiders that night."[25]

It is not known, but Rogers might have reflected back briefly on his childhood days before the red dawn of October 4, which might be his last, illuminated this infamous place along the St. Francis River. Was he destined to die tragically like his Ireland-born father, James Rogers, who had been shot dead by a neighbor in the winter twilight because he had worn a bearskin hat and was mistaken for an approaching black bear? This tragedy, like the death of brother Richard while serving God and country, never left Rogers.[26]

Finally, at the quiet edge of the pine forest, destiny itself now called to Rogers like a siren's song, because this was his time at long last. The long-awaited moment finally came about a half hour before sunrise, which would happen around 5 a.m., after the pale light of the nighttime moon had begun to fade away and just before the full chorus of morning sounds of the natural world enlivened the surrounding pine forests. But now all that was heard were the first gentle notes of songbirds and perhaps a cawing crow in the distance in the direction of the St. Francis River.

As noted, after Rogers had led his men in stealthy fashion to the edge of the wide clearing where they stood aligned in a wide semicircle, he remained in close striking distance of his target, which still showed no signs of life. Basking in having caught the enemy completely by surprise while the cold morning mists still hung over the land of the Abenaki, the major briefly stood before the wide field, now bare of cornstalks after the recent harvest, and hoped to win his most impressive victory.

All the while, Rogers saw that St. Francis still lay quiet in the biting chill of predawn—which told him that winter was on its way to the St. Lawrence River country, as did the chevron-shaped flocks of Canadian geese heading south at a brisk pace in the autumnal skies—and realized that he had a rendezvous with a special destiny on the early morning of October 4, 1759.

ROGERS'S SIGNAL TO ADVANCE ACROSS THE OPEN FIELD

Major Rogers, especially eager to unleash his men before any accidental discovery of their presence, which might occur at any moment when now so close to St. Francis, wasted little time in reflection or contemplation with precious seconds ticking away, because it was time to strike as hard as possible. And, of course, this first meant getting his men across the open field shrouded in darkness and the lingering mists of this cold morning as quickly as possible. Hence, the major's eagerness to strike just before the arrival of the early October dawn brightened the eastern horizon to illuminate St. Francis. There was no time to send out scouts or flankers because the time to attack had come.

Just as the Abenaki of St. Francis had long delivered unstoppable blows upon the New England settlements and isolated log cabins nestled in the pristine beauty of the wilderness, Rogers was now finally about to mount the same kind of attack that had long proved so devastating in the annals of frontier warfare. And now, just before the arrival of the red Quebec dawn over St. Francis, he wanted to reap the dividends of his determination, good fortune, and sheer audacity. In the face of so many past setbacks and frustrations, the major's willpower had now placed his command of eager Rangers and volunteers in the most advantageous of positions to strike a punishing blow.

All the while, the Rangers, Provincials, and Britons were chomping at the bit and ready to pounce. A lengthy line of fully prepared men with fixed bayonets stood silently in the cold darkness at the edge of the pine forest before the cleared ground, awaiting Rogers's signal to surge across the wide field on the double—a risky enterprise if they would be charging headlong into an ambush, which still might be the case. In their eagerness, these hardened veterans felt like hungry wolves ready to pounce on a sleeping lamb.

To all appearances, a completely vulnerable St. Francis was still wrapped in strange and inexplicable silence, which was only the calm before the storm.

At around 4:30 a.m. Rogers gave the signal to attack, one that his 142 eager men had been waiting for seemingly all their lives. In the haunted blackness of early morning, rather than firing a flintlock pistol, as often alleged, which would jeopardize the element of surprise, Rogers gave the cry of a hawk, or the cawing of a crow, or the sharp-sounding hoot of a great horned owl: a familiar signal like that given by Abenaki warriors in so many attacks across the frontier. Then, all of a sudden, about "a half hour before sunrise," the Rangers, Provincials, and British Regulars surged out of the tall pines in a lengthy line in the form of a semicircle, heading on the double, with fixed bayonets and high hopes for success, across the open field that lay covered in a light mist.

CLOSING THE CIRCLE OF DEATH LIKE A VISE

In many ways, this was one of the most symbolic attacks in the blood-stained history of the New England frontier, because it was launched primarily to save hundreds of innocent men, women, and children in the future, especially in the Connecticut and Merrimack River Valleys: a compensation of sorts, as least in the major's eyes, for his harsh order to his men to show no mercy for the Abenaki, when history had come full circle and hell itself finally came to St. Francis.

Thousands of prayers from all across New England were now about to be answered by Major Rogers and his men, including the heartfelt words of Thomas Williams, a physician with a Provincial regiment, which had been heard ten thousand times across the frontier for generations: "I trust a righteous God will one day avenge their barbarous rage, cruelty & malice against us."[27]

Rogers no doubt rejoiced in another psychological advantage that has been overlooked by historians in regard to its overall importance: the major and his men possessed a look—ragged, bearded, and with revenge in their eyes—that was terrifying to the Abenaki. As a migratory people originally from Asia millions of years before, the Abenaki and other Native Americans did not have facial hair and possessed a distinctive cultural distaste and "hatred" for the beard on a man's face. As noted, Rogers men now wore beards in colors of brown, red, black, and blond to appear like avengers from hell to the Abenaki, who were about to see the fleeting figures of white hairy demons before receiving their death strokes.[28]

Finally, after so many years, an awful Judgment Day had arrived at St. Francis, and the Abenaki people would never be the same. October 4 was viewed as the glorious day that generations of New Englanders had long prayed to God for when their boys would march far to the North to deliver a long-deserved vengeance without any mercy whatsoever. Rogers's signal to attack was given around 4:30 a.m., a half hour before sunrise amid the cold darkness and before the arrival of another beautiful autumn dawn in Quebec. In one bold rush, the Rangers, Provincials, and British Regulars of three designated columns, each commanded by the most reliable officer, continued to surge forward in unison in the biting chill of the early morning darkness. In front as usual, the major led his men onward in the three columns in a disciplined advance over the wide stretch of open ground lying before the silent buildings of St. Francis, which stood poised on the high ground of a bluff overlooking the river's wide waters. In total, ninety-seven Rangers (mostly from New Hampshire), ten Stockbridge Ranger "Wolves," fourteen British Regulars, and twenty-one Provincials (mostly from Massachusetts and Connecticut) dashed as one over the outer edge of the open field, moving at a brisk pace in the cold darkness with fixed steel bayonets that now reflected no glare in the dim moonlight.

In the words of one of Rogers's 142 followers from a letter, "At Half between Day-break and Sun-rise, they march'd [toward] the Town," which was not only bathed in a haunting stillness but also still unguarded by any Abenaki, Canadian, or Frenchman: all of which meant that in overall tactical terms, Rogers had achieved the impossible—complete tactical surprise—as he had envisioned in his mind for years, verifying that the gods of war were still smiling upon him with a special fondness.[29]

Moving at a fast pace across the wide-open space, a former cornfield that had long given sustenance to the town, without the usual clatter of accoutrements, as would have been the case had they been Regular soldiers on a conventional battlefield, Rogers's men charged through the predawn darkness on a mission of death and destruction, while gaining momentum with each yard gained in the open field. No moonlight glimmered off any gear or weapons, especially steel bayonets, because the moon, not yet full, had moved below the horizon with the dawn's near arrival, although the night's coldness still lingered as if it were early November in New England.

Advancing on the double across the wide field near the St. Francis River and just below the St. Lawrence, the major's troops moved together like a well-oiled machine, as if these Rangers, Provincials, and Britons had served together for years. Rogers's unique leadership style and the forge of adversity had molded these men together as one in a remarkably short time. Rogers's soldiers, whose worn clothing and uniforms provided little protection from the morning's cold, were reminded that it was crucial to complete their mission at St. Francis as soon as possible and then immediately head south to the relatively warmer Connecticut River country to escape the inevitable pursuers. But that was all in the future. First and foremost, the onrushing men needed to get across the open field before St. Francis as soon as possible.

Demonstrating a strict adherence to the major's last words, not a single Ranger yelled the traditional "Indian hollow [holler]" or cheered in an excessive display of enthusiasm to break the heightened tension that had mounted to a crescendo, because silence was now still a vital ingredient to success, if the Rangers were to catch the Abenaki completely by surprise. Consequently, silence was golden during the rapid sprint across the wide field covered in the corn stubble left from the harvested crop, which was a good one this year. Only the onrushing feet of 142 men surging across the open field, covered in a layer of mist to give the attackers a ghostly appearance, were now heard just before the October dawn.

Moving with stealth through the slowly lifting mist, Rogers led his troops with a silent and confident ease across the open ground on the double. No obstacle whatsoever was encountered, much to everyone's relief. Still no fire erupted from the darkened houses of St. Francis, which still stood silent. All the while, Rogers's onrushing men descended en masse upon the sleeping town in a long, thin line. In a sprawling formation that extended across the open field as far as the eye could see in the shadowy half-light of early morning, the Rangers, Provincials, and British Regulars closed in on the town from three sides at a fast pace. Meanwhile, Rogers's luck continued to hold true. Still no Indian guard or Canadian or French sentry sounded a warning to awaken the sleeping villagers—mostly women, children, and the respected elders in Abenaki society. Each passing second more thoroughly sealed the fate of St. Francis and its inhabitants as the lengthy line of attackers drew ever closer to the most lucrative of targets.

Even the Indian dogs, known to be especially vicious toward whites, were still asleep in the warmth of the French-style houses, having stayed up late with their masters at the festivities inside the large Council House. No Indian domestic animals of any kind betrayed the eerily quiet but swift movements of 142 men of an ad hoc command that was about to engage in its first fight. All the while, the three groups of attackers, who now began to warm up from the night's cold, continued onward with fixed bayonets over the open ground that was free of any ravine or any trees before the quiet town.

The veteran soldiers of different races and ethnic groups who had solidified under Rogers's leadership during the journey north possessed but a single thought while pushing onward across the wide field and directly toward the quiet town: the complete destruction of St. Francis to fulfill Major General Amherst's orders and to make Rogers's most passionate dream a reality. Unlike British officers of the regular army, officers in Major Rogers's command carried no swords in this attack because they were generally considered obsolete in ranging warfare. As the major fully realized and most important, no time could be wasted in getting across the open field, not even a precious second with so much at stake. A barking dog, a warrior coming outdoors to relieve himself, a woman with a headache or menstrual pain, or an unfaithful husband returning to his usual sleeping quarters with his wife before the sunrise might result in the immediate sounding of the much-feared alarm.

While the attack flowed onward across the field like clockwork, with the veterans' sure gait at a rapid pace made steadier by the conviction that they knew they were fully prepared for the grim work that lay ahead, Rogers's dirty and bearded men, looking like devils incarnate, charged onward with fixed bayonets at the ends of muskets, which were gripped with a righteous sense of retribution that burned brightly in the biting cold of this fateful early morning in Quebec. For the Rangers and Provincials, a longing for vengeance had been building up for years to reach an unsustainable peak by this time.

Just ahead, the higher ground of St. Francis beyond the open field lay before them in an almost inexplicable comatose stillness. On the run, Rogers's men neared the dense clusters of Abenaki houses bathed in a perfect silence that now seemed so unnatural and out of place. Rogers's timing could not have been more on target, because the blackness was now starting to turn gray, with dawn drawing near to provide the visibility necessary for the men to take their assigned positions in the town. So far, Rogers's daring plan was working to perfection beyond his wildest dreams.

Remembering every word of the major's last orders to them, the 142 attackers continued to move on the double through the open field and ever closer to the houses of St. Francis without awaking anyone or causing another stir whatsoever. Through the early dawn's gray light, everyone was now rushing onward with a swift determination in a desperate race to gain the town before daybreak yielded too much visibility, and the Abenaki discovered them and sounded the alarm to awaken the entire town. Meanwhile, adrenaline pumped faster through veins and breath came faster to the attackers during the sprint over the open ground. Wiping out St. Francis and its dark legacy dominated every thought and instinct of the swift-moving men, who knew that they had to reach and get into their assigned positions before each house, as ordered by Rogers, as soon as possible. In the major's words, in his typically understated style in regard to catching the enemy by surprise, "At half an hour before sun-rise I surprised the town when they were all fast sleep, on the right, left, and center" of the attackers, who surged through the dirt streets and began to take their assigned positions before the first houses of the town.[30]

In a most revealing letter, one of Rogers's men, who continued to race ever closer to St. Francis in three swift-moving groups, or divisions, wrote, "They march'd up to the Town, where . . . the Indians [were still] all asleep" in a comforting sense of absolute security that was no more.[31] Leading the onrushing troops of the right division that swiftly descended upon the town, Rogers wrote of an amazing tactical achievement that brought a sense of satisfaction in having caught the enemy completely by surprise: "Half an hour before sunrise we surprised the village, approaching it from three divisions, on the right, left, and centre."[32]

A wide line of confident men, arranged in a semicircle divided in three separate parts, surged into St. Francis from three sides in the pale light of early morning, while maintaining a disciplined silence in obeying Rogers's strict orders. At this time, some fast-moving Rangers, Provincials, and British Regulars were surprised to discover that they were charging into a much-feared place that was obviously more of a town than a traditional Indian village in the cool blackness that was just beginning to dissipate with the first faint hint of early autumn light appearing on the eastern horizon to reveal that Rogers's timing had been perfect. In the early morning grayness, the major's men poured onward in an unstoppable tide with fixed bayonets, moving swiftly and in silence with discipline.

Everything still seemed too good to be true. No one had yet emerged from the church, the Council House, or any of the houses, including the French-style residences built of regular wooden boards like a home in Montreal or Quebec. Obtaining their first close look at St. Francis caused some surprise among the attackers, who had previously seen it only in their imaginations. They had expected to see only a traditional Native American village with wigwams, huts, and lengthy longhouses like those of the tribes of the Iroquois Confederacy.

With fixed bayonets at the end of their Brown Bess muskets, Rogers's men raced onward down the narrow dirt streets of St. Francis to gain their assigned positions before each house. Almost brooding in its deathly quiet given the tragedy that was about to play out in full, this agricultural community situated on the wide river was for the most part "regular built with Timber and Boards, in two Rows, with a fine large Church, at the Head of the Town."[33]

On this fateful day of reckoning at St. Francis, the first rays of morning light gradually revealed a disturbing sight that fueled a righteous rage and reminded the breathless Rangers, Provincials, and Britons, who were now inside the town and busily taking assigned positions before the houses, exactly why they viewed this mission as a righteous crusade and divine retribution straight out of the pages of the Old Testament: "We found six hundred scalps hanging upon poles over the doors of their wigwams" and houses, Rogers said of the grisly sight that fueled his motivation on this early October morning in the heart of New France.[34]

In the dawn's pale light and biting cold, Captain Amos Ogden, like his handful of men of the New Jersey Blues, was horrified by the shocking sight of "between 6 or 700 English scalps waving in the air, which were fixed on poles and fastened to the tops of their houses; and their church within was also decorated with the same."[35]

As Rogers's men moved swiftly and silently inside the town with businesslike efficiency, a sufficient amount of light shone for them to ascertain the colors of the long hair hanging down from the circular pieces of darkened skin that had been violently ripped from victims' heads by warriors year after year across the frontier: blond, auburn, red, brunet, and black. However, as if this grisly sight were not sufficiently gory, the greatest of all horrors stunned Rogers's interlopers when they ascertained that a good many of the scalps, mostly belonging to people of the frontier settlements, were smaller than the others.

Of course, these were the scalps of children who never had a chance to grow up or understand why they were so passionately hated and brutally killed by Abenaki warriors. Truly horrifying to Rogers's men, some of the smallest of scalps were those of infants who had been tomahawked in their wooden cradles, ripped out of the stomachs of pregnant mothers with a savage delight, or had their heads smashed against trees by strong warriors who had swung their bodies like baseball bats with full force, hitting the trunk with a dull, sickening thud.

It is not known, but one or more of Rogers's men may have unwittingly seen the scalps of their own children waving above the houses and other structures of St. Francis. In the eerie cold of early morning before the sun rose to shine brightly on an autumnal landscape, the Rangers, Provincials, and British Regulars continued to move deeper into the town without making an excess of noise, almost like stealthy hunters sneaking up on a flock of unaware wood ducks in a quiet forest pond nestled deep in New England's woodlands.

In swift silence and without discovery, more of Rogers's men moved into their assigned positions just beyond the first row of outermost houses in the deadly still community that seemed like a ghost town, while other soldiers continued to push deeper into St. Francis to reach their positions. As ordered by Rogers, "two by two," they placed themselves "severally at each house," in Private Robert Kirkwood's words. All the while, the foremost men stood in silence and ready in the half-light to smash down the wooden doors with musket butts and shoulders, realizing that the darkened house before them was full of the hated Abenaki.

Moving silently with fixed bayonets and tomahawks ready, additional attackers dashed onward in the hope of gaining their assigned positions before other houses in the town's center and before their sleeping victims, who remained unaware of the danger because no guards had been posted anywhere around the town, awakened, and sounded an alarm. Because the festivities at the Council House had lasted so late in the night, everyone in the town was sleeping in. Fine French brandy also contributed to the deep slumber of the relatively few warriors who remained in the village. Here, amid the houses in the morning's gray light, the foremost interlopers in the town stood quietly in the heightened tension and waited for the final moment of truth to arrive. With each second stretching like an eternity, they eagerly anticipated Rogers's pistol-shot signal. All of the men had been informed that "on the firing of a shot by way of signal from Major Rogers, [they] were to fire the town" and begin killing as many Abenaki as they could find in the houses, streets, and open spaces.[36]

With fixed bayonets and muskets loaded with "buck & ball," the foremost soldiers, panting and sucking air from their long sprint across the cleared ground, held their assigned positions before each Abenaki house that stood just behind the church, which was located at the town's head near the bluffs that overlooked the St. Francis River. Meanwhile, other men still pushed through the town with a noiseless ease and an increasing confidence. Finally, they took up their places before the houses throughout the center of town and patiently waited in a disciplined silence.

As quietly as circumstances would allow, additional soldiers continued to race through the dirt streets in the hope of reaching their assigned positions at the outer edges of town. Eager to strike a blow, with soft leather moccasins making no noise on the open streets in the desperate race deeper into town, these tried veterans eased through darker shadows that lay between the French-style houses in an attempt to reach the town's other side as soon as possible. All the while, Rogers's grip on St. Francis continued to close more tightly.

Meanwhile, chosen by Rogers for a special mission of killing Abenaki at longer range than the majority of their comrades with Brown Bess muskets now standing before most of the town's houses, the swiftly moving riflemen, who were all sure shots, reached their objective, as assigned by Rogers. After deploying in prone positions on higher ground to overlook the riverbank where the Abenaki canoes were concentrated side by side on the sandy shore, they took up good firing positions to close the Abenaki escape route to the river, while catching their breath in the early morning cold. Here, in excellent firing positions on commanding terrain, these expert riflemen were ready to shoot down any Abenaki who sought to escape by reaching the canoes on the river once the killing began in earnest upon Rogers's long-awaited signal.

Fortunately for Major Rogers's other men, who continued to move like ghostly shadows farther into the town to take up positions in front of their assigned Abenaki houses, the narrow streets that ran through St. Francis were empty of the fallen red and yellow leaves of autumn, since autumn had not yet peaked, and clear of any morning frost, providing silent dirt avenues of approach. But most of all, these streets—they were more like wide footpaths, dusty from the summer and early autumn heat—were well trodden from generations of use, becoming natural paths for a swift advance of Rogers's soldiers all the way to the very rear of the town.

Of course, this advantage of easy passage down the dirt streets allowed the interlopers to move almost noiselessly through the haunting stillness that still consumed St. Francis like a shroud. Incredibly, no part of the long sprint of Rogers's men through the open field and into the town had been either heard or ascertained by the Abenaki. At this point, the rapid advance into St. Francis seemingly possessed a surreal and ghostlike quality of its own, because it had not been heard or seen by any Abenaki just before dawn shined its bright light over this alien land of New France's fiercest Native American allies.

More men, including the Stockbridge warriors, or "Wolves," moved silently like hungry predators through the silent town to take their assigned positions at the houses near the town's far side. All the while, larger numbers of Rogers's soldiers gained their places before the front door of each house deeper in the town, as the major had ordered. Meanwhile, the last fast-moving soldiers, including the Rangers, who wore their soft, blue Highland bonnets of wool, continued onward in the hope of reaching the last houses on the town's other side, before the major gave his signal for the killing to begin.

During what seemed like an eternity to them, dirt-stained men in tattered uniforms stood in the half-light like stoic silent sentinels with muskets, fixed with bayonets, and steel tomahawks in hand, awaiting Rogers's signal to start a slaughter without remorse or mercy. These hardened veterans realized that if they fired their muskets too early before the major's signal, they would be at a severe disadvantage when, musket now empty, an experienced Abenaki warrior emerged from his house with a loaded musket and determination to kill a Ranger, who had dared to violate the sacred ground of St. Francis.

Therefore, after having endured the longest night of their lives in the dreary pine forest before the open field, these savvy men now knew exactly what to do when about to engage the enemy for the first time during this expedition: a situation that first meant relying on their trusty bayonets and tomahawks so they would not risk having an unloaded musket at the worst time, when they would be the most vulnerable if they encountered large numbers of the enemy. For such reasons, teams of three men often stood before the front doors of houses, with two soldiers holding their Brown Bess flintlocks with fixed bayonets.

Here, they were ready to burst inside the house upon the major's signal, while a third man stood outside in support in case of any emergency to assist his two partners with a loaded musket and trusty tomahawk: an inevitable development once Rogers gave the fateful order to begin the slaughter of a still unknown number of warriors. In consequence, the initial phase of the upcoming combat was destined to be by far the ugliest of a truly hellish morning in every possible way, because it was destined to be almost a mirror image of the brutal attacks of the Abenaki warriors on isolated log cabins and settlements across the frontier.

In this sense on this autumn morning in Quebec, the terrorist attacks of the Abenaki had finally come full circle in a classic, and extremely grim, case of frontier justice that the Rangers especially relished. Consequently, it was now time for the playing out of a great reckoning as if Providence itself had designed Rogers's long-awaited delivery of his own brand of righteous retribution in which there would be no mercy at St. Francis.[37]

Perhaps the greatest symbolism of a cruel justice having come full circle at St. Francis on this early morning was the fact that Rogers's men were fully prepared for the horrific work of chopping down fellow human beings with repeated blows from tomahawks. Appreciating the weapon that he also now carried, like his men, Rogers explained how the tomahawk was highly prized among the Indians, as among the Rangers, and was held with "great esteem and importance" as second to no other hand weapon.[38]

Employed in deadly fashion by the Abenaki thousands of times all across the frontier, the steel tomahawks, in Rogers's admiring words, possessed the power, with a single swift blow to the temple, "to knock men's brains out."[39] This kind of grisly death for the unfortunate victim was about to become the fate of a good many inhabitants of St. Francis on this bloody morning along the St. Francis, because Rogers was ever mindful of Amherst's orders "to chastise these savages with some severity."[40]

However, this traditional explanation for committing a massacre at this town was much too simplistic. While revenge was certainly a leading factor because of Major General Amherst's and Major Rogers's orders, a good many other factors came into play on the most ill-fated morning in the history of the Abenaki nation. The September 13 orders from the Crown Point headquarters aside, the slaughter of almost every Abenaki who came within the sight of Rogers's men was also ensured by factors that brought out an almost primeval response rooted in kill-or-be-killed instincts going back millions of years, once Rogers finally gave the signal: bloodlust and an adrenaline rush in the dim half-light of the lingering predawn darkness; fear of losing one's life in a split second of close-range combat; the knowledge that no risks could be taken when inside St. Francis; confusion resulting from barging into dark houses filled with hostiles; the realization that the traditional rules of warfare no longer applied in the houses and streets; the commonsense practicality of killing first and asking questions later; the realization that a single moment's hesitation might cost one's life; and, last but not least, the need to fight just as the enemy fought and to be as utterly ruthless as the so-called savages, if not more so.

ACCIDENTAL DISCHARGE OF A MUSKET BEGINS A SLAUGHTER

Since everyone in St. Francis was fast asleep in the warmth of the houses just before dawn because of the late night celebrations, almost all of Rogers's men gained their assigned positions throughout the breadth of the town, as ordered and without any difficulties. Then, suddenly, a single shot broke the eerie stillness that shrouded the town like a blanket, echoing through the cold air of the fading night and across the silent town. Every member of Rogers's task force naturally assumed that this shot was the long-awaited signal from the major. However, this was not the case.

This gunshot from an accidentally fired weapon echoed across the river valley. Breaking the stillness, the resounding boom, which had caught everyone (especially the people of St. Francis and Rogers himself) by surprise, was even louder than a shot fired from a rifle or a fowling piece. As fate would have it, the firing of this large-caliber Brown Bess musket by one of Rogers's men immediately awoke a town filled with Abenaki warriors, women, and children to an awful truth: the English "savages" were in their midst when least expected by anyone. To this day, it is not known if a Ranger, Provincial, or British Regular accidently fired the shot.

Indeed, Major Rogers never gave his eagerly awaited pistol shot to shatter the stillness of St. Francis. Because of the time it took for everyone to ease silently into their assigned positions before each house, he had not yet deemed it time to give the signal to attack. Of course, it took the longest for Rogers's rearmost men to reach the houses on the town's outer fringes, after having passed through the dark streets and backyards in the near blackness, which was rapidly fading away. Scotsman Private Kirkwood, who had taken a good position before the front door of a house near the town's foremost edge on the west, said of the alarming fact that Rogers never gave the signal to begin the grim business of killing, "When the morning dawn'd, we went into the town and took our stations by two's, but by accident one of the men's pieces went off, which made us begin [the grim business of killing] without the right signal."[41]

Ironically, the accidental firing of the musket was sufficiently late that it coincided with the arrival of a larger glimmer of morning light when the sun was just easing over the eastern horizon, which increased visibility to allow most of Rogers's men to reach their assigned positions before scores of houses. Most important, Rogers's stationary men (the vast majority) had caught their breath by this time, as could be seen in the gradual decrease in the slight puffs of condensation in the crisp air. It was quite possible that Rogers had been just about to fire his own flintlock pistol to unleash his signal as planned when the accidental musket firing occurred.

If not, then Rogers must have been infuriated by the accidental discharge of the firearm, which caused the killing to begin prematurely. In fact, he was extremely lucky that such an accident, which now alerted the entire town, had not occurred on the previous night or earlier in the morning. Nevertheless, the accidental shot stood in for Rogers's anticipated signal, as the attack needed to begin because it was only a matter of time before an alerted Abenaki unleashed his own shot at the white interlopers, who were swarming all over town. With so many of Rogers's soldiers already in their assigned positions before almost every house in the town, it high time to strike. Eager fighting men, like Scotsman Private Kirkwood, who was evidently near the major and a member of his right column when the accidental musket firing broke the early morning stillness, saw that Rogers had not given the signal.

However, most Rangers, Provincials, and British soldiers simply thought that the major had fired the crucial signal to initiate the attack on the houses.

The shot evidently came from an overly eager soldier who had fired prematurely at a warrior, or perhaps a soldier tripped and fell, resulting in an accidental discharge of a musket. Or maybe one of the inexperienced volunteers from the Provincial or British Regular ranks simply lost his nerve and discipline, firing prematurely at a shadow in the near darkness when deep inside the town. Or an Abenaki warrior might have suddenly emerged from a house to investigate a noise outside, seen to his astonishment that the streets were overflowing with white soldiers, and been shot at. To this day, the true origin of the shot that initiated the killing spree that now began in earnest throughout the town is not known. As if realizing that now was the right time, Rogers then fired his weapon to make sure that everyone, especially his own Rangers of the right division, went to work with zeal in the half-light even before the sun had a chance to bring an early morning warmth to the land.

With the unexpected shot that had echoed like thunder across the entire community of St. Francis, Rogers's men initiated the process of killing as many Abenaki as possible. They immediately began to batter down the light wooden doors with musket butts and shoulders before surging inside darkened houses with tomahawks and fixed bayonets to begin a nightmarish killing spree, when the bloodlust ran high.[42]

With the single shot that had caught Major Rogers completely by surprise, the fighting erupted across the breadth of the town. After the men bashed down doors, they then entered the dark insides of Abenaki houses. Here, inside the residences, they knew that the enemy still lay asleep quietly—just as when Abenaki warriors had smashed through the doors of log cabins all across the frontier to slaughter entire families, including infants, who never awoke from their sleep.

THE HORRIFIC BUSINESS OF KILLING BEGINS

In a letter, one of Rogers's followers described the dramatic moment when the men had achieved complete surprise, after having swarmed "up to the Town, where finding the Indians all asleep, [they] never stood to ask Entrance [to the houses], but burst open their Doors, and saluted them with Tomahawks and Bayonets" in the half-light on the bloodiest morning in Abenaki history.[43]

One of the most accurate accounts of the attack came from Sergeant Thompson Maxwell, who hailed from the town of Milford, New Hampshire. He had turned seventeen in September, on the eve of embarking upon the most harrowing experience of his life. He wrote, "All the warriors were out hunting [and] It became an easy prey for us [because] we found only old men, children, and squaws. Rogers ordered them, without discrimination, to be put to death. This massacre was only done, when the war-whoop was raised in the woods & Rogers told every man to take care of himself."[44]

Rogers's men now brought their own war of terrorism to St. Francis with a vengeance. Raising Indian-like warrior screams and the battle cry "Remember Fort William Henry," which fueled their burning hatred for the Abenaki, Rogers's experienced soldiers conducted the horrific work of killing without mercy with a grim earnestness, releasing a long pent-up rage. In the most vicious of wars in which there was no pity for the unfortunate victims, Rogers's men showed no mercy in part because, in the dawn's half-light and inside darkened houses, combatants could not be distinguished from non-combatants in the hectic confusion and noise. There was simply no way to tell the difference between the two during the excitement of having caught the most hated enemy of all New England completely by surprise. Therefore, Rogers's unleashed men followed the major's orders like good soldiers, based on the grim realities of frontier warfare, killing whomever they found in the houses, which they turned into gory slaughter pens. The ugly work of bayonetting and tomahawking every Abenaki in sight was as swift as it was awful.

The systematic killing by Rogers's men was conducted with a business-like efficiency—professional and mechanical—which only battle-hardened veterans and frontiersmen could perform with utter ruthlessness. Unfortunately for the doomed people of St. Francis, this was a classic case of whites having basically become Indians by waging the same kind of brutal warfare that had long victimized their own people. Under the circumstances and the orders given by Rogers, a wide variety of horrific excesses were inevitable because this was the most hated Indian community in North America.

Gaining access into each house of the sprawling community was quick and relatively easy for these experienced fighting men, who knew that they had to act, move, and kill as swiftly as possible. As mentioned, no one in St. Francis had ever imagined that any white soldiers would have the courage and fortitude to march so deep into the heart of New France to attack St.

Francis. The Abenaki were caught completely by surprise when the two fighting men assigned to each house smashed through the front door, which was not locked or bolted in this communal society, and barged into the main room with war cries and stabbing bayonets.

Because the front doors were relatively flimsy and all but left open, some Rangers, like Sergeant Benjamin Bradley of the Merrimack River country (like Rogers and Stark), burst through with such force that they fell headlong into the midst of Abenaki families sleeping on the dirt floor. Although an experienced Ranger, Sergeant Bradley, from Concord, New Hampshire, was as shaken as the Abenaki inside, whom he had landed upon in full force.

Led by Lieutenant Jacob Farrington, of Andover, Essex County, in northeast Massachusetts, who had been promoted to an officer's rank the previous July, this group of Merrimack River country Rangers, which included Sergeant "Ben" Bradley, who was fated to die of starvation on the long return journey to civilization, promptly killed all inhabitants in a brutal flurry of jabbing bayonets and skull-crushing tomahawk blows. Startled Native American inhabitants awoke to a living nightmare, with the white soldiers among them, turning their homes into scenes of carnage. Some Abenaki never awoke in what had become a hell from which there was no escape when Rogers's men broke into houses to bayonet everyone in sight. Angry bearded men were screaming like madmen and swarming all around the Abenaki, making resistance all but impossible in houses that quickly became gory slaughter pens.

A perfect frenzy of killing played out without restraint, and sheer savagery reached a new high on this bloody morning, in a perfect storm of heightened adrenaline, emotion, and primeval instinct among the Rangers, especially those men whose family members had been killed in the long list of seemingly countless Abenaki raids. The highly combustible situation resulted in a bloodlust among the attackers that ensured not only a slaughter but also a massacre that the Abenaki people never forgot, even to this day.

For the most part, Abenaki women, children, and old men (who were beyond warrior age and mostly the highly respected grandfathers of young men of fighting age) were killed in their sleep or just upon awaking to a nightmarish dawn, because the village was denuded of its young and middle-aged warriors. Unfortunately for the inhabitants of St. Francis, especially the helpless children, the town's warrior protectors were now far away, because no one had believed that any English soldiers, not even the hated Rogers, would be so bold as to cross such a great expanse of an uncharted wilderness and strike St. Francis with impunity.

Inside darkened Abenaki houses, innocent noncombatants were quickly killed in a frantic flurry of vigorous bayonet jabs, close-range musket shots, and steel tomahawk chops that easily crushed skulls in one blow. Survivors responded by fighting back as best they could, while the high-pitched screams of the victims rose like a crescendo through the town, which had become a vast urban killing field. The attackers' terrifying war cries sounded like those from Indian warriors rather than white men to reveal a total acclimation of whites to their brutal wartime environment of frontier warfare.

Rogers's Indian Ranger warriors joined the killing spree like everyone else, while shouting their own distinctive war cries of "Ai-ai-ai!" All of St. Francis was now consumed in a nightmarish chorus of shouts, screams, prayers, unanswered pleas for mercy, and cries of pain. The attackers satisfied their lust for revenge, which burned brightly like the morning sun that continued to rise to dissipate the last vestiges of darkness. In the process, the people and the spirit of St. Francis died ugly deaths in their once secure place that had been turned into hell.

Like an avenging angel who had seen the slaughter of so many settlers in the Merrimack River country, Rogers unleashed his own personal rage, which had been building up year after year while his people on the frontier had been butchered like sheep. And it was a terrible vengeance that knew no bounds. Clearly, the young men and boys in the ranks had taken Rogers's harsh final orders most seriously and obeyed them with an angry zeal, transforming themselves into little more than savage beasts on the most brutal of mornings, which the Abenaki never forgave.

The tomahawks, with broad steel heads that had been made razor sharp just for this occasion, and the long bayonets of Rogers's men were utilized with a bloody finesse that was as efficient as it was gory. These enraged veterans felled one Abenaki after another almost effortlessly in a killing spree that shortly spun out of control until extreme excess became the order of the day. From the beginning, every Abenaki seen by Rogers's men was cut down without mercy. Fortunately, quite a few women and children (including some warriors) found shelter in cellars and lofts, hiding silently to save themselves from Rogers's angry soldiers, who were dedicated to the total destruction of everything.

Inside the dark homes, where puddles of blood and piles of bodies accumulated like red and yellow autumn leaves on a windy fall day in New England, the attackers were not concerned if they encountered an Abenaki man, woman, or juvenile, because everyone inside was considered a hostile. No one was taking any chances: if they saw a moving shadow inside a house, the attackers immediately lunged with bayonets, hacked with steel tomahawks, and unleashed close-range shots that could not miss.

With adrenaline pumping rapidly through their veins during the close-range combat that swirled inside the houses, which was the Rangers' first experience with the nightmare of urban combat, no time existed to ascertain the difference when they suddenly came face-to-face with a woman or a warrior, because it was a case of kill or be killed, which had become the simple law of survival in the combat that consumed St. Francis. Hell itself had descended upon St. Francis on this bloody morning, when Rogers and his men had become the grimmest of reapers, as in an ancient moral tale from the Old Testament.

Major Rogers admitted as much, because everyone realized that this attack was all about killing or being killed in the long-accepted frontier formula that now guaranteed total victory for him. He wrote about how the hard-hitting surprise attack "was done with so much alacrity by both officers and men, that the enemy had no time to recover themselves, or take arms for their own defence, till they were chiefly destroyed, except some few of them who took to the water."[45] Indeed, the battle-hardened major of Scotch-Irish heritage penned in more detail how the success of the attack was based on "so much caution and promptitude on the part" of the attackers, who had obeyed Rogers's orders to the letter.[46]

In a rare compliment to his soldiers for their combat performance on this bloody morning, Rogers also emphasized how "he never saw a better Command of Officers and Men," who performed efficiently, like a well-oiled killing machine at St. Francis, because they knew that they had to prevail. Clearly, this was an elite command of tough fighting men who had risen to the occasion. Rogers, consequently, praised "not only their good Courage and Behaviour, but [also] the Fatigues and Sufferings they have undergone."[47]

However, Rogers failed—for ample good reason—to specify whether the victims were women, old men, and children or young warriors in their prime. The killing of the Abenaki without mercy continued after the first light of dawn, which gradually illuminated a grisly scene of a body-strewn St. Francis. As noted, the special detachment of marksmen had taken a good position on slightly higher ground to cover the open space that led from the town to the river: the fourth side of St. Francis now covered by the brisk fire of sharpshooters who raked the initial trickle of escapees who were running for their lives. Unleashing hot fire on easy targets that they could not miss, these expert Ranger riflemen ensured that all sides of the town were closed and completely in the attackers' hands as ordered by the major.

With the ease of shooting fish in a barrel, these chosen veteran sharpshooters methodically shot down the ever-increasing flow of fleeing Abenaki, who raced for their lives to escape this town of unspeakable horrors. To experienced marksmen from the frontier, these escapees made especially easy targets in their vain attempts to reach the river and push off in canoes, which placed them in an ideal killing field of open water. Here, the St. Francis was a much different river from where Rogers and his men had crossed upriver, when it was swifter and narrower: a much wider and deeper river during its gradual descent into the larger St. Lawrence just to the north.

In a grim tragedy for noncombatants, this longtime river of life to the Abenaki people had now become a river of death, where the corpses of men, women, and children who had been shot by the rifleman or drowned in their panic to escape floated slowly downstream with the northward current that carried these victims toward the St. Lawrence. Rogers explained how these belated escape attempts had only resulted in additional slaughter: "About forty of my people pursued them, who destroyed such as attempted to make their escape that way [to the St. Francis River], and sunk both them and their boats" (or in this case birchbark canoes).[48]

The sloping riverbank located northwest of the town was transformed into a grim killing field from the cracking rifle fire of Rangers, who continued to blast away from good positions on higher ground to cover the dirt paths leading from the town to the river: the "Indians tried to escape by the river, leaping into canoes [but] the blocking force [of riflemen] shot them down, knifed and scalped them in the canoes or in the water, staining the waters of the St. Francis red."[49]

As usual amid the heat of battle, Major Rogers was everywhere at once to encourage his men to work faster and finish the ugly job of completely reducing St. Francis and eliminating its inhabitants as quickly as possible, because time was of the essence. The major's mind was already focused on the necessity of a quick exit from town and escaping southward, because the noise of the attack had alerted the countryside for miles around. One account revealed how "the major, who was never known to be idle in such an Affair, was in every Part of the Engagement encouraging his Men and giving Directions."[50]

Thankfully, the large-scale battle that Rogers had expected and feared because of the small size of his command never erupted at St. Francis. To his credit, although he was guilty of glorying Rogers and whitewashing the dark stain of a massacre in part because he was a proud New Englander like the major, Parkman wrote with understatement that "many of the warriors were absent, and the rest [noncombatants] were asleep [because] Some were killed in their beds."[51]

A more accurate account from the pages of the *Boston Gazette* revealed the swift and efficient work of Rogers's veterans, who once again demonstrated that they were expert killers, because what resulted was a slaughter: "Shot some as they lay in bed, while others attempting to flee by back Ways, were tomahawked or run thro' with Bayonets."[52]

The members of one fortunate Abenaki family were swifter than others. They managed to escape out of the back of the house just in time when Rangers began banging on the front door. With the rest of his family having escaped, the Abenaki father realized that in his haste he had left his infant behind in its wooden cradle. He had then raced back to the house and retrieved the baby just as Rogers's men shattered the sturdy front door to pieces and appeared with fixed bayonets at the ready.[53]

For those Abenaki not killed in their beds, running the gauntlet to the river was not only a vain effort but also a most deadly once, because Rogers had closed his grip completely around the town by this time. After having developed a well-conceived tactical plan in which his semicircular line of attack completed the town's encirclement, Rogers's wise deployment of his finest marksmen continued to pay dividends. These expert riflemen continued their systematic slaughter of the terrorized Abenaki without a break on this bloody morning in hell. This detachment of around forty picked men, who were the command's finest marksmen and handled their rifles with a masterfully lethal effectiveness, systematically cut down an unknown number of Abenaki who were attempting to flee in their panic.[54]

Evidently after her family was slaughtered by the revenge-seeking Rangers, a little dark-haired Abenaki girl, who was so young as to not understand the horrors that she had witnessed swirling around her and why so many angry white men were killing her people with such brutality, ran away along a brushy path. It appeared inevitable that she would become another tragic victim when a warrior suddenly appeared, knelt down, and shot one of Rogers's attacking men, who was dropped but not mortally wounded by the well-placed shot.[55]

The most bitter of ironies for the Abenaki fleeing toward the river was the fact that they were forced to run a deadly gauntlet of musket fire from some of Rogers's best riflemen, who had long shot down game with ease, much as white captives, including John Stark, had been long forced to run a gauntlet of parallel lines of villagers swinging clubs and beating them to a bloody pulp in many cases.[56]

Scotland's Private Robert Kirkwood was an especially revenge-minded volunteer from Colonel Archibald Montgomery's 77th Highland Regiment, which had reached America's shores in 1756. At that time, the Scottish soldiers, who were eager to match their warfighting skills with Native Americans, wore the colorful Highland kilts of the ancient clans. These Celtic warriors were excessively proud of their Scottish Highland roots, which included a distinctive warrior ethos. Private Kirkwood was far more descriptive in regard to the gory details than most participants, including Rogers, about what really happened at St. Francis based on Rogers's orders to "kill every one without mercy," in the Scotsman's words.[57]

After the killing finally ended, leaving the men, panting and covered in sweat and blood, exhausted and numbed by the horror, Rogers planned to shortly issue orders for the burning of the town to begin. In Kirkwood's revealing words about the swiftness of the attack, which wreaked a terrible vengeance at the once beautiful place on the high north bank of the St. Francis River, "In less than a quarter hour the whole town was in a blaze, and the carnage terrible, hardly any of the enemy escaping, those who the flames did not devour, were either shot or tomohawk'd" to death.[58]

All the while, and as throughout the past, Major Rogers had been in the forefront, leading the way in the destruction of the most hated Indian town in America. As one of his men wrote with undying admiration for the dynamic major, who had continued to lead by example in the dirt streets— now strewn with Abenaki bodies—during the Rangers' first taste of urban combat, which was always the most deadly in war regardless of place or time, Rogers "was in every Part of the Engagement" on a nightmarish day that no one would ever forget.[59]

It was all over very quickly, because there was so little resistance and because Rogers's men—the professional killers whom Rogers had nurtured with such loving care over the years, seemingly for this very moment and mission deep in Quebec—had worked smoothly together as a highly efficient killing machine, wiping out everyone in their way with a swift, merciless ease.

Therefore, the growing light on the eastern horizon presented a scene of slaughter throughout the body-strewn town. Major Rogers and his men had completed their job without emotion or remorse because they viewed the slaughter of their most brutal of enemies as nothing more than a mechanical, businesslike procedure that was necessary for the greater good of the overall war effort and the safety of thousands of people along the frontier.

In a strange irony, the Rangers had suffered severely during the three-week trek to St. Francis without the luxury of even a fire for warmth, just for the opportunity to now torch St. Francis on Rogers's orders. In Rogers own words, "A little after sun-rise I set fire to all their houses, except three, in which there was corn, that I reserved for the use of the party."[60]

In an unexpected development, and as a cruel fate would have it, the greatest horror of the raid was yet to come. The tragedy revealed itself after all the wood-frame houses had been set on fire by Rogers's men, who continued to do their work of systematic destruction in a fast, efficient manner, while the major constantly implored them with a sense of frantic urgency to hurry and not waste a single second in spreading fire to every structure. Terrified by the attackers' initial screams and yells, which had suddenly erupted in the cold darkness, mostly women and children had sought safety by hiding underground in food storage cellars and in the lofts of their houses.

Long familiar with enemy trickery in the art of unconventional warfare, which he had mastered like no other American officer, Major Rogers, like his men, almost certainly assumed that these residences contained a good many lurking warriors, which was not the case for the most part. Evidence has revealed that most of the relatively few warriors—like everyone else—had broken for the river instead of remaining inside the houses, which were nothing more than deathtraps, especially when engulfed in flames, and the Indian way of fighting excluded the concept of making defensive stands against impossible odds when no escape or victory was possible on bloody October 4.

Even if they realized that most of these hidden survivors, in both the upper and the lower levels of houses, were women and children, these experienced fighting men felt that they could take no chances in attempting to root out those who had been left behind, because a warrior—and an unknown number in fact remained in these houses—might be hidden among them. The little existing evidence has suggested that a good "many" Indians, in Rogers's words, or perhaps the majority of villagers had remained hidden during the attack, because only a minority had been flushed out of their hiding places inside their houses, including those inhabitants who had raced for the river in the vain hope of reaching the birchbark canoes to escape.

Caught in a grim race with death, these escapees had been riddled with a hail of bullets from the special sharpshooting detachment of marksmen, who shot down quite a few Abenaki who dashed for safety to escape the closing arms of Rogers's ever-tightening tactical vise. Rogers described the most terrible aspect of the attack in rather basic terms, without compassion or emotion, because he felt relatively little for the enemy: "The fire consumed many of the Indians who had concealed themselves in the cellars and lofts of their houses."[61]

Perhaps most revealingly, no estimates were ever made in regard to the number of women and children who died in the flames, but that number was almost certainly high: a suspicious omission from the historical record that might well have been made to disguise the fact that more Abenaki died in the fires that consumed every single house and standing structure in St. Francis than anyone dared to admit.

However, we do know that many Abenaki died in the flames, swept and fanned by the river breeze, that roared to consume the entire town. Indeed, as revealed in a firsthand account that appeared in the pages of the *Boston Evening Post*, the attackers "set fire to the houses [where] many of the enemy . . . had concealed themselves . . . which our men learnt from the crying and shrieking of those" about to be consumed by the raging fire.[62]

In the end, however, this nightmarish ending in a fiery hell for so many inhabitants of St. Francis was inevitable. It revealed how thoroughly the town had been surprised, with very little chance for anyone to escape, because, in Rogers's words, the Abenaki "would not come out."[63]

Distinguished by great understatement, like Rogers's own words, but right to the point, an article in the *Boston Gazette* revealed the extent of the horror when St. Francis was transformed into hell on earth for the Abenaki trapped inside their residences: "Those miserable wretches, when they perceived their houses on fire, and themselves likely to be made the fuel: The sword without, which prevented all escapes, and the fire within rendered their situation most unhappy, most miserable."[64]

During the September 1756 attack by Pennsylvanians on the Native American village of Kittanning, which was located on the Allegheny River and not "denuded of its fighting men," like St. Francis on the morning of October 4, the Indian warriors had been trapped in houses that were then deliberately fired by the attackers, because they had refused to surrender. Then, "as the Fire approached, some began to sing" the song of death.[65]

These determined warriors of Kittanning, when about to die from the raging fires, sang what were essentially traditional prayers to their God just before meeting their maker. But there is no record of anyone singing prayers and warrior songs when about to burn to death at St. Francis. This was additional evidence that mostly women, children, and old men were trapped in lofts and cellars when the fire consumed them, and not warriors, as generally assumed by historians and as emphasized by Major Rogers.

The tragic fates of Indian women and children, caught between warring factions in an especially brutal conflict and burned alive, had been a common theme of frontier warfare for generations: just another grisly chapter of America's brutal warfare, when no mercy was the order of the day for both sides, who waged their own vicious brand of frontier warfare. And, as in all wars, it was always the innocent, women and children, who suffered most, especially with their lives.

When the biblically inspired Puritans and their Mohegan allies had attacked the Pequot village on May 26, 1637, at Mystic, Connecticut, it had resulted in a terrible slaughter on an unprecedented scale—for the first time, genocide against indigenous people had come in full force to America, and it was destined to continue long after the American pioneers reached the Pacific's shores during the so-called winning of the West. What was witnessed at St. Francis was nothing less than a tragic exhibition of the merciless concept of total war: the systematic killing of noncombatants, the burning of dwellings containing both fighting men and women and children, and the thorough destruction of an entire community. But again, this was nothing new.

During America's first genocide at Mystic, Captain John Mason, the die-hard leader of the militia from the Connecticut settlements, had admonished his men when they unsheathed their swords and were about to charge the trapped Pequot, who, enclosed inside their stockade village, had no chance of offering serious resistance, "We should never kill them after that manner [because] WE MUST BURN THEM" to death.[66]

In the same way, Rogers was now waging his own personal holy war against the Abenaki and embracing the genocidal concept that was part of the grim continuum of the slaughter of Native American people for generations. Therefore, when the major had implored his men to "kill every one without mercy," he meant every single word in his heart and soul, continuing a horrific cultural legacy early rooted in the early New England experience. Rogers's harsh order of no mercy was also entirely instinctive, born of an ancient primeval urge that had evolved from deep inside him in a process that was all about simple survival on the northern frontier after having fought a merciless foe for so many years.

Like never before, the bloody morning of October 4 was for Rogers a long-awaited reckoning delivered to the primary tormentors of his people for generations in an apocalyptic day for the unfortunate people of St. Francis. And on his beautiful autumn day in Quebec along the St. Francis River, which now ran with blood and bodies, including drowned Abenaki children, he had orchestrated a terrible vengeance in the name of the Lord for the seemingly countless slaughtered white victims of decades past. These white victims made up a list too long to tabulate, much like the large number of scalps found by Rogers and his men at St. Francis.[67]

BURNING DOWN THE JESUIT MISSION
ROMAN CATHOLIC CHURCH

Major Rogers made no mention in his report to Amherst of having issued orders for the torching of the whitewashed Jesuit Mission Roman Catholic church, located at the head of this missionary town. French-born priests had long promised the salvation of Abenaki souls for the slaughtering of English settlers across the frontier from this house of God.

Consequently, the church was a primary target. The warriors of St. Francis were mission Indians officially known as a "Christianized" people. This so-called civilizing influence by way of Roman Catholicism had done absolutely nothing to tame the warriors' ferocity and savagery when they fell upon white settlers, including women and children, in their lonely cabins and small settlements. In truth, the dictates of Roman Catholicism and the fiery words of the priests had made the warriors even more unmerciful, because their war was also against Protestantism.

Even before the massacre at Fort William Henry, at which the Abenaki had played a leading role, the good priest of St. Francis—Father Pierre-Joseph-Antoine Roubaud—had performed Mass for these warriors before they had engaged in a perfect orgy of hideous crimes against the English and Provincials, including women and children, after the garrison's surrender and parole. The Abenaki had initiated the massacre by attacking the wounded and sick men in the fort's hospital, where they were slaughtered in their beds and dragged outside onto the parade ground to be killed before the shocked prisoners.

As noted, the longtime powerful influence of the Jesuits' hatred of the heretical Protestants, combined with the Abenaki's powerful warrior ethos, had fueled a greater savagery toward New Englanders of every age and sex. In the end, the Jesuits had only brought the old religious hatred and wars with them from Europe to create a more merciless foe. The Abenaki, consequently, fought not only for their ancestral lands, revenge, and the preservation of their people but also to save the Roman Catholic faith. Paradoxically, and in a rather strange development for Rogers and his men, this was not as much a racial war as it was a total war within the context of an international religious conflict transferred from Europe. Therefore, as Rogers and his men saw it, everything standing at St. Francis had to be razed to the ground as symbolic devastation of the Abenaki's own form of genocide, which is often overlooked by politically correct historians of today in a silencing of fundamental truths.

For such distinct reasons, with which he was only too familiar since the days of his youth in the picturesque Merrimack River country, Rogers was determined that the church at St. Francis should be destroyed. He therefore ordered the Catholic church, especially because it was decorated with scalps, to be burned to the ground until nothing remained. In many ways, the apotheosis of Rogers's and his followers' hatred of Catholicism and the evils that had long stemmed from this holy place on the river was represented by the major's order to destroy the Roman Catholic church, which had long served as the center of Abenaki spiritual-political-military life at St. Francis.

On Rogers's direct orders, which were shouted out above the piercing cries of the hapless Abenaki, who were being burned alive while their houses crackled in the rising flames, a squad of bearded Rangers dashed into the one-story wooden church situated at the head of town. This sturdily built wooden house of worship represented everything that they, especially the Scotch-Irish Rangers of the Presbyterian faith, had hated for as long as they could remember, as a cultural legacy. In their holy war, the Scotch-Irish Rangers had long hated Catholicism, Jesuits, and so-called Christianized Indians, who had long slaughtered so many settlers on the New England frontier and brought their prized trophies—hundreds of scalps and prisoners, including women and children—back to St. Francis.

To these Protestant fighting men, especially the Scotch-Irish Presbyterians from Ulster Province, north Ireland, and the sons and grandsons of immigrants, Roman Catholics and Jesuits were ancient enemies who had long sought to roll back the heretical tide of Protestantism. Therefore, it was with great pleasure that the Rangers spread fire with makeshift torches throughout the inside of the church, where Mass had long been conducted by Priest Roubaud every morning and night throughout the week to enlighten the Abenaki about the moral necessity of slaughtering even more Protestant heretics.

Cherished religious icons, holy relics, Jesuit artifacts, and all objects having to do with Roman Catholicism were either stolen or destroyed by incensed Protestant soldiers, who delighted in the venting of their anti-Catholicism. In the passion of the moment, having achieved total victory at St. Francis, they had seemingly reverted back to the motivations that had resulted in so much carnage in Europe's terrible religious wars, which were one reason why their forefathers had first migrated to the New World: ironically, a case of history now having come full circle in the heart of the Canadian wilderness.

Precious religious items, including candlesticks of both gold and silver, incense vessels, a gold-plated incense cup, a large painting of a revered Catholic saint, a copper chalice coated with silver, a large religious banner decorated with gold and silver threads, a gold case, and other valuables, were stolen by Rogers's men. And even the exquisite solid-silver statue of the Virgin Mary was pilfered by greedy men who had never seen such riches before. As noted, this prized statue had been sent to the Abenaki mission by the canon of Chartres, France.

For these Protestants, mostly Scotch-Irish Presbyterians from the New England frontier, the Roman Catholic church represented the greatest symbol of the religious faith that long helped to inspire the Abenaki to strike exceptionally hard at the New England settlements and to show no mercy. Therefore, the Protestants, perhaps laughing and cursing this primary source of so many raids on their homeland, eagerly watched the flames leaping up around the large wooden structure topped with a large wooden cross.

It was only a short time before the flames entirely consumed the modest wood structure, which was so unlike the magnificent cathedrals of stone and brick in Montreal and Quebec, which looked like houses of worship in countless French cities. The church had to be reduced to ashes in the mind of Rogers, who continued to wage his holy war for God, country, and faith. In this regard, St. Francis's fate was much like that the ancient Romans had inflicted upon their commercial rival of Carthage, whose burning to the ground became a beautiful reality for the ancient world's most vigorous imperialists, whose empire rose significantly around the world in consequence.

In many ways, the burning of the Roman Catholic church to the ground was not only the climax of the audacious raid on St. Francis but also the height of Major Rogers's career in true symbolic fashion. Rogers's one-sided success was now symbolically represented in strictly moral terms by the sight of the red and yellow flames engulfing the church. In a moral reckoning, Rogers was truly the White Devil, as the Abenaki came to call him because of his hard-hitting Indian-like ways at St. Francis.

Meanwhile, all around the burning church, thick clouds of black smoke continued to rise higher into a clear October morning sky to display the extent of Rogers's wrath to one and all. Most of all, the church's fiery destruction had deep meaning, because it had long served as a representative symbol of Abenaki power and prestige: ample proof that Rogers's righteous rage had been released in full at the right place, which was destined to bring a great sense of relief in the future to thousands of people in the settlements and towns across America.

Major Rogers, the lowly son of Scotch-Irish immigrants from Ulster Province, must have smiled with delight in viewing the Catholic church wrapped in flames, when he watched its destruction through a traditional Scotch-Irish Presbyterian lens and savored every precious moment: this sacred missionary house of worship was that of the enemies of his own Presbyterian parents, James and Mary Rogers, and his people, mostly Scotch-Irish, of the Merrimack River country.

All the while, the yellow and red flames that consumed the Catholic church and the houses of the conquered town leaped higher and higher into the early autumn sky. The smell of burning pine gave the air a pleasant smell that seemed to mock the scene of absolute destruction and widespread death at this sacred place in the wilderness. The Roman Catholic church finally collapsed into a fiery ball, which no doubt brought a cheer from Rogers's men, who rejoiced in a complete victory.[68]

But to be fair to the no-nonsense major, the complete destruction of the Catholic church was simply a normal feature of conflict during the course of the French and Indian War, which so closely resembled scenes from the devastating Hundred Years' War in Europe. A lengthy list of Protestant churches along the frontier had been torched by Abenaki war parties for as long as anyone could remember. Not only the entire town of St. Francis but also the mission church had been transformed into one vast "smoking funeral pyre" in record time.[69] At least one Gallic man of God died with his burning church like a noble-minded and stoic captain going down with his ship. This defiant French priest "though offered Quarter, chose to perish in the Flames."[70]

All the while, Rogers and his men delighted in the sheer thoroughness of their zealous work of destruction when the church and other structures went down in flames with a crash, basking in their one-sided victory, which could hardly have been more complete. However, some Rangers, including those with Abenaki blood on their hands, bayonets, tomahawks, and what little was left of ragged uniforms, were even more excited by the plunder, which had exceeded all expectations, than by the church's destruction. As revealed in one account, "One Ranger [shortly brought] off 170 guineas and another the silver image [statue of the Virgin Mary] of 10 pounds in weight."[71]

While still shouting orders to his busy men whose efficiency in the work of destruction was a marvel and sight to be seen, the major relished a well-earned sense of satisfaction. After all, Rogers had never forgotten how brother Richard's grave had been dug open by plunder-hungry Abenaki warriors at the soldiers' cemetery at Fort William Henry and his scalp ripped from his head. To Rogers, this outrage was only one example of Abenaki "cruelty and rage" that knew no bounds and had long haunted him day and night.[72]

WANTON DESTRUCTIVENESS

By far, the greatest moral transgression that had been committed by the raiders was the unrestrained bloodlust that had resulted in a massacre. The excess of killing and destruction of the entire community was time-consuming. Additional time, therefore, had been wasted during the killing spree when Rogers and his men should have already withdrawn south in case any Abenaki war parties were returning to the town.

These powerful emotions of Rogers and his soldiers at the height of the killing clouded reason because passions and adrenaline ran so high, resulting in a lack of foresight as additional precious time ticked away. Because of the intensity of the close-range combat, in a case of killed or be killed, there was no time for long-term reasoning by the men in the ranks, because simply surviving this close-quarter fight became the top priority. In this confusing urban-combat situation, Rogers's men had most of all relied on quickness, reflexes, and instincts that had been well honed by this time.

This situation that resulted in an intense focus on the most immediate priorities of killing Abenaki and overwhelming the town as quickly as possible resulted in a great mistake. Most precious reserves of food, such as smoked meat (deer, turkey, moose, fish from the St. Francis River, etc.) and stored vegetables and fruit (fresh and dried), were located in each house, stored in lofts and primarily in the cooler cellars. These were reserves of food for consumption by each Abenaki family to survive the long Quebec winter that lasted around six months. During this postharvest period of early fall, these foodstuffs had already been distributed throughout the community on an equal basis for everyone to consume during the winter.

Because the smoked meats and dried fruits and vegetables were stored in the house cellars and lofts, this large supply of invaluable foodstuffs for the community's survival in winter's depths was lost when the houses went up in flames. Major Rogers and his followers allowed each house to burn to the ground to satisfy revenge and complete the work of destruction without considering the cost when it came to destroyed foodstuffs. This oversight, of course, was a grievous mistake. Given the overall situation during the heat of combat, these supplies of food simply had not been a top priority: killing the Abenaki was more important than anything else when passions ran high and simple survival had been the main priority.

This much-needed food supply—by this time, Rogers's men were out of rations—had not been retrieved because so many, if not all, houses were still occupied by residents when they were torched. Given the prospect of even more bitter urban combat, this procedure seemed to make sense to Rogers and his men, who set the houses on fire in part because they remained occupied by some warriors, perhaps a good many, for all they knew at this time. Evidently, since they had killed relatively few warriors, Major Rogers and his men might have assumed that the vast majority of the warriors were still hidden in the houses, which was not the case. As mentioned, the warriors were absent from St. Francis on various assignments in the service of New France. It was women, children, and elderly Abenaki who remained in their lofts and cellars instead of fighting men.

And in keeping with Rogers's order, the razing of St. Francis to the ground had been the top priority from the beginning, and the major avoided sending his soldiers into the lofts and cellars for fear of losing a good many men in close-quarter fighting in the dark. After all, he was already worried about his depleted command's chances of surviving the upcoming lengthy withdrawal and fighting off pursuers in the weeks ahead. Consequently, every man would be needed for the many challenges that were sure to come. Rogers's command—142 men—was already too small for the mission even before the attack was launched. Thankfully, the vast majority of warriors had been absent to compensate for Rogers's diminutive numbers.

When the houses of St. Francis burned down, large numbers of occupants, who were hiding in the cellars and lofts, died in the fires. As noted, the largest and most valuable supplies of provisions were also destroyed in the flames, however. The remaining Abenaki warriors would have fought back fiercely and to the last breath in these structures, ensuring desperate last stands if Rogers had ordered the search of lofts and storehouses. Therefore, it was absolutely necessary for Rogers to save the lives of his men by immediately burning down the houses to eliminate all resistance, destroy any supplies of black powder and caches of weapons, and save time, which was now of the essence. In addition, the major knew that it would take too long and prove too costly if the houses had to be carried by storm to root out every last resisting warrior in cellars and lofts, ensuring that stored foodstuffs would never be discovered.

Since Rogers could not afford to lose any more men from his small command, the conflagration had been allowed to consume each house and each hidden warrior and family member who remained inside. Therefore, the fires that transformed the town to ashes did a thorough job, completed in record time, when Rogers appreciated the supreme value of time. However, this systematic and thorough destruction came at a frightfully high price, and not just in Abenaki lives, including women and children. After the loss of the large amount of supplies of food in cellars and lofts, all that was now left for Rogers's men for subsistence in the days ahead—the long return trip south to the safety of New England would take more than two months in some cases, after the major divided his command into separate parties—were three wooden storehouses of dried corn on the cob. Thinking ahead as usual, Major Rogers had wisely ordered that the corn storehouses be spared from the flames.

Of course, this supply of corn was entirely inadequate and insufficient for the lengthy journey ahead. Even more, what remained in the three Abenaki corn storehouses was basically nonnutritious (cornmeal ground by Abenaki women), unlike the supplies of better provisions that had been consumed by the flames at St. Francis. Therefore, because of the burning down of all houses, an absolute disaster—including a good many deaths of Rogers's men from starvation and the horrors of cannibalism during the nightmarish return journey—was in the making and destined to claim far more lives of Rogers's soldiers than the assault on St. Francis, where only one Ranger had been killed. As deemed by Rogers, the firing of the houses saved the lives of some of his men, who avoided the risky business of engaging in hand-to-hand combat in dark enclosed spaces. Such close-range struggles to gain hidden provisions in lofts and cellars could not have been more dangerous for Rogers's men, who had been spared in this regard.

Therefore, the rapidly spreading fire that had consumed all of the town's houses in an inferno eliminated not only the remaining Abenaki but also what now was most valuable—the precious supplies of food inside the houses—for Rogers's overall goal of minimizing casualties among a task force that was already too diminutive. In regard to allowing the hidden food-stuffs to go up in flames without Rogers's men having entered the cellars and lofts, one account described how in "the hurry in burning the houses [this situation] could not give many an opportunity of bringing off much."[73]

In a letter, one of the major's soldiers explained the saddest tragedy that occurred at St. Francis, when "they set the Town all in flames, think-ing there was no one left alive [no soldiers had searched the cellars and lofts of the houses because it was far too dangerous]; afterwards we heard the dreadful Cries and Screeches, as though there were Numbers of them in the Flames, who had concealed themselves in their upper Rooms and By-places, thinking to Escape."[74]

Indeed, the sad fact that large numbers of women, children, and old men remained hidden in the houses was a certain death sentence that claimed more lives than Ranger bullets, tomahawks, and bayonets on October 4. The loud cries of victims of the conflagration revealed their presence, when "our men learn't" of their hiding positions in lofts and cellars.[75]

Tragically, there was no escape at all for the secluded Abenaki on this bloody morning in Quebec. The sad fates of the last able-bodied persons—warriors and women, children and the elderly—were sealed at the height of the firestorm that transformed St. Francis into hell on earth. A Celtic soldier from Scotland, Private Kirkwood, whose heart still lay in his distant homeland across the sea, briefly described the bitter end for the relatively few Abenaki who attempted to escape from the burning houses surrounded by Rogers's men, who were ready and waiting for that inevitable eventuality: "Those who the flames did not devour, were either shot or tomohawk'd" when they ran out of houses that had been turned into ovens.[76]

But the systematic and thorough destruction of St. Francis and the killing of men and women were only part of the story when the passions among the attackers were allowed to run wild. The Rangers had been overwhelmed with "the blood lust which had gripped them when they had seen scalp-festooned poles by the huts" and European-style houses. In consequence, the worst of all scenarios and the ultimate tragedy had finally come to the mission community, because the "St. Francis Indians had lived by the sword and they died—men, women, and children—as they had lived, but no harder than had died hundreds of families on the New England frontier" for generations.[77]

To this day, the Abenaki people still tell their children about the green-uniform-clad conqueror who came as a grim avenger on October 4: Rogers, the "Butcher of the Abenaki."[78] But in truth and unknown to the Abenaki, Major Rogers, the consummate soldier who proved that he was the master of the deep raid into the heart of the enemy's country, was simply following the harsh orders of Major General Amherst: "Remember the barbarities that have been committed by the enemy's Indian scoundrels on every occasion, where they had an opportunity of shewing their infamous cruelties on the King's subjects, which they had done without mercy. Take your revenge."[79] In truth, it was Amherst, and not Rogers, who had a good deal of blood on his hands for what was nothing less than a war crime and atrocity, because of the slaughter of the Abenaki, mostly women, children, and elderly rather than warriors.[80]

However, Amherst, thinking almost like a colonial who had been born on American soil, had exactly voiced the feelings of Rogers and his men and the people of New England for generations with pinpoint accuracy. As a Boston journalist explained,

> *The severe treatment which these Indians met with from Rogers and his Party, if upon any occasion such usage can be justified, surely it might be here; for these St. Francois Indians [had committed more attacks and atrocities] than perhaps any tribe on the continent: For proof of this, when our men entering the town, they saw 6 or 700 English scalps waving in the wind upon the tops of poles, which were struck up on their houses and such like eminent places [including the Roman Catholic mission church and the Council House, which were both located near each other at the head of town]:—Wherefore it seems they have now been punished for their cruelty and that a just providence never designed that these blood thirsty heathen should go down to the grave in peace.[81]*

For the dark days ahead during the lengthy withdrawal from St. Francis, and as Rogers's fully appreciated, the most tangible benefit of the last warriors dying in the flames was the saving of Ranger lives and the precious remaining supply of ammunition in case of a large clash with a pursuing enemy in the near future. After all, a good many of the inevitable Abenaki, Canadian, and French pursuers would be lusting to take revenge for St.

Francis's destruction and the deaths of so many noncombatants, including their own relatives. Consequently, the Rangers, Britons, and Provincials had relied on bayonets and tomahawks in the killing spree at St. Francis, which saved a good deal of black powder in powder horns and rounds in leather cartridge boxes.[82]

With regard to the town's destruction, perhaps some of the more religious-minded men in Rogers's ranks recalled how the Lord had commanded Joshua, the great Jewish guerrilla leader, who fought with his heart for possession of the promised land, "Stretch out the spear that is in our hand toward [the hostile city of] Ai, for I will give it into your hand."[83]

Therefore, like Rogers and his men at St. Francis on October 4, Joshua and his Jewish attackers "entered the city and took it, and hurried to the city on fire. . . . And it came to pass when Israel had made an end of slaying all the inhabitants of Ai [and] So it was that all who fell that day, both men and women [were] all the people of Ai."[84]

Father Pierre-Joseph-Antoine Roubaud would finally reach his beloved St. Francis from Trois-Rivières, located southwest of Quebec and down the St. Lawrence River, near midnight on October 4, after Rogers had struck on that same morning—the Pearl Harbor of the Abenaki people that has haunted them for generations and to this day—to stun French leadership almost as much as the tragic victims of Rogers's bloody retribution.

Shocked and horrified by what he saw around him only hours after the thoroughness of the most unexpected of surprise attacks had left Abenaki bodies scattered across the ground and in the town's charred ruins, the saddened Jesuit father wrote, "Nothing was left of the village but embers. My house, the church, everything had been consumed" by the flames. Clearly, the righteous rage of the hard-bitten major from the Merrimack River country had been as complete as it had been thorough in a nightmarish cleansing.[85]

Rogers had carefully attended to the last detail of the complete destruction of the community by adhering to the core tenets of total warfare. But, most of all, the outstanding tactical success in having achieved complete surprise at St. Francis once again revealed the sterling leadership qualities of the Scotch-Irish major, who continued to establish himself as a frontier and combat leader second to none. Finally, the destructiveness and the final flurry of killing that had transformed St. Francis into what appeared to be Dante's Inferno came to an end. At last, when Abenaki victims could no longer be found by the fast-moving Rangers, British Regulars, and Provincials, the terrible bloodlust fizzled out like a hot summer day having faded away into the cool of early fall in a natural, timeless transition.

In Major Rogers's words, "About seven o'clock in the morning the affair was completely over, in which time we had killed at least two hundred Indians, and taken twenty of their women and children prisoners, fifteen of whom I let go on their own way."[86] Interestingly, Rogers revealed his typical modesty by simply referring to the crowning achievement of his distinguished military career as nothing more than an "affair."[87]

Likewise, astounded by the attack's swiftness and destructiveness, one of Rogers's men penned in a letter about the utter precision of the devastation that had laid waste to everything in short order: "In the Space of 2 Hours, we had cleared the whole Town of them, some of which attempted to run off were shot down immediately, others trying to cross the [St. Francis] River in Canoes were killed, and their Boats sunk."[88] The slaughter of Abenaki at the river where their birchbark canoes were located was one of the great tragedies that was played out in full. As later admitted by Captain Amos Ogden to Major General Amherst, a number of Abenaki children were drowned in the melee around the canoes, which had overturned in the panic, when Abenaki men, women, and children had attempted in vain to escape across the river.[89]

However, in truth, the tally of Abenaki warrior lives lost in combat was a gross exaggeration, especially in regard to Rogers's official report. Rather than warriors, far more Abenaki noncombatants had been consumed by fire rather than the bullets, tomahawks, and bayonets of Rogers's men. French accounts, including those of individuals like Father Roubaud, revealed quite a different version that matched the oral history of the Abenaki people. However, as in all their reports, the French deliberately minimized the extent of the disaster and losses for propaganda purposes. French prestige, credibility, and perceived strength were at stake, because leadership had long promised to protect the villages of its mission Indians, as the Abenaki had sincerely believed all the way up until the morning of October 4, in their unholy bargain and alliance: security and protection from the French in return for raiding the frontier settlements, which proved to be a Faustian bargain in the end.

After all, the most alarming of messages could not be allowed to circulate in New France, where morale was now exceptionally low after successive defeats and with Wolfe having recently captured Quebec: that

Rogers had dared to march with impunity so deep into the heart of New France and destroy the home community of the most faithful and lethal Native American allies of the French. And throughout, top French leadership had proved their inability to stop the relentless march of Rogers all the way to St. Francis. Therefore, in this never-ending propaganda war, like the English who had long manipulated losses to their benefit, the French only admitted that thirty Abenaki had been killed at St. Francis, twenty of them women and children.[90]

Presenting a corresponding account that was truthful in regard to the lack of warriors at St. Francis, Captain Pierre Pouchet, who was a member of the *troupes de terre*, wrote how Rogers and his raiders had "found this Abenaki village entirely denuded of its warriors [and] killed around thirty women and old people" on the morning of October 4.[91]

THE BEST PRIMARY EVIDENCE HAS REVEALED A MASSACRE

Of course, every nation in every war since time immemorial has demonized the enemy and glorified its own fighting men and their victories. In this regard, of course, the French and Indian War was no exception to the rule, and the raid on St. Francis was a classic example of this inevitable development of history having been written by the winners. Indeed, because of this natural process of a sanitization and romanticization of history that has been only too commonplace, even massacres have been glorified as great victories by the winners of war since time immemorial.

In fact, the raid on St. Francis has served as still another classic example of this phenomenon, because a massacre of mostly women, children, and the elderly certainly took place, as almost all of the town's warriors were absent. This massacre was revealed in soldier accounts like that of Sergeant Thompson Maxwell. He correctly described the fight as "this massacre," which was first covered up by glowing reports in colonial newspapers.

The ever-predictable process of glorification was then continued by generations of New England historians, as if totally influenced by the ample number of contemporary press reports in newspapers across the colonies and then by Rogers's *Journals*. In the twentieth century, this anti-historical process of romantic glorification was then continued by fiction writer Kenneth Lewis Roberts in his 1937 popular novel *Northwest Passage* and, of course, the 1940 movie based on this immensely popular work of fiction. And this romance and fiction has been widely accepted as fact by generations of Americans, including historians, to this day.

An epic confrontation between good and evil resulting in a great victory at St. Francis has been the standard view of what happened on bloody October 4 among generations of American historians. However, the Abenaki people knew the horrible truth about the raid on St. Francis, which could not be denied, although it was long silenced by white writers, historians, and Hollywood. Indeed, the undeniable facts and ugly truths about the attack on St. Francis told a far different story than has been presented to us for more than two and a half centuries.

Indeed, like so many other such reports for propaganda purposes, which were a behind-the-scenes war in themselves on both sides of the Atlantic, the French estimate of losses was far too low during this inevitable war of words over what had happened at St. Francis, while Rogers's own estimate of Abenaki losses was too high, but not as exaggerated as some historians have claimed in the past. Therefore, the truth of the Abenaki loses might well lay closer to a more middle-ground figure well below Rogers's 200 killed but higher than in French accounts, because they always engaged in a propaganda war to minimize losses and defeat: perhaps around 140–150 Abenaki were killed, as verified by the diary of Ebenezer Dibble, an invaluable primary source of information. Dibble might even have personally counted 140 Abenaki dead—far more noncombatants than warriors—on the morning of October 4.

Indeed, Scotland-born Private Robert Kirkwood, having volunteered from the ranks of Colonel Montgomery's Scottish Highland regiment and sounding almost like a biblical Hebrew holy warrior, was closer to the truth about the extent of the carnage when he wrote candidly about what happened and what he saw around him: "The whole town was reduced to ashes in about an hour, thus the inhumanity of these savages was rewarded with a calamity, dreadful indeed, but justly deserved."[92]

Then, in his vivid account about the devastating raid that was not unlike what had been seen during the English systematic destruction of the Scottish Highlands after failed Highlanders' rebellions, Kirkwood's words about a grim killing field mocked the low estimates by the French propagandists about the losses inflicted by Rogers's men: "This was I believe the bloodiest scene in all America, our revenge being completed."[93]

Clearly, this description by the young Scotsman fits Rogers's estimation of two hundred Abenaki dead: "We had killed at least two hundred Indians," penned the major.[94] In fact, Rogers's words suggested an Abenaki loss of more than two hundred victims, but he meant warriors and not women, children, and the elderly.[95]

Of course, Private Kirkwood's more accurate words have indicated a higher casualty number among the Abenaki than has been generally accepted by American historians, who had long simply dismissed any suggestion of a possible massacre. In the end, and as noted, the distinct possibility certainly existed that Rogers had not exaggerated Abenaki losses as long assumed. The exact number of Abenaki—warriors, women, and children—who died in cellars and lofts with the burning down of around sixty houses is not known. But when the total losses were calculated with those mostly noncombatant Abenaki who had been killed in the burning houses, the figure of dead increased much higher to a number actually very close to Rogers's figure of two hundred Abenaki fatalities.[96]

Agreeing with the views of Private Kirkwood—an honest Scotsman who faithfully reported what he had seen and known to have been truthful without worrying about repercussions from what he had written—about the larger extent of Abenaki losses than previously emphasized by writers and historians to minimize the possibilities of a massacre, one participant of the raid wrote in a letter not long after the attack that "out of between Two and Three Hundred People, old and young, not above Six made their Escape, besides about TWENTY taken Prisoners"—a large-scale massacre in the truest sense of the word.[97]

This estimation was almost certainly too high. But this higher figure was found penned in the diary of Ebenezer Dibble, who wrote that the "Indians that was kild 140 Savadgs [and] 6 Prisoners."[98] Corresponding with such accounts, Governor-General Pierre de Rigaud, the Marquis de Vaudreuil, wrote that "many Indians" were killed at St. Francis.[99]

Perhaps Sergeant Thompson Maxwell, who had advanced from the rank of private because of excellent past performances, said it best in regard to what really happened, with an honest accuracy not seen for more than two centuries after the end of the French and Indian War: "All warriors were out hunting [but mostly out in war parties elsewhere, and therefore St. Francis] was easy prey for us [as] we found only old men, children and squaws. Rogers ordered them, without discrimination to be put to death."[100]

With the town still burning while great clouds of smoke continued to rise, and thinking ahead as usual, Rogers desperately now needed timely information about the whereabouts of the absent Abenaki warriors and their movements. He therefore gained crucial intelligence from interrogating twenty prisoners, including the biracial sons of white chief Joseph-Louis Gill and his Abenaki wife, Marie-Jeanne. Rogers had smartly ordered some prisoners, especially those of mixed race, to be taken to secure timely information and to serve as hostages.

Rogers questioned Gill's two sons, Antoine and Xavier (or Sabattis), and two girls, who were the blood relatives of Eunice Williams. Eunice had been captured during the attack on Deerfield, Massachusetts, in 1704. Father Roubaud and Chief Gill, who acted as a go-between for his people and the France-born priest and now commanded the contingent of St. Francis warriors at Yamaska, had taught his sons well in regard to surviving a crisis situation. They had saved themselves by following Gill's wise instructions to fall to their knees before any English attackers, while shouting "quarter": a surprising development that completely shocked the would-be bearded white killers who had come all the way from Crown Point.[101]

To the surprise of everyone, five white captives were liberated. Even three Rangers were freed. Besides the three lucky Rangers, George Barnes (a New Hampshire soldier) and a Teutonic girl, who had been captured at German Flats situated along the Mohawk River and west of Schenectady, New York, were saved.[102]

To his credit, Rogers ordered no killing of the prisoners after he secured intelligence, benevolently releasing fourteen Abenaki captives. However, just in case he found himself in a tight spot, especially if surrounded at some point during the upcoming lengthy withdrawal all the way to New England, he kept his prize captures—Chief Gill's wife and two sons—for possible future negotiation. All four white captives (three Rangers and one Provincial), three Abenaki girls (including two of mixed race), and the Teutonic girl from German Flats were also to accompany the Rangers south. Clearly, any trace of white blood among the prisoners called not for death but for rescue and a return to white society.[103]

After having arrived from Trois-Rivières around midnight on October 4, after Rogers and his men had departed in a great hurry and as noted, a stunned Father Roubaud would finally get a chance to see his beloved St. Francis in daylight hours on the following morning. He described how "the surprise attack on the village of St. Francois [resulted in] the massacre and reduction of the village to ashes."[104] But, of course, Father Roubaud said nothing about how hundreds of English scalps had also been burned by the raiders to strip the Abenaki forever of their precious trophies, which was a great source of pride among the people.[105]

A SMALL PRICE TO PAY

The best and most accurate primary source material about the raid has indicated that there was a massacre and very little Abenaki resistance of any kind whatsoever on the early morning of October 4. After all, and almost unbelievably, in attacking the very center of the most formidable Native American ally of New France, Major Rogers lost only one man—a single Stockbridge Ranger "Wolf" named Samadagwis. And only one white soldier was seriously wounded, Captain Amos Ogden, who managed to keep his feet and persevere, despite his injuries: a lucky break because no wounded Rangers could be carried south over many miles of wilderness, including mountains covered in virgin timber.

During the combat, a half dozen other raiders were slightly wounded, including one Ranger who was shot by a warrior who had gallantly saved the life of an Abenaki girl, a terrified child, on the run in attempting to escape. The lack of serious losses among the attackers seemed little short of miraculous—the divine hand of Providence in the raiders' minds, which were so often biblically focused. Major Rogers must have been utterly astounded when his officers presented their oral reports to him about losses. Everything that had happened at St. Francis led to one inevitable conclusion: a massacre had taken place, and few warriors had been in the town to offer any kind of resistance.

In addition, no weapons or supplies of black powder were reported to have been captured. Although the entire town of St. Francis was burned to the ground, no hidden supplies of powder had exploded, like in the houses of the Indian village of Kittanning in Pennsylvania. During the September 8, 1756, attack on Kittanning, located around forty miles northeast of Pittsburgh, Pennsylvania, and the burning down of the village, numerous fiery explosions of hidden reserves of black powder had rocked the village. This development never happened at St. Francis, because Abenaki war parties were elsewhere, including one under Chief Gill. Of course, these absent warriors had taken weapons and black powder with them, thereby sparing Ranger lives on October 4 in another lucky break for Rogers and his men.

In consequence, the expected explosions of hidden powder reserves in the houses, especially in the cellars, did not materialize, surprising Rogers and his men. In striking contrast to the relatively quiet burning of St. Francis, when only terrifying screams of the unfortunate victims were heard, when Kittanning, located on the Allegheny River and containing its regular contingent of warriors, went up in flames, the victorious Pennsylvania militia were surprised when the "Indians had a Number of spare Arms in their Houses loaded, which went off in quick Succession, as the Fire came to them; the Quantities of Gun-Powder which had been stored in every House blew up from time to Time, Throwing some of the Bodies a great Height into the Air."[106]

Forgotten High Tally

However, the brutal massacre of mostly Abenaki noncombatants at St. Francis might well have ranked as one of the great slaughters of Native Americans in American frontier history, if the high estimates of high losses are accepted as fact. First and foremost, there was a great discrepancy between the total population of St. Francis, estimated by Father Roubaud to have been around 500 people, and the number of victims of the massacre, estimated at around 140 Abenaki, according to the best primary evidence, including reliable first-person accounts.

What happened to the other 350 or so Abenaki when Rogers struck? Quite simply and as mentioned, the vast majority of the residents, especially warriors, were not in St. Francis when Rogers attacked. How could this be, if St. Francis had been caught by surprise? Ironically, this difference in numbers between residents and victims has stemmed from the fact that one of Rogers's own men had warned the village deep in the night of October 3, probably after Rogers returned from his late-night reconnaissance at around 2:00 a.m.

During this cold period before the dawn, an exhausted Rogers might have catnapped like his soldiers and never noticed the departure and absence of Samadagwis, who had decided to embark on a mission of mercy. He was a Stockbridge Mohican warrior and Rogers's only fatality of the attack. Because this Stockbridge warrior had torn loyalties, since he was related to the people in this hybrid community, he had warned the Abenaki in person that they were about to be attacked by informing a young girl, whom he found just outside the Council House, which contained the adults engaged in dancing and other festivities throughout the night.

However, the tally of 160 Abenaki (140 dead and 20 prisoners taken because Rogers needed information about the strength and location of absent the war parties and the overall strategic situation, including with regard to Wolfe at Quebec) was correct: the adults among them had not believed the young girl due to her age and had stayed in St. Francis. But perhaps as many as 350 people had believed her and departed to find shelter a good distance away in the thickets of the Sibosek Pines, while Rogers and his men rested in the pine woodlands. Here, large numbers of Abenaki had escaped not only Rogers's attack but also discovery.[107]

Ironically, the true author (Major General Jeffery Amherst) of the massacre—Rogers was only obeying his superior's Crown Point–issued orders of September 13 like a good soldier—had attempted to safeguard his own lofty reputation from the inevitable criticism after what was certainly a war crime. Writing for posterity in his early bid to wash his hands of all responsibility and lay blame on Rogers, whom he had told, "Take your revenge," in his public orders (almost certainly the major general's private words at Crown Point headquarters on September 13 had been much different and even more severe), Amherst, the highest-ranking British officer of the Crown in North America, representative of King George II, and the symbol of Great Britain's power, early went to the considerable length of safeguarding his reputation from whatever might happen at St. Francis.

Learning accurate facts from a French officer under a "flag of truce," the general wrote in his journal on November 2, 1759, how the Gallic gentleman in a proper white uniform of Bourbon France "said M. Rogers Party had burnt the settlement of St. Francois, killed some Indians, women & children. I fancy he is mistaken about the women & children."[108]

It was significant that Amherst said nothing of the numbers of noncombatants who had been killed and only casually mentioned that "some" had been killed, suggesting that the total number had been insignificant, which was certainly not the case.[109] Of course, the reality of the overall situation was much different. Even in his September 13 orders to Rogers at Crown Point, Amherst had emphasized "Take your revenge"—the green light to Rogers and America's most hardened fighting men that played a large part in leading to a massacre that was as automatic and inevitable as the setting sun in the end.[110]

MASSACRE VIEWED AS RIGHTEOUS RETRIBUTION AND GOD'S WILL

The editors of English newspapers of God-fearing societies on both sides of the Atlantic faithfully reported the stern measures applied by Rogers and his raiders on the bloody morning of October 4, 1759. As could be expected, they stressed the most important moral reason that justified giving no quarter because the Abenaki fully deserved a cruel punishment, since "a just providence never design'd that those blood-thirsty Heathen should go down to the grave in peace."[111]

But in truth, and as noted, Rogers had unleashed the long-practiced method of total war long adapted by both sides during a brutal conflict in which the winner took all and there was no tomorrow—as there was no mercy, especially for the losers. Quite simply, it was a case of destroy or be destroyed, and this grim feature of a war without garlands or glory had been played out in full at St. Francis.

Ironically, the cagy Native Americans, masters of psychological warfare, had long excelled in part because of their stern warrior ethos and reliance on terrorism as devastating as it was lethal. These warriors had long relied on terror, especially giving no quarter, torturing captives, and disemboweling victims in the vain hope of demoralizing their hated enemy into abandoning the war effort. In this sense, Rogers had acted no differently when he and his men finally obtained the long-awaited opportunity to descend upon St. Francis with revenge in their eyes and hearts, delivering a stunning psychological blow in the hope of eliminating the will of the Abenaki to resist and leading them to abandon their longtime allegiance to New France.

However, as expected, and just as this war of terrorism had backfired to cause the settlers, especially the Scotch-Irish, to fight with greater determination, the same situation resulted from the surprise attack on St. Francis when the war had been brought to the Abenaki as never before. Now the

Abenaki were more determined to wreak their revenge, because nothing was more important to them than the motivational aspects of revenge, much as the Puritans had been obsessed with sin, which they had seen as personified in Native Americans, especially the ill-fated Pequot, who thus had to be destroyed.[112]

Nevertheless, and in brilliant fashion that defied all expectations and odds, Major Rogers had succeeded in his seemingly impossible mission that called for the complete destruction of St. Francis, as emphasized in Amherst's orders to deliver a devastating blow to the Abenaki, or "the enemy's Indian scoundrels," who had long "murdered women and children of all ages" across the frontier. Most important, Rogers had succeeded magnificently in his longtime personal ambition of doing "his utmost to humble that haughty nation" of New France with fire and sword by outsmarting and outwitting the top French leadership in not only Quebec and Montreal but also the garrison towns located in between Canada's two major cities.[113]

In a letter overflowing with a sense of pride in accomplishment and a distinct air of righteousness that was believed to have been heaven sent, like the burning of St. Francis, one of Rogers's soldiers described his elation in Rogers's having finally delivered his tactical masterstroke with ruthless efficiency: "This Nation of [Abenaki] Indians have always been at War with us, and have committed more cruel Barbarities on our poor People, than all the Rest of the Indian Nations in America; and it is the most happy Thing for them, as could have been done, as they cannot commit any more Cruelties."[114]

A true believer in the time-honored severity of Old Testament justice and demonstrating qualities of a homespun philosopher, one Provincial volunteer, Lieutenant Nathan Brigham of Massachusetts, never forgot the slaughter of American soldiers, including many Massachusetts men, after the surrender of ill-fated Fort William Henry. He wrote of the karma that had doomed St. Francis in the end: "And now for their own cruelty [and] In the same manner they must dy."[115]

Indeed, Major Rogers had mastered not only the best of Indian tactics and those of guerrilla, or irregular, warfare but also the core tenets of the modern concept of total war to bring total destruction to the enemy by literally wiping St. Francis off the map. Clearly, in the art of warfighting in what was basically the tenets of guerrilla warfare, Rogers was certainly ahead of his time, and the hard-hit people of St. Francis were the most qualified to reveal the fundamental truths about the major's having mastered these tactical and strategic realities born of the dual wilderness and frontier experience.[116] At long last, the reign of terror that had long been forthcoming from St. Francis had been ended by the rampaging Rogers, or so it seemed to the victors.[117]

Ominously Tolling Church Bells amid the Smoking Ruins

However, on the morning of October 4, something quite unsettling and ominous had unexpectedly happened that reminded the elated raiders that not all was well, and it involved the destruction of "the fine large Church," the most sizeable building in town and the center of Abenaki spiritual life for generations. This mission church had been long operated by the Jesuits at St. Francis, and they considered the Abenaki their own people. The Roman Catholic Church, especially at St. Francis, and Catholicism in general, in the words of one colonial, served as the dark heart of the "Tyranny, Perfidy and Cruelty of the Mongrel Race of French Papists and Indian Barbarians."[118]

As mentioned, and for such reasons, the Jesuit church had early become a primary target of Major Rogers because of its longtime role in inspiring Abenaki war parties to go forth on their hellish raids for nearly a century and because the church itself was decorated with the scalps of a good many settlers.[119] In the minds of Rogers's fighting men, the church's systematic destruction on this brutal morning in early autumn in Quebec represented a blow against "our cruel and crafty Enemy [who] are rushing on us from every Side, brandishing the Sword with insolence" and impunity.[120]

Even at the height of victory and Rogers's apotheosis on this bloody October morning, something strange and a bit unnerving to the major's more religious men had unexpectedly happened to seemingly mock the righteous retribution that had been unleased on St. Francis and its people with a savage vengeance and righteous bloodlust, if not sheer joy. Amid the flames, columns of dark smoke swirled high in the sky, and as the wooden walls of the house of God crackled, the bell in the wooden bell tower of the Catholic church had continued to ring.

Consequently, some superstitious Rangers, who believed fervently in the words of the Holy Bible, had taken this inexplicable development of the loud clanging bell of the church as a dark omen, even on a day when seemingly everything had gone right, according to Rogers's meticulous plan. Sounding the alarm that rang over the St. Francis River country in the hope of securing French assistance, while Abenaki women and children were still being consumed by the flames that engulfed the houses in a fiery hell, the church bell of the spiritual center of Catholicism had continued to loudly clang in a steady rhythm, while the church burned, before it toppled in fiery ruins with a loud crash. The ragged and emaciated Rangers felt a great deal of relief in knowing that this troublesome holy place, where successive Jesuit priests and missionaries had long exhorted the warriors to strike without mercy and to destroy every visible presence of a heretical religion, culture, and civilization, was no more.

Strict Ranger Protestants and Presbyterians, especially the Scotch-Irish from Ulster Province, north Ireland, saw something especially eerie and ominous in the steadily tolling bell of a wooden church engulfed in flames. Especially after the church had been defiled by long-haired Protestant Rangers in dirty buckskins with demonic looks, including men who were stained with the blood of their victims, some victors began to wonder whether the persistent ringing of the bell forecast impending doom for the boldest group of raiders in North America. Impending personal disaster had been likewise symbolically forecast for the doomed American volunteer Robert Jordan during the Spanish Civil War in Ernest Hemingway's classic 1940 novel *For Whom the Bell Tolls*.

Was the clanging of the church bell amid the roaring flames and plumes of smoke a manifestation of the avenging spirit of the Catholic saint Francis of Assisi now delivering a dark curse on those Protestant men who had destroyed the church and the entire missionary town named in his honor? Italy's St. Francis, the town's revered patron saint, had failed to protect this flock in the end as promised by the French Jesuits. Neither the patron saint nor Roman Catholicism had protected the slaughtered Abenaki women and children from Rogers's unleashed men, who were bent on revenge. Consequently, were the town's patron saint and the gods of war now plotting the Rangers' destruction in the days ahead, as some of Rogers's men no doubt feared?

And back in France at the cathedral of Chartres, a magnificent, twin-towered structure known as Our Lady of Chartres, whose construction in the French Gothic style began in 1220, the Abenaki were still considered the spiritual children of the French parishioners. Here, at Chartres, allegedly the veil of the Virgin Mary was kept as a sacred object by generations of French citizens. Therefore, Our Lady of Chartres had long meant something special to the people of St. Francis, despite its far distance from the wilds of Quebec. The canons of Chartres had donated the greatest prize of all, now stolen by Rangers: the solid-silver statue of the Virgin Mary, which was worth a small fortune, weighing ten pounds. Clearly, the Rangers were tempting not only the gods of war but also the Catholic God and saints on October 4.

More than a half century before, the French priests of the beautiful cathedral, which sat on a hilltop above the Eure River, had donated prized religious relics and ornaments, including the silver statue of the Virgin Mary, to the missionary church along the St. Francis River. Greedy Rangers, unmindful of the sacredness of these religious objects, stole whatever looked shiny and valuable, including the holy statue of solid silver. These Protestant transgressors of one of the holiest places in New France broke other sacred items when they desecrated the church.

Rogers's Protestant heretics in green coats, buckskins, and civilian clothing were enraged when inside the church, because they knew that its missionary Indians had been inspired from the pulpit to raid New England's settlements for years in the name of saving the true religion, which equated to destroying Protestant lives. As mentioned, silver and gold candlesticks, cloth-of-gold draperies, and an exquisite silk banner with life-sized painted portraits of Christ and the Virgin Mary, embroidered with silver and gold wire, were stolen. It is not known, but a Catholic Irish soldier might have taken some of these treasures to keep them out of Protestant hands.

Therefore, as some men feared, were St. Francis of Assisi or the ghosts of the dead Abenaki noncombatants now casting curses and bad luck on Rogers's men? Of course, no one knew, but some Rangers began to grow uneasy because of what had happened at St. Francis, especially the massacre of noncombatants and the church's destruction. Some of Rogers's men believed so, because the loud clanging rhythm of the tolling bell seemed to indicate as much, as if offering an eerie warning, while the town burned to the ground: an unnerving and strange, if not bizarre, development that seemed to ordain for the attackers a cruel fate in the days ahead, when the countryside would be swarming with angry Native Americans, Canadians, and French in pursuit.

After all, the enemy lusted for the opportunity to destroy the attackers, especially the famed Ranger chieftain who had led them to a remarkable victory that had defied all the odds and mocked the finest French military leadership. As a cruel fate would have it, the fear of the most superstitious men in Rogers's ranks was destined to prove only too true in the dark days ahead.[121]

Major Rogers and his men had gained a special dual revenge in their holy war against the so-called Papists and Barbarians, who had long ago created their unholy alliance against the Protestants to the south. As mentioned, the struggle of the major and his followers was very much a holy war in which they had now become as religiously oriented and single-minded as the French, Canadians, and Indians, who had long waged their own religious crusade in burning down Protestant churches across the frontier with a righteous Catholic delight. Robert Eastburn realized as much while a captive in Canada, including at Montreal, having seen his captors' almost fanatical hopes of spreading Catholicism by any means: "Prayers were put up in all the churches of Canada, and great processions made, in order to procure success to their arms [and] I saw the English standards (the melancholy trophy of victory) and the French rejoicing at our downfall."[122]

Even more, Rogers and his men realized that the prosperity and wealth that they found in this Indian missionary town in the middle of nowhere stemmed from the most ill gotten of gains: "our poor People's Scalps," in the words of a disgusted journalist of the *New-York Gazette*.[123]

The mysterious ringing of the church bell was almost certainly done by a novice or missionary who had been assigned to St. Francis in the absence of Father Roubaud, who was at Trois-Rivières, which was located on the fertile banks of the St. Lawrence just southwest of Quebec. A Ranger captured one French Jesuit man of God and led him out of the burning church with a rope around his neck like a cow going to the slaughter. But as noted, another French man of God perished in the flames of the collapsing church, after having refused all appeals to surrender.

Therefore, in Father Roubaud's absence, two men of God were at St. Francis when the attack had so suddenly descended upon the sleeping town. But to this day, the names of this captured Jesuit missionary and the Jesuit man of God who died in the flames are entirely unknown, partly because New France was tottering on the verge of collapse, and many official records and documentation were destined to be lost. However, given that St. Francis was the scene of a bloody massacre of mostly noncombatants, the capture of the French missionary sealed his fate, which was a cruel one.

Given that the French priests had long fueled the wrath of the Abenaki to attack and destroy the heretical Protestants along the frontier, the Rangers were in no mood to give mercy to a religious Frenchman. Consequently, this captured Jesuit from France was almost certainly killed, perhaps on Rogers's orders, especially if he believed that the French cleric was the infamous Father Roubaud. After all, and as mentioned, Roubaud had accompanied the warriors of the Abenaki war party that had played a leading role in committing the most infamous massacre of the French and Indian War at Fort William Henry.[124]

The raging fire had consumed not only the Roman Catholic church but also the precious holy relics that had not been stolen by the Rangers. However, as when killing a good many Abenaki that morning along the St. Francis River, the Rangers had been thorough, leaving few valuables behind in their frenzied search, when sheer greed dominated thoughts and actions. However, not everything of value was taken. One religious relic devoured by the flames was a silver shirt in a reliquary. The Rangers, for whatever reason, unlike the heavy silver statue of the Virgin Mary, had not taken this precious item. But the solid-silver statue, which had been donated by the good parishioners the cathedral of Chartres in faraway France as a gift to the Abenaki people to help bind the most unholy of alliances in the name of God, was stolen.[125]

The Jesuit mission church had been reduced to smoking ciders in short order. If he remembered the words from the Holy Bible when he had been a younger man while growing up in his parent's log cabin amid the Merrimack River country, then Rogers might have recalled how the ancient Jewish leader Joshua had led his fighters in the reduction of the hostile city of Ai. At that time, the Hebrew victors had watched with supreme satisfaction as "the smoke of the city ascended to heaven" and toward the one true God who had played the key role in having made a remarkable Jewish victory possible.[126]

As could be expected, Rogers was elated because he had fulfilled the great dream that had consumed him for so long. But there was no time for the young major to celebrate his greatest victory. The low temperatures of the early morning had already informed the keenly observant major that these Canadian days were now shorter, and winter was already on the way. He also knew that fall was briefer in Quebec than in New England. Like the flocks of honking Canadian geese flying high in the early autumnal skies hurriedly winging south in search of a warmer land, it was time for him and his men also to hurry south in a race against the inevitable arrival of much colder weather. Even more, it was now only a matter of time before the arrival of French, Abenaki, and Canadian pursuers, who were sure to come after the raiders, especially after they had spied the columns of black smoke towering in the blue skies above the devastated town.

For Major Rogers, the systematic elimination of the legendary center of countless Abenaki raids and the most infamous place of all to generations of frontier settlers was a high point not only in a military career but also in a most eventful life. Perhaps Rogers now realized as much, which might even have brought a slight sense of an emotional letdown, because a great goal at long last had been obtained. Most of all, Rogers heaved a sigh of relief, because the destruction of St. Francis represented the end of a dream that had lingered for too many years in his estimation, while hundreds of settlers had continued to be killed or taken captive.

A QUICK EXIT FROM THE CHARRED RUINS OF ST. FRANCIS

Knowing that no time should be wasted after the massive destruction had been unleashed in short order, Rogers hurriedly called his men together at around 6:45 a.m., while the dark clouds of smoke continued to rise over the smoldering ruins of St. Francis along with the sickening odor of burned Abenaki bodies that hung heavy in the autumn air. To the dirt-stained Rangers, it seemed almost like the soul of St. Francis had died and was streaming upward in the dense columns of black smoke, vanishing into the blue skies of early October.

In frantic haste, the major formed his men in a line at the head of town to restore discipline and count the final cost, after the orgy of killing and looting that had raged completely out of control. Rogers wrote, "When I paraded my detachment, I found I had Capt. [Amos] Ogden [of the New Jersey Blues with combat experience extending back to 1756 near the war's beginning] badly wounded in his body, but not so as to hinder him from doing his duty. I had also six men slightly wounded, and one Stockbridge Indian killed."[127]

And one of Rogers's men penned in a November 26, 1759, letter about the universal feelings that now dominated the ranks, "The Loss on our Side was one [Stockbridge] Indian killed and six men slightly wounded; besides

Capt. Ogden who was wounded in the Head, and a Ball went through his Body, and his Powder-horn shot from his Side in the Beginning of the Engagement; but it did not hinder him from doing his Duty, he took his Handkerchief and bound it round the Wound in his body; two or three Men being near him, asked him if he was wounded, he answered only scratched, and encouraged them on" during their ugly and messy, but highly effective, work of killing.

Most revealingly, this unexpected boon that cheered Rogers provided additional evidence of light resistance and that relatively few warriors had been in the town. Indeed, all of St. Francis had been "denuded" of fighting men to a surprising degree that had been unexpected. In the astonished words of one raider from a letter, "not above Six made their Escape" from a hell on earth on the bloody morning of October 4, 1759.[128] Like his comrades, especially those men who hailed from New England's frontier, he also delighted in "seeing the Town in ashes."[129]

Private Robert Kirkwood described the final preparations for exiting the smoking ruins of St. Francis with his comrades, who felt fortunate to have survived up to this point: "This being over [the town's complete destruction], we rendevoused [sic] at the place appointed [by Rogers], and to our happiness had not a man missing, only two or three a little hurt."[130] Another member of the expedition penned how besides Captain Ogden, the "Loss on our Side was one Indian [Samadagwis] killed and six men slightly wounded"—partly a testament to Rogers's tactical skill and leadership abilities from beginning to end.[131] Along with a Provincial soldier named George Barnes, who had been captured by the French in 1756, three extremely lucky Ranger prisoners now added much-needed manpower to Rogers's small command to make up for the slight losses.[132]

But the credit for such a one-sided success should not go completely to Rogers because he benefited immeasurably from commanding so many experienced fighting men, especially highly qualified and experienced fellow officers. Major Rogers gave little outward sign of his elation at the astounding success and the light losses because he knew by now that St. Francis's warriors were elsewhere and were sure to descend upon the town when they heard the terrible news. Then the enemy would be motivated by the hope of wreaking a terrible Abenaki revenge for the deaths of mothers, grandfathers, brothers, sisters, fathers, cousins, and close friends.

As could be expected, Rogers was extremely proud of his men, who had performed admirably since having departed Crown Point on September 13. In a letter, one of the raiders wrote of hearing the major emphasize with heartfelt sincerity how "he never saw a better Command of Officers and Men, and thinks no Party of Men ever deserved more [recognition and praise] for the Country Service, not only for their good Courage and Behavior, but [also] the Fatigues and Sufferings they have undergone."[133]

Of course, Rogers conveniently ignored the fact that his men were now loaded with plunder—religious relics from the church, long belts of wampum, and other valuable Indian goods—because he reasoned that they deserved the spoils of war after all they had endured since departing Crown Point three weeks before. By this time, the Rangers had already scampered back to the pine thickets to retrieve their packs, and these were crammed full of their ill-gotten gains, especially from the Roman Catholic church.

In addition, Rogers's men now carried a good many fresh scalps with pride in their grisly achievement, almost as if they were Abenaki warrior themselves on the warpath in New England: a classic example of how such vicious warfare has always succeeded in brutalizing and dehumanizing the average fighting man, regardless of side or cause and despite battling in the name of God and country. Rogers's success was so complete and one-sided that the attack had resulted in a greater than usual share of plunder because the town was a wealthy one.[134]

With few, if any, provisions left in leather haversacks, since most rations had been consumed during the arduous march from Missisquoi Bay, Major Rogers, in his own words, had already "ordered my people to take corn out of the [three] reserved houses for their subsistence home, there being no other provision there; and whilst they were loading themselves [with corn] I examined the prisoners and captives," who were huddled together and under guard.[135]

One of Rogers's hungry men scribbled in a letter, "After the Action was over, they supplied themselves with Corn, as there was no other Provisions to be found; their own being expended three Days before [October 1] they arrived at the Town."[136]

Significantly, Rogers now revealed yet another primary motivation for capturing St. Francis at all costs as a great deal was at stake in logistical terms alone. Now with their provisions at Missisquoi Bay for the return trip destroyed by the enemy along with the sixteen whaleboats, which the French believed heralded the raiders' end, Rogers had known that he had to overwhelm the town as quickly as possible, because he desperately needed a resupply of provisions to replace what already had been expended. If the Abenaki had set fire to the three wooden storehouses of corn, then Rogers and his men would have been without anything for the long return trip to the northernmost military post in the New England frontier, Fort Number Four, around two hundred miles to the south.

Fortunately, the parched corn (dried and hard on the cob) literally saved the day for Rogers's men in logistical terms by providing an immediate and steady source of food for an extended period, representing a significant success in securing a badly needed resupply for the return journey. After all, the harvested corn was light and easily carried by weary men during a lengthy journey south over rugged country. Because it was their "favorite trail food," known as *roheeheg*, the Abenaki warriors had long carried parched corn without the cobs and then pounded it into a flour during their long-distance raids south to hit the New England settlements to provide a reliable source of sustenance over an extended period. And, of course, this basic staple provided for the tribe during the harsh winters. When water was added to the ground cornmeal, it provided good nutrition and expanded in the stomach to feel like a full meal had been recently eaten.[137]

However, the parched corn taken from the three Abenaki storehouses on Rogers's orders had only limited nutritional value, which presented a serious problem in the long term. To reduce weight, because the useless corncobs (far more cob than corn) filled up packs and haversacks, the edible corn kernels should have been separated from the cobs. However, there was simply no time for such time-consuming procedures because enemy war parties were already preparing to concentrate on St. Francis in determined bids to thoroughly punish the raiders.

Instead, most of the filled packs and haversacks carried the weight of corncobs instead of corn kernels since they had not been separated by either the Abenaki or Rogers's men. Even worse, plunder also left less room in packs for food, with many soldiers (especially the greedy ones) not thinking ahead about simply staying alive in the wilderness. Generations of Abenaki at St. Francis had boiled corn kernels picked from parched corncobs by women for the best taste and nutritional value: something that Rogers should have ordered his men or the captives to do before moving out of St. Francis, if he had been able to learn as much from the Abenaki prisoners. Despite Rogers's extensive knowledge about the opposing warriors, he knew relatively little about the women and their chores, especially when it came to preparing meals and Abenaki foods that sustained warriors on long-distance raids.[138]

In addition, even the corncobs—which, of course, Rogers's men did not eat, because it was unthinkable when not starving, unlike when starving—would have provided some limited sustenance if they were ground up like the kernels and then added to the resulting meal to provide additional food, although much more diluted.[139]

In this regard, and like others whom Rogers had taken prisoner, white captive Jane Chandler (who was now more Abenaki than white by this time since she had been captured as a child) kept her Indian secret of survival, which was unknown to the Rangers, including the major, who seemingly knew everything else necessary for survival except this key knowledge of the resourceful Abenaki. For the upcoming journey to Fort Number Four far to the south, Chandler, unlike Rogers's men, smartly filled her Ranger pack or haversack with corn kernels without the heavy corncobs that took up too much of the limited space, a wise procedure that ensured a long-lasting supply of food for this savvy woman. She would then crush the corn kernels between rocks for a ground cornmeal that she ate for full nutritional value to keep her healthy in the weeks ahead, while Rangers around her, including strong men in their prime, starved to death.[140]

Unbeknownst to the Rangers, and as noted, this important nutritional knowledge about the proper way to utilize parched corn for survival during a lengthy trek was the key to explaining how Abenaki war parties had been able to pour south through the same corridor (primarily along the headwaters of the St. Francis River and then cross-country to the headwaters of the Connecticut River, which provided an avenue, or war trail, to attack New England's settlements) for lengthy periods without starving. As cruel fate would have it, dozens of Rogers's men would fall victim to starvation because they did not utilize parched corn like Jane Chandler.

As Major Rogers and his men noticed to their shock, Jane was not only totally acclimated to Abenaki life and culture because of her capture as a young child but also strikingly beautiful. The sight of the attractive Jane, the white beauty of St. Francis, reminded the men of the horrors of racial intermixing, but they looked at her with a bit of a lustful eye because of her attractiveness. In fact, Jane was an Abenaki devil in disguise, because her hatred toward Rangers was as deep at that of an experienced Abenaki warrior.

Rogers and his men, therefore, knew without a doubt that Jane would love nothing more than to stick a knife in the ribs of every Ranger and take his scalp to her immense satisfaction, if she gained the opportunity and could get away with it. Like other men, Second Lieutenant George Campbell, who had joined the Rangers in the spring of 1759, was struck by the seductiveness of Jane's blond and shapely beauty, which she knew how to use to her advantage. Almost as if partly under Jane's spell, which combined the feminine beauty of the Abenaki world with the white world, he wrote in his diary how she was "one of ye finest lookers I ever saw. A very sparkish Wench. Her Indian name was ye full moon, being full ye day she was bro't into ye town as an infant. Her savage mate was kill'd [and she is] like one of ye tribe."[141]

Along with the small group of other captives, including the German girl, who evidently still spoke German and had been captured in the Mohawk River Valley in 1757, and Chief Joseph-Louis Gill's wife and two sons, Jane was closely questioned by Rogers. With a healthy sex drive, like his men, Rogers could not help but also be dazzled by Jane's natural beauty, now in full blossom. However, Rogers was more focused on gaining accurate information, because his life and that of his small command depended on acquiring facts that had to be separated from the lies. As usual, the major adhered to Rule Number V from his wise axioms of ranging service: "If you have the good fortune to take any prisoners, keep them separate, till they are examined" thoroughly and in full.[142]

Another thoughtful individual who ensured his own survival was one especially savvy Ranger, who was thinking ahead in the frontier tradition. He took wise precautions for what was about to come because he was already expecting the worst and knowing that the corn supply was totally insufficient. Instead of filling his pack and haversack with too many useless corncobs with kernels intact—unfulfilling parched corn—to keep him alive in the days ahead like everyone else, he possessed other ideas about what was needed to stay alive.

Unlike his less experienced comrades, this veteran Ranger and frontiersman, who might have hailed from Rogers's Merrimack River Valley, wisely placed a sizeable clump of animal tallow—from either a deer or a moose, or possibly both—in the bottom of his leather knapsack. This invaluable large clump of bone tallow, which would prove a godsend to the resourceful Ranger in the weeks ahead, "supported him on the way home, while many, who had secured plunder, perished with hunger."[143]

Also prudently thinking ahead in regard to the long journey south toward their faraway homeland, other smart Rangers stole leather moccasins from the feet of dead warriors in anticipation of what lay before them, including an inevitable trek across formidable mountains, rivers, swamps, and streams. However, the majority of Rogers's men were more concerned with taking as much valuable plunder as possible, giving relatively little thought to the crucial need to replace their worn-out footwear when it was most needed at this time.[144]

At one house—almost certainly that of Chief Gill before it was torched with all the other residences—one Ranger found the personal papers of Captain James Johnson, who was the husband of St. Francis captive Susanna Johnson. He placed the papers in his pack and eventually returned them to a totally stunned Susanna at Fort Number Four after barely surviving the most harrowing ordeal of his life.[145]

Of course, and as noted, no time could be wasted when the billowing clouds of smoke from the town's burning had been seen far and wide, and this meant leaving the dead inhabitants—now scalped by Rogers's men, who cherished these grisly trophies like the Abenaki—exactly where they had fallen in the houses, in the dirt streets, and on the high riverbank. Other dead bodies, including the Abenaki children who had drowned while attempting to escape, were carried north with the river's current deeper into the heart of Canada.

But even if ample time had existed before Rogers ordered the march south, there would have been no burial of Abenaki, including the many charred bodies now lying in the smoking debris of the burned-down houses. After all, three-quarters of a century of Abenaki raids revealed not a single burial of a white victim by the hard-hitting raiders from the north. Unlike the Abenaki warriors, the Rangers did not mutilate the dead for ritualistic and spiritual reasons because those customs were not part of their European-based culture and society.

However, Rogers knew that the people of St. Francis, upon their return, would bury their dead in ritualistic fashion according to the ancient traditions of the Abenaki people. In Rogers's words, "The Indians generally bury their dead with great decency, and monuments over their graves. They deposit in the grave such things as the deceased had made the greatest use of, and been mo[st] attached to; as pipes, tobacco, bows, arrows, [so] that he may not be in want of any thing when he comes to the other country" forever.[146]

After the Rangers, Provincials, and British volunteers formed up in line for a final head count—only a single Stockbridge Ranger warrior had been killed—the vast majority of these men, tough and hardened veterans, felt little, if any, remorse or guilt for the destruction of St. Francis and its inhabitants. The victors felt like Major Rogers and the thousands of people of the frontier, because the people of St. Francis, in a biblical analogy based on the concept of divine justice, had been doomed since "a just providence never design'd that those bloodthirsty Heathen should go down to the grave in peace," in the words of a writer from a colonial newspaper.[147]

However, this overall situation had been a case of one atrocity inevitably leading to another and usually a more gruesome one, with no end in sight during the horrific cycle of extreme violence throughout the course of this cruel war. The relatives of the dead of St. Francis prayed for their God's wrath to descend upon the ruthless raiders, who had slaughtered without mercy, including women and children, in a massacre.

When not grieving for the lost relatives, the surviving Abenaki prayed for the raiders' destruction with the same passion that the people of New England had long wished for the destruction of St. Francis. For such reasons, in the dark days ahead, the creator of the universe and the gods of war were destined to seemingly conspire against the best efforts of Rogers and his men to survive on the long journey back to safety. Hereafter, everything would change when the fortunes of war turned against the major and his followers with a vengeance. Rogers's lucky streak was about to come to a crashing halt on what would become a journey in hell.

As in ancient times, perhaps the capricious gods had been angered after having bestowed such a sparkling success on young and brash Rogers until it had degenerated into an ugly massacre without any glory whatsoever. All in all, Rogers's unleashed soldiers had behaved like savages in eagerly scalping men, women, and children when their bloodlust had become uncontrollable. Indeed, in the harsh days ahead, during the upcoming long trek south that was destined to become a living nightmare to the conquerors of St. Francis, it was a cruel irony that one of the great prizes—bloody scalps according to the Ranger value system based on frontier customs—taken at St. Francis would be eaten (at least the remaining red flesh along the hairline) by Rangers facing the horrors of starvation in a lonely wilderness far from civilization.[148]

During the upcoming journey to New England, a most unusual source of protein would be utilized by one man after provisions ran out: three human heads were discovered in the knapsack of one Ranger to the horror of Sergeant David Evans, of Concord, New Hampshire. Evans began his Ranger career in in August 1756 and was promoted to sergeant in only six months because of his proven abilities. During his faithful term of service, Evans had never experienced anything remotely resembling what he was about to endure in a lengthy starvation period destined to curse the command and cull the ranks in the upcoming withdrawal.[149]

In the end, and in the ultimate irony, the ravenous eating of human flesh from these three severed heads was partly an inevitable consequence and by-product of sheer greed. Because so much plunder, including from the church, filled knapsacks, haversacks, and packs, not enough precious space was allotted for the parched corn. In some astonishment, Captain Ogden described how St. Francis was "very rich, and if they had not had to[o] far to travel, they might have brought home a thousand pounds worth of Indian goods [including wampum and] The people [of Rogers's command] did bring away considerable plunder."[150]

In total, and as noted, five English captives (including George Barnes, the Provincial soldier from Durham, New Hampshire, who had been captured near Lake George in 1756) were liberated, including three Rangers, whose identities are not known. Naturally, they provided the major with any information that they had gained about the enemy during their captivity, enlightening him about matters of importance.

Based on years of experience, Rogers knew how to extract information from captives in part by interrogating them separately and without cruelty, except for the usual threats, including death, which were not backed up by action in most cases. With a good understanding of French and the Algonquian languages, like Lieutenant George Turner, who was nearby to assist in interpretation because of his fluency in Indian languages, Rogers quickly learned from the prisoners what was necessary to enhance the chances for survival in the days ahead.

Jane Chandler had been adopted by Chief Joseph-Louis Gill, who called her "Wemeghil" in honor of the full moon seen when she first arrived at

St. Francis at the age of five. As noted, she was thoroughly acclimated into Abenaki life and culture by this time. Therefore, the captivating Jane was angered by the mere sight of the hated Rangers, especially after her warrior husband had been killed. Meanwhile, the spirits of the powder-streaked major and his men were lifted even higher when they learned from the captives that a longtime strategic goal had been achieved: mighty Quebec had finally fallen to young General James Wolfe on September 13.[151]

However, the major did not obtain only good news. Rogers learned from the hasty interrogation of prisoners, both white and Indian, what he already knew but was now additionally confirmed: "That a party of 300 French, and some Indians, were about four miles down the river below us; and that our boats were way-laid, which I had reason to believe was true, as they told the exact number, and the place where I left them at: that a party of 200 French and fifteen Indians, had, three days before I attacked the town, gone up the river Wigwam Martinic, supposing that was the place I intended to attack."[152]

In a letter, one of Rogers's men also described what had been learned from the prisoners: "that their [sixteen whale] Boats of the Lake [Champlain] were Way-laid by a large Number of French and Indians . . . and 215 Indians had been out three Days after us up Wigwamortineack [Wigwam Martinique], a River [and Abenaki mission village located] 10 miles on this side St. Francois."[153]

Meanwhile, to Amherst and his soldiers at Crown Point, it seemed as if Rogers and his men had disappeared from the face of the earth. Ironically, on the same day, October 4, as Rogers's most famous attack, a letter from a soldier at Crown Point was printed in the pages of the *Boston News-Letter*: "Major Rogers is gone out with 207 men, towards Montreal; but is not return'd as yet & what success he may have, is yet unknown" to the army.[154] More and more soldiers in Amherst's army never expected to see Rogers and his Rangers ever again. However, they had underestimated the resourcefulness and ingenuity of Major Rogers, just like the French leadership, which had early thought and assumed that he and his command would be easily destroyed.

DIVIDING THE COMMAND BEFORE DEPARTING ST. FRANCIS

Striking like a bombshell, this shocking information gained from the captives about large numbers of a revenge-seeking enemy on the move in pursuit was indeed the most alarming possible news that Rogers could have received. Of course, such timely intelligence called for an immediate exit from the ruined village, even sooner than originally planned by the major. In a hurry, therefore, Rogers called together his officers "to consult the safety of our return, who were of opinion there was of no other way for us to return with safety, but by No. 4 [today's Charlestown, New Hampshire, on the east bank of the] Connecticut River."[155]

In the major's own words, which revealed his customary egalitarian command style in the frontier democratic tradition, "A council of war now concluded that no other course remained for us than to return by [the] Connecticut river to [Fort] Number Four."[156]

As mentioned, and in truth, Rogers's command had been too small for the required mission in the first place, although it had proved astoundingly successful. But the smallness of the task force now increased the danger to new levels. Ironically, as ordered by Major General Amherst, Captain Stark and two hundred Rangers had recently cut a road through the wilderness east from Crown Point to Fort Number Four on the Connecticut River, which had reduced the number of available Rangers for the expedition but also allowed the Provincial and British Regular volunteers in fill the gap in Rogers's task force: thirty-seven men and twenty-one men, respectively.[157]

While the columns of black smoke were pushed by a slight breeze sweeping off the river and continued to tower upward to darken the sky above the town's ruins, Private Robert Kirkwood described how "we then held another council, and it was agreed for our mutual safety, to divide into three parties and so make the best of our way to the English settlement, and as it happened I was one of Rogers's party consisting of 25 men."[158] In a rare letter, another participant in Rogers's masterstroke deep in Quebec wrote about how, with the alarming news gained about the size and nearness of the enemy, "our People was obliged to return by Way of [Fort] Number Four in Connecticut."[159]

Most important, Rogers continued to wisely follow his own Rule Number V for effective ranging service and survival when deep in enemy territory, which now applied to the upcoming withdrawal: "In your return take a different route from that in which you went out, that you may the better discover any party in your rear, and have an opportunity, if their strength be superior to yours, to alter your course, or disperse, as circumstances may require."[160]

At a time when the packs and haversacks of the men were bulging, their leather seams nearly bursting, Rogers planned to march southeast up the St. Francis River and along a course where the river gradually narrowed. This long route of retreat—a daunting distance of more than two hundred miles as the crow flies—all the way to Fort Number Four was almost an automatic decision that the tactically flexible Rogers had first decided upon when the two Stockbridge warriors had told him of the destruction of the whaleboats and provisions at Missisquoi Bay. The wisdom of this decision was reconfirmed by what he learned from his prisoners. This route—up the gradually narrowing St. Francis River to Lake Memphremagog, then south, down the headwaters of the Connecticut River—was basically an Abenaki war trail that led to the New England settlements. Hence, it was well known to Indians and whites, including Rogers.[161]

Clearly, Major Rogers had made the wisest possible decision, which was relatively easy because there was no other choice except to surrender to the French, which, of course, was unthinkable and the antithesis of his credo and ethos as commander of the Rangers. After all, Rogers fully realized that this had long been the easiest natural route for generations of Abenaki warriors to trek south to strike the New England settlements.[162]

Taking no chances and wasting no precious time while the smell of smoke and burnt flesh hung heavy in the air and over what had become a river of death, Rogers hurriedly divided the command into three sections in the open at the town's head: a smart division of force to avoid complete destruction if an ambush was sprung during the immediate push south, because he believed that the enemy might well have set up a blocking force at some point farther up the St. Francis, which descended from higher ground to the southeast during its journey to the St. Lawrence. Later, when Rogers felt that they were safely beyond the most immediate danger, he then prudently planned to reunite his command, but he would later again divide it into smaller parties at Lake Memphremagog to enhance the overall chances of success in the search for food.[163]

Initially dividing the command for the departure from the destroyed village, after sending out flankers and scouts, was something that Rogers had learned from the Native American war parties that had long struck the New England settlements: "breaking up into small parties . . . was their general practice," which guaranteed a safer withdrawal during the return north to their distant homeland, including St. Francis.[164]

As noted, Major Rogers could not afford to make a single mistake at this crucial stage of an expedition that had already been successful beyond expectations, because any misstep might prove fatal to the entire command. He had been incredibly lucky in having not met with any serious opposition at any point during the expedition. Even more, Rogers had profited immensely from the mistakes of his enemies, while having consistently outwitted an experienced opponent in his home territory. Indeed, Governor-General Vaudreuil had played the leading role in formulating the ad hoc French strategy of catching and eliminating the audacious raiders: an overly optimistic plan that had been based on the erroneous concept that Rogers would return by the same route and allow himself to be ambushed where he had left his whaleboats at Missisquoi Bay and along the Yamaska River. Here, on the Yamaska River, less than ten miles southwest of St. Francis, Chief Gill and his Abenaki warriors were waiting in vain to unleash an ambush in the hope of ending Rogers's impressive career. Consequently, by October 4, and as mentioned, "St. Francis had been stripped of [its last] manpower in the misguided bid to ambush the raiders en route to their target."[165]

When informed of the town's destruction by five wounded Abenaki warriors who had escaped Rogers's attack, during a stunning scene in his palatial office at his Montreal headquarters, Vaudreuil believed that a larger force from Amherst's army was on the loose and perhaps now heading northeast and moving toward Trois-Rivières and Quebec. He therefore dispatched additional troops to intercept the expected raiders to eliminate that possibility. But Rogers and his men would be moving in the opposite direction—southeast and not north as the enemy expected.

The French had created a clever trap for Rogers if he had decided to continue north and all the way to the St. Lawrence to raid the Canadian settlements in the St. Lawrence River Valley as ordered by Major General Amherst in an outrageous example of excessive ambition and mission overstretch. However, the planned French ambushes would never be sprung, because Rogers was sufficiently wise to have decided to move in the opposite direction and contrary to the orders that he had received at Crown Point from the overreaching major general.[166]

Clearly, Major Rogers had repeatedly outsmarted his opponent and succeeded in his mission against the odds in one of the most amazing military feats of the French and Indian War and in the annals of American military history. It was no wonder that the American editor of one colonial newspaper, long before the raid on St. Francis but in a truism that now applied more than ever before, although the reaped glory was certainly grim, wrote, "The brave Rogers is acquiring Glory [and] recovering the sunken Reputation of his Country."[167]

Worried about the ominous signs and dark clouds on the horizon, indicating the arrival of a cold rain before nightfall on October 4, Rogers hoped that his good luck—always a quality of a good commander who knew how to win victories and survive against the odds—would somehow hold during the long trek that would take them, if all went according to plan, all the way to Fort Number Four on the northern New England frontier: more than two hundred miles away through an untamed and sprawling wilderness, because these young men and boys, like Rogers, in the ranks still believed that the impossible could be achieved.[168]

CHAPTER EIGHT

The Long Retreat That
Became a Living Nightmare

MAJOR ROGERS KNEW THAT TIME WAS NOT ONLY NOW PRECIOUS BUT ALSO absolutely critical because moving his command at a fast pace now equated to survival. To Rogers, nothing was more important than the time factor, because it meant the difference between life and death now that the enemy was all around him and fully alerted.

From the prisoners and the columns of black smoke swirling up from the destroyed town, the major knew that pursuers were on the way and eager to slaughter Rangers far from all support and reinforcements. Rogers realized that his precise position was pinpointed with a fatal exactness when the rattling of gunfire from nearly 150 muskets first erupted inside the town and then columns of black smoke rolled up into the clear skies over the St. Francis River country and St. Lawrence River country just to the north. All of Rogers's past experiences and well-honed instincts had taught him the hard lesson that he needed to depart the scene of a massacre and the total destruction of a major Native American town in the heart of New France as soon as possible.

At last, after all the packs and knapsacks were loaded full, Rogers ordered his men to move out of the destroyed town. One of the major's soldiers penned in a November 26, 1759, letter that with all of St. Francis now "in ashes, about 11 o'Clock, they set out on their Return back" to civilization with full packs to begin the most ill-fated and costly march in the history of the Rangers of more than two hundred miles. With his haversack, like those of Rogers's other men, crammed full of parched corn on the cob taken from the three Abenaki corn storehouses before they went up in flames like every-

454

thing else in St. Francis, Private Kirkwood wrote about what played out when they shortly intercepted a group of Abenaki when least expected: "We set out immediately on our journey for New-England, and in the evening, fell in with four Indians and a Squaw, loaded with provisions from St. Fransway; we dispatched the four Indians, but spared the Squaw."[1] While Rogers led his command southeast up the shallow valley of the St. Francis River to follow the watercourse, he was most fortunate. He keenly sensed that an "extensive encirclement" had been cleverly orchestrated around him by the French without them ever imagining that he was now on the move southeastward at a rapid pace and farther away from their traps.[2]

However, after three weeks of the most arduous possible service in simply having gained an advanced position to strike St. Francis, even greater and more dangerous challenges lay ahead. The young men and boys of Rogers's command had already suffered for an extended period with stoic fortitude, but the surviving Rangers, Britons, and Provincials believed that they could endure the next great challenge—a dangerous assumption that was entirely illusory. In the end, this significant amount of suffering for months by Rogers's jaded warriors revealed in full that they were "Men of Constitutions like Lions."[3]

What now lay before Rogers was a vast expanse of uncharted wilderness that spanned south for more than two hundred miles. But the New Hampshire major from the frontier knew something about this wild region and its trails, both Abenaki and game paths, which were often one and the same, that cut through the vast expanse of the dense hardwood forests. He knew that these old trails, established by traders, explorers, trappers, war parties, and missionaries and existing for as long as anyone could remember, would lead him south.

Therefore, Rogers was relatively familiar with his escape route—the same one that he had intended to use for his planned 1756 advance on and retreat from St. Francis with the same mission of destroying the town if Lord Loudoun had given him permission—and the general lay of the land all the way to Fort Number Four on the Connecticut River. Also, thanks to Captain John Starks's detailed descriptions, including his hand-drawn map, because he had been taken north as a prisoner along this same route in 1752, Rogers had a distinct advantage during the withdrawal in the days ahead. However, and as noted, this new journey from St. Francis to Fort Number Four was more than two hundred miles as the crow flies and through some of the most rugged territory ever seen by the Rangers.

With some confidence, because of his general familiarity with the wild region so far north of Fort Number Four, therefore, Rogers led his men, including the handful of walking wounded, with confidence through the heavily timbered north bank of the St. Francis. Moving at a good pace, the trekkers, with packs and knapsacks heavy with parched corncobs and all kinds of loot, ascended the generally straight course up the river that gradually began narrower and shallower, while pushing southeastward toward its headwaters for what would be a total of nine torturous days.

Facing a stern challenge beyond his wildest dreams in the weeks ahead, Rogers hoped to reach Fort Number Four on the Connecticut River before his small task force was overwhelmed by a good many angry Abenaki, Canadian, and French pursuers. Warriors had long moved along this same route, following the clear waters of the St. Francis and then the Connecticut River south through a virgin wilderness. As mentioned, one of the warriors' favorite targets had been the northwestern Massachusetts town of Deerfield. The descendants of Deerfield's victims included war-hardened men who now served under Rogers, and they had never forgotten that awful winter day. Sergeant Martin Severance, age forty-one, was one of these Rangers who carried the nightmarish legacy of the Deerfield massacre with them to St. Francis and back, having lost relatives. Deerfield had been struck a half dozen times in the 1690s, before the most famous attack on the ill-fated town on February 29, 1703.

Moving briskly through the tall trees with sharp-eyed flankers and scouts out on higher ground to avoid ambush, Rogers led his party farther up the St. Francis and its narrow valley amid a pristine wilderness that he had never seen before. As fate would have it, the trek was made miserable for the men in the ranks by the arrival of a bone-chilling rain and by extreme cold at night and heat in daytime. Rogers continued to lead his diminutive task force swiftly in a southeast direction, following the river's course, while the land gradually rose higher along the St. Francis.

All the while, Rogers kept everyone going at a rapid pace, knowing full well that he had stirred up a hornet's nest by razing the legendary Abenaki town, which the French, whose legendary pride was now at stake, had long considered untouchable. Already a large number of Canadians, Indians, and

French were in rapid pursuit and eager to run down the raiders. Experienced members of La Marine were now among revenge-seeking pursuers under Major Jean-Daniel Dumas, who had reached the ruins of St. Francis with sixty Canadians, then linked with surviving Abenaki warriors from Trois-Rivières on October 5. Dumas was a hero of the July 1755 destruction of General Edward Braddock's army near the forks of the Ohio. By this time, he was one of the most talented, hard-hitting Canadian partisans and the respected leader of the tough French fighting men of La Marine. He had recently proven his value during the siege of Quebec.

Second in command of this pursuing task force was Captain-Major Degannes (de Ganes). He was the adjutant of the Trois-Rivières garrison and led nineteen French Regulars and thirty-three Canadian militiamen. The St. Francis Abenaki under Chief Joseph-Louis Gill, who had been waiting in vain to ambush Rogers on the Yamaska, also joined the pursuit after they had returned to the devastated town on the St. Francis and been thoroughly stunned by what they saw—the charred remains of inhabitants and the embers of the houses, church, and Council House. Last but not least, after having reached the town late on October 4, Father Roubaud shortly also led his own band of Abenaki southeast along the river trail in pursuit, after having spent two days in galvanizing his scattered warriors in the hope of delivering his own nasty brand of holy retribution.

With flintlock muskets on shoulders and a jaunty step, Rogers's men had already hurriedly passed the relatively shallow place where they had crossed the St. Francis on October 3. More than four thousand miles away from his native Scotland, which he wondered whether he would ever see again, Private Kirkwood wrote, "We marched very hard for four days, knowing well that we would have all the French and Indians in the country after us, when it should come to their knowledge that we had destroyed St. Fransway. We however made so good out of the start we had got, that none ever came up with us, tho' we learned they were upon the pursuit" and on Rogers's tracks.

Finally, at the forks of the Magog River, which drained Lake Memphremagog in the St. Francis River watershed, situated southeast of St. Francis and northwest of the headwaters of the Connecticut River, Rogers held a commander's conference with the leaders of all three detachments, or columns, which had reunited by this time. Here, Rogers and his top lieutenants debated the increasingly desperate situation, after the supplies of corn taken from the three storehouses had been mostly consumed by their men to leave empty haversacks and packs except for the plunder, especially from the Roman Catholic church.[4]

In fact, most corn had been eagerly eaten by October 12, and many of Rogers's men were already in bad overall shape. On October 12, eight days after the attack on St. Francis, Second Lieutenant George Campbell described the lengthy withdrawal in his diary, writing, "All parties first cross'd ye Saint Francois R[iver] to ye west [or south] shore before parting [in groups after another division of force], as Major Rogers wanted us all intact after fording ye river. Ye detachments['] spirits up as they now imagine they will find sufficient game, albeit Major Rogers countenance reveals ye anxiety he suffers at dividing his command. I daresay I must concur with him as he has been our sustaining strength for so long & I have apprehensions of finding our way thru this wilderness without him."[5]

But, in fact, this timely division in force on the cold morning of October 12 was necessary because Rogers's men were facing the grim prospect of starvation, since the supplies of parched corn had been consumed so rapidly, long before anyone expected. Therefore, in total, Rogers's troops divided into eleven groups consisting of a little more than a dozen men each. These separate parties were headed by the best leaders in the command: Captain Joseph Wait, Lieutenants William James Dunbar, George Campbell, James Turner, Jacob Farrington, Abernethy Cargill, Jenkins, and William "Bill" Hendrick Phillips, Ensign Elias Avery, and Sergeants Benjamin Bradley, John Evans, and Stephen Hoit.[6]

For his own group of around twenty-five men, most likely the largest contingent about to go their own way in the uncharted wilderness, Rogers "took with him the Poorest of the Men [the sick, lame, and injured, including the wounded Captain Amos Ogden, who gamely ignored his injuries to somehow keep up with the command], to supply and support them himself" in his usual fatherly way, which had long caused him to be idolized by his men.[7]

Reasoning that a wider separation of groups taking different routes would confuse the pursuers and increase the chances for finding food over an extended area, Rogers assigned three groups, under Captain Wait, Ensign Avery, and Lieutenant Jenkins of Massachusetts, to take the most direct route to Crown Point, while the other groups continued south in the hope of reaching Fort Number Four on the east side of the Green Mountains and on the Connecticut River's east bank.[8]

Quite correctly, Rogers reasoned that the key to his men's survival lay in taking different routes through the wilderness largely devoid of game, including two well-worn Abenaki war trails that continued all the way south to the New England settlements. One of these paths led southeast to the Connecticut River from the waters of the St. Francis River, and the other led south to the Connecticut River country. But the inevitable choice of taking well-established Abenaki war paths that followed the easiest terrain, including ridgetops, was risky, because these well-known avenues would be taken by the eager pursuers of Rogers's command.[9]

With the colder rains of a dying autumn pouring down with more intensity on this rugged land that seemed to have no end, Ensign Avery's contingent was the first to encounter serious trouble on October 14. By this time, Avery's men had fallen upon Rogers's tracks heading straight south across rugged country toward the Wells River and the Connecticut River country, because the major had smartly decided to stay off the main Abenaki war trails. However, as cruel fate would have it, the highly effective team of Dumas and Degannes, who had force-marched their men—with Indian scouts out in front—in following Ranger moccasin tracks, caught up with the raiders under Avery only two days after the command's separation. Not fooled by Rogers's decision to divide his command, Dumas had wisely dispatched an Abenaki war party to follow the tracks of Ensign Avery's party, while he and the main body continued to track the companies that had taken the old Abenaki war trail that led southwestward.

These well-armed Abenaki warriors, eager to avenge the loss of their beloved hometown, knew this area's shortcuts and easier routes through the wilderness, which were unknown to Rogers and his men. In addition, the stamina and energy of the weary members of Avery's party, including half a dozen Connecticut men from Colonel Eleazar Fitch's Third Connecticut Regiment and three Rangers (Jacob or Daniel Lee, Sergeant James Ballard, and John Hewit) who served as guides, had dropped to a new low. Meanwhile, the pursuing French, Indians, and Canadians were invigorated by the prospect of catching up with Rogers's men and unleashing their own brutal brand of justice.[10]

As mentioned, in a smart tactical decision, Dumas and Degannes had divided their forces when their expert Abenaki scouts first distinguished the moccasin tracks of members of Rogers's command, after it had divided in search of food on the premise that small parties were more likely to find game in a land strangely devoid of game. Unfortunately for Ensign Avery and his men, the majority of pursuers under Degannes followed them closely in their unbridled lust to deliver a punishing blow, while the other section, with a lesser number of pursuers, including revenge-seeking Abenaki from St. Francis, under Major Dumas, followed the footprints of the Dunbar-Turner contingent over the rugged terrain at a brisk pace.

Ironically, Ensign Avery's party was so weakened by having lived for the past five days on beech leaves and mushrooms that its exhausted members were lying helpless on the ground when surprised by the St. Francis Abenaki. The warriors suddenly descended upon the famished raiders with muskets ready to blast away at point-blank range. After having received the surprise of their lives, seven unfortunate men were immediately stripped of their uniforms and tied to trees by the gleeful warriors. Fortunately, Ensign Avery and several others had been out hunting for game at this time, while the unguarded bivouac area was easily surprised by Degannes's eager pursuers.

The Abenaki warriors flew into a rage when they saw the blue Scottish bonnets and short green coats of the Rangers, knowing that it was Rogers who had destroyed their homes and perhaps families, while they had been away serving with the French to protect their sacred homeland. Evidently believed by the Abenaki to be the experienced leader of this band of men, Sergeant Ballard was the first victim. While lashed to the tree, he was slashed with a flurry of scalping knives, screaming in pain until he died. As could be expected under the circumstances, the six captives, who felt fortunate that they had not suffered Ballard's tragic fate, were treated roughly when they were eventually marched back to what little remained of St. Francis.

Fearing their fate once they reached St. Francis, Rangers Lee and Hewit managed to escape that night in a stroke of luck. Then, also making a fortunate break, Ensign Avery and his two comrades eventually joined Rogers's contingent. Both were truly miraculous escapes from a certain death if the men had been taken to St. Francis. For whatever reason, but most likely to collect a nice ransom, Sergeant Moses Jones, a Connecticut Provincial of Colonel Fitch's regiment, was not tortured and killed. After a harrowing experience, he was eventually exchanged and lived to tell a remarkable tale of survival on the brink.[11]

In his diary, one Frenchman recorded the tragic fate of Rogers's men who were taken by the Abenaki to St. Francis, "where some of them fell a victim to the fury of the Indian women, notwithstanding the efforts the Canadians could make to save them."[12] Corporal Frederick Curtiss recorded the tragic fate of five of Rogers's men who were escorted back to the scene of a wartime atrocity. Describing the final ordeal, he watched as the Abenaki warriors "went about building their Canoes which was the last place that I saw my fellow prisoners Excepting Moses Jones, as they went off [in] one Canoe Load after another, ours was the Last at the End of five days we got Back again to St. Francis at night having lived nine days on mushrooms and Beech leaves. These prisoners that was Carryed in the day Time was killed" at St. Francis.[13]

Major Rogers described the overall situation after having departed St. Francis at a rapid pace because he knew that an incensed French leadership was determined to catch and punish the raiders:

> *The detachment [now] marched in a body eight days upon that course [south], and, when provisions became scarce, near Memphremagog lake, it was divided into companies [in search of food and to increase better chances for hunting], with proper guides to each, and directed to assemble at the mouth of Ammonoosue river, as I expected to find provisions there for our relief. Two days after our separation, Ensign Elias Avery, of Fitch's [Connecticut] regiment, with his party, fell upon my track, and followed in my rear. The enemy fell upon them, and took seven prisoners, two of whom escaped, and joined me the next morning. Avery and his men soon afterward came up with us, and we proceeded to the Coos intervales [sic], where I left them under the orders of Lieutenant [William] Grant.[14]*

Of course, Rogers was referring to the Lower Coos Meadows.

Providing a far more detailed account than Rogers of the first disaster that befell the sojourners in the wilderness in regard to Ensign Avery's contingent, Frederick Curtiss described the living nightmare of the lengthy journey from St. Francis:

> *After nine days travail in an unknown Wilderness [we] were at the close of the Ninth Day Surprised by a party of Indians about Twenty or Thirty in number*

that had pursued us & watching an opportunity when we were Resting our Selves being much Enfeebled by travail & destitute of provision save mushrooms & Beach [sic] Leaves for four or five days then past [and] Came upon us unperceived till within a few foot of us. Some with their guns presented while others Seised [sic] upon us that we had no opportunity for defense or flight & So made us all prisoners [including Sergeant Moses Jones, Lee, Hewit, and Corporal Frederick Curtiss of Fitch's Regiment and Canterbury, Connecticut] Stript us of our Cloathes & tyed [sic] us to trees save one Ballard whom after binding they stabb'd & killed, afterwards they loosed us from ye tree & carryed [sic] us about two mile: Camped for that night. Two of ye prisoners Escaped vis. Hewet & Lee. The rest of us was Carryed [sic] back & we travail'd together or in Light ye next Day [and eventually] at the End of five days we got Back again to St. Francis at night, having lived nine days on mushrooms and Beach [sic] leaves. These prisoners that was Carryed [sic] in the day Time was killed outright [by a horde of enraged Abenaki women and] five of whom Lay there dead on the Ground [where Rogers had recently won his sparkling success on the banks of the St. Francis River].[15]

As if the lack of provisions and omnipresent dangers were not enough, Rogers wrote, "it [was] impossible to describe the dejected and miserable condition of the [men as they trekked] so long [during a nightmarish] march, over rocky, barren mountains, and through deep swamps."[16]

While most of Ensign Avery's party was fortunate to be taken prisoner instead of being massacred in the initial disaster, the worst was yet to come. After having decided to take the southeastern route to the Connecticut River country, Lieutenant William James Dunbar and Second Lieutenant George Turner's contingent of eighteen men was not so lucky. More than one hundred of the enemy under Major Dumas wiped out most of this contingent of excellent fighting men on fateful October 15. This forlorn party of Rogers's men had followed the clear waters of the north-flowing Coaticook (from the Abenaki word *Koatikeku*) River, east of the Magog River and south of today's Sherbrooke, Quebec, where the St. Francis and Coaticook Rivers intersected, to its spring-fed source at Coaticook Pond.

Here, deep in the woodlands, Dumas sprang his clever ambush at dusk amid the thick underbrush of the swamp at the pond's southern end, which was surrounded by dense clumps of evergreens. In an unmapped wilderness area of southern Quebec, southeast of St. Francis, the next disaster befell the men who were now only trying to get home and had no more fighting on their minds.

Despite making a heroic last stand against the odds and cutting down a number of attackers, the men of Turner and Dunbar's command of Rangers and General Thomas Gage's Britons of the 80th Light Infantry never had a chance against so many veteran Canadians, French, and St. Francis Abenaki under the leadership of revenge-seeking Gill, the white chief of the community that was no more. An infuriated Gill had ample good reason to want to destroy the enemy to the last man, because Rogers had taken his two sons, Antoine and Xavier (or Sabattis), and his own wife, Marie-Jeanne, as hostages during the long withdrawal toward New England.

During this brutal showdown in the unmapped swamps in the wilderness, the badly outnumbered defenders were shortly surrounded by a throng of attackers who wanted nothing more than to take Ranger scalps. Vicious hand-to-hand combat erupted in the heavy underbrush at the pond's southern end, with the Rangers fighting desperately for their lives in a no-quarter battle to the bitter end. Lieutenant Dunbar, who had volunteered from General Thomas Gage's light infantry regiment, and seven of his men were slaughtered and scalped by the victors. After the massacre in the blood-stained swamp in the middle of nowhere, the mangled remains of the victims washed down with the slow-moving current of the Pherrins River after their bodies, without scalps, had been contemptuously thrown into the water.

It is not known, but the possibility does exist that some men, who had been wounded, were scalped alive and then hurled into the water to suffer slow, agonizing deaths by the killers. Meanwhile, the remaining men of the Dunbar-Turner band escaped Chief Gill and his lethal warriors, including a wounded Lieutenant James Turner, who managed to slip away through the underbrush. However, three wounded privates were captured and taken to St. Francis, "where they were butchered with the two captives from Ensign Avery's party."[17]

Despite managing to escape through the thick clumps of evergreens that bordered the swamp and provided a screen, Lieutenant Turner met a most unkind fate in the end. As Second Lieutenant George Campbell recorded still another horror in his diary, "Jane [Chandler] ye [white] captive who escap'd found Turner wounded in ye hills. She nurs'd him to health. They hid out in a hidden gulch [and] They had a grand time sparking [as] I believe Turner had a liking for her, & she him, tho 'tis hard to believe, she was such a savage ungrateful Lass. Ye Witch had told this & how she had poisn'd Turner with Toadstools."[18]

Fortunate to have survived the ambush, although some men were wounded when they had slipped away from their potential killers, who were in a frenzy to gain more Ranger scalps, Sergeant Robert Lewis's small group ran straight into a different kind of danger that was completely unanticipated. In his diary, Second Lieutenant George Campbell described the nightmarish scenario that resulted in the loss of additional Ranger lives. When the party under the capable Sergeant "Bob" Lewis "shot a Moose near a River but it disappear'd in ye woods & they were to [*sic*] weak to track it, except 3 Rangers who came upon ye Moose being attack'd by wolves who turn'd on ye 3 Rangers & kill'd one of them & mortally wd. [and the] other 2 who crawled to Lewis where they died."[19]

Ironically, "Wolves" was the traditional nickname of the Stockbridge Ranger warriors, who were proud of their Mohegan heritage and culture. However, there were no friendly warriors available from western Massachusetts to save the three white Rangers, who discovered that hell itself lurked in the form of these formidable beasts of prey—the top predators of the forests. Like the Abenaki, the wolves were natural killers, especially the alpha males or the leaders of the pack, in this pristine wilderness. In one of the great ironies of the famous raid on St. Francis in another forgotten tragedy, the hungry wolves took more Ranger lives than the defenders of St. Francis on October 4.[20]

Leading the way, Rogers and his party were more fortunate than the Ensign Avery's and Dunbar and Turner's desperate men, who were only attempting to reach safety and eventually home. While some Abenaki warriors hurried their prisoners to St. Francis, Major Dumas—now knowing that the raiders had split up into small groups, making them even more vulnerable, and that they were so weak as to be almost unable to defend themselves—was even more determined to wipe out his exhausted prey. Like every other French commander, Dumas, of course, especially wanted to run down Major Rogers and his small contingent, which was in equally bad shape as the other groups of starving men at this time.

Like a pack of hungry wolves fast on the blood trail in the snow of a gut-shot moose or elk, the relentless Dumas and his fighters found Rogers's trail. Smelling Ranger blood, they swiftly followed the moccasin tracks of the Ranger chieftain. Most of all, these pursuers lusted for the opportunity to deliver a punishing blow that might well make them famous, especially the taking of Rogers's scalp—the ultimate trophy. Wiping out the most esteemed American fighting man and Ranger leader in North America would bestow Major Dumas with endless fame across the breadth of New France and even on the Atlantic's other side.

However, with the sixth sense that had served him so well in the past, especially in the enemy's proximity, rising to the fore, Rogers kept relentlessly pushing his followers ever harder. The increasingly desperate major knew that he had to now outmarch Dumas as he had the vigorous French pursuit from Missisquoi Bay, despite the weakened condition of the hungry men. Major Jean-Daniel Dumas, born in Montauban, France, was no ordinary opponent. He had first joined a French regiment in 1742 and gained plenty of combat experience, including service in Europe. Dumas had journeyed to Canada in 1750 to embark upon a new career and life. Here, in battling for New France, Dumas gained such a fine reputation that he was appointed adjutant general of colonial troops on January 1, 1759. Clearly, he was an ambitious, smart, and talented man on the rise, possessing much potential. Successfully tracking down and eliminating Rogers would be a high point in Major Dumas's career.

However, it would not be easy, because Rogers was utilizing every trick and evasive action in the book to stay ahead of the eager pursuers. Finally, with less than one hundred men and with rations expended, a weary Major Dumas finally gave up his pursuit because of the difficulty in following the trail in the wilderness. Additionally, Rogers was nearing the Connecticut River, where reinforcements from Fort Number Four might have advanced north to threaten the war party now far from French garrisons, as Dumas feared.[21]

The More Fortunate Fate of Major Rogers's Party

As could be expected with the major in charge, the contingent under Rogers, including Captain Ogden, fared better than any other party, which was now bolstered by the survivors of Ensign Avery's Ranger and Provincial groups. The major had wisely decided to lead his men straight south cross-country from Lake Memphremagog in the hope of gaining the Wells River, which led to the Connecticut, and staying off the well-worn Abenaki war trail that led through the wilderness. Following the war trail was much too risky in Rogers's mind because it was tailor-made for ambush: a wise decision that saved Rogers's life and those of his men.

Rogers's group of survivors included some of the command's best men, including Captain Ogden and Lieutenant Grant, who were now the major's top lieutenants. Rogers's decision to head straight south cross-country was a wise one, and his example had been smartly followed by groups under Captain Joseph Wait, Ensign Elias Avery, and Lieutenants Jacob Farrington and Abernethy Cargill—experienced commanders who likewise shared Rogers's caution and wisdom by staying off the main Abenaki war path that led south to the Connecticut River country and posed great danger.

This largest group of survivors included weary Rangers, nine men of the New Jersey Blues, including Captain Ogden, Lieutenant Grant's Massachusetts Provincials, Ensign Avery's Connecticut Provincials, and British Regulars. Chief Gill's son, Sabattis (also known as Xavier, who was nearly killed and eaten by starving members of Lieutenant "Billy" Phillips's contingent of starving men), was also with Rogers's band. With hunger pangs torturing them with every step through an unspoiled wilderness that seemed to stretch before them forever, these desperate men survived by eating whatever they could find, including the leather of cartridge boxes, the fringe from leather leggings and shirts, and their wide leather belts.[22]

Private Kirkwood said of the painful ordeal of Rogers's party of twenty-five men,

We continued this journey for eight days when our provisions being almost spent, we encamped and went to hunt for three days, but we succeeded badly, killing very little, we then removed and made short marches being so much afflicted with the cold and hunger which we now began to feel in an intolerable degree, the deepness of the snow and swampness of the country, made it impossible for us to stir for several days. During this miserable period, we were obliged to scrape under the snow for acorns, and even to eat our shoes and belts, and broil our powder-horns and thought it delicious eating.[23]

Clearly, the living nightmare of the seemingly endless trek south for the men of Rogers's party, who wisely carried less plunder than other contingents, reached new heights of misery. Greedily, the survivors in the major's group had long ago eaten the last morsels of corn until nothing remained of a once-bountiful supply. The parched corn had been consumed much faster than Rogers and his men had anticipated, when at St. Francis it had seemed like they had a considerable surplus of this manna from heaven. Therefore, leather gear had been eagerly devoured by the men of Rogers's contingent.

Fortunately for Rogers's group of survivors, Chief Joseph-Louis Gill's son Sabattis proved invaluable in foraging Indian style in the woodlands for food, and he proved an excellent gatherer of eatables—skills taught to him by his Abenaki mother, Marie-Jeanne, rather than his white father. He pointed out to Rogers some Abenaki secrets about what was necessary for a man to maintain life in the wilderness, including eating groundnuts and acorns and boiling lily roots.[24]

In a letter, one of Rogers's men described the nightmarish ordeal, including the division of the command into numerous small parties, and the almost indescribable misery because of the lack of food and the vain hope of finding game: "They marched eight Days, and then parted themselves into small Parties, as their Corn was almost expended, and every Party took his Way; the Rest of their Corn was soon gone, and they were obliged to live on Roots and Barks, Toad-stools, some old Beaver skins, and [Abenaki] Scalps, as there was but little Game to be had, it was seldom they saw any: They thought themselves well supplied, when they could get on Partridge between 10 Men a Day."[25]

Second Lieutenant George Campbell, the tough Scotsman who was destined to survive this grueling, seemingly endless march ever southward—perhaps because he wrote ancient Celtic prayers and asked for God's forgiveness in his diary—described the depths of depravity and still another horror, when some starving men "who could no longer bear the keen pangs of an empty stomach, attempt[ed] to eat their own excrements."[26]

Wishing that he had never left his native Scotland and the familiar faces of the Campbell clan from the picturesque Highlands, Campbell wrote in his diary, "One Ranger was discover'd eating his own stool which I sought to forbare & was acurs'd by ye [hunger] crazed men."[27]

Commanding his contingent, which had taken the southeastern route to the Connecticut River like the Dunbar-Turner party and the group commanded by Sergeant John Evans, Second Lieutenant Campbell was not guilty of exaggeration when he described the desperate Rangers of his party as "crazed men."[28] The breaking point of Rangers killing other Rangers over food and minor matters was nearly reached due to the stresses of facing starvation. As Campbell penned in his diary, "Rangers . . . Sparrow & [Francis] Hartwell had found some bird eggs in ye bogs & popp'd them raw into their gullets without sharing, which most caused a fight amongst ye party. Ye men are losing their reason for want of food."[29]

Clearly, among the famished Rangers, the powerful instinct—the basest and lowest common denominator among human beings that was most of all primeval—of self-preservation now dominated the daily existence of these famished men, who continued to toil onward in a desperate bid to save their lives and to see their wives, parents, and families once again if they could only escape the hell of the seemingly endless wilderness and a horrible death by starvation. Amid the greatest adversity and misery, simple self-preservation evolved into the most basic motivation of all for the remaining survivors, who were now living by their instincts—a case of simply doing anything and everything in order to stay alive.

Surviving Rangers, including men who now looked almost like skeletons, were trapped in a never-ending nightmare, while living an animal-like existence that was purely primeval. The omnipresent struggle of these men was not only wearily trudging over the most forbidding terrain that these Rangers had ever encountered but also waging an inner battle against the urge to just give up and go no farther. Death to some Rangers now seemed like a restful salvation and a blissful release from the endless suffering. Some men believed that they essentially had been assigned to death row in this endless ordeal and that the ugliest of demises lay inevitably in their future. Indeed, it seemed as if the victors of St. Francis had been cursed and ordained to a cruel fate by a vengeful Abenaki god for having committed a massacre.

THE NIGHTMARISH TREK THROUGH THE WILDERNESS CONTINUES

Meanwhile, Rogers, who was leading the way as usual, and the surviving members of his party continued onward through the seemingly endless evergreen forests and over one towering ridge after another, despite "not knowing where we were," in Private Kirkwood's words, which echoed the fear of dying a horrible death far from home amid the wilderness.[30]

With each passing day, the misery increased among the ragged sojourners long after the corn had been consumed to the very last kernel. More men died because "the extreme fatigue and the want of something to eat brought such weakness among us, that we were forced to leave two or three [exhausted soldiers] behind us every morning, they being unable to proceed any farther."[31]

The attrition increased in Rogers's contingent, despite the major's best efforts in attempting to keep everyone alive and moving onward. One man of Rogers's party described the grim reality that was inevitable due to the lack of food and the rugged terrain of a wilderness seemingly devoid of animal life: "We were forced to leave two or three [men] behind us every morning [but] We always left behind some [supply of kindling and wood], and if there was any thing eatable among us left a part, but this was seldom the case" at this point.[32]

Then, suddenly, the female captive Abenaki Marie-Jeanne, the plump but attractive wife of Chief Joseph-Louis Gill, began to look much better to the starving Rogers—not erotically but as tasty food to keep them alive. In the words of Private Kirkwood, who felt sympathy for this knowledgeable Abenaki women whose wilderness savvy helped to save their lives day after day, "As for the squaw, she bore it nobly and was of infinite service in gathering roots and herbs, which she was the better acquainted with, as she was bred among such hardships, as we could by no means support a long continuance of. She was plump and fat, having more flesh upon her than five of us, and Major Rogers several times proposed to make away with her [to kill her for food], but we would never consent to it."[33]

One victim was a young Abenaki boy, who fell prey to another group of emaciated Rangers, who eagerly devoured him in a true life-or-death situation that had left the starving men with no choice.[34] But in fact, this nightmarish situation for survival was nothing unique. The act of cannibalism can be found throughout the annals of military history, when starving soldiers of many nations and different cultures have found themselves cut down and without the usual food rations for extended periods.

Indeed, to place the Rangers' cannibalism of not only Abenaki captives, male and female, but also eventually their own comrades, in a proper historical perspective, it is important to note that soldiers of other nations in other wars have resorted to cannibalism when starving and facing death in desperate situations. Cannibalism occurred among starving French soldiers who ate the flesh of their own comrades during Napoleon Bonaparte's hellish retreat from Moscow in November 1812. Even modern warriors have resorted to cannibalism to stay alive in the most desperate of situations. An unknown number of the doomed German soldiers of the ill-fated Sixth Army, when besieged and surrounded by a great mass of Russians at Stalingrad, also turned to cannibalism during the awful winter of 1942–1943, when they were cut off from supplies and food for an extended time to seal their fate and eventually force their surrender.[35]

However, Major Rogers, who was most of all concerned about the welfare of his men, who were succumbing fast to starvation, was doing relatively well compared to his followers during this ordeal. In fact, Rogers "alone possessed the physical strength and moral courage to keep his men alive" by any means.[36]

Private Kirkwood, the ultimate survivor who had nine lives, so to speak, throughout his career as a soldier, much like the commander, whom he so greatly admired, marveled that the men were even "jealous of the Major," because "he was stronger, and in better spirits than any of us."[37]

Finally, when his men were on the verge of starving to death, Rogers decided to do what he knew had to be done when it came to Marie-Jeanne, whose easy availability and plump body—she must have caused the major and his famished men to perhaps think of her as a giant ham in human form—was simply too tempting under the most desperate circumstances. As Private Kirkwood explained the nightmarish situation when heightened desperation and the fear of death from starvation finally forced Rogers to commit the most unthinkable of acts, "We were now reduced to ten in number [from the original twenty-five who formed the party], weak and starved in such a manner [and] we were in the greatest extremity, when the major [then] followed the squaw who was gone out to gather roots, and there he kill'd, and cut her up, and brought her to our fire where he divided and cast lots for the shares which were distributed to each an equal part, we then broiled and eat the most of her; and received great strength thereby."[38]

What Rogers did when basically left without a choice was simply another demonstration of his determination to save himself and his men, while revealing his grim expertise in the art of survival. In the deadly Darwinian game of survival of the fittest in the wilderness, Marie-Jeanne fell victim to a horrific fate, but one necessary to keep Rogers and his men alive.

This grisly act committed by Rogers to save his men partly revealed that he thought and acted much like a Native American in supremely pragmatic and realistic terms. However, one important distinction should be made regarding cannibalism. While Rogers and his men ate human flesh for the express purpose of saving themselves to fight another day, many Native American warriors at this time consumed the human flesh of their foes for ritualistic and spiritual reasons rooted in ancient tribal traditions of a mystical nature, including to gain the power and bravery of the enemy warrior, who had garnered their respect before he died.

In his journal, Captain Louis Antoine de Bougainville wrote on June 12, 1757, about the horror of cannibalism after the return of a Delaware and Shawnee war party with a group of gloomy English prisoners and plenty of scalps, revealing the extent of their success. Shocked but knowing that he could never understand the mysterious ways of New France's Native American allies, the highly educated Bougainville wrote, "They have eaten an English officer whose pallor and plumpness tempted them [as in the case of the unfortunate Marie-Jeanne]. Such cruelties are frequent enough among the Indians," who murdered and consumed the flesh of Englishmen and Provincials for the glory of New France.[39]

Captain Bougainville, who was grimly fascinated by the unimaginable horrors, also penned in his journal how warriors had captured English rum in one summer 1757 attack and white prisoners in another successful raid on the frontier settlements: "The Indians immediately drank [the rum which] caused them to commit great cruelties. They put in the pot and ate three prisoners, and perhaps others were so treated. . . . A horrible spectacle to European [French] eyes."[40]

Even more mind-numbingly horrific to defy anything in the Western European belief system and imagination, Captain Bougainville recorded only four days later that "an English corpse came floating by the Indians' camp [and the warriors then] crowded around it with loud cries, drank its blood, and put its pieces in the kettle."[41]

However, and as mentioned, the Rangers only resorted to cannibalism at the point of starvation when their lives were at stake. Ranger Thomas Brown, the smooth-faced teenager from Charlestown, Massachusetts, escaped with "an English lad" from his adopted Canadian family, whom he served deep in the heart of New France, after having been captured at the Second Battle on Snowshoes on March 13, 1758. He and his friend escaped in a desperate bid to reach the safety of the New England settlements, but the long journey through an untamed wilderness took a serious toll on the two young men, when their scanty provisions ran out. Finally, the "English lad" died of starvation.

Brown described the horror that forced him to entertain grisly thoughts that had been unimaginable only a few days before: "I sat down by him [his body], and at first concluded to make a fire ... and eat his flesh, and ... finally came to this resolution: To cut off of his bones as much flesh as I could and tie it up in a handkerchief, and so proceed as well as I could. Accordingly I did so, and buried my companion on the day I left him. . . . Being weak and tired, about 9 o'clock I sat down, but could not eat my friend's flesh [and] I expected soon to die myself." Young Private Brown was eventually rescued by three Canadians, who took him to Crown Point, where he was confined once again by the French.[42]

Clearly, to say the least, the world of Rogers and his men was extremely harsh and, most of all, unforgiving, like nature in the wild, as would especially be the case if the Rangers were captured by the most fanatical warriors of the North American wilderness. As more days passed, the nightmarish retreat from St. Francis brought even more horrors than Captain Bougainville witnessed or heard about during America's most brutal war.

After the surrender of the English-Provincial garrison of Fort William Henry, Bougainville had been horrified by the slaughter of hundreds of garrison members, including wives and camp followers, after they surrendered on honorable terms to the Marquis de Montcalm. Montcalm's able aide-de-camp, Captain Bougainville, wrote of the terrible fate of some English and American captives, after they were marched the long distance to Montreal, situated on the St. Lawrence River. On August 15, 1757, the aristocratic Frenchman wrote of one tragic event that shocked his European sensibilities to the core: "At two o'clock in the presence of the entire town [of Montreal, which possessed distinctive western frontier qualities that were unimaginable in a more cultured and refined Quebec where New France's elite resided and ruled in the aristocratic class tradition of the nobles, the Indians allied with the French] killed one of [the English prisoners from Fort William Henry], put him in a kettle, and forced his unfortunate compatriots to eat him."[43]

Father Pierre-Joseph-Antoine Roubaud, who had been an active part of the Abenaki war party from St. Francis, whose members had played a leading role in initiating the slaughter of many paroled Provincial soldiers after Fort William Henry's surrender, was shocked by the fate of some English prisoners, when they were placed in the cooking pots of the warriors. When the priest protested about the consumption of human flesh because it was a mortal sin in God's eyes, a young Ottawa warrior, streaked in red and black war paint, stopped Roubaud in his tracks by explaining in simple terms the situation that the Jesuit failed to understand: "You have French taste; I have Indian. This is good meat for me."[44] French common soldier Charles Bonin wrote how when the warriors desired a special "feast they have a dog or a prisoner boiled."[45]

Meanwhile, the arduous trek of Rogers's ever-dwindling band of warriors became even more demanding with each passing day, as they encountered more rugged terrain and harsher weather conditions, including falling snow and winter Arctic winds, in the midst of the seemingly endless wilderness. In order for these men to survive their harrowing ordeal, the horror of cannibalism inevitably continued among members of other Ranger contingents, while they were laboriously making their way south through the rugged wilderness seemingly devoid of animal life.

In pushing straight south for the Wells River, Rogers's original party had been reduced when a small group of starving men under Sergeant John Evans broke off in the hope that a lesser number of Rangers could more easily hunt and find food among the strangely silent forests that seemed to have no end. They were shortly joined by a small band under Sergeant Benjamin Bradley, heading steadily south for the safety of the Connecticut River and Fort Number Four. Barely able to place one foot before the others, these survivors kept moving onward in weary fashion, subsisting on a meager diet of birch bark and eating the leather of cartridge boxes, which tasted almost like juicy beef steak in their starving condition. As fate would have it, they then entered the sprawling expanse of the Coaticook swamps, where Lieutenant William James Dunbar and his men had made their defiant last stand against far too many attackers and been defeated by Major Dumas's fierce fighters, who had been bent on a bloody revenge.

One of the greatest of all horrors during the nightmarish withdrawal from St. Francis was played out in full by a group of surviving Rangers when they found the decomposing bodies of First Lieutenant Dunbar and his Britons of Thomas Gage's 80th Light Infantry. Even the lifeless bodies of these Englishmen were ill fated in the end. As mentioned, their mangled, scalped, and butchered bodies had been carried downstream by the swift current of the Pherrins River, until they lodged together on a pile of logs, cut down by beavers for food and to create their den and dam. Here, the bodies became jammed together against the logs at this point in the water-course's headwaters, near where the river met the Coaticook Pond. These grisly remains of mutilated and scalped Englishmen, whose families in Great Britain never knew of their tragic fates, were destined to become a source of much-needed food for the starving Rangers.[46]

Leading his party of hungry men, Second Lieutenant George Campbell, who spoke a distinctive "Scots-Gaelic" dialect and had joined the Rangers in the spring of 1759, was about to experience the surreal horror that had become all but inevitable at this time. Toward the end of an increasingly cold and inclement October, Campbell's contingent had discovered the moccasin tracks of the ill-fated members of Sergeant John Evans's party and followed them toward the Coaticook swamps and the Pherrins River, although initially believing that these were enemy footprints. Once again, even among the most experienced Rangers, including revered officers, at this point, starvation and desperation were effectively counteracting the dictates of reason and the most basic rules of ranging warfare as formulated by Rogers.[47]

In Campbell's group of fortunate survivors, which included Stockbridge Ranger warriors from the Indian town in western Massachusetts of the same name, which was more than one hundred miles from Rogers's homeland of the Merrimack River country to the northeast, a living nightmare was played out in truly horrific fashion:

These were, at one time, four days without any kind of sustenance, when some of them, in consequence of their complicated misery, severely aggravated by their not knowing whither the route they pursued would lead, and, of course, the little prospect of relief that was left to them, lost their senses; while others, who could no longer bear the keen [hunger pangs] of an empty stomach, attempted to eat their own excrements. What leather they had on their catouch-boxes, they had already reduced to a cider, and greedily devoured. At length, on the 28th of October, as they were crossing a small river [Pherrins], which was in some measure dammed up by logs, they discovered some human bodies not only scalped but horribly mangled, which they supposed to be those of some of their own party. But this was not a season for distinctions. On them, accordingly, they fell like Cannibals, and devoured part of them raw [despite the rotting flesh and awful stench]; their impatience being so great to wait the kindling of a fire to dress it by. When they thus abated the excruciating [hunger] pangs they before endured, they carefully collected the fragments, and carried them off. This was their sole support, except roots and a squirrel, till the 4th of November, when Providence conducted them to a boat on the Connecticut River, which Major Rogers had sent with provisions to their relief.[48]

Second Lieutenant George Campbell, who continued to faithfully write about the gory details of the unimaginable excesses in his diary, provided the most revealing account when destiny itself had seemingly brought him and his men to the exact point where First Lieutenant Dunbar's group had fought magnificently against the odds, before being overwhelmed by the tide of screaming French, Canadians, and Indians. In his diary entry for October 28, Campbell wrote about what he would never forget as long as he lived:

As we were crossing a stream [Pherrins River], partly dammed up by fallen Beaver logs we came upon ye most horrible remains I fear of one of ye Majors partys. Ye remains had been stripp'd quite nakid & portions mangled or cut away. Some of ye bodies were headless [cut off by one of Sergeant John Evans's party for consumption] & all ye others scalp'd. I lost control of my men as they fell like wolves upon ye horribly cut up remains & proceeded to cut off strips of flesh & bolt them raw. I fear I most joyn'd them but forebare long enough to order my men to cook ye flesh before partaking it. Ye bodies were near skeletons when ye men had most completely finish'd dressing ye carcases & cooked all ye flesh they could not eat [which provided food in the upcoming days].[49]

Revealing a tragic demise, the mangled bodies of the dead men of the ill-fated group under First Lieutenant William James Dunbar, the capable English officer from Gage's 80th Light Infantry Regiment, proved to be a godsend that ensured the survival of many men, who had reached their physical and mental limits. Despite starving, Sergeant John Evans, a hardened veteran who had joined the Rangers in early August 1756, was so repulsed by his comrades' desperate actions that he initially refused to eat the flesh of any of the rotting bodies of the slaughtered Britons. However, in the end, he may well have saved his own life when he eventually broke down and tossed away all civilized and Christian values from his childhood days, which no longer applied in a life-or-death situation in an unmapped wilderness. He finally took what he needed and then broiled human flesh from the severed head of one Englishman over an open fire. To his shock, Sergeant Evans discovered that the grilled flesh of the Briton was nothing less than the "sweetest morsel he ever tasted."[50]

Most important, and as Major Rogers fully realized, the eating of human flesh saved quite a few of these men, proving to be a godsend when they had been dying of starvation. Quite simply, in bestowing strength and energy when it was most needed, including to the injured Captain Ogden, the gruesome act of cannibalism allowed Rogers and his band to struggle onward and eventually reach the blue waters of the Connecticut River amid the remoteness of the wilderness north of Fort Number Four.[51]

The possibility has arisen that Major Rogers killed another captured Abenaki woman instead of Chief Gill's wife, because a different account exists of Marie-Jeanne's death. However, in much the same way as Rogers's party, the famished members of Provincial Lieutenant Jenkins's party of thirteen men, including two Stockbridge Ranger guides, who led the way southwest through the Green Mountains in the hope of reaching Crown Point, were able to survive by the same horrific means that were appalling in the extreme but absolutely necessary for survival.

According to this account, two prisoners, a teenage Abenaki girl and the attractive wife of Chief Gill, Marie-Jeanne, were among this contingent. Anger toward Marie-Jeanne rose to fever pitch, especially among the two Stockbridge warriors, when she cleverly attempted to trick the two Native American Ranger guides and send the party in the direction (west or northwest depending on their exact location) of the French garrison at Isle-aux-Noix, which was located on the east side of Lake Champlain beyond, or north of, its head. The Ranger warriors wreaked their revenge before Lieutenant Jenkins, who hailed from the Bay Colony and had served in a Massachusetts regiment, could do anything to stop them.

In keeping with their nickname, and despite Marie-Jeanne's good looks and prestigious status as the wife of the chief of St. Francis, the Stockbridge "Wolves" quickly slit her throat with their scalping knives. But this tragic killing of the chief's beloved wife was not just about revenge. The members of Jenkins's party, including the "Wolves," were starving like the rest of Rogers's men. As if they had just killed a deer or a moose for food, the Stockbridge warriors, without a hint of emotion or hesitation, immediately began to butcher Marie-Jeanne's body without noticing its most alluring parts that made her attractive, because she had become an edible object to be devoured by starving men to sustain life.

Then the blood-stained slabs of freshly cut meat of the Abenaki woman were put on the fire and roasted like the tasty steak from a slaughtered cow or hog in the frontier settlements. Reversing the cultural differences when it came to cannibalism, because the Stockbridge's warriors embraced longtime Christian traditions, the whites more eagerly ate Marie-Jeanne's flesh than the Stockbridge warriors. But as could be expected in their emaciated condition, the warriors, nevertheless, eventually partook in the eating of human flesh. As planned, the consumption of the body of Chief Gill's wife gave new strength to totally exhausted men, benefiting them immensely in their darkest hour. However, the life-sustaining flesh was not enough to save Lieutenant Jenkins, who eventually died of starvation far from his Massachusetts home and family.[52]

By this time, the demise of Chief Gill's wife caused no sense of guilt among those men who had consumed her because doing so had given them the precious gift of life. In his diary, Second Lieutenant George Campbell, a strict Calvinist in the Scottish tradition, wrote that he deemed her death a harsh but deserved moral judgment: "Ye [Chief's] wife was a hellon [sic] an[d] an wors [whore]," who deserved death because of her treachery.[53]

In the end, Second Lieutenant George Campbell learned from Rogers of the tragic fate of Lieutenant Jenkins and his men: "Ye Major informs of ye fate of Lieut. Jenkins party attempting to return to Crown Point by journeying south on the west side of the Green Mountains. Poor Jenkins starv'd to death on ye Missiqo [Missisquoi] & his party captur'd later. . . . Ye Chefs [Gill's] wife expired & may have been kill'd by ye Stockbridges [because] She led them toward ye French on Lock [Lake] Champlain. Her flesh kept them alive, except poor Jenkins who did not eat" human flesh like the others.[54]

In addition, the twelve-man Ranger party, which had taken a southwestern route to Crown Point, struggled through the Green Mountains like Lieutenant Jenkins's party, under Second Lieutenant William "Bill"

Hendrick Phillips. As noted, "Billy" Phillips, who hailed from the Colony of New York, was a mixed-race officer of considerable ability. He was also one of the older officers, at around forty, and the son of a loving Indian mother. The Rangers were about to kill one of their captives, perhaps Chief Gill's youngest son, Sabattis (Xavier), when the intended victim was saved at the last minute when the survivors found the rare opportunity to kill a tasty muskrat. Fortunately, the German girl from the Mohawk River Valley and three Abenaki girls were spared by members of "Billy" Phillips's group.[55]

Still another group, of which Ebenezer Dibble was a member, was ambushed by pursuers, who wreaked their revenge for the October 4 slaughter. In his diary, Dibble penned how "one of our Capt[ains] & 20 [men were] lost [and] By the way Coming back [some] 20 [of] the Enymis destroyed one Saml fuard and Jos[eph]" were killed.[56]

Of all the groups that straggled south during what was a living nightmare in a tortuous march over seemingly countless hills and valleys, Captain Wait was the only commander who brought his group of around a dozen men, including his brother Sergeant Benjamin Wait, to safety, after successfully reaching the Connecticut River intact. This remarkable feat was not surprising because of the wise guidance and outstanding leadership abilities of the highly capable Wait. He had served with distinction as Rogers's second in command during the expedition, and he and his brother had long operated as a highly effective team.[57]

The harrowing experience of attempting to survive in a howling wilderness defied the imagination on almost every level. In his typical understated manner, Rogers described the ordeal: "Our distress, our grief and consternation, were truly inexpressible [during] so many days [of] weary march over steep, rocky mountains, or through wet, dirty swamps [and] we saw no hope that we should escape a miserable death by famine."[58]

But when the going got tough, Rogers got going with more grim determination in the most impossible of situations, while additional Rangers of his group had to be left behind and died of starvation the uncharted wilderness. Now the key to survival for himself and his remaining men, the irrepressible major once again adhered to his own Rule Number XXVIII of ranging service that was a key to survival, which called for maintaining "a firmness and presence of mind on every occasion."[59]

Indeed, Rogers once again rose to the challenge in the darkest hour and came to the rescue of his men, who were losing strength and willpower to continue onward while struggling ever southward. On October 20, Rogers successfully led his men to the heavily timbered banks of the Wells River around half a dozen miles from its intersection with the Connecticut River, which was a cause of celebration.

He heard firing to the east in the direction of the point, the intersection of the Wells and Amonoosuc Rivers, where Lieutenant Andrew McMullen had informed Major General Jeffery Amherst to send provisions upriver. Here, Rogers fired his weapon to signal for help, but none was forthcoming. However, Rogers was elated in the extreme, knowing that McMullen had reached Crown Point and Amherst had sent help, as requested.

However, at the mouth of the Wells River, the relief party, under Lieutenant Samuel Stevens, had abruptly returned back down the Connecticut with all of the precious provisions because they feared that the shots meant that an Abenaki war party was in the area. For nearly a week, Rogers and his men waited for the arrival of the relief party with provisions, but it never came. Therefore, with his men starving to death and giving up hope, Rogers knew that he had to take drastic action before it was too late for the men at the ad hoc rendezvous site whose numbers were growing as other parties of famished straggled into the makeshift camp on the Wells River.

Major Rogers described his final bid on October 26 to reach Fort Number Four to secure help at all costs, before his men died of starvation: "I then proceeded with Captain Ogden [who had defied all expectations and kept up with Rogers's contingent after having recovered from his wounds suffered in the attack on St. Francis, as well as with Chief Gill's son Sabattis], and one private, upon a raft, and arrived at this place [Fort Number Four] yesterday [November 4]. Provisions were in half an hour after dispatched up the [Connecticut] river to Mr. [Lieutenant Noah] Grant, which will reach him this night."[60]

Revealing more details about a truly desperate situation, Rogers wrote,

In this emergency, I resolved to make the best of my way to [Fort] Number Four, leaving the remainder of the party, unable to proceed farther, to obtain such wretched substance as the wilderness afforded until I could relieve them, which

I promised to do in ten days. Captain Ogden, myself, a captive Indian boy, embarked on a raft of dry pine trees. The current carried us down the stream, in the middle of which we kept our miserable vessel with such paddles as could be split and hewn with small hatchets. On the second day we reached White River falls, and narrowly escaped running over them. The raft went over and was lost; but our remaining strength enabled us to land, and pass by the falls, at the foot of which Captain Ogden and the ranger killed several red squirrels and a partridge, while I attempted to construct a new raft. Not being able to cut the trees, I burned them down, and burned them off at proper lengths. This was our third day's work after leaving our companions. The next day we floated to Wattoquichie falls, which are about fifty yards in length. Here we landed, and Captain Ogden held the raft with a withe of hazel-bushes, while I went below to swim in, board the raft, and paddle it ashore. This was our only hope of life; for we had not strength to make another raft, should this be lost. I succeeded in securing it, and next morning we floated to within a short distance of [Fort] Number Four. Here [on October 31, when dark skies threatened to unleash their snowy contents] we found several men cutting timber, who relieved and assisted us to the fort.[61]

Here, in the wilderness north of Fort Number Four, these New Hampshire men were garrison members from the fort on the Connecticut River. Thankfully, their fellow New Englanders, in Rogers's words, "gave us the first relief [since having departed Crown Point on September 13] and assisted us to the fort."[62]

Of course, the major's use of the word "assisted" was a considerable understatement by any measure. In fact, when Rogers finally reached the friendly confines of Fort Number Four, "he was scarcely able to walk after his fatigues," which would have resulted in the demise of almost any other man.[63]

After an amazing odyssey and saga second to none in the annals of American military history, Rogers had somehow willed himself onward to finally arrive at Fort Number Four on the last day of October. The incredible news—for Rogers had been given up for dead by friend and foe—spread like wildfire. While heavy snow fell on the Crown Point encampment, and Lake Champlain was frozen over, an Indian arrived to inform Amherst that he had left sixteen Rangers at the mouth of Otter River, and they were on the verge of dying. A relief party from Fort Number Four was immediately ordered north up the Connecticut to this remote place in the dense woodlands and rugged countryside.[64]

All in all, a miracle had occurred in the wilderness, when least expected, to save other survivors who were on the brink of dying. Private Kirkwood related a different version of the happy ending for the fortunate men of Rogers's party of survivors:

> *Our provisions being again out, we were out of all hopes of ever coming to the English settlements; when Major Rogers putting on his rockets or snow shoes, which was the only pair among us, went hunting, in order if possible to procure us some relief [and then] Providence made him the means of bring us a [most thankful and timely] relief [from nearby Fort Number Four, which was the northernmost fort in New England that protected English settlement. After] he was agreeably surprised with hearing a shot, he immediately used all the speed he could, to come up with the person who fired, and by good fortune fell in with a man belonging to [Fort Number Four], who had come out to hunt, and killed a large deer [and] The Hunter was extremely surprised to see a man in such a woeful plight, as the Major was, and could scarcely believe it could be him, having heard that his whole party had perished among the snow.[65]*

Then the major, ignoring his own state of absolute exhaustion, flew into action and made sure that "two hind quarters" were transported up the Connecticut River to his starving men, who were on the verge of dying. As Scotsman Robert Kirkwood explained with considerable understatement, "We were all full of thankfulness to the Almighty" for Rogers's last desperate effort to save his dying men.[66] Rogers described the final relief effort that paid dividends and played a role in saving his men: "Two other canoes, with provisions, have been sent to the mouth of the Ammonoosuc river."[67]

Major Rogers's tireless attempts to save his men continued with frantic efforts to do everything possible within his power. Private Kirkwood wrote, "Next day he brought us (being reduced to ten) on horseback to the Fort, so that during the course of this fatiguing and tedious march, we lost eighteen men. Here we all had a severe fit of sickness [but] by God's assistance we got all safe over it, and in a little time began to gather so much strength as to walk ahead."[68]

A lucky survivor from another group of Rangers, who reached Fort Number Four after Rogers and his party, described his ordeal and Rogers's heroics in a letter written not long afterward: "They arrived at [the] Connecticut River, where Major Rogers left all his Party, except Capt. Ogden and one man, (this was about 80 Miles above [Fort] Number Four). They then made a Raft with some Pieces of Wood and floated down on them, until they came to Number Four, to which Place they arrived in 29 Days from St. Francois, it being between 3 and 400 Miles; through excessive bad travelling. They were 20 Days in a continued Swamp, with their feet in the Mud and water, and could scarcely get a dry Place to sleep on."[69]

However, perhaps Rogers's supreme dedication to his men became evident once again—as throughout the mission to St. Francis—when he told General Amherst from Fort Number Four on November 5, despite a bone-numbing weariness and exhaustion that still overwhelmed him, "I shall go up the [Connecticut] river, to look after my men, and return as soon as possible to Crown Point."[70]

BRITISH HEADQUARTERS EXPECTED THE WORST

At Crown Point, until receiving Rogers's letter, Major General Amherst and his officers and men had worried about the fate of Rogers's and his troops for ample good reason, assuming that they had died in the snowy wilderness. Garrison members at Fort Number Four, which was the northernmost fortified position on the New England frontier, felt the same. As penned by "a Gentleman" (or officer) in an October 19, 1759, letter, "The Truth with respect of Major Rogers is, he has now been gone [from Crown Point] 30 odd Days, and we know not certainly his particular Destination, nor where he is, 'tis supposed he's gone to St. Francis."[71]

An October 26 notice in the *Boston News-Letter* revealed that Amherst's army "had received no account from Major Rogers since he went out with a large Party into the Enemy's Country but expected to hear" shortly from him.[72]

Almost from the beginning, wild rumors had continued to spread about the tragic fate of Rogers and his men, who were widely seen as having perished. As early as September, one soldier from Crown Point penned in a letter, "It is said [that Rogers] himself is either killed or wounded."[73] Ironically, and since it had been widely believed, this rumor about Major Rogers's possible death had cast a long shadow over the possibility of the expedition's failure so far north.[74]

In the *Boston News-Letter*, the first good news about a successful expedition that had achieved its objective in faraway Quebec finally trickled in and was published on November 8: "Maj. Rogers with his party had destroyed St. Francis [as he] was true [to himself and his orders] as to their destroying the Village; but that he only lost 1 Man in the attempt & not 100, as was then said . . . Major Rogers & the Party under his Command, had entirely destroy'd St. Francis" by burning it to the ground.[75]

As published in colonial newspapers in late December, the information was spread from "a Gentleman [who] left [Fort] Number 4 [and mentioned how] the Day he came away, 6 of Major Rogers's Party came in safe, and the Remainder were soon expected."[76] Of course, no one dared to mention that one secret of the survival of Rogers's party had been the "dinner of broiled 'squaw,'" which had given the Rangers much-needed strength to keep going on.[77]

Rogers, as noted, had been the first to reach Fort Number Four on a memorable October 31. One of his men recalled,

> When the Major arrived at this Place, he was scarcely able to walk after his fatigues, as he took with him the Poorest of the Men, to supply and support them himself, and having Capt. Ogden with him, who was wounded, and whom he used often to take on his Back and carry him through Rivers. Immediately after the Majors arrival here, he provided Canoes with Provision, and sent them up the River to the Relief of the Party he had left, and within two days set himself up the River to recollect his wearied Men; the same Day that Capt. Ogden set out for Crown-Point.[78]

Four days later, these provisions had finally reached Rogers's band, with the major fulfilling his sacred promise to his men, whose lives had depended on his doing so. After writing his report to Major General Amherst on the first day of November, just two days later on November 2, despite looking sick and haggard, the still energetic Rogers was off once again, as if he had not recently endured the most harrowing and lengthy journey of his career. He headed north up the Connecticut, leading a convoy of canoes with even more provisions for his men. By a stroke of luck, Second Lieutenant George Campbell's party, which had partly subsisted on "scraps of human flesh" to survive their nightmarish ordeal, flagged down the canoes that Rogers had hurriedly dispatched upriver, before it was too late.[79]

After his journey north up the clear waters of the Connecticut River, the irrepressible major experienced unspeakable joy in having encountered the famished parties of Rangers, who he feared had all died of starvation. These groups of men were led by Sergeant David Evans, Second Lieutenant Jacob Farrington, Lieutenant Noah Grant, Second Lieutenant George Campbell, and Second Lieutenant Abernethy Cargill, who originally hailed from Maine.

An experienced officer of ability, Cargill had first enlisted as a private in Captain John Stark's company on Christmas Day 1757. Because of his demonstrated leadership skills, he had been promoted to a coveted officer's rank in July 1759. These survivors had gathered in a general rendezvous in the wilderness in the hope of increasing the chances of mutual survival and greater safety from a possible attack.[80] Second Lieutenant Campbell, who now loved his native Scotland even more after having gained a new lease on life, described how the ragged and famished survivors now looked much like "ye beggars of Edinburgh."[81]

Clearly, the saving of Rogers's contingent had only been possible because of the major's physical endurance and never-say-die attitude, which had risen to new heights during the moments of greatest crisis, when the situation became more severe than ever before. When everyone else in his group of Rangers had given up all hope and could go no farther, Rogers had always risen to the fore in what seemed like a superhuman effort.

Like almost all of his men, except some exceptional officers like the never-say-die Captain Ogden, who had been part of Rogers's group and had somehow, during the long trek south, recovered from his wounds received at St. Francis, Rogers never became a shell of his former self, despite having almost every possible reason for having become a shattered commander. Throughout all the adversity, he somehow kept his Scotch-Irish humor intact and his spirits up when panic and depression ran rampant through the ranks, knowing that there was no time for self-pity or for second-guessing his own decisions.

During an odyssey of truly staggering magnitude, Rogers had instead served as a beacon of hope and inspiration day after day for his famished men, who were sick and dizzy with weariness and starving to the point of dying. He always implored his Rangers to keeping moving and never give up. If anyone proved the old adage "When the going gets tough, the tough get going," it was Rogers during this grueling ordeal in which the challenges were almost without number and of an unimaginable nature.

Indeed, the grizzled, red-bearded major, who looked much older than his years and haggard from his endless exertions, only became better as an inspirational and motivational leader, when the situation looked the darkest: sterling leadership qualities from which his men drew strength to keep going during both the advance on St. Francis and the long retreat, when it seemed that all hope was lost. From beginning to end, and to his great credit, Rogers never changed as a leader of men and never ceased to inspire his followers. He continued to motivate his men—both Rangers and Provincial and British volunteers—to do not only the impossible but also the unthinkable against all odds.[82] And even at the end of an amazing ordeal that was a classic case of to hell and back, he was still looking "after my men," which meant more than anything else to the fatherlike Rogers, who always looked after his flock like a good shepherd.[83]

On November 6, Rogers had arrived with another canoe of provisions, after again pushing north up the Connecticut with a small party of rescuers. As noted, Rogers and Second Lieutenant George Campbell had previously scoured the area and gathered the relatively few remaining survivors on the Connecticut River. He distributed still another supply of food to Campbell's party, which had earlier gained a load of provisions. At the time of the initial securing of foodstuffs, Campbell described how the famished men, who had consumed too much and too fast, had "bolted food to fast & vomited, bringing curses from ye others for wasting [precious] food."[84]

As mentioned, the Stockbridge warrior who had reached Crown Point saved other Ranger lives, after he had been escorted into General Amherst's headquarters on the afternoon of November 7. After a lengthy interview, the warrior, who proudly carried a bloody scalp, had casually remarked in the middle of his lengthy storytelling—the traditional Native American way of breaking important news with a nonchalant air—that he had left sixteen survivors at the mouth of Otter River.[85]

Finally, on November 8, a soldier at Crown Point recorded in a letter how at long last, in a minor miracle, "Sixteen of Major Rogers's Party, including 3 Prisoners, and one English Captain, came into Crown-Point about 4 Days since."[86]

After overcoming odds that seemed insurmountable, this ragged group of survivors was commanded by Captain Ogden, who had performed magnificently in navigating his men during this incredible journey through the wilderness and keeping his followers alive. Ironically, he and his men reached Crown Point along the same narrow road that Captain Stark and his men had recently built through the hardwood forests. A soldier at Crown Point penned how, despite his wounds suffered at St. Francis, when "Capt Ogden arrived on the 8th instant, he look'd very poor; but well and in good spirits; we have heard nothing since of the Major. Capt. Ogden informs me [that] The people did bring away considerable plunder, but they drop'd them, or the greater part before they arrived at [the] Connecticut River. There are several of the [Stockbridge] Indians come in dres't very fine [in wampum] with their plunder."[87]

These were the sixteen tattered survivors whom Amherst ordered rescued after learning of their presence at the mouth of the Otter River from the seemingly indifferent Stockbridge Ranger on the previous day. The relief party of Rangers then escorted into Crown Point "four Indians, two rangers, one of the released prisoners, and two Indian girls and an Indian boy [Xavier or Sabattis] who were from St. Francis [and] All were loaded with wampum and trinkets plundered from that village."[88] In addition, the fortunate few survivors of Lieutenant William James Dunbar's party succeeded in reaching safety, when least expected by anyone, including Rogers.[89]

November 8, 1759, marked the fifty-sixth day since Rogers had led his men from Crown Point with confidence that they could succeed in what seemed like an impossible mission. These survivors were most fortunate to have successfully passed through their harrowing ordeal with few, if any, parallels in American military history. Like Rogers, these lucky men thanked God that they had not been captured and taken back to St. Francis like some of their unfortunate comrades, in the words of a Frenchman, where they "became victims of the fury of the Indian women."[90]

On November 26, 1759, in the midst of a severe northern frontier winter, nearly two months after the surprise attack on St. Francis, one survivor wrote in a letter, without overstatement or hyperbole, from Fort Number Four, which he had earlier reached safely, "We all here wait impatient for the safe Arrival of all those brave Officers and Men, that have behaved so gallantly in this Affair, and in particular that indefatigable Major, and a happy Recovery of Capt. [Amos] Ogden of his Wounds, such Behavior as only Men of Constitutions like Lions could ever have went through."[91] In another letter written the same day, a soldier wrote that he had met "a Gentleman . . . who told him he left Number 4 . . . and that the Day he came away, 6 of Major Rogers's Party came in safe, and the Remainder were soon expected."[92]

But in truth, nearly half of the men who had boldly marched all the way to St. Francis to deliver a devastating blow would never return from Major Rogers's most daring raid. A total of sixty-nine men were lost, including forty-three who starved to death; seventy-three soldiers survived. Horrified that so many good Rangers—the best and the brightest—were no more, Rogers realized that the terrible cost in lives had been far too high and feared for his reputation in having lost so much of his command.[93]

Arriving at Crown Point on November 7 to bring the first official news of the St. Francis raid to General Amherst with Rogers's report written at Fort Number Four, the seemingly indestructible Captain Amos Ogden, the remarkable New Jersey Blues officer who made a perfect Ranger, proved to be the most durable and strong-minded member of the expedition, after only Major Rogers. He had suffered serious wounds at St. Francis and somehow survived to tell the tale that seemed too incredible to be true. Under the circumstances, it is possible that not another man in the command could have persevered and survived Ogden's almost indescribable ordeal, which was more challenging than for any other member of Rogers's Rangers. By any measure, Captain Ogden, who was a respected leader, was a most remarkable man.

Captain Edward Crofton was another fortunate survivor. Ambitious and confident in his own considerable abilities, he had first come to America in 1757 as a "free lance volunteer" in order to gain promotion and a brighter future. However, the young man's ambitions had backfired when he engaged in serous personal squabbles with a British major of his regiment. Ever mindful of his personal honor and a proud man, an incensed Crofton had then written an appeal to Lord Loudoun to gain official permission to be allowed to duel the major who had insulted him in a manner that he could not ignore.

However, a kind fate had unexpectedly intervened when Lord Loudoun had solved the problem to end the possibility of a duel and to give Crofton a new lease on life. He had then attached Crofton as a volunteer to Rogers's Rangers to serve in the cadet company of promising young men on the rise and destined for the officer's ranks. The fiery Crofton, who was every inch a fighter, was a natural fit in the ranks of the rough-and-tumble Rangers.[94]

Rogers admired Crofton nearly as much as Ogden. As Rogers penned in a letter from Fort Number Four to Major General Amherst about a fine officer, "Captain Ogden can inform you of other particulars respecting this scout, as he was with me through the whole of the expedition, and behaved nobly."[95]

However, unlike Ogden, who survived the war to gain a choice land grant of twenty-five thousand acres in West Florida from the British Crown, Crofton was ill starred. Paradoxically, a tragic fate stalked Captain Crofton after his distinguished service on the St. Francis raid. Rogers had early recognized Crofton's talents and leadership abilities, appreciating all that he had to offer the Rangers. On January 10, 1758, Rogers, who was an excellent judge of men and knew exactly whom to advance in his officer corps, recommended the Briton for promotion to the rank of lieutenant to serve in his own personal company ("Rogers's Own") of elite fighting men. However, Crofton had reservations about the promotion, desiring to serve in a British Regular regiment.[96]

However, Crofton changed his mind, and Loudoun officially bestowed on him a commission to serve as second lieutenant in the ranks of Captain John Stark's company on January 14, 1758. As mentioned, Crofton had then performed with considerable skill and established a reputation as an excellent Ranger officer, as Rogers had early anticipated. He was one of two officers who had somehow survived the slaughter at the Second Battle on Snowshoes on March 13, 1758.[97]

Captain Crofton's almost incredible good luck finally ended when an unkind fate at last caught up with him in February 1761, after he had gained a commission as second lieutenant in a British Regular regiment. The hot-headed Crofton clashed with a fellow British lieutenant over the issue of rank. Deadly serious when it came to matters of rank and personal honor, he then engaged in a duel in Boston with the British officer of his regiment in early February 1760, and it proved an ill-fated decision.[98]

On February 8, 1761, his regimental commander reported to Major General Amherst of the sad ending for a hero of the raid on St. Francis: "Lieutenant Crofton (who had been put into the Regiment by General Wolf over all the Ensigns from being an officer of Rangers) . . . received a Pistol shot, of which he died the Day after."[99]

In the end, nothing could save the brave Captain Crofton, one of Rogers's best top lieutenants, who had especially proved his mettle during the St. Francis expedition and the ordeal of the harrowing retreat, defying the odds for so long. Crofton should have followed the prudent example of Rogers, who was always careful to minimize personal clashes with fellow officers as much as possible and wisely kept his emotions in check for the overall good of himself and the service, despite his personality clashes with others, including commanders and British officers, who detested him far more than he detested them—another secret of his overall success.[100]

Rogers remained haunted by the tragic fate of three of his men captured by a handful of Abenaki warriors in early November: Josiah Malone, a Ranger of Irish descent; James Brown; and Robert Lewis of Sergeant Delanoe's five-man party, which was originally part of Lieutenant Jenkins's contingent. The latter two soldiers were volunteers from General Gage's 80th Light Infantry, which had been partly modeled on Rogers's Rangers.

During the arduous sojourn south, the unlucky members of this group had only survived trekking through the vast expanse of wilderness because they had killed and eaten a captured Abenaki boy, as verified by "an English girl," who had been taken from St. Francis. When some human flesh was found in their packs and knapsacks, the three Rangers had their "throats cut on the spot" by the Abenaki. Two scalps of the unfortunate victims of Lieutenant Jenkins's group were then brought as trophies to the commander of the French garrison at Isle-aux-Noix on the evening of November 7.[101]

The brother of Ranger Sergeant James Ballard of Captain Stark's company, who had been killed at "Rogers's Rock" (Second Battle on Snowshoes on March 13, 1758), Samuel Ballard was another Ranger who suffered the wrath of the infuriated Abenaki, who were determined to avenge the loss of St. Francis. He endured "a horrible death" at the hands of his captors.[102] Watching while tied to a tree, Corporal Frederick Curtiss never forgot "Ballard whom after binding they stabb'd & killed" without mercy.[103]

As could be expected, the large amount of plunder, including religious items stolen from the Catholic church, taken from St. Francis now lay scattered throughout a vast expanse of uncharted wilderness, having been abandoned by Rogers's weary men out of urgent necessity because their lives depended on it. Even the most stubborn Rangers had eventually realized that life was more precious than gold and other riches—a hard-earned lesson that cost the lives of a good many young men and boys in the ranks.

All in all, it almost seemed as if angry Abenaki gods had laid a cruel trap for the victorious Rangers by corrupting their minds with the blind fever of greed to blot out reason and logic in a nasty payback for St. Francis's destruction. They had seemingly laid the golden riches of St. Francis before Rogers's victorious men to allow them to make the fatal mistake of carrying off precious goods instead of food. In this way, it seemed as if the Abenaki gods had wreaked a cruel vengeance in a terrible way by mass starvation that cost the lives of forty-three men, who were some of the finest members of Rogers's Rangers: a tragic loss that haunted Rogers for the rest of his life. In Rogers's words of guilt and sorrow, "The Misfortunes [especially so many deaths by starvation] attending from Retreat from St. Francois causes me great uneasiness [because] the Brave men lost I heartily lament."[104]

Captain Amos Ogden, the former officer of the New Jersey Blues, described the situation that had led to so many deaths in a tragic and unnecessary culling of the ranks when greed raised its ugly head and proved to have been nothing less than a grim reaper of young lives, including some of Rogers's finest men: "The people did bring away considerable plunder, but they drop'd them, or the greater part before they arrived at [the] Connecticut River."[105]

THE PEAK OF A REMARKABLE CAREER

Like few other events, except the fall of Louisbourg and Quebec, the destruction of St. Francis brought a wave of rejoicing and celebration across the colonies, especially in New England and along the northern frontier. And the long-awaited task had been accomplished by one of their own, young Robert Rogers of New Hampshire, who had dared to go where no one else would go by penetrating so deeply into the heart of New France. Indeed, "the whole frontier breathed its relieved thanks" to Major Rogers and his men for achieving the impossible.[106]

A grateful journalist of the *New Hampshire Gazette* captured the representative feeling in Rogers's native state by emphasizing that a great deal of thanks should be delivered to the remarkable man who had destroyed St. Francis and left only ashes as long desired by the colonial people, especially along the frontier.[107]

For such reasons, after the attack on St. Francis, Rogers "was handsomely receiv'd" when he journeyed to Albany and New York in January 1760 to recover from the harrowing ordeal that might well have killed a lesser man.[108]

In eliminating the longtime scourge of the frontier of numerous colonies and wreaking revenge for an entire people, especially the Scotch-Irish, and the large number of dead settlers who had been slaughtered for nearly a century by the seemingly endless war parties from St. Francis, Major Rogers achieved new heights of fame. As could be expected, he basked in the bright "spotlight of celebrity," when colonial newspapers printed the almost unbelievable details of the most daring raid of the French and Indian War. For instance, the editor of the *New-York Mercury* poured lavish praise upon "the indefatigable and brave Major ROGERS" for his "last scout against the St. Francis Indians [which] must be agreeable to our readers."[109]

Another newspaper asked, "What do we owe to such a beneficial Man; and a man of such enterprising genius."[110] Rogers's amazing success in wiping out the hated "nest of Barbarians" that had long vomited forth "Scalping Parties" and thoroughly chastising the Abenaki caused universal rejoicing across the colonies, especially in New England and along the frontier.[111] An account in the pages of the *Boston Evening News* on November 1, 1759, related, "Thus has Major Rogers, with little loss on his own side, almost wholly cut off one tribe" with the most devastating raid ever launched by any fighting men from the British-Provincial Army during the course of the French and Indian War.[112]

Even the amazed enemy, who now possessed more of a grudging respect for the young New Englander, was complimentary because Rogers's remarkable feat fairly boggled the imagination of friend and foe, especially military men educated in conventional European warfare. In disbelief, one Frenchman penned in his diary how "a detachment of about 200 men of Mons. Amherst's army, headed by Captain Rogers, having had the boldness to traverse a pretty extensive tract of country, covered with timber, succeeded, under cover of the surprise, in burning the Indian village of Saint Francois [and] Mons. de Bourlamaque [was] expecting him to return by the same route [to Missisquoi Bay], had him watched, at the passage, by a strong detachment of Canadians and Indians, but Rogers had anticipated all that [and] resolved [to reach safety] by another way" through the wilderness.[113]

However, as could be expected, in continuing to wage a fierce propaganda war, the French had mostly harsh words for the victor of St. Francis. In his memoirs, Pierre Pouchot wrote how Major Rogers "found this Abenaki village deprived of its warriors and killed thirty women and old men, and took away some young persons and prisoners. As he was short of provisions, he separated his troops into several bands [but] All perished of want and famine in the woods except that of Rogers."[114]

Pierre-Joseph-Antoine Roubaud deplored "the massacre and reduction of the village to ashes.... Most of the village was burned to ashes including my house [the rectory of the Jesuit mission church]. Considerable Indian corn and Indians were burned. Ten men and twenty-two women and infants" were killed at St. Francis.[115] Most of all, the leading French officials were astounded by the sheer audacity of the most daring raid of the war, which stunned New France to the core. While they publicly denounced and condemned the raid in the strongest terms, French leaders, nevertheless, could not deny the simple fact that this masterful brainchild of Major Rogers was certainly a "great enterprise," as revealed in the pages of *Lloyd's Evening Post* of London.[116]

But in the end, and as a tragic fate would have it, Rogers had paid a high personal price for winning glory and reaching an even higher level of celebrity across the colonies. After orchestrating one of the greatest wartime odysseys in American history, Rogers was broken down in health, after so much physical and mental exertion, almost superhuman according to the accounts of his men and nothing less than Herculean by any measure. As he penned to General Amherst on April 24, 1760, "I have been in a very bad state of health Ever since the 26th of March last. This being the first day of my walking abroad, but I hope soon to recover to my former health again."[117]

In addition, Rogers had been severely traumatized by the surreal horrors of St. Francis and the loss of so many men (nearly the majority of his command during the harrowing weeks after the attack), and the major would never be quite the same person. In a supreme irony, a traumatized Major Rogers had left his soul behind at St. Francis and in the forgotten places of unbelievable misery amid the wilderness during the long trek home, which had permanently seared his soul to the core.[118]

For him personally, the only bright spot for Rogers had been the initial sight of his surviving men, who he believed had died on the nightmarish trek back to civilization. This was especially the case in regard to the black Ranger "Duke" Jacob. He had been a member of the ten-man contingent, which included Sergeant Stephen Hoit, under the overall command of Sergeant

Benjamin Bradley, who was the senior sergeant and from the Merrimack River country like Rogers.

Like so many others, including most of the sergeant's contingent of ill-starred men, Bradley had died a grisly death from starvation. Finally, only Private "Duke" Jacob, Sergeant Hoit, and Private Robert Pomeroy had remained alive during the nightmarish journey south. A member of "Rogers's Own" who first became a proud Ranger on June 1, 1756, and an experienced woodsman, Sergeant Hoit had gone his own way through the wilderness in the hope of reaching his Merrimack River Valley homeland. However, starvation took the lives of Hoit and Pomeroy until only the irrepressible "Duke" Jacob remained alive.

In the end, a kind Providence or an ancient African god of his ancestors shined upon the lone black Ranger, who became the only lucky survivor of Sergeant Bradley's doomed party when he accidently ran into a hunter along the Baker River: ironically, the same wilderness area where John Stark had been captured by St. Francis Abenaki in 1752 and then taken to St. Francis, where he won the respect of these warriors for his defiant courage. In a most fortunate and timely meeting, the hunter carried the Ranger to his log cabin and revived him; the lucky African American Ranger of a darker hue gradually regained his strength and fully recovered from a living nightmare.

His spirits lifted by the sight of a walking miracle in the form of a most resilient African, Major Rogers could hardly believe his eyes upon the sudden appearance of Private "Duke" Jacob, who was the only survivor of the ill-fated Ranger contingent that had attempted to cross the formidable White Mountains to reach the Merrimack River country through the most rugged of countryside. Indeed, a "gifted fighting man" known for his abilities and resourcefulness, Jacob had defied the odds and lived to tell the tale, including a joyous reunion with his black lover, Rose, who long awaited him in the Colony of New York.[119]

Unlike forty-three of their comrades, who had died of starvation during the trek south from St. Francis, Africa-born "Duke" Jacob, age twenty-six and with tribal markings (or scars) of his native Africa still on his cheeks, and other skeleton-like men were most fortunate to have survived a nightmarish sojourn—a true odyssey with few parallels in American military history—of more than two hundred miles south from St. Francis that continued for two months. One of the New Yorkers who served with distinction in the far-flung raid deep in Quebec, the "Duke" then lived with his black lover and the woman of his dreams, his dusky Rose, who had waited for the return of her Ranger born in Africa.[120]

In the end, Second Lieutenant George Campbell, who hailed from the green hills of Scotland, wrote with a mixture of surprise and astonishment in his diary about the lone surviving black Ranger of the raid on St. Francis: "Ye Major [Rogers] tells that ye Duke [Jacob] was ye only survivor that went toward ye Merrimac" River—a remarkable odyssey of a resilient and resourceful black Ranger, who simply refused to give up and die in the wilderness like the rest of his white comrades of Sergeant Benjamin Bradley's party.[121]

Private "Duke" Jacob was even more fortunate in regard to a horror of which he was not yet aware or perhaps never knew. During this starving time in still another cascade of falling snow that had wrapped the wilderness in a blanket of white, another black Ranger fell victim to a horrific fate. Indeed, in the words of a Ranger named Wood, "a negro soldier died in the night and was cut up in the morning and divided among the soldiers, and [Wood] had one [black] hand for his share [to eat], on which, with a small trout, after being cooked, he made a very good breakfast."[122]

Fortunately, the ever-resourceful Private "Duke" Jacob had avoided suffering such a terrible fate far from the land and the New York woman, Rose, whom he loved like no other.[123]

CHAPTER NINE

Enduring Questions and Controversies to This Day

PERHAPS THE GREATEST IRONY OF THE RAID ON ST. FRANCIS WAS THE FACT that it would have had a larger overall strategic impact to benefit the war effort if Rogers had been unleashed in 1756, as he had carefully planned and proposed to his superior, Lord Loudoun, instead of in 1759. Even more ironically, Rogers's planned invasion route—the same as his recent withdrawal from St. Francis—in 1756 was safer and guaranteed fewer losses than the route taken in 1759, because of the changed strategic situation, especially the fact that the enemy's fighting men had been released after Quebec's fall and joined in the pursuit of the raiders.[1]

Before the raid on St. Francis, Major Rogers was already known for embellishing his battle reports to distort the facts to impress his superiors and enhance his image on both sides of the Atlantic. Like many commanders of the day on both sides, he maximized his own accomplishments and minimized his own losses, while inflating the numbers of opponents who he faced and their losses. Ambitious and smart, consequently, Rogers wrote battle reports to please his superiors in part to enhance his chances for future promotion, and his presentation of what happened at St. Francis was no exception. For example, one historian has recently emphasized how Rogers's report on the Second Battle on Snowshoes on March 13, 1758, where he was badly defeated and his entire command nearly annihilated, was marred by "wild exaggerations."[2] In fact, the "glaring discrepancies in the various reports of the snowshoe fight caused some British commentators to question both Rogers's prowess and his honesty."[3]

What cannot be denied is the fact that there was a massacre at St. Francis, although that disturbing reality has been obscured by Rogers's own words and the writings of generations of admiring New England historians, who have long glorified the audacious raid and the major partly because of an excess of regional pride and because Rogers was a native son. Indeed, what happened at St. Francis was an "uncontrolled massacre" of the ugliest kind because its victims were mostly noncombatants, including children.

Private Robert Kirkwood revealed that his orders from Rogers were to "kill everyone without mercy." With hardly any Abenaki warriors located in the village on that fateful morning in early October, Rogers's men had struck before dawn to catch everyone, mostly women and children, by surprise. Far more women and children were killed in their sleep or in the burning houses than warriors.

To be fair to the Rangers, these men were products of their harsh frontier environment; the French and Indian War was a total war, and their job was to kill. Quite simply, a massacre was inevitable because Rogers's men fought like their opponents in what was basically a war of terrorism and no quarter. This kind of brutality was simply a normal feature of life in an exceptionally cruel world, like the natural world, of many of the New England–born Rangers, since they had been children on the frontier.

The view that the Indians should be exterminated was a common one, especially popular on the frontier, even among Americans, including intellectuals, who had never known the surreal horrors of the wartime frontier experience. Even the refined sage of Monticello, Virginia, Thomas Jefferson, advocated an especially harsh solution for dealing with the Indians of the Upper Ohio region during the American Revolution: "The end proposed should be their extermination, or their removal" farther west.[4]

Meanwhile, across the breadth of New England, the destruction of the "nest of Barbarians" at St. Francis was widely celebrated and hailed as a great victory.[5] After reading Rogers's report disguising the reality of a massacre and as published in colonial newspapers, Major General Jeffery Amherst wrote not only to thank him but also to assure him "of the satisfaction I had on reading it, as every step you inform me you have taken, has been very well judged, and deserves my full approbation."[6]

Therefore, in many ways, the massacre on the morning of October 4 was all but inevitable, because virtually everyone on the British-Provincial side, especially along the frontier, had long desired the destruction of St. Francis. However, one newspaper account revealed the awful truth that cannot be denied: "Orders were to spare all the Women and Children, but they were little attended to" by Rogers's men, whose bloodlust on that terrible morning had been uncontrolled.[7]

However, in truth, after Quebec's fall on September 13, 1759, the daring raid on St. Francis was only a relatively limited success in overall strategic terms and primarily a psychological victory that humiliated New France's power and damaged Abenaki prestige to a degree not previously seen. Because the raid has been long incorrectly portrayed in terms of having wiped out the vast majority of Abenaki warriors (which was certainly not the case) to forever end any possibility of additional threats on the frontier settlements, it has been gloried from the beginning, particularly in New England, especially by historians and popular novelist Kenneth Lewis Roberts in the twentieth century. Everything from history books to novels in the twentieth century have extensively romanticized and glorified the raid, while silencing the ugly truth.

Despite its limited success, Rogers's strike could not have been more audacious, penetrating deep into the heart of French Canada, between Montreal and Quebec, to inflict a devastating blow that increased English and colonial morale. By winning a great moral and psychological victory—more than physical in regard to eliminating warriors, who were surprisingly few—Rogers demonstrated that if New France's most valuable and loyal ally could be punished so severely by the raiders, then no tribe aligned with the French was safe from a hard-hitting reprisal deep in their home territory. This was a powerful message not soon forgotten.[8]

However, "contrary to Rogers' assertions and New England's hopes, St. Francis was not obliterated and the western Abenaki were not destroyed" on the morning of October 4, as the vast majority of warriors had been absent. Therefore, the Abenaki warriors continued to raid, albeit to a lesser degree, because they had not been eliminated by Rogers, directly contradicting the longtime heroic myth of the raid's effectiveness. In fact, the destruction of St. Francis only fueled the Abenaki desire for revenge—ironically, the same motivation that partly fueled Rogers and his men.

As in all wars, a brutal atrocity committed by one side just led to another atrocity, usually a more horrendous one, by the other side, because of the heightened desires for revenge and increased levels of hatred. Quite simply, the most fundamental truth about the raid cannot be denied: Rogers succeeded in destroying only an Abenaki town, not the vast majority of its warriors, which, of course, had been the primary objective of the mission when Major General Amherst dispatched the expedition from Crown Point on September 13.[9]

In the end, Rogers could not even claim the elimination of the great prize of Jesuit Father Roubaud, a native of Avignon, France, in his mid-thirties. He had been absent from St. Francis at Trois-Rivières to the northeast and below Quebec, which came as a great disappointment to the raiders. Fate and God had been kind to Roubaud, who had managed to slip through Rogers's hands, which would have squeezed the life out of Roubaud as they had strangled this wilderness center of Catholicism and source of so many raids on the settlements. After all, this warlike priest had long encouraged and accompanied Abenaki war parties that had slaughtered men, women, and children, including the hapless garrison not long after the surrender of Fort William Henry.[10]

However, an unexpected prize was forthcoming on October 4 with the liberation of captives, including three Rangers, which compensated for having narrowly missed nabbing Father Roubaud, long a wanted man among the Rangers. Hailing from the town of Durham, New Hampshire, George Barnes, a Provincial soldier captured near Lake George in 1756, was liberated by the victors, ending his ordeal in St. Francis. And Barnes's captivity had included a painful running of the gauntlet when he had been "stripped of his clothes and beat with Staves and Clubs" for Abenaki entertainment.[11]

Meanwhile, the Abenaki's war against the English continued with an unabated fury after the destruction of St. Francis. Therefore, in overall strategic terms, Rogers had unleashed what was very much "a pyrrhic campaign against St. Francis" that had little, if any, effect on the overall course of the war. All in all, the raid on St. Francis succeeded against the odds in a true epic, but entirely without long-term strategic results.[12]

In the end, the famous raid on St. Francis should be seen today more as a massacre than as an important strategic strike in a purely traditional sense, as long maintained by historians. Again, to be fair to the Rangers, they behaved at St. Francis in the manner of their enemy and in a way that was not only fully acceptable but also celebrated across New England and the thirteen colonies at the time. After all, Rogers's men were tough and hardened by years of some of the bitterest warfare, including no-mercy combat, ever seen on the North American continent.

For instance, not long after the raid on St. Francis, the Rangers "were waylaid by about 150 French and Indians." As usual, the fortunate survivors, including Rogers, were in an especially foul mood. Therefore, the next morning, when another force of Rangers was sent north from Crown Point to investigate, they discovered "a Squaw, (one of the three) that was shot and proceeding farther, found her Husband, a French Indian, hanging on a Tree, with a Glass close to his Face, supposed to be taken, but just scalped, alive."[13]

In summary, the brutal excesses of Major Rogers and his men at St. Francis must be viewed today in the context of the times and not through a modern lens, without consideration of the place and time in which the value systems of the white world, especially those along the long-suffering frontier, were entirely different to a degree almost unimaginable today. First, Rogers's men had been thoroughly hardened by the wilderness experience, partisan warfare, and deadly struggles for survival, including no-quarter warfare. In their excessively cruel world, in which some of the most hideous tortures had become a pleasurable form of entertainment for Native Americans and some white fighting men, no-quarter warfare was not only a common feature of this conflict but also the norm in the wilderness war. What the average Ranger engaged in year after year in this exceedingly harsh conflict, unlike any other in Europe during this period as part of the Seven Years' War, was in essence an ugly frontier brand of total war—one without mercy or pity—and this brutal reality was demonstrated in full at St. Francis.

Indeed, for a host of reasons, what happened at St. Francis on the early morning of October 4, 1759, should not be interpreted or analyzed from a current-day perspective in terms of the ever-popular political correctness that has automatically condemned every Indian fighter *solely* on racial grounds, because modern readers today cannot understand the true degree of the horror, depravity, and barbarity of this unrestrained war or what generations of America's first settlers experienced across the frontier for generations. After having seen their comrades tortured, butchered like cattle, and scalped alive, their severed heads mounted on poles as trophies, Major Rogers and his men neither asked for nor gave mercy: this was the simple frontier reality and brutal equation of the most vicious conflict in the course of American history.[14]

In truth, even if Rogers had given the order for his men to restrain themselves and not harm any Abenaki women or children at St. Francis, such words would have been quickly forgotten in the heat of combat, with adrenaline pumping in life-and-death situations and bloodlust rising in a war long dominated by surreal horrors.[15]

For such reasons, Major Rogers had no hesitation whatsoever when he ordered his men to "kill every one without mercy"—the most basic rule and law of survival of the fittest in not only the world of nature but also on the embattled northern frontier, where only the strong survived.[16]

But, in the end, there was a method to the madness and the horror that dominated Rogers's boldest attack during the French and Indian War. The slaughter at St. Francis had an overall purpose for the greater good, which was to save settler lives across the breadth of the frontier. The destruction of St. Francis accomplished its goal in one historian's estimation, because Major "Rogers's attack put an end to [the] terrorism" that had descended upon the frontier for generations.[17]

Unacceptable Losses and Glaring Reversals

On October 26, 1759, Governor-General Pierre de Rigaud, the Marquis de Vaudreuil, who had long orchestrated the raids of the hard-fighting defenders of New France with great skill for years, wrote with delight to the minister of France to boast about the elimination of a good many hated Rangers, who had long ago become infamous in French leadership circles: "Forty-six Rangers [actually forty-three men] were killed and ten captured [and] all the rest will starve to death" in the wilderness.[18] Another delighted French leader exaggerated Rogers's loses by claiming, "My savages took prisoners and destroyed three-fourths of the detachment" under Rogers.[19]

Clearly, the destruction of a large percentage of Rogers's command was a propaganda coup for French leadership, which made the most of the opportunity. In this never-ending propaganda war between England and France, nothing bolstered French and Canadian morale more than the exciting news that the hated Rogers had suffered high losses, because the Rangers had been a major thorn in the side of New France year after year.

However, French accounts have proved important in presenting facts not found in English accounts, and they have often come much closer to the truth than English versions of the attack, including from Rogers himself.

After all, much of the glorification of the St. Francis raid does not conform with the facts, because it has become so romanticized and idealized for so long by generations of writers and historians.

In truth, an ample number of "French and Indian accounts provide[d] a rather different picture of the raid from that reported by Rogers, repeated by Amherst, and fictionalized by Kenneth Roberts in his novel [and] Rogers wrote his account of the campaign to impress the British authorities with a view of furthering his own career, and he exaggerated both his own achievements and the impact of the expedition."[20]

To be fair to Rogers, including in regard to his *Journals*, the nature of frontier conflict was so vicious that reports and accounts had to be sanitized because this was official army documentation made palatable to the leading officials and publics on both sides of the Atlantic. Quite simply, on October 4, Rogers never killed two hundred Abenaki warriors at St. Francis, as he claimed to create the illusion that he had permanently eliminated a major threat to the frontier settlements, as was widely assumed then and today.[21]

In truth, Rogers's success at St. Francis was a pyrrhic victory: the cost was entirely too high in regard to lost manpower, which included the flower of the Rangers. In achieving his amazing success at St. Francis, worst of all, Major Rogers lost nearly half his command in the far-flung expedition that covered more than 350 miles round-trip. Only seventy-three men, including Rogers, survived the raid deep into the heart of New France and lived to tell the tale of a true odyssey. But losing such a large percentage of his command, at least 69 of the 142 men who had attacked St. Francis, was nothing new for Major Rogers.

More men had died of starvation (forty-three) than had been killed by the enemy, a total of seventeen men during the entire expedition, including only one, a Stockbridge Ranger, during the attack itself. Of course, the rest of Rogers's men who were killed had been cut down by pursuers during the long withdrawal to New England.

Hiding the awful truth about the frightful cost of destroying St. Francis, the major claimed that he lost only fifty men. In truth, the actual losses of this small task force were so great that Rogers feared for his career and reputation, knowing that he had risked displeasure, if not severe censure, from the high command for losing almost half of his entire task force without ever having fought a battle with large numbers of the enemy.

As a sad fate would have it, and contrary to popular myths, Rogers had lost a sizeable portion of his command in every major confrontation with his opponents, because he was bested by the more experienced Indians and Canadians, especially the highly capable Canadian officers who had been fighting Indian style for most of their lives. Without the propagandist purposes of the raid (which was not a major confrontation in the traditional sense), including excessive romanticization and glorification, and the popular novel by Kenneth Lewis Roberts and the 1940 Hollywood film based on his fiction, Rogers's dismal loss of so many men—nearly 50 percent during the lengthy withdrawal from St. Francis—at a time when conventional battlefield losses were much lower was most alarming by any measure, especially when these were elite fighting men much needed by the British-Provincial Army in the future.

However, the raid's excessive glorification, including by way of Rogers's own self-serving report, has obscured the full extent of these frightful losses, especially of the forty-three men who died from starvation. Rogers's earlier reports also minimized the humiliating defeats suffered by him in large clashes that began in January 1757 during the First Battle on Snowshoes and continued with the Second Battle on Snowshoes in March 1758. Ironically, the victory won at St. Francis so redeemed Rogers's reputation for posterity that the high losses have been long overlooked and considered relatively unimportant by his enthusiastic promoters for generations.

Quite simply, without the daring raid on St. Francis, Rogers would not have become an authentic American hero celebrated to such an extent to this day. Nor would an admiring popular novel and major Hollywood film—presenting him in the most heroic possible light and exactly as he desired to go down in history, which was a chief motivation behind the publication of his *Journals*—have celebrated his exploits. Quite simply, the attack on St. Francis made Major Rogers into an enduring icon, especially in New England, to this day. Without the much-publicized raid on St. Francis that generated so much interest on both sides of the Atlantic, there would have been no publication of Rogers's *Journals* in 1765 and their ensuing popularity.

In the end, an exceptionally large percentage of the Rangers died agonizing deaths in the wilderness because they had believed in Rogers and his tactical abilities, especially in regard to avoiding ambushes and getting them out of tight fixes in emergency situations. But to be fair to Major Rogers, he was simply often outmatched by more experienced leaders and excellent fighting men who were more seasoned and conditioned in Indian fighting and the northern woodlands—after all, the Rangers were interlopers in the enemy's homeland and far from their home forts, which placed them at a severe disadvantage.

Of course, the Indians, who defended their beloved homeland of picturesque hills, pristine rivers, and grassy meadows with their lives, were the best fighting men in the forests of North America for much of the French and Indian War. In addition, the often-overlooked Canadians, who might be more properly described as white Indians (especially in their wilderness knowledge and warfighting skills), often proved superior to the Rangers. While the Rangers were America's best fighting men, they were frequently not as good as the Indians and Canadians in the wilderness that was their home territory—a reality revealed by high Ranger losses over an extended period and long before the attack on St. Francis.

Therefore, in perhaps his greatest achievement, Rogers's real success in this war was simply surviving to fight another day and providing invaluable intelligence to headquarters for years, in contrast to what he accomplished on the battlefield, because he was often outmatched and fighting at a great disadvantage. Most of all, he excelled in the art of reconnaissance and intelligence gathering, having no peer in the British-American army, and these accomplishments were unmatched on either side.

Major Rogers most often only excelled on the battlefield if he faced an opponent of inferior or approximately equal numbers. If he faced a larger force of experienced fighting men on the battlefield (which could be expected since he fought far from support and deep in enemy territory that was far better known to his wily and resourceful opponent), Rogers almost always inevitably met with disaster and lost a large percentage of his men. Given the superior skill and numbers of the French, Canadians, and Indians whom he encountered in the two bloody Battles on Snowshoes, the result was a costly defeat for the Rangers. However, as noted, and most of all, Rogers's greatest victory was simply in surviving to ensure that his command continued to perform as a highly effective combat, intelligence-gathering, and reconnaissance unit and fight another day. Rogers's real success was this rare resiliency not seen in any other commands.

Contrary to romantic legend and myth and fortunately for his reputation, Rogers's most bitter defeats were overshadowed in the historical record by the success at St. Francis. Indeed, an exceptionally large number of Ranger bodies had been left behind in the wilderness across the Lake Champlain strategic corridor before Rogers destroyed St. Francis. Erupting on March 13, 1758, amid the snowy wilderness not far from Fort Carillon, the initial Ranger success gained in the Second Battle on Snowshoes shortly evolved into nothing short of an absolute disaster of unparalleled proportions. The battle evolved into a fiasco for the Rangers, thanks to Ensign Langy's superior leadership and the firepower of the sharpshooting Canadians, who cut down one Ranger after another with astonishing effectiveness to leave the snow splashed in red and covered in bodies. More than 140 men were killed during the greatest disaster ever suffered by the Rangers. In the end, Rogers and those of his men not cut down on this day of slaughter had been fortunate to escape, when the veil of darkness provided the long-awaited opportunity.

As mentioned, the men who served under Rogers paid a frightfully high cost for the privilege of serving with great pride in an elite fraternity as Rangers. The pain of losing so many good men—friends, relatives, and neighbors from the Merrimack River country and across New England—in past fights over the years and then in the raid on St. Francis drove a stake through Rogers's heart, revealing the soft side of a warm and sentimental Scotch-Irishman who never entirely recovered from the horror and trauma. From beginning to end, the most human quality of Rogers was his deep, if not excessive, concern for the welfare of his men, and his pain at losing them was like that of a father losing his own children. As he had no close family of his own at the time, these terrible losses of his beloved Rangers devastated Rogers, torturing his heart and soul for the remainder of his days.

After the Second Battle on Snowshoes on March 13, 1758, when more than 140 Rangers were killed and scalped, Rogers wrote how his Rangers had "behaved with the utmost Bravery, and Coolness" during the most recent disaster.[22] However, Rogers was less truthful in his reports about the battle, which were embellished and distorted to the extent that the major lost credibility.[23]

For good reason, Major Rogers devoted few words to the bloody fiasco in which the Canadians, French, and Indian warriors gained "a great harvest of a hundred and fourteen scalps."[24] In regard to his losses suffered during the St. Francis raid, a grieving Rogers wrote a heartfelt letter to Major General Amherst and bared his soul, which was still tormented: "The misfortunes attending my Retreat from St. Francis causes me great uneasiness, the Brave men lost I most heartily [*sic*] lament, and fear your Excellency's Censure as the going against that place was my own proposal [and he remained haunted by] so many perishing in the woods."25

In fact, the losses suffered year after year by the major in leading his Rangers were so high that they played a part in keeping the average frontiersman of common sense from enlisting in the Rangers. Therefore, partly because of such generally overlooked factors, Ranger recruiters were forced to recruit urbanities from the wharves of Boston—city boys without any wilderness or frontier experience—and far from the frontier.26

Some colonial newspapers faithfully listed the Rangers' high losses, which were a testament to the superior fighting qualities of their opponents. As mentioned, to be fair to Major Rogers, for obvious propaganda purposes and as could be expected, the French leadership likewise hid their own losses, but they were not as high as those of Rogers in larger clashes or in regard to the St. Francis expedition. Naturally, the French wanted to keep this information about their own losses from encouraging the English and lifting morale in a brutal war of attrition not seen in Europe.27

However, the fact remained that serving under Rogers was a risky and extremely dangerous experience, and the high losses suffered during the St. Francis expedition long haunted the major because he knew that the price paid had been far too high. In fact, no British or Provincial unit in North American more consistently lost higher percentages of men than Rogers's command. In both Battles on Snowshoes and during the retreat from St. Francis, Rogers's command suffered a very high percentage of losses, which were enough to have ended his career and the command's existence, if not for his outstanding leadership qualities.28

However, this worst-case scenario did not come to pass for the Rangers largely because the major was needed by the army and because of his ability to resurrect his command without a significant reduction of capabilities. Rogers's leadership skills and abilities ensured the longtime survival of his command, despite high losses that were entirely unacceptable. Time and time again, he successfully resurrected his decimated command from massive losses that seemingly could not be overcome. Consequently, the Rangers continued to function at a high level and make important contributions to the overall war effort year after year: perhaps the most remarkable testament to

Rogers's sterling leadership qualities and abilities. Despite suffering the kind of terrible losses that would typically have ensured the unit's decommissioning, and thanks to the undying willingness of his men to follow him to hell and back if necessary, Rogers continued to lead his Rangers with skill and his usual aggressiveness, contributing to the ultimate victory of England during the struggle for possession of the North American continent.

NAGGING QUESTIONS ABOUT AN ENDURING LEGACY

One modern historian, Walter R. Borneman, was right on target when he concluded about the raid on St. Francis, "Even compared with the most horrendous encounters of the period, this casualty rate was appalling. . . . There is some evidence that both Rogers and General Amherst sought to sweep the figures under the table or at the very least not tally them all in one place."[29]

However, in summary, perhaps historian Colin G. Calloway said it best in regard to the enduring legacy of the most famous raid of the French and Indian War: "The Abenaki called Rogers Wobi Madaondo—the White Devil. Rogers claimed that 200 Abenaki died in the attacks—clearly an exaggeration [but a] fictionalized and biased account of Rogers' raid is provided in Kenneth Roberts's novel *Northwest Passage*, made into a movie in 1940. The popular book and movie *Northwest Passage* both helped perpetuate the common image and enduring racial stereotype of the Abenaki as bloodthirsty savages," who were only deserving of extinction in the traditional metaphysics of Indian hating.[30]

In all wars, especially in the course of American history, the winners have written the history, and Major Rogers's dramatic story of the raid on St. Francis did not deviate from the rule. Therefore, for generations we have been given the winner's version (exaggerated and embellished, as in the major's self-serving reports to his superiors) of the raid on St. Francis, one that was extensively glorified, especially in New England and by historians and writers from this region. And this sanitized version of events came primarily from the carefully crafted words of the man who had the most to gain from it: Rogers.[31]

Of course, and as mentioned, the first example of an inevitable distortion of the historical record that was widely committed by both sides during the French and Indian War came in the form of Rogers's official report, which was printed in colonial newspapers and bolstered the major's legacy.[32] As mentioned, Rogers wrote about the return march in his report about the expedition, and this information that avoided the horrendous losses was received by Major General Amherst at this Crown Point headquarters.[33]

In another letter to Amherst, Rogers wrote in more detail on November 8 to fill in the gaps left in his original report to the major general: "I cannot forbear making some remarks upon the difficulties and distresses which attended the expedition, under my command, against St. Francis, situated within three miles of the river St. Lawrence, in the heart of Canada, half way between Montreal and Quebec [and the troops] proceeded to destroy the town, as before related [in his first report to Major General Amherst], which would probably have been effected, with no other loss than that of the Indian killed in the action, had not our boats been discovered and our retreat that way cut off."[34]

To his credit, historian Francis Parkman seemed almost hesitant to give Rogers his just due to a rather surprising degree because of the controversies surrounding the attack on St. Francis, especially the killing of Abenaki women and children, both intentionally and by accident, and because he knew that very few warriors were present on October 4, 1759. Consequently, Parkman devoted only several pages to the most legendary raid of the French and Indian War in his classic work *Montcalm and Wolfe*. Of course, Parkman had read the contrary and more accurate reports of French officials, whose accounts of the St. Francis raid are now housed in the Archives of the Quebec Archdiocese, Canada, which revealed the truth about a raid that was much less significant in overall strategic terms than claimed by Rogers, local writers, and historians.[35] Indeed, in 1765, Rogers published his famous *Journals* in England "partly to obscure less heroic ventures," in the accurate words and analysis of historian Walter R. Borneman.[36]

Author John F. Ross, in his popular 2011 work titled *War on the Run*, likewise emphasized, "Yet Rogers's journals—what he chooses to tell and what he omits—reveal a man mysterious by design, who left the question of how he did things hanging in the air."[37] Historian Stephen Brumwell described how the "glaring discrepancies" in Rogers's writings and reports "caused some British commentators to question both Rogers' prowess and his honesty."[38] However, Rogers's report about his St. Francis raid was far more honest and accurate than young George Washington's report, containing deliberate falsehoods, to Virginia governor Robert Dinwiddie about his bungling in western Pennsylvania that had started the French and Indian War in July 1754.[39]

One critic of Parkman and his most famous work devoted to the French and Indian War took him to task for rescuing Rogers from historical oblivion by way of glorification and idolization to an excessive degree: "Parkman's great hero Rogers was nothing less than depraved: a brutal braggart, and an unashamed self-publicist whose celebrated raid upon St. Francis amounted to little more than the massacre of defenceless women and children."[40]

Consequently, the real Rogers cannot be seen in the writings of his famous *Journals*, which were polished by his London editors and continue to be reprinted to this day, but in his own words. For example, he described the high personal price that he paid in emotional and psychological terms for having been trapped in the most brutal and dehumanizing of frontier environments and merciless of wars, especially the nagging guilt that came from having lost so many men, including from his own tactical mistakes and errors of judgment, which proved so costly. And, as noted, this situation applied to the recent raid on St. Francis and the withdrawal in which he lost nearly half his entire task force. As Rogers, allowing his softer (or more human) side to show in a rare display of his most heartfelt feelings, penned with sincerity to Major General Amherst, "The Misfortunes attending my Retreat from Saint Francois causes me great uneasiness, the Brave men lost heartily [which I greatly] lament."[41]

Private Robert Kirkwood and his fellow surviving members of the expedition that destroyed St. Francis and reduced it to ashes had gained a proud memory of not only Rogers but also the evil (in their minds) that they had extinguished with a righteous zeal at St. Francis. With religious overtones that revealed his Scottish Calvinist heritage and the biblical lessons that he had learned as a child, Kirkwood wrote in summary of America's most impossible mission in which the war was taken to the Abenaki as never before: "Thank God a period [or end finally] was ... put to their cruelty" that had become legendary for generations across the frontier.[42]

But most important, Rogers and his men had demonstrated that they could do the impossible when very few individuals on either side expected them to be successful in the war's most improbable mission. Rogers and his men exhibited in full at St. Francis how Rogers's Rangers had developed "another tactic still used by modern Rangers—the deep raid—and striking at the enemy in their own area of operation [which] became a Ranger trademark [and] Rangers from the beginning have excelled at terrifying their opponents by striking where and when least expected."[43]

The daring raid on St. Francis was additional proof that Major Rogers and his Rangers were "the most formidable body of men ever employed in the early wars of America [and] To their savage and French foes, they were invincible."[44] Quite simply, Rogers and his crack fighting men, masters of irregular, or Indian, warfare, were most of all professional killers just like their most lethal enemy, and they demonstrated this undeniable truth in full during the surprise attack on St. Francis.

Indeed, in regard to a proper historical perspective, the successes of Rogers and his men represented the first golden age of the American fighting man, when these elite Rangers consistently outperformed and outfought not only the Provincial troops but also British Regulars by an exceedingly wide margin, while making more significant overall contributions to the winning of the French and Indian War. And based on his own set of twenty-eight innovative and timeless axioms about the art of warfighting in the wilderness, the frontier tactical mastermind behind these successes was a bold and resourceful Scotch-Irish commander of lowly antecedents, who had never been trained in a military school or ever read a military manual in the art of war: a true Horatio Alger success story born of both the frontier and Scotch-Irish experience.

Instead of relying on traditional and old-fashioned ways of fighting, Rogers waged war based upon his well-honed insights gained from Native Americans and the wilderness experience to create America's most successful and daring fighting men of his day. And, ironically, this remarkable feat was accomplished by Rogers in the most disadvantageous and negative of environments, when the British military establishment and its aristocratic members held Americans in absolute contempt because they were deemed worthless as soldiers because they were colonials born on the soil of America.

Quite simply, Rogers and his Rangers were the best fighting men—the elite of the elite—that America produced during the entire course of the French and Indian War. Rogers was a shining star in a dark constellation of nonachievers and less talented men among the allegedly superior British military establishment based on politics, class, birth, and the purchasing of officer commissions. Rogers benefited from none of these means that traditional military officers used to get ahead instead of achievements; rather, he relied on his own God-given talents and rare gifts in regard to leadership abilities and in the art of warfighting to accomplish what no one else could have achieved.

Rogers and his twenty-eight rules for conducting ranging warfare in the wilderness played a key role that explained why and how Great Britain ultimately emerged victorious in the French and Indian War: the timely utilization of a combination of hard-hitting traditional army and Ranger methods with the use of large numbers of Rangers and British light troops, who had been modeled on the Rangers. Rogers was an ordinary man of the northern frontier, without formal military training or sufficient education (military or civilian), who achieved extraordinary things in the military realm that no one else could accomplish.

For these reasons, this aspiring son of lowly Scotch-Irish parents of the northern frontier grew to be detested by the top British leadership because he was an unorthodox and unconventional American from the backwoods, far too successful in their traditional minds, and a nonprofessional of the lower class who had risen on his own abilities and merits—all factors galling to the aristocratic members of the British military elite that turned against him and made him their target in the end.

Eventually the aristocratic British elite of the military establishment brought their considerable wrath down on Rogers and destroyed him and his military career, which was something that the Indians, French, and Canadians had been unable to accomplish after years of trying with all their might: the ultimate irony of the unorthodox life and distinguished military career of America's first wartime hero, Robert Rogers.[45]

Epilogue

On February 14, 1757, more than two and a half years before the bloody day of reckoning at St. Francis deep in Quebec, when British-Provincial fortunes were especially bleak, America's first wartime hero rose high like the proverbial phoenix from the ashes of a growing list of British-Provincial defeats and humiliations. One astute journalist of the *Boston Gazette* bestowed the ultimate compliment on America's first true war hero and national celebrity, when British and Provincial forces were losing the war on all fronts. He wrote what could be said of no one else in the British-Provincial Army at the time: "The brave Rogers is acquiring Glory to him-self in the Field, and in some Degree recovering the sunken Reputation of his Country."[1]

In playing a key role in the long and bloody process of the winning of an entire continent, so that Americans "might be free to win their independence from England" in the near future, Rogers and his Rangers "became synonymous with the free spirit stirring through the American colonies [and] personified the new breed of free men"—the Americans who were destined to dominate an entire continent after the winning of the French and Indian War and then embarking upon a westward march that eventually reached the Pacific in America's first Manifest Destiny.[2]

When the fate of a great continent was at stake, Rogers emerged from the depths of his extremely harsh northern frontier environment and a lowly immigrant background of Irish parentage to rise high by excelling in his innovative warfighting ways like no other American of his era to achieve fame on both sides of the Atlantic. He was a saint to many people, especially along the frontier, and a sinner to others. In truth, Rogers, like all men, had a dark side and a more redeeming one, but he was a model inspirational leader in wartime second to none in the eyes of a vigorous new people likewise on the rise—the Americans.

Representing an American Horatio Alger story, the irrepressible Rogers was an ordinary man of the northern frontier, blessed with extraordinary talents and gifts, who rose to the fore during America's cruelest war, which was a vicious struggle for survival, when the English colonies were threatened with subjugation. Out of the tempests and bloodletting of the most horrific conflict seen since the Dark Ages, young Robert Rogers emerged as America's foremost wartime hero across the colonies, while helping to fuel the rise of a distinctive American spirit and a nascent American nationalism of an independent-minded people destined to forever change the world with their own homegrown revolution not long after the French and Indian War's conclusion. Rogers's epic march to St. Francis and back—a true American odyssey—was only one short chapter of a remarkable story about America's hard-fighting Rangers.

In the end, the French and Indian War, which was the greatest world war of the eighteenth century, made not only America but also the American people. And all of these earthshaking events might not have been possible without the contributions of Robert Rogers and his legendary Rangers, who conquered America's first frontier in an unorthodox and unconventional manner all their own.

NOTES

Chapter 1: America's First and Bloodiest Frontier

1. Walter R. Borneman, *The French and Indian War: Deciding the Fate of North America* (New York: HarperCollins, 2006), xxi–29; Jacques Lacoursiere and Robin Philpot, *A People's History of Quebec* (Quebec: Baraka Books, 2002), 10–24; John F. Winkler, *Point Pleasant 1774: Prelude to the American Revolution* (Oxford: Osprey Publishing, 2014), 8–9.

2. Armand Francis Lucier, *French and Indian War Notices Abstracted from Colonial Newspapers*, vol. 2: *1756–1757* (Bowie, MD: Heritage Books, 2007), 1.

3. John E. Ferling, *A Wilderness of Miseries: War and Warriors in Early America* (Westport, CT: Greenwood Press, 1980), 28.

4. Lucier, *French and Indian War Notices*, 2:2–3.

5. Kevin Phillips, *The Cousins' Wars* (New York: Basic Books, 1999), xii–xiii; Lucier, *French and Indian War Notices*, 2:31, 58, 69, 142–45, 181; Ferling, *A Wilderness of Miseries*, 8, 10.

6. Lucier, *French and Indian War Notices*, 2:71.

7. Lucier, *French and Indian War Notices*, 2:31.

8. Lucier, *French and Indian War Notices*, 2:58; Ferling, *A Wilderness of Miseries*, 22.

9. Lucier, *French and Indian War Notices*, 2:181.

10. Ferling, *A Wilderness of Miseries*, 35.

11. Ferling, *A Wilderness of Miseries*, 16.

12. Lucier, *French and Indian War Notices*, 2:142–45.

13. Lucier, *French and Indian War Notices*, 2:69.

14. Borneman, *The French and Indian War*, 29.

15. Borneman, *The French and Indian War*, 289–90.

16. Armand Francis Lucier, *French and Indian War Notices Abstracted from Colonial Newspapers*, vol. 3: *January 1, 1758–September 17, 1759* (Bowie, MD: Heritage Books, 1999), 2–4.

17. Lucier, *French and Indian War Notices*, 3:2–4.

18. Lucier, *French and Indian War Notices*, 3:25.

19. Lucier, *French and Indian War Notices*, 2:256–57.

20. Ferling, *A Wilderness of Miseries*, 49.

21. Ferling, *A Wilderness of Miseries*, 49–50.

22. Ferling, *A Wilderness of Miseries*, 31.

23. Lucier, *French and Indian War Notices*, 2:69–71.

24. Lucier, *French and Indian War Notices*, 2:69–71.

25. Wendy Warren, *New England Bound* (New York: W. W. Norton and Company, 2016), 1–151.

26. Warren, *New England Bound*, 1–151; Lucier, *French and Indian War Notices*, 2:69–71.

27. Warren, *New England Bound*, 9.

28. Warren, *New England Bound*, 1–83, 139; Lucier, *French and Indian War Notices*, 2:69–71; George C. Daughan, *Lexington and Concord: The Battle Heard Round the World* (New York: W. W. Norton and Company, 2018), 201–2; Phillips, *The Cousins' Wars*, xii–xiii.

29. Warren, *New England Bound*, 161.

30. Warren, *New England Bound*, 1–14, 31, 34–81, 90–113.

31. Warren, *New England Bound*, 7.

32. Warren, *New England Bound*, 7.

33. Fred Anderson, *The War That Made America* (New York: Penguin Books, 2005), 90–91.

34. Ferling, *A Wilderness of Miseries*, 20.

35. Scott Weidensaul, *The First Frontier: The Forgotten History of Struggle, Savagery, and Endurance in Early America* (Boston: Houghton Mifflin Harcourt, 2012), 60, 117–22; Mir Bahmanyar, *Shadow Warriors: A History of the US Army Rangers* (Oxford: Osprey Publishing, 2005), 9–13; Ferling, *A Wilderness of Miseries*, 16; Serge Courville, *Quebec: Historical Geography*, trans. Richard Howard (Vancouver, BC: UBC Press, 2008), 35, 46; Phillips, *The Cousins' Wars*, xii–xiii.

36. Ferling, *A Wilderness of Miseries*, 10.

37. Weidensaul, *The First Frontier*, xviii–xix, 128–29, 132, 136–67, 174, 192, 211; Warren, *New England Bound*, 83–113; John R. Cuneo, *Robert Rogers of the Rangers* (New York: Richardson and Steirman, 1987), 3–7, 11; Eric Hinderaker and Peter C. Mancall, *At the Edge of Empire: The Backcountry in British North America* (Baltimore: Johns Hopkins University Press, 2003), 1–3; John Demos, *The Unredeemed Captive: A Family Story from Early America* (New York: Vintage Books, 1994), 3–4, 25, 27; Robert W. Black, *Ranger Dawn: The American Rangers from the Colonial Era to the Mexican War* (Mechanicsburg, PA: Stackpole Books), 30, 32, 53–54; Ferling, *A Wilderness of Miseries*, 3–54; Rene Chartrand, *Raiders from New France: North American Forest Warfare Tactics, 17th–18th Centuries* (Oxford: Osprey Publishing, 2019), 42–43, 46–47; Lucier, *French and Indian War Notices*, 2:13, 25, 74; Jim Hobbs, *What You May Not Know about Roger's Rangers* (Columbia, SC: private printing, 2019), 3; Shepard Ritkin, *The Savage Years* (Greenwich, CT: Fawcett Publications, 1967), 41, 46, 48; Michael Johnson, *Indian Tribes of the New England Frontier* (Oxford: Osprey Publishing, 2006), 12, 18–18; Colin G. Calloway, *The Scratch of a Pen: 1763 and the Transformation of North America* (Oxford: Oxford University Press, 2006), 4; Stephen Brumwell, *White Devil: A True Story of War, Savagery, and Vengeance in Colonel America* (New York: Da Capo Press, 2004), 102; Gary Stephen Zaboly, *A True Ranger: The Life and Many Wars of Major Robert Rogers* (New York: Royal Blockhouse, 2004), 14, 16–19, 21, 23, 32–34, 202.

38. Robert Rogers, *A Concise Account of North America* (London: J. Millan, 1765), 49, in Hobbs, *What You May Not Know about Roger's Rangers*.

39. Zaboly, *A True Ranger*, 33.

40. Rogers, *A Concise Account of North America*, in Hobbs, *What You May Not Know about Rogers Rangers*, 55.

41. Hobbs, *What You May Not Know about Roger's Rangers*, 53.

42. Black, *Ranger Dawn*, 30, 32, 54; Zaboly, *A True Ranger*, 36.

43. Anderson, *The War That Made America*, 4–5; Zaboly, *A True Ranger*, 36.

44. Anderson, *The War That Made America*, 36.

45. Lucier, *French and Indian War Notices*, 2:4–6.

46. Lucier, *French and Indian War Notices*, 3:2–3.

47. Ferling, *A Wilderness of Miseries*, 35.

48. Edward P. Hamilton, ed. and trans., *Adventures in the Wilderness: The American Journals of Louis Antoine de Bougainville, 1756–1760* (Norman: University of Oklahoma Press, 1964), 41.

49. Lucier, *French and Indian War Notices*, 3:11.

50. Ferling, *A Wilderness of Miseries*, 34.

51. Weidensaul, *The First Frontier*, 174.

52. Ferling, *A Wilderness of Miseries*, 45.

53. Ferling, *A Wilderness of Miseries*, 46.

54. Ferling, *A Wilderness of Miseries*, 36, 46.

55. Hamilton, *Adventures in the Wilderness*, xi, 45; Brumwell, *White Devil*, 78–79.

56. James Carty, *Ireland: From the Flight of the Earls to Grattan's Parliament* (Dublin: Cahill and Company, Ltd., 1957), 38, 67; Cuneo, *Robert Rogers of the Rangers*, 3–7; Johnson, *Indian Tribes of the New England Frontier*, 7; Michael Kammen, *Colonial New York: A History* (Millwood, NY: KTO Press, 1975), 178–79.

57. Allan Kulikoff, *Tobacco and Slaves: The Development of Southern Cultures in the Chesapeake, 1680–1800* (Chapel Hill: University of North Carolina Press, 1986), 207.

58. Ferling, *A Wilderness of Miseries*, 35.

59. J. W. Meader, *The Merrimack River: Its Sources and Its Tributaries* (Boston: B. B. Russell, 1871), 9; Cuneo, *Robert Rogers of the Rangers*, 6–7; James Webb, *Born Fighting: How the Scots-Irish Shaped America* (New York: Broadway Books, 2004), 32–119.

60. Webb, *Born Fighting*, 89.

61. David Hackett Fischer, *Albion's Seed: Four British Folkways in America* (New York: Oxford University Press, 1989), 612.

62. Weidensaul, *The First Frontier*, 129–30.

63. Meader, *The Merrimack River*, 9, 11; Webb, *Born Fighting*, 32–119.

64. Zaboly, *A True Ranger*, 202.

65. Burt Garfield Loescher, *The History of Rogers' Rangers*, vol. 4: *The St. Francis Raid* (Bowie, MD: Heritage Books, 2002), 3.

66. Bahmanyar, *Shadow Warriors*, 14, 16; Francis Parkman, *Montcalm and Wolfe: The French and Indian War* (New York: Da Capo Books, 1984), 200.

67. Lucier, *French and Indian War Notices*, 2:280.

68. Zaboly, *A True Ranger*, 44.

69. Webb, *Born Fighting*, 9–162; Ferling, *A Wilderness of Miseries*, 50.

70. Ferling, *A Wilderness of Miseries*, 34–35, 49–50.

71. Lucier, *French and Indian War Notices*, 2:244–45.

72. Lucier, *French and Indian War Notices*, 2:130.

73. Lucier, *French and Indian War Notices*, 3:74.

74. Lucier, *French and Indian War Notices*, 3:50.

75. Lucier, *French and Indian War Notices*, 3:55–56.

76. Lucier, *French and Indian War Notices*, 2:257–58.

77. Lucier, *French and Indian War Notices*, 2:286.

78. Lucier, *French and Indian War Notices*, 2:287.

79. Warren, *New England Bound*, 9, 216.

80. Lucier, *French and Indian War Notices*, 2:288.

81. Lucier, *French and Indian War Notices*, 2:295; David R. Starbuck, "The 'Massacre' at Fort William Henry," *Expedition* 50, no. 1 (2008), www.penn.museum/sites/expedition/the-massacre-at-fort-william-henry.

82. Zaboly, *A True Ranger*, 69.
83. Lucier, *French and Indian War Notices*, 3:348.
84. Hamilton, *Adventures in the Wilderness*, 21.
85. Lucier, *French and Indian War Notices*, 2:156.
86. Black, *Ranger Dawn*, 41–42; Borneman, *The French and Indian War*, 13.
87. Zaboly, *A True Ranger*, 187–88.
88. Brumwell, *White Devil*, 197, 243–44.
89. Rogers, *A Concise Account of North America*, 139, in Hobbs, *What You May Not Know about Roger's Rangers*.
90. Hamilton, *Adventures in the Wilderness*, 9.
91. Hamilton, *Adventures in the Wilderness*, 118.
92. Hamilton, *Adventures in the Wilderness*, 332; Calloway, *The Scratch of a Pen*, 6.
93. Dan Snow, *Death or Victory: The Battle of Quebec and the Birth of an Empire* (New York: Penguin Book Group, 2009), xxiii.
94. Snow, *Death or Victory*, 48–49.
95. Robert Eastburn, Rufus Putnam, and John Hawks, *Narratives of the French and Indian War*, Eyewitness to War Series (Duffield, UK: Leonaur, 2008), 27, 39–44.
96. Borneman, *The French and Indian War*, 8–13, 17.

Chapter 2: Quebec's Infamous Jesuit Missionary Town of St. Francis

1. Edward Pierce, *Pitt the Elder: Man of War* (London: Pimlico Publishing, 2011), 211–25; J. Watts De Peyster, *Expedition of the British and Provincial Army, under Major General Jeffrey Amherst, against Ticonderoga and Crown Point, 1759* (Albany: J. Munsell, 1857), 70–119; Zaboly, *A True Ranger*, 218, 260–65.
2. Rene Chartrand, *The Forts of New France in Northeast America, 1600–1763* (Oxford: Osprey Publishing, 2008), 25.
3. Chartrand, *The Forts of New France*, 25.
4. Chartrand, *The Forts of New France*, 25.
5. Hamilton, *Adventures in the Wilderness*, 83; Peter N. Moogk, *La Nouvelle France: The Making of French Canada—a Cultural History* (East Lansing: Michigan State University Press, 2000), 29.
6. Adirondack Life, *Lake Champlain: A Celebration of America's Most Historic Lake: An Illustrated History* (New York: Adirondack Life, 2000), 101; Hamilton, *Adventures in the Wilderness*, 83–84.
7. Hamilton, *Adventures in the Wilderness*, 84; Caleb Stark, *Memoir and Official Correspondence of Gen. John Stark* (Concord, NH: Edison C. Eastman, 1877), 11–13.
8. Andrew Gallup, *Memoir of a French and Indian War Soldier, "Jolicoeur" Charles Bonin* (Westminster, MD: Heritage Books, 2007), 167–68.
9. Colin G. Calloway, *The Western Abenakis of Vermont, 1600–1800: War, Migration, and the Survival of an Indian People* (Norman: University of Oklahoma Press, 1994), 95; Cuneo, *Robert Rogers of the Rangers*, 11; Courville, *Quebec*, 28; Moogk, *La Nouvelle France*, 36; Johnson, *Indian Tribes of the New England Frontier*, 6–7; Brumwell, *White Devil*, 211–12.
10. John Demos, *The Unredeemed Indian Captive: Family Story from Early America* (New York: Vintage Books, 1994), 15; Moogk, *La Nouvelle France*, 36; Richard V. Polhemus and John F. Polhemus, *Stark: The Life and Wars of John Stark, French and Indian War Ranger,*

Revolutionary War General (Delmar, NY: Black Dome Press Corporation, 2014), 5; Johnson, *Indian Tribes of the New England Frontier*, 6–7; Chartrand, *Raiders from New France*, 42–43; Burt Garfield Loescher, *The History of Rogers' Rangers*, vol. 3: *Officers and Noncommissioned Officers* (Bowie, MD: Heritage Books, 2002):17, 75; Clifton La Bree, *New Hampshire's General John Stark, Live Free or Die: Death Is Not the Worst of Evils* (New Boston, NH: Peter E. Randall Publisher, LLC, 2007), 40; Johnson, *Indian Tribes of the New England Frontier*, 7.

11. Demos, *The Redeemed Indian Captive*, 15.

12. Robert Rogers, *Journals of Robert Rogers of the Rangers* (Duffield, UK: Leonaur, 2005), 121; Cuneo, *Robert Rogers of the Rangers*, 7; Hinderaker and Mancall, *At the Edge of Empire*, 58–59; Colin G. Calloway, *The Abenaki* (New York: Chelsea House Publishers, 1989), 56–57; Brumwell, *White Devil*, 45; Demos, *The Unredeemed Captive*, 6–7; Ferling, *A Wilderness of Miseries*, 10–54; Calloway, *The Western Abenakis of Vermont*, 16–18, 26, 30, 48–49, 69, 79, 87–88, 90–92, 135, 166–68, 247.

13. Cuneo, *Robert Rogers of the Rangers*, 7; Hinderaker and Mancall, *At the Edge of Empire*, 1–4; Brumwell, *White Devil*, 51–52, 102–3; Courville, *Quebec*, 44–45.

14. Zaboly, *A True Ranger*, x.

15. Brumwell, *White Devil*, 82, 102; Zaboly, *A True Ranger*, 93–288; John F. Ross, *War on the Run: The Epic Story of Robert Rogers and the Conquest of America's First Frontier* (New York: Bantam Books Trade Paperback, 2011), 156–262.

16. Ross, *War on the Run*, 463.

17. Loescher, *The History of Rogers' Rangers*, 3:14–15; Brumwell, *White Devil*, 92–96.

18. Brumwell, *White Devil*, 130–31, 140, 159–60; Zaboly, *A True Ranger*, 238–65; Loescher, *The History of Rogers' Rangers*, 3:14–15.

19. Cuneo, *Robert Rogers of the Rangers*, 101.

20. Lucier, *French and Indian War Notices*, 2:13, 74, 105, 113, 177.

21. Johnson, *Indian Tribes of the New England Frontier*, 6–7; Borneman, *The French and Indian War*, xxi–xxii; Calloway, *The Western Abenakis of Vermont*, xvi–xviii, 14, 48–49, 63, 94–95, 103; Colin G. Calloway, *Indians of the Northeast* (New York: Facts on File, Inc., 1991), 7–11, 17, 50, 54–55; Ross, *War on the Run*, 248; Parkman, *Montcalm and Wolfe*, 452; Zaboly, *A True Ranger*, 280; Calloway, *The Abenaki*, 13–16, 41–49; Courville, *Quebec*, 27–32, 44–45; Brumwell, *White Devil*, 166–67; Ferling, *A Wilderness of Miseries*, 4–54.

22. Susanna Johnson, *A Narrative of the Captivity of Mrs. Johnson* (Bowie, MD: Heritage Books, 1990), 76–77; Calloway, *The Western Abenakis of Vermont*, 27–28, 63; Johnson, *Indian Tribes of the New England Frontier*, 6–7; La Bree, *New Hampshire's General John Stark*, 40; Ferling, *A Wilderness of Miseries*, 11–92; Ian McCulloch and Timothy Todish, eds., *Through So Many Dangers: The Memoirs and Adventures of Robert Kirk, Late of the Royal Highland Regiment* (Fleischmanns, NY: Purple Mountain Press, 2004), 66; Warren, *New England Bound*, 3–113.

23. Johnson, *A Narrative of the Captivity of Mrs. Johnson*, 28.

24. Johnson, *A Narrative of the Captivity of Mrs. Johnson*, 29.

25. Johnson, *A Narrative of the Captivity of Mrs. Johnson*, 36.

26. Lucier, *French and Indian War Notices*, 3:1–2.

27. Johnson, *A Narrative of the Captivity of Mrs. Johnson*, 67; Calloway, *The Western Abenakis of Vermont*, 30.

28. Johnson, *A Narrative of the Captivity of Mrs. Johnson*, 68; Calloway, *The Western Abenakis of Vermont*, 30.

29. Johnson, *A Narrative of the Captivity of Mrs. Johnson*, 71; Calloway, *The Western Abenakis of Vermont*, 30; Brumwell, *White Devil*, 47, 193.
30. Parkman, *Montcalm and Wolfe*, 452–53.
31. Parkman, *Montcalm and Wolfe*, 453.
32. Johnson, *A Narrative of the Captivity of Mrs. Johnson*, 63.
33. Lucier, *French and Indian War Notices*, 3:1–2.
34. Brumwell, *White Devil*, 237.
35. Brumwell, *White Devil*.
36. Parkman, *Montcalm and Wolfe*, 452–53; Calloway, *The Abenaki*, 22.
37. Moogk, *La Nouvelle France*, 41, 45.
38. Calloway, *The Abenaki*, 25, 41–49.
39. Calloway, *The Abenaki*, 27–29, 39; Johnson, *A Narrative of the Captivity of Mrs. Johnson*, 76–77; Calloway, *The Western Abenakis of Vermont*, 161; Lucier, *French and Indian War Notices*, 3:89.
40. Ross, *War on the Run*, 240; Polhemus and Polhemus, *Stark*, 17; Demos, *The Unredeemed Captive*, 35.
41. Zaboly, *A True Ranger*, 271.
42. Meader, *The Merrimack River*, 78; La Bree, *New Hampshire's General John Stark*, 3–7.
43. Meader, *The Merrimack River*, 78; Cuneo, *Robert Rogers of the Rangers*, 61–62, 79; La Bree, *New Hampshire's General John Stark*, 7, 17–41.
44. Calloway, *The Western Abenakis of Vermont*, 29; Loescher, *The History of Rogers' Rangers*, 3:17; Polhemus and Polhemus, *Stark*, 17–18.
45. Franklin B. Hough, introduction to *Journals of Robert Rogers of the Rangers* (Monee, IL: Arcadia Press, 2020), 27.
46. Eastburn, Putnam, and Hawks, *Narratives of the French and Indian War*, 27, 42.
47. Demos, *The Unredeemed Captive*, 4; Weidensaul, *The First Frontier*, 302–4.
48. Weidensaul, *The First Frontier*, 302–4.
49. McCulloch and Todish, *Through So Many Dangers*, 13–45.
50. McCulloch and Todish, *Through So Many Dangers*, 42.
51. McCulloch and Todish, *Through So Many Dangers*, 45.
52. McCulloch and Todish, *Through So Many Dangers*; Hamilton, *Adventures in the Wilderness*, 21.
53. McCulloch and Todish, *Through So Many Dangers*, 45.
54. McCulloch and Todish, *Through So Many Dangers*, 16, 42, 57–58, 62, 64.
55. Eastburn, Putnam, and Hawks, *Narratives of the French and Indian War*, 13; Loescher, *The History of Rogers' Rangers*, 3:15–16.
56. Eastburn, Putnam, and Hawks, *Narratives of the French and Indian War*, 13–14.
57. Eastburn, Putnam, and Hawks, *Narratives of the French and Indian War*, 19–20.
58. Eastburn, Putnam, and Hawks, *Narratives of the French and Indian War*, 11, 21, 23.
59. Rogers, *Journals of Robert Rogers of the Rangers*, 122.
60. Brumwell, *White Devil*, 95–96.
61. *Boston Gazette*, November 26, 1759.
62. La Bree, *New Hampshire's General John Stark*, 40.
63. Stark, *Memoir and Official Correspondence of Gen. John Stark*, 11–16; Cuneo, *Robert Rogers of the Rangers*, 10–44; Lucier, *French and Indian War Notices*, 2:10–13, 17, 22, 29–30; Webb, *Born Fighting*, 131–60.

Chapter 3: The Most Audacious Raid of the French and Indian War

1. Rogers, *Journals of Robert Rogers of the Rangers*, 35–36; Ross, *War on the Run*, 36; Cuneo, *Robert Rogers of the Rangers*, 44; *Maryland Gazette*, October 4, 1759.

2. Zaboly, *A True Ranger*, 147–48.

3. Lucier, *French and Indian War Notices*, 2:13, 74, 105, 113, 177; Ross, *War on the Run*, 236; Ferling, *A Wilderness of Miseries*, 29, 43; Loescher, *The History of Rogers' Rangers*, 3:17, 75.

4. Rogers, *Journals of Robert Rogers of the Rangers*, 35–36, 120; Chartrand, *Raiders from New France*, 48.

5. Rogers, *Journals of Robert Rogers of the Rangers*, 23; Demos, *The Unredeemed Captive*, 19; Gary S. Zaboly, *American Colonial Ranger: The Northern Colonies 1724–64* (Oxford: UK: Osprey Publishing, 2004), 19; Cuneo, *Robert Rogers of the Rangers*, 8–9; Ferling, *A Wilderness of Miseries*, 4–54; Polhemus and Polhemus, *Stark*, 8, 43.

6. Rogers, *Journals of Robert Rogers of the Rangers*, 25.

7. Rogers, *Journals of Robert Rogers of the Rangers*, 23, 25, 35–36; Demos, *The Unredeemed Captive*, 19.

8. Cuneo, *Robert Rogers of the Rangers*, 33; Brumwell, *White Devil*, 166–67.

9. Lucier, *French and Indian War Notices*, 2:53–54; Loescher, *The History of Rogers' Rangers*, 3:1–2.

10. Rogers, *Journals of Robert Rogers of the Rangers*, 120; Brumwell, *White Devil*, 104; Cuneo, *Robert Rogers of the Rangers*, 38–39; Zaboly, *American Colonial Ranger*, 4.

11. Hough, *Journals of Robert Rogers of the Rangers*, 27.

12. Stark, *Memoir and Official Correspondence of Gen. John Stark*, 444n; Loescher, *The History of Rogers' Rangers*, 3:8.

13. Ferling, *A Wilderness of Miseries*, 47; Zaboly, *American Colonial Ranger*, 8.

14. Robert J. Brugger, *Maryland: A Middle Temperament, 1634–1980* (Baltimore: Johns Hopkins University Press, 1996), 94.

15. Gallup, *Memoir of a French and Indian War Soldier*, 108–9.

16. Chartrand, *Raiders from New France*, 60.

17. Chartrand, *Raiders from New France*, 60.

18. Chartrand, *Raiders from New France*, 60.

19. Christopher B. Matheney, "In Defense of Major Robert Rogers: An Answer to His Critics Regarding His Tactics at the First and Second Battles on Snowshoes," *On the Trail* 10, no. 5 (September/October 2003): 43.

20. Rogers, *Journals of Robert Rogers of the Rangers*, 90; Brumwell, *White Devil*, 109.

21. Parkman, *Montcalm and Wolfe*, 255.

22. Brumwell, *White Devil*, 114.

23. Harrison Clark, *All Cloudless Glory: Life of George Washington, from Youth to Yorktown* (Washington, DC: Regnery Books, 1998), 1: 47.

24. Calloway, *The Western Abenakis of Vermont*, 115; Ferling, *A Wilderness of Miseries*, 47.

25. Ferling, *A Wilderness of Miseries*, 47.

26. Ross, *War on the Run*, 36.

27. Calloway, *The Abenaki*, 54–55.

28. Black, *Ranger Dawn*, 30–31; Johnson, *Indian Tribes of the New England Frontier*, 6.

29. Black, *Ranger Dawn*, 30–31.

30. Hamilton, *Adventures in the Wilderness*, 142.

31. Gallup, *Memoir of a French and Indian War Soldier*, 108.

32. Brumwell, *White Devil*, 95.

33. Lucier, *French and Indian War Notices*, 3:247.

34. Lucier, *French and Indian War Notices*, 2:181.

35. Weidensaul, *The First Frontier*, 82.

36. Holland, *Persian Fire*, 193, 249, 261–62.

37. Shiamin Kwa and Wilt L. Idema, *Mulan: Five Versions of a Classic Chinese Legend and Related Texts* (Indianapolis: Hackett Publishing Company, 2010), 42.

38. Brumwell, *White Devil*, 75, 81–83; Rogers, *Journals of Robert Rogers of the Rangers*, 35–36.

39. Cuneo, *Robert Rogers of the Rangers*, 47; Brumwell, *White Devil*, 83–84; Rogers, *Journals of Robert Rogers of the Rangers*, 45–49, 60; Polhemus and Polhemus, *Stark*, 55–58; Eastburn, Putnam, and Hawks, *Narratives of the French and Indian War*, 12.

40. Ian Castle, *Fort William Henry, 1755–57: A Battle, Two Sieges, and Bloody Massacre* (Oxford: Osprey Publishing, 2013), 83–87.

41. Calloway, *The Scratch of a Pen*, xi.

42. McCulloch and Todish, *Through So Many Dangers*, 46.

43. McCulloch and Todish, *Through So Many Dangers*, 45.

44. Loescher, *The History of Rogers' Rangers*, 4:3, 10; Brumwell, *White Devil*, 133–43, 160.

45. Brumwell, *White Devil*, 133–34, 160.

46. Lucier, *French and Indian War Notices*, 2:70–71.

47. J. C. Long, *Lord Jeffrey Amherst: A Soldier of the King* (New York: Macmillan Company, 1933), 90, 93–94; Zaboly, *A True Ranger*, 147–48, 268–70; Loescher, *The History of Rogers' Rangers*, 3:49–50, 4:21; Brumwell, *White Devil*, 146–55.

48. Anderson, *The War That Made America*, 107–10, 114; Loescher, *The History of Rogers' Rangers*, 4:21.

49. Rogers, *Journals of Robert Rogers of the Rangers*, 36, 116; Calloway, *Indians of the Northeast*, 21, 31, 49; Anderson, *The War That Made America*, 192; Hamilton, *Adventures in the Wilderness*, 58; Loescher, *The History of Rogers' Rangers*, 4:21.

50. Anderson, *The War That Made America*, 192; Calloway, *The Western Abenakis of Vermont*, 121.

51. Calloway, *The Abenaki*, 58; Loescher, *The History of Rogers' Rangers*, 4:21.

52. Parkman, *Montcalm and Wolfe*, 423.

53. Rogers, *Journals of Robert Rogers of the Rangers*, 7–8, 116; Zaboly, *American Colonial Ranger*, 4.

54. Rogers, *Journals of Robert Rogers of the Rangers*, 116; Brumwell, *White Devil*, 157–58, 168, 195.

55. Calloway, *The Western Abenakis of Vermont*, 106; Brumwell, *White Devil*, 168.

56. Rogers, *Journals of Robert Rogers of the Rangers*, 116.

57. Brumwell, *White Devil*, 159.

58. Rogers, *Journals of Robert Rogers of the Rangers*, 115–16; Brumwell, *White Devil*, 160–61.

59. Calloway, *The Western Abenakis of Vermont*, 30; Zaboly, *A True Ranger*, 270, 281; Ross, *War on the Run*, 231; Brumwell, *White Devil*, 195.

60. Borneman, *The French and Indian War*, 227.

61. Johnson, *A Narrative of the Captivity of Mrs. Johnson*, 13; Brumwell, *White Devil*, 39; Stark, *Memoir and Official Correspondence of Gen. John Stark*, 372–73; Loescher, *The History of Rogers' Rangers*, 3:17–18.

62. Ross, *War on the Run*, 240.

63. Johnson, *A Narrative of the Captivity of Mrs. Johnson*, 63.

64. Johnson, *A Narrative of the Captivity of Mrs. Johnson*, 62, 65.

65. Johnson, *A Narrative of the Captivity of Mrs. Johnson*, 70–71.

66. Calloway, *The Abenaki*, 20–21; Brumwell, *White Devil*, 30–33.

67. Hamilton, *Adventures in the Wilderness*, 136.

68. *Maryland Gazette*, October 11, 1759.

69. Brumwell, *White Devil*, 134, 141–44.

70. Rogers, *Journals of Robert Rogers of the Rangers*, 116; Ross, *War on the Run*, 236; Parkman, *Montcalm and Wolfe*, 451; Zaboly, *A True Ranger*, 268; Borneman, *The French and Indian War*, 226; Zaboly, *American Colonial Ranger*, 26; Loescher, *The History of Rogers' Rangers*, 4:1–2; Brumwell, *White Devil*, 146–49.

71. Borneman, *The French and Indian War*, 226; Ross, *War on the Run*, 236; Brumwell, *White Devil*, 153; Calloway, *The Western Abenakis of Vermont*, 175.

72. Ross, *War on the Run*, 236; Brumwell, *White Devil*, 133–34, 153, 158–59.

73. Brumwell, *White Devil*, 158–59.

74. Brumwell, *White Devil*, 158–59.

75. Brumwell, *White Devil*, 159.

76. Lucier, *French and Indian War Notices*, 2:295; Ross, *War on the Run*, 236–37; Castle, *Fort William Henry*, 77–87; Anderson, *The War That Made America*, 184–85, 189; Brumwell, *White Devil*, 82–83, 157–59, 166–68; Hamilton, *Adventures in the Wilderness*, 158–73.

77. Brumwell, *White Devil*, 201.

78. Hamilton, *Adventures in the Wilderness*, 172–74.

79. Hamilton, *Adventures in the Wilderness*, 174.

80. Black, *Ranger Dawn*, 27–29; Castle, *Fort William Henry*, 55, 74, 86; Brumwell, *White Devil*, 91–93.

81. Castle, *Fort William Henry*, 83.

82. Castle, *Fort William Henry*, 83; *New York Mercury*, July 30, 1759.

83. Rogers, *Journals of Robert Rogers of the Rangers*, 35; Brumwell, *White Devil*, 165; Calloway, *The Western Abenakis of Vermont*, 170.

84. Ross, *War on the Run*, 236–37; Rogers, *Journals of Robert Rogers of the Rangers*, 36; Lucier, *French and Indian War Notices*, 2:13, 74, 105, 113, 177.

85. Rogers, *Journals of Robert Rogers of the Rangers*, 51.

86. Parkman, *Montcalm and Wolfe*, 255; Calloway, *The Western Abenakis of Vermont*, 114.

87. Rogers, *Journals of Robert Rogers of the Rangers*, 32.

88. Stark, *Memoir and Official Correspondence of Gen. John Stark*, 387; Brumwell, *White Devil*, 102.

89. Stark, *Memoir and Official Correspondence of Gen. John Stark*, 387.

90. Hough, *Journals of Robert Rogers of the Rangers*, 79; Zaboly, *A True Ranger*, 254.

91. Hough, *Journals of Robert Rogers of the Rangers*, 80.

92. Moogk, *La Nouvelle France*, 14; Anderson, *The War That Made America*, 193.

93. Gallup, *Memoir of a French and Indian War Soldier*, 170–71.

94. Parkman, *Montcalm and Wolfe*, 442; Anderson, *The War That Made America*, 189–91.

95. Rogers, *Journals of Robert Rogers of the Rangers*, 36, 116; Ross, *War on the Run*, 231.

96. Anderson, *The War That Made America*, 184–85, 189; Parkman, *Montcalm and Wolfe*, 442–43; Rogers, *Journals of Robert Rogers of the Rangers*, 116.

97. Anderson, *The War That Made America*, 184–85, 189; Parkman, *Montcalm and Wolfe*, 445; Borneman, *The French and Indian War*, 225–26; *Maryland Gazette*, October 25, 1759.

98. *Maryland Gazette*, November 8 and 15, 1759; Parkman, *Montcalm and Wolfe*, 442–46, 451; Borneman, *The French and Indian War*, 225–26; Brumwell, *White Devil*, 133–34, 160, 244–45; Anderson, *The War That Made America*, 189–205; Rogers, *Journals of Robert Rogers of the Rangers*, 116.

99. Rogers, *Journals of Robert Rogers of the Rangers*, 116; Brumwell, *White Devil*, 179–80.

100. *Maryland Gazette*, October 11, 1759.

101. Rogers, *Journals of Robert Rogers of the Rangers*, 116; Cuneo, *Robert Rogers of the Rangers*, 101.

102. *Maryland Gazette*, October 4, 1759.

103. *Maryland Gazette*, October 4, 1759; Parkman, *Montcalm and Wolfe*, 251.

104. *Maryland Gazette*, October 4, 1759.

105. *Maryland Gazette*, October 4, 1759.

106. *Maryland Gazette*, October 4, 1759.

107. *Maryland Gazette*, October 4, 1759.

108. *Maryland Gazette*, October 4, 1759.

109. *Maryland Gazette*, October 11, 1759.

110. *Boston Gazette*, October 1, 1759.

111. McCulloch and Todish, *Through So Many Dangers*, 66–67; Zaboly, *A True Ranger*, 283.

112. Stark, *Memoir and Official Correspondence of Gen. John Stark*, 18–27; Lucier, *French and Indian War Notices*, 2:13, 74, 105, 113, 177; La Bree, *New Hampshire's General John Stark*, 38; Loescher, *The History of Rogers' Rangers*, 4:3–4; Zaboly, *A True Ranger*, 271.

113. Stark, *Memoir and Official Correspondence of Gen. John Stark*, 18–27.

114. Zaboly, *A True Ranger*, 271–72; Lucier, *French and Indian War Notices*, 2:13, 17, 105, 113, 177; La Bree, *New Hampshire's General John Stark*, 40; Loescher, *The History of Rogers' Rangers*, 3:14–15, 4:3–4, 8–9; Stark, *Memoir and Official Correspondence of Gen. John Stark*, 346.

Chapter 4: Final Preparations for the Odyssey North to St. Francis

1. Loescher, *The History of Rogers' Rangers*, 4:4; Brumwell, *White Devil*, 166–67; Cuneo, *Robert Rogers of the Rangers*, 100–102.

2. Brumwell, *White Devil*, 166–67.

3. Ross, *War on the Run*, 2; Stark, *Memoir and Official Correspondence of Gen. John Stark*, 387; Borneman, *The French and Indian War*, 227; Ross, *War on the Run*, 17; Loescher, *The History of Rogers' Rangers*, 4:4, 183; Parkman, *Montcalm and Wolfe*, 257–59; Zaboly, *American Colonial Ranger*, 62; Brumwell, *White Devil*, 82–83, 161, 163; La Bree, *New Hampshire's General John Stark*, 38; Polhemus and Polhemus, *Stark*, 104.

4. *New-York Gazette*, November 26, 1759; Loescher, *The History of Rogers' Rangers*, 4:4–5, 183; Brumwell, *White Devil*, 163.

5. Loescher, *The History of Rogers' Rangers*, 4:5.

6. Loescher, *The History of Rogers' Rangers*, 4:5.

7. Ross, *War on the Run*, 216–17.

8. Loescher, *The History of Rogers' Rangers*, 4:4; Brumwell, *White Devil*, 163.

9. Loescher, *The History of Rogers' Rangers*, 4:4.

10. Loescher, *The History of Rogers' Rangers*, 3:56.

11. Brumwell, *White Devil*, 103–4, 116, 135, 161–62; Loescher, *The History of Rogers' Rangers*, 4:183.
12. Loescher, *The History of Rogers' Rangers*, 4:4–5; Stark, *Memoir and Official Correspondence of Gen. John Stark*, 11–27.
13. Loescher, *The History of Rogers' Rangers*, 3:7–77.
14. Loescher, *The History of Rogers' Rangers*, 3:23, 4:5, 117, 231n31; Brumwell, *White Devil*, 162.
15. Loescher, *The History of Rogers' Rangers*, 3:23, 4:5; Brumwell, *White Devil*, 162.
16. Loescher, *The History of Rogers' Rangers*, 3:53, 4:5–6, 120.
17. Loescher, *The History of Rogers' Rangers*, 4:5–6.
18. Loescher, *The History of Rogers' Rangers*, 3:3–77.
19. Loescher, *The History of Rogers' Rangers*, 4:5; Stark, *Memoir and Official Correspondence of Gen. John Stark*, 464; Lucier, *French and Indian War Notices*, 2:18–19; Family Tree and Genealogy, Hiram S. Grant, WikiTree, internet; Brooks D. Simpson, *Ulysses S. Grant: Triumph over Adversity, 1822–1865* (Boston: Houghton Mifflin Company, 2000), 1, 266–436; Zaboly, *A True Ranger*, 114–15.
20. Stark, *Memoir and Official Correspondence of Gen. John Stark*, 459, 461–62; Zaboly, *A True Ranger*, 143.
21. Zaboly, *A True Ranger*, 137.
22. Loescher, *The History of Rogers' Rangers*, 3:12–13; Brumwell, *White Devil*, 162.
23. Loescher, *The History of Rogers' Rangers*, 3:14, 4:4–5; Parkman, *Montcalm and Wolfe*, 223; Brumwell, *White Devil*, 135, 161–63.
24. Ross, *War on the Run*, 240; Loescher, *The History of Rogers' Rangers*, 3:44, 4:6, 119; Stark, *Memoir and Official Correspondence of Gen. John Stark*, 431n; Brumwell, *White Devil*, 135, 162.
25. Brumwell, *White Devil*, 162.
26. Loescher, *The History of Rogers' Rangers*, 4:x, 14–16; Zaboly, *A True Ranger*, 273.
27. Bornaman, *The French and Indian War*, 227; Loescher, *The History of Rogers' Rangers*, 4:7.
28. Loescher, *The History of Rogers' Rangers*, 4:6–7.
29. Loescher, *The History of Rogers' Rangers*, 4:6.
30. Loescher, *The History of Rogers' Rangers*, 3:14–15, 4:4–5, 183; Zaboly, *American Colonial Ranger*, 19; Brumwell, *White Devil*, 162–64, 180–81, 199; Ross, *War on the Run*, xix, 171; Zaboly, *A True Ranger*, 270.
31. Hough, *Journals of Robert Rogers of the Rangers*, 45.
32. Hough, *Journals of Robert Rogers of the Rangers*, 46.
33. Cuneo, *Robert Rogers of the Rangers*, 75; Brumwell, *White Devil*, 165–66; Zaboly, *A True Ranger*, 149, 272; *Maryland Gazette*, October 11, 1759.
34. Zaboly, *American Colonial Ranger*, 9, 46; Stark, *Memoir and Official Correspondence of Gen. John Stark*, 346.
35. Webb, *Born Fighting*, 23–119.
36. Webb, *Born Fighting*, 23–119; Brumwell, *White Devil*, 163–64; Zaboly, *A True Ranger*, 202.
37. Zaboly, *A True Ranger*, 202; Brumwell, *White Devil*, 102.
38. Brumwell, *White Devil*, 102; Zaboly, *A True Ranger*, 202.
39. Zaboly, *A True Ranger*, 202.
40. McCulloch and Todish, *Through So Many Dangers*, 14–15; Brumwell, *White Devil*, 163–64.

41. Parkman, *Montcalm and Wolfe*, 397; Zaboly, *A True Ranger*, 202; Brumwell, *White Devil*, 102.

42. Stark, *Memoir and Official Correspondence of Gen. John Stark*, 346; Webb, *Born Fighting*, 23–119, 160; Brumwell, *White Devil*, 102; Zaboly, *A True Ranger*, 202.

43. Webb, *Born Fighting*, 24–36, 89.

44. Lacoursiere and Philpot, *A People's History of Quebec*, 57.

45. Zaboly, *A True Ranger*, 201.

46. Zaboly, *A True Ranger*.

47. Cuneo, *Robert Rogers of the Rangers*, 75; Brumwell, *White Devil*, 103.

48. Cuneo, *Robert Rogers of the Rangers*, 75; Brumwell, *White Devil*, 103.

49. Patrick Mileham, *The Scottish Regiments: 1633–1996* (New York: Sarpedon Publishers, 1996), 13.

50. Adirondack Life, *Lake Champlain*, 101.

51. Parkman, *Montcalm and Wolfe*, 244–45.

52. Brumwell, *White Devil*, 169.

53. Ross, *War on the Run*, 451.

54. Brumwell, *White Devil*, 171; Zaboly, *A True Ranger*, 268–70; Loescher, *The History of Rogers' Rangers*, 4:8.

55. *Boston News-Letter*, September 27, 1759.

56. Stark, *Memoir and Official Correspondence of Gen. John Stark*, 450.

57. Ross, *War on the Run*, 231; Loescher, *The History of Rogers' Rangers*, 3:14, 4:71; Zaboly, *A True Ranger*, 348.

Chapter 5: Relying on the Stealth of New England's Sturdy Whaleboats

1. Ross, *War on the Run*, 231, 461; Loescher, *The History of Rogers' Rangers*, 4:183, 185.

2. McCulloch and Todish, *Through So Many Dangers*, 9, 65; Zaboly, *A True Ranger*, 272–73.

3. Ross, *War on the Run*, 465.

4. *New-York Gazette*, November 26, 1759; Brumwell, *White Devil*, 168; Cuneo, *Robert Rogers of the Rangers*, 75.

5. *Maryland Gazette*, October 4, 1759.

6. *Maryland Gazette*, October 4, 1759.

7. *Maryland Gazette*, October 11, 1759.

8. Ross, *War on the Run*, 465; Zaboly, *A True Ranger*, 272–73.

9. Ross, *War on the Run*, 465.

10. Eric Jay Dolin, *Leviathan: The History of Whaling in America* (New York: W. W. Norton and Company, 2007), 41–125; Loescher, *The History of Rogers' Rangers*, 3:44, 4:183, 185, 232n35; De Peyster, *Expedition of the British and Provincial Army*, 113–14; Ross, *War on the Run*, 232; Polhemus and Polhemus, *Stark*, 46; Zaboly, *A True Ranger*, 131; Edward P. Hamilton, *Fort Ticonderoga: Key to a Continent* (New York: Fort Ticonderoga, 1995), 17; Brumwell, *White Devil*, 101–2, 135, 161; Cuneo, *Robert Rogers of the Rangers*, 102; Warren, *New England Bound*, 1–151.

11. Hamilton, *Fort Ticonderoga*, 17.

12. Loescher, *The History of Rogers' Rangers*, 3:44.

13. De Peyster, *Expedition of the British and Provincial Army*, 162.

14. Brumwell, *White Devil*, 104–5.

15. *New-York Gazette*, November 26, 1759; Brumwell, *White Devil*, 168; McCulloch and Todish, *Through So Many Dangers*, 65; Adirondack Life, *Lake Champlain*, 20, 58.

16. *New-York Gazette*, November 26, 1759.

17. Ross, *War on the Run*, 231; Loescher, *The History of Rogers' Rangers*, 3:71, 4:13–14; Zaboly, *A True Ranger*, 133, 272–73.

18. Loescher, *The History of Rogers' Rangers*, 4:14–15; Zaboly, *A True Ranger*, 272–73; Brumwell, *White Devil*, 171–72.

19. Loescher, *The History of Rogers' Rangers*, 4:x, 10–11, 14; Zaboly, *A True Ranger*, 273, 277–78n52; Brumwell, *White Devil*, 264–65.

20. Zaboly, *A True Ranger*, 273, 277–78n5; Loescher, *The History of Rogers' Rangers*, 4:15.

21. *New York Mercury*, October 1, 1759.

22. Loescher, *The History of Rogers' Rangers*, 4:16.

23. Brumwell, *White Devil*, 171–75; Zaboly, *A True Ranger*, 273, 275.

24. Ross, *War on the Run*, 233–34.

25. Brumwell, *White Devil*, 172–73, 176–77.

26. Zaboly, *A True Ranger*, 160, 268; Brumwell, *White Devil*, 171–77.

27. Brumwell, *White Devil*, 171–77; Zaboly, *A True Ranger*, 160.

28. Ross, *War on the Run*, 237; Zaboly, *A True Ranger*, 272.

29. Brumwell, *White Devil*, 171, 177; Zaboly, *A True Ranger*, 272–73.

30. Loescher, *The History of Rogers' Rangers*, 4:16; Zaboly, *A True Ranger*, 273; Brumwell, *White Devil*, 177.

31. Ross, *War on the Run*, 237; Brumwell, *White Devil*, 177–78; Loescher, *The History of Rogers' Rangers*, 4:16.

32. Ross, *War on the Run*, 238; Loescher, *The History of Rogers' Rangers*, 3:39, 4:16–17; Zaboly, *A True Ranger*, 273.

33. Rogers, *Journals of Robert Rogers of the Rangers*, 120; McCulloch and Todish, *Through So Many Dangers*, 65; Ross, *War on the Run*, 238; Parkman, *Montcalm and Wolfe*, 453; Ross, *War on the Run*, 238–39; Adirondack Life, *Lake Champlain*, 62, 70–73, 82; Brumwell, *White Devil*, 170–72, 177–79; Zaboly, *A True Ranger*, 131, 273; Cuneo, *Robert Rogers of the Rangers*, 103–4; Loescher, *The History of Rogers' Rangers*, 4:17.

34. Adirondack Life, *Lake Champlain*, 60.

35. *New-York Gazette*, November 26, 1759.

36. Dolan, *Leviathan*, 94; Cuneo, *Robert Rogers of the Rangers*, 104.

37. Adirondack Life, *Lake Champlain*, 102; Zaboly, *A True Ranger*, 273; Ross, *War on the Run*, 239.

38. Brumwell, *White Devil*, 156, 323.

39. Borneman, *The French and Indian War*, 227–28; Rogers, *Journals of Robert Rogers of the Rangers*, 120; Zaboly, *American Colonial Ranger*, 15; Ross, *War on the Run*, 239; Brumwell, *White Devil*, 172–75, 179–81; Parkman, *Montcalm and Wolfe*, 453; Cuneo, *Robert Rogers of the Rangers*, 104; Bob Bearor, *The Battle on Snowshoes* (Bowie, MD: Heritage Books, 1997), xiii, 25, 35–41; Loescher, *The History of Rogers' Rangers*, 4:15–17; Zaboly, *A True Ranger*, 272–73.

40. Rogers, *Journals of Robert Rogers of the Rangers*, 120; Zaboly, *A True Ranger*, 273.

41. Loescher, *The History of Rogers' Rangers*, 4:15; Brumwell, *White Devil*, 181; Parkman, *Montcalm and Wolfe*, 453.

42. McCulloch and Todish, *Through So Many Dangers*, 65; Adirondack Life, *Lake Champlain*, 62–63; Cuneo, *Robert Rogers of the Rangers*, 101–2, 104; Zaboly, *A True Ranger*, 274; Ross, *War on the Run*, 239; Brumwell, *White Devil*, 178, 184; Loescher, *The History of Rogers' Rangers*, 4:86.

43. *New-York Gazette*, November 26, 1759; Zaboly, *A True Ranger*, 274; Ross, *War on the Run*, 239.

44. Brumwell, *White Devil*, 169; Zaboly, *A True Ranger*, 280.

45. Stark, *Memoir and Official Correspondence of Gen. John Stark*, 450.

46. Loescher, *The History of Rogers' Rangers*, 4:xiv–xv.

47. Brumwell, *White Devil*, 181–82, 321.

48. Zaboly, *A True Ranger*, 274; Brumwell, *White Devil*, 181–82.

49. Lucier, *French and Indian War Notices*, 2:196; Brumwell, *White Devil*, 182; Zaboly, *A True Ranger*, 274.

50. McCulloch and Todish, *Through So Many Dangers*, 35–36, 65; Ross, *War on the Run*, 244; Borneman, *The French and Indian War*, 228; Brumwell, *White Devil*, 183–84; Zaboly, *American Colonial Ranger*, 58; La Bree, *New Hampshire's General John Stark*, 37; Loescher, *The History of Rogers' Rangers*, 4:86.

51. Ross, *War on the Run*, 461.

52. Rogers, *Journals of Robert Rogers of the Rangers*, 120.

53. Rogers, *Journals of Robert Rogers of the Rangers*, 120; Lucier, *French and Indian War Notices*, 3:78; Zaboly, *A True Ranger*, 274.

54. Rogers, *Journals of Robert Rogers of the Rangers*, 120; Ross, *War on the Run*, 239–44; Borneman, *The French and Indian War*, 228; Bearor, *The Battle on Snowshoes*, xiii, 25, 35–41; Brumwell, *White Devil*, 12, 82–83, 113, 180–81, 184–88; Lucier, *French and Indian War Notices*, 2:13; Loescher, *The History of Rogers' Rangers*, 4:20–22; Zaboly, *A True Ranger*, 274; Cuneo, *Robert Rogers of the Rangers*, 104.

55. Loescher, *The History of Rogers' Rangers*, 4:21.

56. Rogers, *Journals of Robert Rogers of the Rangers*, 120–21; Loescher, *The History of Rogers' Rangers*, 4:20–21.

57. Rogers, *Journals of Robert Rogers of the Rangers*, 120–21; Borneman, *The French and Indian War*, 228; Ross, *War on the Run*, 13–15; Brumwell, *White Devil*, 184–86; Bearor, *The Battle on Snowshoes*, xiii, 25, 35–41; Johnson, *Indian Tribes of the New England Frontier*, 7; Cuneo, *Robert Rogers of the Rangers*, 104; Loescher, *The History of Rogers' Rangers*, 3:31–32, 45, 4:20–23, 86, 131; Zaboly, *A True Ranger*, 274–75; Jacques Boisvert, "Major Rogers and the Abenakis' Treasures," *Sherbrooke Daily Record* (Sherbrooke, QC, Canada), March 20, 1987.

58. Loescher, *The History of Rogers' Rangers*, 4:15–16; Zaboly, *A True Ranger*, 275.

59. Zaboly, *A True Ranger*, 275; Cuneo, *Robert Rogers of the Rangers*, 105.

60. Rogers, *Journals of Robert Rogers of the Rangers*, 121.

61. McCulloch and Todish, *Through So Many Dangers*, 65; Loescher, *The History of Rogers' Rangers*, 4:20, 86.

62. Brumwell, *White Devil*, 159, 166, 183–88; Ted Spring and George A. Bray III, *The Highlanders and Provincial Rangers*, Sketchbook 56, vol. 3 (Osseo, MN: Track of the Wolf, Inc., 1991), 12; Bearor, *The Battle on Snowshoes*, xiii, 25, 35–41; Adirondack Life, *Lake Champlain*, 72; Zaboly, *A True Ranger*, 274–75; Loescher, *The History of Rogers' Rangers*, 4:9, 21–22.

63. Andrew Gallup and Donald F. Shaffer, *La Marine: The French Soldier in Canada, 1745–1761* (Westminster, MD: Heritage Books, 2008), 80.

64. Brumwell, *White Devil*, 190.

65. Gallup and Shaffer, *La Marine*, 16.

66. Loescher, *The History of Rogers' Rangers*, 4:22; Zaboly, *A True Ranger*, 275.

67. Loescher, *The History of Rogers' Rangers*, 4:22; Brumwell, *White Devil*, 323.

68. Brumwell, *White Devil*, 190–91; Zaboly, *A True Ranger*, 274–75; Loescher, *The History of Rogers' Rangers*, 4:20–23.

69. Zaboly, *American Colonial Ranger*, 4, 9, 44–46, 62; Brumwell, *White Devil*, 248.

70. Brumwell, *White Devil*, 248.

71. Lucier, *French and Indian War Notices*, 2:295.

72. Lucier, *French and Indian War Notices*, 2:149.

73. Lucier, *French and Indian War Notices*, 2:13, 74, 177; Zaboly, *American Colonial Ranger*, 8–9, 44, 47.

74. Loescher, *The History of Rogers' Rangers*, 3:18; Zaboly, *A True Ranger*, 270.

75. Loescher, *The History of Rogers' Rangers*, 3:23, 53, 4:78–80.

76. Phillips, *The Cousins' Wars*, xii–xiii; Gallup and Shaffer, *La Marine*, 11–18, 32; Loescher, *The History of Rogers' Rangers*, 4:xvi–xvii, 22; Brumwell, *White Devil*, 82–83.

77. Lucier, *French and Indian War Notices*, 2:13, 74, 105, 113, 177; Black, *Ranger Dawn*, 70, 87.

78. Black, *Ranger Dawn*, 70; Lucier, *French and Indian War Notices*, 2:13, 74, 105, 113, 177.

79. Rogers, *Journals of Robert Rogers of the Rangers*, 121; Cuneo, *Robert Rogers of the Rangers*, 106; Brumwell, *White Devil*, 183, 187.

80. Rogers, *Journals of Robert Rogers of the Rangers*, 121; Brumwell, *White Devil*, 187; Zaboly, *American Colonial Ranger*, 44; Cuneo, *Robert Rogers of the Rangers*, 105–6; Adirondack Life, *Lake Champlain*, 16; Zaboly, *A True Ranger*, 274–75; Loescher, *The History of Rogers' Rangers*, 4:26.

81. Rogers, *Journals of Robert Rogers of the Rangers*, 121; Brumwell, *White Devil*, 187–88; Zaboly, *A True Ranger*, 275; Loescher, *The History of Rogers' Rangers*, 4:26.

82. Brumwell, *White Devil*, 188,

83. Loescher, *The History of Rogers' Rangers*, 4:19–22; Zaboly, *A True Ranger*, 275; Brumwell, *White Devil*, 187–88.

84. Zaboly, *A True Ranger*, 169.

85. Rogers, *Journals of Robert Rogers of the Rangers*, 121; Zaboly, *A True Ranger*, 275; Brumwell, *White Devil*, 184–88; Loescher, *The History of Rogers' Rangers*, 4:26.

86. Loescher, *The History of Rogers' Rangers*, 4:26.

87. Cuneo, *Robert Rogers of the Rangers*, 105.

88. *New-York Gazette*, November 26, 1759.

89. Loescher, *The History of Rogers' Rangers*, 4:25.

90. Loescher, *The History of Rogers' Rangers*, 4:27.

91. Loescher, *The History of Rogers' Rangers*, 4:26; Zaboly, *A True Ranger*, 275.

92. Zaboly, *A True Ranger*, 275–76; Loescher, *The History of Rogers' Rangers*, 4:30, 86; Brumwell, *White Devil*, 181, 188–89; Stark, *Memoir and Official Correspondence of Gen. John Stark*, 11–14.

93. Loescher, *The History of Rogers' Rangers*, 4:29–30; Zaboly, *A True Ranger*, 275–76.

94. Rogers, *Journals of Robert Rogers of the Rangers*, 121; Borneman, *The French and Indian War*, 228–29; Parkman, *Montcalm and Wolfe*, 453; Bearor, *The Battle on Snowshoes*, xiii, 25, 35–41; Zaboly, *A True Ranger*, 276; Loescher, *The History of Rogers' Rangers*, 4:26, 29–33; Cuneo, *Robert Rogers of the Rangers*, 75; Brumwell, *White Devil*, 188–89.

RANGER RAID

95. Rogers, *Journals of Robert Rogers of the Rangers*, 121; Zaboly, *A True Ranger*, 276.

96. Rogers, *Journals of Robert Rogers of the Rangers*, 121; Brumwell, *White Devil*, 189, 191–92; Zaboly, *A True Ranger*, 275–76; Loescher, *The History of Rogers' Rangers*, 4:30–33.

97. Ross, *War on the Run*, 461.

98. Rogers, *Journals of Robert Rogers of the Rangers*, 51.

99. *Maryland Gazette*, October 11, 1759.

100. McCulloch and Todish, *Through So Many Dangers*, 62.

101. McCulloch and Todish, *Through So Many Dangers*, 42.

102. Eastburn, Putnam, and Hawks, *Narratives of the French and Indian War*, 11, 15.

103. McCulloch and Todish, *Through So Many Dangers*, 64.

104. McCulloch and Todish, *Through So Many Dangers*, 64; Stark, *Memoir and Official Correspondence of Gen. John Stark*, 346.

105. Brumwell, *White Devil*, 82–83, 97–118.

Chapter 6: Rogers Determined to Fulfill His Special Destiny in the St. Francis River Country

1. McCulloch and Todish, *Through So Many Dangers*, 65.

2. *New-York Gazette*, November 26, 1759; Rogers, *Journals of Robert Rogers of the Rangers*, 117; Borneman, *The French and Indian War*, 229; Demos, *The Unredeemed Captive*, 17; Stark, *Memoir and Official Correspondence of Gen. John Stark*, 448–49; Zaboly, *A True Ranger*, 275–76; Brumwell, *White Devil*, 189–91, 202, 207–8; Hough, *Journals of Robert Rogers of the Rangers*, 7; Loescher, *The History of Rogers' Rangers*, 4:33.

3. *New-York Gazette*, November 26, 1759.

4. Rogers, *Journals of Robert Rogers of the Rangers*, 117; Cuneo, *Robert Rogers of the Rangers*, 56; Calloway, *The Abenaki*, 18.

5. Stark, *Memoir and Official Correspondence of Gen. John Stark*, 11–15, 346, 448, 450, 460; Borneman, *The French and Indian War*, 227; Calloway, *The Western Abenakis of Vermont*, 48; Rogers, *Journals of Robert Rogers of the Rangers*, 117; Parkman, *Montcalm and Wolfe*, 279; Brumwell, *White Devil*, 91–92; Cuneo, *Robert Rogers of the Rangers*, 106; Gallup and Shaffer, *La Marine*, 207.

6. David Humphreys, *The Life and Heroic Exploits of Israel Putnam, Major-General, in the Revolutionary War* (Hartford, CT: Silas Andrus and Son, 1847), 27.

7. *New-York Gazette*, November 26, 1759; Brumwell, *White Devil*, 51–54, 82–83, 101–3, 172, 202; Gallup and Shaffer, *La Marine*, 85, 220–28; Stark, *Memoir and Official Correspondence of Gen. John Stark*, 11–15, 346, 448, 451–52.

8. *New-York Gazette*, November 26, 1759; Moogk, *La Nouvelle France*, 15, 50, 53–60; Stark, *Memoir and Official Correspondence of Gen. John Stark*, 448.

9. McCulloch and Todish, *Through So Many Dangers*, 65–66.

10. Stark, *Memoir and Official Correspondence of Gen. John Stark*, 448.

11. Stark, *Memoir and Official Correspondence of Gen. John Stark*, 387.

12. *New-York Gazette*, November 26, 1759; Stark, *Memoir and Official Correspondence of Gen. John Stark*, 448.

13. Brumwell, *White Devil*, 193; Stark, *Memoir and Official Correspondence of Gen. John Stark*, 448.

14. *New-York Gazette*, November 26, 1759; Stark, *Memoir and Official Correspondence of Gen. John Stark*, 448.

15. Zaboly, *A True Ranger*, 279.

16. Rogers, *Journals of Robert Rogers of the Rangers*, 116–17; *New-York Gazette*, November 26, 1759; Borneman, *The French and Indian War*, 229; Brumwell, *White Devil*, 91–94, 195; Parkman, *Montcalm and Wolfe*, 295–98, 423, 454; Johnson, *Indian Tribes of the New England Frontier*, 22; Bearor, *The Battle on Snowshoes*, 49–66.

17. *New-York Gazette*, November 26, 1759.

18. Rogers, *Journals of Robert Rogers of the Rangers*, 117; Brumwell, *White Devil*, 192; Ross, *War on the Run*, 248; Loescher, *The History of Rogers' Rangers*, 4:8; Zaboly, *A True Ranger*, 379; Cuneo, *Robert Rogers of the Rangers*, 106.

19. Ross, *War on the Run*, 462.

20. Rogers, *Journals of Robert Rogers of the Rangers*, 117; Brumwell, *White Devil*, 82–83.

21. *New-York Gazette*, November 26, 1759.

22. Stark, *Memoir and Official Correspondence of Gen. John Stark*, 448; Ross, *War on the Run*, 248; Brumwell, *White Devil*, 103.

23. Ross, *War on the Run*, 248; Loescher, *The History of Rogers' Rangers*, 3:46, 4:37; Brumwell, *White Devil*, 202.

24. Zaboly, *A True Ranger*, 279.

25. Loescher, *The History of Rogers' Rangers*, 4:43, 224.

26. Stark, *Memoir and Official Correspondence of Gen. John Stark*, 448.

27. *New-York Gazette*, November 26, 1759; Zaboly, *A True Ranger*, 279; Parkman, *Montcalm and Wolfe*, 453; McCulloch and Todish, *Through So Many Dangers*, 65–66.

28. *New-York Gazette*, November 26, 1759; McCulloch and Todish, *Through So Many Dangers*, 56–66; Stark, *Memoir and Official Correspondence of Gen. John Stark*, 346; Parkman, *Montcalm and Wolfe*, 453; Loescher, *The History of Rogers' Rangers*, 4:31; Brumwell, *White Devil*, 46–51.

29. *New-York Gazette*, November 26, 1759; Brumwell, *White Devil*, 82–83, 159–60; Stark, *Memoir and Official Correspondence of Gen. John Stark*, 448; Parkman, *Montcalm and Wolfe*, 453–54; Cuneo, *Robert Rogers of the Rangers*, 106; Loescher, *The History of Rogers' Rangers*, 4:33.

30. *New-York Gazette*, November 26, 1759; Rogers, *Journals of Robert Rogers of the Rangers*, 36, 117–18; Stark, *Memoir and Official Correspondence of Gen. John Stark*, 448; Loescher, *The History of Rogers' Rangers*, 4:208; Cuneo, *Robert Rogers of the Rangers*, 44; Borneman, *The French and Indian War*, 226–27; Ross, *War on the Run*, 2–3, 12–14; Brumwell, *White Devil*, 11–12, 190–95.

31. *New-York Gazette*, November 26, 1759.

32. McCulloch and Todish, *Through So Many Dangers*, 66.

33. *New-York Gazette*, November 26, 1759; Fischer, *Albion's Seed*, 620; Brumwell, *White Devil*, 101–4.

34. Loescher, *The History of Rogers' Rangers*, 4:37.

35. Gallup, *Memoir of a French and Indian War Soldier*, 42–43; Cuneo, *Robert Rogers of the Rangers*, 107.

36. Stark, *Memoir and Official Correspondence of Gen. John Stark*, 387, 448; Brumwell, *White Devil*, 196; Zaboly, *American Colonial Ranger*, 62; Loescher, *The History of Rogers' Rangers*,

4:4–5; Ben Hubbard, *Troy: An Epic Tale of Rage, Deception, and Destruction* (London: Amber Books, 2018), 13–143.

37. Ross, *War on the Run*, 462.

38. *New-York Gazette*, November 26, 1759.

39. McCulloch and Todish, *Through So Many Dangers*, 66.

40. Cuneo, *Robert Rogers of the Rangers*, 101.

41. Stark, *Memoir and Official Correspondence of Gen. John Stark*, 451.

42. Ferling, *A Wilderness of Miseries*, 18.

43. McCulloch and Todish, *Through So Many Dangers*, 66.

44. Stark, *Memoir and Official Correspondence of Gen. John Stark*, 451–52.

45. Lucier, *French and Indian War Notices*, 2:69.

46. Phillips, *The Cousins' Wars*, xiii.

47. John MacArthur, *The MacArthur Study Bible* (Dallas, TX: Thomas Nelson, 1997), 313.

48. Hamilton, *Adventures in the Wilderness*, 191.

49. Eastburn, Putnam, and Hawks, *Narratives of the French and Indian War*, 18.

50. Eastburn, Putnam, and Hawks, *Narratives of the French and Indian War*, 20.

51. Eastburn, Putnam, and Hawks, *Narratives of the French and Indian War*, 13; Loescher, *The History of Rogers' Rangers*, 3:15–16.

52. Eastburn, Putnam, and Hawks, *Narratives of the French and Indian War*, 15.

53. Michael Ruse, *The Problem of War: Darwinism, Christianity, and Their Battle to Understand Human Conflict* (Oxford: Oxford University Press, 2018), 49; Phillips, *The Cousins' Wars*, xii–xiii.

54. Phillips, *The Cousins' Wars*, xii–xiii; Fischer, *Albion's Seed*, 18, 20.

55. McCulloch and Todish, *Through So Many Dangers*, 66.

56. *Boston Gazette*, November 26, 1759.

57. Zaboly, *A True Ranger*, 280.

58. Zaboly, *A True Ranger*, 280; Brumwell, *White Devil*, 195.

59. Loescher, *The History of Rogers' Rangers*, 4:36, 42; Bearor, *The Battle on Snowshoes*, ix, xiii, xxiii, 25, 35–41.

60. Rogers, *A Concise Account of North America*, 148, in Hobbs, *What You May Not Know about Roger's Rangers*; Zaboly, *A True Ranger*, 187–88; Hough, *Journals of Robert Rogers of the Rangers*, 13–14; Ferling, *A Wilderness of Miseries*, 39–40.

61. Zaboly, *A True Ranger*, 188.

62. Zaboly, *A True Ranger*, 188.

63. Rogers, *A Concise Account of North America*, 62, in Hobbs, *What You May Not Know about Roger's Rangers*; Hough, *Journals of Robert Rogers of the Rangers*, 13–14.

64. Rogers, *A Concise Account of North America*, in Hobbs, *What You May Not Know about Roger's Rangers*, 65.

65. Rogers, *A Concise Account of North America*, in Hobbs, *What You May Not Know about Roger's Rangers*, 158.

66. McCulloch and Todish, *Through So Many Dangers*, 66.

67. MacArthur, *The MacArthur Study Bible*, 313; Phillips, *The Cousins' Wars*, xii–xiii.

68. McCulloch and Todish, *Through So Many Dangers*, 66.

69. Moogk, *La Nouvelle France*, 13–189; Lucier, *French and Indian War Notices*, 2:31, 69–71, 3:2–3.

70. Lucier, *French and Indian War Notices*, 3:2.

71. Chartrand, *Raiders from New France*, 4, 8, 26–27.
72. Brumwell, *White Devil*, 191–92; Zaboly, *A True Ranger*, 275.
73. Cuneo, *Robert Rogers of the Rangers*, 57, 60; Borneman, *The French and Indian War*, 227; Rogers, *Journals of Robert Rogers of the Rangers*, 117; Zaboly, *A True Ranger*, 280; Brumwell, *White Devil*, 101–4, 161, 195–96; Calloway, *The Abenaki*, 18; Zaboly, *American Colonial Ranger*, 30, 59–60.
74. Rogers, *Journals of Robert Rogers of the Rangers*, 60.
75. Rogers, *Journals of Robert Rogers of the Rangers*, 62; Zaboly, *American Colonial Ranger*, 62.
76. Ferling, *A Wilderness of Miseries*, 38.
77. Brumwell, *White Devil*, 196.
78. Loescher, *The History of Rogers' Rangers*, 3:9, 17, 57, 64, 75, 4:37; Long, *Lord Jeffrey Amherst*, 10; Brumwell, *White Devil*, 166–67.
79. Lucier, *French and Indian War Notices*, 3:55.
80. Zaboly, *A True Ranger*, 125.
81. Cuneo, *Robert Rogers of the Rangers*, 6–7; Ruse, *The Problem of War*, 51; MacArthur, *The MacArthur Study Bible*, 313; Loescher, *The History of Rogers' Rangers*, 4:40.
82. MacArthur, *The MacArthur Study Bible*, 313.
83. Johnson, *Indian Tribes of the New England Frontier*, 6–7, 19.
84. Loescher, *The History of Rogers' Rangers*, 3:44, 66, 4:8.
85. Loescher, *The History of Rogers' Rangers*, 3:46, 4:6.
86. Loescher, *The History of Rogers' Rangers*, 3:12–13, 40, 4:6.
87. Loescher, *The History of Rogers' Rangers*, 3:37.
88. Loescher, *The History of Rogers' Rangers*, 3:18, 39, 4:6.
89. Zaboly, *A True Ranger*, ix.
90. Daughan, *Lexington and Concord*, 18–19; Loescher, *The History of Rogers' Rangers*, 3:xv.
91. Rogers, *Journals of Robert Rogers of the Rangers*, 47–49; Cuneo, *Robert Rogers of the Rangers*, 48–50; Zaboly, *American Colonial Ranger*, 12, 49, 60; McCulloch and Todish, *Through So Many Dangers*, 66; Brumwell, *White Devil*, 101–3; *New-York Gazette*, November 26, 1759; Webb, *Born Fighting*, 132, 147; Anderson, *The War That Made America*, 58; Loescher, *The History of Rogers' Rangers*, 3:xv, 15–16.
92. Rogers, *Journals of Robert Rogers of the Rangers*, 90; Brumwell, *White Devil*, 111–15; Zaboly, *American Colonial Ranger*, 46.
93. Brumwell, *White Devil*, 115.
94. Calloway, *The Western Abenakis of Vermont*, 12, 164.
95. Calloway, *The Western Abenakis of Vermont*, 166; Lucier, *French and Indian War Notices*, 2:13, 74, 105, 113, 115, 174, 177.
96. Hamilton, *Adventures in the Wilderness*, 82.
97. Brumwell, *White Devil*, 207; Loescher, *The History of Rogers' Rangers*, 3:9, 17, 57, 64, 75; Zaboly, *A True Ranger*, 280.
98. Hamilton, *Adventures in the Wilderness*, 41.
99. Rogers, *Journals of Robert Rogers of the Rangers*, 116.
100. Rogers, *Journals of Robert Rogers of the Rangers*, 116.
101. Brumwell, *White Devil*, 201, 210; Stark, *Memoir and Official Correspondence of Gen. John Stark*, 11–15; Loescher, *The History of Rogers' Rangers*, 3:9, 17, 57, 64; Zaboly, *A True Ranger*, 280; Parkman, *Montcalm and Wolfe*, 241; Hamilton, *Adventures in the Wilderness*, 29–30.
102. Brumwell, *White Devil*, 201; Weidensaul, *The First Frontier*, 83.

103. Lucier, *French and Indian War Notices*, 2:13, 74, 105, 113, 177; Webb, *Born Fighting*, 160; Bearor, *The Battle on Snowshoes*, xiii, 35–41, 66; Zaboly, *A True Ranger*, 6.

104. Lucier, *French and Indian War Notices*, 2:13, 74, 105, 113, 177; Brumwell, *White Devil*, 166–67, 171–72, 201.

105. *New-York Gazette*, November 26, 1759; Brumwell, *White Devil*, 162; Lucier, *French and Indian War Notices*, 2:13, 74, 105, 113, 177.

106. *Boston Evening Post*, November 1, 1759.

107. *Pennsylvania Journal*, November 29, 1759; Loescher, *The History of Rogers' Rangers*, 3:14.

108. Loescher, *The History of Rogers' Rangers*, 4:43–44, 183.

109. Loescher, *The History of Rogers' Rangers*, 4:44, 176.

110. Johnson, *A Narrative of the Captivity of Mrs. Johnson*, 71; Anderson, *The War That Made America*, 153–54; Zaboly, *American Colonial Ranger*, 62; Snow, *Death or Victory*, 48.

111. Johnson, *A Narrative of the Captivity of Mrs. Johnson*, 72; Brumwell, *White Devil*, 119–20; Johnson, *Indian Tribes of the New England Frontier*, 36.

112. Johnson, *A Narrative of the Captivity of Mrs. Johnson*, 75.

113. Ross, *War on the Run*, 36.

114. Parkman, *Montcalm and Wolfe*, 249.

115. Calloway, *The Western Abenakis of Vermont*, 48; Brumwell, *White Devil*, 199; Borneman, *The French and Indian War*, 229.

116. Lacoursiere and Philpot, *A People's History of Quebec*, 9; Phillips, *The Cousins' Wars*, xii–xiii.

117. Brumwell, *White Devil*, 199; Enrique Meseguer, "The Children's Crusade: Mission of the Masses," *National Geographic History* 6, no. 2 (May/June 2020): 63.

118. Cuneo, *Robert Rogers of the Rangers*, 4, 6, 9, 42; Brumwell, *White Devil*, 51–54, 102–3; Meader, *The Merrimack River*, 189; Rogers, *A Concise Account of North America*, 148–50, in Hobbs, *What You May Not Know about Roger's Rangers*; Loescher, *The History of Rogers' Rangers*, 4:1–78; Webb, *Born Fighting*, 25–161.

119. Borneman, *The French and Indian War*, 227; Calloway, *The Western Abenakis of Vermont*, 48, 138, 161; Spring and Bray, *The Highlanders and Provincial Rangers*, 60; Brumwell, *White Devil*, 51–52, 102–3; Carty, *Ireland*, 38–95; Webb, *Born Fighting*, 73–101; Loescher, *The History of Rogers' Rangers*, 3:1–78; Zaboly, *American Colonial Ranger*, 8–9, 46.

120. Calloway, *The Western Abenakis of Vermont*, 162; Brumwell, *White Devil*, 51–52, 102–3; Stark, *Memoir and Official Correspondence of Gen. John Stark*, 372–74; Loescher, *The History of Rogers' Rangers*, 3:17–19.

121. Brumwell, *White Devil*, 91–92.

122. Brumwell, *White Devil*, 91–92; Zaboly, *American Colonial Ranger*, 47.

123. Demos, *The Unredeemed Captive*, 4; Brumwell, *White Devil*, 47–48, 193, 196–98.

124. Weidensaul, *The First Frontier*, xv–xvi, xix; Ferling, *A Wilderness of Miseries*, 3–54; Meader, *The Merrimack River*, 189; Zaboly, *American Colonial Ranger*, 261; Loescher, *The History of Rogers' Rangers*, 3:30; McCulloch and Todish, *Through So Many Dangers*, 42–43; Brumwell, *White Devil*, 31, 45–49.

125. Parkman, *Montcalm and Wolfe*, 355; McCulloch and Todish, *Through So Many Dangers*, 66.

126. Moogk, *La Nouvelle France*, xix; Brumwell, *White Devil*, 31–34, 38, 48–50.

127. Parkman, *Montcalm and Wolfe*, 355, 372–73.

128. McCulloch and Todish, *Through So Many Dangers*, 64.

129. McCulloch and Todish, *Through So Many Dangers*, 65.

130. Parkman, *Montcalm and Wolfe*, 170–71, 372–73.

131. Parkman, *Montcalm and Wolfe*, 373.

132. Parkman, *Montcalm and Wolfe*, 171.

133. Ross, *War on the Run*, 76.

134. Eastburn, Putnam, and Hawks, *Narratives of the French and Indian War*, 27, 39–41.

135. Eastburn, Putnam, and Hawks, *Narratives of the French and Indian War*, 49n12.

136. Gallup, *Memoir of a French and Indian War Soldier*, 98–99; Anderson, *The War That Made America*, 45–52.

137. Gallup, *Memoir of a French and Indian War Soldier*, 105n2.

138. Lucier, *French and Indian War Notices*, 3:88–89.

139. Rogers, *A Concise Account of North America*, 149, in Hobbs, *What You May Not Know about Roger's Rangers*.

140. Spring and Bray, *The Highlanders and Provincial Rangers*, 58; McCulloch and Todish, *Through So Many Dangers*, 65.

141. Gallup and Shaffer, *La Marine*, 80–83; Brumwell, *White Devil*, 51–53, 101–5, 195–96; Phillip Thomas Tucker, *The South's Finest: The First Missouri Confederate Brigade from Pea Ridge to Vicksburg* (Mechanicsburg, PA: White Mane Publishing Company, 1993), vii; Zaboly, *A True Ranger*, 280; Loescher, *The History of Rogers' Rangers*, 3:1–78; Lucier, *French and Indian War Notices*, 2:13, 74, 105, 113, 177; A. Hamish Ion and Keith Neilson, *Elite Military Formations in War and Peace* (Westport, CT: Praeger Publishing, 1996), 1–41, 93–111.

142. Zaboly, *A True Ranger*, 149.

143. Brumwell, *White Devil*, 102.

Chapter 7: Final Nighttime Approach to the Most Tempting of Targets

1. Webb, *Born Fighting*, 23–161; Brumwell, *White Devil*, 82; Lucier, *French and Indian War Notices*, 2:13, 74, 105, 113, 177; Stark, *Memoir and Official Correspondence of Gen. John Stark*, 346, 387; Lucier, *French and Indian War Notices*, 2:3; Calloway, *The Western Abenakis of Vermont*, 66.

2. Ferling, *A Wilderness of Miseries*, 38, 43–44; Brumwell, *White Devil*, 181–91.

3. Ferling, *A Wilderness of Miseries*, 38, 43–44; Ephraim Kam, *Surprise Attack: The Victim's Perspective* (Cambridge, MA: Harvard University Press, 2004), 1–10; Brumwell, *White Devil*, 181–91.

4. Johnson, *Indian Tribes of the New England Frontier*, 6–7, 40; Loescher, *The History of Rogers' Rangers*, 4:38.

5. Loescher, *The History of Rogers' Rangers*, 3:8; Zaboly, *A True Ranger*, 273; Brumwell, *White Devil*, 75–131.

6. Lacoursiere and Philpot, *A People's History of Quebec*, 17.

7. Ross, *War on the Run*, 249–50; Brumwell, *White Devil*, 104.

8. Rogers, *Journals of Robert Rogers of the Rangers*, 117; Loescher, *The History of Rogers' Rangers*, 4:70, 120, 122, 204; Zaboly, *American Colonial Ranger*, 9, 19, 26, 46, 57–60, 62; Ross, *War on the Run*, 17, 249; Parkman, *Montcalm and Wolfe*, 454; McCulloch and Todish, *Through So Many Dangers*, 66; Brumwell, *White Devil*, 11–12, 104, 166, 226; *New York Mercury*, July 30, 1759; Hamilton, *Adventures in the Wilderness*, 175; Cuneo, *Robert Rogers of the Rangers*, 106–7; Stark, *Memoir and Official Correspondence of Gen. John Stark*, 346; Zaboly, *A True Ranger*, 202, 280; Lucier, *French and Indian War Notices*, 3:2; Philippe Girard, *Haiti: The Tumultuous History— from Pearl of the Caribbean to Broken Nation* (New York: Palgrave Macmillan, 2010), 23–25.

9. *New-York Gazette*, November 26, 1759; Rogers, *Journals of Robert Rogers of the Rangers*, 90, 117; "Rogers' Raid According to the Research of Gordon Day (1981)," Ne-Do-Ba (Friends): Exploring and Sharing the Wabanaki History of Indians of New England, August 1998, internet; McCulloch and Todish, *Through So Many Dangers*, 66; Parkman, *Montcalm and Wolfe*, 454; Zaboly, *A True Ranger*, 273, 283; Bahmanyar, *Shadow Warriors*, 15.

10. Calloway, *The Abenaki*, 22–23; Brumwell, *White Devil*, 91–92; McCulloch and Todish, *Through So Many Dangers*, 42, 45; Loescher, *The History of Rogers' Rangers*, 4:131; Hamilton, *Adventures in the Wilderness*, 133.

11. Parkman, *Montcalm and Wolfe*, 454.

12. Brumwell, *White Devil*, 195; McCulloch and Todish, *Through So Many Dangers*, 66.

13. *New-York Gazette*, November 26, 1759; Loescher, *The History of Rogers' Rangers*, 4:131.

14. Stark, *Memoir and Official Correspondence of Gen. John Stark*, 448.

15. Stark, *Memoir and Official Correspondence of Gen. John Stark*, 11–13; Loescher, *The History of Rogers' Rangers*, 4:35.

16. Ross, *War on the Run*, 13; Rogers, *Journals of Robert Rogers of the Rangers*, 44–45, 117; Brumwell, *White Devil*, 86, 95–96; Loescher, *The History of Rogers' Rangers*, 3:14–15; Zaboly, *A True Ranger*, 202; Lucier, *French and Indian War Notices*, 2:13, 74, 105, 113, 177.

17. Brumwell, *White Devil*, 96; Loescher, *The History of Rogers' Rangers*, 3:14–15.

18. Stark, *Memoir and Official Correspondence of Gen. John Stark*, 452.

19. Demos, *The Unredeemed Captive*, 12.

20. Lucier, *French and Indian War Notices*, 3:54.

21. Lucier, *French and Indian War Notices*, 3:54.

22. Brumwell, *White Devil*, 200.

23. McCulloch and Todish, *Through So Many Dangers*, 46, 66; Brumwell, *White Devil*, 166–67.

24. Rogers, *Journals of Robert Rogers of the Rangers*, 35–36; McCulloch and Todish, *Through So Many Dangers*, 66; Zaboly, *A True Ranger*, 47; Cuneo, *Robert Rogers of the Rangers*, 8–9.

25. Zaboly, *A True Ranger*, 280.

26. Zaboly, *A True Ranger*, 60.

27. McCulloch and Todish, *Through So Many Dangers*, 66; Ross, *War on the Run*, 77; Hough, *Journals of Robert Rogers of the Rangers*, 89; Zaboly, *A True Ranger*, 280; Brumwell, *White Devil*, 196.

28. Eastburn, Putnam, and Hawks, *Narratives of the French and Indian War*, 47.

29. *New-York Gazette*, November 6, 1759; Cuneo, *Robert Rogers of the Rangers*, 107.

30. Rogers, *Journals of Robert Rogers of the Rangers*, 117; Moogk, *La Nouvelle France*, 25; Brumwell, *White Devil*, 106, 196; Zaboly, *A True Ranger*, 280; Parkman, *Montcalm and Wolfe*, 454; Cuneo, *Robert Rogers of the Rangers*, 142–279.

31. *New-York Gazette*, November 26, 1759.

32. Stark, *Memoir and Official Correspondence of Gen. John Stark*, 448; Ross, *War on the Run*, 249.

33. *New-York Gazette*, November 26, 1759; Brumwell, *White Devil*, 202; Stark, *Memoir and Official Correspondence of Gen. John Stark*, 460; Parkman, *Montcalm and Wolfe*, 454; Zaboly, *A True Ranger*, 281.

34. Stark, *Memoir and Official Correspondence of Gen. John Stark*, 452.

35. *Pennsylvania Journal*, November 29, 1759; Loescher, *The History of Rogers' Rangers*, 3:14.

36. McCulloch and Todish, *Through So Many Dangers*, 66; Lucier, *French and Indian War Notices*, 2:244, 295.

37. McCulloch and Todish, *Through So Many Dangers*, 66; Spring and Bray, *The Highlanders and Provincial Rangers*, 60; Brumwell, *White Devil*, 103–4, 196; Zaboly, *A True Ranger*, 280.

38. Rogers, *A Concise Account of North America*, 155, in Hobbs, *What You May Not Know about Roger's Rangers*.

39. Rogers, *A Concise Account of North America*, 155, in Hobbs, *What You May Not Know about Roger's Rangers*.

40. Loescher, *The History of Rogers' Rangers*, 4:3.

41. McCulloch and Todish, *Through So Many Dangers*, 66; Brumwell, *White Devil*, 104.

42. McCulloch and Todish, *Through So Many Dangers*, 66; Zaboly, *A True Ranger*, 281; Cuneo, *Robert Rogers of the Rangers*, 107.

43. *New-York Gazette*, November 26, 1759.

44. Loescher, *The History of Rogers' Rangers*, 4:121, 140.

45. *New-York Gazette*, November 26, 1759; Rogers, *Journals of Robert Rogers of the Rangers*, 117; Brumwell, *White Devil*, 195–98; McCulloch and Todish, *Through So Many Dangers*, 66; Loescher, *The History of Rogers' Rangers*, 4:69, 70–71, 3:40, 64; Zaboly, *A True Ranger*, 281.

46. Stark, *Memoir and Official Correspondence of Gen. John Stark*, 448; Zaboly, *A True Ranger*, 281.

47. *New-York Gazette*, November 26, 1759.

48. Rogers, *Journals of Robert Rogers of the Rangers*, 117–18; Zaboly, *A True Ranger*, 281.

49. Black, *Ranger Dawn*, 73; Ross, *War on the Run*, 250; Loescher, *The History of Rogers' Rangers*, 4:240.

50. Ross, *War on the Run*, 250; McCulloch and Todish, *Through So Many Dangers*, 66.

51. Stark, *Memoir and Official Correspondence of Gen. John Stark*, 460; Parkman, *Montcalm and Wolfe*, 454.

52. Ross, *War on the Run*, 250.

53. Zaboly, *A True Ranger*, 281.

54. *New-York Gazette*, November 26, 1759; Brumwell, *White Devil*, 196, 198.

55. Zaboly, *A True Ranger*, 281.

56. Zaboly, *A True Ranger*, 202; Polhemus and Polhemus, *Stark*, 17.

57. McCulloch and Todish, *Through So Many Dangers*, 66.

58. McCulloch and Todish, *Through So Many Dangers*, 66.

59. *New-York Gazette*, November 26, 1759.

60. Rogers, *Journals of Robert Rogers of the Rangers*, 118.

61. Rogers, *Journals of Robert Rogers of the Rangers*, 118; Borneman, *The French and Indian War*, 229; Zaboly, *A True Ranger*, 281.

62. *Boston Evening Post*, November 1, 1759.

63. Stark, *Memoir and Official Correspondence of Gen. John Stark*, 448.

64. Brumwell, *White Devil*, 198.

65. Loescher, *French and Indian War Notices*, 2:137–38; Brumwell, *White Devil*, 195.

66. Ross, *War on the Run*, 250; Ferling, *A Wilderness of Miseries*, 46.

67. Brumwell, *White Devil*, 196–202; Zaboly, *A True Ranger*, 280–81.

68. Rogers, *Journals of Robert Rogers of the Rangers*, 118; *Pennsylvania Journal*, November 29, 1759; Calloway, *The Abenaki*, 58–59; Johnson, *A Narrative of the Captivity of Mrs. Johnson*, 70; Ross, *War on the Run*, 13; Brumwell, *White Devil*, 51–52, 102–3, 199, 201–2; Webb, *Born Fighting*, 42–119; Loescher, *The History of Rogers' Rangers*, 3:53,75; Zaboly, *A True Ranger*, 280; Boisvert, "Major Rogers and the Abenakis' Treasures."

69. Cuneo, *Robert Rogers of the Rangers*, 108; Brumwell, *White Devil*, 92–95.

70. *South Carolina Gazette* (Charles Town), December 1, 1759.

71. *Boston Evening Post*, November 1, 1759.

72. Brumwell, *White Devil*, 96.

73. *Boston Evening Post*, November 1, 1759; Brumwell, *White Devil*, 195.

74. Brumwell, *White Devil*, 197; *New-York Gazette*, November 26, 1759; McCulloch and Todish, *Through So Many Dangers*, 66.

75. *Boston Evening Post*, November 1, 1759.

76. McCulloch and Todish, *Through So Many Dangers*, 66.

77. Cuneo, *Robert Rogers of the Rangers*, 108.

78. Raymond Pibunki Awasos LeMay, "Why British Major Robert Rogers Does Not Deserve a Statue nor a Days Ceremony nor a Park in His Namesake," Tripod, May 30, 2005, internet.

79. Brumwell, *White Devil*, 167.

80. Brumwell, *White Devil*, 195–97.

81. *Boston Evening Post*, November 1, 1759.

82. *New-York Gazette*, November 26, 1759.

83. MacArthur, *The MacArthur Study Bible*, 313.

84. MacArthur, *The MacArthur Study Bible*, 313.

85. Brumwell, *White Devil*, 91–94, 210.

86. Rogers, *Journals of Robert Rogers of the Rangers*, 118.

87. Rogers, *Journals of Robert Rogers of the Rangers*, 118.

88. *New-York Gazette*, November 26, 1759.

89. Zaboly, *A True Ranger*, 281.

90. "Rogers' Raid According to the Research of Gordon Day (1981)," Ne-Do-Ba (Friends): Exploring and Sharing the Wabanaki History of Indians in New England, August 1998, internet; Pierre Pouchet, *Memoirs in the Late War in North America between France and England* (Niagara, NY: Old Fort Niagara Association, 1994), 249; Borneman, *The French and Indian War*, 229; Brumwell, *White Devil*, 210.

91. Pouchet, *Memoirs in the Late War*, 249; Brumwell, *White Devil*, 92.

92. McCulloch and Todish, *Through So Many Dangers*, 66; Loescher, *The History of Rogers' Rangers*, 4:140, 144; Brumwell, *White Devil*, 195–97; Hough, *Journals of Robert Rogers of the Rangers*, 89.

93. McCulloch and Todish, *Through So Many Dangers*, 66; Snow, *Death or Victory*, 25.

94. Hough, *Journals of Robert Rogers of the Rangers*, 89.

95. Hough, *Journals of Robert Rogers of the Rangers*, 89.

96. McCulloch and Todish, *Through So Many Dangers*, 66; *New-York Gazette*, November 26, 1759; Hough, *Journals of Robert Rogers of the Rangers*, 89.

97. *New-York Gazette*, November 26, 1759.

98. Loescher, *The History of Rogers' Rangers*, 4:144.

99. Zaboly, *A True Ranger*, 283.

100. Loescher, *The History of Rogers' Rangers*, 3:72, 4:140.

101. Brumwell, *White Devil*, 198; Zaboly, *A True Ranger*, 281.

102. Zaboly, *A True Ranger*, 281–82.

103. Zaboly, *A True Ranger*, 282.

104. Loescher, *The History of Rogers' Rangers*, 4:174; Zaboly, *A True Ranger*, 281; Brumwell, *White Devil*, 210.
105. Zaboly, *A True Ranger*, 282.
106. Lucier, *French and Indian War Notices*, 2:137–38; Brumwell, *White Devil*, 200; Theophile Panadis, interview recorded by Gordon Day in 1966, Reel 27, Side 1, internet.
107. Brumwell, *White Devil*, 195–97; Loescher, *The History of Rogers' Rangers*, 4:207–8.
108. Loescher, *The History of Rogers' Rangers*, 4:159; Brumwell, *White Devil*, 167, 195–97.
109. Brumwell, *White Devil*, 167, 195–97.
110. Brumwell, *White Devil*, 167, 195–97.
111. Brumwell, *White Devil*, 200–201.
112. Ferling, *A Wilderness of Miseries*, 50; Brumwell, *White Devil*, 244–45.
113. Rogers, *Journals of Robert Rogers of the Rangers*, 51; Cuneo, *Robert Rogers of the Rangers*, 101; Brumwell, *White Devil*, 189–90.
114. *New-York Gazette*, November 26, 1759.
115. Brumwell, *White Devil*, 201–2.
116. Ross, *War on the Run*, 2–3.
117. Zaboly, *A True Ranger*, 283.
118. *New-York Gazette*, November 26, 1759; Loescher, *The History of Rogers' Rangers*, 4:42; Lucier, *French and Indian War Notices*, 2:69.
119. Brumwell, *White Devil*, 201.
120. Lucier, *French and Indian War Notices*, 2:256.
121. Loescher, *The History of Rogers' Rangers*, 4:42; Brumwell, *White Devil*, 48, 199–200; Zaboly, *A True Ranger*, 281–82.
122. Eastburn, Putnam, and Hawks, *Narratives of the French and Indian War*, 49n12, 55–56; Lucier, *French and Indian War Notices*, 2:4.
123. Brumwell, *White Devil*, 198.
124. Loescher, *The History of Rogers' Rangers*, 4:42; Zaboly, *A True Ranger*, 282; Brumwell, *White Devil*, 91–92, 195–99.
125. Brumwell, *White Devil*, 199.
126. MacArthur, *The MacArthur Study Bible*, 313.
127. Rogers, *Journals of Robert Rogers of the Rangers*, 118; Zaboly, *A True Ranger*, 283; Ross, *War on the Run*, 239, 250–51; Brumwell, *White Devil*, 162–63.
128. *New-York Gazette*, November 26, 1759.
129. *New-York Gazette*, November 26, 1759.
130. McCulloch and Todish, *Through So Many Dangers*, 66–67.
131. *New-York Gazette*, November 26, 1759.
132. Brumwell, *White Devil*, 203.
133. *New-York Gazette*, November 26, 1759.
134. Brumwell, *White Devil*, 199–200; Zaboly, *A True Ranger*, 283.
135. Rogers, *Journals of Robert Rogers of the Rangers*, 118.
136. *New-York Gazette*, November 26, 1759.
137. *New-York Gazette*, November 26, 1759; Rogers, *Journals of Robert Rogers of the Rangers*, 118; Zaboly, *American Colonial Ranger*, 32; Brumwell, *White Devil*, 192, 204; Zaboly, *A True Ranger*, 105.
138. Eastburn, Putnam, and Hawks, *Narratives of the French and Indian War*, 48–49, 54; Loescher, *The History of Rogers' Rangers*, 4:50–51.

139. Edwin S. Redkey, ed., *A Grand Army of Black Men* (Cambridge: Cambridge University Press, 1992), 60.

140. Loescher, *The History of Rogers' Rangers*, 4:66.

141. Loescher, *The History of Rogers' Rangers*, 3:39, 4:244n99.

142. Ross, *War on the Run*, 462; Brumwell, *White Devil*, 203.

143. Loescher, *The History of Rogers' Rangers*, 4:141.

144. Loescher, *The History of Rogers' Rangers*, 4:50.

145. Brumwell, *White Devil*, 237.

146. Rogers, *A Concise Account of North America*, 151, in Hobbs, *What You May Not Know about Roger's Rangers*; Zaboly, *A True Ranger*, 281.

147. Brumwell, *White Devil*, 201.

148. Brumwell, *White Devil*, 195–97, 233.

149. Loescher, *The History of Rogers' Rangers*, 3:66; Brumwell, *White Devil*, 229.

150. *Boston Evening Post*, November 1, 1759.

151. Loescher, *The History of Rogers' Rangers*, 4:42–43.

152. Rogers, *Journals of Robert Rogers of the Rangers*, 118.

153. *New-York Gazette*, November 26, 1759.

154. *Boston News-Letter*, October 4, 1795.

155. Rogers, *Journals of Robert Rogers of the Rangers*, 118.

156. Stark, *Memoir and Official Correspondence of Gen. John Stark*, 449.

157. Loescher, *The History of Rogers' Rangers*, 4:183; La Bree, *New Hampshire's General John Stark*, 38.

158. McCulloch and Todish, *Through So Many Dangers*, 66.

159. *New-York Gazette*, November 26, 1759.

160. Ross, *War on the Run*, 462.

161. Ross, *War on the Run*, 121; Calloway, *The Western Abenakis of Vermont*, 81; Brumwell, *White Devil*, 204.

162. Calloway, *The Western Abenakis of Vermont*, 87–88, 94–95.

163. *New-York Gazette*, November 26, 1759; McCulloch and Todish, *Through So Many Dangers*, 66.

164. John Greenleaf Whittier and Benjamin L. Mirick, *The History of Haverhill, Massachusetts* (Haverhill, MA: A. W. Thayer, 1832), 96.

165. Loescher, *The History of Rogers' Rangers*, 4:36, 42, 44; Brumwell, *White Devil*, 207–9.

166. Loescher, *The History of Rogers' Rangers*, 4:46–47.

167. *Boston Gazette*, February 14, 1757.

168. Brumwell, *White Devil*, 204; Zaboly, *A True Ranger*, 284.

Chapter 8: The Long Retreat That Became a Living Nightmare

1. Brumwell, *White Devil*, 204; McCulloch and Todish, *Through So Many Dangers*, 67.

2. Loescher, *The History of Rogers' Rangers*, 4:49.

3. Ross, *War on the Run*, 231.

4. Borneman, *The French and Indian War*, 231; Brumwell, *White Devil*, 82–84, 189, 204–5, 209–10, 222; Loescher, *The History of Rogers' Rangers*, 3:75, 4:22, 37, 46, 51, 86; Zaboly, *A True Ranger*, 284; Demos, *The Unredeemed Captive*, 6–7; Stark, *Memoir and Official Correspondence of Gen. John Stark*, 11–15; McCulloch and Todish, *Through So Many Dangers*, 66–67.

5. Loescher, *The History of Rogers' Rangers*, 4:53; Zaboly, *A True Ranger*, 284.

6. Loescher, *The History of Rogers' Rangers*, 4:53–54.

7. Zaboly, *A True Ranger*, 285.

8. Loescher, *The History of Rogers' Rangers*, 4:53–54; Zaboly, *A True Ranger*, 285.

9. Zaboly, *A True Ranger*, 285.

10. Loescher, *The History of Rogers' Rangers*, 3:63, 4:55–56, 121; Zaboly, *A True Ranger*, 285.

11. Loescher, *The History of Rogers' Rangers*, 4:56–57, 260n206.

12. Loescher, *The History of Rogers' Rangers*, 4:173.

13. Loescher, *The History of Rogers' Rangers*, 4:143.

14. Stark, *Memoir and Official Correspondence of Gen. John Stark*, 449.

15. Cuneo, *Robert Rogers of the Rangers*, 109–10; Loescher, *The History of Rogers' Rangers*, 4:56–57, 123.

16. Stark, *Memoir and Official Correspondence of Gen. John Stark*, 452.

17. Zaboly, *A True Ranger*, 285; Loescher, *The History of Rogers' Rangers*, 4:58–59; Brumwell, *White Devil*, 203.

18. Loescher, *The History of Rogers' Rangers*, 4:260n206.

19. Zaboly, *A True Ranger*, 285; Loescher, *The History of Rogers' Rangers*, 4:59–60.

20. Loescher, *The History of Rogers' Rangers*, 4:59–60; Brumwell, *White Devil*, 200.

21. "Dumas, Jean-Daniel," *Dictionary of Canadian Biography*, www.biographi.ca/en/bio/dumas_jean_daniel_4E.html; Loescher, *The History of Rogers' Rangers*, 4:60–61; Lucier, *French and Indian War Notices*, 2:13, 74, 177.

22. Loescher, *The History of Rogers' Rangers*, 4:83; Zaboly, *A True Ranger*, 285, 287.

23. McCulloch and Todish, *Through So Many Dangers*, 66–67.

24. Loescher, *The History of Rogers' Rangers*, 4:83, 92.

25. *New-York Gazette*, November 26, 1759.

26. Loescher, *The History of Rogers' Rangers*, 3:39, 4:67; Brumwell, *White Devil*, 228.

27. Loescher, *The History of Rogers' Rangers*, 4:67.

28. Loescher, *The History of Rogers' Rangers*, 4:67.

29. Loescher, *The History of Rogers' Rangers*, 4:67.

30. McCulloch and Todish, *Through So Many Dangers*, 67.

31. McCulloch and Todish, *Through So Many Dangers*, 67.

32. Zaboly, *A True Ranger*, 286.

33. McCulloch and Todish, *Through So Many Dangers*, 66.

34. Brumwell, *White Devil*, 229.

35. Maurice De Tasche, *Campaigning for Napoleon: The Diary of a Napoleonic Cavalry Officer 1806–1813*, ed. and trans. Rosemary Brindle (South Yorkshire, UK: Pen and Sword, 2006), 184; Reinhold Busch, *Survivors of Stalingrad: Eyewitness Accounts from the Sixth Army, 1942–1943* (London: Frontline Books, 2018), 187, 262.

36. Brumwell, *White Devil*, 231.

37. McCulloch and Todish, *Through So Many Dangers*, 67.

38. McCulloch and Todish, *Through So Many Dangers*, 66–67.

39. Hamilton, *Adventures in the Wilderness*, 114.

40. Hamilton, *Adventures in the Wilderness*, 142–43.

41. Hamilton, *Adventures in the Wilderness*, 150.

42. Eastburn, Putnam, and Hawks, *Narratives of the French and Indian War*, 15, 21–22.

43. Hamilton, *Adventures in the Wilderness*, 174; Lucier, *French and Indian War Notices*, 2:295.

44. Parkman, *Montcalm and Wolfe*, 281, 296.

45. Gallup, *Memoir of a French and Indian War Soldier*, 128n4.

46. Loescher, *The History of Rogers' Rangers*, 4:59, 61–62, 67; Zaboly, *A True Ranger*, 285, 287.

47. Loescher, *The History of Rogers' Rangers*, 4:65, 67–68.

48. Loescher, *The History of Rogers' Rangers*, 3:39, 4:65; Cuneo, *Robert Rogers of the Rangers*, 110–11.

49. Loescher, *The History of Rogers' Rangers*, 4:67–68.

50. Loescher, *The History of Rogers' Rangers*, 4:63, 120.

51. Loescher, *The History of Rogers' Rangers*, 4:62–62.

52. Zaboly, *A True Ranger*, 285; Loescher, *The History of Rogers' Rangers*, 4:101–3.

53. Loescher, *The History of Rogers' Rangers*, 4:247n118.

54. Loescher, *The History of Rogers' Rangers*, 4:259n202.

55. Loescher, *The History of Rogers' Rangers*, 3:44, 4:97, 137; Zaboly, *A True Ranger*, 285.

56. Loescher, *The History of Rogers' Rangers*, 4:144.

57. Loescher, *The History of Rogers' Rangers*, 4:78–80.

58. Allen Nevins, *Ranger: The Adventurous Life of Robert Rogers of the Rangers* (Duffield, UK: Leonaur, 2011), 50.

59. Ross, *War on the Run*, 455; Zaboly, *A True Ranger*, 286.

60. Stark, *Memoir and Official Correspondence of Gen. John Stark*, 449–50; Zaboly, *A True Ranger*, 287–88.

61. Stark, *Memoir and Official Correspondence of Gen. John Stark*, 452–53; Cuneo, *Robert Rogers of the Rangers*, 113.

62. Zaboly, *A True Ranger*, 288.

63. Zaboly, *A True Ranger*, 292.

64. Cuneo, *Robert Rogers of the Rangers*, 114.

65. McCulloch and Todish, *Through So Many Dangers*, 67.

66. McCulloch and Todish, *Through So Many Dangers*, 67.

67. Stark, *Memoir and Official Correspondence of Gen. John Stark*, 450.

68. McCulloch and Todish, *Through So Many Dangers*, 67.

69. *New-York Gazette*, November 26, 1759.

70. Stark, *Memoir and Official Correspondence of Gen. John Stark*, 450.

71. *Maryland Gazette*, November 22, 1759.

72. *Boston News-Letter*, October 26, 1759.

73. *Maryland Gazette*, October 4, 1759.

74. Zaboly, *A True Ranger*, 273.

75. *Boston News-Letter*, November 8, 1759.

76. *Maryland Gazette*, December 20, 1759.

77. Zaboly, *A True Ranger*, 287.

78. *New-York Gazette*, November 26, 1759.

79. Brumwell, *White Devil*, 232.

80. Loescher, *The History of Rogers' Rangers*, 3:39, 4:99–100; Brumwell, *White Devil*, 232.

81. Loescher, *The History of Rogers' Rangers*, 4:99.

82. McCulloch and Todish, *Through So Many Dangers*, 66–69.

83. Stark, *Memoir and Official Correspondence of Gen. John Stark*, 450.

84. Loescher, *The History of Rogers' Rangers*, 4:99.

85. Brumwell, *White Devil*, 239.

86. *Maryland Gazette*, November 20, 1759.

87. *Pennsylvania Journal*, November 29, 1759; Zaboly, *A True Ranger*, 292.

88. Cuneo, *Robert Rogers of the Rangers*, 114.

89. Susannah Johnson, *A Narrative of the Captivity of Mrs. Johnson* (Springfield: H. R. Hutting, 1870), 133–34; Brumwell, *White Devil*, 232.

90. Parkman, *Montcalm and Wolfe*, 455.

91. *New-York Gazette*, November 26, 1759.

92. *Maryland Gazette*, December 20, 1759.

93. Brumwell, *White Devil*, 243; Loescher, *The History of Rogers' Rangers*, 4:180, 183–85.

94. Loescher, *The History of Rogers' Rangers*, 3:27; Brumwell, *White Devil*, 239–40.

95. Stark, *Memoir and Official Correspondence of Gen. John Stark*, 450.

96. Loescher, *The History of Rogers' Rangers*, 3:14, 27–28.

97. Loescher, *The History of Rogers' Rangers*, 3:28.

98. Loescher, *The History of Rogers' Rangers*, 3:28.

99. Loescher, *The History of Rogers' Rangers*, 3:28.

100. Loescher, *The History of Rogers' Rangers*, 3:28.

101. Brumwell, *White Devil*, 234–35; Loescher, *The History of Rogers' Rangers*, 4:101–4.

102. Loescher, *The History of Rogers' Rangers*, 3:63, 4:8.

103. Loescher, *The History of Rogers' Rangers*, 4:143.

104. Brumwell, *White Devil*, 243–44; Loescher, *The History of Rogers' Rangers*, 4:180.

105. *Pennsylvania Journal*, November 29, 1759; Loescher, *The History of Rogers' Rangers*, 3:14, 4:180.

106. Nevins, *Ranger*, 48.

107. *New Hampshire Gazette*, February 8, 1760.

108. *Pennsylvania Journal*, January 24, 1760.

109. Brumwell, *White Devil*, 240–41.

110. Loescher, *The History of Rogers' Rangers*, 4:107.

111. Loescher, *The History of Rogers' Rangers*, 4:152, 162.

112. *Boston Evening Post*, November 1, 1759.

113. Loescher, *The History of Rogers' Rangers*, 4:173.

114. Loescher, *The History of Rogers' Rangers*, 4:173–74, 215.

115. Loescher, *The History of Rogers' Rangers*, 4:174.

116. Loescher, *The History of Rogers' Rangers*, 4:258n198.

117. Loescher, *The History of Rogers' Rangers*, 4:262n215.

118. Brumwell, *White Devil*, 241–44; Loescher, *The History of Rogers' Rangers*, 4:280.

119. Stark, *Memoir and Official Correspondence of Gen. John Stark*, 11–15; Loescher, *The History of Rogers' Rangers*, 3:71, 4:7, 69–75.

120. Loescher, *The History of Rogers' Rangers*, 4:7, 74–75, 104, 180, 232n35.

121. Loescher, *The History of Rogers' Rangers*, 4:250n140.

122. Zaboly, *A True Ranger*, 287.

123. Loescher, *The History of Rogers' Rangers*, 4:7.

Chapter 9: Enduring Questions and Controversies to This Day

1. Loescher, *The History of Rogers' Rangers*, 4:110–11; Brumwell, *White Devil*, 82–83.

2. Brumwell, *White Devil*, 118.

3. Brumwell, *White Devil*, 119.

4. Rogers, *Journals of Robert Rogers of the Rangers*, 118; Parkman, *Montcalm and Wolfe*, 423, 454; "Rogers' Raid According to the Research of Gordon Day (1981)," Ne-Do-Ba (Friends): Exploring and Sharing the Wabanaki History of Indians in New England, August 1998, internet; Borneman, *The French and Indian War*, 229; Ferling, *A Wilderness of Miseries*, 3–54; Brumwell, *White Devil*, 195–98; Woody Holton, *Forced Founders: Indians, Debtors, Slaves, and the Making of the American Revolution in Virginia* (Chapel Hill: University of North Carolina Press, 1999), 214.

5. Calloway, *The Western Abenakis of Vermont*, 177.

6. Zaboly, *A True Ranger*, 292.

7. Brumwell, *White Devil*, 197–98.

8. Brumwell, *White Devil*, 244–45.

9. Calloway, *The Western Abenakis of Vermont*, 178.

10. Brumwell, *White Devil*, 91–92, 199.

11. Loescher, *The History of Rogers' Rangers*, 4:43; Brumwell, *White Devil*, 203.

12. Calloway, *The Western Abenakis of Vermont*, 178–82.

13. *Maryland Gazette*, March 13, 1759.

14. *Maryland Gazette*, March 13, 1759; Ferling, *A Wilderness of Miseries*, 3–54; Ross, *War on the Run*, 131–32; Zaboly, *American Colonial Ranger*, 47–49.

15. Ferling, *A Wilderness of Miseries*, 3–54; Zaboly, *American Colonial Ranger*, 47–48; *Maryland Gazette*, March 13, 1759; Ross, *War on the Run*, 131–32.

16. McCulloch and Todish, *Through So Many Dangers*, 66.

17. Zaboly, *A True Ranger*, 283.

18. Loescher, *The History of Rogers' Rangers*, 4:172, 180.

19. Loescher, *The History of Rogers' Rangers*, 4:174.

20. Calloway, *The Western Abenakis of Vermont*, 177.

21. Zaboly, *American Colonial Ranger*, 55.

22. Calloway, *The Western Abenakis of Vermont*; Rogers, *Journals of Robert Rogers of the Rangers*, 77; Brumwell, *White Devil*, 118–19, 241–44; Zaboly, *A True Ranger*, 215; Borneman, *The French and Indian War*, 233; Loescher, *The History of Rogers' Rangers*, 4:104–5; Zaboly, *American Colonial Ranger*, 47.

23. Brumwell, *White Devil*, 119.

24. Brumwell, *White Devil*, 115–16; Borneman, *The French and Indian War*, 233.

25. Loescher, *The History of Rogers' Rangers*, 4:105.

26. Brumwell, *White Devil*, 135.

27. Brumwell, *White Devil*, 241–46; Demos, *The Unredeemed Captive*, 25; Loescher, *The History of Rogers' Rangers*, 4:280.

28. Brumwell, *White Devil*, 241–46; Loescher, *The History of Rogers' Rangers*, 4:280.

29. Borneman, *The French and Indian War*, 233; Brumwell, *White Devil*, 241, 243.

30. Calloway, *The Abenaki*, 59.

31. Calloway, *The Abenaki*, 59; Calloway, *The Western Abenakis of Vermont*, 177; Brumwell, *White Devil*, 118–19.

32. Stark, *Memoir and Official Correspondence of Gen. John Stark*, 448–49.

33. Stark, *Memoir and Official Correspondence of Gen. John Stark*, 448–50.

34. Stark, *Memoir and Official Correspondence of Gen. John Stark*, 450–51.

35. Parkman, *Montcalm and Wolfe*, 452–55; "Rogers' Raid According to the Research of Gordon Day (1981)," Ne-Do-Ba (Friends): Exploring and Sharing the Wabanaki History of Indians in New England, August 1998, internet.

36. Borneman, *The French and Indian War*, 233.

37. Ross, *War on the Run*, 226.

38. Brumwell, *White Devil*, 119.

39. Anderson, *The War That Made America*, 48–49.

40. Brumwell, *White Devil*, 18.

41. Brumwell, *White Devil*, 243–44; Loescher, *The History of Rogers' Rangers*, 4:280.

42. McCulloch and Todish, *Through So Many Dangers*, 65.

43. Bahmanyar, *Shadow Warriors*, 16.

44. La Bree, *New Hampshire's General John Stark*, 13.

45. Zaboly, *A True Ranger*, 250, 367–406; James Flexner, *Mohawk Baronet: A Biography of Sir William Johnson* (Syracuse, NY: Syracuse University Press, 1990), xiv; Daughan, *Lexington and Concord*, 20–52, 58.

Epilogue

1. *Boston Gazette*, February 14, 1757; Lucier, *French and Indian War Notices*, 2:13, 74, 105, 113, 177; *New-York Gazette*, November 26, 1759.

2. Loescher, *The History of Rogers' Rangers*, 4:xv–xvi.

About the Author

Phillip Thomas Tucker, PhD, is the award-winning author of nearly seventy books of history. He received his PhD from St. Louis University, St. Louis, Missouri, in 1990. Tucker has long specialized in producing groundbreaking history in many fields of study, including women's history and African American history. He has been recently recognized as the "Stephen King of History" after more than three decades of authoring important books of unique distinction.